SOMETHING ABOUT THE AUTHOR

SOMETHING ABOUT THE AUTHOR

Facts and Pictures about Authors

and Illustrators of Books for Young People

Anne Commire

VOLUME 15

GALE RESEARCH
BOOK TOWER
DETROIT, MICHIGAN
48226

Also Published by Gale

CONTEMPORARY AUTHORS

*A Bio-Bibliographical Guide to Current Writers in
Fiction, General Nonfiction, Poetry, Journalism,
Drama, Motion Pictures, Television,
and Other Fields*

(Now Covers Nearly 54,000 Authors)

Associate Editor: Agnes Garrett

Assistant Editors: Helga McCue, Linda Shedd

Consultant: Adele Sarkissian

Sketchwriters: Dianne H. Anderson, Rosemary DeAngelis Bridges,
Catherine Coray, D. Jayne Higo, Gail Schermer,
Susan L. Stetler

Research Assistant: Elisa Ann Sawchuk

Library of Congress Catalog Card Number 72-27107

ISBN 0-8103-0096-6

Table of Contents

Introduction

Beginning with this volume, the time span covered by *Something about the Author* is being broadened to include major children's writers who died before 1961, which was the former cut-off point for writers covered in this series. This change will make *SATA* even more helpful to its many thousands of student and professional users.

Authors who did not come within the scope of *SATA* have formerly been included in *Yesterday's Authors of Books for Children,* of which Gale has published two volumes.

It has been pointed out by users, however, that it is inconvenient to have a body of related materials broken up by an arbitrary criterion such as the date of a person's death. Also, some libraries are not able to afford both series, and are therefore denied access to material on some of the most important writers in the juvenile field.

It has been decided, therefore, to discontinue the *YABC* series, and to include in *SATA* at least the most outstanding among the older writers who had been selected for listing in *YABC*. Volumes 1 and 2 of *YABC* will be kept in print, and the listings in those two volumes will be included in the cumulative *SATA* index.

GRATEFUL ACKNOWLEDGMENT

is made to the following publishers, authors, and artists, for their kind permission to reproduce copyrighted material. ■ **AMERICAN ARTIST.** Sidelight excerpts from an article entitled "The Whimsical Illustrations of Hilary Knight," by Joan Hess Michel, in *American Artist,* March, 1963. Copyright © 1963 by Billboard Publications Inc. Reprinted by permission of *American Artist* magazine. ■ **ATHENEUM PUBLISHERS.** Illustration by Marcia Sewell from *The Squire's Bride* by P.C. Asbjörnsen. Copyright © 1975 by Marcia Sewell./ Jacket illustration by Richard Cuffari from *Hew Against the Grain* by Betty Sue Cummings. Copyright © 1977 by Betty Sue Cummings./ Illustration by Trina Schart Hyman from *The Marrow of the World* by Ruth Nichols. Copyright © 1972 by Ruth Nichols. All reprinted by permission of Atheneum Publishers. ■ **BLACKIE AND SON, LTD.** Illustration by Henry Matthew Brock from *The Old Curiosity Shop* by Charles Dickens. Reprinted by permission of Blackie and Son, Ltd. ■ **JOHN F. BLAIR, PUBLISHER.** Illustration by Mary Walker Sparks from *Taffy of Torpedo Junction* by Nell Wise Wechter. Copyright © 1957 by John F. Blair. Reprinted by permission of John F. Blair, Publisher. ■ **THE BOBBS-MERRILL CO.** Illustration by Wladeplau T. Benda from *A Girl of the Limberlost* by Gene Stratton-Porter. Copyright 1909 by Doubleday and Page & Co. Reprinted by permission of The Bobbs-Merrill Co. ■ **BRADBURY PRESS, INC.** Illustration by Diane Goode from *The Selchie's Seed* by Shulamith Oppenheim. Copyright © 1975 by Diane Capuzzo Goode./ Illustration by Christopher Brooker from *The Boat in the Reeds* by A.C. Stewart. Copyright © 1960 by Bradbury Press, Inc. All reprinted by permission of Bradbury Press, Inc. ■ **BROADSIDE PRESS.** Illustration by Ademola Olugebefola from *It's a New Day* by Sonia Sanchez. Copyright © 1971 by Sonia Sanchez. Reprinted by permission of Broadside Press. ■ **CHATTO AND WINDUS, LTD.** Illustration by Patricia Drew from *Elephants Don't Sit on Cars* by David Henry Wilson. Illustrations copyright © 1977 by Patricia Drew. Reprinted by permission of Chatto and Windus, Ltd. ■ **WILLIAM COLLINS AND WORLD PUBLISHING CO.** Illustration by Rainey Bennett from *The Secret Hiding Place* by Rainey Bennett. Copyright © 1960 by Rainey Bennett./ Illustration by Bruno Munari from *Bruno Munari's Zoo.* Copyright © 1964 by Bruno Munari./ Illustration by Bill Geldart from *Garranane* by Tom Ingram. Copyright © 1971 by Tom Ingram./ Illustration by Douglas Hall from *The Pit* by Reginald Maddock. Copyright © 1966 by William Collins Sons & Co. Ltd. All reprinted by permission of William Collins and World Publishing Co. ■ **COWARD, McCANN AND GEOGHEGAN, INC.** Illustration by Charles Fracé from *The Wolf* by Dr. Michael Fox. Copyright © 1973 by Dr. Michael W. Fox./ Illustration by Elizabeth Schmidt from *What Did the Dinosaurs Eat?* by Wilda S. Ross. Text copyright © 1972 by Wilda S. Ross. Illustrations copyright © 1972 by Elizabeth A. Schmidt./ Illustration by Jane Paton from *Hello I'm Karen* by Margaret Sutherland. Text copyright © 1974 by Margaret Sutherland. Illustrations copyright © 1974 by Methuen Children's Books, Ltd. All reprinted by permission of Coward, McCann and Geoghegan, Inc. ■ **THOMAS Y. CROWELL CO., INC.** Illustration by Marjorie Bauernschmidt from *Remember Me When This You See* by Lillian Morrison. Illustrations copyright © 1961 by Marjorie Bauernschmidt./ Illustration by Barbara Cooney from *A White Heron* by Sarah Orne Jewett. Illustrations copyright © 1963 by Barbara Cooney./ Drawing by K.M. Peyton from *Pennington's Heir* by K.M. Peyton. Copyright © 1973 by K.M. Peyton. All reprinted by permission of Thomas Y. Crowell Co., Inc. ■ **CROWN PUBLISHERS, INC.** Illustration by Alexandra Wallner from *Trudy's Straw Hat* by Martha Gamerman. Text copyright © 1977 by Martha Gamerman. Illustrations copyright © 1977 by Alexandra Wallner. Reprinted by permission of Crown Publishers, Inc. ■ **DELACORTE PRESS.** Illustration by Leigh Grant from *What If a Lion Eats Me and I Fall Into a Hippopotamus' Mud Hole* by Emily Hanlon. Illustrations copyright © 1975 by Leigh Grant./ Illustrations from *Come On Out, Daddy!* by Inger and Lasse Sandberg. Copyright 1969, 1971 by Inger and Lasse Sandberg. Both reprinted by permission of Delacorte Press/Seymour Lawrence. ■ **J.M. DENT AND SONS.** Illustration by Hans Baumhauer from *The Further Adventures of Nils* by Selma Lagerlöf. Copyright 1911 by Doubleday & Co./ Illustrations by

Garth Williams./ Illustration by Maurice Sendak from *No Fighting, No Biting!* by Else Holmelund Minarik. Text copyright © 1958 by Else Holmelund Minarik. Illustrations copyright © 1958 by Maurice Sendak./ Illustration by Emily McCully from *Sea Beach Express* by George Panetta. Text copyright © 1966 by George J. Panetta. Illustrations copyright © 1966 by Emily McCully./ Illustration by Robert L. Dickey from *A Dog Named Chips* by Albert Payson Terhune. Copyright, 1931, by Albert Payson Terhune./ Illustration by Marguerite Kirmse from *My Friend the Dog* by Albert Payson Terhune. Copyright 1926 by Albert Payson Terhune./ Picture by Garth Williams from *By the Shores of Silver Lake* by Laura Ingalls Wilder. Copyright 1939, as to text, by Harper & Brothers. Copyright, 1953, as to pictures, by Garth Williams./ Illustration by Garth Williams from *Little House on the Prairie* by Laura Ingalls Wilder. Pictures copyright 1953 by Garth Williams./ Illustration by Garth Williams from *The Long Winter* by Laura Ingalls Wilder. Picture copyright 1953 by Garth Williams./ Sidelight excerpts and photograph from *On the Way Home: The Diary of a Trip from South Dakota to Mansfield, Mo. in 1884* by Laura Ingalls Wilder, with a setting by Rose Wilder Lane. Copyright 1962 by Roger Lea MacBride./ Illustrations by Garth Williams from *These Happy Golden Years* by Laura Ingalls Wilder. Picture copyright 1953 by Garth Williams./ Sidelight excerpts from *West from Home: Letters of Laura Ingalls Wilder.* Copyright © 1974 by Roger Lea MacBride. All reprinted by permission of Harper and Row, Publishers, Inc. ■ **GEORGE HARRAP & CO., LTD.** Illustration by Willy Pogany from *The Children of Odin* by Padraic Colum. Copyright 1920 by Macmillan Publishing Co., Inc. Renewed 1948 by Willy Pogany. Reprinted by permission of George Harrap & Co., Ltd. ■ **HASKELL HOUSE PUBLISHERS, LTD.** Sidelight excerpts from *Reminiscences of My Father* by Charles Dickens. Reprinted by permission of Haskell House Publishers, Ltd. ■ **WILLIAM HEINEMANN, LTD.** Sidelight excerpts from *Arthur Rackham, His Life and Work* by Derek Hudson. Copyright © 1960 by Derek Hudson./ Illustration by Edward Ardizzone from *Complete Poems for Children* by James Reeves. Copyright © 1973 by James Reeves and Edward Ardizzone. Both reprinted by permission of William Heinemann, Ltd. ■ **HODDER AND STOUGHTON, LTD.** Illustration by Kay Nielson from *East of the Sun and West of the Moon* by P.C. Asbjörnsen. Reprinted by permission of Hodder and Stoughton, Ltd. ■ **HOLT, RINEHART AND WINSTON.** Illustration by Nonny Hogrogrian from *Always Room for One More* by Sorche Nic Leodhas. Copyright © 1965 by Leclaire G. Alger. Illustrations copyright © 1965 by Nonny Hogrogrian./ Illustration by Margaret Ayer from *Mark Twain: His Life* by Catherine O. Peare. Copyright © 1954 by Catherine Owens Peare. Both reprinted by permission of Holt, Rinehart and Winston. ■ **THE HORN BOOK, INC.** Sidelight excerpts from the acceptance paper by Ludwig Bemelmans "And So Madeline Was Born" in *Caldecott Medal Books: 1938-1957,* edited by Bertha Mahony Miller and Elinor Whitney Field. Copyright 1954 by The Horn Book, Inc./ Sidelight excerpts from *Writing and Criticism: A Book for Margery Bianco* edited by Anne Carroll Moore and Bertha Mahony Miller./ Sidelight excerpts from an article entitled "Patterns for the Imagination" by Padraic Colum in *The Horn Book Magazine,* February, 1962. Copyright © 1962 by The Horn Book, Inc./ Sidelight excerpts from an acceptance paper by Rachel Field in *Newbery Medal Books: 1922-1955* edited by Bertha Mahony Miller and Elinor Whitney Field. Copyright © 1930 by The Horn Book, Inc./ Sidelight excerpts from *The Hewins Lectures 1947-1962* edited by Siri Andrews. Copyright © 1963 by The Horn Book, Inc./ Sidelight excerpts from "Hugh Lofting: 1886-1947" by Helen Dean Fish, *Newbery Medal Books: 1922-1955* edited by Bertha Mahony Miller and Elinor Whitney Field. Copyright © 1957 by The Horn Book, Inc./ Sidelight excerpts from "A Letter from Laura Ingalls Wilder," The *Horn Book Magazine,* December, 1953. Copyright © 1953 by The Horn Book, Inc. All reprinted by permission of The Horn Book, Inc. ■ **HOUGHTON MIFFLIN CO.** Illustration by Anthony Colbert from *Round About and Long Ago* by Eileen Colwell. Text copyright © 1972 by Eileen Colwell. Illustrations copyright © 1972 by Longman Young Books./ Illustrations by Holling C. Holling from *Seabird* by Holling C. Holling. Copyright 1948, © renewed 1975 by Holling Clancy Holling./ Sidelight excerpts and photographs from *Sarah Orne Jewett* by Francis Otto Matthiessen. Copyright 1929 & 1957 by Francis Otto Matthiessen. All reprinted by permission of Houghton Mifflin Co. ■ **ALFRED A. KNOPF, INC.** Illustration by Leo and Diane Dillon from *Dark Venture* by Audrey White Beyer. Copyright © 1968 by Audrey White Beyer./ Illustration by Rosekrans Hoffman from *Anna Banana* by Rosekrans Hoffman. Copyright © 1975 by Rosekrans Hoffman. Both reprinted by permission of Alfred A. Knopf, Inc., a division of Random House, Inc. ■ **J.B. LIPPINCOTT CO.** Illustration by Hilary Knight from *Mrs. Piggle-Wiggle* by Betty MacDonald. Illustration copyright © 1957 by J.B. Lippincott Co./ Illustrations by Hugh Lofting from *Doctor Dolittle's Caravan* by Hugh Lofting. Copyright 1924, 1925, 1926, by Hugh Lofting./ Illustration by Katherine Milhous from *Through These Arches* by Katherine Milhous. Copyright © 1964 by Katherine Milhous./ Photograph by Jane Miller from *Birth of a Foal* by Jane Miller. Copyright © 1977 by Jane Miller./ All reprinted by permission of J.B. Lippincott Co. ■ **LITTLE, BROWN AND CO.** Illustration by Douglas Hall from *The Pit* by Reginald Maddock. Copyright © 1966 by Reginald Maddock. Reprinted by permission of Little, Brown and Co. ■ **LOTHROP, LEE AND SHEPARD.** Illustration by Bette J. Davis from *Musical Insects* by Bette J. Davis. Copyright © 1971 by Bette J. Davis./ Illustration by Andrée Golbin from *Minnows* by Elizabeth Shepherd. Copyright © 1974 by Elizabeth Shepherd./ Art concept of photographs by Lou Jacobs, Jr. from *Skateboards,*

Against Buster the Dog by Gordon Boshell. Text copyright © 1972 by Gordon Boshell. Illustrations copyright © 1972 by Pat Dypold. Reprinted by permission of J. Philip O'Hara. ■ **OXFORD UNIVERSITY PRESS (London).** Sidelight excerpts and illustrations from *American Notes and Pictures from Italy* by Charles Dickens./ Sidelight excerpts from *The Speeches of Charles Dickens* edited by K.J. Fielding. Copyright © 1960 by Oxford University Press./ Illustration by K.M. Peyton from *Pennington's Heir* by K.M. Peyton. Copyright © 1973 by K.M. Peyton. All reprinted by permission of Oxford University Press (London). ■ **PANTHEON BOOKS.** Illustration by Peggy Wilson from *Ananse the Spider* by Peggy Appiah. Copyright © 1966, by Peggy Appiah./ Illustration by Charles Keeping from *Flood Warning* by Paul Berna. Copyright © 1962 by The Bodley Head Co. Copyright © 1960 by Paul Berna./ Illustrations by Hans Baumhauer from *The Wonderful Adventures of Nils* by Selma Lagerlöf. Copyright 1947 by Pantheon Books, Inc./ All reprinted by permission of Pantheon Books. ■ **PARENTS' MAGAZINE PRESS.** Illustration by Denman Hampson from *Never Tease a Weasel* by Jean Conder Soule. Copyright © 1964 by Parents' Magazine Press. Reprinted by permission of Parents' Magazine Press. ■ **PENGUIN BOOKS, LTD.** Illustration by Anthony Colbert from *Round About and Long Ago* by Eileen Colwell. Text copyright © 1972 by Eileen Colwell. Illustrations copyright © 1972 by Longman Young Books./ Illustration by Ludek Pesek from *The Ocean World* by Peter Ryan. Illustrations © 1973 by Ludek Pesek. Both reprinted by permission of Penguin Books, Ltd. ■ **S.G. PHILLIPS, INC.** Jacket design by Simon Jeruchim from *Ossian House* by A.C. Stewart. Copyright © 1976 by S.G. Phillips, Inc. Reprinted by permission of S.G. Phillips, Inc. ■ **PRENTICE-HALL, INC.** Illustration by Bruce Waldman from *Skunks* by Bernice Kohn Hunt. Copyright © 1973 by Bernice Kohn Hunt. Illustrations © 1973 by Prentice-Hall, Inc. Reprinted by permission of Prentice-Hall, Inc. ■ **G.P. PUTNAM'S SONS.** Illustration by Tran Mawicke from *Major Andre: Brave Enemy* by Lois Duncan. Copyright © 1969 by Lois Duncan./ Illustration by Portia Takakjian from *Pocahontas* by Patricia Miles Martin. Illustrations © 1964 by Portia Takakjian. Both reprinted by permission of G.P. Putnam's Sons. ■ **RAND McNALLY AND CO.** Illustration by Milo Winter from *A Christmas Carol* by Charles Dickens. Copyright 1922 by Rand McNally & Co./ Illustration by Leonard Vosburgh from *Billy Yank and Johnny Reb: How They Fought and Made Up* by Earl Schenck Miers. Copyright © 1959 by Earl Schenck Miers. Copyright 1959 under International Copyright Union by Earl Schenck Miers. Both reprinted by permission of Rand McNally and Co. ■ **RANDOM HOUSE, INC.** Illustration by Michael K. Frith from *Animals Do the Strangest Things* by Leonora and Arthur Hornblow. Copyright © 1964 by Random House./ Illustration by Carolyn Cather from *The Shy One* by Dorothy Nathan. Copyright © 1966 by Dorothy Nathan./ Illustration by Carolyn Cather from *Women of Courage* by Dorothy Nathan. Copyright © 1964 by Dorothy Nathan. All reprinted by permission of Random House, Inc. ■ **HENRY REGNERY CO.** Sidelight excerpts from *Laura: The Life of Laura Ingalls Wilder* by Donald Zochert. Copyright © 1976 by Donald Zochert. Reprinted by permission of Henry Regnery Co. ■ **ROUTLEDGE AND KEGAN PAUL, LTD.** Illustration by Dorothy P. Lathrop from *Hitty: Her First Hundred Years* by Rachel Field. Copyright, 1929, by Macmillan Publishing Co. Copyright renewed 1957 by Arthur S. Pederson. Reprinted by permission of Routledge and Kegan Paul, Ltd. ■ **CHARLES SCRIBNER'S SONS.** Illustration by Thomas Fogarty from *People from Dickens* arranged by Rachel Field. Copyright, 1935, by Charles Scribner's Sons./ Sidelight excerpts from *Arthur Rackham, His Life and Work* by Derek Hudson. Copyright © 1960 by Derek Hudson./ Drawing by Lise Gladstone from *The Guess and Spell Coloring Book* by May Swenson. Copyright © 1976 by May Swenson. All reprinted by permission of Charles Scribner's Sons. ■ **SIMON AND SCHUSTER, INC.** Sidelight excerpts from *Charles Dickens: His Tragedy and Triumph* by Edgar Johnson (vol. 1). Copyright, 1952, by Edgar Johnson./ Illustration by F.A. Fitzgerald from *The Tenth Life of Osiris Oaks* by Wally Cox and Everett Greenbaum. Text copyright © 1972 by Wally Cox and Everett Greenbaum. Illustrations copyright © 1972 by F.A. Fitzgerald. Both reprinted by permission of Simon and Schuster, Inc. ■ **SOUTHERN ILLINOIS UNIVERSITY PRESS.** Sidelight excerpts from *Padraic Colum: A Biographical-Critical Introduction* by Zack Bowen. Copyright © 1970 by Southern Illinois University Press. Reprinted by permission of Southern Illinois University Press. ■ **STANMORE PRESS.** Illustration by Simon Stern from *Grummit the Dragon* by Honour Stern. Copyright © 1965 by Honour Stern. Reprinted by permission of Stanmore Press. ■ **STERLING PUBLISHING CO.** Illustration by Joyce Behr from *Biggest Riddle Book in the World* by Joseph Rosenbloom. Copyright © 1976 by Joseph Rosenbloom. Reprinted by permission of Sterling Publishing Co. ■ **THE VANGUARD PRESS.** Illustration by Louis Slobodkin from *Peter the Great* by Nina Brown Baker. Copyright 1943 by Nina Brown Baker./ Illustration by Helene Carter from *The Gulf Stream* by Ruth Brindze. Copyright © 1945, 1972 by Ruth Brindze./ Illustration by Louis Slobodkin from *The Magic Fishbone* by Charles Dickens. Copyright 1953 by Louis Slobodkin and Vanguard Press, Inc. All reprinted by permission of The Vanguard Press. ■ **THE VIKING PRESS.** Sidelight excerpts from *Father, Dear Father* by Ludwig Bemelmans./ Sidelight excerpts from *Hotel Bemelmans* by Ludwig Bemelmans./ Illustration by Ludwig Bemelmans from *Madeline* by Ludwig Bemelmans. Copyright 1939 by Ludwig Bemelmans. Copyright renewed 1967 by Madeleine Bemelmans and Barbara Bemelmans Marciano./ Illustration by Ludwig Bemelmans from *Madeline and the Bad Hat* by Ludwig Bemelmans. Copyright 1956 by

Ludwig Bemelmans./ Illustration by Arthur Rackham from *Mother Goose Nursery Rhymes.* Published in 1975 by The Viking Press. All reprinted by permission of The Viking Press. ■ **FRANKLIN WATTS, INC.** Illustration by Charles Keeping from *Weirdies, Weirdies, Weirdies,* selected by Helen Hoke. Copyright © 1973 by Franklin Watts, Ltd./ Illustration by Ted Schroeder from *Politics* by Patricia Maloney Markun. Copyright © 1970 by Franklin Watts, Inc. Both reprinted by permission of Franklin Watts, Inc. ■ **WEATHERVANE BOOKS.** Illustrations by Arthur Rackham from *Tales from Shakespeare* by Charles and Mary Lamb. Copyright © 1975 by Crown Publishers. Reprinted by permission of Weathervane Books (a division of Barre Publishing Co., Inc.) ■ **ALBERT WHITMAN AND CO.** Illustration by Fred Irvin from *Best in Camp* by Mike Neigoff. Copyright © 1969 by Albert Whitman & Co./ Illustration by Judith Vigna from *The Little Boy Who Loved Dirt and Almost Became a Superslob* by Judith Vigna. Text and illustrations copyright © 1975 by Judith Vigna. Both reprinted by permission of Albert Whitman and Co. ■

Illustration by Richard Bennett from *Where the Winds Never Blew* by Padraic Colum. Copyright, 1940 by Padraic Colum. Reprinted by permission of Mr. Emmett Greene./ Illustration by Hugh Lofting from *Doctor Dolittle in the Moon,* told by Hugh Lofting. Copyright 1928 by Frederick A. Stokes Co. Reprinted by permission of Christopher Lofting./ Photograph from *Beauty Millionaire--The Life of Helena Rubinstein* by Maxine Fabe. Copyright © 1972 by Maxine Fabe. Reprinted by permission of Helena Rubinstein, Inc./ Sidelight excerpts from *The Book of Sunnybank* by Albert Payson Terhune. Copyright, 1934, by Albert Payson Terhune./ Sidelight excerpts from *To the Best of My Memory* by Albert Payson Terhune. Copyright, 1930, by Albert Payson Terhune./ Both reprinted by permission of Albert Payson Terhune, Inc./ Illustration from *Historical Catastrophes: Earthquakes* by Billye Walker Brown and Walter R. Brown. Text copyright © 1974 by Billye Walker Brown and Walter R. Brown. Illustrations copyright © 1974 by The U.S. Geological Survey Library. Reprinted by permission of The U.S. Geological Survey Library./ Illustration by Arthur Rackham from *Aesop's Fables.*/ Illustration by Arthur Rackham from *Poor Cecco* by Margery Bianco./ Illustration by Arthur Rackham from *Alice's Adventures in Wonderland* by Lewis Carroll. Published by Doubleday, Page, 1907./ Photograph from *Arthur Rackham* by Fred Gettings. Copyright © 1975 by Fred Gettings./ Illustration by Arthur Rackham from *A Christmas Carol* by Charles Dickens./ Illustration by Arthur Rackham from "The Robber Bridegroom" in *Grimm's Fairy Tales,* translated by Mrs. Edgar Lucas./ Illustration by Arthur Rackham from "Old Sultan" in *Grimm's Fairy Tales,* translated by Mrs. Edgar Lucas./ Illustration by Arthur Rackham from *Rip Van Winkle* by Washington Irving./ Illustrations by Arthur Rackham from *Mother Goose, The Old Nursery Rhymes.* Published by Heinemann, 1913 (also published in 1975 by the Viking Press as *Mother Goose Nursery Rhymes.*)/ Illustration by Arthur Rackham from *The Night Before Christmas* by Clement C. Moore. Published by J.B. Lippincott, Philadelphia./ Illustration by Arthur Rackham from *Peter Pan in Kensington Gardens* by J.M. Barrie. Copyright © 1975 by Barre Publishing Co./ Illustration by Arthur Rackham from *Some British Ballads.* All reprinted by the kind permission of Mrs. Barbara Edwards.

We want to extend special thanks to Marilyn Horowitz and Claire K. Leishman of The Terhune Sunnybank Memorial Fund for the use of photos and movie stills of Albert Payson Terhune.

PHOTOGRAPH CREDITS

J.R.L. Anderson: Ivor Fields; Ludwig Bemelmans: Tony Venti; Joanne E. Bernstein: Michael Bernstein; Anthony Colbert: Cliff Hopkinson; Billye Walker Cutchen: Paul Cutchen; Monica Hughes: John E. Brownlee Studios; Hope Jordan: Dave Jordan; Hilary Knight: Otto Maya; Carol Korty: Jamie Cope; William Lipkind: William Vandivert; Seon Manley: Gogo Lewis; Robert W. McKay: *Columbus Dispatch*; Katherine Milhous: Free Library of Philadelphia; Don Miller: Suzanne Poor; Else Holmelund Minarik: Bradford Bachrach; Tunie Munson: Ken Munson; Ruth Nichols: *The Citizen*; Ademola Olugebefola: Norma McMichael; George Panetta: Jay Folb; May Swenson: Martha Sanders.

SOMETHING ABOUT THE AUTHOR

LECLAIRE ALGER

ALGER, Leclaire (Gowans)   1898-1969
(Sorche Nic Leodhas)

PERSONAL: Born May 20, 1898, in Youngstown, Ohio; daughter of Louis Peter Gowans; married Amos Risser Hoffman, 1916 (died, 1918); married second husband several years later; children: (first marriage) Louis. *Education:* Graduated from Carnegie Library School, 1929.

CAREER: Author and librarian. Began writing as a child; started as a page with the Carnegie Library of Pittsburgh, 1915; worked for the New York Public Library, 1921-25; later employed as a librarian in several branches of the Carnegie Library, 1929-66; retired as a librarian to devote her full time to a writing career, 1966. *Awards, honors:* Runner-up for Lewis Carroll Shelf Award, 1962, for *Thistle and Thyme;* runner-up for Newbery Medal, 1963, for *Thistle and Thyme; All in the Morning Early,* illustrated by Evaline Ness, was a runner-up for the Caldecott Medal, 1964; *Always Room for One More,* illustrated by Nonny Hogrogian won the Caldecott Medal, 1966.

WRITINGS: Jan and the Wonderful Mouth Organ (illustrated by Charlotte Becker), Harper, 1939; *Dougal's Wish* (illustrated by Marc Simont), Harper, 1942; *The Golden Summer* (illustrated by Aldren Watson), Harper, 1942.

Under pseudonym Sorche Nic Leodhas: (Editor) *Heather and Broom: Tales of the Scottish Highland* (illustrated by Consuelo Joerns), Holt, 1961; (editor) *Thistle and Thyme: Tales and Legends from Scotland* (illustrated by Evaline Ness), Holt, 1962; *All in the Morning Early* (illustrated by E. Ness), Holt, 1963; *Gaelic Ghosts* (illustrated by Nonny Hogrogian), Holt, 1963; *Ghosts Go Haunting* (illustrated by N. Hogrogian), Holt, 1965; *Always Room for One More* (illustrated by N. Hogrogian), Holt, 1965; (editor) *Claymore and Kilt: Tales of Scottish Kings and Castles* (illustrated by

They wailed for a while in the heather, as glum as a grumpetie grouse. ■ (From *Always Room for One More* by Sorche Nic Leodhas. Illustrated by Nonny Hogrogian.)

Leo and Diane Dillon), Holt, 1967; *Sea-Spell and Moor Magic: Tales of the Western Isles* (illustrated by Vera Bock), Holt, 1968; *Kellyburn Braes* (illustrated by E. Ness), Holt, 1969; *The Laird of Cockpen* (illustrated by Adrienne Adams), Holt, 1969; (editor) *A Scottish Song Book* (illustrated by E. Ness), Holt, 1969; (editor) *By Loch and by Lin: Tales from Scottish Ballads* (illustrated by V. Bock), Holt, 1969; *Twelve Great Black Cats, and Other Eerie Scottish Tales* (illustrated by V. Bock), Dutton, 1971.

SIDELIGHTS: Many of Leclaire Alger's writings were based on old Scottish folk tales passed down through oral tradition. The author preferred to collect and retell folklore which had never been previously published. Her skill in researching and adapting the tales into modern English has been highly praised by literary critics. In reviewing her first collection of folklore, *Heather and Broom,* a critic for the *Chicago Sunday Tribune* noted, "Even television has not

learned to spin richly imaginative adventures to match those . . . from the storyteller's heart. . . ." One year later, Alger came out with *Thistle and Thyme,* a second collection of tales from Scotland. "In a worthy companion to her *Heather and Broom,*" wrote a *Library Journal* critic, "the author tells further Scottish legends. . . . The same deft artistry, magical elements, humor, and suspense season these nicely woven stories. . . ."

In addition to Gaelic folklore, the author's works have also been influenced by folk songs from Scotland. Alger's *Room for One More* was derived from the Scottish folk song about Lachie MacLachlan whose kind hospitality and open heart proved more than his small house could hold. Alice Dalgliesh, writing for the *Saturday Review* noted, "This amusing song with its music has a wisely modified dialect. . . . Children should have fun with the song." Alger gathered information from old Scottish ballads for her *By Loch and by*

Lin. "These good yarns of braw lads and bonnie lasses gleam with lessons, magic, chivalry, trickery, wisdom and adventure," commented a critic for the *Christian Science Monitor.*

Alger's last work was *Twelve Great Black Cats and Other Eerie Scottish Tales.* A *Horn Book* reviewer observed, "[The tales] are told with a fine feeling for the dramatic as well as for the eerie, and with a rhythm and swing that makes them excellent for storytelling. . . . [The] tales are varied, readable, and tellable." In reviewing the same book, a critic for *Library Journal* wrote, "Some of the stories . . . are spine-tingling; others . . . are characterized by rowdy humor. All are the work of an accomplished storyteller."

FOR MORE INFORMATION SEE: Doris de Montreville and Donna Hill, editors, *Third Book of Junior Authors,* H. W. Wilson, 1972.

(Died November 14, 1969)

ANDERSON, J(ohn) R(ichard) L(ane) 1911-

PERSONAL: Born June 17, 1911, in Georgetown, British Guiana; son of James H. E. and Gertrude M. L. (Hanbury) Anderson; married Phyllis E. Huggins, 1933 (divorced); married Helen Elizabeth Matthews, June 12, 1954; children: (first marriage) Richard; (second marriage) David, Timothy, Ricarda Jane. *Education:* Educated at St. Edmund's School, Canterbury, England. *Politics:* "No party politics." *Religion:* Church of England. *Home:* Wick Cottage, Charney Bassett, Wantage, Oxfordshire, England. *Agent:* George Greenfield, John Farquharson Ltd., 15 Red Lion Sq., London W.C.1, England.

CAREER: Journalist on *News Chronicle,* London, then on *Guardian* (formerly *Manchester Guardian*) in Manchester; returned to London for *Guardian,* and became assistant editor; retired, 1967. *Military service:* British Army, Royal Artillery, 1939-41, seconded to Royal Garhwal Rifles, Indian Army, 1941-44, war correspondent attached to Supreme Headquarters, Allied Expeditionary Force, Europe, 1944-45; became captain.

WRITINGS: The Lost Traveller, Elkin Matthews, 1931; (editor) *History on the Road,* Hamish Hamilton, 1954; *The Greatest Race in the World,* Hodder & Stoughton, 1964; *Vinland Voyage,* Funk, 1967; *East of Suez,* Hodder & Stoughton, 1969; *The Ulysses Factor,* Hodder & Stoughton, 1970, Harcourt, 1971; *The Upper Thames,* Methuen, 1971; *Reckoning in Ice,* Gollancz, 1972; *Death on the Rocks,* Gollanz, 1973, Stein & Day, 1975; *The Discovery of America* (juvenile), Penguin, 1973; *The Vikings* (juvenile), Penguin, 1974; *Death in the Thames,* Gollanz, 1974 Stein & Day, 1975; *The Nine-Spoked Wheel,* Gollanz, 1974; *Death in the North Sea,* Gollanz, 1975, Stein & Day, 1976; *The Ridgeway,* Wildwood House, 1975; *Discovering History* (juvenile), Gollancz, 1975; *Redundancy Pay,* Gollanz, 1976, published in the United States under the title, *Death in the Channel,* Stein & Day, 1976; *Death in the Desert,* Gollanz, 1976; *Death in the City,* Gollanz, 1977; *Death in the Caribbean,* Gollanz, 1977.

SIDELIGHTS: "I write, I suppose, mainly to earn a living, but there is more to it than that. I had a rather lonely childhood, being sent to England to go to school while my parents were in South America, and I kept myself going by telling

J.R.L. ANDERSON

myself stories. These were mostly adventure stories of one sort and another, and my novels are simply this kind of story brought up to date. I didn't write a novel until I was sixty. I didn't have time because I was working as assistant editor of *The Guardian* newspaper, and being involved in a newspaper I didn't so much need to tell myself stories. I retired from the paper in 1967 because I wanted time to write some books—not then novels, but my topographical, historical and somewhat philosophical books. The novels came after them.

"My children's books are all historical, and are written from the experience of helping to bring up my own four children. History has always seemed to me the most fascinating subject in the world, but the children used to complain that the history they learned at school was dull. My books try to make bits of history interesting for children. I'm particularly proud that my book on *The Vikings* (written by a Scots-Englishman, I am half and half) has been translated into Danish and Swedish, and my *Discovery of America* into Italian."

Anderson, who has sailed small boats all his life, set out from England in a 44-foot cutter with a crew of five during the summer of 1966 to duplicate the first Norse colonizing voyage of Leif Ericson to North America. *Vinland Voyage* is an account of the 4,000-mile trip via Iceland and Greenland to Martha's Vineyard off Cape Cod.

APPIAH, Peggy   1921-

PERSONAL: Born May 21, 1921, in England; daughter of Stafford (a British cabinet minister) and Isobel (Swithenbank) Cripps; married Joe E. Appiah (a barrister and solicitor), July 18, 1954; children: Anthony, Isobel, Adwoa, Abena. *Education:* Attended Maltman's Green School and Whitehall Secretarial College. *Religion:* Christian. *Home*

When he saw the lizard he was very surprised, for no one had thought the lizard capable of finding out anything. The Chief spoke through his linguist: "You have come to claim the hand of my daughter. If you are wrong in naming her, the executioner is ready to chop off your head." ■ (From *Ananse the Spider* by Peggy Appiah. Illustrated by Peggy Wilson.)

address: P.O. Box 829, Kumasi, Ashanti, Ghana. *Agent:* David Higham Associates, 76 Dean St., London W.1, England.

CAREER: Worked as research assistant in British Ministry of Information, London, England, as secretary for Racial Unity, London, and as youth representative for the British Council of Churches, London; Kumasi Children's Home, Kumasi, Ashanti, Ghana, chairman of advisory committee, 1968—. *Member:* Zonta International (Kumasi unit), Ghana Historical Society, Ghana Wildlife Society, Society for the aid of Mentally Retarded Children, Ashanti branch of Ghana Worker's Association.

WRITINGS: Ananse the Spider (folk tale), Pantheon, 1966; *Tales of an Ashanti Father* (folk tales), Deutsch, 1967; *The Pineapple Child and Other Tales from Ashanti,* Deutsch, 1969; *Children of Ananse,* (juvenile), Evans Brothers, 1969; *A Smell of Onions,* Longmans, Green, 1971; *Why Are There So Many Roads?* Pilgrim Books (Nigeria), 1972; *Gift of the Mmoatia* (children's book) Ghana Publishing Corp., 1973; *A*

Dirge too Soon, Ghana Publishing Corp., 1976; *Ring of Gold* (juvenile), Deutsch, 1976; *Why the Hyena Doesn't Care for Fish, and other Tales from Ashanti Gold Weights,* Deutsch, 1977.

WORK IN PROGRESS: Ashanti Goldweights, their proverbs and folk lore for the Ghana Publishing Corporation.

SIDELIGHTS: "During my life I have been lucky to visit many parts of the world. As a child I went to Jamaica with my family and spent holidays in Ireland, Scotland and Germany. I studied history of art in Italy before the last world war and during the war travelled to Russia where my father was Ambassador, crossing Canada with a stop in the Rocky Mountains, and going through Japan and Korea and across the trans-Siberian railway to Moscow. Later, when the Germans attacked Russia, I worked for the army which was running the Iranian railways. After the war, I travelled in France, Switzerland and Denmark. I went with my mother to China, travelling some 30,000 miles and going from the corner of the Gobi desert, to Moukden, Peking, Shanghai and many other places. We visited Mao Tse Tung's headquarters, then in Yenan. On our way back we stayed in Delhi where we met Jawarlal Nehru and his daughter Indira Gandhi. Everywhere I made friends. Some have managed to visit us here in Ghana, others I have kept in touch with or met on my travels back to England.

"On visiting a new country the first thing I really want to do is to explore the country-side. I love all the small details, seeing where plants grow and working out which ones are growing in the wrong place. I love the excitement of wondering what is round the next corner when one explores a new bit of forest or woodland. I can never be bored in the country or a garden.

"When I first came to Ghana I was disappointed by the flowers though the flowering trees were beautiful. On the ground, most of the flowers are small and hidden in the leaves which shoot up at a terrific speed. But the insects are wonderful and there are such a variety from brilliant butterflies and moths to tiny creatures that look so like seeds that you have to push them to see what they are; there is the voracious preying mantis and big spiders, black and orange like a tiger. One can spend hours watching ants of every size; tiny bees make honey in the window frames and ghekos hunt moths on the ceiling.

"My main hobby is collecting Ashanti goldweights, their stories and proverbs. They are made of brass in every possible shape from animals to guns, birds to insects, peanuts to people, sieves to spades and were used for weighing the gold which was the main form of currency until the introduction of money. I started going to the villages to ask questions about them. I love going into the compounds and seeing all the details of village life. The old people are wonderful storytellers and their best stories are about animals and birds. When they start talking all the children gather round, the chickens run in and out between legs and the whole courtyard rocks with laughter. Everyone is important, which is one reason why I like them so much. In town some people get sort of lost.

"I find writing stories something like life in a village. There are not too many people at a time and one can keep track of their movements. I usually start my story with some incident which strikes me; then the people take over, as they do in real life. Sometimes they don't do at all what I expect. I find it difficult to cut down on the incidents and in deciding which to keep. Just as in real life one's characters are doing things all the time and you have to pick out the relevant actions. I'm always being told 'keep to the story.' But stories in life don't have a beginning and an end!

"Sometimes I play with the children a game which is great fun. We start with a sentence like 'the red-haired woman crossed the road on a camel.' Then we each have to go on with the story, deciding why she was there, where she came from, where she was going and what for—building up a whole imaginary world. This keeps one's imagination flexible and able to use any incidents that turn up.

"Ghana is good for writing because one never knows what is going to happen from day to day. The unexpected is always turning up and life sometimes takes on the quality of a grown-up fairy story. I have always loved fairy stories and folk tales, so I'm never surprised by events. One learns to laugh with people over all sorts of things, even if one should not, and to enjoy even what is sad because it is shared with other people. The main pleasure in life is sharing things with people and that is why I enjoy writing.

"My four children are now growing up. Anthony is a philosopher and poet, Isobel is studying economics, Adwoa, science, and Abena, the youngest, hopes to be a nurse. Although we are often apart, we are a united family. My husband is an expert on foreign affairs and works for the Government as a commissioner and special adviser to the Head of State. He has always encouraged me to write. The house has always been full of children and young people so that I can try out my ideas and it is the children who have enabled me to keep alive the sense of wonder and enjoyment which makes me able to write."

HOBBIES AND OTHER INTERESTS: Arts, crafts, handwork, history, social anthropology, social welfare, church work, studying Asante culture and history, encouraging school drama, and the working in every way for international understanding and peace and the improvement of human and race relationships.

FOR MORE INFORMATION SEE: Christian Science Monitor, May 4, 1967; *Times Literary Supplement,* October 16, 1969.

ASBJÖRNSEN, Peter Christen   1812-1885

PERSONAL: Surname is pronounced As-*byurn*-sen; born January 15, 1812, in Kristiania (now Oslo), Norway; died January 1, 1885, in Kristiania, Norway; son of Anders (a glazier) and Thurine Elizabeth (Bruun) Asbjörnsen. *Education:* Attended the local University (now Oslo University), beginning, 1837; later studied forestry in Germany and Austria, 1856-58.

CAREER: Folklorist, zoologist, and naturalist. Became a private tutor, 1833; began collecting folklore with his friend, Jörgen Möe, 1837; later travelled throughout Norway as a marine zoologist; served as a chief forester, Trondheim district (Norway), 1860-64; retired from forestry, 1876.

WRITINGS—Folktales, except as noted: (And editor with Jörgen Möe) *Nor,* [Kristiania, Norway], 1837; (editor with J. Möe) *Norske Folkeeventyr* ("Norwegian Folk Tales"), [Kristiania], 1841-44, revised edition, 1851; *Norske Huldreeventyr og Folkesagn* ("Norwegian Fairy Tales and Folk

PETER CHRISTEN ASBJÖRNSEN

Legends"), [Kristiania], 1845-47; *Jule: Traeet for 1852,* [Kristiania], 1852; *Juletraeet 1866,* J. Dybwad (Kristiania), 1866; *Anton Rosing* (biography), C. Johnsen (Kristiania), 1869; *Eventyrbog for Boern,* [Kristiania], 1883-97, translation by Hans Lien Braekstad published as *Fairy Tales from the Far North* (illustrated by Erik Werenskiold and Theodor Kittelsen), D. Nutt, 1897, Blue Ribbon Book, circa 1932.

Collected editions of folktales in English translation appear in variously titled editions, including the following: *Popular Tales from the Norse* (translated by George Webbe Dasent), D. Appleton, 1859, reprinted, Johnson Reprint, 1970 [another edition illustrated by William Stobbs, Bodley Head, 1969]; *Tales from the Fjeld* (translated by G. W. Dasent), Chapman & Hall, 1874 [another edition illustrated by John Moyr Smith, Putnam, 1908, reprinted, Blom, 1970]; *'Round the Yule Log: Christmas in Norway* (translated by H. L. Braekstad), Sampson Low, 1881, Estes & Lauriat, 1895; *Christmas Fireside Stories: Norwegian Folk and Fairy Tales,* Sampson Low, 1923; *Norwegian Folk Tales* (translated by Pat Shaw Iversen and Carl Norman; illustrated by E. Werenskiold and T. Kittelsen), Viking Press, 1960; *Favorite Fairy Tales Told in Norway* (edited by Virginia Haviland; illustrated by Leonard Weisgard), Little, Brown, 1961; *A Time for Trolls: Fairy Tales from Norway* (edited and translated by Joan Roll-Hansen), J. G. Tanum (Oslo), 1962.

Single tales published separately or as title stories of collections: *Princess of Glass Hill, and Other Fairy Stories* (ed-

He had heard tell of a maiden who was both comely and fair, excellent at keeping house, and a great hand at cooking. ▪ (From *Norwegian Folk Tales* by Peter Christen Asbjörnsen and Jörgen Möe. Illustrated by Erik Werenskiold.)

"Well, mind and hold tight by my shaggy coat, and then there's nothing to fear," said the Bear, so she rode a long, long way. ■ (From *East of the Sun and West of the Moon* by P.C. Asbjörnsen. Illustrated by Kay Nielsen.)

"Look here, lasses," he said; "you must go upstairs and dress the bay mare as a bride. I expect the master wants to give the guests a laugh." ■ (From *The Squire's Bride* by P.C. Asbjörnsen. Illustrated by Marcia Sewell.)

ited and translated by G. W. Dasent), J. Birch, 1905; *The Blue Belt, and More Fairy Stories* (edited and translated by G. W. Dasent), J. Birch, 1906; *Shortshanks: The Giant Killer, and Other Fairy Stories* (edited and translated by G. W. Dasent), J. Birch, 1906; *East o' the Sun and West o' the Moon* (edited by Gudran Thorne Thomsen; illustrated by Frederick Richardson), Row, Peterson, 1912, revised edition, 1946 [another edition edited and translated by G. W. Dasent, Hodder & Stoughton, 1914, Putnam, 1917; other editions illustrated by Kay Nielsen, Doran, 1922; Hedwig Collin, Macmillan, 1923; Ingri and Edgar Parin d' Aulaire, Viking, 1938, reissued, 1969; Walter Seaton, Junior Deluxe Editions, 1957].

Mother Roundabout's Daughter (translated by G. W. Dasent), Oxford University Press, 1918; *The Sheep and the Pig Who Went into the Woods to Live by Themselves,* C. E. Graham, 1929; *"Doodle Doo" the Rooster Who Fell into the Pea Soup,* C. E. Graham, 1929; *The Three Billy Goats Gruff* ("De Tre Bukkne Bruse"; adapted by Alice

O'Grady and Frances Throop; illustrated by Tony Brice), Rand McNally, 1940 [other editions illustrated by Marcia Brown, Harcourt, 1957; Dale Maxey, Whitman Publishing, 1966; William Stobbs, McGraw, 1968; Paul Galdone, Seabury, 1973]; *The Christmas Visitors: A Norwegian Folktale* (adapted and illustrated by Jeanette Winter), Pantheon, 1968; *The Man Who Was Going to Mind the House* ("Manden Som Skulde Stelle Hjemme"; adapted and illustrated by David McKee), Abelard, 1973; *The Squire's Bride* (illustrated by Marcia Sewall), Atheneum, 1975.

Also author of numerous scholarly papers and textbooks in the field of natural science, forestry, peatmaking, and dietetics.

ADAPTATIONS—Movies and filmstrips: "Peer Gynt" (motion pictures), Oliver Morosco Photoplay Co., 1915, David Bradley, starring Charlton Heston, 1941, revised edition, 1965; "Peer Gynt Suite" (motion picture; Music to Remember series), Columbia Pictures, 1950; "Peer Gynt"

(From "The Three Billy Goats Gruff" by P.C. Asbjörnsen, produced by Weston Woods.)

(filmstrip), Jam Handy Organization, 1953; "Peer Gynt: Suites 1 and 2 by Edvard Grieg" (filmstrip; with teacher's guide and phonodiscs), Educational Audio Visual, 1963.

"The Three Billy Goats Gruff" (filmstrips), Curriculum Films (with teacher's guide), 1946, revised edition, Curriculum Materials Corp., 1957, Jam Handy Organization, 1955, Weston Woods Studios, 1963, Society for Visual Education (with teacher's guide and phonodisc), 1966, Brunswick Productions (language teaching films in French and Spanish), 1967, Educational Projections Corp. (with teacher's guide), 1968, Cooper Films and Records (with teacher's guide and phonodisc), 1968, Universal Education and Visual Arts (with teacher's guide), 1969, Coronet Instructional Films (with teacher's guide and phonodisc), 1970, Encyclopaedia Britannica Educational Corp. (with teacher's guide and phonodisc), 1973.

Other adaptations: Henrik Ibsen, *Peer Gynt: Et Dramatisk Digt,* [Kjoebenhavn, Norway], 1867, translation by William and Charles Archer, published as *Peer Gynt: A Dramatic*

Poem, Walter Scott, 1892, new edition, edited by James W. McFarlane, Oxford University Press, 1970; "Peer Gynt Suites I and II," composed by Edvard Grieg, 1876; first performed in Kristiania, Norway, February 24, 1876.

SIDELIGHTS: **January 15, 1812.** Born in Kristiania (now Oslo), Norway. Went to school in the capital, but he was rather lazy and much preferred to watch life in nature.

1827. Sent to a private school in Ringerike to study towards his matriculation examination. There Asbjörnsen met and formed a life-long friendship with Jörgen Möe (who later became a lyric poet and Bishop of Kristiansand). The two were entirely different types; Möe was nervous, sensitive, and inclined to melancholy, while Asbjörnsen was jovial and easygoing.

During their teen years, they developed an intense interest in the collection of local folk tales and fairy stories. A collaboration of research resulted in a collection of hundreds of traditional tales during their fishing and walking tours in the mountains, valleys and pastures of their native

(From the stage production of "Peer Gynt" by P.C. Asbjörnsen, adapted by Henrik Ibsen, and starring Joseph Schildkraut. Courtesy of the N.Y. Public Library Theatre Collection.)

Norway. Möe's sense of style and Asbjörnsen's instinct for oral tradition provided a happy combination and was to earn them the title of "Fathers of Norwegian Literature."

Asbjörnsen's studies were delayed by his father's bankruptcy and the ensuing miserable living conditions of the family.

1833. Passed his examination, after which he held positions as a private tutor in the province.

1837. *Nor* published. Asbjörnsen contributed some folk tales and Möe a poem.

Enrolled at the University in the capital where he studied mostly natural sciences.

1841. First volume of their *Norske Folkeeventyr* (Norwegian Folk Tales) appeared. A new volume was added each year through 1844.

1856-58. Studied forestry in Germany and Austria.

1860-64. Served as chief forester in the Trondheim district.

January 1, 1885. Died in Kristiania, Norway.

FOR MORE INFORMATION SEE: (For children) Elizabeth Rider Montgomery, *Story behind Great Stories,* Mc-

Bride, 1947; Stanley J. Kunitz, editor, *European Authors: 1000-1900,* H. W. Wilson, 1967; Brian Doyle, editor, *Who's Who of Children's Literature,* Schocken, 1968; *Children's Book Illustration,* Graphis Press, 1975.

ATWATER, Montgomery Meigs 1904-

PERSONAL: Born October 21, 1904, in Baker City, Oregon; son of Maxwell W. (a mining engineer) and Mary (a writer and designer; maiden name, Meigs) Atwater; married Joan Hamill, May, 1956. *Education:* Harvard University, B.S., 1926.

CAREER: Author and avalanche specialist. Began writing after graduating from college; held various jobs as athletic director, fur farmer, cattle rancher, and guide; joined the U.S. Forest Service to research avalanche control at the end of the second World War; retired from the Forest Service to become a private consultant on snow and avalanche problems, 1964. *Military service:* Joined the U.S. Army, 1942; supervised a military ski and winter warfare school, 10th Mountain Division, Camp Hale, Colorado; commanded a reconnaissance unit in Europe, 87th Infantry Division.

WRITINGS: Government Hunter (illustrated by Fred C. Rodewald), Macmillan, 1940; *Flaming Forest* (illustrated by R. Farrington Elwell), Little, Brown, 1941; *Ski Patrol,* Random House, 1943; *Hank Winton, Smokechaser* (illustrated by E. Joseph Dreany), Random House, 1947; (with Sverre Engen) *Ski with Sverre: Deep Snow and Packed Slope Ski*

MONTGOMERY MEIGS ATWATER

Technique, New Directions, 1947; *Smoke Patrol,* Random House, 1949; *Avalanche Patrol,* Random House, 1951; *Rustlers on the High Range,* Random House, 1952; *Cattle Dog,* Random House, 1954; *The Trouble Hunters,* Random House, 1956; *The Ski Lodge Mystery,* Random House, 1959; *Snow Rangers of the Andes,* Random House, 1957; *The Avalanche Hunters* (introduction by Lowell Thomas), Macrae Smith, 1968; *The Forest Rangers,* Macrae Smith, 1969.

Also author (with F. C. Koziol) of *The Alta Avalanche Studies* and the *Avalanche Handbook,* United States Forest Service, 1953.

SIDELIGHTS: A *New York Times* book review said of Atwater's *Avalanche Patrol,* "[with its elements of] . . . mystery and up-to-date outdoor adventure . . . should have wide appeal." In reviewing the same book, the *Saturday Review* noted that the author's background knowledge plus ". . . an ability to create convincing characters make this an unusually good adventure tale." The *Library Journal,* however, in reviewing *Ski Lodge Mystery* found that it had ". . . good information about the snow phase of the Ranger Service, but [that] the characters lack depth . . ."

FOR MORE INFORMATION SEE: Muriel Fuller, editor, *More Junior Authors,* H. W. Wilson, 1963; Frances Valentine Wright, editor, *Who's Who among Pacific Northwest Authors,* Pacific Northwest Library Association, 1969.

AYER, Margaret

PERSONAL: Born in New York City; daughter of Ira (a physician) and Louise (Foster) Ayer; married A. Babington Smith. *Education:* Educated at the Philadelphia Museum School of Industrial Art, and in private studios in Paris and Rome. *Home:* Castro Valley, Calif.

CAREER: Author and illustrator of books for young people. *Member:* Society of Illustrators, Women's National Book Association, and the Artist's Guild (past vice-president).

WRITINGS—All self-illustrated: *Magic Window,* Crowell, 1933; *The Wish That Went Well,* Abelard Press, 1952; *Getting to Know Thailand,* Coward-McCann, 1959, reissued, 1972; *Made in Thailand,* Knopf, 1964; *Animals of Southeast Asia,* St. Martin's, 1970.

Illustrator: Phyllis A. Sowers, *Under the Japanese Moon,* Page, 1937; Walter C. Fabell, *Nature Was First,* Grosset, 1939; Mary B. Hollister, *Pagoda Anchorage: A Story of the Tea Clipper Days in China,* Dodd, 1939; P. A. Sowers, *Lin Foo and Lin Ching: A Boy and Girl of China,* Cadmus, 1940; Julia L. Hahn, editor, *Story Way,* Houghton, 1940; P. A. Sowers, *Sons of the Dragon,* Whitman, 1942; Siddie J. Johnson, *New Town in Texas,* Longmans, Green, 1942; Dorothy Christian and R. C. Wheeler, *Rainbow Stories,* Pacific, 1943; Anna C. Chandler, *Dragons on Guard,* Lippincott, 1944; Margaret Landon, *Anna and the King of Siam,* Day, 1944; Martha L. Poston, *Girl without a Country,* Nelson, 1944; Jean Bothwell, *Little Boat Boy: A Story of Kashmir,* Harcourt, 1945; D. Christian and R. C. Wheeler, *Around the World Stories,* Pacific, 1945.

J. Bothwell, *River Boy of Kashmir,* Morrow, 1946; Maribelle Cormack and P. L. Bytovetzski, *Underground Retreat,* McKay, 1946; J. Bothwell, *Thirteenth Stone: A Story of Rajputana,* Harcourt, 1946; Frances F. Wright, *Secret of*

MARGARET AYER

the Old Sampey Place, Abingdon-Cokesbury, 1946; Judith Ish-Kishor, *Adventure in Palestine: The Search for Aleizah,* Messner, 1947; J. Bothwell, *Star of India,* Morrow, 1947; (for children) M. Landon, *Anna and the King,* Day, 1947; Grace W. McGavran, *Fig Tree Village,* Friendship Press, 1947; Marie McSwigan, *Juan of Manila,* Dutton, 1947; Ethel T. Anderson, *Scarlet Bird,* Nelson, 1948; J. Bothwell, *Empty Tower,* Morrow, 1948; F. F. Wright, *Number Eleven Poplar Street,* Abingdon-Cokesbury, 1948; Elizabeth L. Reed, *Let's Go to Nazareth,* Presbyterian Board of Christian Education, 1948; Robbie Trent, *Star Shone,* Presbyterian Board of Christian Education, 1948; P. A. Sowers, *Elephant Boy of the Teak Forest,* Messner, 1949; J. Bothwell, *Little Flute Player,* Morrow, 1949; Genevieve Cross, *Fawn and the White Mountain Press,* Cross, 1949; Muriel Fuller, editor, *Favorite Old Fairy Tales,* Nelson, 1949.

E. T. Anderson, *Rainbow Campus,* Nelson, 1950; J. Bothwell, *Onions without Tears,* Hastings House, 1950; J. Bothwell, *Peter Holt,* Harcourt, 1950; Chester Bryant, *Lost Kingdom,* Messner, 1951; J. Bothwell, *Paddy and Sam,* Abelard-Schuman, 1952; F. F. Wright, *Poplar Street Park,* Abingdon-Cokesbury, 1952; J. Bothwell and P. A. Sowers, *Golden Letter to Siam,* Abelard-Schuman, 1953; J. Bothwell, *Borrowed Monkey,* Abelard-Schuman, 1953; J. Bothwell, *Red Barn Club,* Harcourt, 1954; Malcolm Hyatt and W. Fabell, *Gilbert and Sullivan Song Book,* Random House, 1955; J. Bothwell, *Cal's Birthday Present,* Abelard-Schuman, 1955; J. Bothwell and P. A. Sowers, *Ranch of a Thousand Horns,* Abelard-Schuman, 1955; Catherine O. Pears, *Jules Verne: His Life,* Holt, 1956; Eight books, color illustrations, biblical subjects, for C. R. Gibson Co., 1953-1954. Ayer also wrote many short stories, serials, and articles for children's magazines.

SIDELIGHTS: "My husband and I owned a home near Westport, Conn., on three acres, bordered by a stream,

The Clemens children had the whole out-of-doors to run in—barefoot. No shoes all summer! ▪ (From *Mark Twain: His Life* by Catherine O. Peare. Illustrated by Margaret Ayer.)

where we went to live when my husband retired. When the winters became too much for his health we came to California. I still live there in Castro Valley since his death.

"At present I am not writing or illustrating, but am painting pictures which I sell through a gallery.

"My full color illustrations are in water color or flat color separations on acetate, as are my book jackets. The black and white pictures are often pen and ink as it is the cheapest to reproduce, or crayon pencil, reproduced either as line cut or full tone. The pictures vary from full page illustrations to chapter headings and decorative spots.

"In reading a book to illustrate, I keep notes of where to find descriptions of characters and objects when I need them when I select the parts to illustrate. These should be well spaced and the pictures, when finished, should all be in proportion to each other. And they should be on time as promised."

Margaret Ayer spent most of her childhood in Mexico and the Philippine Islands, where her father was a doctor. She always wanted to be an artist, and considered the box of paints she received from her mother to be the best gift ever. Many of her paintings were exhibited in Bangkok where she lived when her father was advisor in Public Health to Thailand, Penang, and Singapore, and several were purchased by the King of Siam. The money she earned from these paint-

ings brought her to New York to do free-lance illustrations. Her special knowledge of the Orient helped her to get started in that field.

FOR MORE INFORMATION SEE: Bertha M. Miller and others, compilers, *Illustrators of Children's Books, 1946-1956,* Horn Book, 1958; (for children) Muriel Fuller, editor, *More Junior Authors,* H. W. Wilson, 1963; *Horn Book,* August 1964.

BAKER, Nina (Brown) 1888-1957

PERSONAL: Born December 31, 1888, in Galena, Kansas; died September 1, 1957, in Brooklyn Heights, New York; daughter of Frank and Belle (Warren) Brown; married Sydney J. Baker (a business executive), 1915; children: Berenice, Nina. *Education:* University of Colorado, student, 1909-11. *Home:* Brooklyn, New York.

CAREER: Author. Began working as a teacher in Galena, Kansas; later taught for one year in a small Colorado town; worked for a short time in an insurance office; began her literary career by contributing short stories to magazines; worked briefly at writing scenarios for silent films. *Member:* Authors' Guild, Women's National Book Association.

WRITINGS—Fiction; all published by Lothrop, except as noted: *The Secret of Hallam House: A Mystery Story for Girls* (illustrated by F. J. Butters), 1931; *The Chinese Riddle: A Mystery Story for Girls* (illustrated by J. Clemens Gretta), 1932; *The Ranee's Ruby* (illustrated by Erick Berry), 1935; *The Luck of the Salabars,* W. A. Wilde, 1937; *Inca Gold,* W. A. Wilde, 1938; *The Cinderella Secret,* 1938; *Mystery at Four Chimneys* (illustrated by Ruth King), 1939.

NINA BROWN BAKER

Nonfiction: *He Wouldn't Be King: The Story of Simon Bolivar* (illustrated by Camilo Egas), Vanguard, 1941 [adaptation published as *Simon Bolivar*, edited by William Kottmeyer, Webster, 1947]; *Juarez: Hero of Mexico* (illustrated by Marion Greenwood), Vanguard, 1942 [adaptation under same title by W. Kottmeyer, Webster, 1949, reissued, 1972]; *Peter the Great* (illustrated by Louis Slobodkin), Vanguard, 1943; *Garibaldi* (illustrated by L. Slobodkin), Vanguard, 1944; *Lenin* (illustrated by L. Slobodkin), Vanguard, 1945; *Sun Yat-sen* (illustrated by Jeanyee Wong), Vanguard, 1946; *William the Silent*, Vanguard, 1947; *Robert Bruce: King of Scots*, Vanguard, 1948; *Ten American Cities: Then and Now* (illustrated by Josephine Haskell), Harcourt, 1949.

Sir Walter Raleigh, Harcourt, 1950; *Cyclone in Calico: The Story of Mary Ann Bickerdyke*, Little, Brown, 1952; *The Story of Abraham Lincoln* (illustrated by Warren Baumgartner), Grosset, 1952; *The Story of Christopher Columbus* (illustrated by David Hendrickson), Grosset, 1952; *Pike of Pike's Peak* (illustrated by Richard Powers), Harcourt, 1953; *Nickels and Dimes: The Story of F. W. Woolworth* (illustrated by Douglas Gorsline), Harcourt, 1954; *Texas Yankee: The Story of Gail Borden* (illustrated by Alan Moyler), Harcourt, 1955; *Amerigo Vespucci* (illustrated by Paul Valentine), Knopf, 1956; *Big Catalogue: The Life of Aaron Montgomery Ward* (illustrated by A. Moyler), Harcourt, 1956; *Nellie Bly* (illustrated by George Fulton), Holt, 1956, reissued, Scholastic Book Service, 1972; *Juan Ponce de Leon* (illustrated by Robert Doremus), Knopf, 1957; *Henry Hudson* (illustrated by G. Fulton), Knopf, 1958.

SIDELIGHTS: **Born December 31, 1888.** Born in Galena (a lead-mining camp), Kansas, of pioneer covered-wagon stock. Went to public school in Galena.

1907. Sold a story to *Good Housekeeping* for $25. The check was accompanied by a letter asking for more of her work. But after a second story was rejected, Baker gave up the idea of becoming a short-story writer.

1909-1911. Attended the University of Colorado "just long enough to get the credits I needed for a teacher's certificate.

"I thought it would be fun to teach a rural school in western Colorado. I was engaged by letter and arrived to find that the tiny mountain town consisted of a school, a general store, and a blacksmith shop. The pupils rode in on horseback from ranches as much as twelve miles away. The first day of school was also my first day on a horse. I rode seven miles from the ranch that had taken me in, but I walked home, leading the creature. I didn't know how to get on him by myself, and I thought it would impair my dignity to ask the children for help. I'd thought the Western life would be fun, and after I got used to it, it was. But it took some getting used to."

Her experiences at Alison included living in a one-room shack, chopping wood for her stove, and carrying water from a frozen pond, with the temperature at 22 degrees below zero.

Attended a business school in Kansas City with the idea of teaching shorthand and typing in her home town later. Her first taste of city life, however, settled her future; she never went back to Galena.

The clown pranced up, seized General Shein's beard, and snipped it off. ■ (From *Peter the Great* by Nina Brown Baker. Illustrated by Louis Slobodkin.)

1915. Married Sydney J. Baker, a business executive, and settled in the Midwest. It was during her life in Omaha, while her husband was traveling and her children were small, that Baker began to write in earnest. "I'd always meant to be a writer some day, but I didn't begin very early. It's so much easier just to talk about it! Then one Christmas my husband gave me a portable typewriter, and I had no more excuses. So I started, as almost everyone does, with short stories and rejections and tears. If there's an easier way, I didn't find it. I sold my first story to a church school magazine, and after that I had pretty good luck. But I found I liked writing books better than short stories, so I concentrated on them. I wrote seven mystery stories for young people before I began the series of biographies I'm doing now."

1931. *The Secret of Hallam House*, a mystery story for girls, published.

1938. Moved to New York with family.

1941. First biography, *He Wouldn't Be King*, published, which won the Intra-American Award of the Society for the Americas. "I like biographies best of all. I particularly

Over the shirts went homemade jackets of thick wool, cut down from Father's old ones! Hand-knitted stocking caps and mittens and enormous wool neckscarves completed the picture. ■ (From *Nickels and Dimes: The Story of F.W. Woolworth* by Nina Brown Baker. Illustrated by Douglas Gorsline.)

like the subjects I've chosen, heroes of other lands. I think it's really necessary, if we're to have One World, for us to know how other nations got the way they are, what their people are like, and what they want. To me the most interesting way to acquire this knowledge is through the lives of their great men, because that way you get a good story too.''

1943. *Peter the Great* published. Phyllis A. Whitney considered it ''lively and entertaining every inch of the way. There is a magic, to Nina Brown Baker's storytelling that whisks you swiftly into another age and country and carries you into the very feeling of another day.''

The author put a tremendous amount of research into each of her books, reading for six months before she began to write. She made an outline of dates and events, and studies of the characters ''who are going to be around all the way through.'' Then for some four months she spent the best part of the day at the typewriter. There was one revision.

September 1, 1957. Died in Brooklyn Heights, New York.

FOR MORE INFORMATION SEE: Current Biography Yearbook 1947; Stanley J. Kunitz, editor, *Junior Book of Authors,* revised edition, H. W. Wilson, 1951; *Obituaries—New York Times,* September 3, 1957; *Publishers Weekly,* September 16, 1957; *Wilson Library Bulletin,* November, 1957; *Current Biography Yearbook 1957.*

BAUERNSCHMIDT, Marjorie   1926-

PERSONAL: Born November 19, 1926, in Baltimore, Md.; daughter of John G. and Rena (Henzler) Bauernschmidt; married Edward F. Barnhart (a telecommunications engineer), September 4, 1948; children: Nancy (Mrs. Michael Barron), Katherine (Mrs. James O'Brien). *Education:* Wilson College, Chambersburg, Pa., B.A., 1947. *Home:* 1849 Loudon Heights Road, Charleston, W. Va. 25314.

CAREER: Hamburgers Men's Department Store, Baltimore, Md., assistant advertising manager, 1949-55; Westerville Public Library, Westerville, Ohio, assistant librarian, 1969-70; Richard's Book Nook, Columbus, Ohio, sales clerk, 1974-75.

ILLUSTRATOR: Elizabeth Hudnut, *You Can Always Tell a Freshman,* Dutton, 1948; Lillian Morrison, *Yours Till Niagara Falls,* Crowell, 1950; Peggy Goodin, *Take Care of My Little Girl,* Dutton, 1950; Lillian Morrison, *A Diller, A Dollar,* Crowell, 1955; Lillian Morrison, *Remember Me When This You See,* Crowell, 1961.

MARJORIE BAUERNSCHMIDT

SIDELIGHTS: "My first illustrations were self-portraits, decorating letters to friends while I was recovering from a serious bout with pneumonia. The emaciated little character conceived of then became the basis for illustrations for *You Can Always Tell a Freshman,* which Elizabeth Hudnut and I created during our senior year at Wilson College. I have had no professional art training and do not think of myself as an artist. 'Seeing the funny side of things' has been a great help to me in my career as a housewife and mother . . . as well as in the side-line of book illustration."

FOR MORE INFORMATION SEE: Illustrators of Children's Books, 1946-1956, Horn Book, 1958.

What brings the monster's babies?
Frankenstork.
▪ (From *Biggest Riddle Book in the World* by Joseph Rosenbloom. Illustrated by Joyce Behr.)

BEHR, Joyce   1929-

PERSONAL: Born December 18, 1929, in New York, N.Y., *Education:* Attended Cartoonists and Illustrators School (now School of Visual Arts), New York, N.Y., 1948; Pratt Institute, 1949-51. *Office:* 159 West 33rd Street, New York, N.Y. 10001.

CAREER: Free-lance cartoonist, 1949-54; free-lance illustrator, 1955—. *Exhibitions:* Society of Illustrators, 1960. *Awards, honors:* Society of Illustrators Yearbook, "Illustrators '60."

ILLUSTRATOR: Joseph Rosenbloom, *Biggest Riddle Book in the World,* Sterling, 1976; Joseph Rosenbloom, *Dr. Knock-Knock's Official Knock-Knock Dictionary,* Sterling, 1976; Steve Morgenstern, *Calculator Puzzles Tricks and Games,* Sterling, 1976; Joseph Rosenbloom, *Daffy Dictionary: Funabridged Definitions From Aardvark to Zuider Zee,* Sterling, 1977; Deidra Sanders and other, *Would You Believe This Too?,* Sterling, 1977; Eckstein and Gleit, *The Best Joke Book for Kids,* Avon, 1977; Joseph Rosenbloom, *The Gigantic Joke Book,* Sterling, 1977. Work has appeared in *Times, Sports Illustrated, Ladies' Home Journal, Reporter, New York Times.*

SIDELIGHTS: "I work in line, or line and color. I was influenced by many artists at different periods and for different assignments."

BEMELMANS, Ludwig   1898-1962

PERSONAL: Born April 27, 1898, in Meran, Tirol, Austria (now part of Italy); came to United States in 1914, naturalized in 1918; died October 1, 1962; buried in Arlington, Virginia; son of Lambert (a Belgian painter) and Frances (Fisher) Bemelmans; married Madeline Freund, November, 1935; children: Barbara. *Education:* Attended public and private schools in Austria before dropping out at age sixteen. *Home:* New York City.

CAREER: Writer, humorist, illustrator, painter, and author of books for children. Worked in hotels and restaurants, 1914-17 and after World War I, finally becoming a waiter, and later part owner of Hapsburg House on New York's East Side. Designed settings for a Broadway play and did an

Remember the moon
Remember the stars,
Remember the night
We smoked cigars.
▪ (From *Remember Me When This You See* by Lillian Morrison. Illustrated by Marjorie Bauernshmidt.)

LUDWIG BEMELMANS

unsuccessful comic strip for the New York *World*. *Military service:* U.S. Army during World War I, as an attendant in a mental hospital and instructor of German-speaking recruits. *Awards, honors:* Caldecott Medal, 1953, for *Madeline's Rescue; New York Times* Choice for Best Illustrated Children's Books of the Year, 1953, for *Madeline's Rescue,* and 1955, for *Parsley; New York Herald Tribune* Children's Spring Book Festival Award, 1950, for *Sunshine,* and 1957, for *Madeline and the Bad Hat; Golden Basket* was a runner-up for the Newbery Medal, 1937; *Madeline* was a runner-up for the Caldecott Medal, 1940; all of the "Madeline" books have been selections of the Junior Literary Guild and included in *Children's Catalog.*

WRITINGS: *Small Beer,* Viking, 1939, reissued, Capricorn Books, 1961; *At Your Service: The Way of Life in a Hotel,* Row, Peterson, 1941; *Hotel Splendide,* Viking, 1941, reissued, 1963; *Rosebud,* Random House, 1942; *I Love You, I Love You, I Love You* (short stories), Viking, 1942; *Now I Lay Me Down to Sleep* (novel), Viking, 1943; *Hotel Bemelmans* (autobiographical short stories), Viking, 1946; *Dirty Eddie* (novel), Viking, 1947; *A Tale of Two Glimps,* Columbia Broadcasting System, 1947; *The Eye of God* (novel), Viking, 1949; *Father, Dear Father* (autobiographical), Viking, 1953; *To the One I Love Best,* Viking, 1955; *The World of Bemelmans: An Omnibus,* Viking, 1955; *The Woman of My Life,* Viking, 1957; *My Life in Art,* Harper, 1958; *How to Have Europe All to Yourself,* European Travel Commission, 1960; *Are You Hungry, Are You Cold,* World Publishing, 1960; *Marina,* Harper, 1962; *On Board Noah's Ark,* Viking, 1962; *The Street Where the Heart Lies,* World Publishing, 1963.

All self-illustrated: *My War with the United States,* Viking, 1937; *Life Class,* Viking, 1938; *The Donkey Inside,* Viking, 1941; *The Blue Danube,* Viking, 1945; *The Best Times: An Account of Europe Revisited,* Simon & Schuster, 1948; *How to Travel Incognito,* Little, Brown, 1952; *The Happy Place,* Little, Brown, 1952; *The High World,* Harper, 1954; *Italian Holiday,* Houghton, 1961.

For children; all self-illustrated: *Hansi,* Viking, 1934, reissued, 1966; *The Golden Basket,* Viking, 1936; *Quito Express,* Viking, 1938, reissued, 1965; *The Castle Number Nine,* Viking, 1937; *Madeline,* Simon & Schuster, 1939, reissued, Viking, 1969; *Fifi,* Simon & Schuster, 1940; *Sunshine: A Story about the City of New York,* Simon & Schuster, 1950; *Madeline's Rescue,* Viking, 1950, reissued, 1973; *Parsley* (an earlier version appeared in *Womans Day* under the title, "The Old Stag and the Tree"), Harper, 1955; *Madeline and the Bad Hat,* Viking, 1956, reissued, 1968; *Madeline and the Gypsies,* Viking, 1959, reissued, 1973; *Madeline in London,* Viking, 1961, reissued, 1972.

Other: (Illustrator) Munro Leaf, *Noodle,* F. A. Stokes, 1937, reissued, Four Winds, 1969; (illustrator) Leonard J. Mitchell, *Lüchow's German Cookbook,* Doubleday, 1952; (contributor) *Best of Modern Humor,* edited by Pelham G. Wodehouse and Scott Meredith, Washburn, 1952; (contributor) "In Defense and Praise of Brooklyn: II," in *Empire City: A Treasury of New York,* edited by Alexander Klein, Rinehart, 1955; (compiler and illustrator) *Holiday in France,* Houghton, 1957; (contributor) "The Borrowed Christmas," in *Hallmark Christmas Festival,* edited by Carl Beier, Compass Productions, 1959; *Welcome Home!* (from a poem by Beverley Bogert; originally appeared in *Mademoiselle* under the title, "Randy"), Harper, 1960; *La Bonne Table* (selections), edited by Donald and Eleanor Friede, Simon & Schuster, 1964.

Contributor of articles and stories to periodicals, including *New Yorker, Vogue, Town and Country,* and *Stage.*

ADAPTATIONS—Movies and filmstrips: "Yolanda and the Thief" (motion picture), Metro-Goldwyn-Mayer, 1945; "Madeline" (motion pictures; 35mm), Columbia Pictures, 1952, re-released in 16mm, International Film Bureau, 1955; "Madeline's Rescue" (motion picture; both 35mm and 16mm), Rembrandt Films, 196?; "Madeline's Rescue" (filmstrip; color, with picture-cued text), Weston Woods Studios, 1961; "Madeline and the Bad Hat" (motion picture), Rembrandt Films, 1960, released by Macmillan Films, 1973; "Madeline and the Gypsies" (motion picture), Rembrandt Films, 1960, released by Macmillan Films, 1973; "Madeline and the Gypsies" (filmstrip; color, sound version in both record and cassette, with a teacher's guide), H. M. Stone Productions, 1972; "Sunshine" (motion picture), Rembrandt Films, 1960, released by Macmillan Films, 1973.

Recordings: "Hansi, Parsley, Marina and Welcome Home," four stories read by Carol Channing, Caedmon, 1977.

SIDELIGHTS: **April 27, 1898.** Born in Meran, Tirol, Austria. Father, **L**ambert Bemelmans, a painter. Mother, Frances Fisher, daughter of a wealthy brewery owner.

Due to his father's frequent absences Bemelmans was raised by his mother's family. "I was born in a hotel in Meran, a small city in Tirol, and I spent the first years of my life in a beer garden. An old maitre d'hôtel was my nurse, and the chef himself made up my formula. The beer garden was in Regensburg. Regensburg is a Bavarian city on the banks of the Danube, and it possesses one of the finest Gothic cathedrals. When I was little it had about sixty thousand inhabitants, first among whom was the Duke of Thurn und Taxis. He lived in a castle which it took fifteen minutes to pass; it stood in a park that encircled the city. The Duke retained the Spanish etiquette at his court; his servants wore livery and powdered wigs; he rode about in gilded coach cradled in saffron leather and drawn by white horses. He supported several jewelers, the city's theater, a private orchestra, and the race track.

"Grandfather's brewery stood on a square facing the Duke's theater, in the oldest part of the town. His daughter, my mother, was born in Regensburg and was educated at the convent at Alt Oetting. Grandfather loved the city.

"My father did not. He called it the cloaca of the world, but with a broader, more Bavarian word, which in Regensburg is used frequently as a term of rough endearment among friends. And so he went to Munich whenever he could escape from Regensburg; and when he could not, he walked out to the railroad station at least one evening a week. When all the other people went to the breweries, he would walk up and down the station platform until the signal bell announced the approach of the fast train from Paris. This train stopped for three minutes in Regensburg, and in that time my father would lean over the iron barrier and look into the bright windows of the dining car, over which brass letters spelled out the elegant phrase Compagnie des Wagons-Lits et Express Europeens, and under which were a coat of arms and the word Mitropa, in carved wood. There he hung, drinking in the perfume, looking at the furs, at the few fortunate people who were walking up and down and climbing into the carmine-upholstered compartments. He would wait until the red signal lamp at the end of the train had slid down over the narrowing rails and disappeared around a curve on its way to Vienna. When he came back he would complain of Regensburg's houses, its people, its way of life.

"He was not altogether wrong, for it was a small provincial town, slow and gossipy. Regensburg went to sleep at nine in the evening, its surrounding country was without much excitement or good scenery, and I disliked it chiefly because I had to attend the Lyceum there and all my professors came to eat in the restaurant of Grandfather's brewery, so that he was always informed that I would not pass the examinations, that I was unruly, impertinent, never serious, always late, and kept bad company." [Ludwig Bemelmans, *Hotel Bemelmans,* Viking, 1946.[1]]

After unsuccessful attendance at the Lyceum in Regensburg and a private academy in Rothenburg, he was taken out of school and "apprenticed out" to his hotel-owning uncle. This experiment was also unsuccessful. His final confrontation was a hotel manager who struck him. Bemelmans retaliated with assault with a gun. His family then gave him the choice of reform school or immigration to America. At sixteen years of age, he chose America.

1914. Arrived in the United States armed and ready for hostile Indians. "I had read of them in the books of Karl May and Fenimore Cooper, and intently hoped for their presence without number on the outskirts of New York City.

(From the movie "Yolanda and the Thief," starring Fred Astaire and Lucille Bremer. Copyright 1945 by Metro-Goldwyn-Mayer.)

"I wanted to paint New York as soon as I arrived at Ellis Island. . . . Then, one day I came upon a child painting in Gramercy Park—he was painting in the spirit of sheer fun. I had discovered the secret."

Worked in the dining rooms of exclusive New York Hotels—the Astor, the McAlpin, the Ritz-Carleton. Constantly drawing everything that surrounded him.

"My first job in New York, at the Hotel Astor, did not last long. I filled water bottles and carried out trays with dishes, until I broke too many. So with my uncle's second letter I went to the Hotel McAlpin, where I got a job that lasted a year, at the end of which I spoke passable English, though I was still little better than a bus boy.

"Here I wore for breakfast a white suit, yellow shoes, and, suspended in front of me on a thick leather strap, a silver machine, hot and the size of a baby's coffin. For three hours every morning I walked around the men's cafe, with the heavy silver coffin hanging before me. It contained in a lower compartment two heated bricks, and above on a wire net an assortment of hot cross buns, muffins, biscuits, croissants, and every other kind of rolls, soft and hard."[1]

A co-worker suggested: "For God's sakes, don't stay a waiter! If you can't be a cartoonist, be a streetcleaner, a dishwasher, anything. But don't be an actor or a waiter. It's the most awful occupation in the world. The abuse I have taken, the long hours, the smoke and dust in my lungs and eyes, and the complaints—ah, c'est la barbe, ce métier. My boy, profit by my experience. Take it very seriously, this cartooning."[1]

And lo and behold, the former Barbarian
Turned into a Vegetarian.
■ (From *Madeline and the Bad Hat* by Ludwig Bemelmans. Illustrated by the author.)

He bought a *"how-to"* book on cartooning. "The book said keep a number of sharpened, very soft pencils handy for your work. I did, and for a while I was almost the only waiter who had a pencil when a guest asked for one. 'And remember,' said the book, 'you can never be expert in caricaturing people unless you shake off the fear of drawing people.' I tried to shake off the fear. 'Most people like to have their own pictures drawn,' Mespoulets read solemnly. 'Regular-featured people should be avoided, as they are too simple to draw. Your attention should be concentrated on the faces with unique features.'"[1]

Studied at a German artist's studio. "Thaddeus was a splendid teacher. Many of his students were poor and paid him no money, but he was equally attentive to all of them. He would go rapidly from pupil to pupil, explaining constructions, pointing out a wrong line, sketching large graphic models of nose, lips, ear, to help them understand. He never made fun of a student no matter how bad the drawing. To a man in front of a sheet of paper containing a scribbly design of a broken stick with five fingers on the end of it, he would say slowly: 'Look, it's an arm; its bones are here and there, here they meet; here is muscle; here are veins and ligaments; this is soft shoulder; here is a joint—you can lift a rock with it and throw it, you can scratch your back with it, push the hair back from your forehead, lean on it, you can talk with it and with the fingers on the end of it. Think about all that, and try again.' If, after all the trying, nothing came of it, and the pupil was not a beautiful girl, Thaddeus told him quietly and definitely to go and try no more, that it was hopeless.

"My happiest moment every morning was when I came here from the hotel. I felt as if I had come on a little vacation to the mountains. Thaddeus spoke my language, he understood me and offered me refuge from the hotel. Here was freedom and integrity and good work. All my troubles would leave me on the ride down to the studio. But also this work was making my other life, the life of the Splendide, tolerable, for I was learning to see.

"For in the hotel too there is design; not in its elegant rooms, not in the fashionable people, but in the shoes of Otto Brauhaus, in such guests as the wife of the Steel Judge, in our frightened old waiters, in the hands of cooks—fat fingers sliding around the inside of pots buttering them, sitting together on a carrot and slowly feeding it to the chopping knife. There is color in the copper casseroles and in the back of Kalakobé, the Senegalese Negro who scrubs them in a white-tiled scullery.

"All this I was learning to see for the first time as I spent my mornings in the studio, and that is all I did there. For I never drew a line in that art class. I couldn't. I saw my picture clearly, simply; I saw it finished with my line and with my colors; but the moment I started to draw, a paralysis overcame me; the fear of doing it wrong made a knot of me inside.

"Thaddeus understood this; he had looked at all my work before I came to his school; he knew my problem, and he said: Just sit and look, drink it up and don't worry. It will form itself.

It is finished inside of you. I can't help you much, nobody can. The colors, the design, the line, are all your own, you yourself must get them out.'

"This was a bitter pleasure, a fragile, glasslike feeling. The urge to give something form would run down to my elbows

or my wrists and get stuck there the moment my hand tried to work. But sometimes in the middle of the night, or at a moment when I was not thinking of effort, as when I waited for an elevator in the hotel and was scribbling something simple on the wall—a chair, a table, a shoe, a face—then it was suddenly there, right and good. I needed no one to tell me that it was so. But down in the studio I would be frozen again. Though I watched the model for three hours every morning and could draw her from memory, I was never able to break the spell."[1]

1918. Became a naturalized U.S. citizen.

Enlisted in the U.S. Army during the First World War and was sent to Camp Gordon, Georgia. Attendant in a mental hospital and instructor of German-speaking recruits.

1925. Operated his own restaurant in New York City, Hapsburg House, for three years. Gradually won some success as an artist, illustrating books.

1934. *Hansi,* his first book, published. A story of the Austrian Tyrol.

He often said his writing was the direct result of insomnia and if he could sleep well he would never write again.

1935. Married Madeline Freund. Did settings for a Broadway play.

1937. *Quito Express* published—as a result of a trip to Ecuador.

1939. *Madeline* published. "There is one life that is more difficult than that of the policeman's and that is the life of the artist.

"I have repeatedly said two things that no one takes seriously, and they are that first of all I am not a writer but a painter, and secondly that I have no imagination. It is very curious that, with my lack of these important essentials, the character of Madeline came to be. It accounts perhaps for her strength; she insisted on being born. Before she came into the world, I painted. That is, I placed canvas or paper on an easel before me and made pictures. I found in this complete happiness and satisfaction.

"The unfortunate thing about painting is that the artist must exhibit, and at exhibitions, along with his work, exhibit himself; that he has to see his work, which is as his children, sold; see it wrapped up and taken away. I felt sorry for many of my pictures and those of other painters. I wish that there were a way of acquiring dogs or paintings other than by walking into a store and paying for them. The art market, then, the faces of the people who come and look at pictures, the methods of arriving at success, which entail self-advertisement and the kissing of hands, were not my dish.

"I looked for another way of painting, for privacy; for a fresh audience, vast and critical and remote, to whom I could address myself with complete freedom. I wanted to do what seemed self-evident—to avoid sweet pictures, the eternal still lifes, the pretty portraits that sell well, arty abstractions, pastoral fireplace pictures, calendar art, and surrealist nightmares.

"I wanted to paint purely that which gave me *pleasure,* scenes that interested me; and one day I found that the audience for that kind of painting was a vast reservoir of impres-

In two straight lines they broke their bread. ▪ (From *Madeline* by Ludwig Bemelmans. Illustrated by the author.)

sionists who did very good work themselves, who were very clear-eyed and capable of enthusiasm. I addressed myself to children.

"You will notice in *Madeline* that there is very little text and there is a lot of picture. The text allows me the most varied type of illustration: there is the use of flowers, of the night, of all of Paris, and such varied detail as the cemetery of *Père la Chaise* and the Restaurant of the *Deux Magots*. All this was there waiting to be used, but as yet Madeline herself hovered about as an unborn spirit.

"Her beginnings can be traced to stories my mother told me of her life as a little girl in the convent of Altoetting in Bavaria. I visited this convent with her and saw the little beds in straight rows, and the long table with the washbasins at which the girls had brushed their teeth. I myself, as a small boy, had been sent to a boarding school in Rothenburg. We walked through that ancient town in two straight lines. I was the smallest one, but our arrangement was reversed. I walked ahead in the first row, not on the hand of Mademoiselle Clavel at the end of the column.

"All this, as I said, for many years hung in the air and was at the back of my mind. Madeline finally began to take shape in France, where I had gone to paint. My daughter Barbara was about Madeline's age when we went to the Isle d'Yeu for a summer vacation. This was then an island without pretensions, and has since become famous as the place of detainment of Marshal Pétain. There was the usual *Hôtel des Voyageurs* and the *Café de la Marine*. The house we rented was twenty-five dollars for the season. It had its own private beach and the beds were always full of sand. A few miles away lived a man who owned a few lobsterpots and a fishing boat, and I bicycled there regularly to buy the makings of a *bouillabaisse* or a fish stew.

"One day, pedaling along the road home with the sack of seafood over my shoulder, both hands in my pockets, and tracing fancy curves in the roadbed, I came to a bend which was hidden by some pine trees. Around this turn, coming the other way, raced the island's only automobile—a four horse-power Super Rosengart belonging to the baker of Saint Sauveur, the capital village on the island. This car was a fragrant, flour-covered breadbasket on wheels. I collided with it, and it threw me in a wide curve off the bicycle into a bramble bush. I had taken the car's doorhandle off with my arm and I was bleeding. I asked the baker to take me to the hospital in Saint Sauveur, but he said that according to French law, a car that has been involved in an accident has to remain exactly where it was when the crash occurred so that the gendarmes can make their proper deductions and see who was on the wrong side of the road. I tried to change his mind, but he said: 'Permit me *alors, Monsieur;* if you use language like that it is no use at all to go on with this conversation.'

"Having spoken, he went to pick up his *pain de ménage* and some *croissants* that were scattered on the road, and then he spread the branches of the thicket to look for the handle of his Super Rosengart. I took my lobsters and went to the hospital on foot.

"After I had waited for a time, an old doctor came, with a cigarette stub sticking to his lower lip. He examined my wound, cleaned it, and then with a blunt needle he wobbled into my arm. '*Excusez moi,*' he said, 'but your skin is very, very tough.' I was put into a small, white, carbolicky bed, and it took a while for my arm to heal. Here were the stout

sister that you see bringing the tray to Madeline, and the crank on the bed. In the room across the hall was a little girl who had had an appendix operation, and, standing up in bed, with great pride she showed her scar to me. Over my bed was the crack in the ceiling 'That had the habit, of sometimes looking like a rabbit.' It all began to arrange itself. And after I got back to Paris I started to paint the scenery for the book. I looked up telephone numbers to rhyme with appendix. One day I had a meeting with Léon Blum, and if you take a look at the book, you will see that the doctor who runs to Madeline's bed is the great patriot and humanitarian Léon Blum.

"And so Madeline was born, or rather appeared by her own decision.

"[In the] sequel . . . Madeline shares the pages with a dog. This dog came about in a strange way. My wife's parents live in Larchmont, and in a house next door to them is a family of outwardly respectable folk—that is, no one in that solid community would suspect that this quiet and respectable surburban house was occupied by a poet. Her name is Phyllis McGinley and she writes for *The New Yorker*.

"She has two little girls, and they said, 'Why don't you write another *Madeline?*' So I offered them fifty cents apiece if they would give me an Idea, for I was paralyzed with lack of imagination. The children did not even go out of the room. They came with hands held out, and after I paid them they stated the plot: 'There's a dog, see—Madeline has a dog. And then the dog is taken away but it comes back again, maybe with puppies so all the girls can have dogs.'

"That was right and clever dramatic construction, and now there remained the dog to find. I said, 'What kind of a dog?'

"'Oh, any kind of a dog.'

"I went back to Paris and started to look for any kind of a dog. And of that breed Genevieve is a member.

"I had a studio at the time in a house on the Seine at number one *Git de Coeur,* and I walked down to the quay and promenaded along there. Under one of the bridges there lived an old man with his dog. He loved it very much and he combed its fur with the same comb he did his own hair, and they sat together watching the fishermen and the passing boats. I started to draw that dog, and observed it. It loved to swim.

"I now had the dog and I sat along the Seine, and thought about the new book. But as yet there wasn't a plot I could use, and the little girls who might have done it for me were in America.

"Then one day something happened. An object was floating down the Seine, and little boys ran along the quay, and as the object came near it turned out to be an artificial leg. One of the little boys pointed at it and said, '*Ah, la jambe de mon Grandpère!*'

"At that same moment a long line of little girls passed over the bridge *des Arts,* followed by their teacher. They stopped and looked, holding onto the iron rails with their white-gloved hands. The leg was now very close, and the dog jumped into the Seine and retrieved it, struggling ashore and pulling it from the water by backing up the stones.

"There suddenly was a great vision before me. The plot was perfect." [*Caldecott Medal Books: 1938-1957,* edited by

(From "Madeline" by Ludwig Bemelmans, produced by Learning Corporation of America.)

Bertha Mahony Miller and Elinor Whitney Field, The Horn Book, Inc., 1957.[2]]

1946. On a trip in the Austrian Tyrol with his young daughter, he was taken seriously ill. "One day, as I was slowly recuperating, lying quietly and covered with blankets in my chair on the terrace, Barbara said, 'Poppy, if you had died, would you have wanted to be buried here?'

"I said, 'No, I don't want to be buried here. I want to be cremated and taken to America.'

"''And what would you want to have done with the ashes?'

"''The ashes you can put in a shoebox and take back to New York with you, and then one very cold and freezing day you can take them and spread them over the ice on the sidewalk in front of Lane Bryant's or any other good maternity shop.'

"Children don't like levity in matters of life and death—she ran off to play with the dogs." [Ludwig Bemelmans, *Father, Dear Father,* Viking, 1953.[3]]

On another occasion—a European train trip—she questioned his ethics. "'. . . you fall in love with your characters,

and they all turn mushy and nobody is really bad—they're just odd. In fact, sometimes the bad are much more lovable than the good. And now that I come to think of it, almost always. Anyway, it's not social satire.'

"''Well, maybe it's not social satire but comedy of manners—and in a world in which there are less and less manners, especially among the young, it's a very hard thing to write. As for hating people, I'm sorry, but I find it hard to hate anybody, and impossible to hate anybody for long.'

"''That's what Mother says. She says you love too many people.'

"''What else does Mother say?'

"''She says that you're very fortunate.'

"''Why?'

"''Because everything that makes you happy can be bought.'

"I listened to the 'ta-dang, ta-dang, ta-dang' of the wheels and hoped Barbara would go to sleep.

"'Poppy, are you still awake?'

"'Yes. What else?'

"'Oh, nothing. I was only thinking about what other kinds of people you write about, and I remembered. It's bums and crooks, and they always come out all right too. So you write about the bottom and the top, but never about the between.'

"'The people in between?'

"'Yes. What's wrong with them—the normal people, the people—'

"'The lighthouse was flashing again.

"'We passed several minor stations while I busily searched my mind for plain people that might have appeared in any of my works.

"'The lighthouse said, 'Come to think of it, even the animals are strange in your books, like that little dog that belonged to the magician in *Hotel Splendide.*'

"'Well, a magician wouldn't be satisfied with an ordinary dog.'

"'What are you thinking about, Poppy?'

"'Ordinary people.'

"'Well, what's wrong with them?'

"'Nothing's wrong with them. I love them, and I'm sure I've written about them with understanding—sometime, somewhere.'

"'Your common people, Poppy, are all headwaiters with Cadillacs, and valets and gardeners.' A few seconds passed, and then she added, 'Or French.'

"'I admire the French, because they refuse, the lowest and middlest of them, to be caught by life.'

"'What do you mean by "caught?"'

"'Oh, to lead lives of quiet desperation.'

"'Who leads lives of "quiet desparation?"'

"'Well, the phrase comes from a writer by the name of Thoreau.'

"'French?'

"'No, he was American.'

"'And who was he talking about?'

"'The mass of men.'

"'Did he travel in Europe?'

"'No, darling, he was born in Concord, New Hampshire, and stayed around there all his life.'

"'What was he like?'

"'Well, ask Mother when we get back. All I know is he lived in the woods all alone and he wrote a book called *Walden,* which is very popular in Europe, because I read it there when I was a boy.'

"'What was the name of the book?'

"'*Walden.*'

"She yawned—at last—and asked, 'He wrote a book about Waldi?'

"I said, 'Yes,' and thought, Thank God, she is falling asleep.

"'Poppy—how can you justify a man like that Signor Patrizzi, who lives off the fat of the land and never does anything?'

"'Look, darling, in the circle in which I have responsibility, in which I function, toward the people who are dependent on me, I am responsible and fair. I am kind to everybody and as generous as I can afford to be. I pay my taxes, I don't commit any crimes. Beyond that I have dragged your dog around the world, I have put up with all kinds of nonsense, I have joined all kinds of societies—and if everybody would behave the way I do, the world would be a paradise.'

"'That is not enough.'

"'Darling Barbara, if a man today, especially a married one and a father, goes through life without ending up in the electric chair, in a strait jacket, or a suicide, he has already done enough. In fact, he is a tremendous success, a hero, an accomplished and perfect specimen. And now shut up and go to sleep.'

"'Ta-dang, ta-dang,' went the Rome Express."[3]

In Italy, the questioning continued. "It was time to go out, and I said, 'Hurry up, Barbara.'

"Gathering up her books, she said, 'Poppy, will you ever learn that it's not "hairy ape" but "hurry up?"'

"I am at times astonished myself that I have been unable to shake off my Austrian accent. I, of course, cannot hear myself, but since I have lived in America from the age of seventeen, it is curious how strong the accent still is. Only a year ago I went to England, and I used some royalties that had accumulated there to buy myself a complete British outfit—Lobb boots, a Briggs umbrella, a Lock homburg, and a conservative suit and topcoat made by a recommended tailor. I also had my throat examined by a Harley Street specialist. In this British makeup I took a walk with Barbara on my return to New York. We were in Central Park, and a man approached us. He asked what time it was. I hung the Briggs umbrella on my left arm, opened my London topcoat, and reached into my waistcoat pocket for my watch.

'Quarter to one,' I said—and that is all I said.

"The man smiled, 'Oh, *Sie sprechen Deutsch,*'

"'You see, Poppy, you don't believe it when I tell you,' said Barbara after he had left. 'Do you think in German?'

"'That's another thing that puzzles me—no, I don't.'

"'In English?'

"'No, I don't think in either. I think in pictures, because I see everything in pictures, and then translate them into English. I tried to write in German; I can't. I made an attempt to translate one of my books, and it was very difficult and sounded awful. Then the Swiss publishers Scherz engaged an old lady, the widow of a German general, to translate the book, and when I read it I said to myself, "How odd! It's another book." I liked it, but I could never have done it myself.'

"'What do you mean by pictures?'

"'Well, when I write, a man comes in the door. I see it as a movie—I see the door, precisely a certain kind of a door, and I see the man.'

"'In color? Do you dream in color?'

"'That depends on the subject. Happy dreams are usually in color, especially flying dreams.'

"'How do they go?'

"'They are the best, and I have them after indigestion sometimes, when I eat late and heavily. I am like a bird, and I fly all over and see everything from high up, which is my favorite perspective.'

"'And you have no vertigo?'

"'None whatever. I fly at will low over the ground and swing up and sit on the edges of high buildings, and visually it is the greatest pleasure.'

"'You love painting more than writing?'

"'Yes, I would rather paint than write, for writing is labor.'

"'Do you think you could be a great painter?'

"'Yes, the very best.'

"'But why aren't you?'

"'Because I love living too much. If I were unhappy as Toulouse-Lautrec was, or otherwise burdened, so that I would turn completely inward, then I would be a good painter. As is, I'm not sufficiently devoted.'

"'Is it the same with writing?'

"'Well, yes. My greatest inspiration is a low bank balance. I can perform then.'

"'To make money?'

"'Yes, to make money.'

"'But that's awful!'

"'Well, it has motivated better people than I.'

"'For example, whom?'

"'For example, Shakespeare.'

"'And if you had all the money in the world would you just be a café society playboy and waste it?'

"'At such turns in the conversation I impose silence.

"'Poppy—'

"'Yes, what now?'

"'About the people you write about.'

"'We've had that argument before, and I'll run through my little piece again for you. I was born in a hotel and brought up in three countries—when I was six years old I couldn't speak a word of German, because it was fashionable in Europe to bring up children who spoke nothing but French. And then I lived in other hotels, which was a very lonesome life for a child, and the only people you met were odd ones, below stairs and upstairs. In my youth the upstairs was a collection of Russian grand dukes and French countesses, English lords and American millionaires. Backstairs there were French cooks, Rumanian hairdressers, Chinese manicurists, Italian bootblacks, Swiss managers, English valets. All those people I got to know very well. When I was sent to America to learn the hotel business here, I ran into the same kind of people, and these I know very well and I can write about them, and one ought to write about what one knows. I can write about you, or Mimi, or a few other people, but I can't write about what you call 'ordinary people' because I don't know them well enough. Besides, there are so many people who do, and who write about them well.'

"'Could you write about German ordinary people?'

"'I can write about Tyroleans, and Bavarians, whom I have known in my youth, woodchoppers, teamsters, boatmen, peasants, and the children of all these people.'

"'But how did you find out about them, and understand them, when you didn't speak their language?'

"'Oh, I understood them, as a foreigner does.'

"'When you were older?'

"'Oh no, in my childhood; or better, when I started living and occasionally ran away from the hotel.'

"'And did you like that more than the hotel?'

"'Of course. The hotel was like an all-day theater performance and one played along, but the other was real and important and something you never forget. I ran away often and played with other children, but I was always brought back.'

"'Do you speak German with an accent too?'

"'Yes, of course.'

"'Do you speak any language correctly?'

"'Well, I have the least accent in French, or else the French are very polite, for they always say how very well I speak it for a foreigner.'

"'That's all rather sad, Poppy.'

"'Well, it has its advantages. It's like being a gypsy, belonging everywhere and nowhere. When you are in Paris you want to be in New York and vice versa. You are made up of fragments—and just now it occurs to me it's a good thing that you know what you want to be, an American, that you speak your own language well. Stay that way, and don't let anybody change it—and now we really must hurry up.'

"'Poppy, try saying "Hurry up."'"

"'Hurry up.'

"'That's better.'"[3]

1947. Wrote *Dirty Eddie,* the result of working in Hollywood.

1952. "My trouble is that I have always set out to write in a book a very bitter social satire. But I have a great leaning toward people who are a little larcenous. By the time I'm halfway through the book I fall in love with my characters. I just can't seem to hate the people I write about."

Wrote stories, articles and drew illustrations for leading magazines—*Harper's Bazaar, Fortune, Town and Country, Vogue, Holiday,* etc.

October 1, 1962. Died, buried in Arlington, Virginia. "The portrait of life is the most important work of the artist and it is good only when you've seen it, when you've touched it, when you know it. Then you can breathe life onto canvas and paper."[2]

FOR MORE INFORMATION SEE: Bertha E. Mahony and others, compilers, *Illustrators of Children's Books, 1744-1945,* Horn Book, 1947; Henry C. Pitz, "Ludwig Be-melmans," *American Artist,* May, 1951; Harry R. Warfel, *American Novelists of Today,* American Book Co., 1951; May Massee, "Ludwig Bemelmans," *Horn Book,* August, 1954; "Bemelmans' 'Madeline's Rescue' Wins Caldecott Medal for 1953," *Publishers Weekly,* March 20, 1954; Stanley J. Kunitz, editor, *Twentieth Century Authors,* first supplement, Wilson, 1955; M. Massee, "Ludwig Bemelmans," in *Caldecott Medal Books: 1938-1957,* Horn Book, 1957; S. L. Root, "Ludwig Bemelmans and His Books for Children," *Elementary English,* January, 1957; B. E. Mahony and others, compilers, *Illustrators of Children's Books, 1946-1956,* Horn Book, 1958.

"Story of Bemelmans' Madeline," *Publishers Weekly,* November 14, 1960; (for children) Muriel Fuller, editor, *More Junior Authors,* H. W. Wilson, 1963; P. Groff, "Children's World of Ludwig Bemelmans," *Elementary English,* October, 1966; Brian Doyle, editor, *Who's Who of Children's Literature,* Schocken Books, 1968; Lee Kingman and others, compilers, *Illustrators of Children's Books, 1957-1966,* Horn Book, 1968; Miriam Hoffman and Eva Samuels, *Authors and Illustrators of Children's Books,* R. R. Bowker, 1972; (for children) Norah Smaridge, *Famous Author-Illustrators for Young People,* Dodd, 1973.

Obituaries: *New York Times,* October 2, 1962; *Publishers Weekly,* October 8, 1962; *Time,* October 12, 1962; *Illustrated London News,* October 13, 1962; *Newsweek,* October 15, 1962; *Wilson Library Bulletin,* November, 1962; *Current Biography,* December, 1962; *Current Biography Yearbook 1962; Americana Annual 1963; Britannica Book of the Year 1963.*

(From *The Secret Hiding Place* by Rainey Bennett. Illustrated by the author.)

BENNETT, Rainey   1907-

PERSONAL: Born July 26, 1907, in Marion, Indiana; son of William Rainey and Ethel (Clark) Bennett; married Ann Port, October 4, 1936; children: Pamela, Renee, Anthony. *Education:* University of Chicago, Ph.B., 1930; later studied at several art schools. *Home:* Chicago, Illinois.

CAREER: Artist and illustrator. Became interested in art as a college student; did free-lance work for book publishers, 1931-33; supervisor of the Federal Art Project, Chicago, 1935-38; through project exhibits he developed an association with the Downtown Gallery, 1936-52; commissioned by Nelson Rockefeller to paint watercolors for the Standard Oil Company in Venezuela, 1939; later, advertising work for a major Chicago department store led to career as a book illustrator. His works have been exhibited in many museums, including the Art Institute of Chicago and the Museum of Modern Art, New York; has also painted murals for buildings in many cities in the United States and South America. *Awards, honors:* New York Herald Tribune award, 1960, for *The Secret Hiding Place; After the Sun Goes Down* was selected by the American Institute of Graphic Arts for their 1961-62 Children's Book Show.

WRITINGS:—All self-illustrated: *What Do You Think?,* World Publishing, 1958; *The Secret Hiding Place,* World Publishing, 1960; *After the Sun Goes Down,* World Publishing, 1961.

Illustrator: Sylvia Cassedy, *Little Chameleon,* World Publishing, 1966; Rowena (Bastin) Bennett, *The Day Is Dancing, and Other Poems,* Follett, 1968; Edna Mitchell Preston, *The Temper Tantrum Book,* Viking, 1969; May Hill Arbuthnot, editor, *The Arbuthnot Anthology of Children's Literature,* third edition, Scott, Foresman, 1971; Countee Cullen, *My Lives and How I Lost Them,* Follett, 1971; Carla Stevens, *Hooray for Pig!,* Seabury, 1974; Adeline Corrigan, editor, *Holiday Ring: Festival Stories and Poems,* Albert Whitman, 1975; Bernice Chardiet, *Monkies and the Water Monster,* Scholastic, 1976; Edith H. Tarcov, *Three Famous Stories,* Scholastic, 1976; Carla Stevens, *Pig and the Blue Flag,* Seabury, 1977.

SIDELIGHTS: In many of Bennett's earlier book illustrations, he applied a combination of pen-and-ink drawings and a water-color wash technique. Although used in his award-winning picture book, *Secret Hiding Place,* the *Library Journal* found it ". . . an interesting and effective technique, but not strong enough to make the book as a whole above average in quality and appeal." A reviewer for the *Chicago Sunday Tribune,* in commenting about the same book, said, ". . . he has transformed the homely hippo into a captivating creature who will win all hearts." Bennett again used the same wash-line drawing technique in his *After the Sun Goes Down.* Alice Dalgliesh, writing for *Saturday Review,* compared this story to being ". . . light as a soap bubble, but amusing with interesting pictures."

FOR MORE INFORMATION SEE: Lee Kingman, editor, *Illustrators of Children's Books: 1957-1966,* Horn Book, 1968; Doris de Montreville and Elizabeth D. Crawford, editors, *Fourth Book of Junior Authors and Illustrators,* Wilson, 1978.

BERNA, Paul   1910-

PERSONAL: Born February 21, 1910, in Hyeres, France; son of a chemical engineer; married Jany Saint-Marcoux (a

PAUL BERNA

writer); children: Bernard, Philippe. *Education:* Studied at Villa Saint-Jean, Fribourg, Switzerland. *Home:* Paris, France.

CAREER: Author. Worked as an accountant, insurance man, secretary, film distributor and at other various jobs before starting a full-time writing career; reporter for a suburban Paris newspaper, 1930-36; accepted a position with the French Ministry of Communications at the end of the second World War. *Awards, honors:* The Mystery Writers of America awarded Berna a scroll for *The Secret of the Missing Boat* as one of the top juvenile mysteries of 1967.

WRITINGS: Le Piano a Bretelle (illustrated by Pierre Dehay), Editions G.P. (Paris), 1956, translation by John Buchanan-Brown published as *The Street Musician,* Bodley Head, 1960; *Le Carrefour de la Pie,* Editions G.P., 1957, translation by Helen Woodyatt published as *Magpie Corner,* Hamish Hamilton, 1966; *Le Cheval sans Tete,* 1955, translation by J. Buchanan-Brown published as *A Hundred Million Francs,* Bodley Head, 1957, published in America as *The Horse without a Head,* Pantheon, 1959; *Le Kangourou Volant* (illustrated by Pierre Le Guen), Editions G.P., 1957, translation by H. Woodyatt published as *The Golden Fish,* Hamish Hamilton, 1963; *Millionaires en Herbe* (illustrated by G. de Sainte-Croix), Editions G.P., 1958, translation by J. Buchanan-Brown published as *The Knights of King Midas,* Pantheon, 1961; *Les Pelerins de Chiberta* (illustrated by G. de Sainte-Croix), Editions G.P., 1958, translation by J. Buchanan-Brown published as *The Mystery of the Cross-Eyed Man,* Bodley Head, 1965; *La Porte des Etoiles* (illustrated by Geraldine Spence), translation by J. Buchanan-Brown published as *Threshold of the Stars,* Bodley Head, 1958, Abelard, 1961; *Le Champion* (illustrated by P. Le Guen), Editions G.P., 1959; *Le Continent du Ciel,* transla-

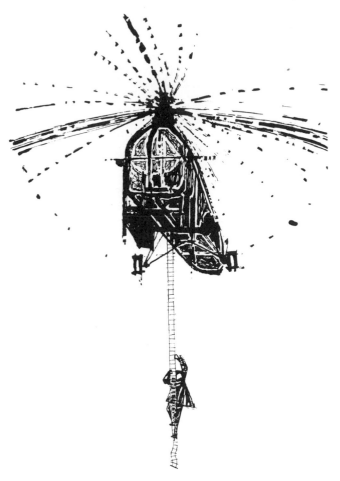

He found it easy to pull himself up rung by rung, his hands gripping the nylon ropes firmly. ■ (From *Flood Warning* by Paul Berna. Illustrated by Charles Keeping.)

tion by J. Buchanan-Brown published as *Continent in the Sky,* Bodley Head, 1959, Abelard, 1963.

La Grande Alerte (illustrated by Jacques Pecnard), Editions G.P., 1960, translation by J. Buchanan-Brown published as *Flood Warning,* Bodley Head, 1962, Pantheon, 1963; *La Piste du Souvenir,* translation by J. Buchanan-Brown published as *The Mystery of Saint-Salgue,* Bodley Head, 1963, Pantheon, 1964; *Le Temoignage du Chat Noir* (illustrated by Daniel Dupuy), Editions G.P., 1963, translation by J. Buchanan-Brown published as *The Clue of the Black Cat,* Bodley Head, 1964, Pantheon, 1965; *La Volle Rouge,* translation by J. Buchanan-Brown published as *The Secret of the Missing Boat,* Bodley Head, 1966, Pantheon, 1967; *Le Commissaire Sinet et le Mystere de l'Autoroute Sud* (illustrated by D. Dupuy), Presses de la Cite (Paris), 1967, translation by J. Buchanan-Brown published as *The Mule on the Motorway,* Bodley Head, 1967, published in America as *The Mule on the Expressway,* Pantheon, 1968; *Le Commissaire Sinet et le Mystere des Poissons Rouges* (illustrated by D. Dupuy), Presses de la Cite, 1968, translation by J. Buchanan-Brown published as *A Truckload of Rice,* Pantheon, 1970; *L'Epave de la Berenice,* Editions G.P., 1969; *Un Pays sans Legende,* translation by J. Buchanan-Brown published as *They Didn't Come Back,* Pantheon, 1970; *Le Grand Rallye de Mirabal,* translation by J. Buchanan-Brown published as *The Vagabonds Ashore,* Bodley Head, 1973; *Les Vagabonds du Pacifique,* translation by J.

Buchanan-Brown published as *Vagabonds of the Pacific,* Bodley Head, 1973; *La Derniere Aube,* Editions G.P., 1974.

Also author of *Le Bout du Monde* and *Operation Oiseau-Noir,* both published by Editions G.P.

SIDELIGHTS: Reviews of Paul Berna's *Threshold of the Stars* range from that of a *Kirkus* critic who called it "good adventure, and so well translated . . . [with] . . . a number of characters who have a thoroughly adult quality and the ideas of what the future hold are made credible," to the comment by a *New York Herald Tribune* writer who described it as, "both dull and inaccurate."

The description of the flood in *Flood Warning* ". . . is handled with mounting suspense, but without sensationalism," according to the *Christian Science Monitor,* ". . . [with] emphasis not on material destruction, but rather on human re-construction. . . .

The London *Times Literary Supplement* described *The Clue of the Black Cat* as, "from the mystery angle, Paul Berna's best work. . . ." *New York Times Book Review* called it a "charming and lively story. . . ."

The sequel to *The Clue of the Black Cat* was *The Mule on the Expressway.* The *Young Readers' Review* critic termed it ". . . a bit more far fetched than [its predecessor], but . . . just as suspenseful and just as cleverly plotted. The riddle unfolds slowly, but the action is fast and readers will be mystified until the very end. . . . This book has a dry humor which is not every child's cup of tea, but it is a superior mystery and one which is worth the reading. . . ."

FOR MORE INFORMATION SEE: Doris de Montreville, editor, *Third Book of Junior Authors,* H. W. Wilson, 1972.

JOANNE E. BERNSTEIN

You may feel many different ways when a person you love dies. ▪ (From *When People Die* by
Joanne E. Bernstein and Stephen V. Gullo. Photographs by Rosmarie Hausherr.)

BERNSTEIN, Joanne E(ckstein)   1943-

PERSONAL: Born April 21, 1943, in New York; daughter
of Murray (a lawyer) and Mildred (a teacher; maiden name,
Weckstein) Eckstein; married Michael J. Bernstein (a
teacher of physics), June 9, 1965; children: Robin, Andrew.
Education: Brooklyn College of the City University of New
York, B.A., 1963; Pratt Institute, M.L.S., 1966; Columbia
University, Ed.D., 1971. *Home:* 3848 Maple Ave., Brook-
lyn, N.Y. 11224. *Office:* School of Education, Brooklyn
College of the City University of New York, Brooklyn,
N.Y. 11210.

CAREER: Kindergarten teacher in a public school in Brooklyn, N.Y., 1963-67; substitute teacher for elementary and
secondary schools in New York, N.Y., 1967-69; Pace College, New York City, adjunct lecturer in education, 1970;
New York Community College, New York City, adjunct
lecturer in education, 1971; Brooklyn College of the City
University of New York, Brooklyn, N.Y., assistant professor of education, 1971—. *Member:* International Reading
Association, Association for Childhood Education International, National Council of Teachers of English, National

Association for the Education of Young Children, Foundation of Thanatology.

WRITINGS: Loss: And How to Cope with It (juvenile),
Seabury, 1977; (with Stephen Gullo) *When People Die,* Dutton, 1977; *Books To Help Children Cope with Separation
and Loss,* Bowker, 1977. Reviewer of juvenile books for
Young Children, 1973-77.

WORK IN PROGRESS: A book about immigrant families;
a book of riddles.

SIDELIGHTS: "My entire professional career—as teacher, reviewer, writer—is wrapped up in the world of publishing for children. I couldn't be more delighted with the direction life has taken!"

BIANCO, Margery (Williams)   1881-1944

PERSONAL: Born July 22, 1881, in London, England; died
September 4, 1944, in New York, New York; daughter of a
barrister, who was also a distinguished classical scholar;

MARGERY WILLIAMS BIANCO

married Francisco Bianco (a dealer in rare books and manuscripts), 1904; children: Cecco (son), Pamela (Mrs. Robert Schlick; an artist and illustrator of children's books). *Education:* Her father believed that children were better educated with little formal schooling; she attended the Convent School in Sharon Hill, Pennsylvania, for two years. *Home:* Greenwich Village, New York.

CAREER: Novelist, translator, and author of books for children. *Awards, honors:* Runner-up for the Newbery Medal, 1937, for *Winterbound.*

WRITINGS—All for children, except as noted: *The Late Returning* (adult novel), Macmillan, 1902; *Spendthrift Summer* (adult novel), W. Heinemann, 1903; *The Price of Youth* (adult novel), Macmillan, 1904; *Paris* (travel and description; illustrated by Allan Stewart), A. & C. Black, 1910; *The Thing in the Woods,* Duckworth, 1913; *The Velveteen Rabbit; or, How Toys Became Real* (illustrated by William Nicholson), G. H. Doran, 1922 [another edition illustrated by Marie Angel, A. Colish, 1974]; *Poor Cecco* (illustrated by Arthur Rackham), G. H. Doran, 1925; *The Little Wooden Doll* (illustrated by daughter, Pamela Bianco), Macmillan, 1925, reissued, 1967; *The Apple Tree* (illustrated by Boris Artzybasheff), G. H. Doran, 1926; *The Skin Horse* (illustrated by P. Bianco), G. H. Doran, 1927; *The Adventures of Andy* (illustrated by Leon Underwood), G. H. Doran, 1927; *The Candlestick* (illustrated by Ludovic Rodo), Doubleday, Doran, 1929; *All About Pets* (illustrated by Grace Gilkison), Macmillan, 1929; (with Harold Hutchinson) *Out of the Night: A Mystery Comedy in Three Acts* (play), [New York], 1929.

The House That Grew Smaller (illustrated by Rachel Field), Macmillan, 1931; *A Street of Little Shops* (illustrated by Grace Paull), Doubleday, Doran, 1932; *The Hurdy-Gurdy Man* (illustrated by Robert Lawson), Oxford University Press, 1933; *More About Animals* (illustrated by Helen Torrey), Macmillan, 1934; *The Good Friends* (illustrated by G. Paull), Viking, 1934; *Green Grows the Garden* (illustrated by Paull), Macmillan, 1936; *Winterbound,* Viking, 1936, reissued, 1966; (with James Cloyd Bowman) *Tales from a Finnish Tupa* (illustrated by Laura Bannon), A. Whitman, 1936, reissued, 1964 [tales published separately include *Seven Silly Wise Men* (illustrated by John Faulkner), A. Whitman, 1965; *Who Was Tricked?* (illustrated by Faulkner), Whitman, 1966]; *Other People's Houses,* Viking, 1939; (with Gisella Loeffler) *Franzi and Gizi,* J. Messner, 1941; *Bright Morning* (illustrated by Margaret Platt), Viking, 1942; (with Marjory Collison) *Penny and the White Horse,* J. Messner, 1942; *Forward, Commandos!* (illustrated by Rafaello Busoni), Viking, 1944; (with others) *Herbert's Zoo and Other Favorite Stories* (illustrated by Julian), Simon & Schuster, 1949.

Translator: Blaise Cendrars, pseudonym of Frederic Sauser, *The African Saga,* Payson & Clarke, 1927; B. Cendrars, *Little Black Stories for Little White Children,* Payson & Clarke, 1929; Georges Oudard, *Four Cents an Acre: The Story of Louisiana under the French,* Brewer & Warren, 1931.

ADAPTATIONS: "The Velveteen Rabbit" (motion picture; 19 minutes, sound, color), LSB Productions, 1974.

SIDELIGHTS: **July 22, 1881.** Born in London, England, the younger of two daughters. Her father was a barrister, distinguished scholar of the classics and a newspaper man. "My father believed children should be taught to read early and then have no regular teaching until they were ten years old. . . . My favorite book in my father's library was Wood's *Natural History* in three big green volumes, and I knew every reptile, bird and beast in those volumes before I knew the multiplication table." [*Writing and Criticism: A Book for Margery Bianco,* edited by Anne Carroll Moore and Bertha Mahony Miller, Horn Book, 1951.[1]]

1888. Father died.

1890. First visited America. Spent summer in New York, mostly in Central Park, then moved to a farm in Pennsylvania. A year later she went to a day school in Philadelphia. She spent an occasional year or so back in England, without schooling.

1896-1898. Spent two happy years in the Convent School, Sharon Hill, Pennsylvania, the last schooling she received. The next few years were spent between England and America.

1902. First novel, *The Late Returning,* which she had written at seventeen, published in England by Heinemann.

1904. Second novel, *The Price of Youth,* published by Macmillan.

1904. Married Francesco Bianco, a graduate of the University of Turin. He was a lover of books and fine arts and finally became manager of the rare book department of Brentano's in Paris.

1904-1907. Lived in London.

August 15, 1905. Son, Cecco, born.

1906. *The Bar* published in England by Methuen.

December 31, 1906. Daughter, Pamela, born.

June, 1907. Family went to live in Paris.

1910. "Peeps at Great Cities," series published.

1911. Family returned to live in London.

1914-1918. Settled in Turin, Italy during World War I. Francesco was called to serve in the Italian army and became a captain.

Summer, 1919. "The war was newly over, there was a sense of life and the whole world beginning afresh; one could dare to feel gladness without the instant after-tug of fear, and into this time of heightened intensity and awareness came the fresh and poignant beauty of Walter de la Mare's poetry. *The Listeners, Songs of Childhood* and *Peacock Pie*—those were the three books that make that summer so vivid in memory, and never did three little books fill a summer so completely. We were living in San Remo. Pamela was making those drawings which later—though she had no faintest idea of it then—were to be her part of *Flora*. For five years we had seen little or nothing of the new English books, and it was almost a shock to realize that poems so gay, so tender, so full of lovely and unexpected imagery, existed. They were read again and again till we all but knew them by heart.

"Looking back over the years since *Songs of Childhood* and *Peacock Pie* first became widely known, one can only now begin to realize how great has been Walter de la Mare's influence upon the whole field of imaginative literature for children, and the full significance of his contribution. Poetry of and for childhood there had always been, but never poetry like this. He brought not only beauty but something rarer and even more vital, the perception of beauty. His poetry is intensely visual. He is concerned with the living quality of things, their shapes and colors, their texture. When he speaks of a tree, a bird, a flower, it is as though one were seeing it—really seeing it—for the first time, through the eyes of one who is sensitive to beauty in whatever form, even under the guise of what is called ugliness.

"To speak of 'the eyes of a child' may sound hackneyed and sentimental but that is because most adults have forgotten what that clear and unspoiled vision is really like. A child does see an object clearly because he is looking at it for the first time and he sees it with all the elements of wonder and miracle. De la Mare is among those happy few who can recapture, or perhaps have never wholly lost, the keenness of that vision, which is of the spirit as much as of the physical eye. In 'Maria-Fly' he describes the almost unbearable wonder with which a small child looks, for the first time consciously, at a house-fly. Something extraordinary has happened to her; she wants to share, instantly, the wonder that she feels, and all she can explain is that she has just seen a fly, *really* seen it. But no one understands, and in her failure to express just what she means by 'seeing' one feels the whole tragic gulf that lies between child and adult.

"In *The Memoirs of a Midget,* Miss M., speaking of her childhood, tells how 'My eyes dazzled in colors. The smallest of the marvels of flowers and flies and beetles and pebbles, and the radiance that washed over them, would fill me with a mute pent-up rapture almost unendurable.' All through the book this sense of visual miracle persists, and we are enthralled by the strangeness, loveliness and sometimes terror of a world seen through almost microscopic eyes.

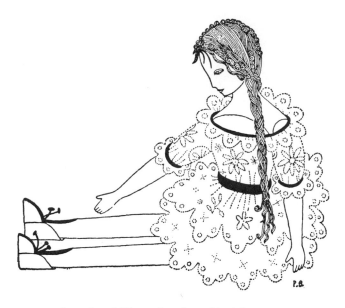

. . .when the child awoke, she rubbed her eyes and stared, for there on the chair by her bedside sat the little wooden doll, watching her. ∎ (From *The Little Wooden Doll* by Margery Williams Bianco. Pictures by Pamela Bianco.)

"Beauty and the transience of beauty is the essence of De la Mare's poetry. His cry is always for the grasping, even for a fleeting moment, of that which can never be held."[1]

1919. Family returned to England and Pamela, who drew from a very early age, had her drawings exhibited at the Leicester Galleries in London.

1921. Francesco and Pamela went to New York for an exhibit of Pamela's work at the Anderson Galleries. Soon after, Margery and Cecco followed. Cecco attended the Donaldson School in Maryland for two years then went to Columbia University.

1922. *The Velveteen Rabbit,* her first children's book, published. "I disliked everything I had written before. I wanted to do something different but did not know what it should be.

"It was by a sort of accident that *The Velveteen Rabbit* became the beginning of all the stories I have written since. . . . By thinking about toys and remembering toys, they suddenly became very much alive—Poor Cecco and all the family toys that had been so much a part of our lives; toys I had loved as a little girl—my almost forgotten Tubby who was the rabbit, and old Dobbin the Skin Horse, the toys my children had loved.

"Nothing is easier than to write a story for children; few things harder, as any writer knows, than to achieve a story that children will really like. Between the two lies that great mass of literature, often charmingly written, instructive, attractive, containing apparently every element that should appeal to the child mind yet destined, for no reason that its creators can see, to remain nicely kept upon the nursery or library shelves, while the public for whom it is intended thanks us politely and returns to the comic strips.

"It isn't that children are not easily pleased. They are the most eager and receptive audience that anyone can have. They are pleased, as any adult knows, by the most absurd and ridiculous things; and being pleased by these things

(From *Poor Cecco* by Margery Bianco. Illustrated by Arthur Rackham.)

Summer Days.
■ (From *The Velveteen Rabbit* by Margery Williams. Illustrated by William Nicholson.)

once, they will continue to enjoy them to the end of time—but they are not always pleased by the very thing that we think is going to please them. For this reason, one is inclined to believe that the really successful children's book is just a thing that happens; that it is very rarely the result of deliberate plan or foresight or, if it began that way, that it took, somewhere, a mysterious turn of its own in the making. Just as we might imagine our actor, if he were a good actor and his play any sort of real play, becoming so engrossed in it that at a certain point he would forget all efforts to please his audience, would consign it to oblivion, and simply go ahead and do the thing to please himself, only to find perhaps at the end that his audience was for the first time really with him.

"Children are extraordinarily quick to detect any effort to engage their attention. They have at times an almost diabolical clairvoyance and skepticism regarding the grown-up's intention; they are eternally suspicious and ready to jump the other way. Say to any intelligent person of four or five years, 'Look at the pretty flower!' and he will, unless he is a hypocrite or hampered by mere politeness, give you a blank pitying stare or else turn his back. Not that he doesn't appreciate the flower; it is simply that, approached directly, his instinct is to question your motive and suspect some design on his personal liberty. To engage children's interest in anything you have to be keenly interested in that thing yourself; if you are not, if you are merely pretending or playing up to them, they will promptly catch you out."[1]

1925. *Poor Cecco* published.

1925. *The Little Wooden Doll,* illustrated by Pamela, published. "There is a very real satisfaction in writing for children. They are both deeply appreciative and highly critical. Before them the author is put on his mettle. They refuse to be sidetracked by any mere exercise of art. All those skilful embroiderings and unessentials, the nice picking of phrases and building up of 'atmosphere' which he may fall back upon to cover an awkward gap or to get away with a story which he knows to be fundamentally weak, are perfectly useless; through them all his emptiness will be revealed. To these critics style means very little. They care more for the thing itself than for how it is done, and they are the one audience whom you cannot hoodwink nor deceive. Unless your story is there no ingenious juggling with words is going to save the situation for you. If it is, and it's a good story from their point of view, and if you have once got their confidence, then there is established magically that cooperation which almost amounts to a conspiracy between storyteller and audience, by which they will be willing to forgive you almost any shortcoming and bear with you through all vicissitudes to the end.

"A wise child! That is all there is to writing a story. It is the believing in it and the keeping at it that are important."[1]

1937. Met Valenti Angelo, whose first book she was editing. They became good friends.

Anxious Times.
■ (From *The Velveteen Rabbit* by Margery Williams. Illustrated by William Nicholson.)

From her earliest years she had a great interest in natural history and a wonderful understanding of animals. She regarded one of her cats, Monkey, "as a perfect barometer, for the nights he decides to sleep indoors I know that I must let the faucets drip and fill the stove well."[1]

Of another cat, Dear Old Peoplecat, she noted: "People has no illusions about going out in unpleasant weather. Rain he loves but not cold."[1]

She referred to a canary she gave her grandson: "Who (with five rooms in the house) lives naturally and inevitably on my desk, where he is a great comfort even though he scatters seed industriously all over papers and floor, and, unless I bestir myself, it will just as naturally proceed to take root. Then I shall have a beautiful green bower all around me and no need of going to the country!"[1]

At one point she wrote with her feet in a chair because: "Lorenzo's [her grandson's] white rat, full of the spring, was too interested in bare toes."[1]

And again, about their bulldog, Caxton: "Poor Caxton has rheumatism badly, can hardly walk, and has to be lifted in and out of chairs. Cecco and I went for a walk up San Vito on Tuesday (without Caxton, for we had to bring him home when we reached the Mauriziano) and found quite a lot of primroses and some blue flowers and snowdrops. It was very hot up there, and we ate tea in the field at the top. There a bee kept buzzing around, so first we gave it chocolate and it ate some, and then Cecco made a paper cup of water for it and it drank a lot, and kept coming back every little while to drink again."[1]

Her daughter remarked that her mother treated their toys as real as if they were her own. She once wrote Pamela: "The Tubbies are very well and happy. As a matter of fact, they are in Tubbyland now, as Jensina's mother telephoned to ask if they couldn't stay over Wednesday, so as to go to a picnic which she had arranged—with dancing afterwards, and I felt sure you wouldn't mind."[1]

Her philosophy on children: "It is so enthralling to watch them grow up and they do it so quickly. Already I no longer recognize the baby [Lorenzo] of half a year past.

"There have been repeated efforts to draw a line, in imaginative literature, between the child's range and the adult's. Actually no such line exists; children certainly have always disregarded it. It will be a good thing when we cease once and for all to puzzle whether a certain book is 'for children' or 'about children,' and leave the young to choose for themselves.

"God to the child is an extension of the parent ... God is a child's only natural and satisfying expansion of the universe, a personal God, some one at the head of things. A paper on religion for children today cannot be written at all without touching the particular problem which worries a great many children. If God is beneficent, how come there are wars and massacres and all the disasters of today? This, it seems to me, is the point that must be faced and accounted for somehow. Too many parents at this moment are probably murmuring, 'W-ell, my dear,' ... and 'When you are a little older,' ... etc. If you feel that these things are due to man's not keeping faith with God, or to his own greed and misunderstanding, come right out and say so. It is an urgent issue.

"Death should be treated naturally. You don't have to educate children about death. Speak of it as a natural occurrence and they will do the same.

"More than ever, I think, children need imaginative literature as an interpretation. Nature does not resist discouragement and not only in the young. The impulse is always toward life and the future. Children are taken up with war and the excitement of it, but it doesn't mean to them what it means to us, unless we make it so. Their own imagination, I think, tends to make of it something like a highly exciting game. It is a defense and like all Nature's defenses, wise.

"There is no privacy deeper or more precious than that in which the spirit finds its inner nourishment . . . I doubt if any child, nurtured on imaginative tales, was ever seriously handicapped in facing the actual world. . . ."[1]

1939. *Other People's Houses* published. *"Other People's Houses* is just a plain story of everyday life. It has no trimmings, almost no plot, and it concerns the experience of a girl who wants to earn her living in a city and is willing to try anything that turns up, domestic jobs included, rather than give in.

"All over the country there are girls very much like Dale in this book. They are girls who haven't got college degrees or a chance of getting them and have no special training for careers. They aren't likely to blossom out into successful artists or writers overnight, to discover lost wills hidden in old furniture, to inherit odd pieces of property and convert them into thriving business concerns within a year on no capital, to unravel mysteries, save impossible situations through heroism or meet strangers who turn out to be wealthy long-lost uncles. Just what would they do if they wanted to earn a living, and what sort of a time would they have trying it out?

"That was the starting point of the story and I have tried to work it out in the way it very probably would happen. I was trying to get away from the average success story which I never felt is playing fair to the reader."[1]

September 4, 1944. Died after an illness of three days. "Imagination is only another word for the interpretation of life. It is through imagination that a child makes his most significant contacts with the world about him, that he learns tolerance, pity, understanding and the love for all created things."[1]

FOR MORE INFORMATION SEE: Anne C. Moore and Bertha M. Miller, editors, *Writing and Criticism: A Book for Margery Bianco,* Horn Book, 1951; (for children) Stanley J. Kunitz and Howard Haycraft, editors, *Junior Book of Authors,* 2nd edition revised, H. W. Wilson, 1951; Brian Doyle, editor, *Who's Who of Children's Literature,* Schocken Books, 1968.

BLACKBURN, John(ny) Brewton 1952-

PERSONAL: Born August 19, 1952, in Nashville, Tenn.; son of George Meredith (in business) and Betty (a teacher; maiden name, Brewton) Blackburn. *Education:* Attended University of Tennessee, 1971-72. *Religion:* "Self-Realization Fellowship Church." *Home address:* P.O. Box 006, Kingston Springs, Tenn. 37082.

CAREER: Musician, 1971—; farmer, 1972—.

WRITINGS: (Compiler with grandmother, Sara Brewton, and grandfather, John Brewton;) *Of Quarks, Quasars, and Other Quirks: Quizzical Poems for the Supersonic Age,* Crowell, 1977.

WORK IN PROGRESS: Songs of Love: Becoming and Being.

SIDELIGHTS: "I enjoy farming and the lifestyle which it brings; it gives me the freedom to pursue my songwriting, and being out in nature is a great source of inspiration. I am participating in an intense love affair with the source of all beauty; therefore, most of my writings are love songs. I've been a vegetarian for seven years now and practice Raja Yoga with great interest. My ultimate goal is non-material, but rather a higher state of 'awareness.'"

BOSHELL, Gordon   1908-

PERSONAL: Born in 1908, in Blackburn, Lancashire, England; son of Thomas (an assistant superintendent) and Ada (Roberts) Boshell; married Margaret Hazel Nisbet, 1961; children: (by previous marriage) David, Toby. *Education:* Attended grammar school in Batley and Burnley, England; Bradford Technical College, 1925-27. *Home:* 17 St. Osmund Close, Yetminster, Sherborne, Dorset DT9 6LU, England. *Agent:* Gill Coleridge, Anthony Sheil Associates Ltd., 2/3 Morwell St., London WC1B 3AR, England.

CAREER: Yorkshire Observer, Bradford, England, reporter, 1926-30; sub-editor for provincial newspapers in England, 1930-33; insurance salesman, 1933; *Daily Express,* Manchester, England, journalist, 1933-36; Reuters Features Service, London, England, assistant editor, 1944-45; *Daily Mirror,* London, England, features editor, 1945-49; *Daily Herald,* London, England, features editor, 1949-51; BBC-Radio, London, England, scriptwriter, 1940-41, editor of "Marching On," and "War Report"; World Health Organization, Geneva, Switzerland, information officer, 1951-57, founder and editor of *World Health,* information officer for Southeast Asia in New Delhi, India, 1957-63, for Western Pacific Region in Manila, Philippines, 1963-64, and for headquarters in Geneva, 1964-67; free-lance writer, 1967—.

WRITINGS: My Pen My Sword (verse), Hodder & Stoughton, 1941; *John Brown's Body* (novel), Secker & Warburg, 1942; *My Country 'Tis of Thee* (verse), W. H. Allen, 1943; *Dog's Life* (novel), Secker & Warburg, 1945; *It Happened to Me* (with own photographs), Orient Longman, 1958; *Nepal Today* (with own photographs), Orient Longman, 1960; *A Day in Ceylon* (with own photographs), Orient Longman, 1961.

Children's books: *Captain Cobwebb,* Chatto & Windus, 1967; *Captain Cobwebb's Cowboys,* Chatto & Windus, 1969; *Captain Cobwebb's Cobra,* Chatto & Windus, 1971; *The Plot against Buster the Dog,* J. Philip O'Hara, 1972; *Captain Cobwebb's Adventurers,* Macdonald & Co., 1973; *Captain Cobwebb and the Red Transistor,* Macdonald & Co., 1974; *The Secret Guardians: The Black Mercedes,* Bailey Brothers & Swinfen, 1974; *The Secret Guardians: The Million-Pound Ransom,* Bailey Brothers & Swinfen, 1975; *The Boy from Black Marsh,* Bailey Brothers & Swinfen, 1975; *Captain Cobwebb and the Crustaks,* Macdonald & Jane's, 1975; *Captain Cobwebb and the Chinese Unicorn,* Macdonald & Jane's, 1976; *The Secret Guardians: The Mendip Money-Makers,* Bailey Brothers & Swinfen, 1976; *Captain Cobwebb and the Mischief Man,* Macdonald &

Jane's, 1977; *Captain Cobwebb and the Quogs,* Macdonald & Jane's, 1978, *Captain Cobwebb and the Magic Drops,* Macdonald & Jane's, 1979.

WORK IN PROGRESS: Grey Tom, a sci-fi adventure.

SIDELIGHTS: "I was born in 1908 in Blackburn, Lancashire, England and educated at the Batley and Burnley Grammar Schools. At age fifteen I started working in the office of the *Yorkshire Observer.* I became a reporter and then left for roving life as sub-editor on a number of provincial papers in England.

"Closure of newspapers during the depression led to a spell of trying to sell insurance in an area where three out of five people were workless. I got back into journalism on the *Daily Express* in Manchester and from there went to Fleet Street, London, and worked for fifteen years on various dailies. I was assistant editor for Reuter Features Service; features editor for the *Daily Mirror,* and features editor for the former *Daily Herald.*

"I took a breather from newspapers during World War II to become script-writer, then editor of BBC Radio's dramatized war-feature series, "Marching On," and later editor on BBC's front-line reportage programme "War Report." Went back to Fleet Street in 1945 for feature editor jobs mentioned above, but in 1951 I left for Geneva, Switzerland, to join headquarters of the World Health Organization as Information Officer. Was founder and editor of its monthly journal, *World Health.* In 1957 I took over as information officer, covering seven countries of the World Health Organ-

GORDON BOSHELL

He was so startled that his jaw dropped and he sat there staring without even the tiniest growl.
■ (From *The Plot Against Buster the Dog* by Gordon Boshell. Illustrated by Pat Dypold.)

ization's South-East Asia Region, operating from New Delhi; later moved to WHO's Western Pacific Region with headquarters in Manila, Philippines. I returned to Geneva in 1964.

"I retired in 1967 when the first children's book, *Captain Cobwebb* was published and settled down to write in the West Country.

"The first children's book was written as a result of a constant loud-voiced demand 'tell us a story' by two brothers, aged seven and five, when told to tuck up, shut up and go to sleep. These stories vanished night after night into thin air, so at last I decided to write one down.

"I took a fortnight's holiday and I wrote all day, hidden away in a remote office. Each chapter was submitted to my young editors in the evening as a continuing bed-time story. It was all very hilarious . . . and since that story got into print, it has been joined by many others."

Three of Boshell's books, *Captain Cobwebb, Captain Cobwebb's Adventurers,* and *The Boy from Black Marsh,* have been translated into German and made into record albums in that country. Eight of the "Captain Cobwebb" series have been published in Dutch by Spectrum, Utrecht, Holland. His books have also been published in Norwegian.

CARTER, Helene   1887-1960

PERSONAL: Born in 1887, in Toronto, Ontario, Canada; died December 31, 1960, in New York City. *Education:* Attended Ontario School of Art, Canada, 1903-07; studied at Art Students League, and Roerich Academy of Art, New York, beginning 1914. *Home:* New York City.

CAREER: Illustrator. Began working for an advertising agency in Toronto, around 1907; traveled to Italy to work on book illustrations in 1921 and again in 1930; later collaborated with Raymond L. Ditmars to do illustrations for

There was Columbus standing at the rail of his flagship, the "Santa Maria," looking down at the water. ■ (From *The Gulf Stream* by Ruth Brindze. Illustrated by Helene Carter.)

nature books. *Member:* Artist Guild, Society of Illustrators, Women's National Book Association. *Awards, honors:* Helene Carter illustrated *Gulf Stream* by Ruth Brindze which won the New York Herald Tribune Spring Festival Award, 1945.

ILLUSTRATOR: Carl Spitteler, *Two Little Misogynists,* Holt, 1922; Carolyn Della Chiesa, *The Three of Salu: Around the World in Northern Italy,* World Book, 1923; Arthur Ransome, *Swallows and Amazons,* Lippincott, 1931; Gertrude Baldwin Linnell, *Behind the Battlements,* Macmillan, 1931; William Wordsworth, *Wayside Flowers,* Macmillan, 1931; A. Ransome, *Swallowdale,* Lippincott, 1932; Raymond L. Ditmars, *Book of Zoography,* Lippincott, 1934; A. Ransome, *Winter Holiday,* Lippincott, 1934; R. L. Ditmars, *Book of Prehistoric Animals,* Lippincott, 1935; R. L. Ditmars, *Book of Living Reptiles,* Lippincott, 1936; Jannette May Lucas, *Earth Changes,* Lippincott, 1937; J. M. Lucas, *Where Did Your Garden Grow?,* Lippincott, 1939; (and author) *Smoky and Pinocchio,* Lippincott, 1940; J. M. Lucas, *Fruits of the Earth,* Lippincott, 1942; R. L. Ditmars, *Twenty Little Pets from Everywhere,* Messner, 1943; Ruth Brindze, *Gulf Stream,* Vanguard, 1944; J. M. Lucas, *Indian Harvest: Wild Food Plants of America,* Lippincott, 1945; Rita Kissin, *Desert Animals,* McKay, 1947; R. Brindze, *Story of Our Calendar,* Vanguard, 1949; Mary Regina Walsh, *Water, Water Everywhere,* Abingdon-Cokesbury, 1953.

"First Book" series; published by F. Watts: Maribelle Cormack, *First Book of Trees,* 1951; Albert B. Tibbets, *. . . of Bees,* 1952; Alice D. Hoke, *. . . of Prehistoric Animals,* 1954; Virginia Kirkus, *. . . of Gardening,* 1956; Helen L. Hoke, *. . . of Tropical Mammals,* 1958.

SIDELIGHTS: **1887.** "More years ago than I care to remember, I was born in Toronto, Canada, and I verily believe I arrived with a pencil in my hand, all ready to go to work. Even as a small child I was fascinated with all kinds of living things—dogs, horses, cows, raccoons, and cats. Most of all *cats.* These animals were all a part of my childhood. Frogs, too, played an important part. Very seriously, I made pants and jackets for the frogs which I kept in the rain barrel and tried to make them look like "The Frog Who Would A-Wooing Go." Mother did not share my love for these pets and would exclaim, "Oh-oh! Take the nasty thing away!" But I thought they were beautiful.

"My growing years were torn between drawing and the violin, but at the ripe old age of sixteen I decided that the violin was out as a means of earning my living—which I was determined to do. So on my sixteenth birthday I was enrolled in the Ontario School of Art, where for four happy years I not only studied art but the theater also.

"The school was quartered on the floors above the old Princess Theatre, which made it mighty easy to see all of the really great people of the stage—from seats in the top balcony for twenty-five cents. This privilege became, and has always been, a great source of pleasure and stimulation to me—just the memory of such people as Ellen Terry, Sarah Bernhardt, Forbes-Robertson, and Gertrude Elliott, Nazimova and many, many others.

"After four years at the art school, I worked in the studio of a leading advertising agency in Toronto, where I learned the mechanics of reproduction and commercial illustration.

1914. "I came to New York, primarily to study, but ultimately to remain. I went to Italy in 1921 to make the illustrations for two books, one of which was written by the Swiss novelist, Carl Spitteler. In 1930 I returned to Italy, via France, where I gathered the material to illustrate a book on Mont Saint Michel, Carcassonne, and Avignon entitled, *Behind the Battlements.*

"My work with the late Raymond L. Ditmars brought me into the field of natural history, a collaboration which I have always felt to be rare privilege. This collaboration has been entirely responsible for the kind of illustration I have done in recent years. These books have, almost without exception, required considerable research but it was through my work with Dr. Ditmars that I found the combination of illustration and research a pleasurable one, albeit exasperating on many occasions."

December 31, 1960. Died in New York City.

FOR MORE INFORMATION SEE: Muriel Fuller, editor, *More Junior Authors,* H. W. Wilson, 1963.

COLBERT, Anthony   1934-

PERSONAL: Born July 17, 1934, in Isle of Wight, England; son of William Edward (a chemist) and Nita (Roberts) Colbert; married Angela Trollope (a secretary) in 1964; children: Amanda, Gemma, Laurence. *Education:* West Sussex College of Art & Crafts, Worthing, England, M.S.I.A., 1953. *Religion:* Catholic. *Home:* 42 Burton Road, Kingston-On-Thames, Surrey, England. *Agent:* B. L. Kearley, Ltd., 33 Chiltern St., London, England.

CAREER: Illustrator. *Exhibitions:* AIA Gallery (one-man show), London, England; Medical Aid for Vietnam, Hampstead, London; "Four Illustrators" Exhibitions, "The Workshop," London, England; Claud Gallery, London, England. *Member:* D.A.D.A.

WRITINGS—All self-illustrated: *Amanda Has a Surprise,* Macmillan (London), 1971; *Amanda Goes Dancing,* Macmillan, 1972.

Illustrator: Tony Parker, *Five Women,* Hutchinson, 1965; Tony Parker, *People of the Streets,* Cape, 1968; Maxim Gorky, *The Spy,* Heron, 1969; George Eliot, *Adam Bede,* Heron, 1969; H. G. Wells, *The Research Magnificent,* Heron, 1969; D. H. Lawrence, *The Lost Girl,* Heron, 1969; Anne Brontë, *The Tenant of Wildfell Hall,* Heron, 1969; Eileen Colwell, *Round About and Long Ago: Tales From the English Countries,* Longman Young, 1972, Houghton, 1974; *My England* (anthology), Heinemann, 1973; Edward Hyams, *The Changing Face of England,* Kestrel, 1973; Rupert Furneaux, *Buried and Sunken Treasure,* Penguin, 1974; Robert Furneaux, *Volcanoes,* Kestrel, 1974; Eileen Colwell, *Tales From the Islands,* Kestrel, 1975; Vadim Netchayev, *Petya and His Dog,* Kestrel, 1975; Jim Riordan, *Tartar Tales,* Kestrel, 1977; Neil Grant, *Stagecoaches,* Kestrel, 1977. Illustrations have appeared in *Radio Times, Spectator, Times, Times Educational Supplement.* Fifty additional full-color illustrations produced for "Jackanary" television series, 1978.

SIDELIGHTS: "I grew up in a small seaside town (Littlehampton) in Sussex. From my bedroom you could see across a farm and fields to the smaller Cathedral town of

ANTHONY COLBERT

Arundel, four miles away, and in these fields reflected the unending cycle of seasons from harvest, through muck-spreading, ploughing, sowing to harvest again.

"My mother, while the rest of us were out walking, tried once or twice to make watercolours of various aspects of this view. (She had no art training and was accustomed only to copying drawings, cartoons and so on, and this always by candlelight when alone at night.)

"The harvesting (with small tractor and binder) was for me, as for the farmer, the high point of the season and I, with an everchanging assortment of young contemporaries, would follow the binder round and round the ever-decreasing square of standing corn, as clouds of gulls would follow and had followed, the plough at another point in the cycle.

"We had the second-to-last house at the end of the road. Building had ceased at the coming of the war and the road stayed in this petrified state until the coming of peace and the ending of my childhood. But meanwhile the derelict land between road and farm was to become 'the dumps'—a wonderland of tall grass, mounds and 'camps' which we dug to a depth of five feet and covered with wood and iron bedsteads before replacing the turf on top of them. We covered the earth floor with scraps of carpeting and cooked potatoes in the hot ashes of fires made in the makeshift fireplaces at the opposite end from the entrance.

"With home-made weapons, we would play out the war that was being waged over our heads by absent fathers. Later a tank trap was dug and, filling with water, afforded a natural environment for the newts, tadpoles and minnows that mi-

raculously arrived. They were an oft-recurring preoccupation as we fished and brought food to feed them, as long as they would survive life in jam jars. Many years later these newts, or rather their descendants, were found living free in the garden.

"The other great love was the sea and the river Arun flowing fast and treacherous between chalked banks, winding its eight miles through Ford aerodrome to Arundel and then beyond my horizon. The war and its measly mines kept us from the sea and beaches, but we were left just a small patch of sand at the mouth of the river where I narrowly escaped drowning and learned to swim.

"The nearby airfield attracted a lot of attention from enemy aircraft and columns of black solid smoke were often seen rolling across the Downs after we had watched the 'dog fights' high above. I suppose we should have been sheltering inside, but I'm glad that my parents and neighbours never left me with the legacy of fear that would have been passed on from a perhaps more prudent sheltering. There was only the old 'table shelter' which was a steel cage in the living room, from which we ate our meals, and I can't remember being in it more than once, soon after its arrival. I remember very clearly a picture of a German aircraft low over the garden (could even see the pilot) with its great black crosses under the wings, banking before a great fountain of hymn sheets bomblasted from the local church. It was Sunday afternoon, just before the local Sunday School service. I was sitting on the back doorstep making a 'galleon' from matchboxes, matchsticks and cotton. 'Tone,' my mother called, 'you'd better come in!'

"School was a Victorian building which I now see as a much smaller 'human scale' and attractive building than when I was there. It was still heated by the old tortoise cast-iron stoves, and it's this scale and detail that I now enjoy drawing from memory whenever occasion permits. I feel that most of the material that an artist finds later committed to memory is that which he has collected from the ages of six to ten. After that it is a much harder and more conscious process.

"Though I've always had a love of books and pictures I was late and slow at learning to read, though a mental block seemed suddenly to be removed before eight when I realised the pleasure it could bring. My father was a dispensing chemist who also had a love of books, and it was his one ambition to own a 'wall of books.' He could never afford to realise this ambition, though he collected many by browsing in second-hand shops. Thereby came a small number of quite remarkable volumes, some of which, being illustrated (and hand coloured) were made available to me. So I learned early a love and admiration for the wood engravings of Bewick and John Farleigh (whose blocks for Shaw's *A Black Girl in Search of God* are still a source of wonder). Many other, much earlier anonymous engravers and cutters formed the basis for inspiration and imitation much later when the rude and ready medium of high-speed newsprint became available to me. It was then, after *Treasure Island* that I knew that I wanted to draw pictures in books.

"I was brought up a Catholic and my school was closely related to and built close beside the church. The duty of serving early mass during my weekly turn was rewarded sometimes by the peace and quiet of those early mornings, summer and winter, when there were few in the congregation and by the sense of being involved in some solemn and fitting rite, celebrating the secret magic of the early dawn.

No giant appeared, for everyone in the castle was asleep, but Jack hammered boldly on the gate.
■ (From *Round About and Long Ago* by Eileen Colwell. Illustrated by Anthony Colbert.)

"At this time my worldly aspirations were embodied in the shape of an old black bike. An object of wonder and desire, long anticipated, it became friend and vehicle not only of my person, but also of an interior life. I found then, and have since rediscovered, that when I am in this mode as the 'cartesian centaur' that thoughts rise and mature from somewhere deep within. Long distance runners, I believe, are also sustained in the same way.

"The prospect of leaving school saw me ill-equipped for a career of any ambition. The only thing I seemed to do well was to draw, so I drew my way into West Sussex Art College by means of an examination that included among other tasks the drawing of a bucket and brush. This paid fees and travel. It was at the college and within the local library (Worthing) that I feel my real education began, and from being a big fish in a small tank I learned to grow among bigger fish in a larger pond. There were then the last of the postwar 'mature students' with the privilege of further education on 'demob.' These older students were a great asset as incentive to me and my young contemporaries as they were well motivated and dedicated (as we 'war kids' were) to the 'work ethic.'

"During the summer holidays I worked on the land on local farms and later, after National Service in the Army, it was to this work I returned while completing a portfolio to help me find a job. It seemed a pity to me to do nothing but go straight into teaching as many contemporaries did, without trying first to do something with this 'parcel' of knowledge that we had been three or four years amassing, rather than turn and pass it on as if that was all it was for. So I decided to try and 'take my parcel to market' to see if I could put it to some purpose at someone else's disposal.

"After initial studio and agency work I joined the editorial staff of *The Observer* where after a time I was able to do (apart from the many menial tasks) some of my first published illustration. It was also a time of further and useful training in print, processing layout and design, which was to prove useful when I went free-lance and later into teaching.

"Gouache resist and similar techniques possess factors, important in themselves, that lead me to prefer these means to direct drawing: the instantaneous arrival of the image on the page as in printing (the technique of offset drawing, a sort of monoprint, is useful here); the invitation of the 'controlled accident'; the element of surprise and discovery, as with pictures in the fire.

"Another factor that has influenced the weight or density of my drawings is that of materials and context—high speed newsprint, for instance, and the advertising, editorial headings and such-like that might accompany my work.

"Then the conception that white is synonymous (as regards the activity of perception and drawing) with light, positive, information and knowledge, as black is with shadow, obscurity, ignorance or lack of knowledge, leads me to prefer to make each mark read as a positive (white) statement on a negative (black) field. But this point of view, for which relief printing (with its activity of cutting and engraving being concentrated in statements of 'light in the dark') is eminently suitable, becomes more difficult when one is simply making a mark on paper. For it is so much easier to make a black mark on white ground than white on black. So one's thinking and observation become to some extent compromised by convention, and the convenience of 'dark on light.'

"In order to keep the medium as simple as possible I prefer to use a brush. But as it is impossible to make an absolutely white mark on black without repeated endorsement, I add to the brushwork the use of resist techniques which give, at a stroke, the contrast that I (and the process camera) require.

"The use of this slightly roundabout method of producing an image (only one stage shorter than printmaking) invites in turn the elements of chance and surprise, as when one removes the black ink one comes face to face with the most completed image FOR THE FIRST TIME, instantaneously. There is the excitement of risk or failure, and a mind open at the suggestion of those elements that have appeared by chance. There is, however, a danger of finding oneself relying or 'hiding' behind a technique or process that comes between the viewer/reader and the autographic line.

"An illustration, as distinct from drawing from life, the abstract element or skeleton that carries the flesh of information is really a 'thought' which one must get down with the least possible interference or compromise. To see this 'thought' trail out of the end of pen or brush over a period of time, and subject to the continual process of appraisal, assessment and self-criticism, is a prospect I would rather avoid being too conscious of in the initial stages.

"After all, the thought is something abstract, a feeling perhaps that springs from an unconscious source, so the further one can allow this to develop as an image, with minimum conscious intervention, before it finds the light of day and has to meet the limitations imposed by being an explicit and coherent statement, the better.

"So I like to just keep throwing the 'coins' and constructing the 'lines' till the 'trigram' image has formed, before I face the picture and together we decide how much needs to be done to 'deliver' it into the light of day.

"And now after twenty years of endeavour and trying to found and support a family by drawing and teaching, I long to release the pressure on this one facility, and to embrace the implications of a simpler broader-based economy which would involve the more wholesome division of labour between drawing/thinking and growing/seeing. This means a move to the country for my goal is to find and found a simple life based on an equity of physical and mental labour in earth of mind and spirit, and by unity of this means support this life, find God, and prepare for the next."

FOR MORE INFORMATION SEE: Arts Review, August 19, 1967; *The Tribune*, September 1, 1967.

COLUM, Padraic   1881-1972

PERSONAL: Born December 8, 1881, in Longford, Ireland; emigrated to the United States in 1914; son of Padraic (a warehouse master) and Susanna (MacCormack) Colum; married Mary Gunning Maguire (a writer), 1912 (died, 1957). *Education:* Educated at local schools. *Religion:* Catholic.

CAREER: Playwright, essayist, novelist, poet, and author of books for children. Colum worked briefly for a railroad, but by the time he was twenty, he had gone to Dublin and was writing in earnest. Was a founder of the Irish National Theatre (later known as the Abbey), and co-founder and editor for a time of the *Irish Review*. Visited Hawaii, 1923, at the request of its legislature to reshape the island's traditional stories. *Member:* Irish Academy of Literature, American Academy of Arts and Letters, Poetry Society of America (president, 1938-39). *Awards, honors:* Runner-up for the Newbery Medal for *The Golden Fleece and the Heroes Who Lived before Achilles,* 1922, *Voyagers,* 1926, and *Big Tree of Bunlahy,* 1934; American Academy of Poets Award, 1952; Gregory Medal of the Irish Academy of Letters, 1953; Regina Medal, 1961; Boston Arts Festival Poet, citation, 1961; Georgetown University 175th Anniversary Medal of Honor, 1964; Litt. D. from Columbia University, 1958, and Trinity College, Dublin, 1958.

WRITINGS—Children's stories: *A Boy in Eirinn,* Dutton, 1913 [another edition illustrated by Jack B. Yeats, Dutton, 1929]; *The King of Ireland's Son* (illustrated by Willy Pogany), Holt, 1916, reissued, Macmillan, 1967; (editor) Jonathan Swift, *Gulliver's Travels* (an abridged edition for children; illustrated by W. Pogany), Macmillan, 1917, reissued, 1964; *The Adventures of Odysseus* [and] *The Tale of Troy* (illustrated by Pogany), Macmillan, 1918, reissued as *The Children's Homer: The Adventures of Odysseus* [and] *The Tale of Troy,* 1962; *The Boy Who Knew What the Birds Said* (illustrated by Dugald S. Walker), Macmillan, 1918; *The Girl Who Sat by the Ashes* (illustrated by D. S. Walker), Macmillan, 1919 [another edition illustrated by Imero Gobbato, Macmillan, 1968]; *The Children of Odin* (illustrated by W. Pogany), Macmillan, 1920, reissued, 1962; *The Boy Apprenticed to an Enchanter* (illustrated by D. S. Walker), Macmillan, 1920 [another edition illustrated by Edward Leight, Macmillan, 1966].

The Golden Fleece and the Heroes Who Lived before Achilles (illustrated by W. Pogany), Macmillan, 1921, reissued, 1962; *The Children Who Followed the Piper* (illustrated by D. S. Walker), Macmillan, 1922; (editor) *A Thousand and One Nights: Tales of Wonder and Magnificence,* Macmillan, 1923; *The Six Who Were Left on a Shoe,* Macmillan, 1923 [another edition illustrated by Joseph Schindelman, McGraw-Hill, 1968]; *The Peep-Show Man* (illustrated by Lois Lenski), Macmillan, 1924; *The Forge in the Forest* (illustrated by Boris Artzybasheff), Macmillan, 1925; *The Voyagers* (illustrated by Wilfred Jones), Macmillan, 1925; *The Fountain of Youth* (illustrated by Jay Van Everen), Macmillan, 1927, excerpt from *The Fountain of Youth* published separately as *Story Telling New and Old* (illustrations from J. Van Everen), Macmillan, 1968; *Three Men: A Tale,* Matthews & Marrot, 1930; *The Big Tree of Bunlahy* (illustrated by J. Yeats), Macmillan, 1933; *The White Sparrow* (illustrated by Lynd Ward), Macmillan, 1933 [another edition illustrated by Joseph Low, McGraw-Hill, 1972]; *Where the Winds Never Blew and the Cocks Never Crew* (illustrated by Richard Bennett), Macmillan, 1940; *The Stone of Victory, and Other Tales* (illustrated by Judith Gwyn Brown), McGraw-Hill, 1966.

Poems: *Heather Ale: A Book of Verse,* [Dublin], 1907; *Wild Earth: A Book of Verse,* Maunsel (Dublin), 1907; *Wild Earth, and Other Poems,* Holt, 1916; (editor) *Poems of the Irish Revolutionary Brotherhood,* Small, Maynard, 1916; *Dramatic Legends, and Other Poems,* Macmillan, 1922; (editor) *An Anthology of Irish Verse,* Boni & Liveright, 1922, reissued, Liveright, 1972; *Creatures* (illustrated by B. Artzybasheff), Macmillan, 1927; *Old Pastures,* Macmillan, 1930; *Poems,* Macmillan, 1932, revised edition published as *Collected Poems,* Devin-Adair, 1953; *Flower Pieces,* Orwell Press, 1938; *The Vegetable Kingdom,* Indiana University Press, 1954; *Irish Elegies,* Dolmen Press (Dublin), 1958, reissued, Dufour, 1965; *The Poet's Circuits,* Oxford University Press, 1960; (editor) Samuel Ferguson, *Poems,* Dufour, 1963; (editor) *Roofs of Gold: Poems to Read Aloud,*

PADRAIC COLUM

Macmillan, 1964; *Images of Departure,* Dolmen Press, 1969.

Plays: *The Land* (three-act), Maunsel, 1905; *The Fiddler's House* (three-act), Maunsel, 1907; *Thomas Muskerry* (three-act), Maunsel, 1910; *Three Plays: The Fiddler's House, The Land, Thomas Muskerry,* Little, Brown, 1916, reissued, Dufour, 1963; *Mogu, the Wanderer; or, The Desert* (three-act), Little, Brown, 1917; *The Miracle of the Corn,* Theatre Arts, 1925; *Balloon,* Macmillan, 1929; (with wife, Mary Colum) *Moytura: A Play for Dancers,* Oxford University Press, 1963.

Other: *My Irish Year* (autobiography), J. Pott, 1912; (editor) *Broad-Sheet Ballads,* Maunsel, 1913; *Castle Conquer* (novel), Macmillan, 1923; *At the Gateways of the Day* (Hawaiian legends; illustrated by Juliette M. Fraser), Yale University Press, 1924; *The Island of the Mighty* (retold from the Mabinogion), Macmillan, 1924; *The Bright Islands* (Hawaiian legends; illustrated by J. M. Fraser), Yale University Press, 1925; *The Road round Ireland,* Macmillan, 1926; (contributor) "Poetry of the Gael," in *Book of Modern Catholic Prose* (edited by Theodore Maynard), Holt, 1928; *Orpheus: Myths of the World* (illustrated by B. Artzybasheff), Macmillan, 1930; *Cross Roads to Ireland,* Macmillan, 1930; *A Half-Day's Ride; or, Estates in Corsica* (essays), Macmillan, 1932, reprinted, Books for Libraries, 1969; *The Legend of Saint Columba* (illustrated by Elizabeth MacKinstry), Macmillan, 1935; *The Frenzied Prince* (Irish legends; illustrated by W. Pogany), McKay, 1943; (editor) *A Treasury of Irish Folklore,* Crown Publishers, 1954, reissued, 1967; *The Flying Swans* (novel), Crown Publishers, 1957, reissued, A. Figgis (Dublin), 1969; (with M. Colum) *Our Friend James Joyce,* Doubleday, 1958; *Ourselves Alone! The Story of Arthur Griffith and the Origin of the Irish Free State,* Crown Publishers, 1959 (published in Ireland as *Arthur Griffith,* Browne & Nolan, 1959).

SIDELIGHTS: **December 8, 1881.** Born in Longford, Ireland, the eldest child of Padraic and Susanna (MacCormack) Colum. "... I was born in a workhouse and knew common speech from my birth. I always say I was born in a workhouse to make a romantic story; the fact is, my father was the master of a workhouse, which isn't *quite* so good, not being quite so bad.

"There is in Ireland a great feeling for character, not character as the modern novelists conceive it, mere psychological material, but for character living, breathing, moving—in a word acting. There is too a real aptitude for dialogue; newspapers and drawingroom conversation have not taken colour out of speech made by peasants and workpeople." [Zack Bowen, *Padraic Colum: A Biographical-Critical Introduction*, Southern Illinois University Press, 1970.[1]]

"Almost everyone in Ireland is badly fed, and this is not because food is scarce, but because food is overlooked. A farmer will start for the Fair at an early hour in the morning, having taken for breakfast only tea and bread. He will stay at the Fair all day without taking a meal, but stimulating his energies with two or three glasses of whisky. If you meet him in the evening, the man will appear drunk. Day after day he takes the same dinner; potatoes, cabbage, American or Russian bacon. Soup is never made in his house, and cabbage is the only vegetable grown for his household. There is no longer the supply of milk and butter that there used to be, when the churning was done in the house. The people have ceased to make porridge for breakfast and supper. Tea is taken at every hour in the day. In the country towns, one cannot get proper food properly cooked, the ordinary dinner served to men in the eating-house is a hard beef-steak with bread and tea." [Padraic Colum, *My Irish Year*, James Pott & Co., 1912.[2]]

Colum's religious devotion and Catholic upbringing were expressed in several poems, especially in "Fuchsia Hedges in Connacht."

"I think you came from some old Roman land—
Most alien, but most Catholic are you:

"Your purple is the purple that enfolds,
In Passion Week, the Shrine,
Your scarlet is the scarlet of the wounds:
You bring before our walls, before our doors
Lamps of the Sanctuary."[1]

1888. Colum's father, a man of considerable thirst, fell into debt, was forced to resign his workhouse duties, and sojourned to America. The remaining family went to live with Colum's grandmother in County Cavan. "... While I was still a child I left the town I was born in and went to live in the next county. There, in my grandmother's house, I heard stories before I could read them, and songs and scraps of poetry before I had to learn any at school."

"I must not give the impression I was a solitary child, one of these youngsters who have to be adopted into their elder's circle. I was eager to listen to their discourse, and I was receptive. But I had employments. I was included in a fairly large household that was my grandmother's. There were my mother, my two brothers, and a sister. There were my aunt, her husband, and their children, who were my contemporaries. And there was another, my mother's younger brother, who went and came as different employments took him here or there. When attached to the house, he slept in the loft or attic. We are farmers—that is to say, we rent acres, grow potatoes, cabbage, a patch of oats, have a pasture field for two cows, keep several pigs in a sty, but no one in the house takes an interest in farming in the way that some of our neighbors do.

"... My grandmother was 'out' with the two families that neighbored us. Not only did they never visit us nor we them, but we never spoke to them if we encountered members of either household in our goings and comings. They did not have to pass our house, but we had to pass theirs without a look into the yards or at the open doors. What reason there was for this ban we children did not know, but we observed it faithfully. Passing the first or second house with someone in the yard before the door, or actually on the lane, we made no acknowledgement of their presence. The consequence of this aloofness was that we rarely had evening visitors. The only one who came to the door with the time-honored 'God save all here' was ... Charlie MacGauran.

"He seemed a survivor—or I will say that to me his dress seemed old-fashioned enough to belong to a bygone time, the frieze coat in a shape that was known as 'swallowtail.' But it was more than that. He was a survivor because he was the spokesman of a period that was further back than my mother's time. He talked of the burning of our nearby village. Like all stories that have the burning of habitations in them, his recollection of the burning of Ballinagh seemed epical. 'The village of the Ford of the Steeds,' he called it, and I had not known until then that the name of the little place had such epical overtones. The Orangemen were charged with that destructiveness. Perhaps there was a counteraction. A ballad that a member of our household had in which there was a memorable line—'And on the hill of Cleggan we'll plant our laurel tree'—may have celebrated a reprisal. The fact that he was the historian of this momentous event made the man who sat at Anne Connolly's [Colum's grandmother] hearth a venerable figure for me.

"But it is right and proper I should look back on Charlie MacGauran as a man of note. He was, in fact, the last in that part of the country to have the office so important in rural Ireland, the shanachie—the local storyteller, the local historian. In times further back—my mother or my aunt told me this—there used to be a *mahil*, a cooperative piece of work, done on the farm or in the house. Sometimes the *mahil* in the house would be spinning. On a certain evening the girls would come to a designated house and do the spinning of the neighborhood there. To entertain them there would be the shanachie with his stories. And so one can say that storytelling in the Irish countryside survived as an economic adjunct. Well, Charlie MacGauran, though his office was now unrecognized, had been the shanachie of my grandmother's generation.

"But in Anne Connolly's I never heard a regular story from him. Once, however, I was sent to his cabin with a present of candles. I imagine that candlelight was not a usual illumination; that the solitary householder did his evening chores by the light of the turf fire, with pieces of whin bush or bog deal to add something of a blaze. Boys and girls were gathered there—it may have been some special occasion—and after some bantering requests to him the old man signified his willingness to tell a story. And what was the story? One of a hundred of the same pattern—a king's son, an enchanter or a king's daughter, a steed that had some magical endowment. It was a story and that was sufficient. But looking back on the scene in after times I could judge that Charlie MacGauran's was a performance, and an accomplished performance. As he sat by the hearth, he held a stick or a staff in

Once upon a time there was an Old Woman who made brooms (only she called them besoms) out of the heather that grew on the mountain. To the very top of this mountain she went one day, gathering her heather; and when she looked down, the other side of the mountain seemed so much nicer than the side she lived on that the Old Woman kept going down and never turning back. And when she got to the bottom, she found friends there; and they treated her so well that she had no need to gather heather nor to make and sell besoms any more. ■ (From *Where the Winds Never Blew* by Padraic Colum. Illustrated by Richard Bennett.)

his hand. His raising it was a sign that he was about to begin. His face took on a firmer expression. When he came to a significant passage he would say suddenly and imperatively, 'Hear me! Hear me!' The conventional descriptions that are in such narratives—in this particular one I remember there was a description of a ship putting out to sea—were given rapidly, with a distinctive rhythm. These were the 'runs' that were to rest the storyteller and the audience.

''In transferring a story of the kind I heard then to the pages of a collection, elements are lost, many elements—the quietness of the surroundings, the shadows on the smoke-browned walls, the crickets chirping in the ashes, the corncrake in the near meadow or the more distant crying of the snipe or curlew, and (for a youngster) the directness of statement or, simply, the evocation of wonder.

''What age was the head of our household when, with my mother, two brothers, and a sister, I came to live with her? Fifty or somewhat over it, I think. My grandmother had not reconciled herself to the loss of that attractiveness which, as I gathered from things said here and there, she was known to have possessed. Once, as I was leaving the pasture field with her, a man on horseback drew by to speak to her. I said something that brought in the word 'grandmother' as the man rode off. 'You must never call me grandmother,' she told me angrily.

''I remember her as a woman of whims. In houses such as hers it was usual for the family to recite the Rosary before bedtime. It was pious routine. My grandmother's was not such a house. We'd have the Rosary not every night; not even on some particular night. We'd be sitting round the fire,

a group of the household, when suddenly my grandmother would order us to kneel for the Rosary. Now, the floor was very uneven; kneeling there for any length of time was an ordeal. The 'Five Glorious Mysteries,' the 'Five Sorrowful Mysteries,' and we would be requested to meditate on the 'Mystery of the Annunciation' or the 'Mystery of the Parting of Mother and Son.' But even if we had any faculty for it, there was no scope for meditation. We went into the decades of the Mysteries as into an ice-cold stream, our object being to reach the bank as soon as we could. There were moments of release when appeal was made to something nascently poetic in me. What had been arid flowered when I repeated the epithets in the Litany—'Tower of Ivory,' 'House of Gold,' 'Ark of the Covenant,' 'Gate of Heaven.' Then we were at the end of the Rosary proper. But we still grounded our knees for my grandmother's whim. She might offer up petitions that would be as lengthy as the Rosary. How many souls in Purgatory would be remembered! How many relatives at home or abroad—uncles, cousins—would have their welfare dutifully prayed for! Sometimes the petitions would be numerous, and sometimes we would conclude the Rosary without one petition.

''I have brought them to the same fireside, my grandmother and Charlie MacGauran. Alone with them I am trying to learn some elementary lesson by candlelight. They have fallen into that ancient form of discourse, the *seanchus*—partly reminiscence, partly local history, partly traditional lore. The mound I had climbed the year before, the Moat of Granard, is mentioned. 'They carried the clay in bags on their backs to build it,' Charlie MacGauran relates. 'Oh, you may be sure it was the Catholics who had to do it.' The sentence stayed in my mind long enough for me to ex-

For two days and two nights he was tossed about on the waters. ■ (From *The Adventure of Odysseus and the Tale of Troy* by Padraic Colum. Illustrated by Willy Pogany.)

amine it with a mind that had some instruction in history. The Moat of Granard is a mound that goes back to prehistoric times. The man beside the hearth was speaking out of a memory—not far back, indeed—when the Catholics of Ireland were politically and socially oppressed. And he was also speaking out of an ancient tradition. The 'Fir Bolg,' the 'Men of the Bag,' had to build fortresses for their conquerors, transporting earth in bags to make ramparts. How did the tradition, I wonder now, come down to the man who sat by Anne Connolly's hearth? Did some scholar who had read manuscript history tell some predecessor of Charlie's about the Men of the Bag who were in Ireland before the Gaels, whose stock remained apart from the Gaelic or mingled with it? They did not get their name from carrying bags of earth—that, obviously, was a contemptuous term given them by a racial ascendancy, to express their servile position at one time. But 'Bolg' may have been their own name for themselves, the name they had brought from the Continent—'the Belgae.'

"The tradition that existed in my grandmother's house was fragmented. There was a fragment that related the household to the people who had built the mounds—a belief in magic, charms, omens. My grandmother believed—but there are degrees in belief—that one might go on churning and churning and get no good of one's labor because some beldame three or four fields away was charming the butter into her own churn. There were omens one met on the wayside. A child walking in his sleep was not addressed by his proper name but by the name of someone outside the house, lest malignant powers get possession of him.

"Out of this particular stratum came a few items that have stayed in my memory. I have come with my grandmother

into the barn where poultry are roosting. How well the sleepy murmur of hens and chickens fits in with the nightfall! And like the child in the folk story, I ask my grandmother what the murmur signifies. 'They are telling where the Danes hid their treasures when they left Ireland.' I couldn't have got an answer that would be richer in traditional implications." [*The New Yorker,* from an article entitled "The Tradition That Existed in My Grandmother's House," December 23, 1967.[3]]

"That side of my education, the traditional side, was developed by another person who lived with us. He was my aunt's husband, and his business was to attend the markets in the towns around and buy fowl from farmers' wives and daughters, sending them to a bigger market for export. On days when I did not have to go to school he would let me come with him to different markets. We went on his cart to destinations that seemed far away. On the street of the town we came into there was always a ballad-singer singing, or rather bawling, a 'come-all-ye' (so-called because one would begin, 'Come all ye tender Christians and listen to me while' or 'Come all, ye true born Irishmen'—one would be pathetic and the other rousing). The ballad-mongers still had ballads in which the Napoleonic cause was celebrated under the figure of 'The Green Linnet.' 'The Bunch of Roses.' 'The Ould Grey Mare.' My uncle-in-law had a great repertoire of such ballads and, jogging homeward, while I ate out of a bag of gingersnaps, would sing a dozen or so of them. And so I received my early literary instruction. I was conditioned to the oral element in literature . . . a story is to be told to a group, a play something that has to be talked into existence." [*New York Herald Tribune Book Review,* from an article entitled "Some Important Fall Authors Speak for Themselves," October 11, 1953.[4]]

". . . Poetry is not just for the eye alone, poetry is for the ear as well—it is for the sounds. . . ." [*The Horn Book Magazine,* from an article entitled "Patterns for the Imagination," February, 1962.[5]]

Attended Glasthule national school in Sandy Cove until seventeen. "I, aged six, and my brother, aged five, are going to school. Before us or alongside of us are a ragged family—father, mother, a boy, and maybe a girl. They have come through the gate of a large-sized building that is our home. That building is the workhouse of the district. My father is master there. The family alongside my brother and me have had a night's shelter there. They are itinerants of some kind, and after doing some jobs on the way—the man may be a tinker or a basketmaker—will spend the night in another workhouse.

"I suppose that for several mornings as my brother and I went to school in a convent I saw such characters. But never before (and, I may add, never since) did I see a white crow on the shoulder of a boy whose day was to be on the long road that led to towns whose names were captivating. And here were we, lesson books in hands, going to stand in classes. . . ."[4]

On a return to the school in his later years, Colum offered the following sketch: "When the stranger enters the school there is a tumult of children rising to their feet in acknowledgment of the visit. The schoolroom recalls a peasant interior: the children are mannerly but not obtrusively disciplined, the walls are bare except for maps and tablets, the floor is broken, the desks and benches are without ease or elegance. A turf fire burns in the grate, and this fire is made up of a toll exacted from the children. (In the morning you might have seen some of them on their way to school, a turf from the home rick under the arm.) We are in the boys' school; about thirty pupils are present, and of these only a few are over sixteen. The schoolmaster, Mr. Jeremiah Kerrigan, comes forward. He is a man of forty, with a foxy beard, sunken cheeks, and alert eyes. If you add to bluffness and a caustic humour something of command and a consciousness of learning you have the main indications of his character. He is of the village, and so his clothes are baggy and his hair is untrimmed.

"Mr. Kerrigan takes us round the classes. The normal subjects are English (including grammar and composition), arithmetic, and geography. Some extra subjects—music, Irish as a foreign language, and mathematics—are also taught. Twenty-two hours per week are given to secular instruction. the hours are from 9:30 A.M. to 3 P.M., and children attend school between the ages of six and seventeen. After sixteen the boys stay at home on the farm, go into business, or emigrate. Mr. Kerrigan calculates that thirty per cent of his pupils go to America.

". . . The Irish schools may be defined as secular institutions under clerical control. In their rules and regulations the Commissioners inform us that the object of their system is 'to afford combined literary and moral and separate religious instruction to children of all persuasions as far as possible in the same school, upon the fundamental principle that no attempt shall be made to interfere with the peculiar religious tenets of any description of Christian pupil.' This regulation is strictly observed, though in the main each school is attended by pupils of the same religious faith. No religious emblems are shown, and religious instruction is outside routine. Clear notice of such instruction is given, and the pupils of a faith different from the majority have permission to withdraw. The parish schools under Catholic, Protestant, or Presbyterian managers are practically autonomous.

". . . Considering the standard of living in an Irish village, Mr Jeremiah Kerrigan is well off. What influence has he on the community? All his pupils can read, figure, and write an expressive letter. It should be noted that the system which he serves does not aim at making the peasantry more effective on the land. The tradition of good agriculture is lapsing in many parts of Ireland, and the schools have done nothing to make farming interesting. Our friend sometimes teaches agriculture as an extra subject; he expounds text-books, making the subject as remote as political economy. He teaches arithmetic, but not arithmetic as applied to farming. The peasants never know where they are economically; they sell their pigs at 4d. per lb. and buy American or Russian bacon at 9d. per lb. Intelligent children attend school for eight or nine years, and they receive a course of instruction that is mainly literary. Afterwards they read the newspapers and take an interest in politics."[2]

"Now, I consider that if we have been educating children in what I hold as most important—and that is the pattern that exists in everything—then teaching [a] sonnet, having a child learn it by heart, makes the pattern evident, and leaves both pattern and poem impressed in the mind of the child. And he will see in his mind how the sonnet is built up, he will see it line by line, quatrain by quatrain, then finally in the sestet, and ultimately in the last line—he will see the climax reached."[5]

Colum's father returned to Ireland after his abortive fortune seeking tour in America. He secured employment as a clerk

The Sea-Maiden who became a Sea-Swan

(From *The Boy Who Knew What the Birds Said* by Padraic Colum. Illustrated by Dugald Stewart Walker.)

in the Sandy Cove Railway Station and eventually worked his way up to station master.

1897. Colum and brother, Fred, were hired to deliver packages for the railway. "At that time (if anyone wants to know), I was sixteen or thereabouts, and living in a suburb of Dublin. My father was in charge of a little railway station, and my brother and I, after school, had the job of delivering parcels that came by train to the various residences around—down avenues, along terraces, or to houses that had drives leading up to them." [*The New Yorker,* from an article entitled, "Another World From Mine," October 10, 1970.[6]]

"I was fortunate in being able to help my brother deliver parcels because it took me away from what might have been that introspective [preoccupation]. I think that I had a tendency towards melancholy. If I hadn't been taken away from that and put on the streets and the roads and went around meeting people and other boys and gangs I would have been—God knows what—I don't."[1]

1897. Mother died. Younger children went to live with relatives in the country and in America. Colum spent much of his time visiting with brothers and sisters in rural Ireland. These visits later resulted in such poems as "The Plougher" and "The Drover." His poetic philosophy is best described in "The Poet."

"But close to the ground are reared
The wings that have widest sway,
And the birds that sing best in the wood. . . .
Were reared with breasts to the clay."[1]

1901. Co-founder of the Irish National Theatre (later known as the Abbey). "I entered the group in which were Yeats, Lady Gregory, A.E., and J. M. Synge, and had a play produced when I was twenty. . . ."

Colum eventually cut his connection with the theatre over disagreement with the drama company's policy.

1903. Awarded a scholarship for promising Irish writers from Thomas Hughes Kelly, son of a wealthy American banker.

1905. *The Land* produced in the Abbey Theatre. "The first popular success the Abbey Theatre had had. . . .

"The passion for the land that motivates the first play is not likely to be responded to in days when farms are being abandoned and when the men who knew the oppression of landlordism as Murtagh Cosgar and Martin Douras did are not to be met with in the flesh. If staged these days *The Land* would have to be played as an historical piece and for character parts. However another issue could give relevancy—the revolt of the young against parental possessiveness."[1]

With David Houston, James Stephens, and Thomas MacDonagh, Colum founded the *Irish Review*. "David Houston was an outgoing, enthusiastic, hospitable man, with a tinge of Orangism that was provocative. Now his house open on Sunday afternoons was crammed with Irish Revivalists. Thomas MacDonagh from the school down the road appeared amongst them. So did James Stephens, who was now a cherished guest at every reception in Dublin. I would come with M.C.M. [Molly; his future wife], who was a favourite in the Houston household.

"One evening the sanguine householder announced to the four of us that he had the establishment of an Irish monthly in mind. It is a measure of the faith that obtained in those days that this disclosure was discussed, not merely seriously, but eagerly. Houston, MacDonagh, Stephens and myself were to conduct it. We named the future publication—at my suggestion, I think—*The Irish Review*. M.C.M. was to have the office of critic-in-chief. And the Review, mind you, was not to be quarterly, but monthly, with the same number of pages as a quarterly of today, and to be sold for sixpence.

"In a couple of weeks we had assembled the first number of *The Irish Review*. James Stephens' contribution to its contents was outstanding: It was the story he had just finished, his first important one, *The Charwoman's Daughter*, which he bestowed on the publication as a serial. George Moore, A.E. and Padraic Pearse gave us material."[1]

1912. Married writer and literary critic Mary Catherine Gunning Maguire ("Molly").

Mary's account of Colum's proposal of marriage revealed their relationship. "I did not have any taste for exchanging the independent and interesting life I was living for pottering around a kitchen, planning meals, hanging curtains, and so on, and I let my young men friends know my sentiments about this. One of them, however, declined to listen to me and kept assuring me that he was the person Heaven had destined me to marry and that I could not escape my fate. I always thought, as he was a very fine and courageous person, that he would be a nice man for somebody else to marry, which was what eventually happened—in fact he married before I did. But he made one final determined effort before dropping me. He called at my little flat, armed with an engagement ring, and told me in a very cave-man manner that he had arranged everything, that I was to marry him on a certain date in a certain church, and that I had better accept my destiny. The argument that ensued reduced me to a state of panic such as I had never known, for I was afraid I might be unable to hold out, especially as he said I had encouraged him and ought to have some sense of responsibility about it. But I managed to be strong-minded, and the harassing interview ended with tears on both sides, with his throwing the ring into the fire and leaving in a high state of emotion. I was stretched out in a condition of copious weeping when, some minutes later, another of my young men friends, a well-known Abbey author, Padraic Colum, called. Tearfully I told him of my ordeal; the ring was still lying unconsumed in a corner of the grate; he fished it out with a tongs, left it on the hearthstone to cool so that it could be mailed back to the young man who had brought it; then he settled himself gravely in an armchair and proceeded to lecture me. 'I think,' said he, 'that to save yourself trouble, you should marry me. Then these fellows will all leave you alone and you won't have to go through any more of these scenes.' He pursued this train of reasoning, and eventually I dried my eyes and said, 'All right, Colum; maybe that would be best.'

"At the end of this scene I think he was a very sober young man at finding himself engaged to be married, for I imagine he had pondered on the marriage state about as little as I had."[1]

1914. ". . . I came to America for the first time. It was there that I began to write stories for children, growing out of translation of a long folk-story from the Irish."

"The story-teller must have respect for the child's mind and the child's conception of the world, knowing it for a complete mind and a complete conception. If a story-teller have that respect he need not be childish in his language in telling stories to children. If the action be clear and the sentences clear one can use a mature language. Strange words, out-of-the-way words do not bewilder children if there be order in the action and in the sentences. They like to hear such words.

"It is more important to let a child's imagination develop than it is to labor to inculcate in him or her some correct ethical point of view.

"It would be well if the modern and metropolitan story-teller could do what that story-teller's art permitted him to do—to make certain descriptions purely conventional—the description of a ship sailing the sea, for instance; the description of a castle or of a lonely waste. . . . When he set his ship sailing upon the sea, when he set this hero wandering through a wilderness, the audience rested and the story-teller rested, not because there was nothing happening, but because what was happening was regular and anticipated."[1]

1923. ". . . On the invitation of the Hawaiian legislature, I went to the Islands to make a survey of their traditional stories and reshape them so as to bring the imaginative past of the Polynesian people to the newer groups in the Islands. . . ."

There was Sindri in his glowing forge, working with bellows and anvil and hammers beside him, and around him masses of metal. ■ (From *The Children of Odin* by Padraic Colum. Illustrated by Willy Pogany.)

''Through the children's stories I became an authority on folklore without ever telling anybody I was one. . . .

''We were in Paris. And we took a boat from Paris to New York. We took a train from New York to San Francisco. We took a liner from San Francisco to Honolulu and when we got there they put a lei on our necks. They got us a little cottage down on Waikiki, and we settled down without thinking of anything beyond that. And then one evening I went into Honolulu; I remember great winds blowing, coconuts knocking me on the head along the street, and I suddenly realized: 'What the hell am I doing here? What do I expect to do? Where is it? I don't know a word of the language; I don't know the history of the people; and here I am, going to write about them!' It was then I told Molly we'd better slip off to Australia, that I had a brother there who'd cover up for me. 'No.' she said. She was always of the opinion that I had this self-confidence that should be pricked at some time or another. 'Now's the time to get your self-confidence. That should show you what t'will lead you to. No, you are not going to Australia. You'll have to stay here.' So I did and worked it out.

''It was curious and interesting too how I got started on it. I was groping around and I went into the Bishop Museum; that's the museum of Polynesian stuff in Honolulu. I didn't notice anything very interesting as I was going along. Then I saw the feathered capes. You know the high chieftains wore what you'd call now a stole just around their shoulders, and it was made of feathers, feathers stitched on tapa and it went over the shoulders. They were generally in black, yellow, red, and they were only permitted to take one feather out of a bird and let it go, so it must have taken twenty years to make a cape of that kind. It was that that gave me the im-

pression that I wanted of this strange civilization that was trying to matter, and then I began to learn some of the language. The very fact that there was a civilization in which a man would spend twenty years trying to make a cape . . . that's what impressed me. So that's how it happened. In three months I was lecturing the Hawaiian Academy on their traditions. Now isn't that something? My self-confidence still lasted. After that terrible discovery of mine that I knew nothing, to have enough self-confidence left to lecture to the Hawaiian Academy on the traditions—why my god! When I think about it! Molly used to say that I'd undertake to do anything except earn a living.

''. . . But the idea of my setting myself up as a folklorist or a mythologist is nonsense. I didn't set myself up, but the Hawaiian legislature thought I was the man. The main thing was my ability to write these stories and an interest in them. After all you could get a real field worker in folklore who couldn't do that and would be less good to them.

''I made it my main task to understand the background of the stories given in that collection, and to hear as many of them as possible from the lips of the surviving custodians of the Polynesian tradition in Hawaii.

''I have had to condense, expand, heighten, subdue, rearrange—in a word, I have had to retell the stories, using the old romances as material for wonder-stories. The old stories were not for children; they gave an image of life to kings and soldiers, to courtiers and to ruling women. As in all stories not originally intended for children, much has had to be suppressed in retelling them for a youthful audience.

PADRAIC COLUM

"And retelling them has meant that I have had to find a new form for the stories. The form that I choose to give them is that of the European folk-tale."[1]

1929. Attempted another fling with the theater by having his play, *Balloon,* produced. "I wrote a play for Broadway, called *Balloon.* It's still called the most famous unproduced play on Broadway. It was bought by Michael Myerberg. He had just put on Thornton Wilder's *Our Town.* He was enterprising and avant-garde. He got my play and put it on over in Ogunquit—experimentally—and it was a success. It ran not only for a week but for two weeks, which had never happened before. And then after I had imagined myself as making money on Broadway it never went on. The usual disappointment. . . . So I'm a foiled, frustrated dramatist."[1]

1930. A stipend from Macmillan Company came to an end. "Your letter and telegram mean that Macmillan Co. are leaving me, an author who has given them twenty books, without any income whatever. And on what pretence? That I have a deficit of 2709 dollars. . . . I shall not forget that the Macmillan Co. are more anxious to take a stand on their auditors' report rather than on their author's interest. I should like to remind them that publishers live by authors, not by auditors. If their authors get disgusted with them or are forced into other ways of earning a living, what good will their auditors be to them? . . . If Macmillans withhold the total earnings on my books I shall have the matter debated in the literary journals of America and Europe. . . . I propose that you make me an allowance of one hundred dollars per month with a thousand dollars advance on my new book, *Other Roads In Ireland.* If you are willing to do this cable me on receipt of this letter."[1] A small stipend was forthcoming.

1930. During a six month stay in Paris, a memorable association with James Joyce culminated in Colum's and his wife's joint effort in the biography, *Our Friend James Joyce.*

1938. President of the Poetry Society of America.

1939. Joined faculty at Columbia. Colum and wife taught a course in comparative literature. "We were teaching in Columbia, Molly and I, in the Philosophy Department . . . and it wasn't philosophy at all. I'm not a good teacher . . . I was never meant to be a teacher because I had no training. Molly was the good teacher. She had good training in teaching. I would come in and talk to them informally rather than formally. Well, I could always teach them poetry, you know. The business of teaching poetry is to make them interested in it, isn't it? Not about the meters which I never could understand."[1]

1940. Medal, Poetry Society of America.

1951. Honorary Doctorate, National University of Ireland.

1952. Fellowship Award, Academy of American Poets.

1953. Lady Gregory Award, Academy of Irish Letters.

1957. His wife died. "I am on the eleventh floor of an apartment house on Central Park. I look across the Park to the great houses of Fifth Avenue. The music that I wanted to listen to has come to an end, and I am conscious that in the apartment that my wife and I lived in for twenty years I am alone. . . ."[2]

1958. Honorary Doctorate, Columbia University.

1961. Regina Medal, Catholic Library Association.

Returned to the theater with a series of Irish plays utilizing the Noh play form. "I wanted to write something short; I wanted to write something with poetry in it; and I wanted to write drama, which I'm always writing anyway."[1]

1963. Membership, American Academy of Arts and Letters.

January 12, 1972. Died of a stroke in Enfield, Conn.

FOR MORE INFORMATION SEE: E. A. Boyd, "Impulse to Folk Drama: J. M. Synge and Padraic Colum," in *Contemporary Drama of Ireland,* Little, Brown, 1917; A. E. Morgan, "Irish Dramatists," in *Tendencies of Modern English Drama,* Scribner, 1923; "Padraic Colum," in *Literary Spotlight,* edited by John C. Farrar, Doran, 1924; Calvert Alexander, "Poetry," in *Catholic Literary Revival,* Bruce Publishers, 1935; Gerald Griffin, "Padraic Colum," in *Wild Geese,* Jarrolds, 1938; A. E. Malone, "Rise of the Realistic Movement," in *Irish Theatre,* edited by Lennox Robinson, Macmillan, 1939; (for children) Stanley J. Kunitz and Howard Haycraft, editors, *Junior Book of Authors,* second revised edition, H. W. Wilson, 1951; Leonard A. G. Strong, "Padraic Colum," in his *Personal Remarks,* Liveright, 1953; Louise S. Bechtel, "Padraic Colum: A Great Storyteller of Today," *Catholic Library World,* December, 1960; (for children) Laura Benét, *Famous Storytellers for Young People,* Dodd, 1968; Zack R. Bowen, *Padraic Colum: A Biographical-Critical Introduction,* Southern Illinois University Press, 1970.

Obituaries: *New York Times,* January 12, 1972; *Newsweek,* January 24, 1972; *Time,* January 24, 1972; *Commonwealth,* February 11, 1972; *Publishers Weekly,* February 21, 1972; *Britannica Book of the Year 1973.*

CUMMINGS, Betty Sue 1918-

PERSONAL: Born July 12, 1918, in Big Stone Gap, Va.; daughter of Howard Lee (a mining accountant) and Hattie (Bruce) Cummings; *Education:* Longwood College, B.S., 1939; University of Washington, Seattle, M.A., 1949. *Residence:* Titusville, Fla. *Agent:* Virginia Kidd, P.O. Box 278, Milford, Pa. 18337.

CAREER: English teacher in junior high schools in Norton, Va., 1939-41, Richmond, Va., 1942-43, and high school in Thermopolis, Wyo., 1950-57; Brevard County School Board, Titusville, Fla., English teacher and counselor, 1957-73; writer, 1973—. *Military service:* U.S. Coast Guard, 1942-45; became ensign. *Member:* American Pen Women (Cape Canaveral branch), Writers in Company. *Awards, honors:* Rollins College Writers Conference Short Story award, 1973; nominated for National Book Award for Children's Literature, for *Hew Against the Grain.*

WRITINGS: Hew Against the Grain, Atheneum, 1977; *Let a River Be,* Atheneum, 1978.

War is never pretty. And the worst of what it does is to the spirit of people. Only the strongest can fight—can hew against the grain. ■ (From *Hew Against the Grain* by Betty Sue Cummings. Jacket illustration by Richard Cuffari.)

BETTY SUE CUMMINGS

WORK IN PROGRESS: A book tentatively titled *Now, Ameriky!;* research on modern prostitution for an adult novel.

SIDELIGHTS: "For many years I have been concerned that the bulk of literature available to young people has stereotyped males as brave and females as cowardly, or at least frivolous toward their responsibilities. My own observation told me that this was not true, and I have begun a pursuit of courage in the women of history, not famous women, but rather the average women who endured. *Hew Against the Grain* is a story about a young woman who endured the terrible happenings along the Virginia-West Virginia border during the Civil War. *Let a River Be* is a story about an old woman, poor and crippled with arthritis, whose work is to save Indian River from pollution."

FOR MORE INFORMATION SEE: New York Times Book Review, April 24, 1977.

CUTCHEN, Billye Walker 1930-
(Billye Walker Brown)

PERSONAL: Born April 23, 1930, in Oklahoma City, Okla.; daughter of William Lafayette (an accountant) and Naomi (Armstrong) Walker; married Walter Reed Brown, September 2, 1949 (divorced, August, 1971); married Paul O. Cutchen (a naval officer), April 18, 1974; children: Susan

BILLYE WALKER CUTCHEN

Merle (Mrs. Dennis Kresmer), Elizabeth Ann, Cynthia Lee (Mrs. Brook West). *Education:* Attended Oklahoma College for Women, 1946-47, University of Oklahoma, 1947-48, and Florida State University, 1959-60. *Residence:* Monrovia, Liberia. *Address:* 111 South Jamaica St., Warrington, Fla. 32507.

CAREER: Writer, 1966—.

WRITINGS—Adult books; under name Billye Walker Brown: (Editor with Kenneth Croft, and contributor) *Science Readings,* McGraw, 1966; *Research Ideas for Science Projects,* U.S. Agency for International Development, 1968; (with Walter R. Brown) *Science Teaching and the Law,* National Science Teachers Association, 1969; (editor) Mary Manoni, *The Black American,* Michie Co., 1969; (editor) Herbert Appenzeller, *From the Gym to the Jury,* Michie Co., 1969; (editor) William Bolmeier, *Legal Authority Over the Pupil,* Michie Co., 1970; (editor) Bolmeier, *Legal Issues in Education,* Michie Co., 1970; (editor) Palmer and Poulter, *The Legal System of Lesotho,* Michie Co., 1972; (editor) Wilfred Bunch and others, *Modern Management of Myelomeningocele,* Warren H. Green Association, 1972; (editor) Jaji N.A. Noor Muhammed, *The Legal System of Somalia,* Michie Co., 1973.

Children's books; under name Billye Walker Brown: (Editor) James Haggerty, *Man's Conquest of Space,* Scholastic Book Services, 1965; (with Walter R. Brown) *Historical Catastrophes: Volcanoes,* Addison-Wesley, 1970; (with W. R. Brown) *Historical Catastrophes: Hurricanes and Tornadoes,* Addison-Wesley, 1972; (with W. R. Brown) *Historical Catastrophes: Earthquakes,* Addison-Wesley, 1974; (editor) Lane Mitchell, *Ceramics: Stone Age to Space Age,* National Science Teachers Association, 1963; (editor) Harold Simon,

Microbes and Men, National Science Teachers Association, 1963; (editor) Catherine Hoffman, *Chemistry of Life,* National Science Teachers Association, 1964; (editor) Van Overbeek, *The Lore of Living Plants,* National Science Teachers Association, 1963; (editor) Olaf Michelsen, *Nutrition, Science, and You,* National Science Teachers Association, 1964; (editor) Moffat, *Life Beyond the Earth,* National Science Teachers Association, 1965. Contributor to science journals, juvenile and popular magazines, and newspapers, including *Jack and Jill* and *Mr.* Associate editor of *Vista of Science,* National Science Teachers Association, 1962-64.

Children's books; under name Billye W. Cutchen: (with W. R. Brown) *Historical Catastrophies: Floods,* Addison-Wesley, 1975.

WORK IN PROGRESS: Villingilli, a suspense novel set in the Maldives; collecting information and photographs of Sri Lanka.

SIDELIGHTS: "When I was in school, it never occurred to me that I might one day write anything for publication. Mathematics and science were my first loves, and English grammar was something to be endured, just to get through school. Fortunately, I was a conscientious student, because that subject has been a very useful tool in my work as a writer and editor of science books for students.

"When Addison-Wesley approached my former husband and me about writing a series of books for junior high school

One tall house leans on its neighbor that seems not to have been affected by the 1906 earthquake. ■ (From *Historical Catastrophes: Earthquakes* by Billye Walker Brown and Walter R. Brown.)

students, we started looking for a series. We were having trouble agreeing on a subject when our daughter complained to us that she was supposed to write a report on the volcanic eruption of Krakatoa in 1883. She could find information about it in the library, but nothing that was really interesting to her. When I went to the library to help her, I found that there was some really fascinating information about this volcano, but it was written long ago in the archaic fashion of the time. So we hit upon the series, 'Historical Catastrophes.'

"It was an interesting series to write, in that it was an adventurous learning experience. Library research and interviews were important, but travel to Iceland, to see Surtsey, and Italy, to see Vesuvius and Pompeii, gave me the feeling for the people who were really present when these events took place. Probably the most interesting experience of this sort was a flight, on a U.S. Navy aircraft, into the eye of a hurricane. In addition to being able to describe the storm itself, this flight gave me the opportunity to see how the crew of the plane treated the penetration of such a storm as a routine, fact-gathering mission. Their competence and good humor were enough to make the trip intensely interesting, but not frightening."

DAVIS, Bette J. 1923-

PERSONAL: Born April 18, 1923, in Joplin, Mo.; daughter of Clyde Wilbur (an engineer) and Opal (Morgan) Davis. *Education:* Pratt Institute, Brooklyn, N.Y., B.F.A., 1944. *Politics:* Liberal. *Religion:* Catholic. *Home and office:* R.F.D. 1, Box 1, Chester, N.H. 03036.

CAREER: Illustrator. U.S. Signal Corps Publication Agency, Fort Monmouth, New Jersey, illustrator, 1948-54; Norcross Greeting Card Co., New York, N.Y., designer, 1956-58; White Pines College, Chester, N.H., instructor of design, director of publicity, 1974-77. *Military service:* U.S. Marine Corps, Woman's Reserve, 1944-46, sergeant in spe-

Hours of laborious work, after seventeen years in the ground—all for a few weeks of life. This is the cicada's life story. ■ (From *Musical Insects* by Bette J. Davis. Illustrated by the author.)

cial services. *Member:* Society of Children's Book Writers, National Wildlife Federation, Audubon Society. *Awards, honors: Winter Buds* received an Outstanding Science Book Award from National Science Teachers Association, 1973.

WRITINGS—All self-illustrated: *Animals with Pockets,* Random House, 1968, *Working Animals,* Random House, 1969; *Mole From the Meadow,* Lothrop, 1970; *Musical Insects,* Lothrop, 1971; *Freedom Eagle,* Lothrop, 1972; *Winter Buds,* Lothrop, 1973; *World of Mosses,* Lothrop, 1975.

Illustrator: Elizabeth Hamilton, *First Book of Caves,* Watts, 1956; Solveig P. Russell, *From Rocks to Rockets,* Rand McNally, 1960; Charles and Martha Shapp, *Let's Find Out About Birds,* Watts, 1967; Charles and Martha Shapp, *Let's Find Out About Animals of Long Ago,* Watts, 1968; Kathy Darling, *Ants have Pets,* Garrard, 1977; Mary Adrian, *Wildlife in the Antartic,* Messner, 1978. Has also illustrated many other books.

SIDELIGHTS: "I work almost exclusively with contact art—black and white—that is, pencil (prismacolor) on mylar material. I am strictly a natural history author and artist—mainly animals—occasional botany.

"I was an apprentice to Franci Criss (a painter) for one year, and to Marshall Simpson (a painter) for one year."

BETTE J. DAVIS

DELULIO, John 1938-

PERSONAL: Surname rhymes with "Leo;" born March 29, 1938; son of Albert F. (a postal clerk) and Vonda (Swol) Delulio; married Cynthia Christopher (an executive editor), October 21, 1973. *Education:* Attended Pratt School of Design, 1961-63; American Academy of Art, 1964; Elmhurst College, 1966-67. *Home and office:* 1901 S. Voss, #60, Houston, Tex. 77057.

CAREER: Artist. Norm Ulrich Studios, Chicago, Ill., contemporary graphics and layout artist, 1963-64; International Harvester Co., Chicago, Ill., graphic artist, industrial design, 1964-65; Chicago Bridge and Iron Co., Chicago, Ill., graphic arts manager, 1965-67; Coca-Cola Export Corp., New York, N.Y., senior staff artist, 1967-69; owner of a studio/gallery in Great Barrington, Mass. and Houston, Tex., 1969—. *Military service:* U.S. Navy, 1957-61.

ILLUSTRATOR: Donata Delulio, *The Day the Animals Left the Zoo,* Doubleday, 1972; Aileen Paul, *Kids Camping,* Doubleday, 1973; Aileen Paul, *Kids Cooking Complete Meals: Menus, Recipes, Instructions,* Doubleday, 1975; Aileen Paul, *Kids Gardening,* Doubleday, 1978; Aileen Paul, *Kids Diet Cookbook,* Doubleday, 1979. Delulio has also illustrated three stories (from Russia, Peru, and Africa) for *Tales of Many Lands,* a film and workshop project for schools basic reading programs produced by the Educreative Systems.

SIDELIGHTS: "I create for only a few reasons: number one for myself, number two for those who truly appreciate, and lastly for the future, so they will not believe us all barbarians. As one goes through life many pebbles are crossed, but very few marked stones."

FOR MORE INFORMATION SEE: Register-Star, Hudson, N.Y., February 10, 1975.

(From *Kids Cooking Complete Meals* by Aileen Paul. Illustrated by John Delulio.)

JOHN DELULIO

DICKENS, Charles (John Huffam)   1812-1870
(Boz)

PERSONAL: Born February 7, 1812, in Landport, near Portsmouth, England; died June 9, 1870, in Gadshill, near Rochester, England; buried in the Poet's Corner of Westminster Abbey, London; son of John Dickens (a government clerk); married Catherine Hogarth, 1836 (separated, 1858); children: ten. *Education:* Had little formal education. *Home:* Gadshill Place, England.

CAREER: Novelist, writer of stories, travel books, and sketches. Began working at age twelve in a blacking warehouse after his father was imprisoned for debt; at fifteen, worked as an attorney's clerk and later as a reporter for the *True Sun*, 1832, and the *Morning Chronicle*, 1835; first editor of the London *Daily News*, 1846; founder and editor of the magazines, *Household Words*, 1833-35, and *All the Year Round*, 1859-70. Acted in amateur theatricals beginning in 1845; performed public readings of his works beginning in 1858 and continuing on his second trip to America, 1867-68. All of Dickens' novels and much of his later writings first appeared in serial form in such periodicals as the *Monthly Magazine, Evening Chronicle,* and *Bell's Life of London.*

WRITINGS—Novels; most early editions under the pseudonym Boz: *Sketches by Boz,* three volumes (illustrated by George Cruikshank), J. Macrone, 1836-37, new edition, with an introduction by G. K. Chesterton, Dutton, 1968 [another edition illustrated by Frederick D. Barnard, Chapman & Hall, 1870]; *The Posthumous Papers of the Pickwick Club* (illustrated by Robert Seymour and Phiz, pseudonym of Hablot Knight Browne), Chapman & Hall, 1837, reissued, Penguin Books, 1972 [other editions illustrated by John Gilbert, Appleyard, 1847; Cecil Aldin,

Chapman & Hall, 1910; Frank Reynolds, Hodder & Stoughton, 1912; Charles E. Brock, Harrap, 1930; John Austen, Oxford University Press, 1933; Gordon Ross, Heritage Press, 1936; Donald McKay, Modern Library, 1943; Broom Lynne, Coward-McCann, 1950]; *Oliver Twist; or, The Parish Boy's Progress* (illustrated by G. Cruikshank), R. Bentley, 1838, reissued, Heron Books, 1970 [other editions illustrated by Felix Darley, W. A. Townsend, 1861; J. Mahoney, Chapman & Hall, 1870; W. M. Berger, Macmillan, 1932; Barnett Freedman, Heritage Press, 1939, reissued, 1966; adaptations for children include an edition illustrated by Lawrence B. Smith, Junior Deluxe Editions, 1956; an edition abridged and edited by David Holbrook, Cambridge University Press, 1965; and an edition illustrated by Whitear (simplified by Margaret Maison and Michael West), Longmans, Green, 1967].

The Life and Adventures of Nicholas Nickleby (illustrated by Phiz), Chapman & Hall, 1838-39, reprinted, Scholar Press, 1972-73 [other editions illustrated by F. Barnard, Chapman & Hall, 1838; C. S. Rinehart, Harper, 1873; C. E. Brock, Dodd, 1931; Steven Spurrier, Heritage Press, 1940]; *The Old Curiosity Shop* (illustrated by George Cattermole and Phiz), Chapman & Hall, 1841, reissued, Penguin, 1972 [other editions illustrated by Thomas Worth, Harper, 1872; H. M. Brock, Gresham, 1901; Frank Reynolds, Hodder & Stoughton, 1913; Rowland Wheelwright, Dodd, 1930]; *Barnaby Rudge: A Tale of the Riots of 'Eighty* (illustrated by G. Cattermole and Phiz), Chapman & Hall, 1841, reprinted, Penguin, 1973 [other editions illustrated by F. D. Barnard, Chapman & Hall, 1870; R. Wheelwright, Dodd, 1931; James Daugherty, Heritage Press, 1941; Brian Wildsmith, Ginn, 1965]; *Master Humphrey's Clock* (illustrated by Cattermole and Phiz), Chapman & Hall, 1841.

The Life and Adventures of Martin Chuzzlewit (illustrated by Phiz), Chapman & Hall, 1843-44, reissued, Penguin, 1968 [other editions illustrated by F. D. Barnard, Chapman & Hall, 1870; C. E. Brock, Dodd, 1935; H. M. Brock, Dodd, 1944]; *Dealings with the Firm of Dombey and Son, Wholesale, Retail, and for Exportation* (illustrated by Phiz), Bradbury & Evans, reissued as *Dombey and Son,* Penguin, 1970 [other editions illustrated by F. D. Barnard, Chapman & Hall, 1870; W. L. Sheppard, Harper, 1873]; *The Personal History of David Copperfield* (illustrated by Phiz), Bradbury & Evans, 1850, reprinted, Macmillan, 1962 [other editions illustrated by F. D. Barnard, Chapman & Hall, 1870; William H. Rainey, Gresham, 1900; F. Reynolds, Hodder & Stoughton, 1911; Gertrude D. Hammond, Dodd, 1921; J. Austen, Heritage Press, 1935; Everett Shinn (edited by W. Somerset Maugham), J. C. Winston, 1948; Fritz Kredel, Scott, Foresman, 1951; adaptations for children include *Young David Copperfield* (abridged by Loretta Sidlowski), Greenwich Book Publishers, 1956; an edition adapted by Robert J. Purdy and edited by Ann Price, Laidlaw Brothers, 1956; an edition edited by C. G. Ford, Houghton, 1958; an edition illustrated by N. M. Bodecker, Macmillan, 1962; and an edition edited by Trevor Blount, Penguin, 1966].

Bleak House (illustrated by Phiz), Harper, 1853, reissued, Macmillan, 1963 [other editions illustrated by F. D. Barnard, Chapman & Hall, 1870; Robert Ball, Heritage Press, 1942]; *Hard Times,* T. L. McElrath, 1854, new edition (edited by George Ford and Sylvere Monod), Norton, 1966 [other editions illustrated by Frederick Walker, Chapman & Hall, 1863; Charles Raymond, Heritage Press, 1966]; *Little Dorrit* (illustrated by Phiz), Bradbury & Evans, 1855-

57, reissued, Oxford University Press, 1966 [other editions illustrated by J. Mahoney, Chapman & Hall, 1870; Mimi Korach, Heritage Press, 1956]; *A Tale of Two Cities* (illustrated by Phiz), Chapman & Hall, 1859, reissued, Penguin, 1970 [other editions illustrated by John McLenan, Peterson, 1859; F. D. Barnard, Chapman & Hall, 1870; F. H. Townsend, Putnam, 1898; Harvey Dunn, Cosmopolitan Book Corp., 1921; R. Wheelwright, Dodd, 1925; Donald Teague, Dodd, 1925; Rene Ben Sussan, Heritage Press, 1938, reissued, 1962; adaptations for children include an edition illustrated by Rafaello Busoni, Grosset & Dunlap, 1948; an edition illustrated by Richard M. Powers, Macmillan, 1962; an edition edited by Helen J. Estes and Lee Wyndham, Prentice-Hall, 1962; an edition illustrated by Richard Sharp, Dent, 1973; and an edition edited by Naunerle Farr, Pendulum Press, 1974].

Great Expectations (illustrated from original designs by John McLenan), T. B. Peterson, 1961, reissued, Harper, 1965 [other editions illustrated by Marcus Stone, Chapman & Hall, 1863; Francis A. Fraser, Chapman & Hall, 1870; Charles Green, Chapman & Hall, 1870; G. Ross (with a preface by George Bernard Shaw), R. & R. Clark, 1937; Edward Ardizzone, Heritage Press, 1939, reissued, 1962; adaptations for children include an edition edited by Angus Calder, Penguin, 1965; an edition illustrated by F. W. Pailthorpe and abridged by Anthony Toyne, Oxford University Press, 1967; and an edition illustrated by Gareth Floyd and abridged by Rosemary Manning, American Education Publications, 1970]; *Our Mutual Friend* (illustrated by M. Stone), Chapman & Hall, 1865, reissued, Oxford University Press, 1963 [other editions illustrated by J. Mahoney, Chapman & Hall, 1871; Lynd Ward, Heritage Press, 1957]; *The Mystery of Edwin Drood* (illustrated by S. L. Fildes), Chapman & Hall, 1870, reissued, Oxford University Press, 1964 [another edition illustrated by Everett Shinn, Heritage Press, 1941].

Christmas stories: *A Christmas Carol* (illustrated by John Leech), G. Routledge, 1843, reprinted, Dover, 1971 [other editions illustrated by Sol Eytinge, Jr., Fields, Osgood, 1869; George T. Tobin, F. A. Stokes, 1899; Frederick Simpson Coburn, Putnam, 1900; Charles Pears, Library Press, 1905; C. E. Brock, Dutton, 1905, reprinted, 1960; A. C. Michael, Hodder & Stoughton, 1911; Milo K. Winter, Rand, McNally, 1912; Spencer Baird Nichols, F. A. Stokes, 1913; Arthur Rackham, Lippincott, 1915, reissued, 1964; Harold Copping, Tuck, 1920; G. Ross (with an introduction by Stephen Leacock), Merrymount Press, 1934; H. M. Brock, Dodd, 1935; Dorothy Bayley, Appleton-Century, 1936; Everett Shinn, J. C. Winston, 1938; Erwin L. Hess and F. D. Lohman, Whitman, 1939; William Mark Young, Grosset & Dunlap, 1939; Philip Reed, Atheneum, 1940, reissued, 1966; Fritz Kredel, Peter Pauper Press, 1943; Maraja, Grosset & Dunlap, 1958, reissued, 1963; Ruth McCrea, Peter Pauper Press, 1966; Charles Mozley, F. Watts, 1969; adaptations for children include an edition illustrated by Robert Ball, Macmillan, 1950, reissued, 1960; an edition illustrated by Arthur Rackham, Lippincott, 1952; an edition abridged and edited by Philo Calhoun, Colby College Press, 1954; and an edition illustrated by John Groth, Macmillan, 1963].

The Chimes (illustrated by Daniel Maclise, Richard Doyle, J. Leech, and Clarkson Stanfield), Chapman & Hall, 1845 [other editions illustrated by George Alfred Williams, Baker & Taylor, 1908; Frederick S. Coburn, Putnam, 1911; Hugh Thomson, Hodder & Stoughton, 1913; A. Rackham, G. W. Jones, 1931]; *The Cricket on the Hearth* (illustrated

by R. Doyle, E. H. Landseer, J. Leech, and C. Stanfield), Bradbury & Evans, 1846, reissued, Chapman & Hall, 1962 [other editions illustrated by F. S. Coburn, Putnam, 1900; G. C. Widney, Rand, McNally, 1902; C. E. Brock, Dent, 1905; F. D. Bedford, Harper, 1927; H. Thomson, Golden Cockerel Press, 1933]; *The Battle of Life,* Bradbury & Evans, 1846; *The Haunted Man [and] The Ghost's Bargain* (illustrated by J. Tenniel, J. Leech, C. Stanfield, and F. Stone), Bradbury & Evans, 1848 [another edition illustrated by C. E. Brock, Dutton, 1907]; *Seven Poor Travelers,* T. B. Peterson, 1855 [other editions illustrated by Arthur Hogg, Sisler, 1908; Doris M. Palmer, C. Palmer, 1920]; (with Wilkie Collins) *The Holly-Tree Inn,* T. B. Peterson, 1856 [another edition illustrated by H. M. Brock, Hodder & Stoughton, 1911].

Mr. Lirriper's Lodgings, Office of the Daily Advertiser and Register, 1864; *Dr. Marigold's Prescriptions,* Harper, 1866 [other editions illustrated by C. E. Brock, T. N. Foulis, 1970; Robin Jacques, Westhouse, 1945]; *A Child's Dream of a Star* (illustrated by Hammatt Billings), Fields, Osgood, 1871; *Christmas Stories from Household Words and All the Year Round,* Chapman & Hall, 1871 [another edition with illustrations from Frederick Walker, F. A. Fraser, H. French, E. G. Dalziel, J. Mahoney, Townley Green, and Charles Green, Scribner, 1911]; *Tom Tiddler's Ground,* G. Munro, 1878; *Mugby Junction,* G. Munro, 1878; (with Wilkie Collins) *The Lazy Tour of Two Idle Apprentices,* F. W. Lovell, 1884.

Captain Boldheart, Constable, 1912; *The Trial of William Tinkling* (illustrated by S. Beatrice Pearse), Constable, 1912; *The Magic Fishbone,* Constable, 1912 [other editions illustrated by F. D. Bedford, F. Warne, 1922; Louis Slobodkin, Vanguard Press, 1953; Pablo Ramirez, Bobbs-Merrill, 1961; Faith Jacques, Harvey House, 1969]; *A Christmas Tree,* New Era Printing Co., 1913; (with W. Collins) *The Perils of Certain English Prisoners,* T. Nelson, 1923; (with Collins) *The Wreck of the Golden Mary,* Blackie, 1935 [another edition illustrated by John Dugan, A. Barker, 1955]; *Mrs. Orange* (illustrated by Robert Stewart Sherriffs), H. Jenkins, 1948.

Plays: *Mr. Nightingale's Diary: A Farce* (one-act), privately printed, 1851; (with W. Collins) *A Message from Sea* (three-act), G. Holsworth, 1861; (with Collins and Charles A. Fechter) *No Thoroughfare* (five-act; based on Dickens' story), Office of All the Year Round, 1867; *The Village Coquettes: A Comic Opera* (two-act; music by John Hullah; first produced in London, December 6, 1836), R. Bentley, 1836; *The Strange Gentleman* (two-act; first produced in London at the St. James Theatre, September 29, 1836), Chapman & Hall, 1837; *Is She His Wife? or, Something Singular* (one-act; first produced at the St. James Theatre, March 6, 1837), J. R. Osgood, 1877; *The Lamplighter* (one-act), [London], 1879.

Other: *Sunday under Three Heads* (illustrated by Phiz), Chapman & Hall, 1836; *Sketches of Young Gentlemen* (illustrated by Phiz), Chapman & Hall, 1838; (editor) *Memoirs of Joseph Grimaldi,* two volumes (illustrated by G. Cruikshank), R. Bentley, 1838, reissued, Stein & Day, 1968; *Sketches of Young Couples* (illustrated by Phiz), Chapman & Hall, 1840; (editor and co-author) *The Pic-Nic Papers* (illustrated by G. Cruikshank and Phiz), Ward, Lock, 1841 (includes *The Lamplighter's Story*); *American Notes for General Circulation,* Harper, 1842, reissued, Limited Editions Club, 1975; *Pictures from Italy* (illustrated by Samuel Palmer), Bradbury & Evans, 1846, reissued,

Dickens, age 27.

Coward-McCann, 1974; *To Be Read at Dusk,* privately printed, 1852; *A Child's History of England,* Bradbury & Evans, 1852-54, reissued, Dutton, 1970 [other editions illustrated by A. deNeuville, Emile Bayard, F. Lix, and others, Estes & Lauriat, 1886; from photographs by Clifton Johnson, Houghton, 1898; M. Stone and J. Mahoney, Scribner, 1910]; *Reprinted Pieces* (from *Household Words* and *All the Year Round*), Chapman & Hall, 1858.

A Curious Dance round a Curious Tree, [London], 1860; *The Uncommercial Traveler,* Chapman & Hall, 1861, reissued, Dutton, 1969 [other editions illustrated by M. Stone, Macmillan, 1896; Harry Furniss, Scribner, 1898, reissued, Heron Books, 1969; G. J. Pinwell and W. M. London, Scribner, 1911]; *Hunted Down,* J. C. Hotten, 1871; *The Mudfog Papers,* R. Bentley, 1880; *Gone Astray* (illustrations from Ruth Cobb), Chapman & Hall, 1912; (with William H. Wills) *A Plated Article,* W. T. Copeland, 1930; *The Life of Our Lord* (written by Dickens for his children, 1846-49, and kept as a family secret for 85 years; illustrated by Gustave Doré), United Feature Syndicate, 1934, reissued, Collins, 1970 [another edition illustrated by Everett Shinn, Garden City Publishing, 1939].

Collections: *The Works of Charles Dickens,* 20 volumes, Hearsts' International Library, 1867; *Dickens' Works,* 14 volumes, Ticknor and Fields, 1867; *The Charles Dickens Edition,* 21 volumes, Chapman & Hall, 1867-75; *Speeches, Literary and Social,* J. C. Hotten, 1870; *The Excelsior Edition of the Works of Charles Dickens,* 14 volumes (illustrations from Darley, Gilbert, Cruikshank and others), Hurd & Houghton, 1870; *The Household Edition of the Works of Charles Dickens,* 21 volumes, Chapman & Hall, 1871-79; *The Globe Edition of the Works of Charles Dickens,* 15 volumes (illustrations from Darley and Gilbert), Houghton, Osgood, 1879; *The Letters of Charles Dickens,* three volumes, edited by Georgina Hogarth and Mary Dickens, Scribner, 1879-81; *The Plays and Poems of Charles Dickens,* two volumes, edited by Richard Herne Shepherd, W. H. Allen, 1882; *The Complete Works of Charles Dickens,* 16 volumes (illustrations from F. Barnard and others), Gebbie, 1892-94; *The Standard Library Edition of the Writings of Charles Dickens,* 32 volumes (illustrations from Phiz, Cruikshank, Leech, and others), Houghton, 1894.

The Gadshill Edition of the Works of Charles Dickens, 36 volumes, Scribner, 1897-1908; *The Temple Edition of the Works of Charles Dickens,* 35 volumes, edited by Walter Jerrold, Doubleday & McClure, 1898-1903; *The Works of Charles Dickens,* 17 volumes, T. Nelson, 1899-1916; *The Complete Works of Charles Dickens,* 30 volumes (illustrations from Cruikshank, Phiz, M. Stone, and others; edited by Richard Garnett), Chapman & Hall, 1900; *The Autograph Edition of the Complete Works of Charles Dickens,* 15 volumes, edited by Frederic G. Kitton, G. D. Sproul, 1902; *The Biographical Edition of the Works of Charles Dickens,* 19 volumes, edited by Arthur Waugh, Chapman & Hall, 1902-03; *The Poems and Verses of Charles Dickens,* edited by F. G. Kitton, Harper, 1903, reprinted, Milford House, 1974; *The Authentic Edition of the Works of Charles Dickens,* 21 volumes, Scribner, 1901-05; *The National Edition of the Works of Charles Dickens,* 40 volumes, edited by B. W. Matz, Chapman & Hall, 1906-08.

The Booklovers Edition of the Works of Charles Dickens, 30 volumes, edited by John H. Clifford, with a life of Dickens by Mamie Dickens and others, introductions by Charles Dickens, Jr. and Edward Everett Hale, essays by F. G. Kitton, University Society (New York), 1908; *The*

Harry Furniss Dickens, 14 volumes, J. T. Gleason, 1910; *The Anniversary Edition of the Works of Charles Dickens,* 25 volumes, P. F. Collier, 1911; *The Waverley Edition of the Works of Charles Dickens,* 30 volumes, Waverley Book Co., 1913-15; *The National Library Edition of the Complete Writings of Charles Dickens,* 40 volumes, C. E. Lauriat, 1923.

The Nonesuch Dickens, 23 volumes, Nonesuch Press, 1937-38; *The New Oxford Illustrated Dickens,* 21 volumes (illustrations from Phiz), Oxford University Press, 1951-59; *The Collected Speeches,* University Microfilms, 1957; *Speeches,* edited by J. K. Fielding, Clarendon Press, 1960; *Letters,* edited by Madeline House and Graham Storey, Clarendon Press, 1965; *Uncollected Writings from Household Words, 1850-59,* edited by Harry Stone, Indiana University Press, 1968; *Complete Plays and Selected Poems of Charles Dickens,* Vision, 1970.

Selections: *Readings from the Works of Dickens as Arranged and Read by Himself,* Chapman & Hall, 1907; *The Best Short Stories of Charles Dickens,* edited by Edwin Valentine Mitchell, Scribner, 1947; *The Bedside Dickens: An Anthology for Pleasure* (illustrated by Leo Vernon; edited by J. W. Garrod), Souvenir Press, 1954, new edition (illustrated by Bill Geldart), Spring Books, 1969; *Stories from Dickens Edited for Young Readers* (illustrated by Susanne Suba; edited by J. Walker McSpadden), Junior Deluxe Editions, 1957; *Stories from Dickens,* retold for children by Helena Power, Exposition Press, 1959; *Best Stories,* edited by Morton D. Zabel, Hanover House, 1959; *More Stories from Dickens,* retold for children by Helena Power, Exposition Press, 1961; *The Dickens Theatrical Reader,* edited by Edgar and Eleanor Johnson, Little, Brown, 1964; *Dickens' London: Selected Essays* (illustrations from G. Cruikshank; edited by Rosalind Vallance), Folio Society, 1966; *Charles Dickens, 1812-1870: An Anthology,* edited by Lola L. Szladits, New York Public Library, 1970; *The Short Stories of Charles Dickens* (illustrated by E. Ardizzone; edited by Walter Allen), Limited Editions Club, 1971; *A Dickens Anthology* (illustrated by Bridge Jackson; edited by H. Pluckrose and F. Peacock), Norwood Editions, 1973.

ADAPTATIONS—Movies and filmstrips; based on *A Christmas Carol:* "Scrooge" (motion picture), Big A Features, 1913; "Right to Be Happy" (motion picture), Bluebird Photoplays, 1916; "Scrooge" (motion picture), Paramount Pictures, 1935; "What the Dickens Have They Done to Scrooge?" (motion picture; a promotional film for the 1970 version of "Scrooge"; also produced in a Spanish version), National General Pictures, 1970; "Scrooge" (musical motion picture), starring Albert Finney and Alec Guinness, Waterbury Films, Ltd., 1907; "A Christmas Carol" (motion pictures), starring Reginald Owen and Gene Lockhart, Metro-Goldwyn-Mayer, 1938, Teaching Film Custodians, excerpts for school use from the Metro-Goldwyn-Mayer movie, 1946, United Artists, 1951, Productions Unlimited, narrated by Vincent Price, 1959, Coronet Instructional Films, narrated by Fredric March and starring Basil Rathbone, 1962; "A Christmas Carol" (filmstrips), Society for Visual Education, 1953, revised (15 minutes, color, with a teacher's guide), 1966, Encyclopaedia Britannica (color, with captions), 1955, Popular Science Publishing (color, with a teacher's guide), 1968, United Productions of America (color, sound, with the animated character, Mr. Magoo), 1972, Brunswick Productions (color, with captions), 1973, Teaching Resources Films (color, sound, with a teacher's guide), 1974.

Stave I.

Marley's Ghost.

Marley was dead: to begin with. There is no doubt whatever about that. The register of his burial was signed by the clergyman, the clerk, the undertaker, and the chief mourner. Scrooge signed it; and Scrooge's name was good upon 'change, for anything he put his hand to. Old Marley was as dead as a door-nail.

Mind! I don't mean to say that I know, of my own knowledge, what there is particularly dead about a door-nail. I might have been inclined, myself, to regard a coffin-nail as the deadest piece of ironmongery in the trade. But the wisdom of our ancestors is in the simile; and my unhallowed hands shall not disturb it, or the country's done for. You will therefore permit me to repeat, emphatically, that Marley was as dead as a door-nail.

Scrooge knew he was dead? Of course he did. How could it be otherwise? Scrooge and he were partners for I don't know how many years. Scrooge was his sole executor, his sole administrator, his sole assign, his sole residuary legatee, his sole friend and sole mourner. And even Scrooge was not so dreadfully cut up by the sad event, but that he was an excellent man of business on the very day of the funeral, and solemnised it with an undoubted bargain.

The mention of Marley's funeral brings me back to the point I started from. There is no doubt that Marley was dead. This must be distinctly understood, or nothing wonderful can come of the story I am going to relate. If we were not perfectly convinced that Hamlet's Father died before the play began, there would be nothing more remarkable in his taking a stroll at night, in an easterly wind, upon his own ramparts, than there would be in any other middle-aged gentleman rashly turning out after dark in a breezy spot — say Saint Paul's Churchyard for instance — literally to astonish his son's weak mind.

Scrooge never painted out old Marley's name. There it ...

(Title and first page of the manuscript of *A Christmas Carol* by Charles Dickens. Illustrated by John Leech.)

"Dolly Varden" (motion picture), based on a portion of *Barnaby Rudge,* Thomas A. Edison, Inc., 1913; "Martin Chuzzlewit" (motion picture), starring Alan Hale, Biograph, 1914; "The Old Curiosity Shop" (motion pictures), Albert Blinkhorn, 1914, Welsh, Pearson, 1921; "Barnaby Rudge" (motion picture), Hepworth American Film Corp., 1915; "Oliver Twist" (motion pictures), Jesse L. Lasky Feature Play Co., 1916, Sol L. Lesser, starring Jackie Coogan and Lon Chaney, 1922, Monogram Pictures, 1933, United World Films, starring Robert Newton and Alec Guinness, 1948; "Oliver Twist" (filmstrips), Jam Handy chool Service (color, with captions and sound), 1968, Educational Dimensions Corp. (color, sound, with a teacher's guide), 1972; Based on *Oliver Twist*—"Oliver Twist, Jr." (motion picture), William Fox, 1921; "Oliver!" (musical motion picture), starring Oliver Reed and Harry Secombe, Columbia Pictures, 1968.

"A Tale of Two Cities" (motion pictures), William Fox, 1917, Metro-Goldwyn Mayer, starring Ronald Colman, 1935, Teaching Film Custodians, excerpts for school use from the Metro-Goldwyn-Mayer movie, 1945, Argyle Enterprises and Telemated Motion Pictures (with a teacher's guide, both color and black and white versions), 1967; "A Tale of Two Cities" (filmstrips), United World Films (black and white, with a teacher's guide), 1959, Brunswick Productions (color, with captions), 1967, Educational Audio Visual (sound, with a teacher's guide), 1968; "The Only Way" (motion picture), based on *A Tale of Two Cities,* Herbert Wilcox Productions, Ltd., 1926.

"Great Expectations" (motion pictures), Famous Players Film Co., 1917, Universal Pictures, starring Jane Wyatt, 1934, Teaching Film Custodians, excerpts from the Universal Pictures movie, 1946, General Film Distributors, starring John Mills and Jean Simmons, 1947; "Great Expectations" (filmstrip; 56 minutes, black and white, sound), Educational Audio Visual, 196?; Based on *Great Expectations*—"The Novel: Great Expectations, 1" (motion picture; 35 minutes, with a teacher's guide, available in both color and black and white versions), Encyclopaedia Britannica Films, 1962; "The Novel: Great Expectations, 2" (motion picture; 34 minutes, with a teacher's guide, available in both color and black and white versions), Encyclopaedia Britannica Films, 1962; "Miss Havisham" (motion picture; 25 minutes, black and white, sound, with a teacher's guide), Coronet Instructional Films, 1963.

Based on *David Copperfield*—"David Copperfield" (motion picture), Associated Exhibitors, 1923; "The Personal History, Adventures, Experience, and Observations of David Copperfield, the Younger" (motion picture), starring Freddie Bartholomew, W. C. Fields, Lionel Barrymore, and Maureen O'Sullivan, Metro-Goldwyn-Mayer, 1935; "David Copperfield, the Man" (motion picture; excerpts from the Metro-Goldwyn-Mayer movie), Teaching Film Custodians, 1946; "David Copperfield, the Boy" (motion picture; excerpts from the Metro-Goldwyn-Mayer movie), Teaching Film Custodians, 1946; "Uriah Heep" (motion picture; 25 minutes, sound, black and white, with a teachers guide), Coronet Instructional Films, 1963; "David and Mr. Micawber" (motion picture; 25 minutes, sound, black and white, with a teacher's guide), Coronet Instructional Films, 1963; "David and His Mother" (motion picture; 25 minutes, sound, black and white, with a teacher's guide), Coronet Instructional Films, 1965; "David and Dora" (motion picture; 25 minutes, sound, black and white, with a teacher's guide), Coronet Instructional Films, 1965; "David and Betsey Trotwood" (motion picture; 25 min-

utes, sound, black and white, with a teacher's guide), Coronet Instructional Films, 1965; "David and Dora Married" (motion picture; 25 minutes, sound, black and white, with a teacher's guide), Coronet Instructional Films, 1965; "The Old Soldier" (motion picture; 25 minutes, sound, black and white, with a teacher's guide), Coronet Instructional Films, 1965; "David Copperfield" (motion picture; 12 minutes, sound, color, with a teacher's guide), Argyle Enterprises and Telemated Motion Pictures, 1967; "David Copperfield" (filmstrip; color, with captions), Brunswick Productions, 1972.

"Our Mutual Friend" (motion picture), Martin G. Chandler, 1921; "The Cricket on the Hearth" (motion picture), Paul Gerson Pictures, 1923; "Rich Man's Folly" (motion picture), based on *Dombey and Son,* Paramount Publix, 1931; "The Mystery of Edwin Drood" (motion pictures), Universal Pictures, starring Claude Rains, 1935, Teaching Film Custodians, excerpts for school use from the Universal Picture movie, 1947; "Nicholas Nickleby" (motion picture), starring Cedric Hardwicke and Sally Ann Howes, Universal-International, 1947.

Based on *The Posthumous Papers of the Pickwick Club*—"The Pickwick Papers" (motion picture; 109 minutes, sound, black and white), starring Nigel Patrick and Hermione Gingold, Brandon Films, 1955; "A Charles Dickens Christmas" (motion picture; 22 minutes, sound, with a film guide, available in both color and black and white versions), Encyclopaedia Britannica Films, 1956; "Mr. Pickwick's Dilemma" (motion picture; 25 minutes, sound, with a teacher's guide), Coronet Instructional Films, 1963; "Sam Weller and His Father" (motion picture; 25 minutes, sound, black and white, with a teacher's guide), Coronet Instructional Films, 1965; "Mr. Jingle at Dingley Dell" (motion picture; 25 minutes, sound, black and white, with a teacher's guide), Coronet Instructional Films, 1965; "Bardell vs. Pickwick" (motion picture; 25 minutes, sound, black and white, with a teacher's guide), Coronet Instructional Films, 1965; "Uneasy Dreams" (motion picture; 26 minutes, sound, color), Films Incorporated, 1971.

"The Runaways" (motion picture; 25 minutes, sound, black and white, with a teacher's guide), based on *The Holly Tree,* Coronet Instructional Films, 1965; "The Signal Man" (filmstrip; color, with captions), Brunswick Productions, 1969.

Plays: Adaptations of *The Posthumous Papers of the Pickwick Club*—William T. Moncreiff, *Sam Weller; or, The Pickwickians* (three-act), [London], 1837; William L. Rede, *Peregrinations of Pickwick* (three-act), [London], 1837; Edward Stirling, *The Pickwick Club; or, The Age We Live In!* (three-act), [London], 1837; Frank E. Emson, *The Weller Family* (one-act), A. Boardman, 1872; W. T. Moncrieff, *The Pickwickians; or, The Peregrinations of Sam Weller* (three-act), [London], 1872; Robert Pollitt, librettist, *The Great Pickwick Case* (operetta), Heywood, 1884; Jane Marsh Parker, *An Evening with Pickwick,* H. Roorbach, 1889; Francis C. Burnard, *Pickwick* (one-act cantata; music by Edward Solomon), Booset, 1889; Cosmo Hamilton and Frank C. Reilly, *Pickwick* (three-act), Putnam, 1927; Stanley Young, *Mr. Pickwick,* Random House, 1952.

Adaptations of *Nicholas Nickleby*—E. Stirling, *Nicholas Nickleby* (two-act), [London], 1838; Stirling, *The Fortunes of Smike; or, A Sequel to Nicholas Nickleby* (two-act), [London], 1840; Harry Simms, *Nicholas Nickleby* (four-

(From the movie musical "Oliver!" starring Ron Moody and Jack Wild. Copyright © 1968 Columbia Pictures.)

act), [London], 1883; H. Horncastle, *The Infant Phenomenon; or, A Rehearsal Rehearsed* (one-act), [London], 1884; Isabelle M. Pagan, *The Gentleman in the Next House* (three-act), Dent, 1900; John Hampden, *Over the Garden Wall* (one-act), Gowans & Gray, 1927; Norman T. Carrington, *Disinherited* (one-act), E. Mathews & Marrot, 1936.

Charles Z. Barnett, *Oliver Twist; or, The Parish Boy's Progress* (three-act), [London], 1838; George Almar, *Oliver Twist* (three-act), [London], 1839; Thomas Hailes Lacy, *Oliver Twist; or, The Parish Boy's Progress,* [London], 1857; F. E. Emson, *Bumble's Courtship* (one-act; adaptation of Oliver Twist), [London], 1873; John D. Ravold, *Oliver Twist* (three-act), Samuel French, 1936; William McCallum Clyde, *Oliver Twist,* Oliver & Boyd, 1938; George H. Holroyd, editor and dramatist, "Oliver Twist," in *Plays from Literature,* G. Philip, 1958.

Frederick F. Cooper, *Master Humphrey's Clock* (two-act), J. Duncombe, 1840; Charles Selby and Charles Melville, *Barnaby Rudge* (three-act), [London], 1841; Thomas Higgie, *Barnaby Rudge; or, The Murder at the Warren* (three-act; adaptation of the play by Selby and Melville), T. H. Lacy, 1856; E. Stirling, *Martin Chuzzlewit!* (three-act), [London], 1844; T. Higgie and Thomas H. Lacy, *Martin Chuzzlewit; or, His Wills and His Ways* (three-act), [London], 1872; Joseph J. Dilley and Lewis Clifton, *Tom Pinch* (three-act; adaptation of *Martin Chuzzlewit*), S. French, 1884; H. Simms, *Martin Chuzzlewit* (four-act), [London], 1886; I. M. Pagan, *Mr. Pecksniff's Pupil* (five-act; adaptation of Martin Chuzzlewit), Dent, 1904.

E. Stirling, *The Old Curiosity Shop; or, One Hour from Master Humphrey's Clock* (two-act), T. H. Lacy, 1844; G. Lander, *The Old Curiosity Shop* (four-act), [London], 1883; Mark Lemon and Gilbert A. a'Beckett, *The Chimes* (four-act), [London], 1845; W. T. Townsend, *The Cricket on the Hearth* (three-act), [London], 1846; E. Stirling, *The Cricket on the Hearth,* [London], 1846; Albert R. Smith, *The Cricket on the Hearth* (three-act), S. French, 1880; A. M. Willner, librettist, *The Cricket on the Hearth* (three-act opera; music by Carl Goldmark), E. Ascherberg, 1900; John Wallace, Jr., *The Cricket on the Hearth* (three-act), Simpkin, Marshall, 1914; Gilmor Brown, *The Cricket on the Hearth,* S. French, 1934; Helen Jerome, *The Cricket on the Hearth* (three-act), S. French, 1948.

E. Stirling, *The Battle of Life* (three-act), [London], 1847; A. R. Smith, *The Battle of Life* (three-act), [London], 1888; Tom Taylor, *A Tale of Two Cities* (two-act), [London], 1860; Henry J. Rivers, *The Tale of Two Cities* (three-act), Davidson, 1862; F. Cooper, *The Tale of Two Cities; or, The Incarcerated Victim of the Bastille,* J. Dicks, 1886; Freeman C. Wills and Frederick Langbridge, *The Only Way* (four-act; adaptation of *A Tale of Two Cities*), F. Muller, 1942; Orpheus C. Kerr (pseudonym of Robert H. Newell), *The Cloven Foot* (adaptation of *The Mystery of Edwin Drood*), Carleton, 1870; Eric Jones-Evans, *John Jasper's Secret* (four-act; adaptation of *The Mystery of Edwin Drood*), S. French, 1951.

Under the Earth; or, The Sons of Toil (three-act; adaptation of *Hard Times*), J. Dicks, 1871; F. Cooper, *Hard Times* (three-act), J. Dicks, 1886; C. Z. Barnett, *A Christmas Carol; or, The Miser's Warning!* (two-act), [London], 1871; Francis A. Hibbert, *A Christmas Carol,* [London], 1928; Sidney N. Sedgwick, *Old Scrooge* (two-act; adaptation of *A Christmas Carol*), H. B. Skinner, 1934; Sarah G. Clark, lyricist, *A Christmas Carol* (musical; music by

Bryeeson Treharne), Willis Music Co., 1936; Cora Wilson Greenwood, *A Christmas Carol* (one-act), S. French, 1938; T. Dowell, *A Christmas Carol* (musical; music by F. W. Wadely), Boosey, 1938; Shaun Sutton, *A Christmas Carol* (three-act), S. French, 1949; Kenelm Foss, *A Christmas Carol* (three-act), S. French, 1949; Harold H. S. Jackson, *A Christmas Parable* (three-act; adaptation of *A Christmas Carol*), Epworth Press, 1951.

William S. Gilbert, *Great Expectations* (three-act), [London], 1871; Shafto Scott, *My Unknown Friend* (three-act; adaptation of *Great Expectations*), [London], 1883; Wilbur Braun, *Great Expectations* (three-act), S. French, 1948; Marion Louise Johnson, *Great Expectations* (three-act), Dramatic Publishing, 1948; Alice Chadwicke, *Great Expectations* (three-act), S. French, 1948; G. H. Holroyd, editor and dramatist, "Great Expectations," in *Plays from Literature,* G. Philip, 1958; G. Lander, *Bleak House; or, Poor Jo* (four-act), [London], 1883; John Palgrave Simpson, *Lady Dedlock's Secret* (adaptation of *Bleak House*), S. French, 1885; John Brougham, *A Message from the Sea* (four-act), [London], 1883; Brougham, *Dombey and Son* (three-act), [London], 1885.

Brougham, *David Copperfield* (three-act), [London], 1885; J. D. Ravold, *David Copperfield* (three-act), S. French, 1935; Louis Lequel, *No Thoroughfare,* [London], 1899; I. M. Pagan, *Mr. Boffin's Secretary* (four-act; adaptation of *Our Mutual Friend*), Dent, 1902; Aimée Beringer, *Holly Tree Inn* (one-act; adaptation of *The Holly Tree*), [New York], 1905; Benjamin N. Webster, *Holly Tree Inn* (one-act), [London], 1907; H. Parry, *Boots at the Holly Tree* (one-act; adaptation of *The Holly Tree*), R. James, 1932.

SIDELIGHTS: **February 7, 1812.** Born at Portsmouth, England. Second of eight children.

1814-1822. Family lived in London and Chatham. Educated at home by mother and at preparatory day-school. Read widely. "My father had left a small collection of books in a little room upstairs, to which I had access (for it adjoined my own) and which nobody else in our house ever troubled. From that blessed little room, *Roderick Random, Peregrine Pickle, Humphrey* [sic] *Clinker, Tom Jones, The Vicar of Wakefield, Don Quixote, Gil Blas,* and *Robinson Crusoe,* came out, a glorious host, to keep me company. They kept alive my fancy, and my hope of something beyond that place and time,—they, and the *Arabian Nights,* and the *Tales of the Genii. . . .*

"It is astonishing to me now, how I found time, in the midst of my porings and blunderings over heavier themes, to read those books as I did. It is curious to me how I could ever have consoled myself under my small troubles (which were great troubles to me), by impersonating my favourite characters in them—as I did. . . . I have been *Tom Jones* (a child's *Tom Jones,* a harmless creature) for a week together. I have sustained my own idea of *Roderick Random* for a month at a stretch, I verily believe. I had a greedy relish for a few volumes of *Voyages and Travels*—I forget what, now—that were on those shelves; and for days and days I can remember to have gone about my region of our house, armed with the centrepiece out of an old set of boot-trees—the perfect realisation of Captain Somebody, of the Royal British Navy, in danger of being beset by savages, and resolved to sell his life at a great price." [Autobiographical scene from *David Copperfield.*[1]]

Dickens, 1849, daguerrotype by Maynall.

Family experienced financial difficulties. "I know my father to be as kindhearted and generous a man as ever lived in the world. Everything that I can remember of his conduct to his wife, or children, or friends, in sickness or affliction, is beyond all praise. By me, as a sick child, he has watched night and day, unweariedly and patiently, many nights and days. . . . He was proud of me, in his way, and had a great admiration of the comic singing. But in the ease of his temper, and the straitness of his means, he appeared to have utterly lost at this time the idea of educating me at all, and to have utterly put from him the notion that I had any claim upon him in that regard, whatever. So I degenerated into cleaning the boots of a morning, and my own; and making myself useful in the work of the little house; and looking after my younger brothers and sisters (we were now six in all); and going on such poor errands as arose out of our poor way of living." [John Forster, *Life of Charles Dickens*, William Clowes and Sons, Ltd.[2]]

Dickens' mother attempted to open a school. "Nobody ever came to the school, nor do I recollect that anybody ever proposed to come, or that the least preparation was made to receive anybody." [Edgar Johnson, *Charles Dickens: His Tragedy and Triumph*, Volume I, Simon & Schuster, 1952.[3]]

1822-24. Family moved again to London. Father, impoverished, arrested for debt and sent to debtor's prison, Marshalsea. Young Charles sent to work at a blacking warehouse for six months. "It is wonderful to me how I could have been so easily cast away at such an age. It is wonderful to me, that, even after my descent into the poor little drudge I had been since we came to London, no one had compassion enough on me—a child of singular abilities, quick, eager, delicate, and soon hurt, bodily or mentally—to suggest that something might have been spared, as certainly it might have been, to place me at any common school. Our friends, I take it, were tired out. No one made any sign. My father and mother were quite satisfied. They could hardly have been more so, if I had been twenty years of age, distinguished at a grammar-school, and going to Cambridge."[2]

"The blacking-warehouse was the last house on the left-hand side of the way, at old Hungerford Stairs. It was a crazy, tumble-down old house, abutting of course on the river, and literally overrun with rats. Its wainscoted rooms, and its rotten floors and staircase, and the old gray rats swarming down in the cellars, and the sound of their squeaking coming up the stairs at all times, and the dirt and decay of the place, rise up visibly before me, as if I were there again. The counting-house was on the first floor, looking over the coal-barges and the river. There was a recess in it, in which I was to sit and work. My work was to cover the pots of paste-blacking; first with a piece of oil-paper, and then with a piece of blue paper; to tie them round with a string; and then to clip the paper close and neat, all round, until it looked as smart as a pot of ointment from an apothecary's shop. When a certain number of grosses of pots had attained this pitch of perfection, I was to paste on each a printed label, and then go on again with more pots. Two or three other boys were kept at similar duty downstairs on similar wages. One of them came up, in a ragged apron and a paper cap, on the first Monday morning, to show me the trick of using the string and tying the knot. His name was Bob Fagin and I took the liberty of using his name, long afterwards, in *Oliver Twist*.

"Our relative had kindly arranged to teach me something in the dinner-hour; from twelve to one, I think it was; every day. But an arrangement so incompatible with counting-house business soon died away, from no fault of his or mine; and, for the same reason, my small work-table, and my grosses of pots, my papers, string, scissors, paste-pot, and labels, by little and little, vanished out of the recess in the counting-house, and kept company with the other small work-tables, grosses of pots, papers, string, scissors, and paste-pots down-stairs. It was not long before Bob Fagin and I, and another boy whose name was Paul Green, but who was currently believed to have been chrisened [sic] Poll (a belief which I transferred, long afterwards again, to Mr. Sweedlepipe, in *Martin Chuzzlewit*), worked generally, side by side. Bob Fagin was an orphan, and lived with his brother-in-law, a waterman. Poll Green's father had the additional distinction of being a fireman, and was employed at Drury Lane theatre; where another relation of Poll's, I think his little sister, did imps in the pantomimes." [*When I Was a Child* (edited by Edward Wagenknecht), Dutton, 1946.[4]]

"No words can express the secret agony of my soul as I sunk into this companionship; compared these every day associates with those of my happier childhood; and felt my early hopes of growing up to be a learned and distinguished man, crushed in my breast. The deep remembrance of the sense I had of being utterly neglected and hopeless; of the shame I felt in my position; of the misery it was to my young heart to believe that, day by day, what I had learned, and thought, and delighted in, and raised my fancy and my emulation up by, was passing away from me, never to be brought back any more; cannot be written. My whole nature was so penetrated with the grief and humiliation of such considerations, that even now, famous and caressed and happy, I often forget in my dreams that I have a dear wife and children; even that I am a man; and wander desolately back to that time of my life.

"My mother and my brothers and sisters (excepting Fanny in the Royal Academy of Music) were still encamped, with a young servant-girl from Chatham work-house, in the two parlors in the emptied house in Gower Street north. It was a long way to go and return within the dinner-hour, and usually I either carried my dinner with me, or went and bought it at some neighboring shop. In the latter case, it was commonly a saveloy and a penny loaf; sometimes, a four-penny plate of beef from a cook's shop; sometimes, a plate of bread and cheese, and a glass of beer, from a miserable old public-house over the way: the Swan, if I remember right, or the Swan and something else that I have forgotten. Once, I remember tucking my own bread (which I had brought from home in the morning) under my arm, wrapped up in a piece of paper like a book, and going into the best dining-room in Johnson's alamode beef-house in Clare Court, Drury Lane, and magnificently ordering a small plate of alamode beef to eat with it. What the waiter thought of such a strange little apparition, coming in all alone, I don't know; but I can see him now, staring at me as I ate my dinner, and bringing up the other waiter to look. I gave him a halfpenny, and I wish, now, that he hadn't taken it.

"I know I do not exaggerate, unconsciously and unintentionally, the scantiness of my resources and the difficulties of my life. I know that if a shilling or so were given me by anyone, I spent it in a dinner or a tea. I know that I worked, from morning to night, with common men and boys, a shabby child. I know that I tried, but ineffectually,

The best among us have their failings, and it must be conceded of Mrs. Prig, that if there were a blemish in the goodness of her disposition, it was a habit she had of not bestowing all its sharp and acid properties upon her patients (as a thoroughly amiable woman would have done), but of keeping a considerable remainder for the service of her friends. ■ (From *Martin Chuzzlewit* by Charles Dickens. Illustrated by "Phiz.")

not to anticipate my money, and to make it last the week through; by putting it away in a drawer I had in the counting-house, wrapped up in six little parcels, each parcel containing the same amount, and labelled with a different day. I know that I lounged about the streets, insufficiently and unsatisfactorily fed. I know that, but for the mercy of God, I might easily have been, for any care that was taken of me, a little robber or a little vagabond.''[2]

Since the elder Dickens was sent to Marshalsea Prison because of bad debts, Charles' mother and her encampment in Gower Street north broke up and also went to live in the Marshalsea. ''The key of the house was sent back to the landlord, who was very glad to get it; and I (small Cain that I was, except that I had never done harm to any one) was handed over as a lodger to a reduced old lady, long known to our family, in Little College Street, Camdentown, who

(A rare movie still from the 1934 version of "Great Expectations," with Valerie Hobson, who was originally slated to play Estella, then chosen to play Biddy, but was edited out of the final version. The role of Estella went to Jane Wyatt, but Hobson did play it in the 1947 remake. Also pictured are Phillip Holmes and Francis Sullivan.)

(From the movie "Great Expectations," starring Jean Simmons and John Mills. Copyright 1947 by Universal-International.)

(From the movie "David Copperfield," starring W.C. Fields and Freddie Bartholomew. Produced by Metro-Goldwyn-Mayer, 1934.)

(From the movie "David Copperfield," starring Susan Hampshire. Produced by 20th Century-Fox, 1972.)

(From the movie "A Christmas Carol," starring Terry Kilburn as Tiny Tim. Produced by Metro-Goldwyn-Mayer, 1938.)

(From the movie "A Christmas Carol," starring Alistair Sim. Produced by United Artists, 1951.)

(From the movie "A Christmas Carol," starring Reginald Owen. Produced by Metro-Goldwyn-Mayer, 1938.)

(From the movie "Scrooge," the musical adaptation of *A Christmas Carol*, starring Albert Finney and Alec Guinness. Copyright © 1970 Cinema Center Films.)

(From the movie "A Tale of Two Cities," starring Dirk Bogarde. Produced by J. Arthur Rank, 1957.)

(From the movie "A Tale of Two Cities." Produced by Metro-Goldwyn-Mayer, 1935.)

(From the movie "The Pickwick Papers." Copyright 1952 by Renown Pictures.)

Ebenezer Scrooge and the ghost of Christmas yet to come in Richard Williams' adaptation of
A Christmas Carol. Produced by ABC Television.

(From the movie "Oliver Twist," starring Dickie Moore. Produced by Monogram Pictures, 1933.)

(From the movie musical "Oliver!" starring Mark Lester as Oliver Twist. Copyright © 1968 by Columbia Pictures.)

(From the movie "Oliver Twist," starring Robert Newton, Alec Guinness and Kay Walsh.
Produced by United Artists, 1951.)

(From the movie "Oliver Twist," starring Robert Newton. Produced by United Artists, 1951.)

took children in to board, and had once done so at Brighton; and who, with a few alterations and embellishments, unconsciously began to sit for Mrs. Pipchin in *Dombey* when she took in me.

"She had a little brother and sister under her care then; somebody's natural children, who were very irregularly paid for; and a widow's little son. The two boys and I slept in the same room. My own exclusive breakfast, of a penny cottage loaf and a pennyworth of milk, I provided for myself. I kept another small loaf, and a quarter of a pound of cheese, on a particular shelf of a particular cupboard; to make my supper on when I came back at night. They made a hole in the six or seven shillings, I know well; and I was out at the blacking-warehouse all day, and had to support myself upon that money all the week. I suppose my lodging was paid for, by my father. I certainly did not pay it myself; and I certainly had no other assistance whatever (the making of my clothes, I think, excepted), from Monday morning until Saturday night. No advice, no counsel, no encouragement, no consolation, no support, from any one that I can call to mind, so help me God.

"Sundays, Fanny and I passed in the prison. I was at the academy in Tenterden Street, Hanover Square, at nine o'clock in the morning, to fetch her; and we walked back there together, at night.

"I was so young and childish, and so little qualified—how could I be otherwise?—to undertake the whole charge of my own existence, that in going to Hungerford Stairs of a morning, I could not resist the stale pastry put out at half-price on trays at the confectioners' doors in Tottenham Court Road; and I often spent in that the money I should have kept for my dinner. Then I went without my dinner, or bought a roll, or a slice of pudding. There were two pudding-shops between which I was divided, according to my finances. One was in a court close to St. Martin's Church (at the back of the church) which is now removed altogether. The pudding at that shop was made with currants, and was rather a special pudding, but was dear: two penn'orth not being larger than a penn'orth of more ordinary pudding. A good shop for the latter was in the Strand, somewhere near where the Lowther Arcade is now. It was a stout, hale pudding, heavy and flabby; with great raisins in it, stuck in whole, at great distances apart. It came up hot, at about noon every day; and many and many a day did I dine off it.

"We had half an hour, I think, for tea. When I had money enough, I used to go to a coffee-shop, and have half a pint of coffee, and a slice of bread-and-butter. When I had no money, I took a turn in Covent Garden market, and stared at the pineapples. The coffee-shops to which I most resorted were, one in Maiden Lane; one in a court (non-existent now) close to Hungerford market; and one in St. Martin's Lane, of which I only recollect that it stood near the church, and that in the door there was an oval glass plate, with COFFEE-ROOM painted on it, addressed towards the street. If I ever find myself in a very different kind of coffee-room now, but where there is such an inscription on glass, and read it backward on the wrong side MOOR-EEFFOC (as I often used to do then, in a dismal reverie), a shock goes through my blood.

"But I held some station at the blacking-warehouse too. Besides that my relative at the counting-house did what a man so occupied, and dealing with a thing so anomalous, could, to treat me as one upon a different footing from the rest, I never said, to man or boy, how it was that I came to be there, or gave the least indication of being sorry that I was there. That I suffered in secret, and that I suffered exquisitely, no one ever knew but I.

"How much I suffered, it is, as I have said already, utterly beyond my power to tell. No man's imagination can overstep the reality. But I kept my own counsel, and I did my work. I knew from the first that, if I could not do my work as well as any of the rest, I could not hold myself above slight and contempt. I soon became at least as expeditious and as skillful with my hands as either of the other boys. Though perfectly familiar with them, my conduct and manners were different enough from theirs to place a space between us. They, and the men, always spoke of me as 'the young gentleman'. A certain man, (a soldier once) named Thomas, who was the foreman, and another named Harry, who was the carman and wore a red jacket, used to call me 'Charles' sometimes, in speaking to me; but I think it was mostly when we were very confidential, and when I had made some efforts to entertain them over our work with the results of some of the old readings, which were fast perishing out of my mind. Poll Green uprose once, and rebelled against the 'young gentleman' usage; but Bob Fagin settled him speedily.

"My rescue from this kind of existence I considered quite hopeless, and abondoned as such, altogether; though I am solemnly convinced that I never, for one hour, was reconciled to it, or was otherwise than miserably unhappy. I felt keenly, however, the being so cut off from my parents, my brothers and sisters, and, when my day's work was done, going home to such a miserable blank; and *that,* I thought, might be corrected. One Sunday night I remonstrated with my father on this head, so pathetically, and with so many tears, that his kind nature gave way. He began to think that it was not quite right. I do believe he had never thought so before, or thought about it. It was the first remonstrance I had ever made about my lot, and perhaps it opened up a little more than I intended. A back-attic was found for me at the house of an insolvent-court agent, who lived in Lant Street in the borough, where Bob Sawyer lodged many years afterwards. A bed and bedding were sent over for me, and made up on the floor. The little window had a pleasant prospect of a timber-yard; and when I took possession of my new abode I thought it was a Paradise."

Part of the pleasure of his new abode was its bringing him again within the circle of home. From this time he used to breakfast "at home" (Marshalsea). Since his father's income was still going on, the family lived more comfortably in prison than they had done for a long time out of it. Besides breakfast, he had supper also in prison, and got his lodging generally at nine o'clock. The gates closed always at ten.

Suffering from old attacks of spasm, he related a similar illness one day in the warehouse: "Bob Fagin was very good to me on the occasion of a bad attack of my old disorder. I suffered such excruciating pain that time, that they made a temporary bed of straw in my old recess in the counting-house, and I rolled about on the floor, and Bob filled empty blacking-bottled with hot water, and applied relays of them to my side, half the day. I got better, and quite easy towards evening; but Bob (who was much bigger and older than I) did not like the idea of my going home alone, and took me under his protection. I was too proud to let him know about the prison, and, after making several efforts to get rid of him, to all of which Bob Fagin in his

Dickens at work.

A sketch of Dickens by George Cruikshank, 1836.

goodness was deaf, shook hands with him on the steps of a house near Southwark Bridge on the Surrey side, making believe that I lived there. As a finishing piece of reality in case of his looking back, I knocked at the door, I recollect, and asked, when the woman opened it, if that was Mr. Robert Fagin's house.

At the discharge from the Marshalsea, a petition was drawn up by the elder Dickens praying for the boon of a bounty to the prisoners to drink his majesty's health on his majesty's forthcoming birthday.

"When I went to the Marshalsea of a night, I was always delighted to hear from my mother what she knew about the histories of the different debtors in the prison; and when I heard of this approaching ceremony, I was so anxious to see them all come in, one after another . . . that I got leave of absence on purpose, and established myself in a corner, near the petition. It was stretched out, I recollect, on a great ironing-board, under the window, which in another part of the room made a bedstead at night. The internal regulations of the place, for cleanliness and order, and for the government of a common room in the ale-house; where hot water and some means of cooking, and a good fire, were provided for all who paid a very small subscription; were excellently administered by a governing committee of debtors, of which my father was chairman for the time being. As many of the principal officers of this body as could be got into the small room without filling it up, supported him, in front of the petition; and my old friend Captain Porter (who had washed himself, to do honour to so solemn an occasion) stationed himself close to it, to read it to all who were unacquainted with its contents. The door was then thrown open, and they began to come in, in a long

file; several waiting on the landing outside, while one entered, affixed his signature, and went out. To everybody in succession, Captain Porter said, 'Would you like to hear it read?' If he weakly showed the least disposition to hear it, Captain Porter, in a loud sonorous voice, gave him every word of it. I remember a certain luscious roll he gave to such words as 'Majesty—gracious Majesty—your gracious Majesty's unfortunate subjects—your Majesty's well-known munificence'—as if the words were something real in his mouth, and delicious to taste; my poor father meanwhile listening with a little of an author's vanity, and contemplating (not severely) the spikes on the opposite wall. Whatever was comical in this scene, and whatever was pathetic, I sincerely believe I perceived in my corner, whether I demonstrated or not, quite as well as I should perceive it now. I made out my own little character and story for every man who put his name to the sheet of paper. I might be able to do that now, more truly, not more earnestly, or with a closer interest. Their different peculiarities of dress, of face, of gait, of manner, were written indelibly upon my memory. I would rather have seen it than the best play ever played; and I thought about it afterwards, over the pots of paste-blacking, often and often. When I looked, with my mind's eye, into the Fleet Prison during Mr. Pickwick's incarceration, I wonder whether half-a-dozen men were wanting from the Marshalsea crowd that came filing in again, to the sound of Captain Porter's voice!"[2]

When the family left the Marshalsea they all went to lodge with the lady in Little College Street, a Mrs. Roylance, who has obtained unexpected immortality as Mrs. Pipchin; and they afterwards occupied a small house in Somerstown. "I am not sure that it was before this time, or after it, that the blacking-warehouse was removed to Chandos Street, Covent Garden. It is no matter. Next to the shop at the corner of Bedford Street in Chandos Street are two rather old-fashioned houses and shops adjoining one another. They were one then, or thrown into one, for the blacking-business; and had been a butter-shop. Opposite to them was, and is a public-house, where I got my ale, under these new circumstances. The stones in the street may be smoothed by my small feet going across to it at dinner-time, and back again. The establishment was larger now, and we had one or two new boys. Bob Fagin and I had attained to great dexterity in tying up the pots. I forget how many we could do in five minutes. We worked, for the light's sake, near the second window as you come from Bedford Street; and we were so brisk at it that the people used to stop and look in. Sometimes there would be quite a little crowd there. I saw my father coming in at the door one day when we were very busy, and I wondered how he could bear it.

"Now, I generally had my dinner in the warehouse. Sometimes I brought it from home, so I was better off. I see myself coming across Russell Square from Somers-town, one morning, with some cold hotch-potch in a small basin tied up in a handkerchief. I had the same wanderings about the streets as I used to have, and was just as solitary and self-dependent as before; but I had not the same difficulty in merely living. I never, however, heard a word of being taken away, or of being otherwise than quite provided for.

"At last, one day, my father, and the relative so often mentioned, quarreled; quarreled by letter, for I took the letter from my father to him which caused the explosion, but quarreled very fiercely. It was about me. It may have had some backward reference, in part, for anything I know, to my employment at the window. All I am certain of is, that, soon after I had given him the letter, my cousin (he

Dickens' Swiss chalet, erected at Gad's Hill, 1865.

was a sort of cousin, by marriage) told me he was very much insulted about me, and that it was impossible to keep me after that. I cried very much, partly because it was so sudden, and partly because in his anger he was violent about my father, though gentle to me. Thomas, the old soldier, comforted me, and said he was sure it was for the best. With a relief so strange that it was like oppression, I went home.

"My mother set herself to accommodate the quarrel, and did so next day. She brought home a request for me to return next morning, and a high character of me, which I am very sure I deserved. My father said I should go back no more, and should go to school. I do not write resentfully or angrily; for I know how all these things have worked together to make me what I am; but I never afterwards forgot, I never shall forget, I never can forget, that my mother was warm for my being sent back.

"From that hour until this at which I write, no word of that part of my childhood which I have now gladly brought to a close has passed my lips to any human being. I have no idea how long it lasted; whether for a year, or much more, or less. From that hour until this my father and my mother have been stricken dumb upon it. I have never heard the least allusion to it, however far off and remote, from either of them. I have never, until I now impart it to this paper, in any burst of confidence with any one, my wife not excepted, raised the curtain I then dropped, thank God.

"Until old Hungerford Market was pulled down, until old Hungerford Stairs were destroyed, and the very nature of the ground changed, I never had the courage to go back to the place where my servitude began. I never saw it. I could not endure to go near it. For many years, when I came near to Robert Warren's in the Strand, I crossed over the opposite side of the way, to avoid a certain smell of the cement they put upon the blackingcorks, which reminded me of what I was once. It was a very long time before I liked to go up Chandos Street. My old way home by the borough made me cry, after my eldest child could speak.

"In my walks at night I have walked there often, since then, and by degrees I have come to write this. It does not seem a tithe of what I might have written, or of what I meant to write."[4]

1824-26. Attended Wellington House Academy.

1827-28. Worked as clerk in attorney's office; studied shorthand at night. "The changes that were wrung upon dots, which in such a position meant such a thing, and in such another position something else entirely different; the wonderful vagaries that were played by circles; the unaccountable consequences that resulted from marks like flies' legs; the tremendous effect of a curve in the wrong place; not only troubled my waking hours, but reappeared before me in my sleep. When I had groped my way, blindly, through these difficulties, and had mastered the alphabet, there then appeared a procession of new horrors, called arbitrary characters; the most despotic characters I had ever known; who insisted, for instance, that a thing like the beginning of a cobweb meant expectation; and that a pen-and-ink skyrocket stood for disadvantageous. When I had fixed these wretches in my mind, I found that they had driven everything else out of it; then, beginning again, I forgot them; while I was picking them up, I dropped the other fragments of the system; in short, it was almost heart-breaking."[2]

1829. Fell in love with Maria Beadnell, later a model for Dora in *David Copperfield*.

1832. Began career as a journalist for London newspapers. "I went into the gallery of the House of Commons as a

Alas for Tiny Tim, he bore a little crutch, and had his limbs supported by an iron frame. ■ (From
A Christmas Carol by Charles Dickens. Illustrated by Arthur Rackham.)

Parliamentary reporter when I was a boy not eighteen, and
I left it—I can hardly believe the inexorable truth—nigh
thirty years ago. I have pursued the calling of a reporter
under circumstances of which many of my brethren at
home in England here, many of my modern successors, can
form no adequate conception. I have often transcribed for
the printer from my shorthand notes, important public
speeches in which the strictest accuracy was required, and
a mistake in which would have been to a young man severely compromising, writing on the palm of my hand, by
the light of a dark lantern, in a post chaise and four, gallop-
ing through a wild country, all through the dead of night, at
the then surprising rate of fifteen miles an hour.

"God bless us every one!" said Tiny Tim, the last of all. ■ (From *A Christmas Carol* by Charles Dickens. Illustrated by John Groth.)

"The very last time I was at Exeter, I strolled into the Castle Yard there to identify, for the amusement of a friend, the spot on which I once 'took,' as we used to call it, an election speech of my noble friend Lord Russell, in the midsts of a lively fight maintained by all the vagabonds in that division of the county, and under such a pelting rain, that I remember two good-natured colleagues, who chanced to be at leisure, held a pocket handkerchief over my notebook after the manner of a state canopy in an ecclesiastical procession.

"I have worn my knees by writing on them on the old back row of the old gallery of the old House of Commons; and I have worn my feet by standing to write in a preposterous pen in the old House of Lords, where we used to be huddled together like so many sheep, kept in waiting, say, until the woolsack might want re-stuffing. I have been, in my time, belated on miry by-roads, towards the small hours, in

a wheelless carriage, with exhausted horses and drunken postboys, and have got back in time for publication. . . ." [*The Speeches of Charles Dickens,* edited by K. J. Fielding, Oxford, Clarendon Press, 1960.[5]]

1833. First published work appeared in the *Monthly Magazine.* "My eyes so dimmed with pride and joy, that they could not bear the street, and were not fit to be seen."[3]

While working as a court reporter, Dickens considered a stage career. "I wrote to Bartley, who was stagemanager, and told him how young I was, and exactly what I thought I could do; and that I believed I had a strong perception of character and oddity, and a natural power of reproducing in my own person what I observed in others. This was at the time when I was at Doctors' Commons as a short-hand writer for the proctors. And I recollect I wrote the letter from a little office had there, where the answer came also.

Joseph Jefferson as "Newman Noggs," in Nicholas Nickleby. Engraved by R.G. Tietze. ■ (From *Rip Van Winkle, The Autobiography of Joseph Jefferson.*)

There must have been something in my letter that struck the authorities, for Bartley wrote to me almost immediately to say that they were busy getting up the 'Hunchback' (so they were), but that they would communicate with me again in a fortnight. Punctual to the time another letter came, with an appointment to do anything of Mathews's I pleased before him and Charles Kemble, on a certain day at the theatre. My sister Fanny was in the secret, and was to go with me to play the songs. I was laid up when the day came with a terrible bad cold and inflammation of the face; the beginning, by-the-bye, of that annoyance in one ear to which I am subject to this day. I wrote to say so, and added that I would resume my application next season. I made a great splash in the gallery soon afterwards; the *Chronicle* opened to me; I had a distinction in the little world of the newspaper, which made one like it; began to write; didn't want money; had never thought of the stage but as the means of getting it; gradually left off turning my thoughts that way, and never resumed the idea. . . . See how near I may have been to another sort of life."[2]

1836. Publication of *Sketches by Boz.* Publication of *The Pickwick Papers,* a huge success. Dickens married Catherine Hogarth. To his future wife: "I have at this moment, got Pickwick, and his friends, on the Rochester coach, and

they are going on swimmingly, in company with a very different character from any I have yet described, who I flatter myself will make a decided hit. I want to get them from the Ball, to their Inn, before I go to bed—and I think that will take me until one or two o'clock, *at the earliest.* The Publishers will be here in the morning, so you will readily suppose I have no alternative but to stick at my desk." [*The Selected Letters of Charles Dickens,* edited by Frederick Dupee, Farrar, Straus, 1960.[6]]

November 1, 1836. "If I were to live a hundred years and write three novels in each, I should never be so proud of any of them as I am of *Pickwick,* feeling as I do, that it has made its own way, and hoping, as I must own I do hope, that long after my hand is withered as the pens it held, *Pickwick* will be found on many a dusty shelf with many a better work."[3]

1837. First child, Charles, born. Mary Hogarth, Dicken's sister-in-law, who had made her home with Charles and Catherine, died. "I presume you heard from my father, that on the Saturday Night we had been to the Theatre—that we returned home as usual—that poor Mary was in the same health and spirits in which you have so often seen her—that almost immediately after she went upstairs to bed she was taken ill—and that next day she died. Thank God she died in my arms, and the very last words she whispered were of me.

"Of our sufferings at the time, and all through the dreary week that ensued, I will say nothing—no one can imagine what they were. You have seen a good deal of her, and can feel for us, and imagine what a blank she has left behind.

(From *Barnaby Rudge* by Charles Dickens. Illustrated by Hablot K. Browne ["Phiz"].)

The first burst of my grief has passed, and I can think and speak of her calmly and dispassionately. I solemnly believe that so perfect a creature never breathed. I knew her inmost heart, and her real worth and values. She had not a fault.''[6]

''You cannot conceive misery in which this dreadful event has plunged us. Since our marriage she has been the peace and life of our home—the admired of all for her beauty and excellence—I could have better spared a much nearer relation or an older friend, for she has been to us what we can never replace, and has left a blank which no one who ever knew her can have the faintest hope of seeing supplied.

''There was no number of *Pickwick Papers* for the end of May, and in the June issue of *Bentley's Miscellany,* instead of an installment of *Oliver Twist,* there was a notice of explanation: 'Since the appearance of the last number of this work the editor has to mourn the sudden death of a very dear young relative to whom he was most affectionately attached and whose society has been for a long time the chief solace of his labours.''[3]

The Marchioness only shook her head mournfully and cried again, whereupon Mr. Swiveller (being very weak) felt his own eyes affected likewise. ■ (From *The Old Curiosity Shop* by Charles Dickens. Illustrated by Henry Matthew Brock.)

It was plain that some extraordinary grudge was working in Miss Brass's gentle breast, and that it was this which impelled her, without the smallest present cause, to rap the child with the blade of the knife, now on her hand, now on her head, and now on her back, as if she found it quite impossible to stand so close to her without administering a few slight knocks. ■ (From *The Old Curiosity Shop* by Charles Dickens. Illustrated by Rowland Wheelwright.)

1838. Birth of second child, Mary. Publication of *Oliver Twist* caused controversy. In reply to Mrs. J. P. Davis: ''I must take leave to say, that if there be any general feeling on the part of the intelligent Jewish people, that I have done them what you describe as 'a great wrong,' they are a far less sensible, a far less just, and a far less good-natured people than I have always supposed them to be. Fagin, in *Oliver Twist,* is a Jew, because it unfortunately was true of the time to which that story refers, that that class of criminal almost invariably was a Jew. But surely no sensible man or woman of your persuasion can fail to observe—firstly, that all the rest of the wicked *dramatis personæ* are Christians; and secondly, that he is called a 'Jew,' not because of his religion, but because of his race. If I were to write a story, in which I described a Frenchman or a Spaniard as 'the Roman Catholic,' I should do a very indecent and unjustifiable thing; but I make mention of Fagin as the Jew, because he is one of the Jewish people, and because it conveys that kind of idea of him which I should give my readers of a Chinaman, by calling him a Chinese.

''The enclosed is quite a nominal subscription towards the good object in which you are interested; but I hope it may serve to show you that I have no feeling towards the Jewish people but a friendly one. I always speak well of them, whether in public or in private, and bear my testimony (as I ought to do) to their perfect good faith in such transactions as I have ever had with them; and in my Child's History of England, I have lost no opportunity of setting forth their cruel persecution in old times.—Dear Madam—faithfully yours.''[6]

1839. Publication of *Nicholas Nickleby.*

1841. Had the single honor of being granted the Freedom of the City of Edinburgh. Publication of *Barnaby Rudge* and *The Old Curiosity Shop.* Little Nell resembled Mary Hogarth.

''TO JOHN FORSTER

[London] *Friday 7th January 1841*

''. . . Done! done!!! Why bless you, I shall not be done till Wednesday night. I only began yesterday, and this part of the story is not to be galloped over. I can tell you. I think it will come famously—but I am the wretchedest of the wretched. It casts the most horrible shadow upon me, and it is as much as I can do to keep moving at all. I tremble to approach the place a great deal more than Kit; a great deal more than Mr. Garland; a great deal more than the Single Gentleman. I shan't recover it for a long time. Nobody will miss her like I shall. It is such a very painful thing to me, that I really cannot express my sorrow. Old wounds bleed afresh when I only think of the way of doing it: what the actual doing it will be, God knows. I can't preach to myself the schoolmaster's consolation, though I try. Dear Mary died yesterday, when I think of this sad story. I don't know what to say about dining to-morrow—perhaps you'll send up to-morrow morning for news? That'll be the best way. I have refused several invitations for this week and next, determining to go nowhere till I had done. I am afraid of disturbing the state I have been trying to get into, and having to fetch it all back again. . . .''[6]

1842. Dickens and wife traveled to America in January, returned to England in June. *American Notes* published in October. ''It is the third morning. I am awakened out of my sleep by a dismal shriek from my wife, who demands to know whether there's any danger. I rouse myself, and look out of bed. The water-jug is plunging and leaping like a lively dolphin; all the smaller articles are afloat, except my shoes, which are stranded on a carpet-bag, high and dry, like a couple of coal-barges. Suddenly I see them spring into the air, and behold the looking-glass, which is nailed to the wall, sticking fast upon the ceiling. At the same time the door entirely disappears, and a new one is opened in the floor. Then I begin to comprehend that the state-room is standing on its head.

''Before it is possible to make any arrangement at all compatible with this novel state of things, the ship rights. Before one can say 'Thank Heaven!' she wrongs again. Before one can cry she *is* wrong, she seems to have started forward, and to be a creature actually running of its own accord, with broken knees and failing legs, through every variety of hole and pitfall, and stumbling constantly. Before one can so much as wonder, she takes a high leap into the air. Before she has well done that, she takes a deep dive into the water. Before she has gained the surface, she throws a summerset. The instant she is on her legs, she rushes backward. And so she goes on staggering, heaving,

wrestling, leaping, diving, jumping, pitching, throbbing, rolling, and rocking: and going through all these movements, sometimes by turns, and sometimes altogether: until one feels disposed to roar for mercy.'' [Charles Dickens, *American Notes and Pictures From Italy,* Oxford University Press, 1957.[7]]

''I can give you no conception of my welcome here. There never was a king or emperor upon the earth so cheered and followed by crowds, and entertained in public at splendid halls and dinners, and waited on by public bodies and deputations of all kinds. I have had one from the Far West—a journey of two thousand miles! (If I go out in a carriage, the crowd surround it and escort me home; if I go to the theatre, the whole house (crowded to the roof) rises as one man, and the timbers ring again. You cannot imagine what it is. I have five great public dinners on hand at this moment, and invitations from every town and village and city in the States.'' [*Charles Dickens, Letters and Speeches,* Volume I, Hurst's International Library, 1893.[8]]

''The people are affectionate, generous, open-hearted, hospitable, enthusiastic, good-humoured, polite to women, frank and candid to all strangers, anxious to oblige, far less prejudiced than they have been described to be, frequently polished and refined, very seldom rude or disagreeable. I have made a great many friends here, even in public conveyances, whom I have been truly sorry to part from. In the towns I have formed perfect attachments. I have seen none of that greediness and indecorousness on which travellers have laid so much emphasis. I have returned frankness with frankness; met questions not intended to be rude, with answers meant to be satisfactory; and have not spoken to one man, woman, or child of any degree who has not grown positively affectionate before we parted. In the respects of not being left alone, and of being horribly disgusted by tobacco chewing and tobacco spittle, I have suffered considerably. The sight of slavery in Virginia, the hatred of British feeling upon the subject, and the miserable hints of the impotent indignation of the South, have pained me very much! on the last head, of course, I have felt nothing but a mingled pity and amusement; on the other, sheer distress. But however much I like the ingredients of this great dish, I cannot but come back to the point upon which I started, and say that the dish itself goes against the grain with me, and that I don't like it.''[6]

Visited many American institutions. ''In the outskirts, stands a great prison, called the Eastern Penitentiary; conducted on a plan peculiar to the state of Pennsylvania. The system here, is rigid, strict, and hopeless solitary confinement. I believe it, in its effects, to be cruel and wrong.

''In its intention, I am well convinced that it is kind, humane, and meant for reformation; but I am persuaded that those who devised this system of Prison Discipline, and those benevolent gentlemen who carry it into execution, do not know what it is that they are doing. I believe that very few men are capable of estimating the immense amount of torture and agony which this dreadful punishment, prolonged for years, inflicts upon the sufferers; and in guessing at it myself, and in reasoning from what I have seen written upon their faces, and what to my certain knowledge they feel within, I am only the more convinced that there is a depth of terrible endurance in it which none but the sufferers themselves can fathom, and which no man has a right to inflict upon his fellow-creature. I hold this slow and daily tampering with the mysteries of the brain, to be immeasurably worse than any torture of the body: and because its

(From *Oliver Twist* by Charles Dickens. Illustrated by George Cruikshank.)

(From the movie "Nicholas Nickleby," starring Sir Cedric Hardwicke. Copyright 1947 by Ealing Studios, Ltd. Released in the U.S. by Universal-International.)

ghastly signs and tokens are not so palpable to the eye and sense of touch as scars upon the flesh; because its wounds are not upon the surface, and it extorts few cries that human ears can hear; therefore I the more denounce it, as a secret punishment which slumbering humanity is not roused up to stay."[6]

Visited an institution for the blind. "If the company at a rout, or drawing-room at court, could only for one time be as unconscious of the eyes upon them as blind men and women are, what secrets would come out, and what a worker of hypocrisy this sight, the Loss of which we so much pity, would appear to be!

"The thought occurred to me as I sat down in another room, before a girl, blind, deaf, and dumb; destitute of smell; and nearly so of taste: before a fair young creature with every human faculty, and hope, and power of goodness and affection, inclosed within her delicate frame, and but one outward sense—the sense of touch. There she was, before me; built up, as it were, in a marble cell, impervious to any ray of light, or particle of sound; with her poor white hand peeping through a chink in the wall, beckoning to some good man for help, that an Immortal soul might be awakened.

"Long before I looked upon her, the help had come. Her face was radiant with intelligence and pleasure. Her hair, braided by her own hands, was bound about a head, whose intellectual capacity and development were beautifully expressed in its graceful outline, and its broad open brow; her dress, arranged by herself, was a pattern of neatness and simplicity; the work she had knitted, lay beside her; her writing-book was on the desk she leaned upon.—From the mournful ruin of such bereavement, there had slowly risen up this gentle, tender, guileless, grateful-hearted being.

"Like other inmates of that house, she had a green ribbon bound round her eyelids. A doll she had dressed lay near upon the ground. I took it up, and saw that she had made a green fillet such as she wore herself, and fastened it about its mimic eyes.

"She was seated in a little enclosure, made by school-desks and forms, writing her daily journal. But soon finishing this pursuit, she engaged in an animated communication with a teacher who sat beside her. This was a favourite mistress with the poor pupil. If she could see the face of her fair instructress, she would not love her less, I am sure.

"I have extracted a few disjointed fragments of her history, from an account, written by that one man who has made her what she is. It is a very beautiful and touching narrative; and I wish I could present it entire. Her name is Laura Bridgman.

"Leaving Cincinnati at eleven o'clock in the forenoon, we embarked for Louisville in *The Pike* steamboat. . . .

"There chanced to be on board this boat, in addition to the usual dreary crowd of passengers, one Pitchlynn, a chief of the Choctaw tribe of Indians, who *sent in his card* to me, and with whom I had the pleasure of a long conversation.

"He spoke English perfectly well, though he had not begun to learn the language, he told me, until he was a young man grown. He had read many books; and Scott's poetry appeared to have left a strong impression on his mind: especially the opening of the Lady of the Lake, and the great battle scene in Marmion, in which, no doubt from the congeniality of the subjects to his own pursuits and tastes, he had great interest and delight. He appeared to understand correctly all he had read; and whatever fiction had enlisted his sympathy in its belief, and done so keenly and earnestly. I might almost say fiercely. He was dressed in our ordinary every-day costume, which hung about his fine figure loosely, and with indifferent grace. On my telling him that I regretted not to see him in his own attire, he threw up his right arm, for a moment, as though he were brandishing some heavy weapon, and answered, as he let it fall again, that his race were losing many things besides their dress, and would soon be seen upon the earth no more: but he wore it at home, he added proudly.

"He told me that he had been away from his home, west of the Mississippi, seventeen months: and was now returning. He had been chiefly at Washington on some negotiations pending between his Tribe and the Government: which were not settled yet (he said in a melancholy way), and he feared never would be: for what could a few poor Indians do, against such well-skilled men of business as the whites? He had no love for Washington; tired of towns and cities very soon; and longed for the Forest and the Prairie.

"I asked him what he thought of Congress? He answered, with a smile, that it wanted dignity, in an Indian's eyes.

"He would very much like, he said, to see England before he died; and spoke with much interest about the great things to be seen there. When I told him of that chamber in the British Museum wherein are preserved household memorials of a race that ceased to be, thousands of years ago, he was very attentive, and it was not hard to see that he had a reference in his mind to the gradual fading away of his own people.

"This lead us to speak of Mr. Catlin's gallery, which he praised highly: observing that his own portrait was among the collection, and that all the likenesses were 'elegant.' Mr. Cooper, he said, had painted the Red Man well; and so would I, he knew, if I would go home with him and hunt buffaloes, which he was quite anxious I should do. When I told him that supposing I went, I should not be very likely to damage the buffaloes much, he took it as a great joke and laughed heartily.

"He was a remarkably handsome man; some years past forty, I should judge; with long black hair, an aquiline nose, broad cheek-bones, a sunburnt complexion, and a very bright, keen, dark, and piercing eye. There were but twenty thousand of the Choctaws left, he said, and their number was decreasing every day. A few of his brother chiefs had been obliged to become civilised, and to make themselves acquainted with what the whites knew, for it was their only chance of existence. But they were not many; and the rest were as they always had been. He dwelt on this: and said several times that unless they tried to assimilate themselves

(From the movie "Mr. Quilp," the musical adaptation of Charles Dickens' *The Old Curiosity Shop*, starring Sarah Jane Varley, Michael Hordern, Anthony Newley and David Hemmings. Produced by Avco Embassy Pictures Corp.)

In half a minute Mrs. Cratchit entered—flushed, but smiling proudly—with the pudding, like a speckled cannon ball, so hard and firm, blazing in half of half a quartern of ignited brandy, and bedight with Christmas holly stuck into the top. ■ (From *A Christmas Carol* by Charles Dickens. Illustrated by Maraja.)

to their conquerors, they must be swept away before the strides of civilised society.

"When we shook hands at parting, I told him he must come to England, as he longed to see the land so much: that I should hope to see him there, one day: and that I could promise him he would be well received and kindly treated. He was evidently pleased by this assurance, though he rejoined with a good-humoured smile and an arch shake of his head, that the English used to be very fond of the Red Men when they wanted their help, but had not cared much for them, since.

"He took his leave; as stately and complete a gentleman of Nature's making, as ever I beheld; and moved among the people in the boat, another kind of being. He sent me a lithographed portrait of himself soon afterwards; very like, though scarcely handsome enough; which I have carefully preserved in memory of our brief acquaintance.''[7]

"I have come at last, and it is time I did, to my life here, and intentions for the future. I can do nothing that I want to do, go nowhere where I want to go, and see nothing that I want to see. If I turn into the street, I am followed by a multitude. If I stay at home, the house becomes, with callers, like a fair. If I visit a public institution, with only one friend, the directors come down incontinently, waylay me in the yard, and address me in a long speech. I go to a party in the evening, and am so inclosed and hemmed about by people, stand where I will, that I am exhausted for want of air. I dine out, and have to talk about everything, to everybody. I go to church for quiet, and there is a violent rush to the neighbourhood of the pew I sit in, and the clergyman preaches *at* me. I take my seat in a railroad car, and the very conductor won't leave me alone. I get out at a station, and can't drink a glass of water, without having a hundred people looking down my throat when I open my mouth to swallow. Conceive what all this is! Then by every post, letters on letters arrive, all about nothing, and all demanding an immediate answer. This man is offended because I won't live in his house; and that man is thoroughly disgusted because I won't go out more than four times in one evening. I have no rest or peace, and am in a perpetual worry. . . .''[6]

"By-the-way, whenever an Englishman would cry 'All right!' an American cries 'Go ahead!' which is somewhat expressive of the national character of the two countries.''[7]

1843-44. Publication of *Martin Chuzzlewit* and *A Christmas Carol.* Dickens family in Italy.

1845-46. Dickens family abroad.

1846-50. *Dombey and Son* and *Christmas Stories* published. Dickens acted in amateur theater.

Opposed to capital punishment, Dickens wrote to the editor of the *Times:*

"DEVONSHIRE TERRACE, *Tuesday, Thirteenth November,* 1849.

"SIR,—I was a witness of the execution at Horsemonger Lane this morning. I went there with the intention of observing the crowd gathered to behold it, and I had excellent opportunities of doing so, at intervals all through the night, and continuously from daybreak until after the spectacle was over. I do not address you on the subject with any intention of discussing the abstract question of capital punishment, or any of the arguments of its opponents or advocates. I simply wish to turn this dreadful experience to some account for the general good, by taking the readiest and most public means of adverting to an intimation given by Sir G. Grey in the last session of Parliament, that the Government might be induced to give its support to a measure making the infliction of capital punishment a private solemnity within the prison walls (with such guarantees for the last sentence of the law being inexorably and surely administered as should be satisfactory to the public at large), and of most earnestly beseeching Sir G. Grey, as a solemn duty which he owes to society, and a responsibility which he cannot for ever put away, to originate such a legislative change himself. I believe that a sight so inconceivably awful as the wickedness and levity of the immense crowd collected at that execution this morning could be imagined by no man, and could be presented in no heathen land under the sun. The horrors of the gibbet and of the crime which brought the wretched murderers to it faded in my mind before the atrocious bearing, looks, and language of the assembled spectators. When I came upon the scene at midnight, the *shrillness* of the cries and howls that were raised from time to time, denoting that they came from a concourse of boys and girls already assembled in the best places, made my blood run cold. As the night went on, screeching, and laughing, and yelling in strong chorus of parodies on negro melodies, with substitutions of 'Mrs. Manning' for 'Susannah,' and the like, were added to these. When the day dawned, thieves, low prostitutes, ruffians, and vagabonds of every kind, flocked on to the ground, with every variety of offensive and foul behaviour. Fightings, faintings, whistlings, imitations of Punch, brutal jokes, tumultuous demonstrations of indecent delight when swooning women were dragged out of the crowd by the police, with their dresses disordered, gave a new zest to the general entertainment. When the sun rose brightly—as it did—it gilded thousands upon thousands of upturned faces, so inexpressibly odious in their brutal mirth or callousness, that a man had cause to feel ashamed of the shape he wore, and to shrink from himself, as fashioned in the image of the Devil. When the two miserable creatures who attracted all this ghastly sight about them were turned quivering into the air, there was no more emotion, no more pity, no more thought that two immortal souls had gone to judgment, no more restraint in any of the previous obscenities, than if the name of Christ had never been heard in this world, and there were no belief among men but that they perished like the beasts.

"I have seen, habitually, some of the worst sources of general contamination and corruption in this country, and I think there are not many phases of London life that could surprise me. I am solemnly convinced that nothing that ingenuity could devise to be done in this city, in the same compass of time, could work such ruin as one public execution, and I stand astounded and appalled by the wickedness it exhibits. I do not believe that any community can prosper where such a scene of horror and demoralisation as was enacted this morning outside Horsemonger Lane Gaol is presented at the very doors of good citizens, and is passed by unknown or forgotten. And when in our prayers and thanksgivings for the season we are humbly expressing before God our desire to remove the moral evils of the land, I would ask your readers to consider whether it is not a time, to think of this one, and to root it out. I am, Sir, your faithful Servant.''[8]

1848. Death of Dickens' sister, Fanny.

"TO JOHN FORSTER

[London] Fifth July 1848

. . . A change took place in poor Fanny, about the middle of the day yesterday, which took me out there last night. Her cough suddenly ceased almost, and, strange to say, she immediately became aware of her hopeless state; to which she resigned herself, after an hour's unrest and struggle, with extraordinary sweetness and constancy. The irritability passed, and all hope faded away; though only two nights before, she had been planning for 'after Christmas.'

"She is greatly changed. I had a long interview with her to-day, alone; and when she had expressed some wishes about the funeral, and her being buried in unconsecrated ground,

I asked her whether she had any care or anxiety in the world. She said No, none. It was hard to die at such a time of life, but she had no alarm whatever in the prospect of the change; felt sure we should meet again in a better world; and although they had said she might rally for a time, did not really wish it. She said she was quite calm and happy, relied upon the mediation of Christ, and had no terror at all. She had worked very hard, even when ill; but believed that was in her nature, and neither regretted nor complained of it.

"TO JOHN FORSTER [*1849*]

"Burnett had been always very good to her; they had never quarrelled; she was sorry to think of his going back to such a lonely home; and was distressed about her children, but

One day the king was going to the office, when he stopped at the fishmonger's to buy a pound and a half of salmon not too near the tail. ■ (From *The Magic Fishbone* by Charles Dickens. Illustrated by Louis Slobodkin.)

"There!" said Richard, putting the plate before her. "First of all, clear that off, and then you'll see what's next." ■ (From *People From Dickens* arranged by Rachel Field. Illustrated by Thomas Fogarty.)

not painfully so. She showed me how thin and worn she was; spoke about an invention she had heard of that she would like to have tried, for the deformed child's back; called to my remembrance all our sister Letitia's patience and steadiness; and, though she shed tears sometimes, clearly impressed upon me that her mind was made up, and at rest. I asked her very often, if she could ever recall anything that she could leave to my doing, to put it down, or mention it to somebody if I was not there; and she said she would, but she firmly believed that there was nothing—nothing. Her husband being young, she said, and her children infants, she could not help thinking sometimes, that it would be very long in the course of nature before they were reunited; but she knew that was a mere human fancy, and could have no reality after she was dead. Such an affecting exhibition of strength and tenderness, in all that early decay, is quite indescribable. I need not tell you how it moved me. I cannot look round upon the dear children here, without some misgiving that this sad disease will not perish out of our blood with her; but I am sure I have no

selfishness in the thought, and God knows how small the world looks to one who comes out of such a sick-room on a bright summer day. I don't know why I write this before going to bed. I only know that in the very pity and grief of my heart, I feel as if it were doing something. . . ."[6]

1849. Publication of *David Copperfield,* Dickens' favorite book.

1850. *Household Words,* weekly publication edited by Dickens, began.

1851-53. Monthly numbers of *Bleak House.*

1854. Publication of *Hard Times.*

October, 1854. "TO JOHN FORSTER

[*Boulogne*]

. . . I have had dreadful thoughts of getting away somewhere altogether by myself. If I could have managed it, I think possibly I might have gone to the Pyreennees (you know what I mean that word for, so I won't re-write it) for six months! I have put the idea into the perspective of six months, but have not abandoned it. I have visions of living for half a year or so, in all sorts of inaccessible places, and opening a new book therein. A floating idea of going up above the snow-line in Switzerland, and living in some astonishing convent, hovers about me. If *Household Words* could be got into a good train, in short, I don't know in what strange place, or at what remote elevation above the level of the sea, I might fall to work next. *Restlessness,* you will say. Whatever it is, it is always driving me, and I cannot help it. I have rested nine or ten weeks, and sometimes feel as if it had been a year—though I had the strangest nervous miseries before I stopped. If I couldn't walk fast and far, I should just explode and perish. . . ."[6]

1855. Publication of *Little Dorritt.* Met Maria Beadnell Winter again.

"TO MARIA BEADNELL WINTER

Tavistock House,
Saturday, Tenth February 1855

I constantly receive hundreds of letters in great varieties of writing. . . . As I was reading by my fire last night, a handful of notes was laid down on my table. I looked them over, and, recognising the writing of no private friend, let them lie there and went back to my book. But I found my mind curiously disturbed, and wandering away through so many years to such early times of my life, that I was quite perplexed to account for it. There was nothing in what I had been reading, or immediately thinking about, to awaken such a train of thought, and at last it came into my head that it might have been suggested by something in the look of one of those letters. So I turned them over again—and suddenly the remembrance of your hand came upon me with an influence that I cannot express to you. Three or four and twenty years vanished like a dream, and I opened it with the touch of my young friend *David Copperfield* when he was in love.

"There was something so busy and so pleasant in your letter—so true and cheerful and frank and affectionate—that I read on with perfect delight until I came to your mention of your two little girls. In the unsettled state of my thoughts, the existence of these dear children appeared such a prodigious phenomenon, that I was inclined to suspect myself of being out of my mind, until it occurred to me, that perhaps I had nine children of my own! Then the three or four and twenty years began to rearrange themselves in a long procession between me and the changeless Past, and I could not help considering what strange stuff all our little stories are made of.

"I fancy—though you may not have thought in the old time how manfully I loved you—that you may have seen in one of my books a faithful reflection of the passion I had for you, and may have thought that it was something to have been loved so well, and may have seen in little bits of 'Dora' touches of your old self sometimes and a grace here and there that may be revived in your little girls, years hence, for the bewilderment of some other young lover—though he will never be as terribly in earnest as I and *David Copperfield* were. People used to say to me how pretty all that was, and how fanciful it was, and how ele-

vated it was above the little foolish loves of very young men and women. But they little thought what reason I had to know it was true and nothing more nor less.

"But nobody can ever know with what a sad heart I resigned you, or after what struggles and what conflict. My entire devotion to you, and the wasted tenderness of those hard years which I have ever since half loved, half dreaded to recall, made so deep an impression on me that I refer to it a habit of suppression which now belongs to me, which I know is no part of my original nature, but which makes me chary of showing my affections, even to my children, except when they are very young. A few years ago (just before *Copperfield*) I began to write my life, intending the manuscript to be found among my papers when its subject should be concluded. But as I began to approach within sight of that part of it, I lost courage and burned the rest. I have never blamed you at all but I have believed until now that you never had the stake in that serious game which I had.

"I have always believed since, and always shall to the last, that there never was such a faithful and devoted poor fellow as I was. Whatever of fancy, romance, energy, passion, aspiration and determination belong to me, I never have separated and never shall separate from the hard-hearted little woman—you—whom it is nothing to say I would have died for, with the greatest alacrity! I never can think, and I never seem to observe, that other young people are in such desperate earnest or set so much, so long, upon one absorbing hope. It is a matter of perfect certainty to me that I began to fight my way out of poverty and obscurity, with one perpetual idea of you. This is so fixed in my knowledge that to the hour when I opened your letter last Friday night I have never heard anybody addressed by your name, or spoken of by your name, without a start. The sound of it has always filled me with a kind of pity and respect for the deep truth that I had, in my silly hobbledehoyhood, to bestow upon one creature who represented the whole world to me. I have never been so good a man since, as I was when you made me wretchedly happy. I shall never be half so good a fellow any more."[6]

1856. Bought Gad's Hill, his last home. "Down at Gad's Hill, near Rochester, in Kent—Shakespeare's Gad's Hill, where Falstaff engaged in the robbery—is a quaint little country-house of Queen Anne's time. I happened to be walking past, a year and a half or so ago, with my sub-editor of *Household Words,* when I said to him: 'You see that house? It has always a curious interest for me, because when I was a small boy down in these parts I thought it the most beautiful house (I suppose because of its famous old cedar-trees) ever seen. And my poor father used to bring me to look at it, and used to say that if I ever grew up to be a clever man perhaps I might own that house, or such another house. In remembrance of which, I have always in passing looked to see if it was to be sold or let, and it has never been to me like any other house, and it has never changed at all.' We came back to town, and my friend went out to dinner. Next morning he came to me in great excitement, and said: 'It is written that you were to have that house at Gad's Hill. The lady I had allotted to me to take down to dinner yesterday began to speak of that neighbourhood. "You know it?" I said; "I have been there to-day." "O yes," said she, "I know it very well. I was a child there, in the house they call Gad's Hill Place. My father was the rector, and lived there many years. He has just died, has left it to me, and I want to sell it." "So," says the sub-editor, "you must buy it. Now or never!" ' I did, and

"In came little Bob the father, with at least three feet of comforter exclusive of the fringe, hanging down before him; and his threadbare clothes darned up and brushed, to look seasonable; and Tiny Tim upon his shoulder." ■ (From *A Christmas Carol* by Charles Dickens. Illustrated by Jessie Wilcox Smith.)

Only one disagreeable incident occurred. Captain Boldheart found himself obliged to put his Cousin Tom in irons, for being disrespectful. ■ (From *Captain Boldheart* by Charles Dickens. Illustrated by Hilary Knight.)

hope to pass next summer there, though I may, perhaps, let it afterwards, furnished, from time to time.''[7]

1857. Gave his first public reading. Made numerous speeches to raise funds for worthy charities. "And now, ladies and gentlemen, perhaps you will permit me to sketch in a few words the sort of school that I do like. It is a school established by the members of an industrious and useful order, which supplies the comforts and graces of life at every familiar turning in the road of our existence; it is a school established by them for the Orphan and Necessitous Children of their own brethren and sisterhood; it is a place of education where, while the beautiful history of the Christian religion is daily taught, and while the life of that Divine Teacher who Himself took little children on His knees is daily studied, no sectarian ill will nor narrow human dogma is permitted to darken the face of the clear heaven which they disclose. It is a children's school, which is at the same time no less a children's home, a home not to be confided to the care of cold or ignorant strangers, nor, by the nature of its foundation, in the course of ages to pass into hands that have as much natural right to deal with it as the peaks of the highest mountains or with the depths of the sea, but to be from generation to generation administered by men living in precisely such homes as those poor children have lost; by men always bent upon making that replacement, such a home as their own dear children might find a happy refuge in if they themselves were taken early away. . . . ''[5]

"Some years ago, being in Scotland, I went with one of the most humane members of the humane medical profession, on a morning tour among some of the worst-lodged inhabitants of the old town of Edinburgh. In the closes and wynds of that picturesque place—I am sorry to remind you what fast friends picturesqueness and typhus often are—we saw more poverty and sickness in an hour than many people would believe in a life. Our way lay from one to another of the most wretched dwellings—reeking with horrible odours—shut out from the sky—shut out from the air—mere pits and dens. In a room in one of these places, where there was an empty porridge-pot on the cold hearth, with a ragged woman and some ragged children crouching on the bare ground near it—where, I remember as I speak, that very light, reflected from a high damp-stained and time-stained house wall, came trembling in, as if the fever which had shaken everything else there had shaken even it—there lay, in an old egg-box which the mother had begged from a shop, a little feeble, wasted, wan, sick child. With his little wasted face, and his little hot worn hands folded over his breast, and his little bright attentive eyes, I can see him now, as I have seen him for several years, looking steadily at us. There he lay in his little frail box, which was not at all a bad emblem of the little body from which he was slowly parting—there he lay, quite quiet, quite patient, saying never a word. He seldom cried, the mother said; he seldom complained; 'he lay there, seeming to wonder what it was a' aboot.' God knows I thought, as I stood looking at him, he had his reasons for wondering—reasons for wondering how it could possibly come to be that he lay there, left alone, feeble and full of pain, when he ought to have been as bright and as brisk as the birds that never got near him—reasons for wondering how he came to be left there, a little decrepit old man, pining to death, quite a thing of course, as if there were no crowds of healthy and happy children playing on the grass under the summer's sun within a stone's throw of him, as if there were no bright moving sea on the other side of the great hill overhanging the city; as if there were no great clouds rushing over it; as if there were no life, and movement, and vigour anywhere

in the world—nothing but stoppage and decay. There he lay looking at us, saying in his silence, more pathetically than I have ever heard anything said by any orator in my life, 'Will you please to tell us what this means, strange man? and if you can give me any good reason why I should be so soon, so far advanced on my way to Him who said that children were to come into His presence, and were not to be forbidden, but who scarcely meant, that they should come by this hard road by which I am travelling—pray give that reason to me, for I seek it very earnestly and wonder about it very much'; and to my mind he has been wondering about it ever since. Many a poor child, sick and neglected, I have seen since that time in this London; many a poor sick child have I seen most affectionately and kindly tended by poor people, in an unwholesome house and under untoward circumstances, wherein its recovery was quite impossible; but at all such times I have seen my poor little dropping friend in his egg-box, and he has always addressed his dumb speech to me, and I have always found him wondering what it meant, and why, in the name of a gracious God, such things should be!''[5]

1858. Separated from wife.

"TO JOHN FORSTER

[September 1857]

. . . Your letter of yesterday was so kind and hearty, and sounded so gently the many chords we have touched together, that I cannot leave it unanswered, though I have not much (to any purpose) to say. My reference to 'confidences' was merely to the relief of saying a word of what has long been pent up in my mind. Poor Catherine and I are not made for each other, and there is no help for it. It is not only that she makes me uneasy and unhappy, but that I make her so too—and much more so. She is exactly what you know, in the way of being amiable and complying; but we are strangely ill-assorted for the bond there is between us. God knows she would have been a thousand times happier if she had married another kind of man, and that her avoidance of this destiny would have been at least equally good for us both. I am often cut to the heart by thinking what a pity it is, for her own sake, that I ever fell in her way. . . .

"I believe my marriage has been for years and years as miserable a one as ever was made. I believe that no two people were ever created, with such an impossibility of interest, sympathy, confidence, sentiment, tender union of any kind between them, as there is between my wife and me. It is an immense misfortune to her—it is an immense misfortune to me—but Nature has put an insurmountable barrier between us, which never in this world can be thrown down.

"We have been virtually separated for a long time. We must put a wider space between us now, than can be found in one house. If the children loved her, or ever had loved her, this severance would have been a far easier thing than it is. But she has never attached one of them to herself, never played with them in their infancy, never attracted their confidence as they have grown older, never presented herself before them in the aspect of a mother. I have seen them fall off from her in a natural—not *un*natural—progress of estrangement, and at this moment I believe that Mary and Katey (whose dispositions are of the gentlest and most affectionate conceivable) harden into stone figures of girls when they can be got to go near her, and have their hearts shut up in her presence as if they were closed by some horrid spring.''[6]

''I know very well that a man who has won a very conspicuous position, has incurred in the winning of it, a heavy debt to the knaves and fools, which he must be content to pay, over and over again, all through his life. Further, I know equally well that I can never hope that anyone out of my house can ever comprehend my domestic story. I will not complain. I have been heavily wounded, but I have covered the wound up, and left it to heal. Some of my children or some of my friends will do me right if I ever need it in the time to come. And I hope that my books will speak for themselves and me, when I and my faults and virtues, my fortunes and misfortunes are all forgotten.'' [Ada Nisbet, *Dickens & Ellen Turnan,* University of California Press, 1952.[9]]

1859. Publication of *Tale of Two Cities.* ''You will not have to complain of the want of humor, as in the *Tale of Two Cities,* I have made the opening, I hope, in its general effect, exceedingly droll.'' [*A Dictionary of Biographies of Authors Represented in the Authors Digest Series,* edited by Rossiter Johnson, Gale Research, 1974.[10]]

1860-61. Publication of *Great Expectations.*

1864-65. Publication of *Our Mutual Friend.*

1867-68. Second visit to the United States. ''. . . to express my high and grateful sense of my second reception in America, and to bear my honest testimony to the national generosity and magnanimity. Also, to declare how astounded I have been by the amazing changes that I have seen around me on every side—changes moral, changes physical, changes in the amount of land subdued and peopled, changes in the rise of vast new cities, changes in the growth of older cities almost out of recognition, changes in the graces and amenities of life, changes in the Press, without whose advancement no advancement can be made anywhere. Nor am I, believe me, so arrogant as to suppose that in five-and-twenty years there have been no changes in me, and that I have nothing to learn, and that I had nothing to learn and no extreme impressions to correct from when I was here first.

''And, gentlemen, this brings me to a point on which I have, ever since I landed here last November, observed a strict silence, though sometimes tempted to break it, but in reference to which I will, with your permission, beg leave to take you now into my confidence. Even the Press, being human, may be sometimes mistaken or misinformed, and I rather think that I have myself, on one or two occasions, in some rare instances, known its information to be not perfectly accurate with reference to myself. Indeed, I have now and again, been more surprised by printed news that I have read of myself, than by any printed news that I have ever read in my present state of existence. Thus, the vigour and perseverance with which I have for some months past been collecting materials and hammering away at a new book on America have much astonished me; seeing that all that time it has been perfectly well known to my publishers on both sides of the Atlantic, that I positively declared that no consideration on earth should induce me to write one. But what I have intended, what I have resolved upon (and this is the confidence I seek to place in you) is, on my return to England, in my own person to bear, for the behoof of my countrymen, such testimony to the gigantic changes in this country as I have hinted at tonight. Also, to record

that wherever I have been, in the smallest places equally with the largest, I have been received with unsurpassable politeness, delicacy, sweet temper, hospitality, consideration, and with unsurpassable respect for the privacy daily enforced upon me by the nature of my avocation here, and the state of my health. This testimony, so long as I live, and so long as my descendants have any legal right in my books, I shall cause to be republished, as an appendix to every copy of those two books of mine in which I have referred to America. And this I will do and cause to be done, not in mere love and thankfulness, but because I regard it as an act of plain justice and honour.''[5]

1868-69. Continued speeches and public readings.

March, 1870. Gave last public reading. ''LADIES and Gentlemen, It would be worse than idle—for it would be hypocritical and unfeeling—if I were to disguise that I close this episode in my life with feelings of very considerable pain. For some fifteen years, in this hall and in many kindred places, I have had the honour of presenting my own cherished ideas before you for your recognition; and, in closely observing your reception of them, have enjoyed an amount of artistic delight and instruction which, perhaps, is given to few men to know. In this task, and in every other which I have ever undertaken, as a faithful servant of the public, always imbued with a sense of duty to them, and always striving to do his best, I have been uniformly cheered by the readiest response, the most generous sympathy, and the most stimulating support. Nevertheless, I have thought it well, at the full floodtide of your favour, to retire upon those older associations between us, which date from much further back than these, and henceforth to devote myself exclusively to that art which first brought us together.

''Ladies and gentlemen, in but two short weeks from this time I hope that you may enter, in your own homes, on a new series of readings, at which my assistance will be indispensable; but from these garish lights I vanish now for evermore, with a heartfelt, grateful, respectful, and affectionate farewell.''[5]

April, 1870. First installment of *Mystery of Edwin Drood.*

June 8, 1870. Suffered stroke and died next day.

June 14, 1870. Buried in Poet's Corner, Westminster Abbey. ''If I had not known long ago that my place could never be held unless I were at any moment ready to devote myself to it entirely, I should have dropped out of it very soon. All this I can hardly expect you to understand—or the restlessness or waywardness of an author's mind. . . . 'It is only half an hour'—'it is only an afternoon'—'it is only an evening'—people say to me over and over again—but they don't know that it is impossible to command one's self sometimes to any stipulated and set disposal of five minutes—or that the mere consciousness of an engagement will sometimes worry a whole day. These are the penalties paid for writing books. Whoever is devoted to an Art must be content to deliver himself wholly up to it, and to find his recompense in it.''[6]

''If you do not yourself believe in what you are describing you will never get your readers to do so. For myself I can as distinctly see before my eyes the scene which I am describing as I can see you now. So much so has this been the case with me that on one occasion, in which I had laid out a certain path which one of my characters was to pur-

(From "The Changing World of Charles Dickens." Produced by the Learning Corporation of America, 1978.)

sue, that character took hold of me and persuaded me to make him do exactly the opposite to what I had originally intended; but I was so sure that he must be right and I wrong that I let him have his own way."[10]

"It is not easy for a man to speak of his own books. I dare say that few persons have been more interested in mine than I; and if it be a general principle in nature that a lover's love is blind, and that a mother's love is blind, I believe it may be said of an author's attachment to the creatures of his own imagination, that it is a perfect model of constancy and devotion, and is the blindest of all. But the objects and purposes I have in view are very plain and simple, and may easily be told. I have always had, and always shall have, an earnest and true desire to contribute, as far as in me lies, to the common stock of healthful cheerfulness and enjoyment. I have always had, and always shall have, an invincible repugnance to that mole-eyed philosophy which loves the darkness, and winks and scowls in the light. I believe that Virtue shows quite as well in rags and patches as she does in purple and fine linen."[5]

"To be numbered among the household gods of one's distant countrymen, and associated with their homes and quiet pleasures; to be told that in each nook and corner of the world's great mass there lives one well-wisher who holds communion with one in the spirit, is a worthy fame indeed, and one which I would not barter for a mine of wealth."[8]

"I never could have done what I have done without the habits of punctuality, order, and diligence; without the determination to concentrate myself on one object at a time, no matter how quickly its successor should come upon its heels. Heaven knows I write this in no spirit of self-laudation. My meaning simply is that whatever I have tried to do in life, I have tried with all my heart to do well; that whatever I have devoted myself to, I have devoted myself to completely; that in great aims and in small, I have always been thoroughly in earnest. Never to put one hand to anything on which I could throw my whole self; and never to affect depreciation of my work, whatever it was; I find, now to have been my golden rules.

"Much better to die, doing. I have always felt of myself that I must, please God, die in harness. How strange it is to be never at rest, and never satisfied, and ever trying after something that is never reached, and to be always laden with plot and plan and care and worry, how clear it is that it

The Chiffonier. ■ (From *The New Oxford Illustrated Dickens: American Notes and Pictures from Italy* by Charles Dickens.)

must be and that one is driven by an irresistible might until the journey is worked out! It is much better to go on and fret, than to stop and fret. As to repose—for some men there's no such thing in this life.'' [Charles Dickens, Jr., *Reminiscences of My Father,* Haskell House, 1972.[11]]

FOR MORE INFORMATION SEE: R. A. Hammond, *Life and Writings of Charles Dickens: A Memorial Volume,* [London], 1871, reprinted, Haskell House, 1972; George Dolby, *Charles Dickens as I Knew Him: The Story of the Reading Tours in Great Britian and America (1866-1870),* T. F. Urwin, 1885, reprinted, Folcroft, 1973; Robert Langton, *Childhood and Youth of Charles Dickens,* Hutchinson, 1891, reprinted, R. West, 1973; G. R. Gissing, *Charles Dickens: A Critical Study,* Dodd, 1898, reprinted, Haskell House, 1974; Frederic G. Kitton, *Dickens and His Illustrators,* G. Redway, 1899, reprinted, AMS Press, 1975; Kitton, *Minor Writings of Charles Dickens,* E. Stock, 1900, reprinted, R. West, 1973; Kitton, *Charles Dickens: His Life, Writings, and Personality,* T. C. & E. C. Jack, 1902, reprinted, R. West, 1973; Gilbert Keith Chesterton, *Charles Dickens: A Critical Study,* Dodd, 1906, reissued, Schocken Books, 1965; Charles Dickens, Jr., *Reminiscences of My Father,* [London], 1908, reprinted, Haskell House, 1972.

S. Adair Fitz-Gerald, *Dickens and the Drama,* Chapman & Hall, 1910, reprinted, R. West, 1973; J. Cuming Walters,

Phases of Dickens: The Man, His Message, and His Mission, Chapman & Hall, 1911, reprinted, R. West, 1973; William G. Wilkins, editor, *Charles Dickens in America,* Chapman & Hall, 1911, reprinted, Haskell House, 1970; Mary Dickens, *Charles Dickens,* Cassell, 1911, reprinted, R. West, 1973; James T. Lightwood, *Charles Dickens and Music,* C. H. Kelly, 1912, reprinted, R. West, 1973; Edgar Browne, *Phiz and Dickens,* J. Nisbet, 1913, reprinted, Haskell House, 1972; Thomas A. Fyfe, *Who's Who in Dickens,* Hodder, Stoughton, 1912, reprinted, Gale, 1971; Walter W. Crotch, *The Pageant of Dickens,* Chapman & Hall, 1915, reprinted, Haskell House, 1972; Crotch, *The Soul of Dickens,* Chapman & Hall, 1916, reprinted, R. West, 1973; Crotch, *The Secret of Dickens,* Chapman & Hall, 1919, reprinted, Haskell House, 1972; J. W. Ley, *The Dickens Circle,* Dutton, 1919, reprinted, Haskell House, 1972.

W. W. Crotch, *The Touchstone of Dickens,* Chapman & Hall, 1920, reissued, R. West, 1973; G. R. Gissing, *Immortal Dickens,* C. Palmer, 1925, reprinted, R. West, 1973; Henry F. Dickens, *Memories of My Father,* V. Gollancz, 1928, reprinted, Haskell House, 1972; John C. Eckel, *The First Editions of the Writings of Charles Dickens,* M. Inman, 1932, reprinted, Haskell House, 1972; Thomas Jackson, *Charles Dickens: Progress of a Radical,* Lawrence, Wishart, 1937, reprinted, Haskell House, 1971; Octavius F. Christie, *Dickens and His Age,* H. Cranton, 1939, reprinted, Phaeton Press, 1974.

William Miller, compiler, *Dickens Student and Collector: A List of Writings Relating to Charles Dickens and His Works, 1836-1945,* Harvard University Press, 1946, reissued, Octagon Books, 1971; C. Dickens and J. Forster, ''Blacking Warehouse,'' in *When I Was a Child,* edited by

(From the television adaptation of Charles Dickens' *Hard Times,* starring Alan Dobie and Ursula Howells. Produced by Granada Television and WNET, New York.)

Edward Charles Wagenknecht, Dutton, 1946; George Orwell, *Dickens, Dali, and Others: Studies in Popular Culture,* Reynal, 1946; Una Pope-Hennessy, *Charles Dickens,* Howell, Soskin, 1946, reprinted, Humanities Press, 1968; W. Somerset Maugham, *Great Novelists and Their Novels,* Winston, 1948; James Robert Cruikshank, *Charles Dickens and Early Victorian England,* Chanticleer, 1949; Hesketh Pearson, *Dickens: His Character, Comedy, and Career,* Harper, 1949, reprinted, R. West, 1973.

Jack Lindsay, *Charles Dickens: A Biographical and Critical Study,* Philosophical Library, 1950; *Heart of Charles Dickens as Revealed in His Letters to Angela Burdett-Coutts,* Little, Brown, 1951; Julian Symons, *Charles Dickens,* Roy Publishers, 1951, reprinted, Haskell House, 1974; Edgar Johnson, *Charles Dickens: His Tragedy and Triumph,* two volumes, Simon & Schuster, 1952; Frank Dubrez Fawcett, *Dickens the Dramatist: On Stage, Screen, and Radio,* Allen, 1952, reprinted, R. West, 1973; K. J. Fielding, *Charles Dickens,* Longmans, Green, 1953, reissued, 1963; Michael Harrison, *Charles Dickens: A Sentimental Journey in Search of an Unvarnished Portrait,* Cassell, 1953, reprinted, R. West, 1973; W. Somerset Maugham, *Art of Fiction,* Doubleday, 1955; George H. Ford, *Dickens and His Readers,* Princeton University Press, 1955, reprinted, Gordian Press, 1974.

(From *A Christmas Carol* by Charles Dickens. Illustrated by Milo Winter.)

Scrooge crept towards it, trembling as he went; and following the finger, read upon the stone of the neglected grave his own name, "EBENEZER SCROOGE." ■ (From *A Christmas Carol* by Charles Dickens. Illustrated by C.E. Brock.)

Elias Bredsdorff, *Hans Andersen and Charles Dickens: A Friendship and Its Dissolution,* Rosenkilde, 1956; William Henry Bowen, *Charles Dickens and His Family: A Sympathetic Study,* Heffer, 1956; Arthur A. Adrian, *Georgina Hogarth and the Dickens Circle,* Oxford University Press, 1957; John Everett Butt and Kathleen Mary Tillotson, *Dickens at Work,* Essential Books, 1958; K. J. Fielding, *Charles Dickens: A Critical Introduction,* Longmans, Green, 1958; Felix Aylmer, *Dickens Incognito,* Hart-Davis, 1959; Joseph Hillis Miller, Jr., *Charles Dickens: The World of His Novels,* Harvard University Press, 1959, reissued, Indiana University Press, 1969.

F. W. Dupee, editor, *Selected Letters,* Farrar, Straus, 1960; George H. Ford and Lauriat Lane, Jr., editors, *The Dickens' Critics,* Cornell University Press, 1961; Charles G. L. Du Cann, *Love-Lives of Charles Dickens,* Muller, 1961, reprinted, Greenwood Press, 1972; A. O. Cockshut, *Imagination of Charles Dickens,* New York University Press, 1962; Myrick Ebben Land, *Fine Art of Literary Mayhem,* Holt, 1962; John Boynton Priestly, *Charles Dickens: A Pictorial Biography,* Viking, 1962, reissued, 1969; John Cowie Reid, *Hidden World of Charles Dickens,* University of Auckland Press, 1962; Dorothy Phoebe Ansle, *Unwanted Wife: A Defense of Mrs. Charles Dickens,* Jarrolds, 1963; Ivor J. C. Brown, *Dickens in His Time,* Nelson, 1963; Colin Clair, *Charles Dickens: Life and Character*, Bruce, 1963; Earle Davis, *Flint and Flame: The Artistry of Charles Dickens*, University of Missouri Press, 1963.

Robert F. Fleissner, *Dickens and Shakespeare: A Study in Histrionic Contrasts*, Haskell House, 1965, reprinted, 1969; Robert Garis, *Dickens Theatre: A Reassessment of the Novels*, Oxford University Press, 1965; Madeline House and Graham Storey, editors, *Letters of Charles Dickens, Volume I: 1820-1839*, Clarendon Press, 1965; E. C. Wagenknecht, *Dickens and the Scandalmongers: Essays on Criticism*, University of Oklahoma Press, 1965; M. Hardwick and M. Hardwick, *Charles Dickens Companion*, Holt, 1966; E. C. Wagenknecht, *The Man Charles Dickens: A Victorian Portrait*, University of Oklahoma Press, 1966, reissued, 1971; John Gross and Gabriel Pearson, editors, *Dickens and the Twentieth Century*, Routledge, 1966; André Maurois, *Dickens* (translated from the French by Hamish Miles), Ungar, 1967; Frank Donovan, *Dickens and Youth*, Dodd, 1968; Sylvere Monod, *Dickens the Novelist*, University of Oklahoma Press, 1968; E. W. Tomlin, editor, *Charles Dickens Centennial*, Simon & Schuster, 1969.

Harvey Sucksmith, *Narrative Art of Charles Dickens: The Rhetoric of Sympathy and Irony in His Novels*, Oxford University Press, 1970; William Oddie, *Dickens and Carlyle: The Question of Influence*, Centenary Press, 1972; Joseph Gold, *Charles Dickens: Radical Moralist*, University of Minnesota Press, 1972; Philip Hobsbaum, *A Reader's Guide to Charles Dickens*, Farrar, Strauss, 1973; M. Hardwick and M. Hardwick, compilers, *The Charles Dickens Encyclopedia*, Scribner, 1973; N. M. Lary, *Dostoevsky and Dickens: A Study of Literary Influence*, Routledge, 1973; John Carey, *Here Comes Dickens: The Imagination of a Novelist*, Schocken Books, 1974; R. W. Long, "The England of Charles Dickens," *National Geographic*, April, 1974; Alfred B. Harbage, *A Kind of Power: The Shakespeare-Dickens Analogy*, American Philosophical Society, 1975.

For children: Elizabeth Rider Montgomery, *Story behind Great Books*, McBride, 1946; Sarah Knowles Bolton, *Lives of Poor Boys Who Became Famous*, Crowell, 1947, reprinted, 1962; E. Montgomery, *Story behind Great Stories*, McBride, 1947; Frederick Houk Law, *Great Lives*, Globe, 1952; John Cournos and H.S.N.K. Cournos, *Famous British Novelists*, Dodd, 1952; Eleanor Graham, *Story of Charles Dickens*, Abelard-Schuman, 1954; Patrick Pringle, *When They Were Boys*, Roy Publishers, 1954; Walter Ernest Allen, *Six Great Novelists*, Hamilton, 1955; J. Bayley, "Charles Dickens: The Life of the Imagination," in *Children's Book of Famous Lives*, edited by Eric Duthie, Odhams, 1958; Howard Jones, *Men of Letters*, Bell, 1959; Catherine Owens Peare, *Charles Dickens: His Life*, Holt, 1959.

P. Pringle, *Young Dickens*, Roy Publishers, 1960; Rhoda Hoff, *Why They Wrote*, Walck, 1961; Hannah Bellis, *They Made History*, Cassell, 1963; P. Pringle, *101 Great Lives*, Ward, Lock, 1963; Lawrence DuGarde Peach, *Charles Dickens*, Wills, 1965; Nora Stirling, *Who Wrote the Classics?*, Day, 1965; Christopher Hibbert, *Making of Charles Dickens*, Harper, 1967; Lettice Cooper, *Hand upon the Time: A Life of Charles Dickens*, Pantheon Books, 1968; Elisabeth Kyle, *Great Ambitions: A Story of the Early Years of Charles Dickens*, Holt, 1968; I. Brown, *Dickens and His World*, Walck, 1970; Patrick Rooke, *Age of Dickens*, Putnam, 1970.

Movies and filmstrips: "Charles Dickens: Background for His Works" (motion picture; 10 minutes, color, with a teacher's guide), Coronet Films, 1949; "Charles Dickens" (filmstrip; color, with a teacher's guide), Eye Gate House, 1952; "Charles Dickens: Characters in Action" (motion picture; 19 minutes, black and white, with a teacher's guide; excerpts from movies of Dickens' works), Teaching Film Custodians, 1958; "Reading Dickens, Part One: Five Literary Forms" (motion picture; 30 minutes, black and white), Anthology Films, 1959; "Reading Dickens, Part Two: Fact into Fiction" (motion picture; 22 minutes, black and white), Anthology Films, 1959.

"The Novel: Early Victorian England and Charles Dickens" (motion picture; 34 minutes, color, with a teacher's guide), Encyclopaedia Britannica Films, 1962; "A Dickens Chronicle, Parts 1 and 2" (motion picture; 54 minutes, black and white), Columbia Broadcasting System, 1963; "Tale of Two Cities" (filmstrip; color, with a teacher's guide), Audio-Visual Division, Popular Science Publishing, 1967; "A Tale of Two Cities: Analysis and Evaluation" (filmstrip; 17 minutes, color, sound, with a teacher's guide), Society for Visual Education, 1967; "Life in the Time of Charles Dickens" (filmstrip; 46 minutes, sound, with a teacher's guide), Educational Audio Visual, 1967.

DILLON, Diane   1933-

PERSONAL: Born March 13, 1933, in Glendale, Calif.; daughter of Adelbert Paul (a teacher) and Phyllis (Worsley) Sorber; married Leo J. Dillon (an artist), March 17, 1957; children: Lee. *Education:* Attended Parsons School of Design, New York, N.Y., four years; School of Visual Arts, New York, N.Y., one year. *Office:* C/o Dial Press, 1 Dag Hammarskjold Plaza, New York, N.Y. 10017.

CAREER: Artist; illustrator. Dave Fris Advertising Agency, Albany, N.Y., staff artist, 1956-57. *Exhibitions:* Black Arts Show, 1960's; Gallery 91, 1974, 1975; Society of Illustrators. *Member:* Society of Illustrators. *Awards, honors:* *Hakon of Rogen's Saga* was on the *Horn Book* Honor List, 1963, and was an ALA Notable Children's Book; *A Slave's Tale* was on the *Horn Book* Honor List, 1966, and was an ALA Notable Children's Book; Hugo Award, 1971, for science fiction illustration of a series of book jackets; *The Hundred Penny Box* was the winner of the *Boston Globe-Horn Book* award, 1975, and received the Newbery Medal; *Why Mosquitoes Buzz in People's Ears: A West African Tale* received the Caldecott Medal, 1975; *Ashanti to Zulu: African Traditions* was on the *Horn Book* honor List, 1977, received *New York Times* Best Illustrated Children's Book Award, the Caldecott Medal, 1977, and the Hamilton King Award, 1977; nominated for the Hans Christian Andersen Award, 1978.

ILLUSTRATOR: Erik C. Haugaard, *Hakon of Rogen's Saga* (ALA Notable Book), Houghton, 1963; Erik C. Haugaard, *A Slave's Tale* (ALA Notable Book), Houghton, 1965; F. M. Pilkington, *Shamrock and Spear*, Holt, 1966; Sorche Nic Leodhas, *Claymore and Kilt: Tales of Scottish Kings and Castles*, Holt, 1967; Erik C. Haugaard, *The Rider and His Horse*, Houghton, 1968; Audrey W. Beyer, *Dark Venture*, Knopf, 1968; John Bierhorst, *The Ring in the Prairie*, Dial, 1970; Alta Jablow, *Gassier's Lute: A West African Epic*, Dutton, 1971; Murray and Thomas (editors), *The Search*, Scholastic, 1971; Erik C. Haugaard, *The Untold Tale*, Houghton, 1971; Verna Aardema, *Behind the Back of the Mountain: Black Folktales From Southern Afri-*

ca, Dial, 1973; Seth Clifford, *Burning Star*, Houghton, 1974; W. Moses Serwadda, *Songs and Stories from Uganda*, Crowell, 1974; Jan Carew, *The Third Gift*, Little, Brown, 1974; Natalie Belting, *Whirlwind is a Ghost Dancing*, Dutton, 1974; Lorenz Graham, *Song of the Boat*, Crowell, 1975; Sharon Bell Mathis, *The Hundred Penny Box*, Viking, 1975; Verna Aardema, *Why Mosquitoes Buzz in People's Ears: A West African Folk Tale*, Dial, 1975; Margaret W. Musgrove, *Ashanti to Zulu: African Traditions*, Dial, 1976; Verna Aardema, *Who's in Rabbit's House? A Masai Tale*, Dial, 1977. Illustrations have appeared in *Ladies' Home Journal*, *The Saturday Evening Post*, and others.

SIDELIGHTS: "Art is a way of life—from illustrating to working on our home. We don't specialize because we don't want to be forced into one category. Media we have worked in, include wood, plastic, clay, oils, guache, watercolor, acrylic, pastels, metal and cloth. Things we admire: Art Nouveau, Diego Rivera, African Sculpture, the Bauhaus School."

DILLON, Leo 1933-

PERSONAL: Born March 2, 1933, in Brooklyn, N.Y.; son of Lionel J. (an owner of a truck business) and Marie (Rodriques; a dressmaker) Dillon; married Diane Sorber (an artist), March 17, 1957; children: Lee. *Education:* Attended Parsons School of Design, four years; School of Visual Arts, one year. *Office:* C/o Dial Press, 1 Dag Hammarskjold Plaza, New York, N.Y. 10017.

LEO and DIANE DILLON

Suddenly he was afraid. Somewhere behind him a twig had snapped, loud over the chattering of the monkeys, sharp above the cry of the birds. ■ (From *Dark Venture* by Audrey White Beyer. Illustrated by Leo and Diane Dillon.)

CAREER: Artist; illustrator. West Park Publishers, New York, N.Y., art editor, 1956-67. *Exhibitions:* Black Arts Show, 1960's; Gallery 91, 1974, 1975; Society of Illustrators. *Military service:* U.S. Navy, 1950-53. *Member:* Society of Illustrators. *Awards, honors: Hakon of Rogen's Saga* was on the *Horn Book* Honor List, 1963, and was an ALA Notable Children's Book; *A Slave's Tale* was on the *Horn Book* Honor List, 1966, and was an ALA Notable Children's Book; Hugo Award, 1971, for science fiction illustration of a series of book jackets; *The Hundred Penny Box* was the winner of the *Boston Globe-Horn Book* award, 1975, and received the Newbery Medal; *Why Mosquitoes Buzz in People's Ears: A West African Tale* received the Caldecott Medal, 1975; *Ashanti to Zulu: African Traditions* was on the *Horn Book* Honor List, 1977, received *New York Times* Best Illustrated Children's Book Award, Caldecott Medal, 1977, and the Hamilton King Award, 1977; nominated for the Hans Christian Anderson Award, 1978.

ILLUSTRATOR: Erik C. Haugaard, *Hakon of Rogen's Saga* (ALA Notable Book), Houghton, 1963; Erik C. Haugaard, *A Slave's Tale* (ALA Notable Book), Houghton, 1965; F. M. Pilkington, *Shamrock and Spear*, Holt, 1966;

Sorche Nic Leodhas, *Claymore and Kilt: Tales of Scottish Kings and Castles,* Holt, 1967; Erik C. Haugaard, *The Rider and His Horse,* Houghton, 1968; Audrey W. Beyer, *Dark Venture,* Knopf, 1968; John Bierhorst, *The Ring in the Prairie,* Dial, 1970; Alta Jablow, *Gassier's Lute: A West African Epic,* Dutton, 1971; Murray and Thomas (editors), *The Search,* Scholastic, 1971; Erik C. Haugaard, *The Untold Tale,* Houghton, 1971; Verna Aardema, *Behind the Back of the Mountain: Black Folktales From Southern Africa,* Dial, 1973; Seth Clifford, *Burning Star,* Houghton, 1974; W. Moses Serwadda, *Songs and Stories From Uganda,* Crowell, 1974; Jan Carew, *The Third Gift,* Little, Brown, 1974; Natalie Belting, *Whirlwind is a Ghost Dancing,* Dutton, 1974; Lorenz Graham, *Song of the Boat,* Crowell, 1975; Sharon Bell Mathis, *The Hundred Penny Box,* Viking, 1975; Verna Aardema, *Why Mosquitoes Buzz in People's Ears: A West African Folk Tale,* Dial, 1975; Margaret W. Musgrove, *Ashanti to Zulu: African Traditions,* Dial, 1976; Verna Aardema, *Who's in Rabbit's House? A Masai Tale,* Dial, 1977. Illustrations have appeared in *Ladies' Home Journal, The Saturday Evening Post,* and others.

DREW, Patricia (Mary) 1938-

PERSONAL: Born September 13, 1938, in Cornwall, England; daughter of Eric Summers (an engineer) and Elsie (a musician; maiden name, Quayle) Drew. *Education:* Portsmouth College of Art, N.D.D., 1960. *Religion:* Christian. *Home:* Howe, Watlington, Oxfordshire, England. *Agent:* Curtis Brown Ltd., 1 Craven Hill, London N.2, England.

PATRICIA DREW

"Jeremy James," said Mummy. "Elephants don't sit on cars."
"Well this one does."
■ (From *Elephants Don't Sit on Cars* by David Henry Wilson. Illustrated by Patricia Drew.)

CAREER: United Turkey Red, Ltd. (textile design studio), London, England, calico printer assistant, 1960-63; free-lance writer and artist, 1977—. Art teacher at Collingham Tutors schools in London, England, 1963—. Art work includes book illustration, commissioned portrait drawings and paintings, and design of greeting cards.

WRITINGS—Self-illustrated children's books: *Hogglespike,* Chatto & Windus, 1971; *Hogglespike and Thistle,* Chatto & Windus, 1972; *Hogglespike in Danger,* Chatto & Windus, 1973; *Spotter Puff,* Chatto & Windus, 1974; *The Dream Dragon,* Chatto & Windus, 1976; *Caramelia,* Benn, 1977. Also designed covers for numerous books.

Illustrator: David Henry Wilson, *Elephants Don't Sit on Cars,* Chatto & Windus, 1977.

WORK IN PROGRESS: Picture books for children.

SIDELIGHTS: "Animals and birds are interesting and I have a great fondness for most of them. This has probably been the reason for the sort of books I write. The way I feel and write is possibly governed by my happy childhood, a fascinating father, and happy home background. I couldn't write a long book; I like compact sentences next to pictures which don't need words, and I find reading poetry helpful. I know I couldn't write for adults. Children's books need pictures and I'm really more artist than author."

DRURY, Roger W(olcott)   1914-

PERSONAL: Born March 3, 1914, in Boston, Mass.; son of Samuel S. (a schoolmaster) and Cornelia F. (Wolcott) Drury; married Virginia Jenney (a sculptor), September 13, 1941; children: Tom, Geoffrey, Daniel, Julia. *Education:* Harvard University, A.B., 1936. *Politics:* Independent. *Religion:* Episcopalian. *Home and office:* Barnum St., Sheffield, Mass. 01257.

CAREER: New York Herald Tribune, New York, N.Y., cub reporter, 1936-37; Macmillan Co. (publishers), New York City, worked in advertising department, 1937-39; worked as assistant director of alternative service camp, as a forester, and in mental hospitals, all for alternative service as a conscientious objector from military service, 1939-46; dairy farmer in Sheffield, Mass., 1946-60; writer, 1960—. Member of Sheffield Planning Board. *Awards, honors:* Christopher Award, 1976, and the Ethical Culture School Book Award, 1977, for *The Champion of Merrimack County.*

WRITINGS—Juvenile: (With father, Samuel S. Drury) *In Pursuit of Pelicans,* privately printed, 1931; *Drury and St. Paul's,* Little, Brown, 1964; *The Finches' Fabulous Furnace,* Little, Brown, 1971; *The Champion of Merrimack County,* Little, Brown, 1976. Editor of Alumnae Horae, 1966—.

WORK IN PROGRESS: More children's books.

SIDELIGHTS: "As a faculty child on the grounds of an independent six-year boys' secondary school, of which my father was headmaster, in the country near Concord, N.H., I grew up in a rather protected atmosphere. I developed few friendships with boys and girls of my own age. Instead, I enjoyed the stimulus of interesting adults coming and going, and spent a great deal of time in books, on woodland walks, and watching building construction, etc. In retrospect, I think of it as a very happy childhood.

"I wrote my first verses when I was eleven, away at boarding school in Massachusetts, and unhappy. From that time, I was hooked on writing. The thrill of discovering that words, with their integration of content, shape, and sound, could be disciplined to become living cells in a web of meaning was an excitement that I have never, since then, wished to live without.

"During my teen years, architecture challenged writing as a possible career. Writing won. Except for a period of fifteen years when our four children were growing up at home, and time was scarce, I have been chiefly absorbed by writing of some sort ever since.

"In my early twenties I was twice a member of mapping-mountaineering expeditions in the St. Elias Mountains of Yukon Territory. A recent trip to Crete and Greece topped all previous travels in England, France, Switzerland, the Middle East, and the American West.

ROGER W. DRURY

"Archaeology and exploration have always had special fascination for me. The discovery of Tutankhamen's tomb when I was eight gave me a push in that direction which never had to be repeated. The unexpected discovery of marvels is a principal theme of my dreams even today, and seems to be the seed of the kind of story for children that I most enjoy unfolding. Along with the pleasure of discovering where any isolated marvelous happening will lead, I find endless delight in observing the reactions of my characters to their encounters with a slightly deranged world.

"Usually the grownups have a prosy tendency to want to straighten the disorder or wish it away, whereas the children enjoy the oddity of it. They play with the world as they find it, while their parents are obsessed with 'fixing' it. My sympathies are mostly with the children!"

HOBBIES AND OTHER INTERESTS: Photography, archaeology, travel (Greece, the Middle East, mountaineering in the Yukon Territory), carpentry and cabinet making.

FOR MORE INFORMATION SEE: Horn Book, August, 1971, April, 1972.

DUGAN, Michael (Gray)   1947-

PERSONAL Born October 9, 1947, in Melbourne, Australia; son of Dennis Lloyd (a journalist) and June (Wilkinson) Dugan. *Education:* Attended high school in Melbourne, Australia. *Home:* 7 Sunbury Cres., Surrey Hills, 3127 Victoria, Australia.

CAREER: Writer. Vice-president of Children's Book Council of Victoria, 1977—. *Member:* International P.E.N., Fellowship of Australian Writers, Melbourne Cricket Club. *Awards, honors:* Commendation from Australian Visual Arts Foundation, 1975.

WRITINGS: Missing People (poetry), Sweeney Reed, 1970; *Returning from the Prophet* (poetry), Contempa, 1972; (editor) *The Drunken Tram* (poetry), Stockland, 1972; (co-editor with John Jenkins) *The Outback Reader* (prose), Outback Press, 1975; *Clouds* (poetry), Outback Press, 1975; *Publishing Your Poems,* Second Back Row Press, 1978.

Juvenile: *Travel and Transport,* Oxford University Press, 1968; *Stuff and Nonsense,* Collins, 1974; *Weekend,* Macmillan, 1976; *Nonsense Places,* Collins, 1976; *Mountain Easter,* Macmillan, 1976; *My Old Dad,* Longmans-Cheshire, 1976; *The Race,* Macmillan, 1976; *The Golden Ghost,* Macmillan, 1976; *True Ghosts,* Macmillan, 1977; *A House in a Tree,* Lion Press, 1978; *Nonsense Numbers,* Thomas Nelson, 1978; *Goal,* Macmillan, 1978; *Dragon's Breath,* Gryphon, 1978; *Hostage,* Hodder & Stoughton, 1978. Book reviewer for *Age* and *Reading Time.* Editor of *Australian Puffin Club* magazine.

WORK IN PROGRESS: Another collection of nonsense poems; a novel for teenagers.

SIDELIGHTS: "My best memories of childhood are of my first eight years which were spent in the country near Melbourne. When my family moved to the suburbs of Melbourne, I took some time to adjust to the change, and it was during this period that I began to write, mainly poems and stories about the country and about my teddy bears and other toys.

"My father was a journalist and my mother wrote occasional articles and poems, so it was not surprising that I grew up wanting to be a writer. My most successful books for children have been collections of nonsense poetry.

"I live and write in a large run-down house near Melbourne which usually has lots of people staying in it or passing through. Often I escape to the country or the coast for a few days and a lot of my time is spent visiting schools to read nonsense poems and talk about what it is like being a writer."

EISEMAN, Alberta   1925-

PERSONAL: Born November 2, 1925, in Venice, Italy; came to the United States in 1941, naturalized citizen, 1947; daughter of Alberto and Xenia (Oreffice) Friedenberg; married Alfred S. Eiseman, Jr. (a printing representative), September 22, 1946; children: Margot, Nicole. *Education:* Cornell University, B.A., 1946; also attended New School for Social Research. *Politics:* "Usually Democrat." *Religion:* Jewish. *Home and office:* 5 Hidden Hill, Westport, Conn. 06880. *Agent:* McIntosh & Otis, Inc., 475 Fifth Ave., New York, N.Y. 10017.

CAREER: Seventeen, editorial staff and editor of a book review column; *New York Times,* New York City, children's book reviewer, 1952-65; free-lance writer for children, 1956—. Member of board of trustees of Westport Pub-

lic Library. *Member:* Authors League of America, American Civil Liberties Union, American Jewish Committee, Save Venice, Inc., Connecticut Trust for Historic Preservation. *Awards, honors:* Award from Seventeenth Summer Literary Competition, 1957, for *Monica.*

WRITINGS—For children: (With Ingrid Sladkus) *Monica,* Dodd, 1957; *Candido,* Macmillan, 1965; (with Sladkus) *Skate to a Mountain Song,* Macmillan, 1966; *The Guest Dog,* Random House, 1968; *From Many Lands* (Junior Literary Guild selection), Atheneum, 1970; *Manana Is Now: The Spanish-Speaking in the United States,* Atheneum, 1973; *Rebels and Reformers,* Doubleday, 1976; *The Sunday Whirligig,* Atheneum, 1977. Author of "The Immigrants" (cassette series), Mass Communications, Inc., 1975. Contributor of articles and reviews to magazines and newspapers, including *Connecticut, Publishers Weekly,* and *New York Times.*

WORK IN PROGRESS: A book with daughter, Nicole Eiseman, publication by Atheneum expected in 1979; historical research for a book.

SIDELIGHTS: "My interests are varied—scattered, I often think. I consider it my great good fortune that I have been able to take a subject that appeals to me, deepen my own knowledge with research, then share it with a young audience. My work is all based on research, even the books I have written for the very young. *The Sunday Whirligig,* for example, was the result of the first folk art exhibit I ever saw. I was intrigued by a group of whirligigs, but it was only after I read up on them—who made them, how they were used, in what part of the country and what period—that a story began to take shape. My books for older readers on the history of immigration and ethnic groups grew out of the re-

ALBERTA EISEMAN

Candido lay down beside him and stretched his neck across the boy's lap. ■ (From *Candido* by Alberta Eiseman. Illustrated by Lilian Obligado.)

alization that my daughters and their friends, elementary and junior high school students at that time, were not sufficiently aware of the wondrously varied backgrounds of their contemporaries. This led to a rethinking of my own years as a refugee, and of American history as it is usually taught. The research that I did produced three books, but more than that, it has given me a far better understanding of the American experience, and of many of today's trends.''

HOBBIES AND OTHER INTERESTS: The outdoors (swimming, sailing, and gardening in the summer; walking and cross-country skiing in the winter), theater, movies, fine architecture, ''good talk with friends and family,'' travel.

FABE, Maxene 1943-

PERSONAL: Born May 22, 1943, in Atlanta, Ga.; daughter of Robert (an artist) and Miriam (Timmer) Fabe. *Education:* Attended Earlham College, 1961-62; University of Cincinnati, B.A. (high honors), 1965; University of Pennsylvania, M.A., 1966. *Home:* 420 East 80th St., New York, N.Y. 10021. *Agent:* Elaine Markson Literary Agency, Inc., 44

Greenwich Ave., New York, N.Y. 10011. *Office:* 1 Bank St., New York, N.Y. 10014.

CAREER: Thomas Y. Crowell Co., New York, N.Y., publicist for children's books, 1968-70; taxicab driver in New York City, 1970-71; writer for horror comic books, 1971-72; Thomas Y. Crowell Co., publicist for children's books, 1972-76; free-lance writer, 1976—. Staff member of Miami University writers workshop, 1974.

WRITINGS: Death Rock (novel), Popular Library, 1972; *Beauty Millionaire: The Life of Helena Rubenstein,* Crowell, 1972; (contributor) Judy Fireman, editor, *The Television Book,* Workman Publishing, 1977; *Game Shows,* Doubleday, 1978. Contributor to magazines and newspapers, including *New Times, Mademoiselle, Village Voice, Creem, Penthouse,* and *Apartment Life.*

WORK IN PROGRESS: A second novel; a feminist psychology book.

SIDELIGHTS: ''Because I think we grow up too truncated from our childhoods, all my work tries to bridge that gap, whether by explaining how our 'lost' childhoods affect us

A wall of portraits by world famous artists—and the original. ■ (From *Beauty Millionaire—The Life of Helena Rubinstein* by Maxine Fabe.)

adults, or by describing the fun things from childhood (games, for example) adults still cling to. In general, I think the best books and the best ideas can't be labeled adult or children's. The core of the best reaches the child in all of us.''

FIAROTTA, Noel   1944-

PERSONAL: Original name, Noel Ficarotta; name not legally changed. Born March 13, 1944, in Meriden, Conn.; son of Anthony (an engineer) and Santa (a secretary; maiden name, Lentini) Ficarotta; married Beatriz Esteban (a teacher). *Education:* Jersey City State College, B.A., 1966; Fairleigh Dickinson University, M.A., 1973. *Politics:* ''Depends on who and what.'' *Religion:* ''I believe in God.'' *Home and office:* Brook Way, Llewellyn Park, West Orange, N.J. 07052.

CAREER: Language arts teacher in elementary school in East Orange, N.J., 1967-74; King Features Syndicate, New York, N.Y., editor of column ''Leisure Craftsman,'' 1972—. Professional singer, 1962-68; director of A. Harry Moore Camp, 1972-74.

WRITINGS—All with sister, Phyllis Fiarotta; all published by Workman Publishing: *A Hundred One Gifts You Can Make at Home*, 1968; *A Hundred One Children's Gifts You Can Make at Home*, 1970; *Sticks and Stones and Ice Cream Cones: The Craft Book for Children*, 1973; *Snips and Snails and Walnut Whales: Nature Crafts for Children*, 1975; *Pin It, Tack It, Hang It: The Big Book of Kids' Bulletin Boards*, 1975; *The You and Me Heritage Tree: Children's Crafts from Twenty-One American Traditions*, 1976; *Banker, Baker, Jewelry Maker*, 1977.

Editor, with Phyllis Fiarotta, and contributor; all published by Workman Publishing: *Sewing Without a Pattern*, 1969; *Children's Parties*, 1971; *Making It with Leather and Beads*, 1971; *Sewing Tricks*, 1971; *How to Make Stuffed Animals*, 1973; *The Complete Treasury of the Decorative Craft*, 1973; *Phyllis Fiarotta's Nostalgia Crafts Book*, 1974.

WORK IN PROGRESS: A pilot television program for children, dealing with crafts and entertainment, with sister, Phyllis Fiarotta.

SIDELIGHTS: "Living is that once in a lifetime opportunity to do everything you really want to do, and so be it with my life. I started writing at the ripe old age of ten, nothing too fancy, just childhood thoughts set to adult situations. Adolescence got the better of this shortlived literary career and the corner candy store replaced the bedroom desk, a pretzel stick took the place of my pencil.

"Caught up in the times, of rock and roll, bebop, customized cars, high school dances, and hanging out, music became my main interest. Everyone wanted to become a rock and roll star, and I was there waiting in line. I headed several rock and roll and folk groups, through my high school and college years, with many minor successes: several TV appearances, the college circuit, the Bitter End, and a couple of not-so unsuccessful records. I even tried producing records, owned a record company called Felicia Records. The music field was getting too crowded and I was looking forward to a new career, an English teacher.

"I taught English in an experimental school in East Orange, N.J. My main concern was teaching the writing skills to grades five through eight, in a little red school house atmosphere. Students were encouraged to undertake a yearly project: to write a novel, collection of poems, essays, etc.

NOEL FIAROTTA

and through their writings they would learn what language arts is all about. The experiment lasted six years, and was replaced by traditional teaching. During the summers I worked at a camp for the physically handicapped and the mentally retarded, and eventually directed the camp for two years. The A. Harry Moore Camp really pointed out the beauty of life. My teaching experiences gave me a good foundation for preparing children's craft books.

"My future plans may possibly include a TV show for children (craft oriented): writing, directing, performing, and producing. I guess I will continue to try to keep quite active and doing it all before my name is added to the dead file with the epitaph, 'He did all he possibly could!' "

FIAROTTA, Phyllis 1942-

PERSONAL: Original name, Phyllis Ficarotta; name not legally changed. Born August 21, 1942, in Meriden, Conn.; daughter of Anthony (an engineer) and Santa (a secretary; maiden name, Lentini) Ficarotta. *Education:* Attended Newark School of Fine and Industrial Arts, 1960-63. *Politics:* Democrat. *Religion:* Roman Catholic. *Home and office:* Brook Way, Llewellyn Park, West Orange, N.J. 07052.

CAREER: Good Housekeeping, New York, N.Y., associate art director, 1965-71; King Features Syndicate, New York, N.Y., author and illustrator of column "The Leisure Craftsman," 1972—. Assistant art director for Pharmaceutical Advertising, 1963-65. Assistant stage manager for International Ladies' Garment Workers' Union Theatre. Guest and demonstrator on more than a hundred television and radio programs.

WRITINGS—All self-illustrated; all with brother, Noel Fiarotta; all published by Workman Publishing: *A Hundred One Gifts You Can Make at Home,* 1968; *Sewing Without a Pattern,* 1969; *Children's Parties,* 1971; *Making It with Leather and Beads,* 1971; *Sewing Tricks,* 1971; *How to Make Stuffed Animals,* 1973; *The Complete Treasury of the Decorative Craft,* 1973; *Phyllis Fiarotta's Nostalgia Crafts Book,* 1974.

Self-illustrated books, with brother, Noel Fiarotta; all published by Workman Publishing: *A Hundred One Children's Gifts You Can Make at Home,* 1970; *Sticks and Stones and Ice Cream Cones: The Craft Book for Children,* 1973; *Snips and Snails and Walnut Whales: Nature Crafts for Children,* 1975; *Pin It, Tack It, Hang It: The Big Book of Kids' Bulletin Boards,* 1975; *The You and Me Heritage Tree: Children's Crafts from Twenty-One American Traditions,* 1976; *Banker, Baker, Jewelry Maker,* 1977. Contributor to popular magazines, including *Woman's Day, Family Circle,* and *Essence.* Art editor of *Good Housekeeping Family Christmas Book,* 1963-65. Illustrator of children's stories appearing in *The Magic Carpet,* Western Publishing, 1966.

WORK IN PROGRESS: Preparing scripts, sets, and puppets for a pilot television program for children, dealing with crafts and entertainment, with brother, Noel Fiarotta.

SIDELIGHTS: "Although I was born in Connecticut and presently live in New Jersey, I will be eternally a New Yorker. I have an intense love affair with this, the greatest city in the world.

"I have a passion for everything that is connected with my precious life, and I reject very little.

PHYLLIS FIAROTTA

''My philosophy of life was summed up by Fred Flintstone of cartoon fame, saying, as he emptied a quart of milk on the floor, 'I laugh at spilt milk.'

''My extreme loves, my mother, father, brother, tacos, Mexican trees of life, opera, my house, landscaping, colors, and *The Grinch That Stole Christmas* keep me busy. My extreme dislike, DYING.''

FIELD, Rachel (Lyman)   1894-1942

PERSONAL: Born September 19, 1894, in New York City; died March 15, 1942, in Beverly Hills, California; buried in Stockbridge, Massachusetts; daughter of Matthew D. (a physician) and Lucy (Atwater) Field; married Arthur S. Pederson (a literary agent), June, 1935; children: Hannah. *Education:* Attended Radcliffe College as a special student, 1914-18.

CAREER: Held several editorial positions in New York City before turning to free-lance writing; novelist, poet, playwright, and writer for children. *Awards, honors:* Drama League of America prize, 1918, for *Rise Up, Jennie Smith;* Newbery Medal (the first awarded to a woman), 1929, for *Hitty: Her First Hundred Years.*

WRITINGS—Stories for children, except as noted: *Calico Bush* (illustrated by Allen Lewis), Macmillan, 1913, reprinted, 1966; *An Alphabet for Boys and Girls* (self-illustrated), Doubleday, Page, 1926; *Eliza and the Elves* (illustrated by Elizabeth MacKinstry), Macmillan, 1926; *The Magic Pawnshop: A New Year's Eve Fantasy* (illustrated by MacKinstry), Dutton, 1927; (editor) Marie Catherine, Comtesse d'Aulnoy, *The White Cat, and Other French Fairy Tales,* Macmillan, 1928, new edition (illustrated by MacKinstry), 1967; *Little Toby* (self-illustrated), Macmillan, 1928; *Polly Patchwork,* Doubleday, Doran, 1928; (editor) *American Folk and Fairy Tales* (illustrated by Margaret Freeman), Scribner, 1929, reprinted, 1957; *Hitty: Her First Hundred Years* (illustrated by Dorothy P. Lathrop), Macmillan, 1929, reprinted, 1968; *Pocket-Handkerchief Park,* Doubleday, Doran, 1929.

The Yellow Shop (self-illustrated), Doubleday, Doran, 1931; *The Bird Began to Sing* (illustrated by Ilse Bischoff), Morrow, 1932; *Hepatica Hawks* (illustrated by Allen Lewis), Macmillan, 1932, reprinted, 1966; *Just Across the Street* (self-illustrated), Macmillan, 1933; *Susanna B. and William C.,* Morrow, 1934; *God's Pocket: The Story of Captain Samuel Hadlock, Junior, of Cranberry Isles, Maine* (fictionalized biography), Macmillan, 1934; (author of lyrics) *Ave Maria: An Interpretation from Walt Disney's "Fantasia,"* Random House, 1940; *Prayer for a Child* (devotional; illustrated by Elizabeth Orton Jones), Macmillan, 1944; *The Rachel Field Story Book* (illustrated by Adrienne Adams), Doubleday, 1958.

Plays for children: *Rise Up, Jennie Smith* (one-act), Samuel French, 1918; *Six Plays,* Scribner, 1924 (contains *Cinderella Married, Three Pills in a Bottle, Columbine in Business, The Patchwork Quilt, Wisdom Teeth,* and *Theories and Thumbs*); *The Cross-Stitch Heart, and Other Plays,* Scribner, 1927 (also contains *Greasy Luck, The Nine Days' Queen, The Londonderry Air, At the Junction,* and *Bargains in Cathay*); *Patchwork Plays* (self-illustrated), Doubleday, Doran, 1930 (contains *Polly Patchwork; Little Square-Toes; Miss Ant, Miss Grasshopper, and Mr. Cricket; Chimney Sweeps' Holiday;* and *The Sentimental Scarecrow* [for the last, also see the following]); *The Sentimental Scarecrow* (one-act), Samuel French, 1957, musical adaptation by S. Charles Shertzer and Nathan Brown, 1970.

Adult fiction: *Time Out of Mind,* Macmillan, 1935, reprinted, 1963; *First Class Matter* (one-act play), Samuel French, 1936; (with husband, Arthur S. Pederson) *To See Ourselves,* Macmillan, 1937; *All This and Heaven Too,* Macmillan, 1938, reprinted, 1968; *All Through the Night,* Macmillan, 1940, new edition (illustrated by Shirley Hughes), 1955; *And Now Tomorrow,* Macmillan, 1942, reprinted, 1966.

Poems: *The Pointed People: Verses and Silhouettes,* Yale University Press, 1924; *Taxis and Toadstools: Verses and Decorations,* Doubleday, Page, 1926, new edition, World's Work (England), 1962; *A Little Book of Days,* Doubleday,

Page, 1927; *Points East: Narratives of New England,* Brewer & Warren, 1930; *Branches Green* (illustrated by Dorothy P. Lathrop), Macmillan, 1934; *Fear Is the Thorn,* Macmillan, 1936; *Christmas Time: Verses and Illustrations,* Macmillan, 1941; *Poems* (self-illustrated), Macmillan, 1957.

Contributor of articles, stories, and verse to various periodicals, including *St. Nicholas, Horn Book, Saturday Review of Literature,* and the *New Yorker.*

ADAPTATIONS—Movies: *All This and Heaven Too,* Warner Brothers, 1940, starring Bette Davis and Charles Boyer; *And Now Tomorrow,* Paramount Pictures, 1944, starring Loretta Young and Alan Ladd; *Time Out of Mind,* United Artists, 1947, starring Phyllis Calvert and Robert Hutton.

SIDELIGHTS: **September 19, 1894.** Born in New York City. Field's early childhood was spent in western Massachusetts, at Springfield and at Stockbridge, the ancestral home of the Field family.

Attended a small private school of about ten children. "Literally I wrote before I could read. It wasn't that I could not have learned to read earlier, I knew the letters and all that, but it was so much pleasanter to have my mother read real

She walked very slowly between the spindly fir trees on the old wood road, for she had no wish to reach the yellow schoolhouse that stood at the crossroads. Every step of the way her feet dragged more and more.
■ (From *The Rachel Field Story Book* by Rachel Field. Illustrated by Adrienne Adams.)

RACHEL FIELD

books to me than to plod through the infantile sort of stuff I could have read myself. I went to a little school kept by two maiden ladies. At the time they seemed old ladies to me, but I know now that they could not have been old. I loved poetry and one of them read us a great deal of poetry. I developed very early a facility for memorizing it. I even got so that when my teacher had read a poem to me once I could repeat it from just that single hearing of it." [*The Hewins Lectures: 1947-1962,* edited by Siri Andrews, The Horn Book, Inc., 1963.[1]]

In this school Field had her first taste of acting—playing such parts as Shylock in *The Merchant of Venice* and Rebecca in *Rebecca of Sunnybrook Farm.*

The theater always meant much to her. Once she wrote: "Something had gone wrong. At this late date I forget the reason, and it probably was a good one, but at all events I was *not* going to the theater with the rest. I must have been eleven or a little older at the time and it mattered terribly. Theaters were few and far betweef and movies practically unknown, so I hoped up to the last minute that a miracle would happen. Sometimes they did, and you found yourself let in at the last, just when you were most despairing. I reminded myself of Cinderella and the ball, an encouraging story to recall on almost any occasion. But on this particular one, it did me no good and I saw the lucky ones setting off. The last minute had come and gone and Fate had done nothing about it. I remember as if it were yesterdaysthe sound of the door closing."[1]

Another interest formed in her early days in Stockbridge was to influence Field throughout her life—her love of islands. "There's something about islands, I don't know what it is, but I simply cannot keep them out of the things I write. I always find them there along with pointed trees, toadstools, children, and patchwork quilts. Even when I was a very little girl and lived among hills with no larger body of water than a brook handy, I made islands of the stones in it. I made islands out of sponges stuck full of ferns and placed conveniently (since the inconsiderate owners of sponges were always calling for their return!) in a garden pool. I even found an island big enough to hold me in the tiny triangle of grass where a signpost pointed the way of three brown country roads. I used to sit there and pretend the roads were ships.

"If once you have slept on an island
    You'll never be quite the same;
You may look as you looked the day before
    And go by the same old name.

You may bustle about in street and shop;
    You may sit at home and sew,
But you'll see blue water and wheeling gulls
    Wherever your feet may go.

You may chat with the neighbors of this and that
    And close to your fire keep,
But you'll hear ship whistle and lighthouse bell
    And tides beat through your sleep.

Oh, you won't know why, and you can't say how
    Such change upon you came,
But—once you have slept on an island
    You'll never be quite the same!"[1]

When asked if she believed in fairies, Field answered: "I believed not so much in them as about them. I was willing to accept them as real characters in some of the stories I loved. When the story was finished the characters vanished just as characters that now come to life out of the pages of a good novel are gone as soon as some other interest takes the place of the novel. As a child I could pop out of Elfland into the kitchen as quick as a wink. A moment after a fairy tale had held all my attention I could be just as deeply entranced in the cook and what she was getting for dinner, and whether or not she was going to let me stir up something to bake in her nice hot oven. I always liked mussing around in the kitchen."[1]

A childhood in Stockbridge gave way to school days in Springfield. "I think I had the best history teacher in the United States. I would not take anything for having had Dr. Jessie M. Law as my teacher of English and American history. She taught me to love history, and made it real and vital."[1]

In her senior year, Field won an essay contest open to pupils in three schools, and a prize of $20.

1914. Admitted to Radcliffe College as a special student because of her excellence in writing.

Three of Field's plays were produced there, "Rise up, Jennie Smith" (1918), "Time Will Tell" (1920), and "Three Pills in a Bottle" (1917). "In plays people never sit side by side for hours and talk. They move about, pick things up and lay them down again, make gestures and the way they

RACHEL FIELD

Sometimes the mice took pity on my sad state and when they were washing off their babies' faces, they would wash mine too. ■ (From *Hitty: Her First Hundred Years* by Rachel Field. Illustrated by Dorothy P. Lathrop.)

RACHEL LYMAN FIELD

mountain ashwood hands right from the start. Her very discovery was in the nature of what some of our ancestors might have called 'a miraculous providence.'

"It is curious how books happen—those who write them often know least about this. Sometimes an idea comes all in a flash, for a whole book, or again one gathers material piece by piece and puts it painstakingly together like a patchwork quilt, or, as in this case, some concrete object will set a whole train of ideas in motion. Nothing was farther from my mind than writing the autobiography of an early American doll, until Dorothy P. Lathrop and I discovered Hitty in an antique shop in New York and found we had each wanted her. But she turned out to be over a hundred years old and a real museum piece as we were told. So we went our separate ways and tried to think no more about her and her very brown and wise old face. Then one day Hitty was gone from the window and I wrote the news regretfully to Miss Lathrop. She replied by return mail, saying that we should have had sense enough to buy her together. 'You could have written her story and I could have illustrated it.' I knew she was right,—and in fact all sorts of ideas about Hitty's past life and adventures began to come to me, so it was a great relief to find she had only been taken out of the window to show a customer. That very night she was ours, with our only clue to her identity a yellowed slip pinned to her dress with 'Hitty' written on it in faded Spenserian handwriting.

do these things helps us to know what they are thinking or what was behind the thought of the playwright."[1]

First job was in the editorial department of Famous Players-Lasky, producers of silent motion pictures. Field wrote synopses of plays and stories, finding spare time for writing verse, short plays, and making an attempt at writing a novel. "It went the rounds, and was turned down as it should have been. But some of the editors wrote me letters about it and they all said that the first part, dealing with the heroine's childhood, was the best."[1]

This encouraged Field to devote her efforts to children's stories. "In writing books for children it is not necessary to have contacts with children. Of course it helps to know children. But if you have it in you to write children's books, you can write them anywhere,—alone on a desert island, if you have enough paper and pencils. . . . It seems to me far more important to be able to remember exactly how a thing impressed you when you were a child than to guess how it may impress another child. Children's natures do not change perceptibly from one generation to another. It is their dress, their speech and their manners that change, not their natures."[1]

1929. *Hitty* published, for which Field received the Newbery Medal. "Hitty, and how the book came to be written. First of all, I want to say that I feel as if I, myself, had very little to do with it. It is as if Hitty took things into her own

You will never find the Magic Pawnshop by deliberately setting out to look for it. That is no use at all. ■ (From *The Magic Pawnshop* by Rachel Field. Illustrated by Elizabeth Mackinstry.)

(From the movie "All This and Heaven Too," starring Bette Davis and Charles Boyer. Produced by Warner Brothers, 1940.)

"By such queer coincidences are books sometimes evolved! Miss Lathrop's pictures are such an integral part of the story that I cannot imagine the text without them. Those of you who have seen the doll's six and one-half inches of wood will realize how impossible it would be to have shown her in proper proportion along with even a human forefinger. This meant much planning and ingenuity on the artist's part to keep the pictures varied and interesting. Then there was another difficulty, that of expression,—dolls must keep the same one all their days—and so Hitty smiles serenely through the most trying circumstances. This meant that the artist must somehow manage to convey her emotion by means of attitude, and as Hitty's pegging is extremely simple and limited to exactly two motions, here were more difficulties.

"My problems in writing the story were of a different sort. They were chiefly connected with the element of time. I soon found that covering a hundred years of American life was more of a piece of work than I had expected. Incidentally, this accounts for the fact that the book is almost as long as a novel and required nearly as much care and research. But this also gave a cumulative effect and I was able to choose certain periods and things I already knew something about. I had for some years past been interested in reading old log books of whaling vessels, so it was natural for me to have Hitty go on a whaling voyage. Then after her New England, Philadelphia and New York days, I wanted to give a feeling of an entirely different life in another part of the country. This accounts for sending her down the Mississippi River and into the South.

"Then there was the matter of style. I felt from the first that Hitty would have had a very prim but spicy way of talking, and so I tried to select every word and phrase carefully, for I think people don't give words half enough credit. Yet they are what really affect readers, children most of all because they are most impressionable. It seems to me we ought to remember what J. M. Synge said about dialogue: that 'every phrase should be finely flavored as a nut or an apple.' So many juveniles today are too evidently written down to children with the words so simplified that all the spirit is lost in commonplaces.

"There is one thing Hitty and the Medal have in common and that is the past. I never get over that such things as old samplers, toys, and little tattered children's books should be here for us to see and touch long after those who made and handled them are gone. There is something singularly moving about them and I know that I can never see an old toy or one of those early chap books without this sense of the past. So perhaps, after all, it is appropriate that a little doll of a hundred years ago should be connected with John Newbery and his bookshop in old London. I cannot help feeling that she possesses qualities of character that would have pleased him and some of his distinguished friends and

Four small children clustered about her, and a baby filled her broad lap. In her full, brown homespun dress and scoop bonnet, Marguerite thought she looked mightily like one of the hens in their coop up forward. ■ (From *Calico Bush* by Rachel Field. Illustrated by Allen Lewis.)

customers—Oliver Goldsmith, Charles and Mary Lamb, and others.

"And since so many things of both the past and the present seem to belong to children, I am sure that the Newbery Medal· has made a great difference in people's thinking about the matter of children's books. I know this must have been in the mind of Frederic Melcher when he planned the award and named it in honor of the first children's bookseller." [*Newbery Medal Books: 1922-1955,* ed. by Bertha Mahony Miller and Elinor Whitney Field, The Horn Book, Inc., 1955[2]]

Field was a master of detail. "Perhaps I have the sort of memory that holds impressions, a camera memory. Anyway I have many pictures in my mind, many impressions that I have carried since my childhood. I was always able to take in details. I loved old houses, and I never entered one for the first time that I did not get an exact picture in my mind of at least one of the rooms. I would know just where the windows were, how the furniture was placed, the position of the rug on the floor, what ornaments there were on the mantel or whatnot. A second visit would verify this impression and prove to me that I saw clearly the first time."[1]

Field illustrated some of her early books with her own drawings or silhouettes, such as *A Little Book of Days, Susanna B. and William C., The Pointed People, Taxis and Toadstools, Little Dog Toby, Patchwork Plays* and others.

American Folk and Fairy Tales published in 1929. "Yet there is this about all folk and fairy tales,—they must possess a certain frankness and simplicity of idea. They must be direct and unhurried, yet also swift of action and salted and peppered liberally with talk and sayings. . . . Then, too, it seems to me there is always an element of the supernatural, or at least of the impossible in all folklore. . . ."[1]

June 20, 1935. Married Arthur S. Pederson, a literary agent. After a honeymoon on Sutton Island, they went to California.

1938. Achieved her greatest popular success with *All This, and Heaven Too,* a fictionalized life of her great-aunt, who before she became the wife of the Rev. Henry M. Field had

(From *Poems* by Rachel Field. Illustrated by the author.)

(From *Poems* by Rachel Field. Decorations by the author.)

been the famous "Mademoiselle D." of Paris, a central figure in the dramatic and still-debated de Praslin murder case. This book was a national best-seller for months and was made into a highly successful moving picture.

1939. Pedersons completed their family with the adoption of eight-week-old Hannah.

March 15, 1942. Died after an operation and brief illness. In a tribute in the *Saturday Review of Literature,* Laura Benét called Field "a tonic and a stay to those who loved her."

FOR MORE INFORMATION SEE: Horn Book, special memorial issue, July, 1942, includes "Of Rachel Field and Letters," by Bertha E. Mahony, "Portrait of a Troubadour," by J. Titzell, "Rachel Field: A Memory," by Laura Benét, and "Rachel Field, 1894-1942," by J. Titzell, the last reprinted in *Newbery Medal Books, 1922-1955,* edited by Bertha E. Mahony Miller and E. W. Field, Horn Book, 1955; Elizabeth R. Montgomery, *Story behind Modern Books,* Dodd, 1949; Margery W. Bianco, "Hitty: Her First Hundred Years," in *Writing and Criticism,* edited by Anne Carrol Moore and Bertha E. Mahony Miller, Horn Book, 1951; Stanley J. Kunitz and Howard Haycraft, editors, *Junior Book of Authors,* Wilson, 2nd edition, 1951; Laura Benét, *Famous Poets for Young People,* Dodd, 1964.

Obituaries: *New York Times,* March 16, 1942; *Publishers Weekly,* March 21, 1942; *Wilson Library Bulletin,* May, 1942; *Current Biography Yearbook 1942.*

FIRMIN, Peter 1928-

PERSONAL: Born December 11, 1928, in Harwich, England; son of Lewis Charles (a railway telegrapher) and Lila (Burnett) Firmin; married Joan Ruth Clapham (a bookbinder), July 29, 1952; children: Charlotte, Hannah, Josephine, Katharine, Lucy, Emily. *Education:* Colchester Art School, diploma, 1947; Central School of Art, diploma, 1952. *Politics:* Socialist. *Home:* Hillside Farm, 36 Blean Hill, Blean, Canterbury, Kent, England.

CAREER: Free-lance book illustrator, puppet maker, and cartoon film artist, 1952—. *Military service:* Royal Navy, 1947-49. *Member:* Canterbury Art Society.

WRITINGS—For children: "Basil Brush" series; all self-illustrated; all published by Kaye & Ward: *Basil Brush Goes Flying,* 1969, Prentice-Hall, 1977; . . . *Goes Boating,* 1969, Prentice-Hall, 1976; . . . *in the Jungle,* 1970; . . . *at the Seaside,* 1970, Prentice-Hall, 1976; . . . *and a Dragon,* 1971; . . . *Finds Treasure,* 1971; . . . *Builds a House,* 1973, Prentice-Hall, 1977; . . . *Gets a Medal,* 1973.

Illustrator of numerous children's books, including the "Noggin" series and "Ivor the Engine" series, both by Oliver Postgate. Also illustrator of *The "Blue Peter" Book of Limericks,* Pan Books, 1972, and *The "Blue Peter" Book of Odd Odes,* BBC Publications, 1976, both by Biddy Baxter.

WORK IN PROGRESS: Illustrating more books for the "Ivor the Engine" series.

SIDELIGHTS: "Most of my work results from the partnership with Oliver Postgate. We have made films, including cartoon and puppet films. I also made various puppets for live television programs, one of which was Basil Brush. I did not write for him for television, but the 'Basil Brush' books are my sole venture so far into writing.

"My family and I have dogs, donkeys, chickens, tortoises, a cat, rabbits, gerbils, ducks, and hamsters on the farm, which

PETER FIRMIN

(A set of twenty, five-minute color cartoon films based on the "Ivor the Engine" series were produced for BBC Television.)

is no longer a real farm, but forms the studios in which the films are made.''

HOBBIES AND OTHER INTERESTS: Walking, sailing, birds, books.

FISHER, John (Oswald Hamilton) 1909-
(Roger Piper)

PERSONAL: Born in 1909, in Surrey, Eng.; married Phyllis Parsons-Smith; children: one son, one daughter. *Education:* Balliol College, Oxford, B.A. *Home:* Flagstones, Chalkdock Lane, Itchenor, Chichester, Sussex, PO2O 7DE, England.

CAREER: Diplomatic correspondent, Thomson Newspapers Ltd.; author.

WRITINGS—Nonfiction: (For children) *The True Book About the Civil War* (illustrated by N. G. Wilson), Muller, 1958; (for children) *The True Book About the Russian Revolution* (illustrated by N. G. Wilson), Muller, 1960; (editor) *Eye-Witness: An Anthology of British Reporting,* Cassell, 1960; *1815: An End and a Beginning,* Harper, 1963 (published in England as *Eighteen Fifteen: An End and a Beginning,* Cassell, 1963); (for children; under pseudonym Roger Piper) *The Big Dish: The Fascinating Story of Radio Telescopes,* Harcourt, 1963; (for children; under pseudonym R. Piper) *The Story of Computers,* Harcourt, 1964, revised edition, Hodder & Stoughton, 1977; (under pseudonym Roger Piper) *The Story of Jodrell Bank,* Hutchinson, 1965; *Six Summers in Paris, 1789-1794,* Harper, 1966 (published in England as *The Elysian Fields: France in Ferment, 1789-1794,* Cassell, 1966); *The Australians from 1788 to Modern*

JOHN FISHER

Times, Hale, 1968; *The Afrikaners,* Cassell, 1969; *That Miss Hobhouse,* Secker & Warburg, 1971; *Paul Kruger: His Life and Times,* Secker & Warburg, 1974; *What a Performance: The Life of Sid Field,* Seeley, 1975; *The World of the Forsytes* (Book Club Associates selection), Universe Books, 1976; *Burgess and Maclean—A New Look at the Foreign Office Spies* (Book Club Associates selection), Hale, 1977.

Sailing: *How to Sail,* Eyre & Spottiswoode, 1952, revised edition, 1959; *Sailing Dinghies,* R. Ross, 1952, 4th edition, J. de Graff, 1961; *Better Small-Boat Sailing,* J. de Graff, 1955; (with Adland Coles and Douglas Phillips-Birt) *Sailing: Handling and Craft,* J. de Graff, 1958; *Starting to Sail* (illustrated by Roy Glanville), J. de Graff, 1958; *Storms,* J. de Graff, 1958; *Catamarans* (illustrated by R. Glanville), A. Coles, 1959, revised edition, 1962; *The New Small Boat Sailing,* J. de Graff, 1959; *Starting to Race,* J. de Graff, 1959.

WORK IN PROGRESS: The Story of Oil for children, to be published by A&C Black.

SIDELIGHTS: ''As a reporter my training has conditioned me to look for the questions I would ask myself if I know nothing about the subject I'm writing about. Sounds 'Irish' but makes sense.''

FOR MORE INFORMATION SEE: New York Herald Tribune Books, May 12, 1963; *New York Times Book Review,* March 26, 1967; *Christian Science Monitor,* May 6, 1967.

FITZGERALD, F(rancis) A(nthony) 1940-

PERSONAL: Born January 13, 1940, in Queens, N.Y.; son of Francis Anthony (a photo-engraver) and Ellen (McGrath) Fitzgerald; married Patricia Ann Cronkite (divorced), December, 1963; married Martha Jane Miller (a computer programer), July 21, 1974. *Education:* Attended School of Visual Arts, New York, N.Y., two years. *Religion:* Christian. *Home and office:* 212 East 89th St., New York, N.Y. 10028.

CAREER: Free-lance illustrator, 1971—. Display Novelties, New York, N.Y., display designer, 1968-72. Member/trainer in the Quaker sponsored Alternative to Violence Project (for prison inmates); produced the New York Alternatives to Violence Project Newsletter. *Exhibitions:* Society of Illustrators Annual, 1972; American Institute of Graphic Artists, 1973. *Military service:* U.S. Navy, photographer, mate third class, 1957-61. *Member:* Association for Research and Enlightenment.

ILLUSTRATOR: Wally Cox and Everett Greenbaum, *The Tenth Life of Osiris Oaks,* Simon and Schuster, 1972; Charles Keller (compiler), *Daffynitions,* Prentice, 1976; Harry Allard, *May I Stay?,* Prentice, 1978.

SIDELIGHTS: ''I have always been an illustrator. As a child I drew comic strips (cowboy fights in saloons/breaking furniture/falling from balconies/exploding six guns, etc.). My best friend, Bobby, drew similar subjects and drew them well. One day it was decided by our buddies that Bobby was the better artist. I did not agree. I knew it was the one thing I did better than him.

''To be a professional artist was not my driving ambition however. I wanted to be an airplane pilot. The 1945-46 skies

Mr. OSWALD KEMPNER

"It's your week to deal first," he said. Then he took his penknife and cut a little hunk out of the table to show him next week was his turn. ■ (From *The Tenth Life of Osiris Oaks* by Wally Cox and Everett Greenbaum. Illustrated by F.A. Fitzgerald.)

over my house were filled with hundreds of planes in formations returning from the war in Europe.

"My passion to soar through the wild blue yonder was dampened when informed that I would need much math and much schooling to be an air-ace. At age seventeen I joined the Navy and was trained as a photographer.

"I had not done much drawing since entering high school, but shortly before my enlistment was up, I tried my hand at cartoons and caricatures. My shipmates thought they were pretty good and encouraged me. After my discharge in 1961, I tried job hunting for a few weeks without success. I then decided to enter art school.

"To gain admittance to the school of my choice, I was required to present a portfolio of my work and be interviewed. I appeared on the appointed day before Mr. Dean (fictitious, his real name escapes me) who examined my work. I had put together a little book of about twelve pages with a single cartoon, line drawn on each page. I used photographic printing paper, generously supplied by the U.S. Navy, for the pages. The emulsion side was too slick for ink so I drew on the back. The Eastman Kodak imprint appeared as a repeated background pattern in each of my creations. My cartoons were crudely drawn and *very* corny.

"Mr. Dean interviewed me, examined my 'portfolio' and for reasons unknown, accepted me as a student.

"Jerome Martin, an illustrator, was a teacher of mine at the School of Visual Arts. I was 'awakened' by his enthusiasm for art and design.

"Much has happened since them. While at school, my interest in art deepened and turned from cartooning to fine art. I decided to become a painter. However, after completing only two years of a three year course, I left school determined to learn 'by doing.'

"Periodically taking odd jobs to support myself, I worked at my art for a number of years. I was seldom satisfied with my creations and one day decided that I had no talent and would never be an artist. I gave up painting.

"This was a difficult time for me. Gradually my attentions turned to other things. I developed an interest in puppetry and made many puppets and puppet toys. They were quite good and I realized it. My self-confidence began to grow.

"I next was attracted to movie making and made a number of 8mm films, some of which were animated with puppet figures. Being quite happy with these new found modes of creativity, I was quite surprised one night years later while visiting an artist friend to find my interest in drawing rekindled. I was drawing again and liking what I drew.

"It's been about ten years since that night and though I feel much better about my work now, I still am often dissatisfied. But these days when things look dark I can think back to the time when there seemed no hope at all and, happily, was proven wrong. I am more patient with myself now.

"I've been illustrating professionally since 1971. My wife Martha and I, together with our dog, Toshiro and cat, Matsu, live in an old apartment building in Manhattan. One room of the apartment serves as my studio.

F.A. FITZGERALD

"My first love is drawing and as a result the majority of my illustrations have been line drawings done in ink with a good deal of 'cross hatching' used to render form. *Daffynitions* was one of the few projects in which I used line and wash. *May I Stay?* was a complicated four-color job. The color was pre-separated (by me) and each illustration required at least four overlays.

"Expecting to have more opportunities to work in color, I practice painting whenever possible. I favor water color, gouache and acrylic paints but am also interested in oil painting. I enjoy making pictures that are fun to look at and hope that they entertain and delight.

"It is all too clear that there are enormous problems in the world, but it is my belief that with God's help they will be solved. It is my greatest wish that the characters I create will do their part to make the world a happier place."

FOX, Michael Wilson 1937-

PERSONAL: Born August 13, 1937, in Bolton, England; married in 1963; children: Michael, Camilla. *Education:* Royal Veterinary College, University of London, B.Vet.Med., 1962; University of London, Ph.D., 1967, D.Sc., 1975.

CAREER: Jackson Laboratory, Bar Harbor, Me., fellow, 1962-64; State Research Hospital, Galesburg, Ill., medical research associate in brain and behavioral development,

Nonchalantly he tore off a willow branch and nibbled at a few leaves while the cubs, huddled together on the sandbank, stared wide-eyed, like curious children. ■ (From *The Wolf* by Dr. Michael Fox. Illustrated by Charles Fracé.)

1964-67; Washington University, St. Louis, Mo., associate professor of biology and psychology, 1967-68, associate professor of psychology, 1968-76; Insitute for the Study of Animal Problems, Humane Society of the United States, Washington D.C., director, 1977—; author. *Member:* Royal College of Veterinary Surgeons, Animal Behavior Society, American Veterinary Medical Association. *Awards, honors:* Christopher Award for *The Wolf;* nominee for Mark Twain Awards for *Sundance Coyote;* best Science Book Award, National Teacher's Association for *Ramu and Chennai.*

WRITINGS: Canine Pediatrics: Development, Neonatal, and Congenital Diseases, C. C Thomas, 1966; (editor) *Abnormal Behavior in Animals,* Saunders, 1968; *Understanding Your Dog: Everything You Want to Know about Your Dog But Haven't Been Able to Ask Him,* Coward, 1971; *Integrative Development of Brain and Behavior in the Dog,* University of Chicago Press, 1971; *Behavior of Wolves, Dogs, and Related Canids,* Cape, 1971, Harper, 1972; (editor) *Readings in Ethology and Comparative Psychology,* Brooks/Cole, 1973; *Understanding Your Cat,* Coward, 1974; *Concepts in Ethology: Animal and Human Behavior,* University of Minnesota Press, 1974; (editor) *The Wild Canids: Their Systematics, Behavioral Ecology, and Evolution,* Van Nostrand, 1974; *Between Animal and Man,* Coward, 1976; (with W. D. Gates) *What Is Your Dog Saying?,* Coward, 1977; (editor, with Richard K. Morris) *On the Fifth Day: Animal Liberation and Human Ethics,* Acropolis, 1977; *Understanding Your Pet,* Coward, 1978; *The Dog: Its Domestication and Behavior,* Garland, 1978.

Fiction for young people: *The Wolf* (illustrated by Charles Frace), Coward, 1973; *Vixie: The Story of a Little Fox* (illustrated by Jennifer Perrott), Coward, 1973; *Sundance Coyote* (illustrated by Dee Gates), Coward, 1974; *Ramu and Chennai: Brothers of the Wild* (illustrated by Michael Hampshire), Coward, 1975; *Wild Dogs Three,* Coward, 1977.

SIDELIGHTS: "I was born in Bolton, England and raised in the Derbyshire hills while attending Buxton College. My earliest ambition was to become a veterinarian. This was accomplished in 1962 at the Royal Veterinary College, London. Interest in behavior development led to a post doctoral fellowship at Jackson Laboratory, Bar Harbor, Maine (1962-64), after a brief post-graduate internship at Cambridge University, School of Veterinary Medicine. Subsequently (1964-67) I was a medical research associate at Galesburg State Research Hospital where an external London University Ph.D. thesis was completed in developmental psychobiology. Then from 1967 to 1976 I was associate professor of psychology at Washington University, St. Louis, Missouri. Research on wild canids led to the completion of research which was awarded the D.Sc. degree in Ethology/Animal Behavior by London University. Basic research led to applied behavioral problems in veterinary medicine and work with wild canids led to a more active involvement in animal conservation and related areas of humane philosophy and education."

In recent years, the writing career of Michael W. Fox has become two-sided. Besides his many technical studies of animals, Fox has also penned several fictional stories for young people.

Behavior of Wolves, Dogs, and Related Canids was called, "a sociology of canine behavior," by a *Book World* critic, who went on to say, "He surveys the wolf's keen senses with the same thoroughness he brings to his analysis of canine body language . . . [It] is a scholarly study, but can aid

MICHAEL WILSON FOX

the dog lover or wild animal enthusiast." A *Choice* reviewer added, "In addition to its academic interest for comparative psychologists and zoologists, the book can enrich the dog-lover's understanding of a pet's behavior." "The most important section of the book," wrote *Science,* "is an account of the comparative aspects of behavior in several canids, with in addition an illuminating comparison of facial expression in canids and primates. The difficult subject is well presented in an easy, flowing style with superb photographs which enable the reader to judge the significance of visual signals . . . much more easily than would be possible from line drawings."

In a review of *Sundance Coyote, Horn Book* observed, "A psychology professor writes about animal behavior with an authority rooted in his raising of coyotes and many other animals; his lively storytelling style sets his life-cycle narration apart from the majority of such fictionalized informational works. . . . Carefully detailed and sometimes lit with humor are the depictions of Sundance's encounters with wild enemies and also with a protective Indian lad who gradually makes a pet of him. At this point, the account becomes pure fiction. Numerous ink-line drawings attractively complement the text. . . ." The *Bulletin of the Center for Children's Books* added, ". . . His coyote is given a name, but there is otherwise no anthropomorphism, and the narrative form is used with skill as Dr. Fox describes the early training of coyote cubs, their social behavior, coping with predators—including man—and their mating patterns. . . ."

Fox's most recent book is *Wild Dogs Three.* A review appearing in *Publishers Weekly* included the following comments: "By a specialist in animal behavior and a well-known author of books for adults and children, this is the affecting story of abandoned pets. While essentially factual, the account has been fictionalized in parts and it's a strong indictment of irresponsible humans, although the author's text is tightly controlled. . . . The book is an appeal to compassion and proof that it's kinder to have an unwanted pet painlessly killed than set 'free'.''

FOR MORE INFORMATION SEE: Book World, May 21, 1972; *Choice,* January, 1973; *Science,* April 6, 1973; *Horn Book,* June, 1973, April, 1974, December, 1974; *Bulletin of the Center for Children's Books,* December, 1974; *Junior Literary Guild,* September, 1975; *Horn Book,* April, 1976; *Publishers Weekly,* April 4, 1977.

FUJIWARA, Michiko 1946-
(Michiko Saito)

PERSONAL: Born December 6, 1946, in Yokohama, Japan; daughter of Tatsuo (a painter) and Kiyoko Saito; married Masami Fujiwara, October 6, 1974; children: Ken, Jun. *Education:* Attended Kuwasawa Design Institute, 1965-68. *Home:* 4-19-15 Kitazawa, Setagaya-ku, Tokyo, Japan.

CAREER: Shufu to Seikatsu (publisher), 3-5 Kyobashi, Chuo-ku, Tokyo, illustrator, 1967-68; Matsukiya Department, Yokohama, Japan, graphic designer, 1968-69; Japan Advertising Center, Tokyo, illustrator, 1969-70; free-lance illustrator and writer, 1970—.

WRITINGS: (Under name Michiko Saito) *Jenny's Journey* (self-illustrated juvenile), McGraw, 1974.

Illustrator: Elizabeth Ando, *Japanese Cooking,* Knopf, 1978.

WORK IN PROGRESS: (With Masako Osodo), *The World is Narrower,* 1978.

SIDELIGHTS: ''I went to New York in August of 1972. At the beginning I planned to stay there three months but was compelled to put it off for two years. Therefore I was able to publish an illustrated book which I had desired to do for a long time. Furthermore, I issued two kinds of Christmas cards.

''I returned to Japan in Autumn of 1974 to marry my present husband. After I arrived here I drew illustrations on book covers at the end of every month and have made animal masks for children's television programs. My remaining hours have been spent originating covers of illustrated books.

''I will visit New York again after collecting a lot of work.''

(From *Trudy's Straw Hat* by Martha Gamerman. Illustrated by Alexandra Wallner.)

MARTHA GAMERMAN

GAMERMAN, Martha   1941-

PERSONAL: Born June 13, 1941, in New York, N.Y.; daughter of Oscar (a realtor and certified public accountant) and Sarah (Berlinsky) Sapir; married Kenneth Gamerman (a producer of educational materials), December 25, 1958; children: Amy, Nancy, Ellen. *Education:* Queens College (now part of the City University of New York), B.A., 1962. *Home:* 257 Barnard Rd., Larchmont, N.Y. 10538.

CAREER: Roslyn High School, Roslyn, N.Y., teacher of English, 1962-64; writer, 1975—. Teacher of writing and poetry workshops for children.

WRITINGS: Trudy's Straw Hat (juvenile), Crown, 1977.

WORK IN PROGRESS: Another picture book and an adventure story for older readers.

SIDELIGHTS: "One winter, when my children were very young, we moved from New York to Chicago. It was cold, and we were lonely, so we spent many hours in the children's room of the local library. We read hundreds of books together that winter. I loved them as much as my children did. And I remained fascinated and delighted long after my children outgrew them. My interest in children's literature had taken firm hold by then.

"I remember my own childhood as a sequence of unadulterated pleasures and uncomfortable dilemmas. And those childhood predicaments are the material for my stories. Wanting things we can't have, trying to find good friends, and being afraid of strangers, are some of the problems I remember and want to explore. I think of my stories as illustrated conversations about those old dilemmas."

GELDART, William   1936-

PERSONAL: Born March 21, 1936, in Chesire, England; son of William Edmund (a decorator) and Edith Gertrude (Cranmer; a factory worker) Geldart; married Anne Mary Wardley (his secretary), August 1, 1958; children: William Wardley, Victoria. *Education:* Attended Regional College of Art, Manchester, England, 1956-57. *Politics:* Centre. *Religion:* Agnostic. *Home:* Spinks House, Chelford Road, Henbury, near Macclesfield, Chesire, England. *Office:* The Geldart Gallery, Spinks House, Chelford Road, Henbury, near Macclesfield, Chesire, England.

CAREER: Artist; designer; typographer. The Whitehorn Press, Ltd., Manchester, England, studio assistant, 1957-62, art editor, 1962-70; free-lance artist, 1970—; owner of gallery, 1974—. Governor of Hyde College of Further Education, 1971-73. *Military service:* Royal Air Force, ciné photographer, 1954-56.

ILLUSTRATOR: Tom Ingram, *Garranane,* Bradbury, 1972; Mary Bowring, *The Animals Come First* (cover), Collins, 1976; Joyce Stranger, *Kym,* Michael Joseph, 1976, Coward, 1977; Ruth Manning-Sanders, *The Three Witch Maidens,* Hamlyn, 1977; Joyce Stranger, *The Fox at Drummers' Darkness,* Farrar, 1977; Joyce Stranger, *A Walk in the Dark* (cover), Michael Joseph, 1978; Arthur Catherall, *Lost in Lapland* (cover), Dent, 1978; Bruce Carter, *Miaow* (cover), Dent, 1978; Frank Walker, *The Lurcher* (cover), Michael Joseph, 1978. Illustrations have appeared in the Sunday *Times, My Weekly, Lancashire Life* and *Chesire Life.*

Kai shielded his eyes with both hands and stared up at the cloud, ball, plate or falcon floating in the sky.
■ (From *Garranane* by Tom Ingram. Illustrated by Bill Geldart.)

WILLIAM GELDART

WORK IN PROGRESS: Illustrations for A. L. Rowse, *Three Cornish Cats* for Weidenfeld & Nicolson Ltd. "Mostly I work to commission—animals, buildings, town scenes, country scenes, trees, etc. I have just finished a series of four drawings of the machinery in an engineering group (and some of the men in the factory), and also a large montage of the three day Badminton Horse Trials, showing horses, personalities and general scenes of the Trials. This was commissioned by the Whitehorn Press who used it in their magazine and published a signed limited edition of prints. In between times I snatch a few moments to work on my decorative dragon (pen and ink), when it's finished I'll make some posters."

SIDELIGHTS: "Although having drawn and painted since the year dot, after leaving Hyde Grammar school I was undecided what to do. I had no aim nor target and a kind of vague ambition to make it as an artist. I was employed by a small printer in my home town of Marple, to do odd jobs about the shop—punching holes for calendars to be strung etc. While I was there I had an interview in Manchester at a Textile design studio, I obviously made a favourable impression for I was offered the job but was shattered when they offered me £1.50p. a week. When I told the elder of the two printers what I was working for, he said I should ring them and say that the 'remuneration wasn't sufficient.' This I did hardly knowing what it meant! Shortly afterwards I left the printshop and moved next door, but one, to a free-lance photographer who was employed in taking wedding photos, engagements and industrial premises. I developed film made prints and dry mounted for him. I remember he had an old convertible car which had to be urged to go up hills, in fact a couple of times I thought he was going to have a heart attack the tension was so severe. I think he could ill afford an assistant because after I'd been there only a short time he told me that he had spoken to a friend who had a textile design studio in Manchester and arranged for me to start there.

"So I was introduced to Sharples & Downes, this comprised of the two directors, two designers (male) and five girls (colourists). My time here was spent mostly in screen printing various colourings for one design on bits of cloth. I found it deadly tedious and tended to mess about a lot—practical jokes, etc. and eventually after one disastrous prank which involved throwing polywog paste across the narrow street (about four floors up) to stick onto the windows of the solicitors opposite. The poor old chaps were dumbfounded by this white fudge dropping from heaven and landing with a dull thud on their windows and clinging there like an alien from a science fiction story. They eventually twigged and the sequel was not so amusing—I was very ashamed of getting the sack and I remember worrying as I went home on the bus how I was going to break the news to my parents.

"Shortly after this episode I was ordered into the Royal Air Force to do my two years National Service. These years I spent mainly in Germany as a cine photographer with 14 squadron—a fighter squadron. I rose to the dizzy heights of a Senior Aircraftsman but I *was* in charge of the photo section! During my service I decided that I would become an art teacher so I applied to the Regional College of Art and after a short interview they said I could start on completion of my military training. In the break between finishing my service and going to art school I met my future wife, Anne, and we started to 'go out' together.

"At the art school—which I used to reach on a motor bike my father had bought while I was in the RAF—the curriculum stated that a student would do two years intermediate, specialize for a couple of years in painting or illustration and then do the teacher training. Unfortunately I had decided by the end of the first year of intermediate—being the grand old age of twenty-one—that I couldn't wait all those years to ask Anne to marry me so at the summer holiday I dropped out of art school and started with a very small advertising agency in Manchester. The owner—very astute—said that I could work the summer holidays to see if I would fit in. For this period he would pay expenses—£3 per week! The time passed and 'fit in' I did for he upped my pay to £6 a week—riches!

"After six months I saw a job advertised for an assistant in the studios of a magazine publisher for which I applied successfully. This was the start of serious training for me in the art of illustration, typography, page design and plate processing, etc. and it gave me a good basics on which I have been building ever since. After eventually taking over as art editor and staying in that post for a few years I started freelancing about eight years ago—opening my own gallery after four years.

"I mostly work in black and white rather than colour although when the opportunity occurs I use gouache for book covers, etc. My preference in black and white work is to use either mapping pen and Indian ink, ballpoint pen or scraperboard (used a lot for my animal studies). Mainly I use the white scraperboard and put in my own ink rather than the already black scraperboard supplied by the manufacturers. I never start a drawing until I have plenty of reference—this is most important—unless the illustrations are for children's fairy stories or ghost stories, then this gives my imagination plenty of scope."

HOBBIES AND OTHER INTERESTS: "Reading anything, music—across the board, walking in the country, watching television, eating out (Chinese food especially)."

GILMAN, Esther 1925-

PERSONAL: Born in 1925, in Cleveland, Ohio; daughter of Joseph (a manufacturer) and Bertha (Tenenbaum) Morgenstern; married Richard Gilman, August 30, 1949 (divorced, 1967); children: Nicholas Alexander. *Education:* University of Michigan, B.S., 1961; also attended Cleveland School of Art, Art Students League of New York, and Columbia University. *Home:* 160 Riverside Drive, New York, N.Y. 10024.

CAREER: Painter, illustrator. Visual consultant for Open Theatre; art consultant and editorial board member for Feminist Press; created theatre sets for ten off-off Broadway productions. *Exhibitions*—Group shows: Museum of Modern Art, Young Printmakers Exhibition, New York, N.Y.; Riverside Museum, New York, N.Y.; National Academy of New York, New York, N.Y.; American Water Color Society, New York, N.Y.; Jersey City Museum, Jersey City, N.J.; Northwest Printmakers, Portland, Ore.; Fourth International Lithographers Annual, Cincinnati, Ohio; Downtown Community School, New York, N.Y.; New York City Center Gallery, New York, N.Y.; Laurel Gallery (two person show), New York, N.Y.; Roko Gallery, New York, N.Y.; Gertrude Stein Gallery, The No Show, New York, N.Y.; Roland de Aenille Gallery, New York, N.Y.; Rochester Festival of Religious Arts, Rochester, N.Y. One-woman shows: Bodley Gallery, New York, N.Y., 1961; Little Gallery, Detroit, Mich., 1962; Simons Rock College, Simons Rock, Mass., 1971; A Show of Hands, New York, N.Y., 1973; Cleveland Institute of Music, Pavillion Gallery, Cleveland, Ohio, 1973; Pentagram Gallery, Charlottesville, Va., 1974; Razor Gallery, New York, N.Y., 1977. Works are in the private collections of Hazel Guggenheim, New York, N.Y.; Mrs. Otto Spaeth, New York, N.Y.; Mr. and Mrs. Irving Berg, Detroit, Mich.; Dr. and Mrs. Maynard Cohen, Chicago, Ill. *Member:* The Art Students League. *Awards, honors:* The Robert Boardman Award, Painters and Sculptors Society of New Jersey, first prize watercolor, 1958; Outstanding Children's Book Illustration for *The Little Girl and Her Mother*, 1963-64; American Institute of Graphic Arts Exhibition, 1965; Rochester Festival of Religious Arts, first award in graphic arts, 1970.

ESTHER GILMAN

ILLUSTRATOR: Beatrice Schenk de Regnier, *The Little Girl and Her Mother*, Vanguard, 1964; Joseph Morgenstern, *I Have Considered My Days*, Ykuf Publishers, 1964; Bobbi Katz, *Nothing But a Dog*, Feminist Press, 1972; Ruth Kraus, *Little Boat Lighter Than a Cork*, Magic Circle Press, 1975. Work has appeared in *Jubilee Magazine* and *Little Magazine*, 1975.

WORK IN PROGRESS: Wouldn't It Be Funny if I Was a Cake, a children's book of verse and pictures.

SIDELIGHTS: "A favorite activity of mine, in my early childhood in Cleveland, Ohio, was to cut out the pictures I loved best from magazines my mother subscribed to, like *Good Housekeeping*. I especially delighted in the pictures of the Campbell's Soup kid, which came every month with a new costume and activity. I still possess an early drawing of her which I copied on a blank leaf of the *Book of Knowledge*, another of my favorite sources of illustrations and photographs.

"I also loved dressing up in costumes which I either made for myself or borrowed from my mother. I was especially fond of Russian peasant clothes which she had kept for me, and richly embroidered peasant blouses which were given to me by our Polish housekeeper. My mother told me of her life in Russia which seemed so colorful and exotic, stirring my imagination.

"I wanted to be an opera singer or a ballet dancer when I grew up. The opera singer idea came from having a couple of opera singers spend a week with us when I was about eight; they seemed glamorous and exciting to me. My mother took me to dance classes and we attended opera, music and dance events together. She talked a lot about Isadora Duncan and Anna Pavlova.

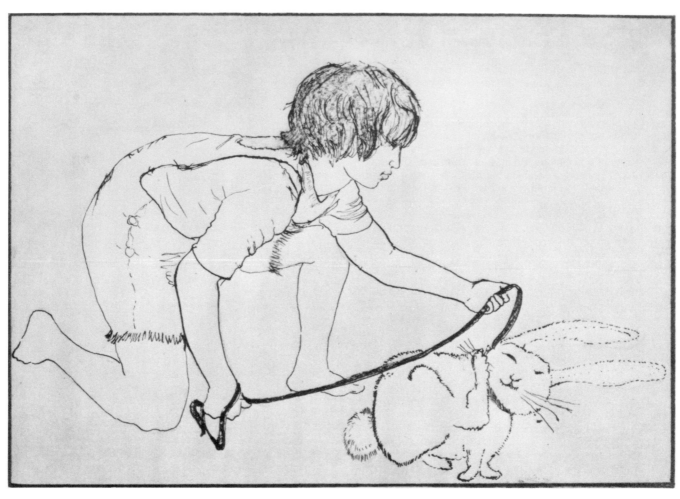

Not a fat bunny called Floyd. . .
■ (From *Nothing But a Dog* by Bobbi Katz. Pictures by Esther Gilman.)

"As I was growing up my mother and I enjoyed embroidery and sewing. In school I once made a doll puppet out of paper maché, sewed a Russian costume for her, and gave her the Russian name Katchinka which I probably got from one of the stories my father read to me. He read stories to me at mealtime and at bedtime, always in Yiddish, from the wealth of Yiddish literature for children.

"There was an Educational Council Alliance near our home which offered creative activities for children, and I took after school art classes there. At the council a wonderful, loving woman, whom I remember as Miss Brown, encouraged me, as well as many other gifted youngsters toward art careers. Much later at Camp Mehia, in Michigan, a counsellor helped me make a final decision to study art seriously and make it my career. Although my mother and my teachers encouraged me in music and athletics, I dropped these activities after a few summers at that camp. After high school I attended the Cleveland School of Art; then wanting to get away from home and be on my own, I transferred to the University of Wisconsin and then to the University of Michigan. During my last year I was advised to further my study in New York and I have been a New Yorker ever since.

"I did not consider illustrating until much later when I was married and had a baby. I happened to do a series of mother and child etchings in which I tried to express my feelings about motherhood. I met Beatrice de Regnier, a children's

book writer and editor of Scholastic Books, who asked me to illustrate a book she had written about a little girl and her mother. In working with her, I found that I drew myself as both the mother and the girl. It was fascinating to do a double self-portrait, recalling myself as a child while at the same time expressing my feelings as a mother.

"In the children's books that I have done since that first one, I have always, when asked to draw animals, little boys or little girls, recalled memories of myself as a child. I find satisfaction in expressing this part of me, and therefore would rather draw children than adults, I like to participate in the lives of children and enjoy having them as my audience."

FOR MORE INFORMATION SEE: The Cleveland Plain Dealer, September 2, 1973.

GOLBIN, Andrée   1923-

PERSONAL: Born June 4, 1923, in Leipzig, Germany; daughter of Owsey (a furrier) and Elsa (Rimathé; a pianist and composer) Golbin; married Ernest Gold, July, 1943 (divorced, 1948); married Don David (an artist), January 8, 1952. *Education:* Parsons School of Art, diploma, 1943; also attended Art Student's League, 1944; Hans Hofmann School of Art, 1952. *Home and office:* 32 East 22nd Street, New York, N.Y. 10010.

CAREER: Illustrator; artist. Gussow & Kahn Advertising, New York, N.Y., art director's assistant, 1943-44; *California Magazine,* Los Angeles, Calif., art director's assistant, 1946-47; *Mademoiselle,* New York, N.Y., promotion art director, 1950-52; Newark School of Fine and Industrial Art, Newark, N.J., instructor, 1971. *Exhibitions*—One person shows: Camino Gallery, New York, N.Y., 1956, 1958; Roko Gallery, New York, N.Y., 1964; Grand Central Moderns Gallery, New York, N.Y., 1964, 1966; Contemporary Arts Gallery, New York University, New York, N.Y., 1971. Group Shows: "Contemporary Painting and Sculpture," Riverside Museum, 1963; New School of Social Research, 1968; Alonzo Gallery, 1969; "Women Choose Women," New York Cultural Center, 1973; Women's Interart Center, 1973; "Works on Paper, Women Artists," Brooklyn Museum, 1975; Noah Goldowsky Gallery, 1976. Work has been represented at the Lending Library of the Museum of Modern Art and has toured around the world through the "Art for Embassies" program. Paintings in private and public collections include: World Trade Center, New York, N.Y.; Eastman Kodak, New York, N.Y.; Wako Securities Co. Ltd., Tokyo, Japan; Industrial Bank of Japan; Klopman Mills, New York, N.Y. *Member:* Artists Equity, Women in the Arts, Inc. *Awards, honors:* Ann Cole Phillips Award for "progressive painting," 1952; *The Cloud Eater* was a Junior Literary Guild selection, 1963.

ILLUSTRATOR: Paul Rothenhäusler, *Amerika Für Anfanger* (written in German), Fretz & Wasmuth Verlag (Zürich), 1952; Leone Adelson, *Fly Away at the Airshow,* Grosset,

But the baby mummichog needs to stay hidden.
■ (From *Minnows* by Elizabeth Shepherd. Illustrated by Andrée Golbin.)

ANDRÉE GOLBIN ●

1962; Oscar Weigle (compiler), *A Treasury of Stories to Read Aloud,* Grosset, 1962; Katherine Reeves, *The Cloud Eater,* Rand McNally, 1963; Elizabeth Shepherd, *Minnows,* Lothrop, 1974.

SIDELIGHTS: "I have always had a special interest in drawing and painting from nature and both my last book *Minnows* and my paintings reflect this (even though the paintings are abstract, they are strongly derived from landscape).

"Several influences have been crucial to my development as an artist: Hans Hofmann's classes, the paintings of Monet and Leon Polk Smith, as well as Erick Hawkins' classes in modern dance.

"I lived in Italy until 1938, went to London, England with my parents for five months and came to this country just before the war in April, 1939. First lived in New York City, where I finished high school and went to art school. Married Ernest Gold in 1943, went to Hollywood, California with him in 1945. Divorced in 1948, returned to New York City in 1948 where I've lived since. Married Don David in 1952. Spent the last eight summers at our little farm in Springbrook, Oregon (near Portland) and I consider it my home also. My career has been divided between painting, illustrating and designing. I speak four languages more or less fluently: English, Italian, French, and German. I have travelled widely here and in Europe."

FOR MORE INFORMATION SEE: New York Times Book Review, December 29, 1963; *New York Times,* 1964; *New York Herald Tribune,* 1964; *Art News,* 1964, 1973; *Arts* Magazine, 1964, 1966; *Art Forum,* March, 1973; *The Nation,* June, 1973.

GOODE, Diane   1949-

PERSONAL: Born September 14, 1949, in New York, N.Y.; daughter of Armand R. (a dentist) and Paule (Guerrini) Capuozzo; married David Goode (a teacher/researcher), May 26, 1973. *Education:* Queens College, B.A., 1972; attended Les Beaux Arts, Aix-en-Provence, France, 1971.

CAREER: Illustrator. New York Public Schools, New York, N.Y., substitute teacher, 1972-73; University of Cali-

On the land above, Marian contrived, despite her chores, to stay within his sight. ■ (From *The Selchie's Seed* by Shulamith Oppenheim. Illustrated by Diane Goode.)

fornia at Los Angeles, Los Angeles, Calif., teacher in workshop in children's book illustration, summers of 1976, 1977, 1978. *Awards, honors:* Received an award from the Southern California Council on Literature for Children and Young People for a "significant contribution to the field of illustration published during 1975." The illustrations were in *The Selchie's Seed* and *Little Pieces of the West Wind.*

ILLUSTRATOR: Shulamith Oppenheim, *The Selchie's Seed,* Bradbury, 1975; Christian Garrison, *Little Pieces of the West Wind,* Bradbury, 1975; Christian Garrison, *Flim and Flam and the Big Cheese,* Bradbury, 1976; Flora Annie Steele, *Tattercoats: An Old English Tale* (ALA Notable Book), Bradbury, 1976; Irene Hunt, *The Lottery Rose* (book jacket), Scribner, 1976; Elizabeth Starr Hill, *Ever-After Island* (book jacket), Dutton, 1977; Madame de Beaumont (translated by the illustrator), *Beauty and the Beast,* Bradbury, 1978; Christian Garrison, *The Dream Eater,* Bradbury, 1978.

WORK IN PROGRESS: A magazine jacket for the Braille Institute of America; collection of current years: children's books translated into Braille.

SIDELIGHTS: "As far back as I can remember, I always loved to draw. Early on I also became an avid reader and through an endless procession of books passing through my hands, developed a fascination for the 'feel' of the book, its weight and texture, and the rhythm of turning pages.

"As a fine arts major at Queens College, I concentrated on drawing and color theory with Marvin Bileck and Herbert Aach. It was then that I made a conscious connection between my own drawing and book illustration.

"Following a sojourn at Les Beaux Arts in France, and substitute teaching in New York, I moved to California where I received my first manuscript, *Little Pieces of the West Wind.*

"The transition from drawing board to story board was a natural one, but I had no experience in commercial art techniques. Thanks to my editors I learned the mechanics of book illustration—how to lay-out, organize, design, and pre-separate a picture book.

"I regard a picture book in its totality. The relationship of illustration to text must be very close with the overall flow and rhythm of the story matched and enhanced visually by the artist. While the relationship between author and artist is spiritually intimate, I, like many other illustrators, have never met the authors of my books.

"Because of the delicate nature of my style, it is sometimes difficult for me to keep the total concept and flow of the story in view while focusing in on, say, a tiny buttonhole. In order to keep the book in perspective, I work at a very long drawing board over which I hang the pictures in progress in page order.

"The soft, delicate line technique I have used exclusively in all my books is achieved by using a very fine brush (000), Japanese stick ink, and parchment paper. Only the brush can create a heavy line and taper off to a mere whisp in a single stroke.

"Many of my illustrations come from personal experiences of places, people, and things. Feelings of friendship, love,

DIANE GOODE

gentleness, and humor are universal. I hope to convey them through my drawings. For me a book must elicit some positive reaction and if it cannot be a reflection of our lives, at least let it be a hope for the future."

GOULD, Marilyn   1928-

PERSONAL: Born February 12, 1928, in Cleveland, Ohio; daughter of Seymour Irving (an executive) and Edith (Eisner) Amster; married Paul Irving Gould (in real estate and building management), January 29, 1950; children: Sheri Ellen (Mrs. Gary Sindell), Melanie Jane (Mrs. Todd Adams), George Marshall. *Education:* University of California at Los Angeles, Associate of Arts, 1948; attended Columbia University, summer, 1948; University of Southern California, B.S., 1950; California State University, teaching credential, 1965. *Home:* 726 Bison Avenue, Newport Beach, Calif. 92260. *Agent:* Bert Briskin, 984 Casiano Drive, Los Angeles, Calif. 90049. *Office:* 407 East Pico Boulevard, Los Angeles, Calif. 90015.

CAREER: Los Angeles City Schools, Los Angeles, Calif., teacher, 1965-75; Allied Crafts Building, Los Angeles, Calif., building management, 1977-78. Lectures in classrooms on writing. *Member:* Society of Children's Book Writers, Southern California Conference on Literature for Children and Young People.

WRITINGS: (With George Gould) *Skateboards, Scooterboards, and Seatboards You Can Make,* Lothrop, 1977; *Playground Sports, A Book of Ball Games,* Lothrop, 1978. Articles have appeared in *Highlights for Children, Bike World,* and *Family Circle.*

Learning to ride a skateboard takes time and practice. It's very much like learning to ride a bicycle. You need balance and nerve while you're in motion. ■ (From *Skateboards, Scooterboards and Seatboards You Can Make* by Marilyn Gould and George Gould. Art concept of photographs by Lou Jacobs, Jr.)

MARILYN and GEORGE GOULD

LEON GREGORI

WORK IN PROGRESS: A Host of Golden Daffodils, a story about a handicapped child.

SIDELIGHTS: ''As a teacher, I found I was always writing my own teaching material which eventually lead to my becoming a full time writer. I write for children because they are 'my thing.' I remember how I felt as a child and I remember the important part books played in my life. I don't feel much differently, now that I've grown up.''

GREGORI, Leon   1919-

PERSONAL: Born June 3, 1919, in Kiev, Russia; son of Abner (an accountant) and Rose (Gore) Gregori; married Katherine Quint, November 25, 1947; children: Mary Ellen, Peter Avery, Michael Scott. *Education:* Pratt Institute, diploma, 1935; attended George Washington University, 1935-36; New York University, B.S., 1941. *Home:* 400 East 56th St., New York, N.Y. 10022. *Office:* Norman, Craig & Kummel, Inc., 919 Third Avenue, New York, N.Y. 10022.

CAREER: Illustrator; designer. Major motion picture companies, assistant art director, 1937-39; free-lance illustrator, 1939-74; Great Neck Public Schools, Great Neck, N.Y., teacher in adult education, 1970; Norman, Craig & Kummel, New York, N.Y., illustrator, designer, 1974—; School for Visual Arts, New York, N.Y., teacher, 1975—. *Military service:* U.S. Maritime Service, Lieutenant in charge of training aids, 1942-46. *Member:* Society of Illustrators, New York Art Directors Club, Baltimore Art Directors Club, Book Publishers Association.

ILLUSTRATOR: George Kramer, *Kid Battery,* Putnam, 1968; R. L. Stevenson, *Child's Garden of Verses,* Airmont,

1969; (joint illustrator with Lynd Ward) Johann Wyss, *Swiss Family Robinson,* Grossett. Has also designed many book jackets for major publishers. Work has appeared in most national publications.

SIDELIGHTS: ''I am currently involved in television art''.

HAMPSON, (Richard) Denman   1929-

PERSONAL: Born March 5, 1929, in San Bernadino, Calif.; son of Richard (a manufacturer) and Kathleen (Caldwell; a childrens' fashion designer) Hampson; married Tonia Wirch (an artist), November 10, 1961. *Education:* Attended Pasadena City College, two years; Art Center School (Los Angeles), two years. *Home and office:* 172 North Salem Rd., Ridgefield, Conn. 06877.

CAREER: Free-lance illustrator.

WRITINGS—Self-illustrated: *What is That?,* Wonder, 1961.

Illustrator: Jean Komaiko and Kate Rosenthal, *Your Family Tree,* Parents' Magazine Press, 1963; Hazel H. Hohn, *The King Who Could Not Smile,* Parents' Magazine Press, 1963; Jean C. Soule, *Never Tease a Weasel,* Parents' Magazine Press, 1964; Doris H. Lund, *Did You Ever,* Parents' Magazine Press, 1965; Polly Berrien (editor), *Games to Play with the Very Young,* Random House, 1967; Margaret Burke, *Look, Listen and Learn* (textbook), Harcourt, 1971; Bobby Seifert, *Games to Play,* Houghton, 1973; Robin B. Cano, *Rebuses,* Houghton, 1973; George Winkler, *Unser Freund/German I* (textbook), Harcourt, 1978.

But never tease a weasel;
This is very good advice.
A weasel will not like it
And teasing isn't nice.

■ (From *Never Tease a Weasel* by Jean Conder Soule. Illustrated by Denman Hampson.)

WORK IN PROGRESS: Unser Freund/German !I (textbook) for Harcourt.

SIDELIGHTS: "Am continually fascinated by the endless variety of ways to communicate visually. The medium I currently work most in is pen line with watercolor.

"I was a student of Francis De Erdely and an admirer of John Piper, Harlow Rockwell and Friso Henstra.

"When not involved with our various work projects, my wife and I spend time restoring the one hundred year old barn that we live in, working in our large (three acre) garden, watching the waterfowl that our pond attracts and generally enjoying country life.

"Our work takes us to New York at least once a month, to Hartford and to Boston occasionally. We were both born and educated in California—we visit our families there and in western Canada.

"As a young man I traveled in Europe taking photographs and doing sketches which are currently part of our vast picture file. One thing we would both like to do is visit Japan. We are both very interested in oriental arts and crafts.''

HANLON, Emily   1945-

PERSONAL: Born April 26, 1945, in New York, N.Y.; daughter of Stuart (a teacher) and Evelyn (Green) Hanlon; married Edward Tarasov, June 25, 1966; children: Natasha, Nicholas. *Education:* Barnard College, B.A., 1967. *Home address:* Chapman Rd., R.F.D. 1, Yorktown Heights, N.Y. 10598. *Agent:* Florence Crowthers, 17 Murchisor Place White Plains, N.Y. 10605.

CAREER: Occupation Day Center, New York, N.Y., teacher of mentally retarded adults, 1972-74; creative writing

teacher at elementary school (volunteer) in Yorktown Heights, N.Y. *Member:* Authors Guild of Authors League of America.

WRITINGS—For children: *What If a Lion Eats Me and I Fall into a Hippopotamus' Mud Hole?* Delacorte, 1975; *How a Horse Grew Hoarse on the Site Where He Sighted a Bare Bear,* Delacorte, 1976; *It's too Late for Sorry* (young adult), Bradbury, 1978.

WORK IN PROGRESS: The Swing, a juvenile novel about a deaf girl.

SIDELIGHTS: "I have been writing ever since I can remember, although I began writing with thoughts of publication about six years ago. My first books were picture books, but I find writing novels for older children and teenagers more satisfying. I also write adult poetry and enjoy gardening.

"As *The Swing* is now under consideration for publication, I am currently working on a young adult book concerning the friendship between two seventeen year-old girls in their senior year of high school. I am trying to capture in this book the essence of a friendship that goes beyond good times and happy days to become a meaningful experience and an influencing force in an individual's life.''

HO, Minfong   1951-

PERSONAL: Born January 7, 1951, in Rangoon, Burma; daughter of Rih-Hwa (an economist) and Lienfung (a chemist and writer; maiden name, Li) Ho; married John Value Dennis, Jr. (a soil scientist), December 20, 1976. *Education:* Attended Tunghai University, 1967-69; Cornell University, B.A. (honors), 1973. *Religion:* Agnostic. *Home:* 7 Leedon Park, Singapore 10, Singapore. *Office:* Multiple Cropping

I have a friend named Stuart. I asked Stuart to go to the zoo with me. But Stuart said, "No." He was afraid. He has never been to the zoo before. ■ From *What If a Lion Eats Me and I Fall Into a Hippopotamus' Mud Hole* by Emily Hanlon. Illustrated by Leigh Grant.)

Project, Faculty of Agriculture, Chiengmai University, Chiengmai, Thailand.

CAREER: Starlight Plywood Factory, Singapore, manual worker, 1973; *Straits Times,* Singapore, journalist, 1973-75; Chiengmai University, Chiengmai, Thailand, lecturer in department of mass transportation, 1976—. Trade union representative, 1973-75. *Awards, honors:* First prize from Council of Interracial Books for Children, 1973, for *Sing to the Dawn.*

WRITINGS: Sing to the Dawn (juvenile), Lothrop, 1975. Author of "Hsin Nu-Ren," a column in Singapore *Sunday Times.* Contributor to economic journals.

WORK IN PROGRESS: Sky on Fire (tentative title), a novel based on the ideals and experiences of Thailand's student movement during the brief "democratic period," 1973-76.

SIDELIGHTS: "Writing, in itself, is like the sound of one hand clapping—incomplete, silent, and without impact. It is only when the writer as the one hand, and the reader as the other, confront each other is there that clap, that spark of communication which makes literature alive.

"When I wrote *Sing to the Dawn,* it was in moments of homesickness during the thick of winter in upstate New York, when Thailand seemed incredibly far away. Writing about the dappled sunlight and school children of home brought them closer to me; it aired on paper that part of me which couldn't find any place in America. The story was not meant to be read—it was only one hand clapping.

"The manuscript was later published (through no effort of mine). Suddenly a whole new dimension of writing opened up to me: it became a communicative rather than cathartic

Dawan turned around, and saw a young girl squatting on the ground. She was surrounded by sparrows in dainty wooden cages, and a white bucket full of lotus buds. The girl was smiling at her. ■ (From *Sing to the Dawn* by Minfong Ho. Illustrated by Kwoncjan Ho.)

activity. I had always written, but now I would have readers!

"Since then I've returned home to Singapore and Thailand, and I've continued to write. I've also worked in prisons and plywood factories; I have transplanted rice seedlings and helped a peasant woman give birth; I have attended trade union meetings in stuffy attics and international conferences in plush hotels. There is so much, so much beauty and so much pain in the world around me which I want to write about—because I want to share it.

"Hopefully, young readers in America will understand better, through some of my stories, the youth around me in Asia. And hopefully too, some lone foreign student stuck in a snowbound university in America somewhere will pick up a copy of my book one day, and in reading it, feel just a shade less homesick. The sound of such claps will be deeply exhilarating."

HOBBIES AND OTHER INTERESTS: Swimming, hiking, growing things.

FOR MORE INFORMATION SEE: Human Values in Children's Books, Racism and Sexism Resource Center for Educators, 1976.

MINFONG HO

It was ten o'clock in the morning. ■ (From *Anna Banana* by Rosekrans Hoffman. Illustrated by the author.)

HOFFMAN, Rosekrans 1926-

PERSONAL: Born January 7, 1926 in Denton, Neb.; daughter of James Charles (a contractor) and Pearl (Hocking) Rosekrans; married second husband, Robert Hoffman (a product manager), 1955. *Education:* University of Nebraska, B.F.A., 1949. *Politics:* "A sometimes democrat." *Home and office:* One Campbell Avenue, Apartment 66, West Haven, Conn. 06516. *Agent:* Helen Wohlberg, Kirchoff/Wohlberg, Inc., 433 East 51st St., New York, N.Y. 10022.

CAREER: Painter; illustrator. *Exhibitions:* Whitney Museum, Brooklyn Museum.

WRITINGS—Self-illustrated: *Anna Banana,* Knopf, 1974.

Illustrator: A. White, *Walter in Love,* Lothrop, 1971; P. Wolcott, *Where Did That Naughty Little Hamster Go?,* Addison, 1972; Dorothy van Woerkom, *Alexandra the Rock Eater,* Knopf, 1978; Christine Tanz, *An Egg is to Sit on,* Lothrop, 1978; Lee Bennett Hopkins, *Go To Bed!: A Book Of Poems* (anthology), Knopf, 1979.

SIDELIGHTS: "I was born in Nebraska and knew the depression days. I can see black and white and a red sun setting on a flat plain.

"I now work primarily with ink on fine pen points and try to turn corners where I have never been.

"I was strongly influenced by a teacher, Kady Faulkner, who taught painting at the University of Nebraska. She was a philosopher in her way, where art was an everyday event. It is a way of life."

HOKE, Helen (L.) 1903-
(Helen Sterling)

PERSONAL: Born in 1903; married John Hoke (an editor); married second husband, Franklin Watts (a publisher), May 25, 1945; children: (first marriage) John Lindsay (an author). *Address:* Apt. 37F, 10 Waterside Plaza, New York, N.Y. 10010.

CAREER: Franklin Watts, Inc., vice-president and editor-in-chief, beginning 1948, later director of international projects; president, Helen Hoke Associates (consulting and publishing firm), 1956—; author and editor of books for children.

WRITINGS: Mr. Sweeney (illustrated by William Wills), Holt, 1940; (with Richard C. Gill) *Paco Goes to the Fair: A Story of Far-Away Ecuador* (illustrated by Ruth Gannett), Holt, 1940; (with R. C. Gill) *Story of the Other America* (illustrated by Manuel R. Regalado), Houghton, 1941; (with Miriam Teichner) *The Fuzzy Kitten* (illustrated by Meg Wohlberg), Messner, 1941; *Major and the Kitten* (illustrated by Diana Thorne), Holt, 1941; (with Natalie Fox) *The Woolly Lamb* (illustrated by Sally Tate), Messner, 1942; *The Furry Bear* (illustrated by S. Tate), Messner, 1943; *Doctor, the Puppy Who Learned* (illustrated by D. Thorne), Messner, 1944; *Shep and the Baby* (illustrated by D. Thorne), Messner, 1944; *The Shaggy Pony* (illustrated by Dick Hart), Messner, 1944; *Mrs. Silk* (illustrated by D. Thorne), Veritas Press, 1945; *The Fuzzy Puppy* (illustrated by D. Hart), Messner, 1945; *Rags' Day* (illustrated by D. Thorne), Veritas Press, 1945; *Grocery Kitty* (illustrated by Harry Lees), Reynal & Hitchcock, 1946; *Too Many Kittens* (illustrated by H. Lees), McKay, 1947; *Factory Kitty* (illustrated by H. Lees), Watts, 1949.

The First Book of Dolls (illustrated by Jean Michener), Watts, 1954; (with Walter Pels) *The First Book of Toys* (illustrated by J. Michener), Watts, 1957; (with son, John Hoke) *Music Boxes: Their Lore and Lure* (illustrated by Nancy Martin), Hawthorn Books, 1957; *The First Book of Tropical Mammals* (illustrated by Helene Carter), 1958; *One Thousand Ways to Make $1,000 in Your Spare Time,* Bantam, 1959; *Arctic Mammals* (illustrated by Jean Zallinger), Watts, 1969; *The Big Dog and the Very Little Cat* (illustrated by D. Thorne), Watts, 1969; *Etiquette: Your Ticket to Good Times* (illustrated by Carol Wilde), Watts,

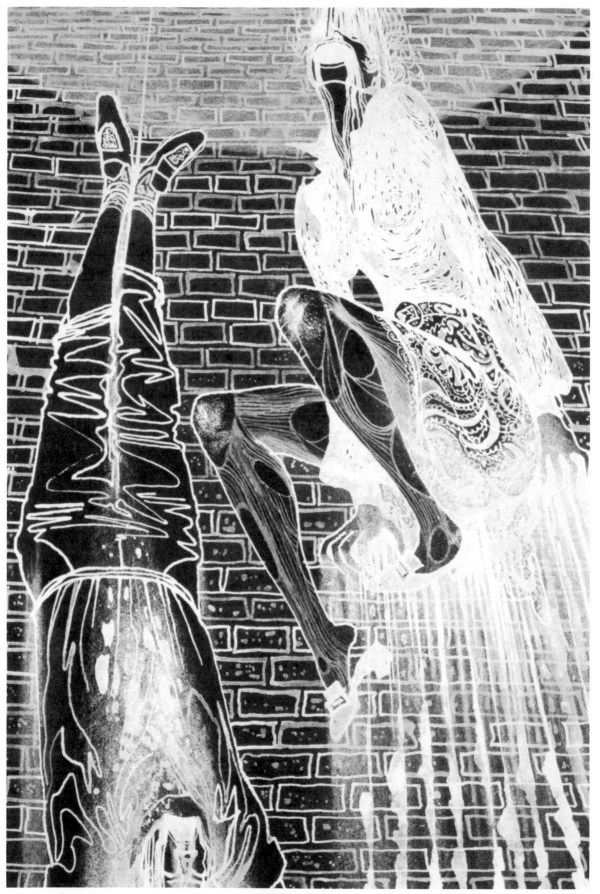

She was lying on her back, dragged across the cobbles by a tentacle caught in her red hair.
■ (From *Weirdies, Weirdies, Weirdies,* selected by Helen Hoke. Illustrated by Charles Keeping.)

1970; *Ants* (illustrated by Arabelle Wheatley), Watts, 1970; *Jokes and Fun* (illustrated by Tony Parkhouse), Watts, 1972; (with Valerie Pitt) *Whales* (illustrated by Thomas R. Funderburk), Watts, 1973; *Hoke's Jokes, Cartoons, and Funny Things* (illustrated by Eric Hill), Watts, 1973; (with V. Pitt) *Fleas*, Watts, 1974; (with V. Pitt) *Owls* (illustrated by Robert Jefferson), Watts, 1974; *Riddle Giggles* (illustrated by T. Parkhouse), Watts, 1975; (with Oliver Neshamkin) *Jokes, Fun, and Folly*, Watts, 1975.

Under pseudonym Helen Sterling: *Little Choo Choo* (illustrated by Denison Budd), Watts, 1944; *The Horse That Takes the Milk Around* (illustrated by Marjorie Hartwell), Watts, 1946; *Little Moo and the Circus* (illustrated by H. Lees), Watts, 1945; *The Biggest Family in the Town* (illustrated by Vance Locke), McKay, 1947.

Editor: *Jokes, Jokes, Jokes* (illustrated by Richard Erdoes), Watts, 1954; *The Family Book of Humor*, Hanover House, 1957; (with Boris Randolph) *Puns, Puns, Puns* (illustrated by Seymour Nydorf), Watts, 1958; *Witches, Witches, Witches* (illustrated by W. R. Lohse), Watts, 1958, reissued, 1966; *Alaska, Alaska, Alaska* (illustrated by R. M. Sax), Watts, 1960; *Nurses, Nurses, Nurses*, Watts, 1961; *Patriotism, Patriotism, Patriotism* (illustrated by Leonard E. Fisher), Watts, 1963; *More Jokes, Jokes, Jokes* (illustrated by R. Erdoes), Watts, 1965; *Spooks, Spooks, Spooks* (illustrated by W. R. Lohse), Watts, 1966; *The Big Book of Jokes* (illustrated by R. Erdoes), Watts, 1971; *Dragons, Dragons, Dragons* (illustrated by C. Barker), Watts, 1972; *Weirdies, Weirdies, Weirdies* (illustrated by Charles Keeping), Watts, 1973; *Jokes, Jests, and Jollies* (illustrated by True Kelley),

HELEN HOKE

Ginn, 1973; *Jokes, Jokes, Jokes, 2* (illustrated by Haro), Watts, 1973, reissued as *Jokes, Giggles, and Guffaws*, 1975; *Monsters, Monsters, Monsters* (illustrated by C. Keeping), Watts, 1974; *Devils, Devils, Devils* (illustrated by C. Baker), Watts, 1976; *More Riddles, Riddles, Riddles* (illustrated by Haro), Watts, 1976; *Ghosts and Ghastlies* (illustrated by Bill Prosser), Watts, 1976.

SIDELIGHTS: Helen Hoke's early career was marked by her stories for children, written under her real name as well as under her pseudonym, Helen Sterling. *Kirkus'* description of *Factory Kitty* included, "This is perhaps the best of the career kitten stories—from the point of view of text. And the Harry Lees pictures are beguiling, too. . . ." The *New York Times* added, "Strong men in action, fascinating machinery, and the engaging calico kitten are dramatized in colorful illustrations which complement the well-told story."

Of *Devils, Devils, Devils*. A *School Library Journal* reviewer observed: "Hoke's new anthology of 13 stories about those supernatural purveyors of evil and temptation—devils—will undoubtedly prove popular with young readers. From France, Finland, Italy, Belgium, the Philippines, Great Britain, and the United States come evil spirits, heathen gods, demons, as well as the familiar devil of Judeo-Christian tradition—Satan. Unfortunately, there are no stories from Africa or the Orient, but a rabbinical folktale and one of Welsh gypsy origin provide diversity. . . . A nice assortment with delightfully weird and macabre illustrations. . . ." *School Library Journal* also reviewed *Ghosts and Ghastlies*, noting: "Hoke has put together another winning collection of ghostly tales. The selection of stories and poems relies heavily on big names such as Saki, Wells, and Bierce; the literary quality of all stories and poems is excellent. There is also a generous dollop of humor—e.g., an inexperienced ghost who is terrified of the whole business of haunting. The numerous full-page illustrations by Bill Prosser are unusual and striking in their eerie graininess."

HOLLING, Holling C(lancy) 1900-

PERSONAL: Original name was Holling Allison Clancy, legally changed in 1925; born August 2, 1900, in Holling Corners, Jackson County, Mich.; son of a superintendent of schools; married Lucille Webster (an artist), 1925. *Education:* Graduated from the School of the Art Institute of Chicago, 1923. *Home:* Pasadena, Calif.

CAREER: Worked as grocery clerk, factory worker, and sailor on a Great Lakes ore boat; Field Museum of Natural History, Chicago, Ill., member of taxidermy department, 1923-26; University World Cruise (sponsored by New York University), art instructor, 1926-27; worked for several years as idea man, artist, and copy writer for a national advertising firm; author and illustrator of books for children; travelled with his wife through remote sections of the United States, Mexico, and Canada to study wildlife and gather information for his books. *Awards, honors:* Runner-up for the Caldecott Medal, 1942, for *Paddle-to-the-Sea;* Commonwealth Club of California Literature Award, 1948, for *Seabird;* runner-up for the Newbery Medal, 1949, for *Seabird,* and 1952, for *Minn of the Mississippi;* Southern California Council on Literature for Children Award, (jointly awarded to wife, Lucille Holling), 1961, for *Pagoo.*

WRITINGS: New Mexico Made Easy (self-illustrated), privately printed, 1923; *Sun and Smoke* (self-illustrated), privately printed, 1923; *Little Big-Bye-and-Bye* (self-illus-

"B-beg pardon, Sir—he's come up!" ■ (From *Seabird* by Holling Clancy Holling. Illustrated by the author.)

His right hand lay in his lap, on his open Bible. ■ (From *Seabird* by Holling Clancy Holling. Illustrated by the author.)

trated), Volland, 1926; *Roll Away Twins* (illustrated by the author with wife, Lucille Holling), Volland, 1927; *Rum-Tum-Tummy,* Volland, 1927; *Claws of the Thunderbird: A Tale of Three Lost Indians* (self-illustrated), Volland, 1928; *Choo-Me-Shoo the Eskimo* (illustrated by the author with L. Holling), Volland, 1928; *Rocky Billy: The Story of the Bounding Career of a Rocky Mountain Goat* (self-illustrated), Macmillan, 1928; *The Twins Who Flew around the World* (self-illustrated), Platt, 1931; *The Book of Indians* (illustrated by the author with L. Holling), Platt, 1935, reissued, 1962; *The Book of Cowboys* (illustrated by the author with L. Holling), Platt, 1936, reissued, 1962; *Little Buffalo Boy* (illustrated by the author with L. Holling), Garden City Publishing, 1939; *Paddle-to-the-Sea* (self-illustrated), Houghton, 1941; *Tree in the Trail* (self-illustrated), Houghton, 1942; *Seabird* (self-illustrated), Houghton, 1943; *Minn of the Mississippi* (self-illustrated), Houghton, 1951; *Pagoo* (illustrated by the author with L. Holling), Houghton, 1957.

Illustrator: (With L. Holling) Watty Piper, editor, *Road in Storyland,* Platt, 1932; (with L. Holling), *The Magic Story Tree: A Favorite Collection of Fifteen Fairy Tales and Fables,* Platt, 1964.

SIDELIGHTS: Holling's interest in nature began when he was a child growing up in the woods of northern Michigan. By the time he was an adolescent, the budding author-artist had made up his mind to write and illustrate books about wildlife for children. To pursue his ambitions, Holling attended the School of the Art Institute of Chicago where he studied draftsmanship and the graphic processes in printmaking. The young artist worked mostly in black and white until his senior year, which he spent at the Taos Art Colony in New Mexico. It was there that Holling discovered the richness and beauty of color in nature.

In addition to the informal education he gained about the outdoors as a child and the formal training he acquired as an art student, Holling also studied privately under Dr. Ralph Linton, a noted anthropologist who was then Sterling Professor at Yale University. By the mid 1920's, the author-illustrator combined his interests and talents to produce the kind of books toward which he had directed his energy since childhood.

One of Holling's most popular books was *Paddle-to-the Sea.* In this book the author described the journey of a carved miniature canoe from its starting point in Lake Nipigon, Canada, through the Great Lakes and the St. Lawrence River to its final destination at sea. "Here is geography presented with freshness and originality and imagination. . . . [A book] that children will enjoy owning that they may look again and again at the pictures whose interest it will be difficult to exhaust," noted a critic for the *New York Times.* A reviewer for the *Christian Science Monitor* wrote, "Traveling with Paddle by story and pictures is good fun . . . and is a fascinating way to learn geography."

In *Seabird* Holling traced the travels of a bird carved from a walrus tusk by sea and by air. A *Saturday Review* critic commented, "This fascinating record of America expanding looks like a picture book because space was needed for the illustrations, reproduced in full color from paintings. They are exciting and beautiful. . . ." In reviewing the same book, a *Horn Book* critic observed, "The subject takes the reader over the globe and provides room for imagination to aid history in vitalizing the period. The beauty of the illustrations gives the book distinction."

The author's *Minn of the Mississippi* told the story of a snapping turtle named Minn and his journey from Minnesota to the Gulf of Mexico via the Mississippi River. "Minn's story—the river's story are of equal fascination as the author weaves them together in this beautiful book. . .," noted a reviewer for the *Chicago Sunday Tribune.* A *New York Herald Tribune* critic wrote, "Young and old will share the

HOLLING C. HOLLING

new book with equal delight in its variety of facts, its stories of the 'River of Dreams' and the contrasting dramas on all the brillant big color pages.''

Holling's latest book, *Pagoo*, was about a hermit Crab. ''This is the story of the life cycle of a hermit crab, told with a sprightly and witty text. . .,'' described a critic for *Saturday Review*. A *New York Times* critic commented, ''Mr. Holling's information about Pagoo and other marine creatures. . .is presented in lively and humorous fashion.''

HOBBIES AND OTHER INTERESTS: Canoeing, archery, hunting, fishing, camping, and woodcraft.

FOR MORE INFORMATION SEE: M. Clyde Armstrong, ''Holling Clancy Holling,'' in *Horn Book*, April, 1955; Lee Kingman, editor, *Illustrators of Children's Books: 1957-1966*, Horn Book, 1968.

HORNBLOW, Arthur, (Jr.) 1893-1976

PERSONAL: Born March 15, 1893, in New York, N.Y.; son of Arthur and Natalie (Lambert) Hornblow; married second wife Leonora Schinasi, November 4, 1945; children: (first marriage) John Terry, (second marriage) Michael. *Education:* Attended Dartmouth College and New York Law School. *Home:* 45 Sutton Pl. S., New York, N.Y. 10022.

CAREER: Admitted to the Bar of New York State, 1917; writer and producer of plays, New York City, 1920-27; assistant managing director, Charles Frohman Co.; Samuel Goldwyn Productions, Hollywood, Calif., supervisor, 1926, writer, 1927; motion picture producer for Paramount, 1933-

42, and Metro-Goldwyn-Mayer, 1942-52; president of Arthur Hornblow Productions; author of books for children. Pictures produced include ''Gaslight,'' 1947; ''The Asphalt Jungle,'' 1950; ''Oklahoma,'' 1955; and ''Witness for the Prosecution,'' 1957. Chairman of the theatre advisory board, Dartmouth College. *Military service:* U.S. Army, Intelligence Corps, counter-espionage section, 1918-19; became first lieutenant; received Etoile Noire de la Legion d'Honneur (France) and U.S. Presidential Citation. *Member:* Dartmouth Club (New York City), Bucks Club (London).

WRITINGS—All with wife, Leonora Hornblow; all published by Random House: *Animals Do the Strangest Things* (illustrated by Michael K. Frith), 1964; *Birds Do the Strangest Things* (illustrated by M. K. Frith), 1965; *Fish Do the Strangest Things* (illustrated by M. K. Frith), 1966; *Insects Do the Strangest Things* (illustrated by M. K. Frith), 1968; *Reptiles Do the Strangest Things* (illustrated by M. K. Frith), 1970; *Prehistoric Monsters Did the Strangest Things* (illustrated by M. K. Frith), 1974.

Also translator of several plays from the French, including Sacha Guitry's ''Pasteur,'' 1925 and Edward Bourdet's ''The Captive,'' 1926.

FOR MORE INFORMATION SEE: (Obituary) *New York Times*, July 18, 1976.

(Died July 17, 1976)

In his jungle home, happy and free, he is a very mild monster. ■ (From *Animals Do the Strangest Things* by Leonora and Arthur Hornblow. Illustrated by Michael K. Frith.)

Sometimes when her work was done
Sybil climbed a maple tree just to rest and think alone.
■ (From *Danbury's Burning* by Anne Grant. Illustrated by Pat Howell.)

HOWELL, Pat 1947-

PERSONAL: Born February 12, 1947, in Glendale, Calif.; daughter of Russell B. (a design engineer) and Kathleen (No-let) Howell. *Education:* Art Center College of Design, Pasadena, Calif., B.F.A., 1970. *Home and office:* Oak Court, 1324 North 3rd. Way, Phoenix, Ariz. 85022.

CAREER: Free-lance illustrator and exhibitor. *Exhibitions:* Benton Convention Center, Winston-Salem, N.C., December, 1974; Willard of Winston Gallery, Winston-Salem, N.C., December, 1974; Northwest Gallery, North Wilksboro, N.C., June, 1975; Wachovia Bank and Trust Co., Winston-Salem, N.C., December, 1976. *Awards, honors:* Received Bank of America Achievement Award in the field of art, 1964.

ILLUSTRATOR: Anne Grant, *Danbury is Burning! The Story of Sybil Ludington,* McKay, 1976. Singular illustrations have appeared in *Catnip Cat, I Used to Live in a Garden,* and *My Ocean Prize,* all by Graham Tether and published by Western Publishing.

SIDELIGHTS: "Art has always been an important part of my life.

"My father is an artist and designer by profession, and has always maintained a studio in our home. I was a constant visitor to the studio as a child. And it was there that my art education began.

"In 1964, I qualified at the University of California at Los Angeles for the Advanced Workshops for Exceptional High School Art Students. The same year I received the Bank of America Achievement Award in the field of art.

"I received my Bachelors of Fine Arts Degree, in illustration from the Art Center College of Design, in Pasadena, California. During my educational years I lived in Europe for a year, touring the countries of Ireland, England, France and Austria. There I did independent study of painting, drawing and art history at the major museums.

"I am currently painting as a free-lance illustrator and exhibitor, specializing in illustrations for children, book illustration, wildlife pencil renderings and line drawings.

"My pen, ink and water color illustrations tend to be full of activity, much like a child's world. I try to relate my work to children as much as possible. I've found that a child will 'read' the illustration long before they have the ability to

PAT HOWELL

read the written word. And I try to convey the author's message in a way the child can relate to.

"In the 50's there was a popular idea among authorities on children, that illustrative art, was for the most part, stifling to the child's imagination and creativity. A new method of illustrating became popular, that of the simple graphic form. I guess you might say that was my motivation in really wanting to become an illustrator of children's books. I for one loathed, with a passion, this form of illustration! I always enjoyed the illustrations of the people like Howard Pyle, Maxfield Parrish, Norman Rockwell, Frank Schoonover, Arthur Frost, N. C. Wycth, Eloise Wilkins and Tasha Tudor just to name a few. If anything a good illustration will spark the imagination not hinder a child's creativity. I hope to carry on the tradition of full rich illustrations that I enjoyed so much as a child."

FOR MORE INFORMATION SEE: The Winston-Salem Journal, December 14, 1976.

HUGHES, Monica 1925-

PERSONAL: Born November 3, 1925, in Liverpool, England; daughter of Edward Lindsay (a mathematician) and Phyllis (Fry) Ince; married Glen Hughes (in city government), April 22, 1957; children: Elizabeth, Adrienne, Russell, Thomas. *Education:* Educated privately in England and Scotland. *Home:* 13816 110-A Ave., Edmonton, Alberta, Canada T5M 2M9.

CAREER: Dress designer in London, England, 1948-49, and Bulawayo, Rhodesia, 1950; bank clerk in Umtali, Rhodesia, 1951; National Research Council, Ottawa, Ontario, laboratory technician, 1952-57; writer, 1975—. *Military service:* Women's Royal Naval Service, 1943-46. *Member:* Alberta Writers Federation, Hand Weavers, Spinners and Dyers of Alberta, Edmonton Weavers Guild.

WRITINGS—For children: *Gold-Fever Trail,* John LeBel, 1974; *Crisis on Conshelf Ten,* Copp, 1975, Atheneum, 1977; *Earthdark,* Hamish Hamilton, 1977; *The Tomorrow City,* Hamish Hamilton, 1978; *The Ghost Dance Caper,* Nelson, 1978.

Work anthologized in *Magook,* McClelland & Stewart, 1977. Author of craft column, "The Craft Corner," in *Edmonton Sunday Sun.*

WORK IN PROGRESS: Science fiction for teenagers.

SIDELIGHTS: "Though born in England, I spent my next six years in Egypt. Then back to London, where I was exposed to all the great museums and art galleries. Then to Edinburgh, where I attended private school and read voraciously, especially science fiction and books of high adventure. Then to boarding school, first in the west of Scotland, and then overlooking the Yorkshire moors—cold and lonely.

"I studied dress designing after the war, but wandering seemed to be in my blood, and I went to Rhodesia, and later to Canada. I worked mostly at testing materials and aircraft, and during (and after) coffeebreaks indulged in much speculation about life on Mars and the pros and cons of flying saucers and ESP. It was great fun, and instead of crossing Canada as I had planned, and then going on to Australia, I stayed on and on.

MONICA HUGHES

"I still wandered, working in Cornwall, Ontario, on the St. Lawrence Seaway and Power Project, then living in London, Ontario, and Toronto. During these years of moving and small babies I wrote sporadically.

"Finally, my husband was transferred to the Prairies, and here in Edmonton all my creative instincts have suddenly jelled. I embroidered, designing wall-hangings that were actually published, and with the proceeds I bought a tapestry loom, on which I have been working for seven years. At about the same time, I read a book on writing for children, discarded all my uncompleted adult novels, and turned to juvenile writing.

"Science fiction is my first love. I cannot write 'ethnic' writing, not about my pioneer roots. I feel like a wanderer, an observer, and I love to speculate—'what if.' I like to explore the feelings, the needs and ideals of young people in the world of tomorrow, hopefully bringing a universality to the specific.

"I care very much about our planet and what we are doing to it, and about the people of the Third World and the underprivileged at home, and what we are doing to them."

HUTCHINS, Pat 1942-

PERSONAL: Born June 18, 1942, in Yorkshire, England; daughter of Edward (a soldier) and Lilian (Crawford) Goundry; married Laurence Hutchins (a film director), July 21, 1965; children: Morgan, Sam. *Education:* Attended Darlington School of Art, 1958-60, and Leeds College of Art, 1960-62. *Home:* 89 Belsize Lane, London N.W.3, England.

CAREER: J. Walter Thompson (advertising agency), London, England, assistant art director, 1963-65; free-lance writer and illustrator, 1965—. *Awards, honors: Changes, Changes* was a Children's Book Showcase Title, 1972; Kate Greenaway Award from Library Association (England), 1974, for *The Wind Blew.*

WRITINGS—for children: *Rosie's Walk,* Macmillan, 1968; *Tom and Sam,* Macmillan, 1968; *The Surprise Party,* Macmillan, 1969; *Clocks and More Clocks,* Macmillan, 1970; *Changes, Changes,* Macmillan, 1971; *Titch,* Macmillan, 1971; *Goodnight, Owl,* Macmillan, 1972; *The Wind Blew,* Macmillan, 1974; *The Silver Christmas Tree,* Macmillan, 1974; *The House That Sailed Away,* Greenwillow, 1975; *Don't Forget the Bacon,* Greenwillow, 1976; *Follow That Bus,* Greenwillow, 1977; *The Best Train Set Ever,* Greenwillow, 1978; *Happy Birthday, Sam,* Greenwillow, 1978.

ADAPTATIONS—Filmstrips: "*Changes, Changes,*" "*Clocks and More Clocks,*" "*Rosie's Walk,*" "*The Surprise Party,*" all produced by Weston Woods.

WORK IN PROGRESS: Picture book about pirates for Greenwillow, publication expected in 1979; a sequel to *Follow that Bus* for Greenwillow, publication expected in 1979.

SIDELIGHTS: Pat Hutchins was born in Yorkshire, England, one of seven children. "Being born and brought up in the country has affected my work enormously. We were surrounded by fields and woods full of wildlife, and spent many hours watching the animals and birds.

"All the important social events took place on the village green: the cricket matches, football matches, gymkhanas,

PAT HUTCHINS

and the annual fair, which was three summer days of fancy-dress parades, archery contests, sack races, egg-and-spoon races, and the children's favorite—the bun-eating competition.

"We were an enormous family—six of us, and quite wild. We roamed around the fields and woods discovering hedgehogs, foxes, stoats, rabbits. Any ailing bird or animal was taken home to be looked after. One bird, a young crow who had fallen from his nest, became a special pet. He stayed with us and refused to fly away. He was quite a well-known character in the village, strutting behind us on walks or sitting on my head, wings outstretched, as I rode my brother's bike."

When she was quite young, Pat Hutchins started drawing pictures of the local countryside. The old Norman churches and stone cottages fascinated her, and still do. At sixteen, she won a scholarship to an art college in Darlington, the nearest town. She studied there for two years and then won a scholarship to Leeds College of Art, graduating two years later with a National Diploma in design. She then went to work as an assistant art director in a large advertising agency in London. There she met Laurence Hutchins and a week after their marriage moved with him to the United States where they stayed for eighteen months. They lived in New York's Greenwich Village, and found time to drive across the country. She says they were stunned by Monument Valley and by the Watts Towers.

(From *Changes Changes* by Pat Hutchins. Illustrated by the author.)

''I'd hankered after illustrating children's books, and in my spare time designed a picture book. I brought my illustrations to New York and thought I'd try my luck at publishing houses. Terrified, I took my work around and to my surprise everyone was terribly kind and encouraging. The Macmillan Company asked me to try my hand at writing a story, a thing I thought I could never do, and *Rosie's Walk* happened.

''I try not to talk down to children. I try to keep my stories logical, even if a story is pure fantasy. I used to get terribly frustrated as a child if I couldn't understand the reasoning behind a plot, if someone waved a wand and everything fell into place with no explanation.

''The basic idea is the most difficult part, to try and do something original. When I have an idea, I sit down and work out the best way of putting the idea across in book form; then I write the story and design the layout. It's very satisfying to

know it's all your own work, from the original idea to the finished artwork.

''To me, the most important thing about a children's picture book is that it should be logical, not only the story, but the layout, too. To a very small child, an opened book is one page, not two—he doesn't see the gutter as a dividing line.

''I like to build my stories up, so the reader can understand what is happening and, in some cases, anticipate what is likely to happen on the next page. I think one can get quite complicated ideas across to small children as long as they are presented in a simple, satisfying way.''

Pat Hutchins and her husband, who is now a film director, live in the Hampstead area of London. She says they are great collectors of junk—''old bottles, quaint books, old toys, and any interesting things we lay our hands on, includ-

Jack knew Chico did not like the idea of having him for a teacher. But Jack liked the idea. He felt Chico should enjoy learning the fun of sailing. Maybe they could share this and become friends during the lesson. ■ (From *Best in Camp* by Mike Neigoff. Illustrated by Fred Irvin.)

ing a flint arrowhead given to us in Arizona by an American Indian.''

FOR MORE INFORMATION SEE: Horn Book, February, 1970, October, 1970, April, 1971, April, 1972, December, 1972, April, 1974, December, 1974.

IRVIN, Fred   1914-

PERSONAL: Born November 19, 1914, in Chillicothe, Mo.; son of Clifford Herbert (a traveling salesman) and Maude (Jarrell; a designer and builder of homes) Irvin; married Betty Smith (an elementary school teacher), September 13, 1947; children: John Maddox, Jarrell Lee. *Education:* Attended Kansas City Art Institute, 1933-34; Chicago Academy of Fine Arts, 1934-35; Art Students League, 1940. *Politics:* Independent. *Religion:* Protestant. *Home and office:* 1702 Hillcrest Rd., Santa Barbara, Calif. 93103. *Agent:* Kirchoff/Wohlberg, Inc., 433 East 51st St., New York, N.Y. 10022.

CAREER: Free-lance illustrator. Charles E. Cooper Art Studios, New York, N.Y., illustrator, 1952-54; Key TV, Santa Barbara, Calif., art director and artist, 1960-63. *Military service:* U.S. Army Signal Corps, 1942-45. *Member:* Society of Illustrators of Los Angeles, Santa Barbara Art Association (treasurer, 1973). *Awards, honors:* Awards in Santa Barbara Art Association shows; artist in residence, Chillicothe, Mo.; Fine Arts Fair, Bicentennial year, 1975.

ILLUSTRATOR—All published by A. Whitman, except as indicated: Mike Niegoff, *Smiley Sherman, Substitute,* 1964; Mike Neigoff, *Dive In,* 1965; Jack Woolgar, *Hot on Ice,* 1965; Mike Neigoff, *Up Sails,* 1966; Mike Neigoff, *Two on First,* 1967; Alice Sankey, *Three-In-One Car,* 1967; Mike Neigoff, *Free Throw,* 1968; Mike Neigoff, *Best in Camp,* 1969; Mike Neigoff, *Goal to Go,* 1970; Alice Sankey, *Music by the Got-Rocks,* 1970; Mike Neigoff, *Hal, Tennis Champ,* 1971; Alice Sankey, *Judo Yell,* 1971; Edna W. Chandler, *Almost Brothers,* 1971; Mike Neigoff, *Ski Run,* 1972; Julian May, *Sea Lion Island,* Creative Educational Society, 1972; Mike Neigoff, *Playmaker,* 1973; Alice Sankey, *Hit the Bike Trail,* 1974; Ferris Weddle, *Tall Like a Pine,* 1974; Mike

Fred Irvin, a self-portrait.

Neigoff, *Terror on the Ice,* 1974; Mike Neigoff, *Runner-up,* 1975; *Macmillan Dictionary for Children,* Macmillan, 1976; Donald Honig, *Hurry Home,* Addison-Wesley, 1976; Clay Graves, *Hurry Up Christmas,* Garrard, 1976. Has also illustrated numerous Little Golden Books for Western Publishing; ten "Cofas Series" (biographies) for Bobbs-Merrill; textbooks for many major publishers. Illustrations have appeared in *Colliers, American Weekly, Reader's Digest, Woman's Home Companion, Elks, Motor Magazine, Family Circle, Woman's Day* and others.

WORK IN PROGRESS: A Little Golden Book; art for Ginn workbooks; character design for Hanna-Barbera Productions.

SIDELIGHTS: "It seems that I never thought of being anything but an artist from a small child on. Being raised in a small town in Missouri, I have a good feeling about people, and like to draw them. Drawing to me is the fun of art. At present, in addition to my book art, I am doing some painting and also preparing several drawings for gallery shows and prints."

JEWETT, Sarah Orne   1849-1909

PERSONAL: Born September 3, 1849, in South Berwick, Maine; died June 24, 1909, in South Berwick; daughter of Theodore Herman (a country doctor) and Caroline Frances (Perry) Jewett. *Education:* Intermittently attended Berwick Academy, but received most of her education from the books in her father's library. *Home:* South Berwick, Maine.

CAREER: Novelist, poet, short story writer, and author of books for children. *Awards, honors:* Litt.D., 1901, from Bowdoin College.

WRITINGS—Short stories; all published by Houghton, Mifflin, except as noted: *Deephaven,* J. R. Osgood, 1877, reissued, College & University Press, 1966 [another edition illustrated by Charles and Marcia Woodbury, 1894]; *Old Friends and New,* Houghton, Osgood, 1879, reprinted, Books for Libraries, 1969; *Country By-Ways,* 1881, reprinted, Books for Libraries, 1969; *The Mate of the Daylight, and Friends Ashore,* 1884, reprinted, 1973; *A White Heron, and Other Stories,* 1886 [another edition illustrated by Barbara Cooney, T. Y. Crowell, 1963]; *The King of Folly Island, and Other People,* 1888; *Strangers and Wayfarers,* 1890, reprinted, 1974; *A Native of Winby, and Other Tales,* 1893, reprinted, Books for Libraries, 1970; *Tales of New England,* 1894, reprinted, Books for Libraries, 1970; *The Life of Nancy,* 1895, reprinted, Books for Libraries, 1969; *The Country of the Pointed Firs,* 1896, reprinted, Scholarly Press, 1974 [other editions include an edition with a preface by Willa Cather, J. Cape, 1939, reissued, Doubleday, 1965, and an edition illustrated by Shirley Burke, Norton, 1968]; *The Queen's Twin, and Other Stories,* 1899, reprinted, Books for Libraries, 1971.

Novels: *A Country Doctor,* Houghton, Mifflin, 1884, reprinted, Literature House, 1970; *A Marsh Island,* Houghton, Mifflin, 1885; *The Tory Lover,* Houghton, Mifflin, 1901, reprinted, Scholarly Press, 1974, also reprinted as *Yankee Ranger,* Norton, 1975.

Other: *Play Days* (for children), Houghton, Osgood, 1878; *The Story of the Normans* (non-fiction), Putnam, 1887; *Betty Leicester: A Story for Girls,* Houghton, Mifflin, 1890 [another edition illustrated by Beatrice Stevens, Houghton, Mifflin, 1929]; *Betty Leicester's Christmas* (for children), Houghton, Mifflin, 1899.

Collections and selections: *Stories and Tales,* seven volumes, Houghton, Mifflin, 1910; *Letters of Sarah Orne Jewett* (edited by Annie Fields), Houghton, Mifflin, 1911; *The Best Stories of Sarah Orne Jewett,* two volumes (edited by Willa Cather), Houghton, Mifflin, 1925, reissued, P. Smith, 1965; *Lady Ferry* (first published in 1879 in *Old Friends and New*), Colby College Press, 1950; *Letters* (edited by Richard Cary), Colby College Press, 1956, enlarged and revised edition, 1967; *The World of Dunnet Landing: A Sarah Orne Jewett Collection* (edited by David B. Green), University of Nebraska Press, 1962, reissued, P. Smith, 1972; *The Uncollected Short Stories of Sarah Orne Jewett* (edited by R. Cary), Colby College Press, 1971.

ADAPTATIONS—Movies: "An Only Son," Realm Television Productions, 1949.

SIDELIGHTS: **September 3, 1849.** Born in South Berwick, Maine. "I have had to go to Exeter several times lately, where I always find my childhood going on as if I had never grown up at all, with my grand-aunts and their old houses and their elm trees and their unbroken china plates and big jars by the fireplaces. And I go by the house where I went to school, aged eight, in a summer that I spent with my grandmother, and feel as if I could go and play in the sandy garden with little dry bits of elm-twigs stuck in painstaking rows. There are electric cars in Exeter now, but they can't make the least difference to me.

The good woman suspected that her granddaughter loitered occasionally on her own account; there never was such a child for straying about out-of-doors since the world was made! ■ (From *A White Heron* by Sarah Orne Jewett. Illustrated by Barbara Cooney.)

(From the movie "The White Heron," produced by Learning Corporation of America.)

"People do not know what they lose when they make away with the reserve, the separateness, the sanctity of the front yard of their grandmothers. It is like writing down the family secrets for any one to read; it is like having everybody call you by your first name and sitting in any pew in church, and like having your house in the middle of a road, to take away the fence which, slight as it may be, is a fortification round your home. More things than one may come in without being asked; we Americans had better build more fences than take any away from our lives." [Francis Otto Matthiessen, *Sarah Orne Jewett,* Peter Smith, 1965.[1]]

She was determined to record the life of the dwindling farms and deserted, shipless harbors of her state. "Nobody has mourned more than I over the forsaken farmhouses which I see everywhere as I drive about the country out of which I grew, and where every bush and tree seem like my cousins. The woods I loved best had all been cut down the winter before. I had played under the great pines when I was a child, and I had spent many a long afternoon under them since. There never will be such trees for me any more in the world. I knew where the flowers grew under them, and where the ferns were greenest, and it was as much home to me as my own house. They grew on the side of a hill, and the sun always shone through the top of the trees as it went down, while below it was all in shadow."[1]

Jewett lived a quiet and happy childhood traveling about the countryside with her country doctor father. She knew his papers, his books, his medicines almost as thoroughly as if she were a doctor herself. Not a corner of his mind or work was foreign to her. "I look upon that generation as the one to which I really belong—I who was brought up with grandfathers and grand-uncles and aunts for my best playmates. They were not the wine one can get for so much the dozen now."[1]

At about age fourteen she began writing down her thoughts, first in the form of rhymes. Then she began telling herself stories which had very fancy titles, such as "The Girl with the Cannon Dresses," and "The Shipwrecked Buttons." She took the bold step of sending them to a children's magazine, *Our Young Folks* or *The Riverside,* but under the assumed name of Alice Eliot. Horace Scudder, the editor of *The Riverside* accepted "The Shipwrecked Buttons."

December, 1869. At the age of twenty, Jewett's story, "Mr. Bruce," appeared in the *Atlantic Monthly.* "I wrote it in two evenings after ten when I was supposed to be in bed and sound asleep, and I copied it in part of another day. That's all the work I 'laid out' on it. It was last August and I was nineteen then, but now I'm twenty.... Do you remember in 'Mr. Bruce,' I made 'Elly' say that like Miss Alcott's 'Jo' she had the habit of 'falling into a vortex'? That's myself, but I mean to be more sensible.... I'm not a bit grown up if I am twenty, and I like my children's books just as well as ever I did, and I read them just the same.... It's a dreadful thing to have been born lazy.... For I might write ever so much; it's very easy for me, and when I have been so successful in what I have written, I ought to study—which I never did in my life hardly, except reading. And I ought to try harder and perhaps by and by I shall know something and can write really well."[1]

October 17, 1871. "I have been writing some children's stories for the *Independent,* and the state of my mind is shadowed forth in the last one, 'Half-done Polly,' which is severely moral. I dare say you will not be able to account

Sarah Orne Jewett, at the age of eight.

for my telling you this, but I suppose it is another illustration of your 'pleasures of autobiography so dear to all of us'—I don't know if I quoted it right, but it made a great impression upon me.... I have grown very ambitious of late and wonder continually if by any possibility I shall write so charmingly by and by. I am diverting myself at present by reading Froude's *History,* but I find myself planning my 'fall campaigns' in the midst of important acts of Parliament and it goes off slowly!"[1]

1873. Had a second story, 'The Shore House,' accepted by the *Atlantic,* four years after 'Mr. Bruce' had appeared in that same magazine. The young writer found her life and her writing opposing each other. "I wish I grew in three or four smooth useful branches instead of starting out here, there and everywhere, and doing nothing of any account at any point. I seem to have so many irons in the fire and I grow worried when I think of it.... It's hard for me to know what to do: ... I have nothing to do with the housekeeping or anything of that kind, but there are bits of work waiting all the time that use up my days. I hate not to do them and I'm afraid of being selfish and shirking—and yet—well, I'll not talk any more about that, but let it wait.

"I am getting quite ambitious and really feel that writing is my work—my business, perhaps; and it is so much better than making a mere amusement of it as I used.... I am really trying to be very much in earnest and to do the best I can.... I have had nothing to complain of, for the editors have never proved to be dragons, and I even find I have achieved a small reputation already. I am glad to have something to do in the world and something which may prove very helpful and useful if I care to make it so, which I certainly do. But I am disposed to longwindedness!"[1]

Sarah Orne Jewett, the author of *Deephaven*.

July 13, 1873. Jewett considered her writing "impulsive" and strove to perfect her ability. "I know I must need [criticism] very much and I realize the disadvantages of never hearing anything about my stories except from my friends, who do not write themselves, and are not unexceptional authorities upon any strictly literary question. . . . I wish to gain as fast as possible and I must know definitely what to do. . . . I think my chief fault is my being too young and knowing so little! . . . Those first stories of mine were written with as little thought and care as one could possibly give to them at all. Lately I have chosen my words and revised as well as I know how: though I always write impulsively—very fast and without much plan. And strange to say this same fault shows itself in my paintings, for the more I worked over pictures the stiffer and more hopeless they grew. I have one or two little marine views I scratched off to use up paint and they are bright and real and have an individuality—just as the 'Cannon Dresses' did. That is the dearest and best thing I ever have written. 'The Shore House' . . . reminds me of it and comes next. I wrote it in the same way and I think it has the same reality.

"But I don't believe I could write a long story. . . . In the first place I have no dramatic talent. The story would have no plot. I should have to fill it out with descriptions of character and meditations. It seems to me I can furnish the theatre, and show . . . the actors, and the scenery, and the audience, but there never is any play! I could write you entertaining letters perhaps from some desirable house where I was in the most charming company, but I couldn't make a story about it. I seem to get very much bewildered when I try to make these come in for secondary parts. And what shall be done with such a girl? For I wish to keep on writing, and to do the very best I can. It is rather discouraging to find I lose my best manner by studying hard and growing older and wiser. Copying one's self has usually proved disastrous. Shall not I let myself alone and not try definitely for this trick of speech or that, and hope that I shall grow into a sufficient respectability as the years go on?

"I do not know how much real talent I have as yet, how much there is in me to be relied upon as original and effective in writing. I am certain I could not write one of the usual magazine stories. If the editors will take the sketchy kind and people like to read them, is not it as well to do that and do it successfully as to make hopeless efforts to achieve something in another line which runs higher? . . . It is not a bread and butter affair with me, though such a spendthrift as I could not fail to be glad of money, which has in most instances been lightly earned. I don't wish to ignore such a great gift as this God has given me. I have not the slightest conceit on the account of it. Indeed I believe it frightens me more than it pleases me."[1]

Spring, 1877. *Deephaven,* a collection of thirteen stories, published. The dedication read: "I dedicate this story of out-of-door life and country people first to my father and mother, my two best friends, and also to all my other friends, whose names I say to myself lovingly, though I do not write them here."[1]

The book sold well and established her reputation and for the next twenty years she published in the best monthlies.

1878. "My dear father died suddenly yesterday at the mountains. It is an awful blow to me. I know you will ask God to help me bear it. I don't know how I can live without him. It is so hard for us."[1]

1879. *Old Friends and New,* another collection of sketches, published. Jewett was very fortunate at this particular period of her life to make acquaintance with Mrs. Annie Fields, the wife of one of the leading editors of the day. They often travelled together and shared enriching relationships with many literary figures.

She was becoming consciously aware of the writing process itself. "You will be amused to hear that the funny old man in the linen duster whom I caught sight of at Chapel Station has really been the making of the 'Atlantic' sketch. I mean to bring him this morning and get well on with him before the girls come. His name is Mr. Teaby, and he is one of those persons who peddle essences and perfumery and a household remedy or two, and foot it about the country with limp enameled cloth bags. What do you think of Mr. Teaby now? Teaby is the name, and he talks with sister Pinkham about personal and civic matters on a depot platform in the rural districts. Don't you think an editor would feel encouraged?"[1]

1882. Left with Mrs. Fields for a long trip to Europe. By far the most impressive event for Jewett was the visit paid to Tennyson. "No two men I have ever seen came up to Grant and Tennyson in GREATNESS. Tennyson, first, I must say that."[1]

1884. *A Country Doctor,* a novel, published.

1886. *A White Heron, and Other Stories,* dedicated to "my dear sister Mary,"[1] published.

1890. One of Jewett's friends whom she admired greatly was Thomas Bailey Aldrich, an editor of *The Atlantic* and successful writer. "I do long to say when I see [Aldrich] in what reverence and admiration I hold [his] great gift and genius of verse. It shines like a star in this world of writers where people go running about with poor candles and lamps with pretty shades. . . . I read [his] poems a great deal and I never take them up without new admiration and a joy at thinking that there will be more to come, and that here is this most beautiful possession new and shining in my hand. . . . I wish that I could tell [him] what a constant pleasure it is to have [him] for my friend and playmate, or how grateful I am for all the help [he has] given me about my work. . . ."

1896. *The Country of the Pointed Firs* published. ". . . When *The Pointed Firs* was printed the few survivors who still said that one had never done anything so good as *Deephaven,* did venture to speak of that!"[1]

September 3, 1897. At forty-eight, on the anniversary of her birth, Jewett exclaimed, "This is my birthday, and I am nine years old."[1] In the same year, her younger sister, Caroline Eastman, died, to whom she had dedicated *The Native of Winby and Other Tales* with the following words: "To my dear younger sister: I have had many pleasures that were doubled because you shared them, and so I write your name at the beginning of this book."[1]

1901. *The Tory Lover* published. "*The Tory Lover* got itself done at last. . . . I grow very melancholy if I fall to thinking of the distance between my poor story and the first dreams of it, but I believe that I have done it just as well as I could."[1]

Summer, 1901. Bowdoin College awarded Jewett the first Litt. D. it had ever bestowed upon a woman. "You can't think how nice it was to be the single sister of so many brothers at Bowdoin, walking in the procession in cap and gown and Doctor's hood, and being fetched by a marshal to the President, to sit on the platform with the Board of Overseers and the Trustees, also the Chief Justice and all the Judges of the Supreme Court, who were in session in Portland, or somewhere near by! And being welcomed by the President in a set speech as the only daughter of Bowdoin, and rising humbly to make the best bow she could. And what was most touching was the old chaplain of the day who spoke about father in his 'bidding prayer,' and said those things of him which were all true. And your SOJ applauded twice by so great an audience! . . ."[1]

That same summer, Jewett was seriously injured when a carriage she was riding in lurched forward unexpectedly and she was thrown out, receiving a dangerous head and spine injury. She suffered a complete loss of balance and was unable to move for weeks. "Perhaps you haven't heard what bad days I have fallen upon—or rather that I fell upon too hard a road the first of last month. I was thrown out of a high wagon and hurt my head a good deal and concussioned my spine, so that I am still not very well mended, and have to stay in bed or lie down nearly all the time. . . . After all these weeks I am still in my room. The trouble was that I came down on my head, and there is apparently

SARAH ORNE JEWETT

some far greater offense in *half* breaking one's neck than in breaking it altogether."[1]

Spring, 1908. Jewett never recovered from her spinal injury and remained an invalid until her death. "Perhaps some day now, in the right place and with the right quietness, I shall find myself beginning all over again; but it will be a timid young author enough! We do have our long years' use of that tool, the pen, to fall back upon, and that must count for something—the wonder and uncertainty is about a 'living spring,' as country people would say, to come out of the hillside with proper water for ink."[1]

Summer, 1908. Too ill to write for any length of time, Jewett ruefully had to take to crocheting. "No story yet, but I do not despair; I begin to dare to think that if I could get a quiet week or two, I could get something done. . . ."[1]

Winter, 1909. That whole winter long she was sustained by an eager interchange of thoughts with all her friends. "To work in silence and with all one's heart, that is the writer's lot; he is the only artist who must be a solitary, and yet needs the widest outlook upon the world."[1]

June 24, 1909. Died in South Berwick, Maine. "I was born here and I hope to die here, leaving the lilac bushes still growing and growing, and all the chairs in their places."[1]

Henry James spoke of her accomplishments in the *Atlantic* after her death. "Her admirable gift, that artistic sensibility in her which rivaled the rare personal, that sense for the finest kind of truthful rendering, the sober and tender note,

(From a short story by Sarah Orne Jewett. Illustrated by Reginald Birch for *St. Nicholas Magazine*, December, 1895.)

the temperately touched, whether in the ironic or the pathetic, would have deserved some more pointed commemoration than I judge her beautiful little quantum of achievement, her free and high, yet all so generously subdued character, a sort of elegance of humility or fine flame of modesty, with her remarkably distinguished outward stamp, to have called forth before the premature and over-darkened close of her young course of production.''[1]

FOR MORE INFORMATION SEE: Francis O. Matthiessen, *Sarah Orne Jewett,* P. Smith, 1929; Carl J. Weber, "Sarah Orne Jewett's First Story," *New England Quarterly,* March, 1946; Weber, "New England through French Eyes Fifty Years Ago," *New England Quarterly,* September, 1947; Clara Weber and C. J. Weber, compilers, *Bibliography of the Published Writings of Sarah Orne Jewett,* Colby College Press, 1949; J. A. Parker, "Sarah Orne Jewett's Boat Song," *American Literature,* March, 1951; Mark A. D. Howe, *Who Lived Here?,* Little, Brown, 1952; Alexander M. Buchan, *Our Dear Sarah: An Essay on Sarah Orne Jewett,* Washington University Press, 1953; F. Bishop, "Henry James Criticizes 'The Tory Lover,'" *American Literature,* May, 1955; E. M. Smith, "Literary Relationship of Sarah Orne Jewett and Willa Sibert Cather," *New England Quarterly,* December, 1956; Richard Cary, editor, *Letters,* Colby College Press, 1956, enlarged and revised edition, 1967; Frank N. Magill, editor, *Cyclopedia of World Authors,* Harper, 1958; R. Cary, *Sarah Orne Jewett,* Twayne, 1962; Louis Auchincloss, *Pioneers and Caretakers,* University of Minnesota Press, 1965;

Margaret Thorp, *Sarah Orne Jewett,* University of Minnesota Press, 1966; (for children) Laura Benét, *Famous New England Authors,* Dodd, 1970; R. Cary, editor, *An Appreciation of Sarah Orne Jewett: Twenty-Nine Interpretative Essays,* Colby College Press, 1973.

JORDAN, Hope (Dahle) 1905-

PERSONAL: Born December 9, 1905, in Mt. Horeb, Wis.; daughter of Otto Bjorn (a merchant) and Bertha (Locke) Dahle; married Claude D. Jordan (a recreational therapist); children: David, Hope (Mrs. Richard Kellman). *Education:* University of Wisconsin, Madison, B.A., 1928; also attended Columbia University, 1930, and the University of Michigan, 1938. *Home:* 625 Kurtis Dr., Elm Grove, Wis. 53122.

CAREER: General Outdoor Advertising Co., New York, N.Y., public relations, 1928-31; writer, 1933—. *Member:* Society of Children's Book Writers, Council for Wisconsin Writers, Fictioneers. *Awards, honors:* Awards from Council for Wisconsin Writers, 1968, for *Haunted Summer,* and 1970, for *Supermarket Sleuth.*

*WRITINGS—*For young people: *Take Me to My Friend,* Lothrop, 1962, reprinted as *Three Dangerous Days,* Scholastic Book Services, 1964; *Haunted Summer,* Lothrop, 1967; *Talk About the Tarchers,* Lothrop, 1968; *Supermarket Sleuth,* Lothrop, 1969; *The Fortune Cake,* Lothrop, 1972,

HOPE JORDAN

reprinted as *Danger at Loud Lake,* Archway, 1974; *Stranger in Their Midst,* Lothrop, 1974. Contributor to popular adult and juvenile magazines, including *Ladies' Home Journal, Seventeen, Reader's Digest, Ingenue,* and *Collier's.*

SIDELIGHTS: "Like most authors, it's easy for me to write about my characters, but so, so difficult to write about myself.

"I was raised in a small Wisconsin town, Mt. Horeb, under ideal conditions, I realize now. Wonderful parents, and grandparents in the home next door—both houses having large libraries crammed with books. My father provided a tennis court, swings, skis, skates, golf clubs, saxophones, drums, piano, typewriter, and every year there was a new 'hired girl' from Norway to help my mother while learning English and finding a husband.

"For me, this meant time to read and read. However, I never meant to write novels. I majored in advertising, went to New York to have a great career, and absolutely loathed the city and was bored by the career.

"It was in my office on Park Avenue that I began writing short stories. Because of my husband's business, we transferred to a number of cities, and this kept me at writing despite discouragements, because I was forever a stranger where we lived, and it was simpler to make friends at the typewriter than in real life.

"My first novel was begun as a short story for *Seventeen* during a heavy Wisconsin snowstorm. It kept snowing, and I

kept writing—and six weeks later I had my novel ready to market. Not even my husband knew I'd written a book until after I'd sold it.

"I thoroughly enjoy writing for young people. It pleases me that they think I'm about sixteen and am writing a true experience (even my first editor thought that)."

HOBBIES AND OTHER INTERESTS: Golf, swimming, hiking, knitting, crocheting, embroidery, travel (especially London).

KALER, James Otis 1848-1912
(James Otis)

PERSONAL: Born March 19, 1848, in Frankfort (now Winterport), Maine; died December 11, 1912, in Portland, Maine; son of a leading hotel man; married Amy L. Scammon, March 1, 1898; children: Stephen, Otis. *Education:* Attended public schools in Maine. *Home:* Portland, Maine.

CAREER: Journalist and author of stories for children; as a teenager began work on the *Boston Journal;* later worked for various newspapers in New York; wrote sermons for a publishing house in Philadelphia; member of the editorial staff of Frank Leslie's *Boys and Girls;* worked for a time as a publicity man for a circus; became superintendent of schools of South Portland, Maine, about 1898.

WRITINGS—"Toby Tyler" series: *Toby Tyler; or, Ten Weeks with a Circus,* Harper, 1881, new edition (illustrated by George Wilson), Grosset, 1967 [other editions illustrated by W. A. Rogers, Harper, 1920; Richard H. Rodgers, Har-

(From *Toby Tyler or Ten Weeks with a Circus* by James Otis Kaler. Illustrated by William A. Rogers.)

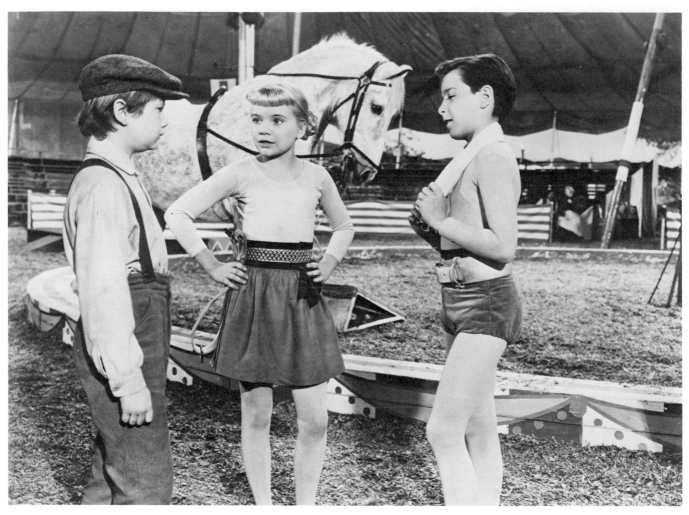

(From the movie "Toby Tyler," starring Kevin Corcoran. Produced by Walt Disney Productions, 1960.)

per, 1930; Everett Shinn, J. C. Winston, 1937; William P. Couse, Saalfield, 1938; Leonard Weisgard, Junior Deluxe Edition, 1958]; *Mr. Stubb's Brother: A Sequel to Toby Tyler* (illustrated by W. A. Rogers), Harper, 1883; *Old Ben, the Friend of Toby Tyler and Mr. Stubbs' Brother* (illustrated by Sarah Noble-Ives), Harper, 1911.

"Stories of American History" series: *The Boys of 1745 at the Capture of Louisbourg*, Estes & Lauriat, 1895; *Ezra Jordan's Escape from the Massacre at Fort Loyall*, Estes & Lauriat, 1895; *An Island Refuge: Casco Bay in 1676*, Estes & Lauriat, 1895; *Neal, the Miller, a Son of Liberty*, Estes & Lauriat, 1895; *Under the Liberty Tree: A Story of the Boston Massacre*, Estes & Lauriat, 1896; *The Signal Boys of '75: A Tale of Boston during the Siege*, Estes & Lauriat, 1897; *When Israel Putnam Served the King*, Estes & Lauriat, 1898; *Off Santiago with Sampson*, D. Estes, 1899; *When Dewey Came to Manila; or, Among the Filipinos*, D. Estes, 1899; *Boston Boys of 1775; or, When We Besieged Boston*, D. Estes, 1900; *When We Destroyed the Gaspee: A Story of Narragansett Bay in 1772*, D. Estes, 1901; *Defending the Island: A Story of Bar Harbor in 1758*, D. Estes, 1904.

"Continental" series; all published by A. L. Burt: *With Lafayette at Yorktown: A Story of How Two Boys Joined the Continental Army*, 1895; *With Washington at Monmouth: A Story of Three Philadelphia Boys*, 1897; *The Capture of the Laughing Mary: A Story of Three New York Boys in 1776* (illustrated by J. Watson Davis), 1898; *With Warren at Bunker Hill: A Story of the Siege of Boston* (illustrated by J. W. Davis), 1898; *At the Siege of Havana: The Experience of Three Boys Serving under Israel Putnam in 1762*, 1899; *The Defense of Fort Henry: A Story of Wheeling Creek in 1777* (illustrated by J. W. Davis), 1900; *Amos Dunkel, Oarsman: A Story of the Whale Boat Navy of 1776* (illustrated by J. W. Davis), 1901.

"Young Patriot" series; all illustrated by J. W. Davis and published by A. L. Burt, except as noted: *A Cruise with Paul Jones: A Story of Naval Warfare in 1778*, 1898; *A Traitor's Escape: A Story of the Attempt to Seize Benedict Arnold after He Had Fled to New York*, 1898, new edition (illustrated by G. G. White), 1899; *Corporal 'Lige's Recruit: A Story of Crown Point and Ticonderoga*, 1898; *Morgan, the Jersey Spy: A Story of the Siege of Yorktown in 1781*, 1898; *Sarah Dillard's Ride: A Story of the Carolinas in 1780*, 1898; *A Tory Plot: A Story of the Attempt to Kill General Washington in 1776*, 1899; *With the Swamp Fox: A Story of General Marion's Young Spies*, 1899; *On the Kentucky Frontier*, 1900; *With the Regulators: A Story of North Carolina in 1768*, 1901; *Across the Delaware: A Boy's Story of the Battle of Trenton in 1777*, 1903; *At the Siege of Detroit: A Story of Two Ohio Boys in the War of 1812*, 1904; *When Washington Served the King: A Boy's Story of Border Warfare in 1754*, 1905.

"Minute Boys" series; all published by D. Estes: *The Minute Boys of the Green Mountains* (illustrated by A. Burnham Shute), 1904; *The Minute Boys of the Mohawk Valley* (illustrated by Shute), 1905; *The Minute Boys of the Wyoming Valley* (illustrated by Shute), 1906; *The Minute Boys of South Carolina: A Story of "How We Boys Aided Marion, the Swamp Fox"* (illustrated by J.W.F. Kennedy), 1907; *The Minute Boys of Long Island: A Story of New York in 1776* (illustrated by L. J. Bridgman), 1908; *The Minute Boys of New York City* (illustrated by Bridgman), 1909; *The Minute Boys of Boston* (illustrated by Bridgman), 1910; *The Minute Boys of Philadelphia* (illustrated by Bridgman), 1911; *The Minute Boys of York Town* (illustrated by Bridgman), 1912.

"Home Life of the Colonists" series; all published by American Book Co., 1910: *Calvert of Maryland: A Story of Lord Baltimore's Colony; Mary of Plymouth: A Story of the Pilgrim Settlement; Peter of New Amsterdam: A Story of Old New York; Richard of Jamestown: A Story of the Virginia Colony; Ruth of Boston: A Story of the Massachusetts Bay Colony; Stephen of Philadelphia: A Story of Penn's Colony.*

"Pioneer" series; all published by American Book Co.: *Antoine of Oregon: A Story of the Oregon Trail*, 1912; *Benjamin of Ohio: A Story of the Settlement of Marietta*, 1912; *Hannah of Kentucky: A Story of the Wilderness Road*, 1912; *Seth of Colorado: A Story of the Settlement of Denver*, 1912; *Martha of California: A Story of the California Trail*, 1913; *Philip of Texas: A Story of Sheep Raising in Texas*, 1913.

Other tales from history: *The Boys of '98* (illustrated by J. Steeple Davis and Frank T. Merrill), D. Estes, 1898; *The Charming Sally, Privateer Schooner of New York: A Tale of 1765*, Houghton, 1898; *Captain Tom, the Privateersman of the Armed Brig Chasseur* (illustrated by J. W. Kennedy), D. Estes, 1899; *With Perry on Lake Erie: A Tale of 1812* (illustrated by William F. Stecher), W. A. Wilde, 1899; *The Armed Ship America; or, When We Sailed from Salem* (illustrated by J. W. Kennedy), D. Estes, 1900; *Fighting for the Empire: The Story of the War in South Africa* (illustrated by F. T. Merrill), D. Estes, 1900; (editor) *The Life of John Paul Jones*, A. L. Burt, 1900; *With Preble at Tripoli: A Story of "Old Ironsides" and the Tripolitan War* (illustrated by W. F. Stecher), W. A. Wilde, 1900.

Our Uncle, the Major: A Story of New York in 1765, Crowell, 1901; *With Porter in the Essex: A Story of His Famous Cruise in Southern Waters during the War of 1812* (illustrated by W. F. Stecher), W. A. Wilde, 1901; *The Story of Old Falmouth*, Crowell, 1901; *The Cruise of the Enterprise: Being a Story of the Struggle and Defeat of the French Privateering Expeditions against the United States in 1779* (illustrated by W. F. Stecher), W. A. Wilde, 1902; *How the Twins Captured a Hessian: A Story of Long Island in 1776*, Crowell, 1902; *The Story of Pemaquid*, Crowell, 1902; *With Rodgers on the President* (illustrated by E. Tailok), W. A. Wilde, 1903; *Dorothy's Spy: A Story of the First Fourth of July Celebration*, Crowell, 1904.

Commodore Barney's Young Spies: A Boy's Story of the Burning of the City of Washington (illustrated by J. W. Davis), A. L. Burt, 1907; *Afloat in Freedom's Cause: The*

(From a story by James Otis Kaler. Illustrated by W.A. Rogers for *St. Nicholas Magazine*, December, 1895.)

Ben held the oars while Jake poised the spear for a cast. ■ (From *The Castaways* by James Otis.)

Story of Two Boys in the War of 1812 (illustrated by J. W. Davis), A. L. Burt, 1908; *The Cruise of the Pickering: A Boy's Story of Privateering in 1780* (illustrated by Davis), A. L. Burt, 1909; *A Struggle for Freedom: The Story of Young Amos Dunkel, Oarsman in the Whale Boat Navy* (illustrated by Davis), A. L. Burt, 1909; *With Grant at Vicksburg: A Boy's Story of the Siege of Vicksburg* (illustrated by Davis), A. L. Burt, 1910; *With Sherman to the Sea: A Boy's Story of General Sherman's Famous March and Capture of Savannah* (illustrated by Davis), A. L. Burt, 1911; *True Adventure Tales from American History in the Stirring Days of the Revolution*, L. C. Page, 1924.

Other writings: *Tim and Tip; or, The Adventures of a Boy and a Dog* (illustrated by W. A. Rogers), Harper, 1883; *Raising the "Pearl,"* Harper, 1884; *Left Behind; or, Ten Days a Newsboy*, Harper, 1885; *Silent Pete; or, The Stowaways*, Harper, 1886; *A Runaway Brig; or, An Accidental Cruise*, A. L. Burt, 1888; *The Castaways; or, On the Florida Reefs*, A. L. Burt, 1888; *Little Joe*, Lothrop, 1888; *The Braganza Diamond*, Penn, 1891; *Jack the Hunchback*, Bradley & Woodruff, 1892; *Jenny Wren's Boarding House: A Story of Newsboy Life in New York* (illustrated by W. A. Rogers), Estes & Lauriat, 1893; *Josiah in New York; or, A*

Coupon from the Fresh Air Fund, A. I. Bradley, 1893; *The Search for the Silver City: A Tale of Adventure in Yucatan*, A. L. Burt, 1893; *The Boys' Revolt: A Story of the Street Arabs of New York* (illustrated by W. P. Hooper), Estes & Lauriat, 1894; *Chasing a Yacht; or, The Theft of the "Gem,"* Penn, 1894.

Jerry's Family: A Story of a Street Waif of New York (illustrated by George Foster Barnes), Estes & Lauriat, 1895; *Andy's Ward; or, The International Museum*, Penn, 1895; *How Tommy Saved the Barn*, Crowell, 1895; *Teddy and Carrots, Two Merchants of Newspaper Row* (illustrated by W. A. Rogers), Estes & Lauriat, 1896; *Admiral J. of Spurwink*, A. I. Bradley, 1896; *The Boy Captain; or, From Forecastle to Cabin*, Estes & Lauriat, 1896; *On Schedule Time*, T. Whittaker, 1896; *A Short Cruise*, Crowell, 1896; *At the Siege of Quebec* (illustrated by F. A. Carter), Penn, 1897; *The Wreck of the Circus*, Crowell, 1897; *An Amateur Fireman*, Dutton, 1898; *A District Messenger Boy and A Necktie Party*, Lothrop, 1898; *Dick in the Desert*, Crowell, 1898; *Joel Harford*, Crowell, 1898; *The Princess and Joe Potter* (illustrated by V. Oakley), Estes & Lauriat, 1898.

Chased through Norway; or, Two Million Dollars Missing, Street & Smith, 1899; *Christmas at Deacon Hacketts: A Sequel to "How Tommy Saved the Barn,"* Crowell, 1899; *Down the Slope*, Werner, 1899; *Messenger No. 48*, Werner, 1899; *Wheeling for Fortune*, Street & Smith, 1899; *Aunt Hannah and Seth*, Crowell, 1900; *Lobster Catchers: A Story of the Coast of Maine*, Dutton, 1900; *Inland Waterways; or, The Cruise of the Restless*, Street & Smith, 1901; *Larry Hudson's Ambition* (illustrated by E. Keen), L. C. Page, 1901; *Reuben Green's Adventures at Yale*, Street & Smith, 1902; *The Treasure of Cocos Island: A Story of the Indian Ocean* (illustrated by J. W. Davis), A. L. Burt, 1902; *Wan Lun and Dandy: The Story of a Chinese Boy and a Dog* (illustrated by Davis), A. L. Burt, 1902; *With the Treasure-Hunters: A Story of the Florida Cays*, Lippin-

(Illustration by W.A. Rogers from *St. Nicholas Magazine*, December, 1895.)

cott, 1903; *Among the Fur Traders* (illustrated by F. T. Merrill), Crowell, 1906; *The Light Keepers: A Story of the United States Lighthouse Service,* Dutton, 1906.

The Wreck of the "Ocean Queen": A Story of the Sea (illustrated by A. O. Scott), L. C. Page, 1907; *Aboard the Hylow on Sable Island Bank,* Dutton, 1907; *The Cruise of the Phoebe: A Story of Lobster Buying on the Eastern Coast* (illustrated by J.W.F. Kennedy), D. Estes, 1908; *Two Stowaways aboard the Ellen Maria,* Crowell, 1908; *Found by the Circus,* Crowell, 1909; *The Sarah Jane, Dicky Dalton, Captain: A Story of Tugboating in Portland Harbor* (illustrated by J.W.F. Kennedy), D. Estes, 1909; *The Cruise of the Sally D.* (illustrated by Hugh A. Bodine), Penn, 1910; *The Wireless Station at Silver Fox Farm* (illustrated by Copeland), Crowell, 1910; *The Camp on Indian Island,* Penn, 1911.

The Aeroplane at Silver Fox Farm (illustrated by Copeland), Crowell, 1911; *Boy Scouts in the Maine Woods* (illustrated by Copeland), Crowell, 1911; *Building an Airship at Silver Fox Farm* (illustrated by Copeland), Crowell, 1912; *"Wanted," and Other Stories,* Harper, 1912; *The Wreck of the Princess* (illustrated by H. A. Bodine), Penn, 1912; *Airship Cruising from Silver Fox Farm* (illustrated by Copeland), Crowell, 1913; *Boy Scouts in a Lumber Camp* (illustrated by Copeland), Crowell, 1913; *The Roaring Lions; or, The Famous Club of Ashbury,* Harper, 1913; *Across the Range, and Other Stories,* Harper, 1914.

Contributor to various periodicals, including *Harper's Young People* and *St. Nicholas.*

ADAPTATIONS—Movies and filmstrips: "Circus Days" (motion picture), adaptation of *Toby Tyler,* Sol Lesser, 1923; "Toby Tyler; or, Ten Weeks with a Circus" (motion picture), Walt Disney Productions, 1959; "Toby Tyler with the Circus" (filmstrip), adaptation of *Toby Tyler,* Encyclopaedia Britannica Films, 1961.

Plays: Richard Young, *Toby Tyler; or, Ten Weeks with a Circus* (three-act), Samuel French, 1941.

FOR MORE INFORMATION SEE: Stanly J. Kunitz and Howard Haycraft, editors, *Junior Book of Authors,* Wilson, 2nd edition, 1951.

KAUFMANN, Angelika   1935-

PERSONAL: Born March 9, 1935, in St. Ruprecht, Austria; daughter of Wilhelm (a farmer) and Irmgard (Schabuss) Kaufmann. *Education:* Academie of Applied Art, Vienna, Austria, diploma, 1958; attended Academie of Fine Art, Cracow, Poland, 1964-65. *Home:* Feldgasse 12/2/23, Vienna, Austria A-1080.

CAREER: Children's author and illustrator. *Exhibitions:* Biennale Der Illustrationen, Bratislava, 1973, 1975, 1977; Kinderbuchmesse, Bologna, 1974, 1975, 1978. *Member:* "Secession Wien," "Internationale Aktionsgemeinschaft Bildender Künstlerinnen. *Awards, honors:* BIB Medal for *Ein Pferd erzählt,* 1973; *Sinclair Sofokles, der Babysaurier* received Illustration Prize of the City of Vienna; *Lollobien* received Prize of the City of Vienna, Austrian State Prize; Certificate of Honor of Hans Christian Andersen Prize for *Komm, sagte die Katze,* 1976.

ANGELIKA KAUFMANN

WRITINGS—All self-illustrated: *Das einsame Schaf* (title means "The Lonely Sheep"), Bad Goisern Neugebauer Press, 1970; *Ein Pferd erzählt* (title means "A Horse Tells"), Bad Goisern Neugebauer Press, 1971; *Verzauberte Geschöpfe* (title means "Enchanted Creatures"), Bad Goisern Neugebauer Press, 1972; *Das ist mein Fenster* (title means "This is My Window"), Bad Goisern Neugebauer Press, 1974; *Anna,* Bad Goisern Neugebauer Press, 1975.

Illustrator: Friederike Mayröcker, *Sinclair Sofokles, der Babysaurier,* Wien Jugend & Volk, 1971, published in America as *Sinclair Sophocles: The Baby Dinosaur,* Random House, 1974; Minna Lachs, *Was raschelt da im Bauernhof?* (title means "What's Rustling on the Farm?") Wien Jugend & Volk, 1973; Brigitte Peter, *Lollobien,* Wien Jungbrunnen, 1973; Mira Lobe, *Komm, sagte die Katze* (title means "Come, Said the Cat"), Wien Jugend & Volk, 1975; Mira Lobe, *Komm sagte der Esel* (title means "Come Said the Donkey"), Wien Jugend & Volk, 1976; Saburo Mutoh, *Ken and the Blue Bird,* Iwasaki Shoten (Tokyo), 1976; Christine Nöstlinger, *Lollipop,* Weinheim Beltz Verlag, 1977; Mira Lobe, *Hoppelpopp,* Dent, 1977.

SIDELIGHTS: "Born in 1935 in the southernmost part of Austria, namely in a little village near Villach, I belong to a generation whose childhood and adolescence were stamped by the war and the post-war period. My parents were farmers, I was the eldest of four children.

"At the age of three, at least I remember it, I drew a picture of my mother. An uncle gave me my first water colours, and

Rhinoceros bicornis, nachdenkend

(From a drawing by Angelika Kaufmann.)

I hoarded paper which had become a rarity during the war wherever I could. Instead of doing my home work, I often drew pictures, veritably taking shelter behind drawing in order to escape doing so many things which seemed unpleasant to me as a child.

"The year 1945 and changing schools for the first time confronted me with an environment for which I was unprepared. In 1950, I chose another school (State School for Occupations of Women) for reasons still unknown to me today. I was correspondingly unhappy there. After completing school, I was faced with the real problem of vocation. I don't remember exactly, but it was probably my drawing teacher who encouraged me to visit the Academy for Applied Art. One thing is certain—I didn't go there because I was so absolutely convinced of my artistic talents. I probably could have just as well become a nurse, sales girl or a stenotypist. I actually completed the Academy and received my diploma and had the opportunity afterwards of working for five months at the Austrian archaeological diggings in Efesos.

"After the following failed attempt as an art teacher, I thought I had found my career as an advertising artist. I earned a great deal, but in time I became conscious of the contradiction between commercial art and what was important to me. I tried to escape by fleeing into free-lance graphics. I tried to draw during every free minute in order to cre-

ate a counter-weight for myself. I was partially successful, an exhibition was planned. Later I received a grant for the Academy in Cracow and began to become interested in printed graphics. At approximately the same time my interest developed in children's book art and illustrations. I quit advertising art, found a part-time job, which I gave up a long time ago. Finally, I also met other artists who have become very important to me. I came to know Friederike Mayröcker, Ernst Jandl and others.

"I cannot deny that the original beginning of my artistic activities was an end in itself. I only believe that in recent years I have found another relationship to myself and my environment. My work has certainly changed due to this. Every now and then I am asked why I illustrate books for children and how I began to do so.

"Of course, I could just simply say because I was trained as a graphic artist. But closer consideration shows me that this answer is not complete. I also learned how to make posters and, in spite of this, I no longer make them today.

"Perhaps I must begin like this in answering this question. Once upon a time there was a child (not my own) named Elisabeth Katharina. One day I wrote and illustrated a book for this child for her birthday entitled *Der Mond für Elisabeth Katharina* (The Moon for Elizabeth Catharina). Elizabeth was three years old then, and she loved this book, which was, of course, never published.

"That was many years ago, maybe ten, at any rate. I saw then that children have no prejudices and that picture books can contribute to a child's formal and artistic development. I was suddenly possessed by the idea that I had to make better books for the children around me, the children of my friends, for all children.

"At first I tried to interest various publishers in my sketches, without success. It took years before I met a publisher who liked my books and who was prepared to print them. And that was the actual beginning.

"Of course, I have learned in the meantime that picture books can not only have a formal and aesthetic influence upon children, but also a social-critical and political one. At the same time I have seen that one should neither overestimate nor underestimate the pedagogical value of a children's book, i.e. this is only a secondary aspect of the educational process and should be considered and evaluated as such.

"In the meanwhile, all the children for whom I originally conceived my books have grown up. But luckily, there will always be more children."

FOR MORE INFORMATION SEE: Salzburger Nachrichten (Austria), December, 1972; *Das Neue Jugendbuch* (Austria), May, 1973.

HILARY KNIGHT

KNIGHT, Hilary   1926-

PERSONAL: Born November 1, 1926, in Hempstead, Long Island, N.Y.; son of Clayton (an artist and writer) and Katharine (also an artist and writer; maiden name Sturges) Knight. *Education:* Attended Art Students League, New York City. *Address:* 300 E. 51st St., New York, N.Y. 10022.

CAREER: Author, illustrator, and designer. Began art career after his drawings were published in *House and Garden* and *Mademoiselle.*

WRITINGS—All self-illustrated: *ABC,* Golden Press, 1961; *Angels and Berries and Candy Canes,* Harper, 1963; *A Christmas Stocking Story,* Harper, 1963; *A Firefly in a Fir Tree,* Harper, 1963; the latter three books were published together with Clement Clarke Moore's *The Night before Christmas* as *Christmas Nutshell Library,* Harper, 1963; *Where's Wallace?,* Harper, 1964; *Sylvia, the Sloth: A Round-about Story,* Harper, 1969.

Illustrator: Kay Thompson, *Eloise,* Simon & Schuster, 1955, reissued, 1969; Patrick Gordon Campbell, *Short Trot with a Cultured Mind through Some Experiences of a Humorous Nature,* Simon & Schuster, 1956; Jan Henry, *Tiger's Chance,* Harcourt, 1957; Betty (Bard) MacDonald, *Hello, Mrs. Piggle-Wiggle,* Lippincott, 1957, reissued, 1976; B. MacDonald, *Mrs. Piggle-Wiggle,* Lippincott, 1957, reissued, 1976; B. MacDonald, *Mrs. Piggle-Wiggle's Magic,* Lippincott, 1957, reissued, 1976; K. Thompson, *Eloise in Paris,* Simon & Schuster, 1957; (from an idea by Max Hess) *Wonderful World of Aunt Tuddy,* Random House, 1958; Dorothea W. Blair, *Roger: A Most Unusual Rabbit,* Lippincott, 1958; K. Thompson, *Eloise at Christmas Time,* Random House, 1958; K. Thompson, *Eloise in Moscow,* Simon & Schuster, 1959.

Evelyn Gendel, *Tortoise and Turtle,* Simon & Schuster, 1960; Cecil Maiden, *Beginning with Mrs. McBee,* Vanguard, 1960; *Hilary Knight's Mother Goose,* Golden Press, 1962, reissued, 1973; C. Maiden, *Speaking of Mrs. McCluskie,* Vanguard, 1962; Margaret Stone Zilboorg, *Jeremiah Octopus,* Golden Press, 1962; E. Gendel, *Tortoise and Turtle Abroad,* Simon & Schuster, 1963; Marie Le Prince De Beaumont, *Beauty and the Beast,* Macmillan, 1963; Clement Clarke Moore, *The Night before Christmas,* Harper, 1963; Charles Dickens, *Captain Boldheart [and] The Magic Fishbone,* Macmillan, 1964; Ogden Nash, *The Animal Garden: A Story,* M. Evans, 1965; Charlotte Zolotow, *When I Have a Little Girl,* Harper, 1965; C. Zolotow, *When I Have a Son,* Harper, 1967; Judith Viorst, *Sunday Morning: A Story,* Harper, 1968; Margaret Fishback, *A Child's Book of Natural History,* Platt & Munk, 1969; Patricia M. Scarry, *The Jeremy Mouse Book,* American Heritage Press, 1969.

Nathaniel Benchley, *Feldman Fieldmouse: A Fable,* Harper, 1971; Duncan Emrich, editor, *The Book of Wishes and Wishmaking,* American Heritage Press, 1971; Janice Udry, *Angie,* Harper, 1971; Adelaide Holl, *Most-of-the-time Maxie: A Story,* Xerox Family Education Services, 1974; Robert Kraus, *I'm a Monkey,* Windmill Books, 1975; Marilyn Sachs, *Matt's Mitt,* Doubleday, 1975; Steven Kroll, *That Makes Me Mad!,* Pantheon, 1976; Lucille Ogle and Tina Thoburn, *The Golden Picture Dictionary: A Beginning Dictionary of More Than 2500 Words,* Western Publishing, 1976; *Six Impossible Things Before Breakfast,* A-W, 1977; *Night Light Calendar 1977,* Windmill, 1977.

SIDELIGHTS: Born on **November, 1926** in Long Island. Knight's parents were both artists. His father, Clayton Knight was an illustrator and writer primarily of aviation books and his mother, Katharine Sturges Knight, was a fashion and book illustrator. Throughout his boyhood his chief

They ate up all the broth, and washed up all the plates and dishes, and cleared away, and pushed the table into a corner, and then they in their cooks' caps, and the Princess Alicia in the smothering coarse apron that belonged to the cook that had run away with her own true love that was the tall but very tipsy soldier, danced a dance of eighteen cooks before the angelic baby, who forgot his swelled face and his black eye, and crowed with joy. ■ (From _Captain Boldheart and the Magic Fishbone_ by Charles Dickens. Pictures by Hilary Knight.)

interest was art. "As a child, I loved to look at a set of books which belonged to my mother. They were illustrated by Edmund Dulac in a romantic, wonderful, detailed manner. I know he has influenced my style." [Joan Hess Michel, "The Whimsical Illustrations of Hilary Knight," *American Artist,* March, 1963.[1]]

Knight attended the Art Students League in New York City before entering the U.S. Navy. Later he studied architectural drafting at Delehanty Institute. To aspiring young artists, Knight advised obtaining the best possible training and using the best materials.

Success in the field of illustration came swiftly and early for Knight. He and Kay Thompson collaborated on a book based on Thompson's imaginary character, *Eloise.* Thompson recalled her first impression of Knight: "A Princetonian young man, shy, gentle and soft-spoken, came in. He seemed terribly impressed with me, which naturally impressed me terribly with him. I noticed his hands, which were slim and artistic, and thought that was a step in the right direction. So I wrote twelve lines on a piece of paper and handed it to him. 'I'm going to write this book,' I said. 'I'll leave this with you. If you're interested, get in touch with me.' Then I spoke a few words of Eloisiana and left.

"That Christmas I received a card from Knight. It was an interesting, beautifully executed and highly stylized picture of an angel and Santa Claus, streaking through the sky on a Christmas tree. On the end of the tree, grinning a lovely grin, her wild hair standing on end, was Eloise. It was immediate recognition on my part. There she was. In person. I knew at once Hilary Knight had to illustrate the book." [Cynthia Lindsay, "McCall Visits Kay Thompson," *McCall's,* January, 1975.[2]]

Intially dedicated to "precocious grownups," *Eloise* became a favorite with children and adolescents as well. "There was the real struggle for me. The success of *Eloise* spoiled me a little. Perhaps I had too much too soon. my technique was not quite mature at the time of *Eloise's* publication. I believe my work has improved since that initial success."[1]

The sequels to *Eloise* afforded Knight the opportunity to visit Europe for "on location" material. Fond of travel, Knight also enjoys zoos. "Wherever I travel, I always make it a point to visit the local zoo.[1] Besides the *Eloise* series, Knight has illustrated many children's books by other authors and has self-illustrated his own books for children.

FOR MORE INFORMATION SEE: New York Herald Tribune Books, November 12, 1961; *New York Times Book Review,* November 12, 1961; J. H. Michel, "Whimsical Illustrations of Hilary Knight," *American Artist,* March, 1963; *Saturday Review,* October 17, 1964; Lee Kingman, editor, *Illustrators of Children's Books: 1957-1966,* Horn Book, 1968.

You see, the Cruel Queen sleeps in my beds every night and inspects them every morning and if *she* finds a single wrinkle, even one as big as a pin, she will have me thrown in a dungeon. ■ (From *Mrs. Piggle-Wiggle* by Betty MacDonald. Illustrated by Hilary Knight.)

KORTY, Carol 1937-

PERSONAL: Born January 4, 1937, in Albany, N.Y.; daughter of Frederick H. (a superviser of accounting departments) and H. Louise (a teacher; maiden name, Herrlich) Tweedie; married John Korty (a filmmaker), March 29, 1958 (divorced, 1964). *Education:* Antioch College, B.A., 1959; Sarah Lawrence College, M.A., 1966; studied dance with top professionals, including Merce Cunningham, Jose Limon, and Martha Graham's school. *Politics:* Socialist. *Religion:* Society of Friends (Quakers). *Home:* 15 Perkins Sq., Jamaica Plain, Boston, Mass. 02130. *Agent:* Alice Bach, 175 East 79th St., New York, N.Y. 10021. *Office:* Department of Theater, Boston University, 855 Commonwealth Ave., Boston, Mass. 02215.

CAREER: Antioch College, Yellowsprings, Ohio, teaching associate in theater and dance, 1966-67; State University of New York College at Brockport, instructor of theater, 1967-68, assistant professor of theater, 1968-71, associate professor of theater, 1971-72; University of Massachusetts, Amherst, associate professor of theater, 1972-75; Children's Museum, Boston, Mass., drama developer, 1975-76; Boston University, Boston, Mass., visiting associate professor of theater, 1977—. Children's theater evaluator for New York State Council on the Arts, 1969-72. Danced with Charles Weidman Dance Co. (solo member), 1961-62; National Co. of "My Fair Lady", 1962-63; New York City Opera, 1963; Music Fair Enterprises, 1963, Merle Marsicano Dance Co. (solo member), 1964-65, and Richard Bull Dance Co., 1970-71.

MEMBER: International Association of Theatre for Children and Young People (member of executive board), University and College Theatre Association, Children's Theatre Association of America, former member of American Guild of Musical Artists and Actors' Equity Association.

CAROL KORTY

WRITINGS—For children: *Plays from African Folktales: With Ideas for Acting, Dance, Costumes, and Music*, Scribner, 1975; *Silly Soup: Ten Zany Plays with Songs and Ideas for Making Them on Your Own*, Scribner, 1977.

Unpublished plays: "The Shape We're In" (one-act), first produced in Brockport, N.Y. at State University College, 1968-69; "Beginnings" (one-act), first produced in Brockport, N.Y. at State Univerity College, 1970-71; "Score for May Fest" (a festival score), first produced in Brockport, N.Y. at State University College, 1971; "Sometimes I'm a Ladybug and Sometimes I'm Angry" (one-act), first produced in Amherst, Mass. at University of Massachusetts, 1974; "If I Were a Kid Back Then . . ." (one-act), first produced in Boston, Mass. at the Children's Museum, 1976.

WORK IN PROGRESS: *Turning Stories into Plays*, publication expected in 1979.

SIDELIGHTS: "I certainly never intended becoming a writer. Although I read a great deal when I was growing up, when it came to choosing a career, I was too busy changing ideas to focus on any one goal. I took a long time to realize you could be interested in a subject without having to consider it your life work: florist, farmer, nurse, politician, teacher, reformer, explorer, artist, historian, anthropologist. By the time I was twenty, however, I knew I wanted to perform professionally in theater as an actress or dancer. I earned a degree in theater and moved to New York City to begin professional study. After a few exciting years of that and a couple more performing, I returned to school to study choreography. I became excited about theater again, and before I knew it, I had picked children's theater as a focus.

"Children's theater was an exciting discovery because it demanded that I use all of myself and incorporated most of the things I'd wanted to do. I got into writing simply because I couldn't find plays that dealt with issues I was interested in. I want a play to make you see yourself in the world in a new way. I also want it to address some of the really important questions of life for which there are no clear answers: questions about birth, death, love, loss, fear, wishes, dreams. I like to try making plays about these things because it helps me understand my own life more clearly. I also love the whole process of getting a play ready, or working collaboratively with other artists, and then of watching an audience enjoy what we have made."

FOR MORE INFORMATION SEE: *Horn Book*, April, 1976.

LAGERLÖF, Selma (Ottiliana Lovisa) 1858-1940

PERSONAL: Born November 20, 1858, in Maarbacka, Värmland, Sweden; died March 16, 1940, in Maarbacka, Sweden; daughter of Erik (an Army officer) and Louisa (Wallroth) Lagerlöf. *Education:* Attended the Royal Women's Superior Training College, Stockholm. *Home:* Falun and Maarbacka, Sweden.

CAREER: Novelist and story-writer. Was a schoolmistress at the Girls' High School, Landskrona, Sweden, 1885-95, and devoted the rest of her life after that to writing. *Member:* Swedish Academy (elected, 1914). *Awards, honors:* Gold Medal of the Swedish Academy, 1904; Nobel Prize for literature, 1909; Ph.D., 1911, from Upsala University. The Nils Holgersson Award (named after the character in *The Wonderful Adventures of Nils*) was first presented in 1950, and is given annually to a Swedish children's author.

WRITINGS—Novels: *Goesta Berlings Saga*, [Stockholm], 1891, translation by Lillie Tudeer published as *Goesta Berlings Saga*, Chapman & Hall, 1898 [another translation by Pauline B. Flach published as *The Story of Goesta Berling*, Little, Brown, 1898; another translation published under the same title by Robert Bly, New American Library, 1962]; *Antikrists Mirakler*, A. Bonnier, 1898, translation by P. B. Flach published as *The Miracles of Antichrist*, Little, Brown, 1899; *Jerusalem*, A. Bonnier, Volume I: *I Dalarne*, 1902, Volume II: *I det Heliga Landet*, 1903, translation of the entire work by Jessie Broechner published as *Jerusalem*, W. Heinemann, 1903, reprinted, Greenwood Press, 1970 [another translation by Velma S. Howard published as Volume I: *Jerusalem*, Doubleday, Page, 1915, Volume II: *The Holy City: Jerusalem*, Doubleday, Page, 1918]; *Liljecronas Hem*, A. Bonnier, 1911, translation by Anna Barwell published as *Liliecrona's Home*, Dutton, 1914; *Kejsarn av Portugallien*, A. Bonnier, 1914, translation by V. S. Howard published as *The Emperor of Portugallia*, Doubleday, Page, 1916; *Bandlyst*, Gyldendal, 1918, translation by William Worster published as *The Outcast*, Gyldendal, 1920; *Loewenskoeldska Ringen*, [Stockholm], 1925, translation published as *The Ring of the Loewenskoelds*, Doubleday, Doran, 1931·(contains three stories, *The General's Ring*, translated by Francesca Martin, and *Charlotte Loewenskoeld* and *Anna Svaerd*, both translated by V. S. Howard).

Tales and legends: *Osynliga Laenkar*, A. Bonnier, 1894, translation by P. B. Flach published as *Invisible Links*, Little, Brown, 1899; *En Herrgaardssaegen*, W. Heinemann, 1899, translation by J. Brochner published as *From a Swedish Homestead*, McClure, Phillips, 1901, reprinted, Books for Libraries, 1970; *Kristuslegender*, [Stockholm], 1904, translation by V. S. Howard published as *Christ Legends*, Holt, 1908; (for children) *Nils Holgersson's Underbara resa Genom Sverige*, translation by V. S. Howard published in two parts as *The Wonderful Adventures of Nils*, Grosset & Dunlap, 1907, and *Further Adventures of Nils* (illustrated by Astri Heiberg), Doubleday, Page, 1911.

Other: *Drottningar i Kungahaella*, A. Bonnier, translation by C. Field published as *The Queens of Kungahaella*, T. W. Laurie, 1917; *Herr Arne's Penningar*, [Stockholm], 1904, translation by Arthur G. Chater published as *Herr Arne's Hoard* (illustrated by Albert Edelfeldt), Gyldendal, 1923 [another translation by A. G. Chater published as *The Treasure*, Doubleday, Page, 1925, reissued, Daughters, Inc., 1973]; *En Saga om en Saga*, [Stockholm], 1908, translation by V. S. Howard published as *The Girl from the Marsh Croft*, Little, Brown, 1910; *Astrid*, Ohlinger, 1910; *Koerkarlen*, A. Bonnier, 1912, translation by William F. Harvey published as *Thy Soul Shall Bear Witness!*, Odhams Press, 1921; *The Legend of the Sacred Image* (translation from the Swedish by V. S. Howard), Holt, 1914; *Troll och Maenniskor*, [Stockholm], 1915; *Schweden*, P. A. Norstedt, 1917; *Toesen Fran Stormyrtorpet*, A. Bonnier, 1918; *Maarbacka* (autobiography), A. Bonnier, Volume I: *Maarbacka*, 1922, Volume II: *Ett Barns Memoarer*, 1930, Volume III: *Dagbok*, 1932, translations by V. S. Howard published as Volume I: *Maarbacka*, Doubleday, Page, 1924, reprinted, Gale, 1974, Volume II: *Memories of My Childhood*, Doubleday, Doran, 1934, reprinted, Kraus Reprint, 1975, Volume III: *The Diary of Selma Lagerlöf*, Doubleday, Doran, 1936, reprinted, Kraus Reprint, 1975; *Dunungen*, A. Bonnier, 1924; *Hoest*, A. Bonnier, 1933, translation by Florence and Naboth Hedin published as *Harvest*, Doubleday, Doran, 1935; *Julberaettelser* (Christmas stories), A. Bonnier, 1938.

Collections: *Skrifter*, 12 volumes, A. Bonnier, 1947-49, reissued, 1961.

ADAPTATIONS—Movies and filmstrips: "The Blizzard" (motion picture), William Fox, 1923; "The Tower of Lies" (motion picture), adaptation of *The Emperor of Portugallia*, starring Lon Chaney, Metro-Goldwyn-Mayer, 1925; "The Shepherd's Gift" (filmstrip; color, with a phonodisc and teacher's manual), adaptation of *Silent Night*, Alexark & Norsim, 1953.

SIDELIGHTS: **November 20, 1858.** Born, the fourth of five children of Lieutenant Erik Gustaf and his wife Louisa, in Värmland, Southern Sweden.

SELMA LAGERLÖF

1862. Suffered an attack of infantile paralysis, resulting in delicate health that lasted throughout most of her childhood.

1863. Grandmother passed away. "When I was five years old, I had a great sorrow, I doubt if I have ever experienced a greater since. That was the death of my grandmother. Every day until then she had sat on the corner sofa in her room and told stories. My one recollection of her is of her sitting there day after day and telling stories from morning till evening while we children had such a time. Of all these stories I have only a dim recollection, except of one about the birth of Jesus, which I remember so well I could re-tell it word for word. . . . It was a great loss when grandmother was gone. I know that something had passed out of life. It was as if the door to a wonderful magic world, in and out of which we had come and gone freely, had been locked, and there was no one now who knew how to open it. I know too, that we children gradually learnt to play like other children, and it might have looked as if we no longer missed grandmother and thought no more of her." [Walter A. Berendsohn, *Selma Lagerlöf: Her Life and Work*, Kennikat Press, 1968.[1]]

Spring, 1868. "We have a nice new governess at Maarbacka. Her name is Aline Laurell. She comes from Karlstad, where her father had been chief surveyor. Aline brought with her a little sister whose name is Emma and

(From *The Wonderful Adventures of Nils* by Selma Lagerlöf. Translated by Velma Swanston Howard.)

who is only ten years old. She is to live here, too, and study with Aline.

"The autumn Aline came to live with us I was in Stockholm attending the Orthopedic Institute. I lived with Uncle Oriel Afzelius and Aunt Georgina at number 7 Klara Strandgata. I had been away the whole winter and did not meet Aline until my return, the following spring. Glad as I was to be back again, at the same time I felt uneasy because of the new governess. For I thought that all governesses were old, and ugly, and cross.

"When I saw Aline I was surprised to find her so young and pretty. I took to her from the first. But Aline must have thought me a pert little Stockholm miss, a spoiled and affected child.

"Having been away so long, I had much to tell, and I talked on and on. I had been to the opera, I told them, and to the Royal Dramatic Theatre, and also the Theatre Intime. I had stood in Deer Park on the first day of May, and had seen King Charles XV and Queen Louise and the little princess. And I told them that Louise Thyselius, who was the prettiest young girl in Stockholm, had gone to the same institute that I had, and her I had seen every day; that the house in which Uncle Oriel lived was owned by a French duke whose name was d'Otrante.

"And all this Aline Laurell had to listen to. I daresay she thought that she could never be friends with a girl who was so conceited. . . .

"The doctor has just been here. Soon after he left, Mamma told us that Papa had inflammation of the lungs. She said that one night while Papa was away from home he had to sleep between damp sheets, which was the most dangerous thing one could do.

"I am wondering all the while what I should do so that God will let my papa live. I should like to ask Aunt Lovisa's advice about this, but I am too shy. . . . It is not anything that I, myself, have thought of; but rather as if someone had whispered into my ear what God would have me do in order that Papa may recover.

"I hesitate at first—the Book is so dreadfully thick. What if it contains only sermons and admonitions?—Well, what matter, if it saves my papa's life? Folding my hands, I make a solemn vow to God that if He spares my father's life I will read the Bible from cover to cover, and not skip a single word.

"Anyhow, I'm glad that Aunt Lovisa does not carry the Bible up to her attic storeroom and lock it away in her wardrobe. I think it was God Who ordered it left on the shelf of the yellow corner cupboard above the trapdoor to the cellar. That cupboard is never locked, and I can take the Book as often as I wish." [Selma Lagerlöf, *Memories of My Childhood,* Doubleday, 1934.[2]]

1868. The *Bible* therapy took—her father lived. "At all events, one fine day Papa received a letter from two gentlemen of Sunne, requesting the presence of himself and family at a buffet supper dance.

"The dance was to be held in the rooms over Nilsson's general store, which they were to have, rent free, for the evening. The gentlemen were to furnish the beverages and the ladies were to bring coffee, tea, and cakes, or whatever else needed for the supper. It was to be a most unpretentious affair; the only outlay would be a few riksdalers for lights and gratuities.

"The day before the dance, as we sat at the dinner table talking about the ball, Papa said: 'I think Selma is big enough now to go along with the others.'

"Papa thought I should be delighted to go to a dance; but indeed I was not. I had been to so many parties in Eäst Amtervik that I knew well enough how I would fare at the dance in Sunne! 'I don't want to go,' I promptly answered.

"I was seized with dread. I did not know of what I was afraid, but I could imagine no worse calamity than having to go to that Sunne ball!

"'My dear child,' said Papa, 'why do you cry when you are going to have a good time?'

"'But I won't have a good time,' I whimpered. 'No one will dance with me because I am lame.'

"I know that Papa hates to see us weep, and that he would be far more likely to let me off if I laughed and looked pleasant. But now I can't stop crying; the tears pour down my cheeks all through the dinner. . . .

"After the promenade polonaise Mamma and the other matrons dance no more, but they go back to the ballroom to watch the young folks dance. Once more the reception room is entirely deserted, save for me and Mamselle Eriksson. We two remain in our seats the whole evening.

"I think it is just as well that no one asks me to dance, for now Papa will know that it is the truth that nobody wants to dance with me. It is small consolation, however, for I am having a dreary time.

"I try to think of all the people who are more unfortunate than I am: the sick; the poor; the blind. Why should you grieve because you are not asked to dance at a ball? What if you were blind?

"Next morning, at the breakfast table, Mamma, Elin Laurell, Emma, and Anna tell Papa of the good time they had at the ball last night, and how well everything went off. I say nothing, for I have nothing to say. When Anna has named all with whom she had danced, Papa asks how Selma fared.

"'Selma wasn't asked to dance,' Mamma replies. 'She is too young, you know.'

"Papa sits musing a while. Then he says: 'Don't you think, Louise, that we should write to Stockholm to see if the Afzeliuses can take Selma another winter and let her attend the institute? She improved so much the last time she was there. I should like to see her well and strong before I die.'

"My eyes nearly pop out of my head. Perhaps Papa feels conscience-stricken because he made me go to the ball last night? Perhaps that is why he wants to send me to Stockholm?

"There's no one so nice as my Papa!"[2]

Easter, 1871. "In the middle of the afternoon of Easter Eve two maids always steal out of the kitchen, each with a bundle of clothing under her arm, and go down to the cow barn. They do it as secretly as possible, so that we children won't notice anything unusual. But we know, all the same, that they are going to make up an Easter witch, because Nurse Maja has told us all about it. . . .

"When the witch is ready, the maids carry her up to the house. They dare not bring her inside, however, but stop at the foot of the steps leading to the porch. They fetch a kitchen chair in which they set her down, and then run over to the brew house for the long oven rake and the broom and place them at the back of the chair; for if the witch has not the oven rake and broom with her, no one will know she is a witch. They also bind securely to her apronstrings a muddy cow horn filled with magic oil, such as witches use when they ride to *Blaakulla,* the Witches' Kitchen. In the horn they stick a long feather, and, last, they hang an old post bag round her neck.

"Then the maids go into the kitchen, and the housekeeper comes up to the nursery to tell us children that one of those horrid witches who ride on a broomstick every Easter Eve has dropped down in the yard at Maarbacka. 'She is sitting just outside the entrance,' says the housekeeper, 'and a hideous-looking creature she is! So you children had better stay in the house until she's gone.'

"But we know what is going to happen and rush past the housekeeper and down the steps to see the Easter witch. Papa of course comes with us; but Mamma and Aunt Lov-

He heard a rustle behind him. ▪ (From *The Further Adventures of Nils* by Selma Lagerlöf. Illustrated by Hans Baumhauer.)

isa say they prefer to remain inside, as they have seen so many Easter witches in their time.

"Coming out on the porch to look for the witch, we see her sitting below, glaring up at us with her coal-black eyes. We pretend to be awfully frightened, and that we think she is really and truly a witch, on her way to the Blaakulla. We know, of course, that she is only a straw witch, but we are supposed to be frightened—that is part of the play. Otherwise, the maids who have gone to the trouble of making the effigy for us would have nothing for their pains.

"When we have gazed at the Easter witch awhile from a safe distance, we creep cautiously down the steps. She holds herself rigidly erect as we approach, until at last one of us thrusts a hand into the bag. The old, discarded post bag is bulging with mail, and we keep a watchful eye on it the whole time. But the one who is the first to thrust a hand into the bag lets out a wild shriek of delight, for the bag is filled with letters. . . .

"We receive many kinds of letters. Some are mere daubs done by small children, while others are in black ink like the usual letter; but always in the middle of the page stands the Old Easter Man or the Old Easter Woman done in colours. It is evident that the grown-ups have helped the children with some of the drawings; for they are not all done equally well, but we don't care. The important thing is to get many letters so we can boast about them when we go to church on Easter Sunday and meet our cousins from Gaardsjö.''[2]

January 20, 1873. Left her home, Maarbacka, to spend the winter in Stockholm visiting relatives and receiving medical treatment for a weak leg. She began keeping a diary of her experiences: ''Elin Laurell gave me a lovely daybook for Christmas. It has a dainty white binding, a blue back and gilt edges. It is such a pretty book it seems almost a pity to write in it.

''I hardly think that I should have kept a diary had I stayed at home, as nothing ever happens in winter at Maarbacka. One day is exactly like another. But now that I'm going to Stockholm, I have put the book in my bag and am taking it with me.

''Elin Laurell says that if one is to become an author one must be thankful for every experience and glad, too, if one meets with trials that are hard to bear, for otherwise one cannot describe how it feels to be unhappy.

''I had fared so well at the home of my uncle five years ago, and the exercises at the Institute had made me well and strong. Anyhow, I am glad to have the company of Daniel [my brother] on the journey. He is going back to Upsala after the Christmas holidays. Daniel is always kind and considerate, and I think the world of him!

''I can't write any more, for when we reached Katrineholm station the student whom Daniel had met at Laaxa came into our compartment in order to have someone to chat with, and it is impossible to write while they sit beside me talking. . . .

''The student and I became the best of friends, and before long he spoke only to me. For Daniel had merely passed through Stockholm on his way to Upsala; so he did not know the city as well as I did.

''If Anna or Hilda Wallroth or Emma Laurell had been sitting here, opposite the student, they would surely have fallen in love with him, for he is so good-looking!

''I thought, too, that when I came to Stockholm it would be a slight matter for me to show Aunt and Uncle that I was neither dull nor unresponsive. All I would have to do would be to sit down and talk to them as easily and frankly as I now talked with the student. Indeed, he did not find me dull; nor did Daniel, who sat chuckling behind his book.'' [*The Diary of Selma Lagerlöf,* translated by Velma Swanston Howard, Doubleday, 1936.[3]]

January 25, 1873. ''I have found that it is no pleasure to keep a diary unless one writes the truth. I had plenty of time to write last evening, but something happened that I was ashamed to set down. I can't understand myself. I seem to have become so wild and unruly that I've lost all control of myself, which is something I have rarely done before. . . .

''One evening when [my uncle] came into the parlour he carried a small, thick book. I wondered what sort of book it could be that was so interesting as to make Uncle forget his newspaper, when he suddenly looked up at me and said:

'''This book you are not to read. Remember that!'

''I wouldn't have touched it, either, had I been my real self. Although I have many faults, I generally keep my word. . . .

''I heard footsteps in the hall; but I am so obtuse nowadays that it didn't occur to me that it might be Uncle. The next moment he was standing in the doorway while I lay reading the forbidden book! I never felt so embarrassed in my life.

''I sprang up and quickly replaced the book on the table; then I begged Uncle's pardon for being so curious to see what sort of book it was that I should not read. Uncle, however, was not so very angry at me.

'''I can understand,' he said, 'that you are the sort who cannot breathe unless you have your nose buried in a book. Hereafter I shall leave the key to my bookcase in the lock so that you may read Sir Walter Scott as much as you like, but you must let the other books alone.'

''It was very kind of Uncle, and I thanked him as graciously as I could. But just the same I feel terribly ashamed. I blush if he only looks at me. I'm afraid he must think me always disobedient, and that no one can rely on any of my promises. He does not know that I am changed and that I am no longer my real self.''[3]

January 27, 1873. ''It began yesterday, shortly after two o'clock, when I stood at the window in the dining room, looking out. Although I had been in Stockholm a whole week I marvelled at the changes that had taken place since I was here five years ago. . . .

''On the other side of the square, directly opposite the Kirstein House, lies the new Central Station. . . . Formerly, one had to drive all the way to the south end of the city to take a train. It is not only convenient to live so near the station, but it is fortunate in another way, too. If, for example, a certain student should decide to come to Stockholm some Sunday, I might catch a glimpse of him as he comes out from the railway station and crosses Centralplan.

''Not that I am in love with that student, oh no! But he was so pleasant, so good-looking, and so kind that it would be a comfort to me just to see him once more. . . .

''But whom should I see just then down on Centralplan but the very Upsala student who had been in the train with Daniel and me when we came to Stockholm! He stood looking up at Klara Strandgata, Number 7, as if he knew it was there I lived.

''Yes, it was surely he. I knew him at once! I tapped on the windowpane very lightly and nodded to him. He glanced up and recognized me instantly. He doffed his hat in greeting and then (it was lucky for me that the Chancellor's wife did not sit by one of the parlour windows), he threw me a kiss! When he did that, no words can describe how blissfully happy I was.''[3]

February 11, 1873. ''After I cross Klara Churchyard I come to a fine large building at the corner of East Klara Kyrkogata and Odingata, which I enter. For it is there that

He had never before seen wild swans at close range. ■ (From *The Wonderful Adventures of Nils* by Selma Lagerlöf. Illustrated by Hans Baumhauer.)

Professor Herman Sätherberg has his Gymnastic Orthopedic Institute.

"After that I go into the gymnasium, which is very large. There, ladders and trapezes and all kinds of gymnastic appliances hang from the walls. On the floor stand a lot of bunks with pillows, and these are the things most utilized in the forenoon by those who take remedial gymnastic treatments. But in the afternoon, I have heard, persons who are well and strong come for regular exercises; it must be then that they climb ladders and swing on trapezes.

"Last autumn when I read *Neighbors,* by Fredrika Bremer, I seemed to recognize the exercises she describes in that book. It would be wonderful if Fredrika Bremer had attended the same gymnasium that I do. But our exercises are not the same as those of her day. We are by no means so strenuous, nor do we have as much fun. We have no fraternities where the patients call each other by ancient Greek names, nor does it occur to us to challenge each other to fight duels.

"It is a pleasure, at all events, to think of Fredrika Bremer as having been here. It is as though it boded good for another who also would write novels.

"There are always many people exercising in the gymnasium. When they are all here, I think there are about a hundred going back and forth, though of course I've never counted them. All are dressed in bloomers and blouses. Some wear fine embroidered blouses, while others look as if they had jumped into a bag. There are old people and children, but the majority are nineteen or twenty years of age. Nearly all have some fault—uneven hips or a clubfoot or a stiff knee or round shoulders. Some are taking gymnastic exercises as a cure for greensickness which they contracted by too much dancing at the Stockholm balls. . . .

"My lame leg has grown stronger already, for which I'm very thankful. Some of the patients who have been exercising all winter are now perfectly well, and they say that Professor Sätherberg is a regular wonder-worker.

"I know that Professor Sätherberg is a poet and that he has written the lyrics to *Sing of the Student's Happiest Days* and *Happy as a Bird,* and that both poems were set to music by Prince Gustaf. But here in the gymnasium I never hear a soul mention our Professor as the author of these splendid verses. Perhaps there is no one here but myself who knows this, but I am positive because I heard it from Uncle Oriel.

"Several days ago, as I stood by the window looking down at Klara Churchyard, Professor Sätherberg came and stood beside me. I thought at first that he wished to ask me something, but he stood there looking out as though he had not seen me. As he was quite near me and no person could hear, I made an attempt to get him to speak about something else than crooked spines. Moving a little nearer, I said as clearly as I could—for I was so nervous over my daring that I could scarcely utter the words:

"'Is it a pleasure to write verse?'

"Professor Sätherberg gave a start and turned to me.

"'How as that?' he said. 'Is there something you wish to ask me, Selma?'

"'I felt so timid that I would gladly have made my escape, but somehow I managed to repeat the query: 'Is it a pleasure to write verse?'

"'Yes,' said the Professor; and from the look he gave me I felt that he must have thought me rather impertinent. Then in a moment he smiled. 'But it is also a pleasure to straighten crooked backs and make stiff joints flexible.'

"Though not at all like Goethe, yet there was the look of a real poet about Professor Sätherberg when he said that. As he evidently did not wish to continue the conversation, he turned from the window and went farther back in the room.

"He had given me a beautiful answer, but I did not think he was right. Now, if I could write poetry I should never care to do anything else."[3]

March 12, 1873. "Now I know what my first book will deal with. It is to be called *The Vision of Charles XI.* In it I shall tell the story of a Swedish king who, as a child, ascended the throne; so that for many years the kingdom was ruled by his guardian.

"But the guardian was a traitor, and was called in Sweden the 'Russian Tsar,' because he had seized possession of the whole country and had taken the young king and all his councillors prisoners and shut them up in the council chamber of the Stockholm palace.

"Then I shall tell how the Russian Tsar had ordered the young men of the realm beheaded in the presence of the boy king and all his councillors (for such things are done in Russia). After that, the Tsar of Russia advises the Swedish king to abdicate so that he himself can be ruler of Sweden. But the boy king refuses to abdicate or allow himself to be persuaded. Then the Tsar will be furious and declare that if he will not abdicate, he must die.

"Then I shall describe with great suspense in my novel how a block is placed in the courtyard of the palace, and how the King of Sweden, blindfolded and bound hand and foot, is carried out and his head laid upon the block. The Russian Tsar's executioner, his sword drawn, stands ready to cut off the King's head, when the Tsar gives a sign to wait, and says that he will ask the Swedish King once more if he will abdicate. And the Swedish King will proudly answer, No.

"At all events, that short delay will save his life. Before the Tsar's executioner can again raise his sword to strike the deathblow, from outside the palace come a deafening noise and shrieks of terror. At the same time trumpets and drums are heard, and the clash of arms. And the servants of the Russian Tsar will come rushing in, shouting that he must flee at once; for the Swedes have taken possession of Stockholm and are marching into the palace.

"And then the Tsar and all his courtiers and warriors will take to their heels, and the executioner will sheathe his long sword, and he, too, will flee. Whereupon a Swedish youth, wearing a student's cap, will rush into the courtyard, fall upon his knees beside the King, and loose his bonds. The student will be followed by great crowds of Swedish men—most of them in peasant garb—and they will shout for joy because their King is alive.

"Then the King will turn to the young student who has freed him of his bonds, and ask the meaning of all this. The

Once there was a boy. He was —let us say—something like fourteen years old; long and loose jointed and towheaded. He wasn't good for much, that boy. His chief delight was to eat and sleep, and after that he liked best to get into mischief. ■ (From *The Wonderful Adventures of Nils* by Selma Lagerlöf. Illustrated by Hans Baumhauer.)

young student will then tell the King that he, like Gustaf Vasa of old, had gone around the country and raised an army of Dalecarlians, Värmlanders, and peasants from all the other provinces of the realm. So now our country is free and there is nothing for the Tsar of Russia to do but to go back to his own country.

''Then the Swedish King will say, for he is a man of honour, that it is his liberator who should rule over Sweden. 'To the Tsar of Russia I would never resign my crown,' (I shall say), 'but to you I will gladly give it. You are more worthy than I to rule over these brave people.'

'''Many thanks, my cousin,' the young man will answer.

'Never shall it be said of me that I would deprive Your Majesty of your crown. But my father, who was your sainted father's brother, and who relinquished his royal rights to marry my mother—I should be most grateful if you would reinstate them, and thereby acknowledge me as your kinsman.'

''That is so noble and so grand—just the thought of it brings the tears to my eyes. But the novel must contain a great deal more, of course, for that is only the end. The rest I shall have to make up when I'm alone and have no lessons to prepare. . . .''[3]

1873. "'If I could only skip the lesson just for once,' I thought. 'I haven't missed a single lesson the whole term; so it wouldn't matter much.'

"The best thing would be to go home and say to Auntie that I felt so ill when I got out on the street that I had to turn back. Which was not untrue. Just the thought of meeting the student made my heart palpitate so fast that I could scarcely move.

"Just then the door of a shop opened and out came a tall, hideous creature in a white tulle dress and white summer hat trimmed with a garland of big red roses. It would be a mistake to say that the dress and the hat were white, for they had turned gray from grime and dirt—they, like the woman, and the veils and ribbons that dangled about her, all looked as though they had been lying in a clay pit.

"I knew at once that the one who went about in a summer hat and tulle dress in midwinter was none other than Ragtag-Fröken, of whom I had heard many times but never had seen before. I had thought there was something romantic about the poor thing, who had gone mad and now went about summer and winter in some kind of bridal array because she had been forsaken by her betrothed.

"At sight of Ragtag-Fröken, I stopped to look at her. She stood outside the shop door, gazing up into space. Of a sudden her face became horribly distorted; she raised her hands toward heaven and broke into blood-curdling shrieks:

"'O God,' she cried, 'that I should love a faithless man!'

"I have never heard anything so frightful. It was not like a human voice, but as if a wild animal—a lion or tiger—had roared. The words in themselves were not so terrifying, but the way in which they were uttered—in one continuous savage cry.

"She shrieked the same words again. Then I could stand no more. I didn't walk, I ran all the way down to the Baroness', and I was only ten minutes late.

"So, you see, I might have got into trouble if I hadn't met Ragtag-Fröken and been frightened back into the straight way."[3]

March 27, 1873. "Day before yesterday was Annunciation Day of the Virgin Mary, and Auntie asked me if I would like to go with her to the Catholic church. It was all the same to me whether I went here or there, and I immediately said, 'Yes.'

"We went in time to get excellent seats far forward, where we could see the priests in their gorgeous robes and the small altar boys who ran back and forth inside the altar railing, moving books, genuflecting, and swinging censers.

"My heart ached for the poor girl who had been so unhappy that she went and drowned herself, and I did not follow the service. I did not even notice when the choir began to sing, for I sat grieving over her death as though I had known and loved her.

"As I was lamenting my loss I heard a high, clear voice reverberating throughout the church. I was astonished, for I had never heard such heavenly music. I had attended the Catholic church before with Auntie, and on coming out she had always praised the beautiful singing. But I myself could

not say that it was beautiful. I wondered at times if there was not something wrong with my ears, that I could not understand what others found so enchanting.

"But now, as I sat there grieving over the dead, I heard every tone distinctly, and marvelled at the beauty of it all. I thought that it was a greeting from the poor suicide. It was she who had caused my ears to be opened that I might hear the song on just that day.

"And I thought, also, that she told me through the song that I should not mourn for her any longer. She heard singing far more glorious than that to which I listened, and she remembered no more the sufferings of her earthly life.

"Auntie saw that I was weeping. She bent down and asked me if I felt ill. I shook my head and tried to whisper that I was crying because the song was so beautiful.

"After that we sat holding hands, Auntie and I, as long as the song lasted."[3]

May 9, 1873. Made the journey from Stockholm to Upsala for a week-end visit to her brother, Daniel. "I packed the daybook in my travelling bag, as it made an excellent 'table' to write upon last winter when I came to Stockholm. And now I am sitting in the corner of the compartment with pencil in hand and book before me just as I did then.

"But think how much has happened in the meantime! So much writing has been crowded into the diary that if I should meet with more adventures in Upsala I fear there would hardly be space left to include them.

"Upsala Cathedral is a majestic structure. It is so grand that I hardly know whether I dare write about it. Perhaps what I may say will be too childish.

"The cathedral is much larger than the churches in Stockholm and is built in an entirely different manner, so that when one steps inside, one stops to draw a deep breath. At least, that's what I did.

"I had never entered a church where the presence of God was so plainly felt; but this was the first time I had been in a cathedral. *Cathedral*—what a beautiful word!

"I had never loved Sweden so much as I loved her then, in the cathedral.

"I can't tell exactly how it came about that I was so moved as they talked of the many who had been great and achieved great things. And now they could lie in the temple where God dwelt—and that was their reward for having served Him and their country.

"I was strengthened and encouraged by my visit to the cathedral. I should like so much to serve God and Sweden, like the great men and heroes who lie buried there!"[3]

May 11, 1873. "When Daniel took me to the train he said that it had been a genuine pleasure to have me at Upsala for a couple of days.

"I was amazed! I couldn't understand what had come over Daniel! But it did me good to hear him say that."[3]

May 13, 1873. "It would be only a few more weeks until I could go home. That thought was a great comfort. My mind had been occupied elsewhere, and I had almost forgotten that Maarbacka existed. It was well that Aunt Lovisa had come to Stockholm, so that Maarbacka loomed large in my thoughts again.''[3]

1880. Went to Stockholm to study at the teacher's Seminary. Began work as a teacher at the High School for Young Girls at Landskrona (Northern Sweden).

1885. Lieutenant Lagerlof, Selma's father, passed away. She was appointed headmistress at the High School for Young Girls.

1888. Family is forced to sell Maarbacka, as a result of financial troubles.

November, 1890. Awarded her first literary prize by the women's paper *Idun*.

December, 1891. First novel, *Gosta Berling's Saga,* published.

1895. Awarded The Royal Travelling Scholarship by King Oskar and Prince Eugen. Left teaching permanently.

1895-96. Visited Italy, Switzerland, Germany and Belgium. Wrote *The Miracles of the Antichrist*.

1898-1900. Travelled to France, Holland, Palestine, Turkey, Greece and Egypt with her friend, Sophie Elkan: "We are in Egypt, away down at Assuan, and we have ridden out early in the morning to see the island of Philæ and the first cataract.

"The road passes through the desert; to the right of us rises a mountain chain, and to the left, a short distance away, we have the Nile. Between the mountain and the river there is nothing but yellow-white desert sand.

"The opposite shore of the Nile is bordered by a row of tall black stones. They have been shaped in the most fantastic way by the river, and as long as I look at them I must ponder over what I can best liken them to. They look like a row of broad pillars which have been driven down into the river bed, but which have been heaved hither and thither, every which way, by some inundation. Or maybe they look more like a long row of fishermen, who in their various postures—sitting, lying, standing, bending out over the river to look at their floats, leaning back to pull the fish out of the water—have all of them been turned to stone in the same instant.

"Beyond the row of black stones extends once more the yellow sand desert, terminated by a range of mountains. Its rocks are dark, but the sand has not failed to powder with yellow its crevices and slopes as far up as it has been able to find something to hold it.

"All this appears to us beautiful; or perhaps it really fascinates us because it is so unusual. We have never before seen a landscape in black and yellow. A setting for fairy tales, it seems to me—for savagery and cruelty. The night before, the Nile, which now is black as a forest river, had lain absolutely red at sundown, like a broad stream of blood. It had looked gorgeous, had provided the touch of red for which nature seems to yearn.

"Since we are in Egypt it is almost unnecessary to say that the weather is wonderful now in the morning, fresh and just

warm enough, with clear air and a sun which has recently risen over the mountain rim and which still acts quite gentle and safe. Wonderful also are the little donkeys which carry us, and the merry, tireless donkey boys who trot ahead of us. Wonderful above all is the feeling of health, of strength, and of contentment which surges through us every day while we travel on the blessed Nile or stay in its vicinity.

"As a matter of fact the river has completely bewitched us. We came to Assuan on a steamboat, but now we contemplate making the return trip to Cairo in the proper way—that is to say, on a river boat. Yesterday we began to negotiate with the owner of a dahabeah about engaging his boat.

"It will be a long boat trip to Cairo, and if the wind is contrary it can stretch out into a month, indeed, perhaps even longer. But that is exactly what we wish. To glide down the river in the fascinating little craft with the fantastic sail and the tidy little cabin, to sit on the brightly polished deck and watch palm groves, and Negro villages, waterworks, and, now and then, a temple ruin pass by—that is what we should like to keep on doing without interruption not only for a month but to the end of life.

"We are completely mad. It is not at all apprehension over the fact that we two women are to set off with an Arab skipper and his crew, without any other European on board, which prevented us from completing the agreement yesterday; neither is it the thought that in this way we shall perhaps not have time to visit Jerusalem, which after all has been the real objective of our trip; nor that we shall be without mail from home for weeks. All these things we consider insignificant in comparison with the chance to see Africa's sparkling sky of stars reflect itself in the Nile night after night, and to see the river, day after day, spread out like a wide breadth of light blue satin, to inhale this marvelous air, which makes existence a blissful intoxication. No, what had hindered us was simply the impossibility of getting a regular contract drawn up yesterday with the skipper. Today was to be dedicated to old Philæ, the morrow again was to be devoted to the drawing up of a contract, to the purchase of a certain amount of food supplies and other necessities such as blankets and comfortable deck chairs.

"No, we feel no anxiety whatever in regard to the good-natured, splendid-looking Arab who is to conduct us. We are not at all afraid of the Orientals. We have made the acquaintance of quite a number in Cairo and Luxor. We have found them quite human, not at all heroic, to be sure, but sympathetic, frank, and naive. We believe we have quite a rare gift of getting on good terms with them, of entering into their feelings and reactions—in a word, of winning their devotion.

"A change in the scenery has taken place. The road has turned in among the mountains, and we have before us quite a wide desert plain, surrounded on all sides by ridges. At the foot of the mountain wall quite close to us stands a mastaba, or tomb of a saint, a small square building covered with a low cupola.

"What luck for us! The tomb does not stand lonely and deserted as it does most of the days in the year. It is surrounded by a fairly large crowd of people already, and more are on their way. There must be some sort of a festival going on there.

"Why is it so beautiful to see the desert people come riding down the sand-covered mountain slopes on horses, camels, and donkeys—whole village groups, men and women, children and old folks? Is it the unexpected in seeing the desert come to life? It is not a colorful crowd. The men wear black cloaks and white turbans, the women are black from top to toe. Not even the saddle beasts are in any way gaudily decorated.

"But that is the way it is under the sky of Egypt. Everything becomes beautiful, but not at all dreamy or melting away in any kind of shadow. Let the eye rejoice at seeing everything outlined definitely and clearly. It is not men and beasts one sees, but a succession of statues in bronze and granite, which come trooping down from the interior of the mountains, bright and shining, molded by a master's hand.

"We give our guide a sign that we would like to stop here a few minutes to see a little more of the desert people, and the next moment we are out of the saddles. Then we walk up toward the mastaba.

"On the ground outside sit a circle of men, easily forty in number, on their crossed legs, singing at the top of their lungs. We have seen similar singing groups before at Cairo, and we assume that here as well as there they sing from the Koran. But here the singing has a few characteristics which are new to us.

"It was, of course, the same howl, forced out through the nose, the same astounding crescendos in high treble, the same total lack of rhythm and melody which had appalled us the first time we had heard singing from the Koran, but now there is added something wild, I should almost say animalistic. It is the roaring of lions and hyenas, the trumpeting of elephants, the bellowing of aurochs, that these singers imitate. In the meantime they devote themselves to their singing with all their might and main. Their eyes protrude from their heads, their cheeks glow, they lean far backward and emit these inhuman sounds with their faces turned toward the sky.

"We stand there absolutely quiet and listen. No one pays the slightest attention to us. Suddenly we nudge each other with the elbows. We have both recognized at the same time the fine-looking captain of the dahabeah who in a few days is to take us down to Cairo. He squats there like the others, completely absorbed in the singing, and to our tortured ears it seems as if he howls and shrieks worse than anyone else.

"Quite unexpectedly we begin to feel a great terror. Everything about us is extremely tranquil. Groups of unveiled women stand all around, visibly enjoying the men's singing. Out of the mountain, new little caravans keep coming; others approach across the desert plain. Some of the new arrivals unload their camels. What is there that is terrifying in all this?

"I hardly know how to explain it. The horror lay in the singing. It must have lain in the fact that these people could enjoy as beauty what to us was ear-splitting noise.

"The horror must have lain in the fact that here opened a wide gulf which separated them from us. The gulf which we had not seen before.

"We had seen that they dressed differently from us, that they ate in a different manner, had another faith, another color of the skin, but all that had seemed to us immaterial. They were nevertheless human beings like ourselves.

"And as human beings we still regarded them; we did not feel superior, but we felt the difference. Here was something we would never understand. If these people were to hear a Mass at St. Peter's, or a symphony by Beethoven, or an opera by Mozart, they would probably feel the same consternation as that which now had seized us. They would be incapable of comprehending that the Occidentals could enjoy these abominable floods of tunes. They would feel separated from us by a yawning, impassable chasm.

"And as it was in one respect, so perhaps it was in all others. We felt consternation before what was alien in these people, and we hurried back to our donkeys to continue our ride.

"The next day we concluded no contract with the captain of the dahabeah, we gave up the long sojourn on the Nile, the starry nights, the delightful life of idlers on the river boat. Our souls ached, but our suspicions had been aroused. To anyone who had sung like that captain, one could not entrust oneself for a whole month on a small Nile boat.

"As soon as this was decided, a hotel employee came up to me and whispered in confidence that the dahabeah which we had intended to hire had shortly before made a veritable death journey. It had had cholera on board.

"And this he told us now for the first time!

"'I no could tell about it before now,' he said, 'now when the ladies don't want to go. If I tell before, I prevent captain make much money. He never forget it.'

"Beyond a doubt no one else in all Assuan would have dared warn us. But the thing that had saved us—was it only chance, or who had been that time the keeper of fools?" [*Great Essays by Nobel Prize Winners,* edited by Leo Hamalian and Edmond Volpe, Noonday Press, 1960.[4]]

1904. Awarded the Swedish Academy's gold medal following the success of her book *Jerusalem*.

1907. Able to purchase the house and garden at Maarbacka.

1909. Received Nobel Prize for Literature, the first woman to be so honored. "A few days ago I was sitting in the train, bound for Stockholm. It was early evening; there was little light in my compartment and none at all outside. My fellow passengers were dozing in their respective corners, and I was very quiet, listening to the rattling of the train.

"And then I began to think of all the other times I had come up to Stockholm. It had usually been to do something difficult—to pass examinations or to find a publisher for my manuscript. And now I was coming to receive the Prize in Literature. That, too, I thought would be difficult.

"All through this autumn I had lived at my old home in Värmland in complete solitude, and now I should have to step forward in the presence of so many people. I had become shy of life's bustle in my solitary retreat and was apprehensive at the thought of facing the world.

"Deep within me, however, was a wondrous joy at receiving this Prize, and I tried to dispel my anxiety by thinking

Maarbacka in the 19th Century, from an old painting.

of those who would rejoice at my good fortune. There were my good friends, my brothers and sisters and, first and foremost, my old mother, who sitting back home, was happy to have lived to see this day.

"But then I thought of my father and felt a deep sorrow that he should no longer be alive, and that I could not go to him and tell him that I had been awarded the Nobel Prize. I knew that no one would have been happier than he to hear this. Never have I met anyone with his love and respect for the written word and its creators, and I wished that he could have known that the Swedish Academy had bestowed on me this great Prize. Yes, it was a deep sorrow to me that I could not tell him.

"Anyone who has ever sat in a train as it rushes through a dark night will know that sometimes there are long minutes when the coaches slide smoothly along without so much as a shudder. All rustle and bustle cease and the sound of the wheels becomes a soothing, peaceful melody. The coaches no longer seem to run on rails and sleeper but glide into space. Well, that is how it was as I sat there and thought how much I should like to see my old father again. So light and soundless was the movement of the train that I could hardly imagine I was on this earth. And so I began to daydream: (Just think, if I were going to meet Father in

Paradise! I seem to have heard of such things happening to other people—why, then, not to myself?) The train went gliding on but it had a long way to go yet, and my thoughts raced ahead of it. Father will certainly be sitting in a rocking chair on a veranda, with a garden full of sunshine and flowers and birds in front of him. He will be reading Fritjof's *Saga,* of course, but when he sees me he will put down his book, push his spectacles high up on his forehead, and get up and walk toward me. He will say, 'Good day, my daughter, I am very glad to see you,' or 'Why, you are here, and how are you, my child,' just as he always used to do.

"He will settle again in his rocking chair and only then begin to wonder why I have come to see him. 'You are sure there is nothing amiss?' he will ask suddenly. 'No, Father, all is well,' I will reply. But then, just as I am about to break my news to him, I will decide to keep it back just a while longer and try the indirect approach. 'I have come to ask you for advice, Father,' I will say, 'for I am very heavily in debt.'

"'I am afraid you will not get much help from me in this matter,' Father will reply. 'One may well say of this place that, like the old estates in our Värmland, it has everything except money.'

"'Ah, but it is not money that I owe, Father.' 'But that's even worse.' Father will say. 'Begin right at the beginning, daughter.'

"'It is not too much to ask that you should help, Father, for it was all your fault right from the beginning. Do you remember how you used to play the piano and sing Bellman's songs to us children and how, at least twice every winter, you would let us read Tegner and Runeberg and Andersen? It was then that I first fell into debt. Father, how shall I ever repay them for teaching me to love fairy tales and sagas of heroes, the land we live in and all of our human life, in all its wretchedness and glory?'

"Father will straighten up in his rocking chair and a wonderful look will come into his eyes. 'I am glad that I got you into this debt,' he will say.

"'Yes, you may be right, Father, but then remember that that is not all of it. Think how many creditors I have. Think of those poor, homeless vagabonds who used to travel up and down Värmland in your youth, playing the fool and singing of those songs. What do I not owe to them, to their mischief and mad pranks! And the old men and women sitting in their small grey cottages as one came out of the forest, telling me wonderful stories of water-sprites and trolls and enchanted maidens lured into the mountains. It was they who taught me that there is poetry in hard rocks and black forests. And think, Father, of all those pale, hollow-cheeked monks and nuns in their dark cloisters, the visions they saw and the voices they heard. I have borrowed from their treasure of legends. And our own peasants who went to Jerusalem—do I owe them nothing for giving me such glorious deeds to write about? And I am in debt not only to people; there is the whole of nature as well. The animals that walk the earth, the birds in the skies, the trees and flowers, they have all told me some of their secrets.'

"Father will smile and nod his head and look not at all worried. 'But don't you understand, Father, that I carry a great burden of debt?' I will say, and look more and more serious. 'No one on earth knows how I can repay it, but I thought that you, in Heaven, would know.' 'We do,' Father will say and be as carefree and relaxed as he used to be. 'Never fear, child, there is a remedy for your trouble.'

"'Yes, Father, but that's not all. I am also heavily in debt to those who have formed and moulded our language into the good instrument that it is, and taught me to use it. And, then, am I not in debt to those who have written in prose and in verse before my time, who have turned writing into art, the torchbearers, the pathfinders? The great Norwegians, the great Russians who wrote when I was a child, do I not owe them a thousand debts? Has it not been given to me to live in an age in which my own country's literature has reached its highest peak, to behold the marble emperors of Rydberg, the world of Snoilsky's poetry, Strindberg's cliffs, Geijerstam's countryfolk, the modern men of Anne-Charlotte Edgren and Ernst Ahlgren, Heidenstam's Orient? Sophie Elkan, who has brought history to life, Fröding and his tales of Värmland's plains, Levertin's legends, Hallström's *Thanatos,* and Karlfeldt's Dalekarlian sketches, and much else that was young and new, all that nourished my fantasy, drove me on to compete, and made the dreams bear fruit—do I not owe them anything?'

"'Yes, yes,' Father will say. 'You are right, yours is a heavy debt but, never fear, we will find a way.'

"'I don't think, Father, that you really understand how hard it is for me. You don't realize that I am also in debt to my readers. I owe them so much—from the old King and his youngest son, who sent me on my apprentice's wanderings through the South, to the small schoolchildren who scribbled a letter of thanks for *Nils Holgersson*. What would have become of me if no one had wanted to read my books? And don't forget all those who have written of me. Remember the famous Danish critic who, with a few words, won me friends all over Denmark! And he who could mix gall and ambrosia in a more masterly fashion than anyone in Sweden had ever done before his time. Now he is dead. Think of all those in foreign lands who have worked for me. I owe them gratitude, Father, both for their praise and for their censure.'

"'Yes, yes,' Father will say, and I shall see him look a little less calm. Surely, he will begin to understand that it will not be easy to help me.

"'Remember all who have helped me, Father!' I shall say. 'Think of my faithful friend, Esselde, who tried to open doors for me when no one dared to believe in me. Think of others who have cared for and protected my work! Think of my good friend and travelling companion, who not only took me south and showed me all the glories of art but made life itself happier and lighter for me. All the love that has come to me, the honours, the distinctions! Do you not understand now that I had to come to you to ask how such debts can be paid?'

"Father has lowered his head and does not look so hopeful any more.

"'I agree, Daughter, it is not going to be easy to find help for you but, surely, there is nothing more you owe anyone?'

"'Yes, Father, I have found it difficult enough to bear all that I owed before, but my biggest debt has not yet come. That is why I had to come to you for advice.' 'I cannot understand how you could owe still more,' Father will say. 'Oh, yes,' I will reply, and then I will tell him all about *this*.

"'I just cannot believe the Academy . . . ,' Father will say but, looking at me and seeing my face, he will know it is all true. And, then, every wrinkle in his face will tremble and tears will come into his eyes.

"'What am I to say to those who put my name up for the Prize and to those who have made the decision—think, Father, it is not only honour and money they are bestowing on me. They have shown that they have trust enough in me to single me out before the whole world. How shall I repay this debt?'

"Father will sit and still no words will come as he thinks. Then, drying tears of joy from his eyes, he will bang down his fist on the arm of the rocking chair and say, 'I will not rack my brains about problems that no one in Heaven or on earth can solve. I am too happy that you have been given the Nobel Prize to worry about anything!'" [*Nobel Lectures Literature, 1901-1967,* edited by Horst Frenz, Elsevier.[5]]

1910. Secured the entire estate at Maarbacka, immediately beginning renovations there.

1914. Invited to become a member of the Swedish Academy, the highest honor her nation could bestow.

August 17, 1919. ''It was the Seventeenth of August, year 1919. I had had a wreath bound, the prettiest that that could be made up at Maarbacka, and with this before me in the victoria, I drove to the church. I was in holiday attire, the victoria shone with a new coat of varnish, and the horses were in their best harness.

''It was a perfect day. The earth lay bathed in sunshine, the air was mild, and across the pale blue sky floated a few white wisps of cloud. Not the slightest breeze blew from any direction. It was a Sunday, and I saw little children in holiday dress playing in the yards, and grown folk in their Sunday best setting off for church. No cows or sheep or chickens were seen in the road, as on weekdays, when the victoria passed through the village of Às.

''The crop that year was so abundant, it seemed as if the good old times were back with us again. The haylofts along the way were so full, shutters and doors could not be closed; the rye fields were decked with close rows of shooks; the apple trees in the front yards hung heavy with reddening fruit, and the fallow fields, newly sown, showed a tender crop just turning green.

''I sat thinking that here was something Lieutenant Lagerlöf—whose centenary it was that day—would have liked to see. Here was prosperity. It was not as in 1918 and 1917 and 1915 and 1914 and 1911—those dreadful years of drouth! How he would have rejoiced at this! He would have nodded to himself, and averred that nowhere in all Värmland could they raise such crops as in his parish.

''During the whole long drive to the church, my father was in my thoughts. On this very road he had driven many and many a time. I pictured with what keen interest he would have noted all the changes. Every house which had been repainted, every new window, every roof where tiling had replaced the old shingles, he would have pointed out and commented upon. The cottage Där Fram at Às, which had remained unaltered, would have delighted him; but he would have been sorry to find Jan Larsson's old house—the finest in the parish in his time—torn down.

''Certainly he had never been opposed to changes and improvements, though there were some time-honoured things he had wished to leave undisturbed. Were he here now, he would think us a shiftless lot to have in this day and age the old crooked, sagging fences that were here in his time. He would be shocked to find the road ditches still choked with weeds, the bridges weak and full of holes, and the dung-yards still lying at the edge of the road.

''When I came to the crossing where the village road runs into the great highway, how I wished I might have pointed out to him the fine health resort among the hills, and told him that Às Springs were now visited every year by hundreds of people. It would have gladdened him to know that his idea—that this would some day be a popular watering-place—had not been so far afield. I could have wished he were beside me in the carriage as I drove across the Ämtan Bridge! It would have been a joy to show him that the river had at last been dredged, and now ran in a straight course, no longer overflowing its banks.

''As I drove by the Ostenby school, I seemed to see him standing on the playground scattering handfuls of pen-

SELMA LAGERLÖF

nies—happy and content as always, when he had a crowd of children about him. I had heard him say, time and time again, that popular education was a calamity, and would bring us to ruin. But all the same, on every examination day, he would drive down to the school to sit for hours while his good friend Melanoz quizzed the children in catechism and history, and let them show how clever they were at arithmetic and composition. I doubt whether there was any one more pleased than he when the youngsters gave correct answers and got good marks and prizes. I had often wondered at this; but now I understand that where children were concerned, all prejudice was thrown to the winds.

''I remembered how it had been in the old days when we drove into the church grove. We were hailed with cheery salutations as folk sprang aside to let our carriage pass, and father sat smiling and raising his hand to the brim of his hat. But when I drove in on the same ground, the place looked so empty and deserted.

''I was alone in the carriage, and among all who had come to the church only I remembered that this was my father's birthday. I stepped out and went over to the churchyard to place the wreath. My sad heart wept over my loved ones who lay sleeping there. Father and Mother, Grandmother, Aunt Lovisa, and the old housekeeper—I had seen them all laid away.

''I longed for them, I wished they might come back and dwell in that Maarbacka which their labours had built up.

"But still, silent, inaccessible, they slept on. They seemed not to hear me. Yet, perhaps they did. Perhaps these recollections, which have hovered round me the last few years, were sent forth by them. I do not know, but I love to think so." [Selma Lagerlöf, *Maarbacka*, translated by Velma Howard, Doubleday, 1924, republished by Gale Research, 1974.[6]]

March 16, 1940. Died at Maarbacka.

FOR MORE INFORMATION SEE: Edwin A. Bjoerkman, "Story of Selma Lagerlöf," in his *Voices of Tomorrow*, Kennerley, 1913; Selma Lagerlöf, *Maarbacka*, Doubleday, Page, 1924, reprinted, Gale, 1974; Annie R. Marble, "Selma Lagerlöf—Swedish Realist and Idealist," in her *Nobel Prize Winners in Literature, 1901-1931*, Appleton-Century, 1931; Walter A. Berendsohn, *Selma Lagerlöf: Her Life and Work* (translated from the German by George F. Timson), I. Nicholson & Watson, 1931, reprinted, Kennikat, 1968; Winifred M. Kirkland and Frances Kirkland, "Selma Lagerlöf, Who Listened and Remembers," in their *Girls Who Became Writers*, Harper, 1933; S. Lagerlöf, *Memories of My Childhood*, Doubleday, Doran, 1934, reprinted, Kraus Reprint, 1975; Hanna A. Larsen, *Selma Lagerlöf*, Doubleday, Doran, 1936, reprinted, Kraus Reprint, 1975; S. Lagerlöf, *The Diary of Selma Lagerlöf*, Doubleday, Doran, 1936, reprinted, Kraus Reprint, 1975; W. Gore Allen, *Renaissance in the North*, Sheed, 1946; (for children) Elizabeth R. Montgomery, *Story behind Great Books*, McBride, 1946.

F. Fleisher, "Selma Lagerlöf: A Centennial Tribute," *American-Scandinavian Review*, September, 1958; Margery Evernden, "Of a Peacock and a Wild Goose," *Horn Book*, December, 1961; Alrik Gustafson, *Six Scandinavian Novelists*, University of Minnesota Press, 1967; Brian Doyle, editor, *Who's Who of Children's Literature*, Schocken Books, 1968; Juan R. Jimenez and others, *Selma Lagerlöf*, Gregory, 1971; Mary J. Moffat and C. Painter, editors, *Revelations: Diaries of Women*, Random House, 1974.

LAND, Myrick (Ebben) 1922-

PERSONAL: Born February 25, 1922, in Shreveport, La.; son of James Arthur and Mary Edna (Fancher) Land; married Barbara Neblett, 1949; children: Robert Arthur, Jacquelyn Myrick. *Education:* University of California, Los Angeles, B.A., 1945; Columbia University, M.S. in Journalism, 1946. *Agent:* Sterling Lord Agency, 660 Madison Ave., New York, N.Y. 10021.

CAREER: American National Red Cross, Washington, D.C., director of information in Europe and North Africa, 1949-52; Scholastic Magazines, New York, N.Y., editor, 1952-55; *This Week*, New York, N.Y., assistant editor, 1955-59; *Look*, New York, N.Y., assistant managing editor, 1959-71; teacher of journalism, University of Queensland, Brisbane, Australia, 1972-76; University of Nevada, assistant professor of journalism, 1971—. *Military service:* U.S. Army Air Forces, 1942-43. *Member:* Columbia Journalism Alumni (president, 1963-65). *Awards, honors:* Pulitzer traveling fellowship, 1946-47.

WRITINGS: Search the Dark Woods (novel), Funk, 1955, published as *The Search*, Dell, 1959; *The Fine Art of Literary Mayhem*, Holt, 1963; (with wife, Barbara Land and

MYRICK LAND

Robert L. Oswald) *Lee: A Portrait of Lee Harvey Oswald by His Brother*, Coward, 1967; *Quicksand*, Harper, 1969; *Last Flight*, Norton, 1975.

Juvenile books with wife, Barbara Land: *Jungle Oil*, Coward, 1957; *The Changing South*, Coward, 1959; *The Quest of Isaac Newton*, Doubleday, 1961.

Contributor of some two hundred articles to *Look, This Week, New York Times Magazine, Cosmopolitan, Script, Coronet, Toronto Star, World, World Week*, and other periodicals and newspapers.

SIDELIGHTS: "When I was eleven years old, my older brother, Tom, introduced me to one of his friends.

"'This is Myrick,' Tom said. 'He's going to be an author.'

"Tom had seen me sneaking away to the post office with large manila envelopes and he had guessed what was in them. The fact that *Liberty, The Saturday Evening Post* and *The Atlantic* had someone waiting to put my short stories into the return envelopes and send them right back, didn't seem important to Tom. I've often felt that his simple announcement of my future that day helped determine how I've spent much of my life.

"One reason it has been a very satisfactory choice is that a writer has a chance to relive those parts of his life which interest him, or please him, or pain him, or puzzle him. You learn that very little of the past is ever lost. An episode which occurred forty years ago in Texas or thirty years in Venezuela becomes as vivid to me when I begin writing about it as what happened last night in Nevada.

"I am finding this particularly true now that I'm writing a novel about Australia. We lived there for four and a half years and while I was there I made occasional notes for a book about that strange country. I believe now, I was too close to Australia to see it clearly. Now that we are twelve thousand miles away, everything I saw and heard and imagined about Australia's past has begun to return far more vividly."

HOBBIES AND OTHER INTERESTS: Painting.

LANDECK, Beatrice   1904-

PERSONAL: Born April 27, 1904, in New York City; married in 1928; children: two. *Education:* B.Arch., Columbia University, 1926; certificate. Dalcroze School of Music, 1934. *Address:* 18 Stevens Lane, Westhampton Beach, N.Y. 11978.

CAREER: Music director, Little Red School House, New York City, 1937-47; head of music department, Mills College, Oakland, Calif., 1948-59; author and lecturer, 1960—. Member of the National Music and Education Committee of Young Audiences, Inc., 1960—; consultant, *Book of Knowledge,* and Grolier Council Educational Research, 1968. *Member:* Music Educational National Conference, National Education Association, National Association of Jazz Education.

BEATRICE LANDECK

WRITINGS: (Editor) *Git On Board: Collection of Folk Songs,* Edward. B. Marks Music Corp., 1944; (editor) *Songs to Grow On: A Collection of American Folk Songs for Children* (illustrated by David S. Martin), Edward B. Marks Music Corp., 1950; *Children and Music: An Informal Guide for Parents and Teachers,* Sloane, 1952; (editor) *More Songs to Grow On: A Collection of Folk Songs for Children* (illustrated by D. S. Martin), Morrow, 1954; *Time for Music: A Guide for Parents,* Public Affairs Committee (New York), 1958; *Echoes of Africa in Folk Songs of the Americas,* McKay, 1961; *Making Music Your Own,* Silver, 1964, revised edition, 1971; (editor with Elizabeth Crook) *Wake Up and Sing! Folk Songs from America's Grass Roots* (illustrated by Bob Blansky), Morrow, 1969; *Learn to Read, Read to Learn: Poetry and Prose from Afro-Rooted Sources* (illustrated by Michael Heming), McKay, 1975.

SIDELIGHTS: "Throughout the years, I have become ever more convinced of the major importance of folklore in children's lives. Experiencing the past of one's own forebears through the lore they have unconsciously created as they worked and played not only gives children security and an innate pride in their roots, but somehow frees the mind from distracting thoughts and opens it to learning. If only teachers who work with underprivileged groups could become aware of the richness of the heritage of these materially poor youngsters, they would draw on the children's ethnic culture as a source for teaching materials, making it a lot easier for themselves as well as for their students."

FOR MORE INFORMATION SEE: Christian Science Monitor, October 7, 1950; *San Francisco Chronicle,* July 20, 1952; *Saturday Review,* November 15, 1952.

LANE, John   1932-

PERSONAL: Born August 12, 1932, in Jefferson City, Mo.; son of Ralph (a cartoonist) and Florence (Naegelin; a fashion illustrator) Lane; married Jane Callinan (a writer), May 30, 1964; children: Matthew John. *Education:* Attended Cleveland Institute of Art, 1950-52. *Office:* Newspaper Enterprise Association, 200 Park Avenue, New York, N.Y. 10017.

CAREER: Artist; illustrator. Newspaper Enterprise Association, New York, N.Y., staff artist, 1956-70, art director, 1970-75, chief editorial cartoonist, 1976—; United Feature Service, art director, 1978—. John Lane's editorial cartoons were distributed to NEA's more than 750 daily newspaper subscribers in North America. *Exhibitions:* Galleries in northern Ohio. *Military service:* U.S. Navy, aircraft mechanic, 1952-54.

ILLUSTRATOR: Bill McCormick, *The Complete Beginner's Guide To Golf,* Doubleday, 1974; Brian L. Denyer, *Basic Soccer Strategy: An Introduction for Young Players,* Doubleday, 1976; *You and Your Body: A Book of Experiments to Perform on Yourself,* Doubleday, 1977; *The Complete Beginner's Guide to Making and Flying Kites,* Doubleday, 1977. Illustrations have appeared in *Business Week, Homelife, Golf Magazine.*

WORK IN PROGRESS: (With Howard Smith) *Giant Animals;* (with Howard Smith) *Animal Olympics,* expected publication in 1979; (with wife, Jane Lane) *Play Places and Secret Hidy Holes,* expected publication in 1979.

Gerald Ford

Henry Kissinger

Nelson Rockefeller

Anwar Sadat

Yitzhak Rabin

Chou En-lai

A collection of Lane's caricatures.

SIDELIGHTS: "I was born in Missouri, grew up in Kansas City and then moved to Orlando, Florida in 1943, where my dad assisted Roy Crane for a couple of years at NEA. My mother was a fashion illustrator so my interest in art came naturally. I attended the Cleveland Institute of Art for a couple of years, and then went into the Navy as an aircraft mechanic in Korea. After discharge, I freelanced for a while and then went to work in Cleveland for a printing company that was going to start an art department. I became their art director. Later I went with NEA.

"John Fischetti was the principal editorial cartoonist for NEA at the time I went with them and I wasn't even interested in doing a weekly political cartoon for them. I guess I

didn't have enough confidence to think that what I was angry about would be what anybody else would care about, and it took me a while to realize that 'I am a People.' In this connection, I had known so many adequate artists who were doing real well because of a lack of confidence, and also some really good artists who went nowhere because they couldn't stand rejection.

"Unlike so many of the men in the field, I was sort of a late-bloomer. I didn't really know that there were other people in the world, I guess, till after I was twenty-five—and I didn't really start to think or be angry at things until after I was thirty or thirty-five. Maybe I was born in reverse—retired until I was thirty-five and now going to work.

"As I was growing up my thoughts and actions were almost entirely centered on my own family, and I didn't think about the so-called 'outside world.' But as time went on, my life was affected very definitely by three important people—one I married. I was impressed by what these three said and thought, and I found myself feeling embarrassed at so many of the things I heard *myself* saying, so that I started reading and wanting to know. I began to get angry at myself and at injustices, and I suddenly realized that my drawing was a tool with which I could make these newfound thoughts known. Another of these important three was Walter Coyne, who was at NEA at the time. The third person who influenced me greatly was Jerry Sheehan who now has his own public relations firm in Paris. I didn't have especially deep conversations with these three—it was just that they made me ashamed and all of a sudden I realized I was like a 350cc. engine that had been idling all the time. I began to feel that I had a potential. I was thirty before I realized there was anybody standing next to me in this world. I started reading, talking, thinking, and caring about everything. I asked for more things to do and wanted more responsibility. I was made assistant art director and then creative art director at NEA.

"I've done a variety of things at NEA. For a while I drew a Sunday comic strip, written by Russ Winterbotham, which was called 'The Good Guys.' All the characters were people at NEA but after awhile it died a natural death. And I sketched at the 1968 Democratic Convention in Chicago, and I can recommend this sort of thing to young cartoonists for the intellectual stimulation one gets from it.

"A caricature can be a bland exaggeration of just the features of a face but it will be much more successful when it conveys your opinion of that person. When doing a caricature of a politican, it's important to have an opinion of him, and this means that caricatures of him by different cartoonists may look somewhat different from each other. You can make a statement with a caricature—something that the reader or viewer can't get out of a photo, or out of a straight drawing or illustration. However, in the case of former President Nixon, things finally got so that every cartoonist was drawing a cliché of Nixon with the ski-nose and all. Probably many of these weren't good caricatures because we'd all gotten used to employing clichés in his case. When I'm doing a caricature, I just use photos as a reference because I might not want my caricature looking the way the photo shows.

"I still do life drawing and sketching and still need practice. In the case of the first few people I draw whenever I go out on a sketching trip, I find that I'm not drawing that particular person's hand but rather a cliché thing because time is always of the essence, and one naturally wants to cut corners and make things as easy as possible for himself. Another thing that I have to make an effort on has to do with the matter of reading—and, as you know, an editorial cartoonist has to do a lot of that. I'd rather do things than read about them—in other words, I'd rather build a boat, which I'm now doing, than read a book about how to do it. I'm not an intellectual, but I realize that more important really than learning to draw is having something to say—and that means reading and talking. A formal education—is probably more important than the art part of the job.

"I use the famous Gillott 290 pen which will produce a fine line or a very thick line for the editorial cartoons, and I use a slick (plate finish) Strathmore because the pen doesn't drag as much as it would with a medium or rougher surface. I

72–74. PUNTING THE BALL.

(From *Basic Soccer Strategy: An Introduction for Young Players* by Brian Lindsay Denyer. Illustrated by John Lane.)

JOHN LANE

don't use a brush on the editorial cartoons. On the science cartoons, I usually use a No. 5 brush.

"I remember particularly one of the gems of wisdom my dad gave me—'Good artists are a dime-a-dozen. They're mechanics, you can buy them. Anyone can learn to draw. But they can't learn to think and to have a flair. That's a talent you're born with—a flair. When you have an artist with an *idea*, you've really got something!' In this connection I think that the cartoonist is really cheating mankind if his art ability gives him the *mechanics* to say something in this world, and he doesn't bother to think about *what* to say but just draw for himself. With our society the way it is, we have to communicate if we want to survive. We're a complex society of many animals together, and if we all try to be an island, we will die."

LIPKIND, William   1904-1974
(Will)

PERSONAL: Born December 17, 1904, in New York, N.Y.; married Maria Cimino (a librarian). *Education:* City College (now City College of the City University of New York), B.A., 1927; Columbia University, M.A., Ph.D., 1937. *Address:* 15 W. 11th St., New York, N.Y.

CAREER: Columbia University, Social Science Research Council, researcher among the Caraja and Javahe Indians of central Brazil, 1937-39; worked for the American Military Government in Germany, following World War II; teacher of anthropology at New York University and of children's literature at Hunter College of the City University of New York; author of books for children, beginning 1947. *Military service:* Served in England with the Office of War Information during World War II. *Awards, honors:* Caldecott Medal, 1952, for *Finders Keepers*, and runner-up, 1951, for *The Two Reds*.

WRITINGS—Under pseudonym Will; all written with and illustrated by Nicolas, pseudonym of Nicolas Mordvinoff; all published by Harcourt: *The Two Reds*, 1950; *Finders Keepers*, 1951, reissued, 1973; *Even Steven*, 1952; *The Christmas Bunny*, 1953; *Circus Ruckus*, 1954; *Chaga*, 1955; *Perry the Imp*, 1956; *Sleepyhead*, 1957; *The Magic Feather Duster*, 1958; *Four-Leaf Clover*, 1959; *The Little Tiny Rooster*, 1960; *Billy the Kid*, 1961; *Russet and the Two Reds*, 1962; *The Boy and the Forest*, 1964.

Other writings: *Winnebago Grammar*, King's Crown Press, 1945; *Boy with a Harpoon* (illustrated by Nicolas Mordvinoff), Harcourt, 1952; *Boy of the Islands* (illustrated by Mordvinoff), 1954; (with Georges Schreiber) *Professor Bull's Umbrella* (illustrated by Schreiber), Viking, 1954; *Days to Remember* (illustrated by Jerome Snyder), I. Obolensky, 1961; *Nubber Bear* (illustrated by Roger Duvoisin), Harcourt, 1966.

SIDELIGHTS: William Lipkind was once described by his collaborator and illustrator, Nicolas Mordvinoff, as an anthropologist by profession, but a poet by inclination. The two met through Lipkind's wife and began a successful partnership that lasted for a decade and a half.

The Two Reds was their first joint effort, and received favorable reviews from critics. Observed the *New York Times:* "The drawing is highly sophisticated, yet it has the forthrightness and humor of a child's viewpoint. The economical text and the vigor of the illustrations make this a notable picture book." *Horn Book* added, "The text is as graphic as the pictures in its choice of words, its keen perception of life, its humor and identification with the compelling interests of a small boy." "Will and Nicolas obviously had a wonderful time creating this new and original picture book," wrote a *Saturday Review of Literature* critic. "There are a zest and freshness in every word and line of it that boys and girls of almost every age will be quick to appreciate." The book was one of the first to depict life in the slums. It was banned in Boston with the claim that it was subversive, despite its runner-up finish for the Caldecott Medal in 1951.

In 1952, the team of Will and Nicolas won the Caldecott Medal for *Finders Keepers*. A *Horn Book* reviewer commented as follows: "The text has the form of a folk tale and its humor [has] an instant appeal. . . . Author, illustrator, and publisher have collaborated to produce a picture book which is as fresh and different in its treatment of the adventures of Nap and Winkle as was *The Two Reds* of 1950." Added the *New York Times*, "[This] story has a good deal of the quality of a traditional fable, yet it is told in crisp modern style. It isn't, to be sure, quite so funny nor so action-filled as their notable picture book, *The Two Reds*. However, both story and pictures are done with great good humor. Nicolas' red, yellow, and black illustrations are bolder in scale and in color than those in *The Two Reds*, but distinguished by the same droll imagination."

Sleepyhead was yet another collaborative effort, described in *Saturday Review* as, "A lively and entertaining picture book. . . . The artist and the author, William Lipkind, work so closely and harmoniously that they always achieve a unity that is usually only possible when an author is also the illustrator of his book. . . ." The *New York Herald Tribune Book Review* noted, "The picture book in tones of pumpkin and soft green ends in a proper way for a bedtime story, but it is really a riotous daytime adventure told in swift-moving delightful rhymes by William Lipkind."

The two Reds got away quickly and sat on a stoop.

(From *The Two Reds* by William Lipkind. Illustrated by Nicolas Mordvinoff.)

WILLIAM LIPKIND

Kirkus called *Magic Feather Duster*, "lyrical in concept and form," and went on to say that, "Nicolas Mordvinoff's expressive drawings and Will Lipkind's chastely moving text work faithfully to achieve that high aesthetic quality which characterizes their work." *Saturday Review* described it as, "A picture book for all who enjoy originality in a provocative and imaginative interpretation of a classic pattern."

FOR MORE INFORMATION SEE: New York Times, August 20, 1950, August 26, 1951, October 3, 1974 (obituary); *Horn Book,* September, 1950, September, 1951; *Saturday Review of Literature,* November 11, 1950; *Saturday Review,* November 16, 1957, November 1, 1958; *New York Herald Tribune Book Review,* November 17, 1957; *Kirkus,* August 15, 1958; Muriel Fuller, editor, *More Junior Authors,* H. W. Wilson, 1963.

(Died October 2, 1974)

LOFTING, Hugh 1886-1947

PERSONAL: Born January 14, 1886, in Maidenhead, Berkshire, England; emigrated to the United States, 1912; naturalized a citizen; died September 26, 1947, in Santa Monica, California; son of John Brien and Elizabeth Agnes Lofting; married Flora Small, 1912 (died, 1927); married Katherine Harrower, 1928 (died, 1928); married Josephine Fricker, 1935; children: (first marriage) Elizabeth, Colin; (third marriage) Christopher Clement. *Education:* Attended Mount St. Mary's College, Chesterfield, Derbyshire; later studied at the Massachusetts Institute of Technology, 1904-05, and at the London Polytechnic, 1906-07. *Home:* Santa Monica, California.

CAREER: Author and illustrator of books for children. Worked for a short time as an architect and later, as a civil engineer in Canada, Africa, and the West Indies. *Military service:* British Army during World War I, serving in Flanders and France, 1917-18. *Member:* Players' Club, Dutch Treat Club, and New York Club. *Awards, honors:* Newbery Medal, 1922, for *The Voyages of Doctor Dolittle.*

WRITINGS—"Doctor Dolittle" series; all self-illustrated: *The Story of Doctor Dolittle, being the History of His Peculiar Life at Home and Astonishing Adventures in Foreign Parts,* F. A. Stokes, 1920; *The Voyages of Doctor Dolittle,* F. A. Stokes, 1922, reprinted, Dell, 1975; *Doctor Dolittle's Post Office,* F. A. Stokes, 1923; *Doctor Dolittle's Circus,* F. A. Stokes, 1924; *Doctor Dolittle's Zoo,* F. A. Stokes, 1925; *Doctor Dolittle's Caravan,* F. A. Stokes, 1926; *Doctor Dolittle's Garden,* F. A. Stokes, 1927; *Doctor Dolittle in the Moon,* F. A. Stokes, 1928, reissued, Penguin, 1968; *Doctor Dolittle's Return,* F. A. Stokes, 1933; *Doctor Dolittle's Birthday Book,* F. A. Stokes, 1935; *Doctor Dolittle and the Secret Lake,* Lippincott, 1948; *Doctor Dolittle and the Green Canary,* Lippincott, 1950; *Doctor Dolittle's Puddleby Adventures,* Lippincott, 1952, reissued, J. Cape, 1966; *Doctor Dolittle's Treasury,* Lippincott, 1967.

Other writings: *The Story of Mrs. Tubbs* (self-illustrated), F. A. Stokes, 1923, reissued, Lippincott, 1968; *Porridge Poetry* (self-illustrated), F. A. Stokes, 1924; *Noisy Nora,* F. A. Stokes, 1929; *The Twilight of Magic* (illustrated by Lois Lenski), F. A. Stokes, 1930, reissued, Lippincott, 1967; *Gub Gub's Book: An Encyclopedia of Food,* F. A. Stokes, 1932; *Tommy, Tilly, and Mrs. Tubbs* (self-illustrated), F. A. Stokes, 1936; *Victory for the Slain* (poem), J. Cape, 1942.

ADAPTATIONS—Movies: "Doctor Dolittle," starring Rex Harrison, Samantha Eggar, and Anthony Newly, Twentieth Century-Fox, 1967.

HUGH LOFTING

(From the movie "Doctor Dolittle," starring Rex Harrison and Anthony Newley. Produced by 20th Century-Fox, 1967.)

Filmstrips: "The Voyages of Dr. Dolittle," Miller-Brody Productions.

SIDELIGHTS: **January 14, 1886.** Born at Maidenhead, in Berkshire, England, of an Irish father, John Brien Lofting, and an English mother, Elizabeth Agnes. There were six children in the family: five boys and a girl.

1894. At the age of eight, Lofting was sent to a boarding school—a Jesuit college, Mount St. Mary—and thereafter (for the next ten years) he saw his family infrequently.

1904. Studied at the Massachusetts Institute of Technology in the United States. He completed his studies later at the London Polytechnic.

1910-1912. Worked as an engineer for the Lagos Railway in West Africa and the United Railways of Havana. Lofting considered himself a bad engineer and hated his profession.

1912. Married Flora Small of New York and settled in the United States.

1916. Joined the Irish Guards during the First World War. Saw service in France and Flanders. It was during this war that Lofting formulated his belief in internationalism, a principle that he was to carry with him until the end of his life. "The war of 1914 began with the murder of the Archduke at Sarajevo. Before that it began with two big empires striving for economic mastery of the world. Going back further still it

began with the misrepresentation of government bureaus and the press. But before all of these it began with the sagas—with the folk-tales, the tribal legends that were purposely designed to keep alive race hatreds combined with a paramount respect for military prowess.

"'Arma virumque cano!'

"The little naked boy listening over the peat fire, or at the door of the tribal tent, grasps his wooden sword, his small frame quivering with ardor! And as the song goes on, telling of the evil deeds of the hereditary enemy, he lifts his toy weapon and shakes it toward the stars. 'I too,' he cries, 'when I am a man, will be a warrior such as the great ones. And woe to any of that tribe who wronged our people if he cross my path!' And the old gray-beards nod approval, saying: 'He is a true son of a martial race. Our enemies shall tremble at his name.'

"That was where the war of 1914 started. And there perhaps is where the most effective work for rational internationalism can . . . begin. By education, by getting the child to realize that the day of the old-fashioned military hero is gone; that war henceforth, if we must have it, will be at best a contest of chemists and machinery design, we shall do more toward laying the foundations of permanent peace than by any devices of statesmanship which run ahead of popular education. If, beginning with the children, we launch a campaign for the right of Peace Preparedness, the working out of governmental plans later will be easier." ["Children and

"It was natural to spring a step that measured six or seven feet." ■ (From *Doctor Dolittle in the Moon,* told and illustrated by Hugh Lofting.)

Internationalism," Hugh Lofting, *The Nation,* Vol. 118, February 13, 1924.[1]]

1917. Wounded and invalided out of the Army. It was during the war that Lofting first created Dr. Dolittle, a character that later changed his life. The character was created for his two children, Elizabeth and Colin. "It was during the Great War and my children at home wanted letters from me—and they wanted them with illustrations rather than without. There seemed very little of interest to write to youngsters from the Front: the news was either too horrible or too dull. And it was all censored. One thing, however, that kept forcing itself more and more on my attention was the very considerable part the animals were playing in the World War and that as time went on they, too, seemed to become Fatalists. They took their chances with the rest of us. But their fate was far different from the men's. However seriously a soldier was wounded, his life was not despaired of; all the resources of a surgery highly developed by the war were brought to his aid. A seriously wounded horse was put out by a timely bullet.

"This did not seem quite fair. If we made the animals take the same chances as we did ourselves, why did we not give them similar attention when wounded? But obviously to develop a horse-surgery as that of our Casualty Clearing Stations would necessitate a knowledge of horse language.

"That was the beginning of the idea: an eccentric country physician with a bent for natural history and a great love of pets, who finally decides to give up his human practice for the more difficult, more sincere, and for him, more attractive therapy of the animal kingdom. He is challenged by the difficulty of the work—for obviously it requires a much cleverer brain to become a good animal doctor (who must first acquire all animal languages and physiologies) than it does to take care of the mere human hypochondriac.

"This was a new plot for my narrative letter for the children. It delighted them. . . ." ["Hugh Lofting 1886-1947," Helen

Dean Fish, *Newbery Medal Books: 1922-1955,* ed. by Bertha Mahony Miller and Elinor Whitney Field, Horn Book, 1955.[2]]

1918. World War I ended, but Lofting firmly believed that the way to lasting peace was through the education of children. "No one would want the supreme sacrifices made by the soldiers who died in the World War to be forgotten. But neither must we forget that the main thing they died for was to make future war impossible, to make peace permanent. And the modern battle-book for children should depict the war of 1914 not as a field on which any individual army showed its sportsmanlike excellence over all others; not as part of the 'good old fighting days'; not as a chance to win medals. But beneath all the braying of the brass bands and the cheering of the girls who lined the streets, it should be displayed as the death throes of two ugly giants, the epochs of Competitive Industrialism and Armed Imperialism. In this great struggle, it should be shown that millions of men gave their lives for ideals which the rest of us, as soon as the armistice was signed, failed to live up to. And whether the giants are to come back to life and have their ugly fight all over again, with still less of the Queensberry code of rules in evidence, rests with them—the children."[1]

Autumn, 1919. Doctor Dolittle became a beloved character to Lofting's two children and his son, Colin, even adopted the name. When the family returned home to America, Lofting had already decided, at his wife's prompting, to turn the letters into a book. The novelist, Cecil Roberts, recalled his meeting with the future author on board ship: "Crossing the Atlantic I had a neighbor [Lofting] in my deck chair. Every evening about six he said he had to disappear to read a bedtime story to Doctor Dolittle. I enquired who Doctor Dolittle might be and he said it was his son. The next day a snub-nosed boy appeared on deck with his mother and thus I made the acquaintance of the original Doctor Dolittle. Later Hugh Lofting at my request showed me some manuscript and he wondered if it would make a book. I was at once struck by the quality of the stories and, enthusiastic about

The Pelican Chorus. ■ (From *Doctor Dolittle's Caravan* by Hugh Lofting. Illustrated by the author.)

their publication, I recommended him to my publisher, Mr. Stokes. I never saw Hugh Lofting again but when his Dolittle book came out, he sent me a copy with a charming inscription."[2]

1920. *The Story of Doctor Dolittle,* with Lofting's own illustrations, was published. Lofting wrote his story so that it could be enjoyed by all ages. "To all children—children in years and children in heart—I dedicate this story." [Hugh Lofting, *The Story of Doctor Dolittle,* J. B. Lippincott Co., 1920, 1948.[3]]

1922. *The Voyages of Doctor Dolittle* published, after the instant success of his first book. "I make no claim to be an authority on writing or illustrating for children. The fact that I have been successful merely means that I can write and illustrate in my own way. There has always been a tendency to classify children almost as a distinct species. For years it was a constant source of shock to me to find my writings amongst 'Juveniles.' It does not bother me any more now, but I still feel there should be a category of 'Seniles' to offset the epithet."

1923. *The Voyages of Doctor Dolittle* awarded the Newbery Medal. Hereafter, Lofting's life was very much that of the professional writer with an assured audience. The Dolittle series were an attempt to create, for children, a new and gentle hero for them to emulate. He aimed to show children that the world must turn to internationalism. "If we make children see that all races, given equal physical and mental chances for development, have about the same batting averages of good and bad, we shall have laid another very substantial foundation stone in the edifice of peace and internationalism."[1]

1927. First wife, Flora Small Lofting, died.

1928. Married Katherine Harrower-Peters, but she died shortly after their marriage that same year.

Mr. and Mrs. Cheapside. ■ (From *Doctor Dolittle's Caravan* by Hugh Lofting. Illustrated by the author.)

"An Enormous Footprint." ■ (From *The Story of Doctor Dolittle* by Hugh Lofting. Illustrated by the author.)

1935. Married Josephine Fricker.

1936. Moved to California where his son, Christopher, was born.

1942. *Victory for the Slain,* Lofting's only serious poem, a poem of passionate despair, was published. The poet imagined war following war ad infinitum:

> When nation against nation
> Shall at last lay down their arms,
> Will class against another come—
> The Reds against the Whites?
> And faiths and races, too . . . ?

[Edward Blishen, *Hugh Lofting,* The Bodley Head Ltd., (London), 1968.[4]]

September 26, 1947. Died in Santa Monica, California at the age of sixty-one.

FOR MORE INFORMATION SEE: Bertha E. Mahony, and others, compilers, *Illustrators of Children's Books, 1744-1945,* Horn Book, 1947; Helen D. Fish, "Doctor Dolittle: His Life and Work," *Horn Book,* September, 1948; H. D. Fish, "Hugh Lofting, 1886-1947," in *Newbery Medal Books, 1922-1955,* edited by B. E. Mahony Miller and E. W. Field, Horn Book, 1955; Roger L. Green, *Tellers of Tales,* rewritten and enlarged edition, F. Watts, 1965; Edward Blishen, *Hugh Lofting,* Bodley Head, 1968; Brian Doyle, editor, *Who's Who of Children's Literature,* Schocken Books, 1968.

For children: Elizabeth Rider Montgomery, *Story behind Great Books,* McBride, 1946; Stanley J. Kunitz and Howard Haycraft, editors, *Junior Book of Authors,* second edition revised, H. W. Wilson, 1951; Carolyn Sherwin Bailey, *Candle for Your Cake,* Lippincott, 1952; Norah Smaridge, *Famous Modern Story-Tellers for Young People,* Dodd, 1969.

HUGH LOFTING

Obituaries: *New York Times*, September 28, 1947; *Newsweek*, October 6, 1947; *Time*, October 6, 1947; *Publishers Weekly*, October 11, 1947; *Wilson Library Bulletin*, November, 1947.

MADDOCK, Reginald (Bertram) 1912-

PERSONAL: Born in 1912, in Warrington, England; married Louisa S. Hawthorn. *Residence:* High Legh, Knutsford, Cheshire, England.

CAREER: Headmaster; author. *Member:* Society of Authors, P.E.N.

WRITINGS—For children: *Rocky and the Lions* (illustrated by Robert Hodgson), Thomas Nelson, 1957; *The Time Maze* (illustrated by R. Hodgson), Thomas Nelson, 1960; *The Last Horizon* (illustrated by Douglas Relf), Thomas Nelson, 1961; *Rocky and the Elephant* (illustrated by R. Hodgson), Thomas Nelson, 1962; *The Willow Wand* (illustrated R. Hodgson), Thomas Nelson, 1962; *The Tall Man from the Sea* (illustrated by R. Hodgson), Thomas Nelson, 1962; *One More River* (illustrated by A. S. Douthwaite), Thomas Nelson, 1963; *The Great Bow*, Collins, 1964 [another edition illustrated by Victor Ambrus, Rand McNally, 1968]; *The Widgeon Gang* (illustrated by Dick Hart), Thomas Nelson, 1964; *The Pit* (illustrated by Douglas Hall), Little Brown, 1966; *Danny Rowley*, Little Brown, 1969; *The Dragon in the Garden*, Little Brown, 1969; *Sell-Out*, Collins, 1969; *Northmen's Fury* (illustrated by Graham Humphreys), Macdonald & Co., 1970; *Thin Ice*, Little, Brown, 1971.

"Corrigan" series; all illustrated by R. Hodgson; all published by Thomas Nelson: *Corrigan and the White Cobra*, 1956; . . . *and the Black Riders*, 1957; . . . *and the Tomb of Opi*, 1957; . . . *and the Yellow Peril*, 1957; . . . *and the Golden Pagoda*, 1958; . . . *and the Dream-Makers*, 1959; . . . *and the Blue Crater*, 1960; . . . *and the Green Tiger*, 1961; . . . *and the Red Lions*, 1962; . . . *and the Little People*, 1963.

SIDELIGHTS: Reginald Maddock's *The Pit* told the story of Butch Reece and how he improved his self-image and his tough kid reputation. "[*The Pit*] is full of exciting incident and good dialogue and does not dawdle in the narration. Underpriviledged American adolescents will readily understand Butch Reece's attitudes, which are not unlike their own," commented a critic for *Book World*. A *Horn Book* reviewer noted, "Butch Reece's story [is] told with gentleness and dignity.... Particularly memorable are the definite, individualistic characters." Similarly, a critic for *Young Readers' Review* wrote, "Mr. Maddock does an outstanding job in bringing this youth to life.... Incorporated into this good adventure story is a fine study of character and reputation that will interest, intrigue, and enlighten readers. This is a very good book with solid substance."

In *Northmen's Fury*, Maddock wove a tale set during the time of the Danish invasion and King Alfred. "It is a straight historical adventure, only saved from mediocrity by the excellent portrayal of its chief character.... The book as a whole fails to convey a proper sense of period.... Change the names and these people could be fighting invaders at any time in history," commented a reviewer for *Books and Bookmen*. A critic for the *Times Literary Supplement* also noted that Maddock failed to provide any "sense of period." However, the London *Times* critic observed other commendable qualities about the book. "[*Northmen's Fury* has] a good climax; it is all plausible, possible and fast-moving. The interests and doings of the little band are woven quite deftly into the larger Alfredian heroic picture."

I'm Butch Reece. My real name's Bernard but only my mother ever dared to use it. ■ (From *The Pit* by Reginald Maddock. Illustrated by Douglas Hall.)

FOR MORE INFORMATION SEE: Young Readers' Review, April, 1968; *Book World,* May 5, 1968; *Horn Book,* June, 1968, October, 1968, October, 1969; *Christian Science Monitor,* November 6, 1969; *Times Literary Supplement,* April 16, 1970; *Books and Bookmen,* May, 1970.

MANLEY, Seon

PERSONAL: Born in Connecticut; sister of Gogo Lewis (an author); married Robert Manley (a management consultant); children: Shivaun (daughter). *Education:* Attended Wellesley College. *Home:* Greenwich, Conn.

CAREER: Manley Management & Marketing Services, senior vice president, 1958-78. Has been employed in bookstores and in publishing company; author and editor.

WRITINGS: Adventures in Making: The Romance of Crafts around the World, Vanguard, 1959; *Rudyard Kipling, Creative Adventurer,* Vanguard, 1965; *Long Island Discovery: An Adventure into the History, Manners, and Mores of America's Front Porch,* Doubleday, 1966; *My Heart's in the Heather* (autobiographical), Funk & Wagnalls, 1968; *Nathaniel Hawthorne: Captain of Imagination,* Vanguard, 1968; (with husband, Robert Manley) *Beaches: Their Lives, Legends, and Lore,* Chilton, 1968; *My Heart's in Greenwich Village* (autobiographical), Funk & Wagnalls, 1969; (with R. Manley) *Islands: Their Lives, Legends, and Lore,* Chilton, 1970; (with Susan Belcher) *O Those Extraordinary Women; or, The Joys of Literary Lib,* Chilton, 1972; *Dorothy and William Wordsworth: The Heart of a Circle of Friends,* Vanguard, 1974; *The Ghost in the Far Garden, and Other Stories,* Lothrop, 1977.

Editor: *James Joyce: Two Decades of Criticism,* Vanguard, 1948, reissued, 1963; *Teen-Age Treasury for Girls,* Funk & Wagnalls, 1958; *Teen-Age Treasury of Good Humor,* Funk & Wagnalls, 1960; (with R. Manley) *The Age of the Manager: A Treasury of Our Times,* Macmillan, 1962.

Editor, with sister Gogo Lewis: *Teen-Age Treasury of Our Science World,* Funk & Wagnalls, 1961; *Teen-Age Treasury of Imagination and Discovery,* Funk & Wagnalls, 1962; *Mystery! A Treasury for Younger Readers,* Funk & Wagnalls, 1963; *Teen-Age Treasury of the Arts,* Funk & Wagnalls, 1964; *Merriment! A Treasury for Young Readers,* Funk & Wagnalls, 1965; *Suspense: A Treasury for Young Adults,* Funk & Wagnalls, 1966; *The Oceans: A Treasury of the Sea World,* Doubleday, 1967; *Magic: A Treasury for Young Readers,* Funk & Wagnalls, 1967; *Polar Secrets: A Treasury of the Arctic and Antarctic,* Doubleday, 1968; *High Adventure: A Treasury for Young Adults,* Funk & Wagnalls, 1968; *To You with Love: A Treasury of Great Romantic Literature,* M. Smith, 1969; *Shapes of the Supernatural,* Doubleday, 1969.

A Gathering of Ghosts: A Treasury, Funk & Wagnalls, 1970; *Ladies of Horror: Two Centuries of Supernatural Stories by the Gentle Sex,* Lothrop, 1971; *Grande Dames of Detection: Two Centuries of Sleuthing Stories by the Gentle Sex,* Lothrop, 1973; *Mistresses of Mystery: Two Centuries of Suspense Stories by the Gentle Sex,* Lothrop, 1973; *Bewitched Beings: Phantoms, Familiars, and the Possessed in Stories from Two Centuries,* Lothrop, 1974; *Baleful Beasts: Great Supernatural Stories of the Animal Kingdom,* Lothrop, 1974; *Masters of the Macabre: An Anthology of Mystery, Horror, and Detection,* Doubleday, 1975; *Ladies of the Gothics: Tales of Romance and Terror by the Gentle Sex,*

SEON MANLEY

Lothrop, 1975; *Ladies of Fantasy: Two Centuries of Sinister Stories by the Gentle Sex,* Lothrop, 1975; *Sisters of Sorcery: Two Centuries of Witchcraft Stories by the Gentle Sex,* Lothrop, 1976; *Women of the Weird: Eerie Stories by the Gentle Sex,* Lothrop, 1976; *Ghostly Gentlewomen: Two Centuries of Spectral Stories by the Gentle Sex,* Lothrop, 1977; *Masters of Shades and Shadows,* Doubleday, 1978.

SIDELIGHTS: "Certain themes run throughout my literary life. I was trained in the world of folklore and have had a great interest in the history of the supernatural story. Because I have worked in both aspects of publishing as a published author and as a working editor, I have had deep interest in the creative process of other authors. My professional life has led me into many aspects of technological advances in the understanding of the environment, and as such often inspires my work in the world of natural history. I write every day for about three quarters of the year."

Seon Manley's literary success has been very diverse. A *Young Readers Review* critique of *Nathaniel Hawthorne: Captain of the Imagination* included, "One strength of the book lies in Seon Manley's evocation of the times during which Hawthorne lived. But its main strength is in its picture of the creative artist as he struggles to put his inward vision on paper. This struggle to create, regardless of 'outside' influences and distractions, is yet dependent upon those very same 'outside' influences. This interaction between the environment and the creative spirit, which transmutes the artist's experiences into a work of art, is shown to the reader so that an appreciation of the difficulties and mysteries involved is inevitable. . . ."

Manley's autobiography, *My Heart's in the Heather,* was reviewed in the *New York Times Book Review:* "The structure of Seon Manley's book is as episodic as memory. Each episode is a delight. Mama is wholly Americanized, a dedicated admirer of the Revolutionary War heroine Molly Pitcher. Papa's heart remains in the heather. He never does take out naturalization papers, though he gives the United

In Scotland, there was a Meg of the Shore whose supernatural powers put her in the same league as the Mistress of Montauk Point. ■ (From *The Ghost in the Far Garden* by Seon Manley. Illustrated by Emanuel Schongut.)

States credit for two world bargains: the Bill of Rights and the five-and-ten. The dialogue, especially between the children is superb.''

With her sister, Seon Manley has edited several anthologies. In reviewing *Teen-Age Treasury of Our Science World,* a *Chicago Sunday Tribune* critic wrote, ''This bright anthology . . . is not a series of dry articles on the state of various sciences today. It is instead, a collection of the warm and witty, live and lively things that have been said about science and scientists and about the people who enlarge the boundaries of knowledge.'' The *New York Times Book Review* added, ''An unconventional, immensely provocative anthology. . . . Certain of the selections seem a little far-fetched, but the volume succeeds admirably in prodding the reader, who may have thought of science as a remote field for geniuses, into a realization of its breadth and immediacy.''

FOR MORE INFORMATION SEE: New York Times Book Review, October 8, 1961 and May 5, 1968; *Chicago Sunday Tribune,* November 12, 1961; *Young Readers Review,* May, 1969; *Horn Book,* February, 1970, October, 1974.

MANNING-SANDERS, Ruth 1895-

PERSONAL: Born in 1895, in Swansea, Wales; daughter of a minister; married George Manning-Sanders (an artist and writer); children: Joan (an artist), David. *Education:* Attended Manchester University. *Residence:* Penzance, Cornwall, England.

CAREER: Poet and novelist prior to World War II, and author of books for children, beginning 1948. Worked for two years with a circus. *Awards, honors:* Blindman International Poetry Prize, 1926, for *The City;* Kate Greenaway Medal, 1959, for *A Bundle of Ballads* (illustrated by William Stobbs).

WRITINGS—Fiction, except as noted: *The Twelve Saints,* E. J. Clode, 1926; *The City* (poem), Dial Press, 1927; *Waste Corner,* Christophers, 1927, E. J. Clode, 1928; *Hucca's Moor,* Faber & Gwyer, 1929; *The Crochet Woman,* Coward-McCann, 1930; *The Growing Trees,* Morrow, 1931; *She Was Sophia,* Cobden-Sanderson, 1932; *Run Away,* Cassell, 1934; *Mermaid's Mirror,* Cassell, 1935; *The Girl Who Made an Angel,* Cassell, 1936; *Elephant: The*

"Oh, my good, funny, dear, kind monster, open your eyes, look at me, tell me you forgive me, don't die, don't leave me, for I love you, my monster, and I will marry you, dear monster, I will be your faithful wife!" ■ (From *A Book of Monsters* by Ruth Manning-Sanders. Drawings by Robin Jacques.)

RUTH MANNING-SANDERS

Romance of Laura (short stories), F. A. Stokes, 1938; *Children by the Sea* (illustrated by Mary Shepard), Collins, 1938, published in America as *Adventure May be Anywhere*, F. A. Stokes, 1939; *Luke's Circus*, Collins, 1939, Little, Brown, 1940; *Mystery at Penmarth* (illustrated by Susanne Suba), McBride, 1941; *The West of England* (nonfiction), B. T. Batsford, 1949; *The River Dart* (nonfiction), Westaway Books, 1951; *Seaside England* (nonfiction), B. T. Batsford, 1951.

Juvenile: *The Circus*, Chanticleer Press, 1948; *Swan of Denmark: The Story of Hans Christian Andersen* (illustrated by Astrid Walford), Heinemann, 1949, McBride, 1950, a later edition published as *The Story of Hans Andersen, Swan of Denmark*, Dutton, 1966; *The English Circus*, Laurie, 1952; *The Golden Ball: A Novel of the Circus*, R. Hale, 1954; *Melissa*, R. Hale, 1957; *Peter and the Piskies: Cornish Folk and Fairy Tales* (illustrated by Raymond Briggs), Oxford University Press, 1958, Roy, 1966; *Circus Boy* (illustrated by Annette Macarthur-Onslow), Oxford University Press, 1960; *Red Indian Folk and Fairy Tales* (illustrated by C. Walter Hodges), Oxford University Press, 1960, Roy, 1962; *Animal Stories* (illustrated by A. Macarthur-Onslow), Oxford University Press, 1961, Roy, 1962; *A Book of Giants* (illustrated by Robin Jacques), Methuen, 1962, Dutton, 1963; *The Smugglers* (illustrated by William Stobbs), Oxford University Press, 1962; *A Book of Dwarfs* (illustrated by R. Jacques), Methuen, 1963, Dutton, 1964; *A Book of Dragons* (illustrated by R. Jacques), Methuen, 1964, Dutton, 1965.

Damian and the Dragon: Modern Greek Folk-Tales (illustrated by William Papas), Roy, 1965; *A Book of Wizards* (illustrated by R. Jacques), Methuen, 1966, Dutton, 1967; *A Book of Mermaids* (illustrated by R. Jacques), Methuen, 1967, Dutton, 1968; *Stories from the English and Scottish Ballads* (illustrated by Trevor Ridley), Dutton, 1968; *A Book of Ghosts and Goblins* (illustrated by Robin Jacques), Methuen, 1968, Dutton, 1969; *The Glass Man and the Golden Bird: Hungarian Folk and Fairy Tales* (illustrated by Victor G. Ambrus), Roy, 1968; *The Spaniards Are Coming!* (illustrated by Jacqueline Rizvi), Heinemann, 1969, Watts, 1970; *Jonnikin and the Flying Basket: French Folk and Fairy Tales* (illustrated by V. G. Ambrus), Dutton, 1969; *A Book of Princes and Princesses* (illustrated by R. Jacques), Methuen, 1969, Dutton, 1970; *Gianni and the Ogre* (illustrated by W. Stobbs), Methuen, 1970, Dutton, 1971; *A Book of Devils and Demons* (illustrated by R. Jacques), Dutton, 1970; *A Book of Charms and Changelings* (illustrated by R. Jacques), Methuen, 1971, Dutton, 1972; *A Choice of Magic* (illustrated by R. Jacques), Dutton, 1971; *A Book of Ogres and Trolls* (illustrated by R. Jacques), Methuen, 1972, Dutton, 1973; *A Book of Sorcerers and Spells* (illustrated by R. Jacques), Methuen, 1973, Dutton, 1974; *A Book of Magic Animals* (illustrated by R. Jacques), Methuen, 1974, Dutton, 1975; *Stumpy: A Russian Tale* (illustrated by Leon Shtainmets), Methuen, 1974; *Old Dog Sirko: A Ukrainian Tale* (illustrated by L. Shtainmets), Methuen, 1974; *Sir Green Hat and the Wizard* (illustrated by W. Stobbs), Methuen, 1974; *Tortoise Tales* (illustrated by Donald Chaffin), Nelson, 1974; *A Book of Monsters* (illustrated by R. Jacques), Methuen, 1975, Dutton, 1976; *Young Gabby Goose* (illustrated by J. Hodgson), Methuen, 1975; *Scottish Folk Tales* (illustrated by W. Stobbs), Methuen, 1976; *Fox Tales* (illustrated by J. Hodgson), Methuen, 1976.

Editor: *A Bundle of Ballads* (illustrated by W. Stobbs), Oxford University Press, 1959, Lippincott, 1961; *Birds, Beasts, and Fishes* (illustrated by Rita Parsons), Oxford University Press, 1962; *The Red King and the Witch* (illustrated by V. G. Ambrus), Oxford University Press, 1964, Roy, 1965; *The Hamish Hamilton Book of Magical Beasts* (illustrated by Raymond Briggs), Hamish Hamilton, 1965, published in America as *A Book of Magical Beasts,* T. Nelson, 1970; *A Book of Witches* (illustrated by R. Jacques), Methuen, 1965, Dutton, 1966; *Festivals* (illustrated by R. Briggs), Heinemann, 1972, Dutton, 1973.

SIDELIGHTS: Because of her close association with the circus, many of Ruth Manning-Sanders' books center around that form of entertainment. *English Circus* discussed the historical origins of the circus. A *Saturday Review* critic wrote, "No one even faintly interested in the circus—its history, traditions, and bizarre personalities—can fail to be interested in this detailed tribute, in spite of a rather uninspired writing style and the inclusion of material that is sometimes irritatingly fragmentary. Mrs. Manning-Sanders, however, more often than not manages to bring to life the glories of 'the art that eternally contemplates the proud enchantment of its own perfection.'" The London *Times Literary Supplement* added, "The book is agreeably and quietly written and contains a large amount of interesting information. Much of it has been gathered from the work of other writers and the book's main fault is that it lacks the freshness and drive of genuine originality."

Later in her career, Ruth Manning-Sanders concentrated mainly on books for children. One of the most recent is *A Book of Sorcerers and Spells.* The London *Times Literary Supplement* commented that, "The frequent use of rhetorical questions and of present-tense narrative makes the style vivid and easy to read aloud, in spite of its dependence on repeated tricks. The selection of stories is pleasantly varied, most of them being the sort of European fairy stories which Lang used so extensively. One exception to this, a tale from the African saga of Anansi the spider, arguably loses some of its effect out of context but in general this is an enjoyable, if unambitious collection."

FOR MORE INFORMATION SEE: Times Literary Supplement, November 14, 1952; *Saturday Review,* April 3, 1954; *Horn Book,* December, 1963, December, 1964, October, 1965, June, 1966, August, 1966, August, 1968, February, 1970, August, 1971, April, 1972; Doris de Montreville and Donna Hill, editors, *Third Book of Junior Authors,* H. W. Wilson, 1972; *Times Literary Supplement,* September 28, 1973.

MARKUN, Patricia M(aloney) 1924-
(Sybil Forrest, Ryan O'Carroll)

PERSONAL: Born August 24, 1924, in Chisholm, Minn.; daughter of Andrew Michael and Helen (Ryan) Maloney; married David J. Markun (an administrative law judge), June 14, 1948; children: Sybil, Meredith, David, Jr., Paul Addam. *Education:* University of Minnesota, B.A. (magna cum laude), 1945. *Politics:* Democrat. *Religion:* Catholic. *Home:* 4405 W. Street, N.W., Washington, D.C. 20007.

The clubs argue that cutting a highway through the refuge would bring an end to one more of the fast-disappearing dwelling places of these creatures. ■ (From *Politics* by Patricia Maloney Markun. Illustrated by Ted Schroeder.)

CAREER: WMFG, Hibbing, Minn., radio writer and announcer, 1942-43; KSTP, St. Paul, Minn., radio newswriter, 1945; WCCO, Minneapolis, Minn., radio newswriter, 1945; Worthington Pump Corp., Minneapolis, Minn., employees' magazine editor, 1945-46; Minneapolis Art Institute, Minneapolis, Minn., public relations writer, 1945-47; Hotel Nicollet, Minneapolis, Minn., advertising and publicity director, 1948; Television show, "Bienvenido" and "Pat Markun Show," 1963-66; Funk & Wagnall's Young Students Encyclopedia, executive editor, 1971-73; Association for Childhood Education International, editorial associate, 1973-75; *Petroleum Today* magazine of American Petroleum Institute, executive editor, 1977—. *Member:* National League of American Pen Women (president, Canal Zone branch, 1954-56), Theta Sigma Phi Alumnae Association, Democratic National Committee (1964-68), Children's Book Guild of Washington (president, 1976-77).

WRITINGS: The Pelican Tree, and Other Panama Adventures, North River Press, 1953; *The First Book of the Panama Canal,* Watts, 1958, 1962; *The Secret of El Baru* (Catholic Children's Book Club selection), Watts, 1958; *The First Book of Mining,* Watts, 1960; *The First Book of Central America and Panama,* Watts, 1963, revised edition, 1972; *The First Book of Politics,* Watts, 1971.

SIDELIGHTS: "I grew up in a little mining town on the Mesabi Iron Range in northern Minnesota—where 7,000 people, mostly immigrants from a variety of countries, went to fourteen different churches (including Russian, Serbian, and Greek churches using the Julian calendar with different Christmas and Easter dates) and spoke so many languages that learning English was the only way to communicate.

"Taxes from the iron ore had brought superb public schools and beautiful libraries to this remote outpost in the coldest part of the contiguous United States, and reading was a constant, ever renewing joy. Other people may remember their first teachers; I remember my first librarians, and the pleasure of wandering undisciplined, unrestrained among the stacks—piling my treasures then on one of the round, golden oak tables, and sitting down to choose which books I would take home.

"The Mesabi Range was a marvelous place to grow up with appreciation of people from many countries, learning their songs and how to cook their foods, doing their dances as a Girl Scout.

"When I married and went to live in the Panama Canal Zone, again I found myself in an environment of more than one culture, and learned Spanish so that we could enjoy spending summers among Spanish speaking Panamanians high in the mountains near the Costa Rican border. Washington has this international flavor, too.

"These various backgrounds have all influenced my writing, plus a fascination with mining and geology and later petroleum that is traceable to the iron mines I grew up among. I enjoy making information interesting to children, and I love writing mysteries."

MARTIN, J(ohn) P(ercival)   1880?-1966

PERSONAL: Born around 1880, in Scarborough, Yorkshire, England; died in March, 1966, in Timberscombe, Somerset, England. *Religion:* Methodist. *Home:* Timberscombe, Somerset, England.

CAREER: Entered the Methodist ministry in 1902; served as a missionary in South Africa; became chaplain during the First World War and worked mainly in Palestine; went into semi-retirement at the end of the Second World War and served the Chapel in Timberscombe, Somerset, England until 1966; author of book's for children.

WRITINGS —All illustrated by Quentin Blake: *Uncle*, J. Cape, 1964, Coward-McCann, 1966; *Uncle Cleans Up*, J. Cape, 1965, Coward-McCann, 1967; *Uncle and His Detective*, J. Cape, 1966; *Uncle and the Treacle Trouble*, J. Cape, 1967; *Uncle and Claudius the Camel*, J. Cape, 1969.

FOR MORE INFORMATION SEE: Brian Doyle, editor, *Who's Who of Children's Literature*, Schocken, 1968.

MAWICKE, Tran   1911-

PERSONAL: Surname is pronounced Mahwick; born September 20, 1911, in Chicago, Ill.; son of Henry J. (a photo engraver) and Margaret (Mann) Mawicke; married Laura Dodge (a real estate agent), February 17, 1939; children: David, Jane (Mrs. David Thomas), Helen (Mrs. Richard Ashley, Jr.), Catherine. *Education:* Attended St. Thomas Academy, St. Paul, Minn.; School of the Art Institute, Chi-

cago, Ill.; American Academy of Art, Chicago, Ill. *Religion:* Roman Catholic. *Home and office:* 452 Golf Villas, Route 1, Johns Island, S.C. 29455.

CAREER: Artist; illustrator. *Member:* Society of Illustrators (president, 1960-61), American Watercolor Society (director, 1962-64, 1971-73).

ILLUSTRATOR: Ralph Moody, *Little Britches*, Norton, 1950; Ralph Moody, *Man of the Family*, Norton, 1951; Ralph Moody, *Fields of Home*, Norton, 1953; Ralph Moody, *Home Ranch*, Norton, 1956; Mary Elting, *Answer Book*, Grosset, 1959; Benjamin Appel *Book About South America*, Grosset, 1960; Mary Elting, *Answers and More Answers*, Grosset, 1961; Ralph Moody, *Mary Emma and Company*, Norton, 1961; Ralph Moody, *Shaking the Nickel Bush*, Norton, 1962; Ralph Moody, *Dry Divide*, Norton, 1963; Marion Talmridge and Iris Gilmore, *Six Great Horse Rides*, Putnam, 1967; Al Schutzer, *Great Civil War Escapes*, Putnam, 1967; Jean Rikoff, *Robert E. Lee: Soldier of the South*, Putnam, 1968; James Norman, *Young Generals*, Putnam, 1968; Paul Rink, *John Paul Jones: Conquer or Die*, Putnam, 1968; Lois Duncan, *Major Andre: Brave Enemy*, Putnam, 1969; *Zachary Taylor*, Putnam, 1969; Carl Malmberg, *America is also Scandinavian*, Putnam, 1970; Sonia Fox, *Chicago Burns*, Putnam, 1971; Burke Davis, *Getting to Know Jamestown*, Coward, 1971; Robert N. Webb, *America is also Irish*, Putnam, 1973; F. L. Devereux, *Famous American Horses*, Devin-Adair, 1975; Lynn Hall, *Captain: Canada's Flying Pony*, Garrard, 1975; Richard

TRAN MAWICKE

By the light of the lantern, John studied the face of the man across from him. ■ (From *Major Andre: Brave Enemy* by Lois Duncan. Illustrated by Tran Mawicke.)

Skolnik, *Our Great Heritage* (Volumes I and XI), Consolidated Book, 1975; Joanne L. Henry, *Robert Fulton: Steamboat Builder*, Garrard, 1975; Edwin P. Hoyt, *The Terrible Voyage*, Pinnacle, 1976.

WORK IN PROGRESS: History of Seabrook and Kiawah Islands.

SIDELIGHTS: "Enjoy historical subjects. I have traveled in Ireland, Spain, Portugal, Brazil, England, France, Morocco, Japan, Taiwan, and the Phillipines. I play golf and painted golf courses all over the United States. Enjoy portrait painting."

FOR MORE INFORMATION SEE: American Artist, July, 1972.

McKAY, Robert W. 1921-

PERSONAL: Born June 4, 1921, in Mayville, N.Y.; son of S. H. and Ebba (Stark) McKay; divorced; children: Robert W., Jr. *Education:* Attended University of Massachusetts. *Home:* 30 Academy St., Mayville, N.Y. *Agent:* Ann Elmo Agency, Inc., 545 Fifth Ave., New York, N.Y. 10017.

CAREER: Free-lance writer. *Military service:* U.S. Army Air Forces, 1943-46; became second lieutenant. *Member:* Nu-Color Bird Association.

WRITINGS: The Way Things Are, Pyramid Books, 1964; *Canary Red*, Hawthorn, 1968; *Dave's Song*, Hawthorn, 1969; *The Troublemaker*, Nelson, 1972; *Skean*, Nelson, 1976; *Bordy*, Nelson, 1977. Contributor of short stories and articles to magazines.

ROBERT W. McKAY

(From *Bordy* by Robert McKay.)

WORK IN PROGRESS: Winning, a novel for young people; a novel dealing with love and chance.

HOBBIES AND OTHER INTERESTS: Fishing.

MILHOUS, Katherine 1894-1977

PERSONAL: Born November 27, 1894, in Philadelphia, Penn.; daughter of Oscar Thomas (a printer) and Katie Arey Daly (a seamstress; maiden name McGuckin) Milhous. *Education:* Attended the Philadelphia Museum School of Industrial Art and the Pennsylvania Academy of Fine Arts. *Residence:* Philadelphia, Penn.

CAREER: Federal Art Project, supervisor, late 1930's; Charles Scribner's Sons, New York, N.Y., book designer, 1945-47; author, illustrator, and designer of books for children. *Member:* Authors League of America, American Institute of Graphic Arts, United World Federalists, Bookseller's Association of Philadelphia, Historical Society of Pennsylvania, Society of Architectural Historians, Independence Hall Association. *Awards, honors:* Caldecott Medal, 1951, for *The Egg Tree;* citation from the Drexel Institute of Technology, 1967.

WRITINGS—All self-illustrated and all published by Scribner, except as noted: *Lovina: A Story of the Pennsylvania Country*, 1940; *Herodia, the Lovely Puppet*, 1942; *Corporal Keeperupper*, 1943; *The First Christmas Crib*, 1944; *Snow over Bethlehem*, 1945; *The Egg Tree*, 1950; *Patrick and the Golden Slippers*, 1951; *Appolonia's Valentine*, 1954; *With Bells On: A Christmas Story*, 1955; *Through These Arches: The Story of Independence Hall*, Lippincott, 1964.

Every hour of the day people strolled up from the Town to see the State House—women with babes in arms, soldiers, sailors, shopkeepers, clergymen, Ben Franklin and the young fellows of his Leathern Apron Club. Indians, when in town, came to marvel. No day was without its group of onlookers, admiring, commenting. ■ (From *Through These Arches* by Katherine Milhous. Illustrated by the author.)

Illustrator; all published by Scribner, except as noted: Alice Dalgliesh, *Once on a Time*, 1938; Dalgliesh, compiler, *Happily Ever After: Fairy Tales*, 1939; Dalgliesh, *Book for Jennifer*, 1940; Dalgliesh, *Wings around South America*, 1941; Mabel L. Hunt, *Billy Button's Buttered Biscuit*, Lippincott, 1941; Hunt, *Peter Piper's Pickled Peppers*, Lippincott, 1942; A. Dalgliesh, *They Live in South America*, 1942; Dalgliesh, *Little Angel*, 1943; Dalgliesh, *The Silver Pencil*, 1944; Dalgliesh, *Along Janet's Road*, 1946; (and adapter) Juliana H. G. Ewing, *The Brownies*, 1946.

SIDELIGHTS: Katherine Milhous' Pennsylvania Dutch heritage played an important part in her career. She designed a series of Pennsylvania Dutch posters that attracted the attention of Scribner's juvenile editor, Alice Dalgliesh, and thus began her career as a children's book illustrator, a vocation which later expanded to include writing as well.

The Pennsylvania Dutch were the subject matter for several of her books. Her first effort, *Lovina: A Story of the Penn-*

sylvania Country, depicted the heroine as a young girl in the beginning and a grandmother at the end. Although this concept is difficult for young readers to grasp, the story is still appealing, according to Elaine Templin, because, "its illustrations are gay and colorful, bold and uncluttered and typical of the native art of the Pennsylvania Dutch. Moreover, her characters are pictured as plain, comfortable-looking, friendly people...." *New Yorker* described the book as, "... an attractive volume with bright postery pictures and a story with the qualities of a folk tale." Added the *Boston Transcript:* "To parents who strive early to imbue in their children a feeling for the antique and a sympathy for different cults and customs, we recommend *Lovina*. Miss Milhous ... authoritatively illustrates her own book with handsome design and striking color. This so-called 'picture' book is a real experience for children and adults as well."

The Egg Tree, a story concerning the Easter customs of the Pennsylvania Dutch, won the Caldecott Medal in 1951. The *New York Herald Tribune Book Review* noted, "The simple

KATHERINE MILHOUS

tale is gently and plainly written but the many colored pictures and designs around the pages enrich it. . . . The artist's bold, simple style is one that would encourage children to try painting themselves." Observed the *New York Times:* "It is a pity the narrative isn't more substantial and that there isn't more use of color words in the text to convey that joy which children have in using colors. But there are lovely illustrations and decorations based on traditional Pennsylvania Dutch designs to stimulate young eyes and young fingers. . . ."

Milhous called *Through These Arches: The Story of Independence Hall* her most important book because her love for the city of Philadelphia and its history are depicted in it. "The History of Philadelphia," wrote a *Horn Book* reviewer, "[is presented] through a kaleidoscope of changing scenes at the site of Independence Hall. . . . The striking, decorative pictures are printed in coral and teal blue, with black, on a light wrapping-paper brown."

According to Elaine Templin, writing in *Elementary English,* Katherine Milhous believed that good art must possess an intangible, indefinable force that is felt instead of seen. "Her work has the sturdy quality of pioneer living. It tells of people who know the joy of creating gifts with their hands, of people who appreciate the wonders and beauties of nature, of people who live simple lives and have close and loving family ties that are made closer through the celebration of holidays and festivals, of people devoted to all things beautiful and to the creators of such beauty."

FOR MORE INFORMATION SEE: Boston Transcript, April 6, 1940; *New Yorker,* May 18, 1940; Bertha E. Mahony and others, compilers, *Illustrators of Children's Books, 1744-1945,* Horn Book, 1947; *New York Times,*

March 19, 1950; *New York Herald Tribune Book Review,* March 26, 1950; (for children) Stanley J. Kunitz and Howard Haycraft, editors, *Junior Book of Authors,* 2nd edition, revised, H. W. Wilson, 1951; "Elizabeth Yates and Katherine Milhous Win Newbery and Caldecott Medals," *Publishers Weekly,* March 10, 1951; Frances Lichten, "Katherine Milhous," *Horn Book,* July, 1951; Elaine Templin, "Enjoying Festivals with Katherine Milhous," *Elementary English,* November, 1957, reprinted in Miriam Hoffman and Eva Samuels, *Authors and Illustrators of Children's Books,* Bowker, 1972; B. M. Miller and others, compilers, *Illustrators of Children's Books, 1946-1956,* Horn Book, 1958; *Horn Book,* August, 1964; Lee Kingman and others, compilers, *Illustrators of Children's Books, 1957-1966,* Horn Book, 1968.

(Died December 5, 1977)

MILLER, Don   1923-

PERSONAL: Born June 30, 1923, in Jamaica, West Indies; son of Claude C. (a school custodian) and Rhena (Newman) Miller; married Julia Guitano (a director of Black studies), June 8, 1952; children: Eric, Craig. *Education:* Cooper Union, certificate, 1949; attended Art Students League,

DON MILLER

The first day, Edgar rode the wheel all the way to Bathsheba, where he saw giant waves of water, so cold it seemed frosted, whip the huge boulders and rocks as they crashed onto the sand.
■ (From *A Bicycle from Bridgetown* by Dawn C. Thomas. Illustrated by Don Miller.)

1950; New School for Social Research, 1967. *Home:* 14 Stanford Place, Montclair, N.J. 07042. *Office:* 363 Bloomfield Avenue, Montclair, N.J. 07042.

CAREER: Illustrator. Chernow Advertising Agency, New York, N.Y., assistant art director, 1950-52; Black Starr and Gorham, New York, N.Y., art director and illustrator, 1952-57; free-lance illustrator, 1957—. Montclair Public Library Board of Trustees, president, 1971-75; Essex County Cultural and Heritage Commission. *Exhibitions*—One-man shows: Madison Public Library, Madison, N.J., 1946; East Orange Public Library, East Orange, N.J., 1960, 1977; Montclair Community Hospital, Montclair, N.J., 1968; Montclair Public Library, Montclair, N.J., 1970, 1974; St. Peters College, Jersey City, N.J., 1973; Annex Gallery, Montclair, N.J., 1973; Bloomsburg State College, Bloomsburg, Pa., 1974; Morristown Community Medical Center, 1976; Double Tree Gallery, Montclair, N.J., 1978. Group Shows: Atlanta University, University of Pennsylvania, University of Connecticut, Trenton State College, Montclair State College, Fairleigh Dickinson, Seton Hall University, Colorado State Museum, New Jersey State Museum, Newark Museum, Montclair Art Museum, Marebesh Museum, American Museum of Natural History. *Military service:* U.S. Army, illustrator on Army newspaper, 1943-46.

Member: National Conference of Artists, Society of Illustrators.

ILLUSTRATOR: Dashielle Hammett (editor), *Windblown and Dripping,* Adakian Press, 1945; Van Wyck Mason, *Himalyan Assignment,* Doubleday, 1952; Charles Dougherty, *Searchers of the Deep,* Viking, 1957; Mark Twain, *Huckleberry Finn,* Scholastic, 1963; Marshall Smelser, Charles McCollester, *Frontiers of Freedom,* Silver Burdett, 1964; (editor) Sidney Seltzer, *Science for Tomorrow's World,* Macmillan, 1965; (editor) Alfred Cain, *American Negro Reference Book,* Negro Heritage Library, 1965; Kathrine Murrey, *Family Laugh Lines,* Prentice-Hall, 1966; David Knight, *Let's Find out About Mars,* Watts, 1966; *Boys Life Book of Sports,* Random House, 1967; David Knight, *Let's Find Out About Telephones,* Watts, 1967; David Knight, *Let's Find Out About Magnets,* Watts, 1967; David Knight, *Let's Find Out About Earth,* Watts, 1968; Jack and Vashti Brown, *Proudly We Hail,* Houghton, 1968; Thomas Johnson; *When Nature Runs Wild,* Creative Education, 1968.

Lewis Fenderson, *Daniel Hale Williams,* McGraw, 1971; Jack and Vashti Brown, *Stronger Than the Rest,* Houghton, 1971; Jack and Vashti Brown, *Above the Crowd,* Houghton, 1971; Jack and Vashti Brown, *Out in Front,* Houghton,

1971; Lucille Clifton, *The Black BC's*, Dutton, 1972; Conrad Schmidt, Protase Woodford, and Randall Marshall, *Learning Spanish the Modern Way*, McGraw, 1972; Conrad Schmidt, Protase Woodford, and Randall Marshall, *Learning German the Modern Way*, McGraw, 1973; Brenda Johnston, *Between the Devil and the Sea: The Life of James Forten*, Harcourt, 1974; *Caring and Sharing*, John Knox, 1974; Alice Walker, *Langston Hughes, American Poet*, Crowell, 1974; Dawn C. Thomas, *Bicycle from Bridgetown*, McGraw, 1975; James Haskins, *The Creoles of Color*, Crowell, 1975; Ernest and Mindy Thompson, *Homeboy Comes to Orange*, Bridgebuilder Press, 1975; Roscoe Brown, *The Little Black Book*, 3 Volumes, Artography, 1976, 1977, 1978; Earl Koger, *Jocko: A Legend of the American Revolution*, Prentice-Hall, 1976; Willis Lindquist, *Haji of the Elephants*, McGraw, 1976.

Illustrations have appeared in *Grolier's Book of Popular Science* and *Book of Knowledge, Collier's Encyclopedia, True Magazine, Grade Teacher Magazine* and *Children's Digest*. Produced visuals for twelve sound filmstrips for McGraw.

SIDELIGHTS: "Although I had illustrated five books prior to 1963, until then I had not focused on book illustration as a major interest. It was during a meeting my wife and I had with my son's second grade teacher that I decided to concentrate on this specialty. We were shown some *Dick and Jane* books used to teach reading. The families illustrated in these books were middle class suburbanite blue-eyed blonds. My son and other black children could not see themselves in these books.

"That same year publishers began to revise illustrations to better reflect our multi-racial society, and my career as a book illustrator was underway."

FOR MORE INFORMATION SEE: Grade Teacher Magazine, September, 1967; *Suburban Life*, March, 1970; *Encore*, April, 1973.

JANE MILLER

Sometimes drops of milk spill all over her face.
■ (From *Birth of a Foal* by Jane Miller. Photographs by the author.)

MILLER, Jane (Judith) 1925-

PERSONAL: Born October 6, 1925, in Sydney, Australia; daughter of Peter and Thelma (Thomson) Lawrence; divorced. *Education:* Educated in Australia. *Residence:* London, England. *Agent:* Jonathan Clowes Ltd., 19 Jeffreys Pl., London N.W.1, England.

CAREER: Free-lance photographer and writer for children, 1965—. *Awards, honors:* Outstanding Science Books for Children for *Birth of a Foal*, 1977.

WRITINGS—For children: *Foxglove Farm*, Dent, 1975; *Birth of a Foal*, Lippincott, 1977; *Lambing Time*, Dent, 1978, Methuen, in press.

WORK IN PROGRESS: More children's books.

SIDELIGHTS: "My other work in photography is with a variety of books, magazines and papers on a free-lance basis. I also supply the natural history pictures for greeting cards, etc. My favourite subjects are animals, where possible in their natural surroundings. I spend hours waiting for the right moment to capture the desired photograph, or often the unexpected one that just happens. You have to be relaxed with your subject and use a form of telepathy. In photographing for my books on animals for children, I first have to get the confidence of the animals just by being with them and talking to them, so that after a time they get used to me and I am able to concentrate on the photography.

"I have lived in Thailand and visited the United States."

ELSE HOLMELUND MINARIK

MINARIK, Else Holmelund 1920-

PERSONAL: Born September 13, 1920, in Denmark; emigrated to the U.S. at age four; married Walter Minarik (died, 1963); married Homer Bigart, 1970; children: (first marriage) Brooke. *Education:* Attended Queens College (now of the City University of New York) and Paltz College of the State University of New York.

CAREER: Has worked as a reporter for a local newspaper and as a teacher during World War II in a rural school in Commack, Long Island; author of books for children. *Awards, honors:* Runner-up for the Caldecott Medal, 1962, for *Little Bear's Visit; Father Bear Comes Home* and *A Kiss for Little Bear* (both illustrated by Maurice Sendak) were listed among the New York Times Choice of Best Illustrated Children's Books of the Year in 1959 and 1968, respectively.

WRITINGS: Little Bear (illustrated by Maurice Sendak), Harper, 1957; *No Fighting, No Biting!* (illustrated by M. Sendak), Harper, 1958; *Father Bear Comes Home* (illustrated by M. Sendak), Harper, 1959; *Cat and Dog* (illustrated by Fritz Siebel), Harper, 1960, reissued, World's Work, 1969; *Little Bear's Friend* (illustrated by M. Sendak), Harper, 1960; *Little Bear's Visit* (illustrated by M. Sendak), Harper, 1961; *The Little Giant Girl and the Elf Boy* (illustrated by Garth Williams), Harper, 1963; *The Winds That Come From Far Away, and Other Poems* (illustrated by Joan P. Berg), Harper, 1964; *A Kiss for Little Bear* (illustrated by M. Sendak), Harper, 1968.

SIDELIGHTS: As a result of her teaching experience, Else Holmelund Minarik became interested in writing for children. When she couldn't find enough books for her first-graders, she responded to their needs by writing books herself.

Commenting on Else Minarik's first book, *Little Bear*, a *New York Times* critic wrote, "It is difficult to be practical about something charming—one wants only to be charmed. Yet this is a book that must be considered on two counts: its joyousness and its usefulness. It passes on both counts. One look at the illustrations and children will grab it. A second look at the short, easy sentences, the repetition of words and the beautiful type spacing, and children will know they can read it themselves." Wrote *New Yorker:* "What makes this book different from all the other children's books in which animals wear clothes and live in houses is that instead of being a tale told to amuse children it all seems to be happening within a child's head. Also the fact that it is so full of love."

Kirkus' comments concerning *No Fighting, No Biting!* included, "Else Holmelund Minarik whose *Little Bear* indicated a uniquely charming talent has outdone herself here, and Maurice Sendak's illustrations reaffirm the impression that he is one of the most gifted illustrators of contemporary children's books." The *New York Times* remarked that, "Mrs. Minarik has wisely not tried to repeat the tender mood of her first book—that was probably inimitable, even by its own author. This new one may not touch the emotions so sensitively and may not be so durable, but children should find very realistic the sketches of two youngsters engaged in one of those timeless routines of pinching, squeezing, and general teasing. . . ."

Most recently, Else Minarik has written *A Kiss for Little Bear*. "In return for a picture he has drawn," wrote *Library Journal,* "grandma sends Little Bear a kiss via several animals until the hen puts a stop to 'too much kissing.' The illustrations are lovely, soft, and charming. The story features less of Little Bear and more of his friends this time but will certainly take its place among the other Little Bear favorites." A *Horn Book* critic commented, "[The story] is slight and almost incidental to the pictures. As in all Little Bear books the artist's imagination complements and greatly extends the text. The illustrations, in muted greenish-yellow and brown, seem filled with an end-of-summer melancholy that is heightened by the expressions of alarm and watchfulness in many of the animals' eyes. There is, however, humor in each animal's reaction, as he or she receives a kiss. The illustrations have splendid touches . . . and Little Bear's kiss at the end shows that he is acquiring savoir-faire." *Commonweal* added, "Little Bear is a creature of love and joy and he spreads it around in this enchanting story. The illustrations are incredibly alive and expressive. This is a good easy reader, the vocabulary is simple but vivid, and the story is well constructed."

HOBBIES AND OTHER INTERESTS: Gardening.

FOR MORE INFORMATION SEE: New York Times, September 8, 1957; *New Yorker,* November 23, 1957; *Kirkus,* July 15, 1958; *New York Times,* October 5, 1958; *Horn Book,* October, 1968; *Commonweal,* November 22, 1968; Lee Bennett Hopkins, *Books Are by People,* Citation Press, 1969; Doris de Montreville and Donna Hill, editors, *Third Book of Junior Authors,* H. W. Wilson, 1972.

"If I could grow little," she said, "we might be playmates." ■ (From *The Little Giant Girl and the Elf Boy* by Else Holmelund Minarik. Illustrated by Garth Williams.)

"**Willy, you sit here, and Rosa, you sit here. Now be still. I want to read.**" ■ (From *No Fighting, No Biting!* by Else Holmelund Minarik. Pictures by Maurice Sendak.)

MUNARI, Bruno 1907-

PERSONAL: Born October 24, 1907, in Milan, Italy; son of a waiter and innkeeper; married wife, Dilma; children: Alberto. *Education:* Attended the Technical Institute of Naples (Italy), but received no formal training in art. *Residence:* Milan, Italy.

CAREER: Painter, sculptor, photographer, illustrator and designer of books, toys, and mobiles. *Awards, honors:* Gold Medal of the Triennale of Milan; several Golden Compasses for industrial designs; *Bruno Munari's ABC* and the *Circus in the Mist* were listed among the New York Times Choice of Best Illustrated Children's Books of the Year in 1960 and 1969, respectively.

WRITINGS: I Libri Munari, Mondadori, 1945; *Nella Notte Buia,* Muggiani, 1956, translation published as *In the Dark of the Night,* G. Wittenborn, 1961; *Alfabetiere Secondo il Metodo Attivo,* Einaudi, 1960; *Il Quadrato* (published with "The Square," a translation by Desmond O'Grady), G. Wittenborn, 1960, translation also published separately as *Discovery of the Square,* G. Wittenborn, 1963; *Vetrine,*

Negozi Italiani: Modern Design For Italian Show-Windows and Shops (text in Italian, English, and German), Editrice L'Ufficio Moderno, 1961; *Good Design* (translation from the Italian), All'Insegna del Pesce D'Oro (distributed by G. Wittenborn), 1963; *Supplemento al Dizionario Italiano* (text in English, French, and German), Muggiani, 1963, also published as *Supplement to the Italian Dictionary,* G. Wittenborn, 1963; *Il Cerchio,* All'Insegna del Pesce D'Oro, 1964, translation by Marcello and Edna Maestro published as *The Discovery of the Circle,* G. Wittenborn, 1965; *Arte come Mestiere,* Laterza, 1966, translation by Patrick Creagh published as *Design as Art,* Penguin, 1971; *Libro Illeggibile,* Museum of Modern Art (New York), 1967; *Design e Comunicazione Visiva,* Laterza, 1968; *Codice Ovvio,* G. Einaudi, 1971; *Artista e Designer,* Laterza, 1971; *Cappuccetto Verde* (illustrated by the author), Einaudi, 1972.

For children; all illustrated by the author: *Lorry Driver,* Harvill, 1953; *What I'd Like to Be,* Harvill, 1953; *Animals for Sale* (translation from the Italian by Maria Cimino), World Publishing, 1957; *Who's There? Open the Door!* (translation from the Italian by M. Cimino), World Publishing, 1957; *Tic, Tac, and Toc* (translation of *Storie di Tre*

The lion
does not fear
anyone.

(From *Bruno Munari's Zoo*. Illustrated by the author.)

Uccellini by M. Cimino), World Publishing, 1957; *The Elephant's Wish* (translation of *Mai Contenti*), World Publishing, 1959; *The Birthday Present* (translation of *L'Uomo del Camion*), World Publishing, 1959; *Jimmy Has Lost His Cap, Where Can It Be?* (translation of *Gigi Cerca il suo Berretto),* World Publishing, 1959; *Bruno Munari's ABC,* World Publishing, 1960; *Bruno Munari's Zoo*, World Publishing 1963; *Nella Nebbia di Milano,* Emme Edizioni, 1968, translation published as *The Circus in the Mist,* World Publishing, 1969; *Da Lontano era un'Isola,* Emme, 1971, translation by Pierrette Fleutiaux published as *From Afar It Is an Island,* World Publishing, 1972; *A Flower with Love* (translation from the Italian by Patricia T. Lowe), Crowell, 1974.

Illustrator: Gianni Rodari, *Filastrocche in Cielo e in Terra,* Einaudi, 1960; G. Rodari, *Il Pianeta degli Alberi de Natale,* Einaudi, 1962; G. Rodari, *Favole al Telefono,* Einaudi, 1962; G. Rodari, *Il Libro degli Errori,* Einaudi, 1964; G. Rodari, *La Torta in Cielo,* Einaudi, 1966; Nico Orengo, *A-Uli-Ule: Filastrocche, Conte, Ninnenanne,* Einaudi, 1972. Also creator of several educational games.

Editor: *Design Italiano: Mobili* (text in English, French, German, and Italian), C. Bestetti, 1968; (with others) *Campo Urbano: Interventi Estetici Nella Dimensione Collettiva Urbana,* C. Nani, 1969. Also edited a collection for children, *Tantibambini,* and a notebook of design, *Quaderni Di Design.* A new book, *Fantasia* (title means, "Fantasy") has been published by Laterza of Bari.

ADAPTATIONS—Filmstrip: "Bruno Munari's ABC," produced by Weston Woods.

SIDELIGHTS: Bruno Munari began his career at age twenty as a member of the Italian Futurist Movement, a group of artists whose efforts were concentrated on giving formal expression to the energy and movement related to mechanical processes. He later became interested in making mobiles, which he calls 'machine inutile'—useless machines.

His work has been exhibited in the United States at the New York Public Library and the Museum of Modern Art in New York City. In 1965 he held a one-man show in Tokyo.

In 1967 Munari was invited by Harvard University to teach Basic Design and Advanced Explorations in Visual Communications. There he experimented with a new method of teaching design which he later published in book form, *Design and Visual Communications.*

He began publishing books for children when his own son was small, and in his opinion, there were no good books for children. All of the illustrations in these books were done in tempera. *Horn Book's* comments on *Bruno Munari's ABC* included, "It is not difficult to imagine an attractive ABC book. Good design with plenty of space, interesting objects skillfully drawn in lovely true colors.... However, Mr. Munari's genius does not let him stop with those essentials. He has made an ABC book that is so truly a work of art that one can look at it again and again and never tire, and it has exuberance and wit as well. Because young children are ready to accept anything we give them, nothing can be too good for them. Beauty now can make them receptive to beauty always. Here is beauty and imagination and fun. No child should miss it." Observed *New Yorker:* "A light-hearted alphabet book full of the surrealistic surprises that one has come to associate with this Italian artist. Each double-page spread is an experiment in balancing colors, textures, and space. It is as if every letter had produced its own mood and color."

In reviewing *The Circus in the Mist,* a *New York Times Book Review* critic wrote: "Bruno Munari is not only an illustrator but an innovator—a master at introducing us to the delights of abstraction by playing with color and form, and he does it superbly in this experiment in bookcraft. The story is simple—a trip through the foggy city when 'birds make only short flights'.... This in black on translucent gray paper evoking a synesthesia of silence till we come to the Grand Circus complete with clowns and the high trapeze where colors are hot and pages laced with cutouts.... The limits are those of your imagination.... Here is the conscious use of skill, taste, and creative imagination. The effect is exquisite perfection in the graphic arts." Zena Sutherland, writing in *Saturday Review* noted, "[This is] a beautifully designed, imaginative book.... The text is free and rambling, often mildly nonsensical." In a review of Bruno Munari's most recent book, *A Flower with Love,* the *Bulletin of the Center for Children's Books* observed: "Handsome color photographs show a dozen examples of ikebana, the Japanese art of flower arrangement. Munari wisely chooses not to stress the technical aspects of balance and design but to show arrangements that exemplify the restraint of ikebana compositions.... Each full page photo-graph is faced by a paragraph of text occasionally adding a line drawing. The book itself is handsome, and it conveys effectively both the idea of choosing a flower lovingly and of expressing love by a gift of inexpensive beauty."

FOR MORE INFORMATION SEE: Bertha Mahony Miller and others, compilers, *Illustrators of Children's Books, 1946-56,* Horn Book, 1958; *Horn Book,* October, 1960; *New Yorker,* November 19, 1960; Lee Kingman and others, compilers, *Illustrators of Children's Books, 1956-66,* Horn Book, 1968; *New York Times Book Review,* December 14, 1969; *Saturday Review,* March 21, 1970; (for children) Doris de Montreville and Donna Hill, editors, *Third Book of Junior Authors,* H. W. Wilson, 1972; *Bulletin of the Center for Children's Books,* April, 1975.

MUNSON(-BENSON), Tunie   1946-

PERSONAL: Born August 15, 1946, in Chicago, Ill.; daughter of George Randall (a painter and decorator) and Violet May (an executive secretary; maiden name, Seaberg) Munson; married Peter Lorimer Benson (a psychologist), June 7, 1969; children: Liv Christina. *Education:* Augustana College, Rock Island, Ill., B.A. (magna cum laude), 1968. *Religion:* Lutheran. *Home:* Minneapolis, Minnesota.

CAREER: Conde Nast Publications, New York, N.Y., junior copywriter for *Vogue,* 1968-69; elementary school teacher in Wallingford, Conn., 1969-70, and Aurora, Colo., 1971-73; free-lance writer, 1973-75; Earlham College, Richmond, Ind., part-time lecturer in children's literature, 1975-77; public lecturer on children's literature 1978—. *Member:* Ann Arbor Writers, Detroit Women Writers, Earlham Writers.

WRITINGS: (Under name Tunie Munson) *A Fistful of Sun* (juvenile), Lothrop, 1974. Contributor to magazines, including *American Baby.* Guest editor-in-chief of *Mademoiselle,* 1968.

BRUNO MUNARI   **TUNIE MUNSON**

"I'm not looking for eggs. I'm looking for Robert Fogarty."

Mrs. Priebe frowned. "If that's the case, you're looking for trouble." ■ (From *A Fistful of Sun* by Tunie Munson. Illustrated by Richard Cuffari.)

WORK IN PROGRESS: 7-8-9! (tentative title), a juvenile picture book.

SIDELIGHTS: "I continue to resist the dubious status of grownup. My happiest hours have been spent with children—my own, students, neighborhood friends—and writing has become a natural extension of my love for them, a way to weave my life into the lives of these special persons, and a rewarding means to that end. A fledgling's attempt at a first book (which has as its setting a loft open to sun and sky, inviting flight) has led me to a loft of my own, where I try my wings and, through writing, believe that someday, I too may 'fly.' I'm a pusher of children's books, and addicted to all kinds. I'm partial to the child within me . . . and others."

HOBBIES AND OTHER INTERESTS: Weaving on a floor loom.

FOR MORE INFORMATION SEE: Mademoiselle, August, 1968.

NATHAN, Dorothy (Goldeen)   ?-1966

PERSONAL: Born in Portland, Oregon; married Paul Nathan (contributing editor to *Publishers Weekly*); children: Janet, Andrew, Carl. *Education:* Graduated from the University of California.

CAREER: Author of books for children.

WRITINGS: Women of Courage (illustrated by Carolyn Cather), Random House, 1964; *The Shy One* (illustrated by C. Cather), Random House, 1966; *The Month Brothers* (adapted from Samuel Marchak's play, *Twelve Months;* illustrated by Uri Shulevitz), Dutton, 1967.

SIDELIGHTS: Published posthumously, Dorothy Nathan's *The Month Brothers* is an adaptation of a Russian play which was based on eastern European folklore. "The story," according to a *Library Journal* review, ". . . has the classic fairy-tale themes and structure, but details of plot are original and imaginative and will intrigue children. . . . There is humor and subtle satire. Illustrations in delicate block-

The hard-packed floor was criss-crossed with sunlight and gave off a most wonderful damp, earthy smell. ■ (From *The Shy One* by Dorothy Nathan. Illustrated by Carolyn Cather.)

One day in April of 1865 Jane came home from play to find the white gateposts of her house draped in American flags and black cloth. ■ (From *Women of Courage* by Dorothy Nathan. Illustrated by Carolyn Cather.)

print style, black across the white pages, evoke wintry Russia and vividly dramatize events and characters.''

FOR MORE INFORMATION SEE: Library Journal, December 15, 1967; Obituaries—*New York Times,* December 23, 1966; *Publishers Weekly,* January 9, 1967.

(Died December 22, 1966)

NICHOLS, (Joanna) Ruth   1948-

PERSONAL: Born March 4, 1948, in Toronto, Ontario, Canada; daughter of Edward Morris and Ruby (Smith) Nichols. *Education:* University of British Columbia, B.A. 1969; McMaster University, M.A. 1972, Ph.D., 1977. *Residence:* Ottawa, Canada.

WRITINGS: A Walk out of the World (fantasy for children). Harcourt, 1969; *Ceremony of Innocence* (novel) Faber, 1969; *The Marrow of The World,* Atheneum, 1972; *Song of the Pearl,* Atheneum, 1976; *The Left-Handed Spirit,* Atheneum, 1978.

WORK IN PROGRESS: Historical novels.

SIDELIGHTS: ''The meaning of experience is the motivation for [my] writing. In other times this would have been a religious quest. It remains so even after the disintegration of Christianity which I think we are witnessing. . . . In my novels it leads me to ask what sources of hope and self-affirmation can be found in everyday experience.''

RUTH NICHOLS

Barkhan himself awaited them. ■ (From *The Marrow of the World* by Ruth Nichols. Illustrated by Trina Schart Hyman.)

FOR MORE INFORMATION SEE: Library Journal, July, 1969; *Horn Book,* August, 1969, February, 1977; *Bulletin of the Center of Children's Books,* March, 1977.

OLUGEBEFOLA, Ademole   1941-

PERSONAL: Born October 2, 1941, in St. Thomas, V.I.; son of Harold Alexander (a maintenance engineer) and Golda (Valencia; a cashier) Thomas, II; married Pat (Davis; a photographer); children: Mona, Monica, Tanyeni, Olori, Khari, Solar. *Education:* Fashion Institute of Technology, Associate Degree, 1961; Pomusicart, Inc., Associate Degree, 1965; attended Yoruba Academy of West African Culture, 1966-68; Weusi Academy of Arts & Studies, Ph.D., 1969. *Home:* 800 Riverside Drive, New York, N.Y., 10032. *Agent:* Tetrahedron, Suite 37, 200 West 72nd St., New York, N.Y. 10023. *Office:* National Arts Consortium, 36 West 62nd St., New York, N.Y. 10023.

CAREER: Artist; designer; gallery curator. Metropolitan Museum of Art (in cooperation with the Weusi Academy of Arts & Studies), New York, N.Y., special research consultant, 1969; New Lafayette Theatre, New York, N.Y., resident designer, associate director, 1969-72; Wesleyan University, Middleton, Conn., instructor, lecturer, fall semesters 1972, 1973, 1974; children's art carnival sponsored

As—Salaam—Alaikum my black prince
the morning awaits u.
■ (From *It's A New Day* by Sonia Sanchez. Illustrated by Ademola Olugebefola.)

ADEMOLA OLUGEBEFOLA

by Museum of Modern Art, New York, N.Y., special instructor (part time), 1973—; Hostos Community College, City University of New York, New York, N.Y., team teacher, cultural consultant, 1974-75; Smithsonian Institution, Washington, D.C., art director, presentor, 1976; art director of the television production of "Infinity Factory," March, 1977; Weusi Academy of Arts & Studies, New York, N.Y., co-director, 1978; National Arts Consortium, board member, 1978. Has also designed and been commissioned as consultant for numerous interiors for private homes and has served the business community as a consultant for interior and efficiency planning. *Member:* National Conference of Artists (vice president, 1973-77).

EXHIBITIONS—Group shows: Brooklyn Museum, Brooklyn, N.Y., 1969; Illinois State Museum, Springfield, Ill., 1971; American Museum of Natural History, New York, N.Y., 1973; "Black Contemporary Artists," African American Pavillion, EXPO '74 WORLD FAIR, Spokane, Wash., 1974; Touring Exhibition of West Germany, 1974; National Conference of Artists, NEW MUSE, Community Museum of Brooklyn, Brooklyn, N.Y., 1975; "Black Family" Exhibition, Arts Center, St. Petersburg, Fla., 1976; Second World Festival of Arts and Culture-International Exhibition, Lagos, Nigeria, West Africa, 1977.

One-man shows: Winston-Salem State University, Winston-Salem, N.C., 1970; School of the Arts Institute of Chicago, Chicago, Ill., 1972; Revelations, Lowe Art Center, Syracuse University, Syracuse, N.Y., 1973; Beyond Orion, Gem Gallery of Fine Art, St. Thomas, U.S. Virgin Islands, 1975; Evolution in Color, New York State Office Building

Gallery, New York, N.Y., 1976; Whitaker Gallery, South Carolina State College, Orangburg, S.C., 1976; Eyes on the Masses, comprehensive exhibition of published graphics, cover designs and illustrations from 1969 to 1977, Museum of Western Art, Washington, D.C.

ILLUSTRATOR: Abayomi Fuju (editor), *Fourteen Hundred Cowries,* Lothrop, 1971; *The New Lafayette Presents* (cover), Doubleday, 1973; Ed Bullins, *The Reluctant Rapist* (cover), Harper, 1973; *It's a New Day,* (poems for children), Broadside Press. Illustrations have appeared in *Art in America, Art Gallery Magazine, Natural History Magazine* and *Impressions.*

SIDELIGHTS: "I can remember as far back as two or three years old when certain significant events left a lasting impression on me. For instance, whenever there is a warm moonlit night, I have recollections of riding along the roads of St. Thomas and the beautiful palm trees swishing in the wind and the warm and friendly people chatting on the bus. I'll never forget my bout with the measles and being confined to my crib. I was terrified by my neighbor's pet monkey who was quite harmless, but at three years old, how was I to know. My mother's close friend, Mrs. Muller, still holds a special place in my heart. She took care of me many days when my mother and father had to work.

"My first plane ride was something to remember. It seemed like forever, but we finally landed in Miami where we changed planes for New York. To this day I remember the excitement of entering my first quick food restaurant (as I remember similar to Nathan's of Coney Island).

"We settled in Brooklyn for about two years and my first school experience, kindergarten, the record snow storm of 1947 (1948?), chickens in my back yard, the old wooden porch, the warm lazy summers and cold winters of my first years in the mainland, U.S.A. All these are memories close to me.

"I was five or six years old when I saw a horse on the streets of Brooklyn and asked my mother to draw it for me. She did it effortlessly and from that moment on, my art career began. I knew from then on I could accomplish anything in the universe that I put my mind to. So here I am today on the way up.

"My approach to illustrations, whether intended for children or adults, is based on strong design and patterns that invigorate the eye and thereby enchant the senses. I am less interested in capturing 'realism' than portraying the endless possibilities of line and form.

"The imagination is a reservoir of infinite chambers of fantasy and unexplored dimensions. My work is a calculated attempt to awaken those 'new worlds' through design.

"I employ collage, pen and ink screens, pencil, etc., towards my objective."

PALMER, Heidi   1948-

PERSONAL: Born September 28, 1948, in Geneva, Switzerland; daughter of Forrest M. (an executive) and Ruth (Kremser; a dental hygienist) Palmer. *Education:* Attended Ecole des Beaux Arts de Montreal, 1965-68; Boston University School of Fine Arts, 1968-69; Pratt Institute, B.F.A., 1971. *Home and office:* 392 Whitney Ave., New Haven,

As the dog and I exchanged greetings, I noticed that his coat was in terrible shape. Dry and patchy. Otherwise, the big poodle looked healthy, and he was hard. ■ (From *Uncle Charlie's Poodle* by Kurt Unkelbach. Illustrated by Heidi Palmer.)

Conn. 06511. *Agent:* Publishers Graphics, 611 Riverside Ave., Westport, Conn. 06511.

CAREER: Free-lance illustrator of children's books, 1971—. *Exhibitions:* Westmount Public Library, Montreal, P.Q., Canada, 1967; Greenwich Public Library, Greenwich, Conn., 1974; Creative Arts Workshop, New Haven, Conn., 1976, 1977, 1978.

ILLUSTRATOR: G. Harris, *Manna, Foods of the Frontier,* 101 Productions, 1972; C. Miller, *Skiing Western America,* 101 Productions, 1972; L. Pilarski, *Tibet: Heart of Asia,* Bobbs-Merrill, 1974; E. Gemmings, *Getting to Know the Connecticut River,* Coward, 1974; M. A. Bourne, *Nelly Custis' Diary,* Coward, 1974; P. Limburg, *What's in the Names of Flowers,* Coward, 1974; W. Trask Lee, *A Forest of Pencils,* Bobbs, 1974; L. Rossner, *Let's Go to a Horse Show,* Putnam, 1975; G. McHargue, *Funny Bananas: The Mystery Up in the Museum,* Holt, 1975; K. Unklebach, *Uncle Charlie's Poodle,* Dodd, 1975; W. Hammond, *The Story of Your Eye,* Coward, 1975; E. Kellner, *Animals Come to My House: A Story Guide to the Care of Small*

Wild Animals, Putnam, 1976; Barbara Girion, *The Boy with the Special Face,* Abingdon, 1978; William Wise, *Animal Rescue: Saving our Endangered Wildlife,* Putnam, 1978; Betty Pousar Reigot, *Wake Up–It's Night,* Scholastic Book Services, 1978. Illustrations have appeared in *Children's Digest Magazine, Clue Magazine, Playmate, Weekend, WOW.* Illustrator of educational material including filmstrips, posters and workbooks.

WORK IN PROGRESS: Two trade books; two grade three workbooks.

SIDELIGHTS: "For illustration I work in pen and ink (crow quill) water color and colored pencil. As a printmaker I do lithography and etching."

HOBBIES AND OTHER INTERESTS: Reading, gardening, modern dance, and travelling.

FOR MORE INFORMATION SEE: Horn Book, February, 1976, April, 1977.

The day wore on into a long, tranquil green evening, and the boats still moved steadily onward.
■ (From *The Huffler* by Jill Paton Walsh. Illustrated by Juliette Palmer.)

PALMER, Juliette   1930-

PERSONAL: Born May 18, 1930, in Romford, Essex, England; daughter of Sidney Bernard (a representative) and Edna (a clerk; maiden name, Harris) Woolley; married Dennis Palmer (a civil engineer), April 12, 1952; children: Albertine. *Education:* South-East Essex School of Art, diploma, 1950; University of London, diploma, 1951. *Religion:* "Humanist." *Home:* Melmott Lodge, The Pound, Cookham, Maidenhead, Berkshire, England.

CAREER: Worked as teacher of arts and crafts, 1952-57; display designer for Metal Box Co., 1957-58; representative of Fleet Street Commercial Art Studio, 1959; free-lance illustrator of children's books, 1959-64; author and illustrator, 1970—.

WRITINGS—Self-illustrated; all published by Macmillan: *Cockles and Shrimps,* 1973; *Mountain Wool,* 1973; *Swan Upping,* 1974; *Stow Horsefair,* 1976; *Barley Sow, Barley Grow,* 1978. Also illustrator of more than fifty children's books.

WORK IN PROGRESS: Barley Ripe, Barley Reap.

SIDELIGHTS: "How far back do the influences count that shape one's direction, one's aptitudes and one's outlook in life? My father's father was a carpenter. My father, one of a large family, was a frustrated artist. After school, aged four-

teen, he was an office boy. Later in the 30's, he enjoyed the 'perks' of a car allowance as a travelling mechanic. The country side of East Anglia was his beat and at the onset of war he bought antiques for next to nothing at country auctions. An older brother was a valet in a wealthy country household which we visited once a year. We three girls and our parents used to explore, with awe, every adjunct to gracious living so unlike life in our small suburban 'semi.' There were chintz and wickerwork teas in the rose-garden summerhouse, a donkey and trap for madam to take air in the grounds, rare and beautiful dogs, a talking parrot, wine cellars and a silver hoard in the butler's pantry. There was a huge panelled dining hall with minstrel gallery, and oval windows in ivied towers.

"I would like to have stayed in the pens with the litters of puppies there. I wished at that time (I was seven years old) to be a dog. At home I became, in spirit, a dog. This passion for dogs had started when I was in my pram, but at seven, I insisted on having my food from a dish on the floor, I lolled my tongue, I wore a dog's collar. My sisters used to plead with me when we played mummies and daddies not to insist on being the dog as I squatted obediently beside the doll's pram.

"My next ambition was to be a kennel maid. I loved horses too. I fearlessly patted the towering beasts with huge feathered feet that pulled the coal-car along our road. I cut my straight hair into a forelock when my mother wasn't looking.

I gripped a pencil like a bit in my teeth. I also read a lot, wrote stories, painted and drew. To draw or write about something is to come near to possessing it, to have it for oneself. I could not have a pony so I drew ponies and wrote pony stories. I guess I have worked out my passion now by keeping two successive ponies for my daughter, attending to them every day and constantly being in conversation with other horsey mums!

"My mother was the granddaughter of an Oxfordshire farmer, whom she visited once or twice in childhood. Her father was the second son (the first son inherited the farm) and a cloth buyer for a clothier in St. Paul's churchyard in the city of London. She became a milliner and was always deft with her needle. Her father died when she was fourteen years old and the family's well-to-do life came to an end. Her mother remained an unemployed ex-soldier of 'The Great War' and at eighteen she was forced to leave home and seek out a very frugal existence in a rented room with no money for heating or shoe-mending or sufficient food. It was not until the 50's when we girls were all married that she visited the village of Spelsburg and discovered in the old churchyards many headstones recording previous generations of Harris. She was delighted at having retraced her roots.

"My mother and father both loved weekend country picnics with a blackened kettle hissing over a wood fire. At the outset of World War II they luckily found a near derelict, primitive little cottage in the farmlands of North Essex to which we escaped from the bombing of London and its suburbs. School holidays and intervals when our other home was blitzed were bliss at the cottage. We rode on the horse-drawn harvest wagons. We roamed the farm. It was fun to collect fallen branches to take home to the fire and smell the sweet wood smoke. My mother cooked over the fire. Tea, bacon, sausages, potatoes were all flavoured with smoke. Water was fetched in a bucket and used sparringly. We washed under protest and then only in a china ewer basin.

"So thereafter, when married, my sisters and I tried to choose rural living in old cottages, if only on the fringe of the town. My husband and I first lived, while I was teaching art in secondary schools, in part of a large Victorian house, facing a village green and pub and overlooking a 'smithy' with neglected orchards behind where I often painted the trees. Indeed, I still paint outdoors producing water colour landscapes with old cottages, farms and barns. Later we bought a pair of unmodernised thatched cottages, medieval in origin and lovingly made a home of them in their overgrown acre where Biddy and friends made tree houses as time went on.

"In 1971 we moved from our native habitat, the county of Essex, to the Royal county of Berkshire to live in the Thames riverside village of Cookham, made famous by the mystical paintings of Sir Stanley Spencer. My third book, *Swan Upping* was born following a meeting with Captain

JULIETTE PALMER (at right)

Turk, the Queen's Swan Keeper who lives in Cookham and arranges the annual traditional event of my title.

"We have enjoyed many holidays in Wales. My husband is a keen mountaineer and spends weekends on the hills and crags. In North Wales I made the sketches leading to the creation of *Mountain Wool!*

"The books I choose to create are about people working closely with nature, utilizing respectfully the natural treasure of their environment. I want children to appreciate and wonder at the phenomena of nature and the ingenuity of man. In these days of instant puddings and packet crisps, they might so easily miss the connection. So the first book was about estuarine fishermen collecting the treasure of cockles and shrimps. The second was about collecting the wealth of wool from sheep living on inhospitable mountains. The third about the ancient ceremony which is part of the management of swans on the River Thames and the fourth about pony business, featuring a true event in the life of our own pony, leading me to the historical origins of a typical British horse fair. The book-in-progress records all I have seen of the work on a field through the seasons with glances into the past and the long struggle to grow food.

"I prepare the art work in three separate solid colours. This method has great limitations. Difficulties arise in trying to reproduce natural subject matter. The colour cannot flow from one tone to the next, merge together or gently fade. I hope that children will, therefore, not find my colour interpretation too strange, but will enjoy making new discoveries through my pages."

PANETTA, George   1915-1969

PERSONAL: Born August 6, 1915, in New York, N.Y.; son of Domenick (a tailor) and Angelina (Panetta) Panetta; married Evelyn Rinder, May 15, 1938; children: one son. *Education:* Attended City College of New York, 1934-36. *Residence:* Brooklyn, N.Y.

CAREER: Was an advertising copywriter before becoming a fiction writer and a playwright. *Member:* Dramatists Guild. *Awards, honors: Village Voice* Off-Broadway (Obie) Award for best comedy, 1957-58, for *Comic Strip.*

WRITINGS—Fiction: *We Ride a White Donkey,* Harcourt, 1944; *Jimmy Potts Gets a Haircut* (illustrated by Reisie Lonette), Doubleday, 1947; *Sea Beach Express* (illustrated by Emily McCully), Harper, 1966; *A Kitchen Is Not a Tree* (illustrated by Joe Servello), Norton, 1970; *The Shoeshine Boys* (illustrated by J. Servello), Grosset, 1971.

Plays: *Comic Strip* (three-act; first produced in New York City at the Barbizon-Plaza, May 14, 1958), S. French, 1958; *Viva Madison Avenue!* (first produced in New York City at the Longacre Theatre, April 6, 1960), Harcourt, 1957; *Kiss Mama* (two-act), S. French, 1965.

Also author of a play, "King of the Whole Damn World!"

SIDELIGHTS: All of George Panetta's stories reflect his Italian-American background. His last book, *The Shoeshine Boys,* was critiqued in the *New York Times Book Review:* "This book presents, without antiseptic distortion, poverty, death, adult failure, and against these realities the special love, trust, and strength of spirit that children want to read about and want to feel exists. George Panetta's style is direct, spare, and without condescension. Since Mac Dougall is black and Tony an Italian, the story demonstrates the values of brotherhood, but where many books preach, this one breathes." *Publishers Weekly* wrote that Joe Servello's illustrations "sparkle with vitality."

FOR MORE INFORMATION SEE: Olga Peragallo, *Italian-American Authors and Their Contribution to American Literature,* Vanni, 1949; *New York Times Book Review,* May 2, 1971; *Publishers Weekly,* May 31, 1971; (obituary) *New York Times,* October 17, 1969.

(Died October 16, 1969)

Then, when Pedro decided to swing around the train pole, and when Tony was up to twenty-two in his count, the train did a very funny thing. It stopped. ■ (From *Sea Beach Express* by George Panetta. Illustrated by Emily McCully.)

GEORGE PANETTA

PEYTON, Kathleen (Wendy) 1929-
(Kathleen Herald; K. M. Peyton)

PERSONAL: Born in 1929, in Birmingham, England; married Michael Peyton (a commercial artist and cartoonist), 1950; children: Hilary, Veronica. *Education:* Attended Kingston School of Art; Manchester Art School, received A.T.D. *Home:* Rookery Cottage, North Fambridge, Essex, England.

CAREER: Art teacher at high school in Northampton, England, 1952-56; writer, 1956—. *Member:* Society of Authors. *Awards, honors: New York Herald Tribune* award, 1965, for *The Maplin Bird;* Carnegie Medal, 1969; *Guardian* award, 1970, for *Flambards, The Edge of the Cloud,* and for *Flambards in Summer.*

WRITINGS—Children's books under name Kathleen Herald: *Sabre: The Horse from the Sea,* A. & C. Black, 1947, Macmillan, 1963; *The Mandrake,* A. & C. Black, 1949; *Crab the Roan,* A. & C. Black, 1953.

Children's books under name K. M. Peyton: *North to Adventure,* Collins, 1959, Platt and Munk, 1965; *Stormcock Meets Trouble,* Collins, 1961; *The Hard Way Home,* Collins, 1962; *Sea Fever* (ALA Notable Book), World Publishing, 1963 (published in England as *Windfall,* Oxford University Press, 1963); *Brownsea Silver,* Collins, 1964; *The Maplin Bird,* Oxford University Press, 1964, World Publishing, 1965; *The Plan for Birdsmarsh,* Oxford University Press, 1965, World Publishing 1966; *Thunder in the Sky,* Oxford University Press, 1966, World Publishing, 1967; *Flambards* (trilogy), Oxford University Press, 1967, World Publishing, 1968; *Fly-by-Night,* Oxford University Press, 1968, World Publishing, 1969; *The Edge of the Cloud,* World Publishing, 1969; *Flambards in Summer* (ALA Notable Book), Oxford University Press, 1969, World Publishing, 1970; *Pennington's Seventeenth Summer,* Oxford University Press, 1970, published as *Pennington's Last Term* (ALA Notable Book), Crowell, 1971; *The Beethoven Medal* (ALA Notable Book), Oxford University Press, 1971, Crowell, 1972; *The Pattern of Roses* (ALA Notable Book), Oxford University Press, 1972, Crowell, 1973; *Pennington's*

Heir, Oxford University Press, 1973, Crowell, 1974; *The Team,* Oxford University Press, 1975; *The Right-Hand Man,* Oxford University Press, 1977; *Prove Yourself a Hero,* Oxford University Press, 1977, Collins, 1978; *A Midsummer Night's Death,* Oxford University Press, 1978, Collins, 1979; *Marion's Angels,* Oxford University Press, 1979.

SIDELIGHTS: "I didn't really start to write just by saying that I was going to write a book. When I was small, I was always writing. I think I was nine when I started my first story which was long enough to call a book. It was all written in longhand, of course, and was called, I remember, *Gray Star, the Story of a Race Horse.* It was in the first person. *I* was the race horse. After that I always had a book going. They used to come out so that they were full-length, quite long books. As soon as I finished one, I started another. Once when I was at school, a teacher asked me to do some illustrations for a book. I said I'd do the illustrations for my own book. She was interested, so she read it. She thought it was good and told me to get it typed. I sent it to a publisher, and it was accepted for publication when I was fifteen."[Cornelia Jones and Olivia R. Way, *British Children's Authors,* American Library Association, 1976.[1]]

Fifteen years ago Peyton and her husband owned a Dutch fishing boat until it proved too big to maintain. This vessel was followed by an eleven-ton, thirty-year-old Norwegian-built gaff cutter in which they sailed the waters of the North Sea. They've owned six boats since.

"There are still quite a lot of fishing boats working from the area, [Maldon, England] and a few of the barges that used to do all of the trading in the old days are still sailing around here. Most of the barges are at least eighty feet. They vary from eighty feet long to one hundred feet. But they are so cleverly designed that two people can manage them, although it can be very, very hard work. There's still one sailing barge now trading, just one. It hasn't got an engine and it's skippered by an old boy called Bob Roberts. You see him still around here. He brings the barge up the Crouch sometimes or up to Maldon or up to London quite a lot, and he's carrying cargo without an engine. He's the only one left now.

"I was interested in barge sailing because you see so much of it around here. When we go sailing, we see these barges sailing in the same waters. They're so picturesque, you can't help but stop and look at them. Most of them still haven't got any engines, and they sail under a huge mainsail and a foresail and a mizzen at the back. They do these fantastic passages, and when the wind blows up they really go very fast. We go and watch when they have a race. There are three races every summer—one on the Thames, one on the Medway, and one up here on the Blackwater. We generally take our boat and sail along with the race. If the weather blows up, it's a wonderful sight to see about twelve barges all racing, sailing as hard as they can go.

"I think every book I've written so far, with perhaps the exception of the one about flying, is definitely written through things I've done. In *The Plan for Birdsmarsh,* for example, where they're testing out that rubber suit, the lifesaving suit that the boy wants to develop—that is all absolutely true. A friend of ours invented this suit and we used to test it for him from our own boat in the middle of winter. He actually swam across the Channel to France in it and came back without any escort boat at all. When he got back to England, he couldn't get in to the shore. The tide kept sweeping him out, and he went up on the Goodwin Sands

KATHLEEN PEYTON

and took refuge on one of these buoys until the tide turned and he could swim in. The funny part was that after all he'd been through crossing the Channel, he got terribly seasick sitting on that buoy.

"I've sailed all that area that comes into the sailing stories. My own experiences definitely went into *Sea Fever* and *The Maplin Bird*. When Emily is frightened on a boat in *The Maplin Bird*, it's very much how I felt a couple of times. We have had some very bad experiences. My husband learned to sail just by sailing. He didn't know how to sail, but we bought a boat and just went off. We had the children with us on one occasion when they were very small, just three and four. We were in the Thames estuary, and we had some rigging failure and the engine wasn't working. We had to run before the winds out of the estuary and there was very rough weather. We had to do what we could. We got out off Harwich, which is quite some way out, and we thought we would be able to point into Harwich, but it happened we couldn't. The wind came around and we were going straight out. It was dark, by this time it was midnight, and I was very worried about the children. In the end we flashed up a ship and a steamer came up and took us off. It was pitch dark and very rough, and it was really quite a frightening experience. But it was very useful afterwards knowing how people feel.

"I bought a pony that was unbroken and very much like *Fly-by-Night* in character. He was a very cocky little pony, not a bit docile. My poor daughter did all the suffering just like Ruth in the book. Of course, the circumstances aren't exactly the same. We didn't have Ruth's money problems exactly, but all the actual experiences with the pony were very much what happened to us. My daughter was frightfully keen to get her pony jumping and going around the course in the hunter trials, which she did in the end. She came third in the trials, which is even better than Ruth did.

"Everything in the background of *Sea Fever* is absolutely authentic, the way these old fishermen lived. In *Thunder in the Sky*, the actual plot of the spying I made up, although it was going on all the time during the war. But all the part of the barges going across the Channel and how the war affected them is perfectly authentic. There are a lot of these barges moored up at Maldon, which is near where I live, and I have been on board them. We know quite a lot of the skippers, and we have sailed on them ourselves. But I also had to do an awful lot of research for that because the technical side of it is very difficult, and I had to have quite a lot of help with it. I wanted it to read so that anyone who had sailed a barge would read it and not say, 'That's wrong. That's wrong. That's wrong.' I was very careful about that. I don't think there are many inaccuracies in it.

"The characters in *The Edge of the Cloud* are fictional, but all that about the way the early flying took place and the adventures they had in flying the Channel is as authentic as I could make it.

"I think that getting help from other people is very necessary because you can't know all these points that arise. For example, I needed medical advice in *Flambards* for the problem of Will breaking his leg. I wanted him to be injured in such a way that he would be fairly active for other things but would not actually be able to ride a horse again. It was very difficult to work something out which would just cover this point, but I did manage it with some medical advice. Then I had some more trouble afterwards when I wanted to write a sequel. It was necessary then that William should be able to fly an airplane, which wasn't easy when he had a stiff leg. I had to have medical advice to see how this leg could be

He wasn't a person; he wasn't Pennington, twenty years old, six-feet-two and two hundred pounds, mixed up, aggressive, gentle, thoughtful, violent, extraordinarily sensitive in some ways and thick as a mule in others. ■ (From *Pennington's Heir* by K.M. Peyton. Drawing by the author.)

She was listing at an angle of about forty-five degrees, and the sea was sweeping her decks so that her hull was all but invisible; the great proud mast looked to Matt like a stag holding a pack of hounds at bay, resisting the seas that leaped to drag her down, dipping and reeling against the black sky. The mizzenmast was gone, and rigging trailed in the sea about her like the hair of a drowning woman. ■ (From *Sea Fever* by K.M. Peyton. Illustrated by Victor G. Ambrus.)

fixed again, which at that period apparently was not a very easy thing to do. But I was assured it was all right, that it could be done in Switzerland. This dictated a part of the plot, really, because it meant he had to go to Switzerland.

"I know fairly well what's going to happen when I start a book. I always know the theme, obviously, and what the whole point of the book is, what the main story line is, where I want to finish. Generally I know that, but sometimes I'm not always clear about how I'm going to develop the middle. Naturally you have to know what you're going to write in the beginning, and I always have the end fairly sure in my head, but sometimes the middle is a little loose. But I always find as I go along that it all falls into place. Not just like that, it doesn't just happen. Obviously it doesn't just happen. I find that sitting on a train I get very good ideas. I don't know why. My husband always thinks his ideas up in the bath. I find that going up to London on the train, which takes fifty minutes, is very productive. If I have a bad problem, I always think, 'Oh, I'll work that one out on the train.' It seems to work.

"I don't start a book saying that I want to develop this character in this particular way. I don't think I'm conscious of it really, but I realize myself that the interest to me in writing books is always in the characters of the people. I find that I use the plots to follow my own interest in the people, so to speak, and I find that the plots grow from the way the people interact one on the other. I don't sit down and write a book and say this is going to be about the growth of this character. But I've heard this said so often about my writings. It must be something about the way I work, the way I like to make out my plots.

"My characters are never anybody I know very well. I sometimes start off on a character perhaps by using somebody I've met once. Winnington, in *The Plan for Birdsmarsh*, was somebody I met on vacation, and I used him. Of course, I didn't really know him. It was only his appearance, really, and his superficial character that came over to me that I used. For example, the character I'm writing about here now is a boy I've seen but have never spoken to. I just thought that that's the type I wanted to write about, just from his looks, but I shall never meet him again. That sort of starts you off. I think my female characters always seem to come out the same, which isn't very satisfactory. Emily in *The Maplin Bird* and Christina in *Flambards* are rather the same character, which annoys me a bit. But on the whole, I don't think I base my characters on real people.

"I don't really have a favorite among my books. I always like the one I'm writing now better than any of the others. Once they are written, I sort of forget about them, really."

HOBBIES AND OTHER INTERESTS: Riding, walking in mountains, sailing, music.

FOR MORE INFORMATION SEE: Horn Book, August, 1969, December, 1969, February, 1971, August, 1971, October, 1972, October, 1973, April, 1975, October, 1976, November, 1976; John Rowe Townsend, *A Sense of Story,* Longmans, 1971; *Children's Literature in Education,* #8, APS Publications, July, 1972, #9, November, 1972; Edward Blishen, *The Thorny Paradise,* Kestrel Books, 1975.

RACKHAM, Arthur 1867-1939

PERSONAL: Born September 19, 1867, in London, England; died September 6, 1939; son of Alfred Thomas (a civil servant; Marshal of the Admiralty Court) and Anne (Stevenson) Rackham; married Edyth Starkie (an artist), July 16, 1903 (died March, 1941); children: Barbara Rackham Edwards. *Education:* Attended Lambeth School of Art. *Home:* Stilegate, Limpsfield, Surrey, England.

CAREER: Artist and illustrator; while studying art in night school, worked in an insurance office, 1885-92; staff artist for the *Westminster Budget* (newspaper), 1892-96; freelance illustrator, 1893—. His drawings are exhibited in public collections in Barcelona, Melbourne, Paris, Vienna, and London. *Awards, honors:* Master of the Art Workers' Guild, 1919; member of the Royal Water-Colour Society; gold medal winner at exhibitions in Milan, Italy, 1906, in Barcelona, Spain, 1911, and in Paris, France, where he was also elected an associate of the Societé Nationale des Beaux Arts, 1912.

ILLUSTRATOR: Anthony Hope (pseudonym of Anthony Hope Hawkins), *The Dolly Dialogues,* Westminster Gazette, 1894; S. J. Adair-Fitzgerald, *The Zankiwank and the Bletherwitch,* Dutton, 1896; Henry Seton Merriman (pseudonym of Hugh Stowell Scott) and S. G. Tallantyre, *The Money-Spinner and Other Character Notes,* Smith, Elder, 1896; H. S. Merriman, *The Grey Lady,* Smith, Elder, 1897; Charles Lever, *Charles O'Malley, the Irish Dragoon,* Putnam, 1897; Maggie Browne (pseudonym of Margaret Hamer Andrewes), *Two Old Ladies, Two Foolish Fairies and a Tom Cat: The Surprising Adventures of Tuppy and Tue,* Cassell, 1897, also published as *The Sur-*

Rackham, 1910.

prising *Adventures of Tuppy and Tue,* 1904; Frances Burney, *Evalina; or The History of a Young Lady's Entrance into the World,* Newnes, 1898; R. H. Barham, *The Ingoldsby Legends; or, Mirth and Marvels,* Dent, 1898, revised edition, Dutton, 1907; Harriet Martineau, *Feats on the Fjord: A Tale,* Dent, 1899; Charles and Mary Lamb, *Tales from Shakespeare,* Dent, 1899, revised edition, Dutton, 1909.

Jonathan Swift, *Gulliver's Travels into Several Remote Nations of the World,* Dent, 1900, revised edition, Dutton, 1909, reprinted, Dent, 1952; Jacob and Wilhelm Grimm, *Fairy Tales* (translated by Mrs. Edgar Lucas), Freemantle, 1900, revised edition, Constable, 1909, twenty-five tales from the 1909 edition reprinted as *Snowdrop and Other Tales,* Dutton, 1920, thirty tales from the 1909 edition reprinted as *Hansel and Gretel and Other Tales,* Dutton, 1920, a later revised edition published as *Grimm's Fairy Tales: Twenty Stories,* Viking, 1973; Agnes Grozier Herbertson, *The Bee-Blowaways,* Cassell, 1900; C. R. Kenyon, *The Argonauts of the Amazon,* Dutton, 1901; B. G. Niebuhr, *The Greek Heroes,* Cassell, 1903; Mrs. Greene, *The Grey House on the Hill,* Thomas Nelson, 1903; Mary Cholmondeley, *Red Pottage,* Newnes, 1904; W. P. Drury, *The Peradventures of Private Paget,* Chapman & Hall, 1904; Henry Harbour, *Where Flies the Flag,* Collins, 1904; Richard Henry Dana, *Two Years before the Mast,* Winston, 1904.

Washington Irving, *Rip Van Winkle,* Doubleday, Page, 1905, reprinted, Lippincott, 1967; A. L. Haydon, *Stories of King Arthur,* Cassell, 1905; (with H. R. Millars and others) Myra Hamilton, *Kingdoms Curious,* Heinemann, 1905; James M. Barrie, *Peter Pan in Kensington Gardens,* Scribner, 1906, reprinted, Brockhampton Press, 1971, also published in an edition retold by May C. Gillington Byron, Scribner, 1930; Rudyard Kipling, *Puck of Pook's Hill,* Doubleday, Page, 1906; Lewis Carroll (pseudonym of Charles L. Dodgson), *Alice's Adventures in Wonderland,*

Doubleday, Page, 1907, reprinted, Watts, 1966; A. E. Bonser, B. Sidney Woolf, and E. S. Buchleim, *The Land of Enchantment,* Cassell, 1907; Eleanor Gates, *Good Night,* Crowell, 1907; William Shakespeare, *A Midsummer-Night's Dream,* Doubleday, Page, 1908; De La Motte Fouque, *Undine* (adapted from the German by W. L. Courteney), Doubleday, Page, 1909.

Maggie Browne, *The Book of Betty Barber,* Duckworth, 1910; Richard Wagner, *The Rhine-gold and the Valkyrie,* Doubleday, Page, 1910; Wagner, *Siegfried* [and] *The Twilight of the Gods,* Doubleday, Page, 1911; Aesop, *Aesop's Fables* (translated by V. S. Vernon Jones), Doubleday, Page, 1912, reprinted, Watts, 1968; Mother Goose, *The Old Nursery Rhymes,* Heinemann, 1913, also published as *Mother Goose Nursery Rhymes,* Viking, 1975; *Arthur Rackham's Book of Pictures,* Century, 1913; Charles Dickens, *A Christmas Carol,* Lippincott, 1915, new edition, Doubleday, Page, 1916; *The Allies' Fairy Book,* Lippincott, 1916, also published as *A Fairy Book,* Doubleday, Page, 1923, and later as *Fairy Tales from Many Lands,* Viking, 1974; J.K.L. and W. K. Grimm, *Little Brother and Little Sister,* Dodd, 1917; Thomas Malory, *The Romance of King Arthur and His Knights of the Round Table* (abridged from Malory's *Morte D'Arthur* by Alfred Pollard),

Shylock was sharpening a long knife. ■ (From *Tales from Shakespeare* by Charles and Mary Lamb. Illustrated by Arthur Rackham.)

Macmillan, 1917; Flora A. Steel, *English Fairy Tales Retold,* Macmillan, 1918; Algernon C. Swinburne, *The Springtide of Life: Poems of Childhood,* Lippincott, 1918; *Cinderella* (retold by Charles Seddon Evans), Lippincott, 1919, reprinted, Viking, 1972; Julia Ellsworth Ford, *Snickerty Nick: Rhymes by Whitter Bynner,* Moffat, Yard, 1919, new edition (with music), Suttonhouse, 1935; *Some British Ballads,* Dodd, 1919.

The Sleeping Beauty (retold by C. S. Evans), Lippincott, 1920, reprinted, Viking, 1972; James Stephens, *Irish Fairy Tales,* Macmillan, 1920, reprinted, 1968; Eden Phillpotts, *A Dish of Apples,* Hodder & Stoughton, 1921; John Milton, *Comus,* Doubleday, Page, 1921; Nathaniel Hawthorne, *A Wonder Book,* G. H. Doran, 1922; Christopher Morley, *Where the Blue Begins,* Doubleday, Page, reprinted, 1925; Margery Williams Bianco, *Poor Cecco,* G. H. Doran, 1925; William Shakespeare, *The Tempest,* Doubleday, Page, 1926; Abbie Farwell Brown, *The Lonesomest Doll,* Houghton, new edition, 1928; Washington Irving, *The Legend of Sleepy Hollow,* McKay, 1928; Oliver Goldsmith, *The Vicar of Wakefield,* McKay, 1929.

Izaak Walton, *The Compleat Angler,* McKay, 1931; Clement C. Moore, *The Night before Christmas,* Lippincott, 1931; Charles Dickens, *The Chimes,* Limited Editions Club, 1931; John Ruskin, *The King of the Golden River,* Lippincott, 1932; Hans Christian Andersen, *Fairy Tales,* McKay, 1932; Christina Rossetti, *Goblin Market,* Lippincott, 1933, reprinted, Watts, 1969; *The Arthur Rackham Fairy Book,* Lippincott, 1933, reprinted, 1950; Robert Browning, *The Pied Piper of Hamelin,* Lippincott, 1934; Edgar Allen Poe, *Tales of Mystery and Imagination,* Lip-

Arthur Rackham, a self-portrait in pastel, 1924.

pincott, 1935, reprinted, Dent, 1972; Henrik Ibsen, *Peer Gynt,* Lippincott, 1936; William Shakespeare, *A Midsummer-Night's Dream,* Limited Editions Club, 1939 (illustrations are not those of the 1908 edition); Kenneth Grahame, *The Wind in the Willows,* Limited Editions Club, 1940, and Heritage Press, 1940, reprinted, 1966.

Contributor of drawings to numerous periodicals, including the *Westminster Gazette, Scraps, Illustrated Bits, Daily Graphic, Pall Mall Budget, The Ladies' Field, Cassell's Magazine, Little Folks, Punch,* and *St. Nicholas.*

SIDELIGHTS: **September 19, 1867.** Born at 210 South Lambeth Road, London, England. Fourth of twelve children, Rackham was raised in a middle class Victorian family and believed in frugality, prudence and self-discipline. As a child, he showed a precocious talent for drawing, particularly outlandish caricatures. "From the first day when I was given, as all little boys are, a shilling paint-box . . . from that day, when I first put my watercolour brush in my mouth, and was told I musn't, this craft has been my constant companion. . . . Looking back I have one long memory of holidays and never one without my faithful friend." [Derek Hudson, *Arthur Rackham, His Life and Work,* Scribners, 1960.[1]]

September, 1879. Entered City of London School. ". . . I went there first at the end of '79. . . . Old Joey [Reverend Joseph Harris] was still in great form, and was my master before the school moved to the Embankment—and a great master he was. Then at the 'New School'—as we then called it, I settled down under Rushy [W. G. Rushbrooke], whose back benches I occupied for a long time—never flying higher. But he and I were friends until his death: and he had a great collection of my drawings—done in unorthodox hours and bagged by him. And even Abbott [the headmaster] turned a blind eye to my delinquencies of that kind. . . ."[1]

The North Wind and the Sun. ■ (From *Aesop's Fables.* Illustrated by Arthur Rackham.)

There was an old woman lived under the hill. ■ (From *Mother Goose, The Old Nursery Rhymes*. Illustrated by Arthur Rackham.)

As I was going to St. Ives.
■ (From *Mother Goose, The Old Nursery Rhymes*. Illustrated by Arthur Rackham.)

The Serpentine is a lovely lake, and there is a drowned forest at the bottom of it. If you peer over the edge you can see the trees all growing upside down, and they say that at night there are also drowned stars in it. ■ (From *Peter Pan in Kensington Gardens* by J.M. Barrie. Illustrated by Arthur Rackham.)

Young Bekie. ■ (From *Some British Ballads*. Illustrated by Arthur Rackham.)

(From *Rip Van Winkle* by Washington Irving. Illustrated by Arthur Rackham.)

January 26, 1884. Left school because his health was delicate and traveled to Australia. Rackham returned in July to London with his health restored.

Autumn, 1884. Entered the Lambeth School of Art.

October, 1884. First crude drawings appeared in *Scraps*. "[W]ith the realisation of more serious artistic intentions I soon gave it up and devoted my time to the severest education."[1]

Years later, Rackham advised another struggling young artist to equip himself with an income independent of art as he had done. "You might perhaps make a precarious living out of such work for *Scraps* . . .—but after a few years of it, you would feel it cramping debasing hack work, killing the art in you, and robbing you of the joy of true art expression which is, after all, the one and only reason for your being an artist at all. The *living* from art is a poor one—for only a very few is it better. For numbers it is dismal failure—for some perhaps who appeared in youth to be really talented and who started with the utmost enthusiasm. And the outlook appears to get steadily worse. As a profession it is one to which no parent would be justified in putting a son without being able to give him a permanent income as well. Then, of course, if he fail, he will have something to live upon: I know several such, and, believe me, their bitter disappointment at their professional failure is only just prevented from being misery by the possession of an independent income."[1]

November, 1884. While pursuing his art studies, Rackham worked in an insurance office. For seven years he divided himself between work and the art school. "[I had] to go out into the world and earn [my] living at the age of seventeen; (and for the next seven years or so I worked as hard as I could out of business hours (9-5) to equip myself as an artist—not being able to embark on a professional career till I was nearly twenty-five, and then for many years getting the barest living from my profession and having to do much distasteful hack work.)"[1]

1892. Left the insurance office and joined the staff of the *Westminster Budget*. His "Sketches from the Life" of public personalities became a popular feature of the paper for the next three years.

1899. "[Then] came the Boer War. That really was a very thin time indeed for me, and may be considered the worst time I ever had. The kind of work that was in demand, to the exclusion almost of all else, was such as I had no liking for and very little aptitude. It was also clear that the camera was largely going to supplant the artist in illustrated journalism, and my prospects were not encouraging. But my work was becoming less immature, and before long my special bent began to be recognised—by artists first. I was elected to membership of one or two exhibiting societies, my work was welcomed, dealers and publishers became interested, and the worst was passed." ["The Worst Time in My Life," *The Bookman*, October, 1925.[2]]

(From "The Robber Bridegroom" in *Grimm's Fairy Tales*, translated by Mrs. Edgar Lucas.
Illustrated by Arthur Rackham.)

1900. *Fairy Tales of the Brothers Grimm* published. The book marked the beginning of Rackham's fame as an illustrator. "In many ways I have more affection for the Grimm drawings than for other sets. (I think it is partly one's childhood affection for the stories.) It was the first book I did that began to bring success. . . ."[1]

February, 1902. Elected an associate of the Royal Water-Colour Society.

July 16, 1903. Married Edyth Starkie.

1908. Only child, Barbara, born. As a child, his daughter posed for her father with Rackham's constant directions: "Go on—get over there—bend over and pick up an apple; hold your skirt out with the other hand—put your leg further in front, no, the other one—and now twist round towards me and shake your hair over your shoulder—that's it—now stay still. All right, you can drop the pose—but now get up on that chair and see if you can be another child throwing the apples down from the tree."[1]

1909. Became a member of the Art-Workers' Guild.

January 31, 1910. Regarded as a leading illustrator, Rackham addressed a gathering at the Author's Club with his views on the art of illustration. ". . . An illustration may legitimately give the artist's view of the author's ideas; or it may give his view, his independent view, of the author's subject. But it must be the artist's view; any attempt to coerce him into a mere tool in the author's hands can only result in the most dismal failure. Illustration is as capable of varied appeal as is literature itself; and the only real essential is an association that shall not be at variance or unsympathetic. The illustrator is sometimes expected to say what the author ought to have said or failed to say clearly, to fill up a shortcoming, and not infrequently he has done so. Sometimes he is wanted to add some fresh aspect of interest to a subject which the author has already treated interestingly from his point of view, a partnership that has often been productive of good. But the most fascinating form of illustration consists of the expression by the artist of an individual sense of delight or emotion aroused by the accompanying passage of literature."[1]

September 21, 1910. Illustrated books for adults as well as for children. "I am kept so busy at home over my books and pictures that I have not time to accept half the kind invitations I receive.

". . . I am rather afraid that the books of mine that are coming out this year and next, which illustrate Wagner's great Music-stories, the *Ring of the Nibelungs,* are not very well suited for those lucky people who haven't yet finished the delightful adventure of growing up. . . ."[1]

1916. Served at home for his country during World War I. "I went to Wandsworth [*where his mother and two sisters*

Hey! Diddle Diddle!
■ (From *Mother Goose, The Old Nursery Rhymes.* Illustrated by Arthur Rackham.)

The Mock Turtle drew a long breath and said, "That's very curious." ■ (From *Alice's Adventures in Wonderland* by Lewis Carroll. Illustrated by Arthur Rackham.)

To this brook Ophelia came. ■ (From *Tales from Shakespeare* by Charles and Mary Lamb. Illustrated by Arthur Rackham.)

1923. Advised a group of high school admirers in Trenton, New Jersey: "If you possibly can, be makers and not dealers. Aim at the highest quality in your work. Go on improving it. Never be satisfied with it. Aim at taking pleasure in work for its own sake, and not for what you can make out of it."[1]

1927. In response to increased admiration from his American supporters, sailed to New York where he stayed at the Yale Club. He found both places uncomfortably noisy. "Oh that brass band—in our hall now. Every third tune is the Wacht am Rhein . . . I imagine Yale must have bagged the tune for a college song. Bang, bang, bang, blare, squeal. [E]verything [is] overdone . . . *much* too much—of everything. To live here *must* vulgarise an artist . . . I could *easily* run off and dump my bags and self on the first ship to Europe. . . . Bang bang bang bash. That man will bust that drum if no one stops him."[1]

Later Rackham was impressed by the warmth his American hosts showed their guest. "Everyone is excessively kind. Everyone was brought up on my work—if young enough—or brought up their families on it if *old enough*. The nature of my work seems to have made my name familiar to so many others than artists: the bookish people—librarians, book-lovers and so on. . . . The artists are extraordinarily friendly, too. I cannot think any American artist coming to our country (except a Whistler or Sargent) could find himself so heartily greeted."[1]

1929. Built a house at Limpsfield, Surrey. His wife was plagued throughout her life with poor health, which continued to deteriorate. He wrote her: "Oh my dear old Edyth, it is so difficult for me to make you feel how close close close, how *one* our lives have been for me. How *outside,* how unrecorded, how without influence my wanderings have been to me. . . . The reality of *my* life has been that with you. . . ."[1]

1931. Visited Denmark with his daughter in an effort to gather illustrations for Andersen's *Fairy Tales,* a project he desired for many years. "It is rather fatiguing. I have to talk so much and behave myself so well all the while, taking notes and notes for dear life. But everyone is most delightfully friendly and anxious to help. Of course Andersen is their great god. And all, and at the bookshop, are greatly interested in what I have to do."[1]

A peasant once had a faithful dog called Sultan who had grown old and lost all his teeth, and could no longer keep fast hold of his prey. ■ (From "Old Sultan" in *Grimm's Fairy Tales,* translated by Mrs. Edgar Lucas. Illustrated by Arthur Rackham.)

lived] yesterday. And right through town from here the road is full of groups of kneeling children with all manner of tools gouging and digging out the shrapnel from the wood pavement. Our guns keep going like hell." He continued to illustrate books during the war years.

1917-18. Active in the Art-Workers Guild.

1919. Held the master's chair for the Art-Worker's Guild.

On one occasion, Rackham went into a pigsty on a Danish farm. "But an indoor pigsty. No good for Andersen's Swineherd. And that's a mercy. For the stench was so appalling that I thought I should be sick.

"I think that my visit to Denmark, which, with all its modern progress, happily preserves in town and country a genial atmosphere of old dignity in comely everday use, did give me just that nearer view of the author's country that I needed—a view that helped me to realise again the sensation I felt as a child when I first read Andersen. This sensation experienced in childhood in foreign fairy tales is a foretaste of that encountering of familiar things in unfamiliar guise which later is one of the joys of foreign travel."[1]

July 27, 1935. His daughter, Barbara, married.

Spring, 1938. While working on *The Wind in the Willows,* Rackham underwent an operation for internal cancer. "I wish I could give a good account of either my wife or myself. My wife has borne up amid great disturbances astonishingly well, but I fear it cannot be said that she is better. And I—well the less said the better. Henceforth life will only be possible for me with the aid of a surgical nurse—whether at home or at the hospital as at present. I wish I could stop losing weight—but I eat with difficulty and haemorrhage is frequent and severe. So I am *very* weak."[1]

ARTHUR RACKHAM

There was an old woman called Nothing-a-tall,
Who rejoiced in a dwelling exceedingly small;
A man stretched his mouth to its utmost extent,
And down at one gulp house and old woman
   went.
■ (From *Mother Goose Nursery Rhymes*. Illustrated by Arthur Rackham.)

Returned home with no illusions. ". . . I am told I must not expect to be able to gauge the future possibilities for my life in less than about a year. It turns on unknown conditions that cannot be got at—due to the capricious behaviour of a gland, that *may* get tired of its misbehaviour, or the reverse—in which case my difficulties will be very great. However, we must wait and see. My best hope is to feed as well as I can (at present a very poor effort) and never tire myself."[1]

1939. Continued, near exhaustion, to finish his drawings for *The Wind in the Willows.* That summer he remarked to his nurse: "How nice it would be if I could die here under the trees!"[1]

September 6, 1939. Died at his home, Limpsfield, Surrey, two weeks before his seventy-second birthday.

Away to the window I flew like a flash,
Tore open the shutters and threw up the sash.
■ (From *The Night Before Christmas* by Clement C. Moore. Illustrated by Arthur Rackham.)

FOR MORE INFORMATION SEE: Eleanor Farjeon, "Arthur Rackham: The Wizard at Home," *St. Nicholas,* March, 1914; Sarah B. Latimore and Grace Clark Haskell, *Arthur Rackham: A Bibliography,* Suttonhouse, 1936, reprinted, B. Franklin, 1970; Anne Carroll Moore, "The Three Owls Notebook: A Christmas Ride with Arthur Rackham," *Horn Book,* November 1939; P. G. Konody, "The Home of the Wee Folk: Where Arthur Rackham Lived and Worked in the Heart of Sussex Downs," *Horn Book,* May, 1940; Robert Lawson, "The Genius of Arthur Rackham," and George Macy, "Arthur Rackham and 'The Wind in the Willows'," both in *Horn Book,* May, 1940, and both reprinted in *A Horn Book Sampler on Children's Books and Reading,* edited by Norma R. Fryatt, Horn Book, 1959; Stanley J. Kunitz and Howard Haycraft, editors, *Junior Book of Authors,* Wilson, 2nd edition, 1951.

What a naughty boy was that
To try to drown poor pussy-cat.
■ (From *Mother Goose Nursery Rhymes*. Illustrated by Arthur Rackham.)

Derek Hudson, *Arthur Rackham: His Life and Work,* Scribner, 1960, reprinted, 1974; Roland Baughman, *The Centenary of Arthur Rackham's Birth, September 19, 1867: An Appreciation of His Genius and a Catalogue of His Original Sketches, Drawings, and Paintings in the Berol Collection,* Columbia University Libraries, 1967; D. Hudson, "Arthur Rackham: The Gentle Humorist," *Connoisseur,* September, 1967; Ellen Shaffer, "Arthur Rackham, 1867-1939," *Horn Book,* Brian Doyle, editor, *The Who's Who of Children's Literature,* Schocken Books, 1968; Margery Darrell, editor, *Once upon a Time: The Fairy-Tale World of Arthur Rackham,* Viking, October, 1967; 1972; G. T. McWhorter, "Arthur Rackham: The Search Goes On," *Horn Book,* February, 1972; David Larkin, editor, *Arthur Rackham,* Bantam, 1975.

Collections of Rackham's work are held in the Berol Collection at the Butler Library of Columbia University, in the Spencer Collection at the New York Public Library, and at the Free Library of Philadelphia.

RADLAUER, Edward   1921-

PERSONAL: Born March 3, 1921, in Kentucky; son of Kurt and Hulda Radlauer; married Ruth Shaw (a writer and editor), 1947; children: David, Robin, Daniel. *Education:* University of California, Los Angeles, B.A., 1947, graduate study, 1949-50; Whittier College, M.A., 1956. *Home:* 620 West Rd., La Habra, Calif. 90631.

CAREER: Employed by California Department of Employment, 1948-49; teacher, reading specialist, and principal, 1950-68; writer, 1968—.

WRITINGS—For children: *Drag Racing: Quarter Mile Thunder,* Abelard, 1966; *Drag Racing* (with own photographs), Bowmar, 1967; *Karting: Fun on Wheels* (with own photographs), Bowmar, 1967; *The Mighty Midget* (with own photographs), Bowmar, 1967; *Slot Car Racing,* Bowmar, 1967; *Surfing* (with own photographs), Bowmar, 1968, revised edition, 1975; *Custom Cars* (with own photographs), Bowmar, 1968, revised edition, 1974; *Drag Racing Funny Cars* (with own photographs), Bowmar, 1968; *Dune Buggy Racing* (with own photographs), Bowmar, 1968; *Dune Buggies* (with own photographs), Bowmar, 1968; *Motorcycles: Whirling Wire Wheels,* Abelard, 1969, revised edition, Bowmar, 1975; *Drag Strip Challenge* (fiction; with own photographs), Elk Grove Press, 1969; *Karting Challenge* (fiction; with own photographs), Elk Grove Press, 1969.

Minibike Challenge (fiction), Elk Grove Press, 1970; *Drag Racing Pix Dix: A Picture Dictionary* (with own photographs), Bowmar, 1970; *Motorcycle Racing* (with own photographs), Bowmar, 1970, revised edition, 1975; *VW Bugs,* Bowmar, 1970; *Snowmobiles,* Bowmar, 1970; *Motorcycle Challenge* (fiction), Elk Grove Press, 1972; *Fast, Faster, Fastest,* Childrens Press, 1973; *Motorcycle Mania,* Childrens Press, 1973; *Motorcyclopedia* (with own photographs), Bowmar, 1973; *Soap Box Racing,* Childrens Press, 1973; *Ready, Get Set, Whoa!,* Childrens Press, 1974; *Wild Wheels,* Childrens Press, 1974; *Flying Mania,* Childrens Press, 1974; *Minibikes* (with own photographs), Bowmar, 1975; *Race Car Drivers School,* F. Watts, 1975; *Pursuit School,* F. Watts, 1975; *Motorcycle Moto Cross School,* F. Watts, 1976; *Rodeo School* (with own photographs), F. Watts, 1976; (with son, David Radlauer) *Model Airplanes,* Childrens Press, 1976; *Racing Numbers,* Childrens Press, 1976; *Cats!,* Bowmar, 1976; *Wheels!,* Bowmar, 1976; *Racing!,* Bowmar, 1976, *Kickoff!,* Bowmar, 1976; *Shark Mania,* Childrens Press, 1977; *Boats,* Childrens Press, 1977; *Model*

It must be the shortest and slowest because it's a unicycle. ■ (From *Fast, Faster, Fastest* by Edward Radlauer.)

Cars, Childrens Press, 1977; (with daughter, Robin Radlauer) *Monkey Mania,* Childrens Press, 1977; *CB Radio,* Childrens Press, 1977; *Soccer,* Childrens Press, 1977; *Some Basics About Bicycles,* Childrens Press, 1978; *Some Basics about Vans,* Childrens Press, 1978; *Some Basics about Skateboards,* Childrens Press, 1978; *Some Basics about Motorcycles,* Childrens Press, 1978.

With wife, Ruth Shaw Radlauer: *About Missiles and Men,* Melmont, 1959; *About Atomic Power for People,* Melmont, 1960; *Atoms Afloat: The Nuclear Ship Savannah,* Abelard, 1963; *Father Is Big,* Bowmar, 1967; *What Is a Community?,* Elk Grove Press, 1967; *Water for Your Community,* Elk Grove Press, 1968; *Horses* (with own photographs), Bowmar, 1968, revised edition, 1975; *Evening,* Bowmar, 1968; *Colors,* Bowmar, 1968; *Whose Tools Are These?,* Elk Grove Press, 1968; *Quarter Midget Challenge* (fiction), Elk Grove Press, 1969.

We Go on Wheels, Elk Grove Press, 1970; *Horses Pix Dix: A Picture Dictionary* (with own photographs), Bowmar; 1970; *Buggy-Go-Round* (with own photographs), F. Watts, 1971; *On the Drag Strip* (with own photographs), F. Watts, 1971; *Scramble Cycle* (with own photographs), F. Watts, 1971; *On the Sand* (with own photographs), F. Watts, 1972; *Horsing Around* (with own photographs), F. Watts, 1972; *Chopper Cycle* (fiction; with own photographs), F. Watts, 1972; *Bonneville Cars* (with own photographs), F. Watts, 1973; *Horse Show Challenge* (fiction; with own photographs), Childrens Press, 1973; *Motorcycle Mutt* (with own

photographs), F. Watts, 1973; *On the Water* (with own photographs), F. Watts, 1973; *Salt Cycle* (with own photographs), F. Watts, 1973; *Foolish Filly* (with own photographs), F. Watts, 1974; *Racing on the Wind* (with own photographs), F. Watts, 1974; *Gymnastics School* (with own photographs), F. Watts, 1976; *Acadia National Park,* Childrens Press, 1978; *Mammoth Cave,* Childrens Press, 1978.

ADAPTATIONS—Filmstrips—all published by Pied Piper in 1977: "Yosemite National Park," "Grand Canyon National Park," "Great Smoky National Park," "Yellowstone National Park".

Also author of six reading board games for Bowmar.

WORK IN PROGRESS: Three titles in the "Ready, Get Set, Go" series and four titles for a reading series, all for Childrens Press; "Starting Line II," the second in a series of reading programs, for Bowmar; *Dinosaur Mania;* (with daughter, Robin Radlauer) *Bicycle Moto Cross;* (with son, David Radlauer) *Model Trains.*

SIDELIGHTS: "Many authors write 'high quality' literature that is incomprehensible to the less academic student, the poor reader, the slow reader, the disappointed student. I try to write for all those who feel left out of the usual college oriented curriculum. One of my great pleasures is to get scathing reviews in snobbish journals since these reviewers demonstrate their utter contempt for the youngster who is not attuned to the mainstream of educational junk."

EDWARD RADLAUER

FOR MORE INFORMATION SEE: Bulletin of the Center for Children's Books, January, 1977.

RADLAUER, Ruth (Shaw) 1926-

PERSONAL: Born August 18, 1926, in Midwest, Wyo.; daughter of Tracy (in industrial relations) and Ruth (a real estate agent; maiden name, Preston) Nichols; married Edward Radlauer (a writer), June 28, 1947; children: David, Robin, Dan. *Education:* Attended University of California, Los Angeles, 1944-47, 1948-50. *Residence:* La Habra, Calif. *Office address:* P.O. Box 1637, Whittier, Calif. 90609.

CAREER: Elementary teacher in Norwalk, Calif., 1950-51; substitute teacher in elementary schools in Norwalk, La Habra, E. Whittier, Calif, 1953-69; special education teacher in La Puente, Calif., 1966-67; adult education teacher of parent education and creative writing, Whittier, Calif., 1968-71; Elk Grove Books (a division of Childrens Press) Whittier, Calif., editor, 1971—. *Member:* Authors Guild, Writers' Club of Whittier.

WRITINGS: Fathers at Work, Melmont, 1958, published as *About Men at Work,* 1967; *Women at Work,* Melmont, 1959; *Of Course, You're a Horse,* Abelard, 1959; *Mothers Are That Way,* Abelard, 1960; *About Four Seasons and Five Senses,* Melmont, 1960; (self-illustrated) *Good Times Drawing Lines,* Melmont, 1961; *Good Times with Words,* Melmont, 1963; *Stein, The Great Retriever,* Bobbs-Merrill, 1964; (with Marjorie Pursel) *Where in the World Do You Live?,* Franklin Publishing, 1965; *From Place to Place,*

Franklin Publishing, 1965; *Food From Farm to Family,* Franklin Publishing, 1965; *Clothes From Head to Toe,* Franklin Publishing, 1965; *What Can You Do With a Box?,* Childrens Press, 1973; *Yellowstone National Park,* Childrens Press, 1975; *Yosemite National Park,* Childrens Press, 1975; *Everglades National Park,* Childrens Press, 1975; *Great Smoky Mountains National Park,* Childrens Press, 1976; *Mesa Verde National Park,* Childrens Press, 1976; *Grand Canyon National Park,* Childrens Press, 1977; *Rocky Mountain National Park,* Childrens Press, 1977; *Glacier National Park,* Childrens Press, 1977; *Olympic National Park,* Childrens Press, 1977; *Acadia National Park,* Childrens Press, 1978; *Mammoth Cave National Park,* Childrens Press, 1978; *Zion National Park,* Childrens Press, 1978.

With husband, Edward Radlauer: *About Missiles and Men,* Melmont, 1959; *About Atomic Power for People,* Melmont, 1960; *Atoms Afloat: The Nuclear Ship Savannah,* Abelard, 1963; *What Is a Community?,* Elk Grove Press, 1967; *Get Ready for School,* Elk Grove Press, 1967; *Whose Tools Are These?,* Elk Grove Press, 1968; *Water for Your Community,* Elk Grove Press, 1968; *Father Is Big,* Bowmar, 1968; *Colors,* Bowmar, 1968; *Evening,* Bowmar, 1968; *Quarter Midget Challenge,* Childrens Press, 1969; *Horses,* Bowmar, 1968, revised edition, 1975; *Horses Pix Dix: A Picture Dictionary,* Bowmar, 1970; *Buggy-Go-Round,* F. Watts, 1971; *On the Drag Strip,* F. Watts, 1971; *Scramble Cycle,* F. Watts, 1971; *Chopper Cycle,* F. Watts, 1972; *Horsing Around,* F. Watts, 1972; *On the Sand,* F. Watts, 1972; *Bonneville Cars,* F. Watts, 1973; *Motorcycle Mutt,* F. Watts, 1973; *On the Water,* F. Watts, 1973; *Salt Cycle,* F. Watts, 1973; *Foolish Filly,* F. Watts, 1974; *Racing on the Wind,* F. Watts, 1974; *Gymnastics School,* F. Watts, 1976.

WORK IN PROGRESS: Hawaii Volcanoes National Park, publication expected in 1979; *Haleakala National Park,* publication expected in 1979.

RUTH RADLAUER

(From *What Can You Do with a Box?* by Ruth Shaw Radlauer. Illustrated by Jay Rivkin.)

SIDELIGHTS: "I had access to a typewriter when I was seven years old, so I started writing plays which were adaptations of *Cinderella* and the like. I did not set out to be a writer until after I'd taught first grade. I couldn't find the books I wanted for my class, especially in the field of social studies. While I preferred to write fantasy or humor in verse, I got my start in social studies books for primary grades.

"When the state of California adopted a series of my books, my sometime collaborator, Ed Radlauer, began to look upon our writing more seriously. As a school administrator, Ed saw a great need, and we set out to supply it: reading material with a high impact of colorful reality and interest, written with a reluctant or non-bookish reader in mind. This led to our 'Reading Incentive Series' and other similar books on subjects like motorcycles, horses, drag racing, and minibikes."

HOBBIES AND OTHER INTERESTS: Horses, music, hiking, and sewing.

REED, William Maxwell   1871-1962

PERSONAL: Born in 1871, in Bath, Maine. *Education:* Attended Harvard University.

CAREER: Harvard University Observatory, research assistant; professor of astronomy, Harvard University and Princeton University; also worked in a large steel mill; author.

WRITINGS—For young people; all published by Harcourt, except as indicated: *The Earth for Sam* (illustrated by Karl Moseley), 1930, revised edition (edited by Paul F. Brand-

wein), 1960; *The Stars for Sam* (illustrated by K. Moseley; edited by Charles E. St. John), 1931, revised edition (edited by P. F. Brandwein), 1960; *And That's Why* (illustrated by K. Moseley; edited by F. C. Brown), 1932, reissued, 1960; (with Wilfrid S. Bronson) *The Sea for Sam* (illustrated by W. S. Bronson; edited by F. C. Brown and Charles M. Breder, Jr.), 1935, revised edition (edited by P. F. Brandwein), 1960; (with Jannette M. Lucas) *Animals on the March* (edited by Edwin H. Colbert), 1937; *America's Treasure* (edited by Carey Croneis), 1939; *The Sky Is Blue* (illustrated by James MacDonald; edited by C. Croneis), 1940; *Patterns in the Sky: The Story of the Constellations* (illustrated by D. F. Levett Bradley), Morrow, 1951.

SIDELIGHTS: William Maxwell Reed's books "for Sam" resulted from letters he wrote to his nephew, Sam, to satisfy the young boy's curiosity. *Outlook* described the first, *The Earth for Sam* as "an interestingly written and exceptionally well illustrated story of the earth, from the beginnings of life to the dawn of history. So many of these simplifications of science for children talk down to their young readers that it is a pleasure to find one which doesn't." The revised edition, appearing thirty years later, in 1960, evoked the following comments from *Library Journal:* "Although it is so carefully done over as to be virtually new, it keeps the original spirit, partly through wise elimination of the dated stylistic letter of the older version. . . ."

FOR MORE INFORMATION SEE: Outlook, January 29, 1930; (for children) Stanley J. Kunitz and Howard Haycraft, editors, *Junior Book of Authors,* 2nd edition revised, H. W. Wilson, 1951.

(Died, 1962)

WILLIAM MAXWELL REED

REEVES, James   1909-

PERSONAL: Born July 1, 1909, in London, England; son of Albert John and Ethel Mary (Blench) Reeves; married Mary Phillips, 1936; children: Stella, Juliet Mary, Gareth Edward. *Education:* Attended Stowe School; Cambridge University, M.A. (honors), 1931. *Home and office:* Flints, Rotten Row, Lewes, Sussex, England. *Agent:* Laura Cecil, 10 Exeter Mansions, 106 Shaftesbury Ave., London W1V 7DH, England (children's books); John Johnson, 3 Albermarle St., London W1, England; Sterling Lord Agency, 75 East 55th St., New York, N.Y. 10022.

CAREER: Teacher in state schools and teachers training college, 1933-52; free-lance author and editor, 1952—. Broadcaster and lecturer.

WRITINGS: The Critical Sense: Practical Criticism of Prose and Poetry, Heinemann, 1956; *Teaching Poetry,* Heinemann, 1958; *A Short History of English Poetry, 1340-1940,* Heinemann, 1961, Dutton, 1962; *Understanding Poetry,* Heinemann, 1965, Barnes & Noble, 1968; (with Norman Culpan) *Dialogue and Drama,* Plays, 1967; *Subsong,* Heinemann, 1969; *Heroes and Monsters* (juvenile), Blackie & Son, 1969; *Mr. Horrox and the Gratch* (juvenile), Abelard-Schuman, 1969; *The Path of Gold* (juvenile), Hamish Hamilton, 1972; *The Voyage of Odysseus* (juvenile), Blackie & Son, 1973; *The Forbidden Forest* (juvenile), Heinemann, 1973; *The Lion That Flew* (juvenile), Chatto & Windus, 1974; *Two Greedy Bears* (juvenile), Hamish Hamilton, 1974; *More Prefabulous Animals* (juvenile), Heinemann, 1975; *The Shadow of the Hawk* (juvenile), Collins, 1975; *The Clever Mouse* (juvenile), Chatto & Windus, 1976; *Quest & Conquest* (juvenile), Blackie & Son, 1976; *The Ballad,* George G. Harrap, 1976.

Poetry: *The Natural Need,* Constable, 1936; *The Imprisoned Sea,* Editions Poetry (London), 1949; *The Wandering Moon* (juvenile), Heinemann, 1950, 2nd edition, 1957, Dutton, 1960; *The Password, and Other Poems,* Heinemann, 1952; *The Blackbird in the Lilac* (juvenile), Dutton, 1952; *A Health to John Patch* (ballad opera for children), Boosey & Hawkes, 1957; *Prefabulous Animiles* (juvenile), Heinemann, 1957, Dutton, 1960; *The Talking Skull,* Heinemann, 1958; *Collected Poems, 1929-1959,* Heinemann, 1960; *Ragged Robin* (juvenile), Dutton, 1961; *Hurdy-Gurdy: Selected Poems for Children,* Heinemann, 1961; *The Questioning Tiger,* Heinemann, 1964; *Rhyming Will* (juvenile), Hamish Hamilton, 1967, McGraw, 1968; *Poems,* Heinemann, 1969; *Commitment to Poetry,* Heinemann, 1969; *How to Write Poems for Children,* Heinemann, 1971; *Complete Poems for Children* (juvenile), Heinemann, 1973.

Children's books, prose: *Mulcaster Market* (play), Heinemann, 1951; *The King Who Took Sunshine* (play), Heinemann, 1954; *Pigeons and Princesses* (stories), Heinemann, 1956; *Mulbridge Manor,* Heinemann, 1958, Penguin, 1963; *Titus in Trouble,* Bodley Head, 1959, Walck, 1960; *Sailor Rumbelow and Britannia,* Heinemann, 1961; *Sailor Rumbelow, and Other Stories* (includes *Pigeons and Princesses),* Dutton, 1962; *The Peddler's Dream, and Other Plays,* Dutton, 1963; *The Story of Jackie Thimble,* Dutton, 1964; *The Strange Light,* Heinemann, 1964, Rand McNally, 1966; *The Pillar-Box Thieves,* Nelson, 1965; *The Trojan Horse,* Hamish Hamilton, 1968, Watts, 1969.

JAMES REEVES

'O Harry, Harry! hold me close—
I fear some animile
It is the horny Catipoce
With her outrageous smile!'
■ (From *Complete Poems for Children* by James Reeves. Illustrated by Edward Ardizzone.)

Editor, poetry: *Poets' World* (anthology), Heinemann, 1948; D. H. Lawrence, *Selected Poems,* Heinemann, 1951; John Donne, *Selected Poems,* Heinemann, 1952, 2nd edition, 1957, Macmillan, 1958; Gerard Manley Hopkins, *Selected Poems,* Heinemann, 1953, Macmillan, 1957; John Clare, *Selected Poems,* Heinemann, 1954, Macmillan, 1957; Robert Browning, *Selected Poems,* Heinemann, 1956, Macmil- lan, 1957; (and author of introduction and commentary) *The Modern Poets' World,* Heinemann, 1957; (with Cecil J. Sharp), *The Idiom of the People: English Traditional Verse,* Macmillan, 1958; Emily Dickinson, *Selected Poems,* Heine- mann, 1959; Samuel Taylor Coleridge, *Selected Poems,* Heinemann, 1959; *The Rhyming River,* four volumes, Hei- nemann, 1959; (and author of introduction and notes) *The*

Everlasting Circle: English Traditional Verse, Macmillan, 1960; *Georgian Poetry,* Penguin, 1962; *The Cassell Book of English Poetry,* Harper, 1965; Jonathan Swift, *Selected Poems,* Heinemann, 1966, Barnes & Noble, 1967; *Homage to Trumbull Stickney,* Heinemann, 1968; *An Anthology of Free Verse,* Basil Blackwell, 1968; *The Poets and Their Critics,* (Vol. III), Hutchinson, 1969; (joint editor with M. Seymour-Smith) *Selected Poems of Andrew Marvell,* Heinemann, 1969; (joint editor with M. Seymour-Smith) *Inside Poetry,* Heinemann, 1970; *Chaucer: Lyric and Allegory,* Heinemann, 1970; *Poems and Paraphrases,* Heinemann, 1972, *Complete English Poems of Thomas Gray,* Heinemann, 1973; *A Vein of Mockery,* Heinemann, 1973; *Collected Poems, 1927-1974,* Heinemann, 1975; *The Reputation and Writings of Alexander Pope,* Heinemann, 1976.

Editor, poetry for children: *Orpheus: A Junior Anthology of English Poetry,* Heinemann, 1950, teacher's book, 1952; *Strawberry Fair,* Heinemann, 1954; *Green Broom,* Heinemann, 1954; *Yellow Wheels,* Heinemann, 1954; *Grey Goose and Gander,* Heinemann, 1954; *The Merry-Go-Round,* Heinemann, 1955; *One's None,* Heinemann, 1968, Watts, 1969.

Editor, poetry and prose: (And author of commentary) *The Speaking Oak,* Heinemann, 1951; *A Golden Land: Stories, Poems, Songs* (juvenile), Hastings, 1958; Robert Graves, *Selected Poetry and Prose,* Hutchinson, 1961.

Editor or adaptor, prose: (With Denys Thompson) J. Bronowski and others, *The Quality of Education,* Muller, 1947; *The Writer's Way: An Anthology of English Prose,* Christophers, 1948; (with Norman Culpan) *Dialogue and Drama,* Heinemann, 1950; *The Holy Bible in Brief* (King James text), Messner, 1954; *English Fables and Fairy Tales, Retold,* Oxford University Press, 1954, Walck, 1960; Jonathan Swift, *Gulliver's Travels,* Heinemann, 1955; Jules Verne, *Twenty Thousand Leagues Under the Sea,* Chatto & Windus, 1956; *Exploits of Don Quixote, Retold,* Blackie, 1959, Walck, 1960; (with Desmond Flower) *The Taste of Courage: The War, 1939-1945,* Harper, 1960; Stephen Leacock, *Unicorn Leacock,* Hutchinson, 1960; *Great English Essays,* Cassell, 1961; Aesop, *Fables,* Blackie, 1961, Walck, 1962; *The First Bible: An Abridgement for Young Readers,* Heinemann, 1962; *Three Tall Tales,* Abelard-Schuman, 1964; *Primrose Winter Witch* (adapted from the Czech), Paul Hamlin, 1964; *The Road to a Kingdom* (stories from the Bible), Heinemann, 1965; *The Secret Shoemakers* (adapted from *Kinder und Hausmaerchen,* by the Brothers Grimm), Abelard-Schuman, 1966; (with M. Seymour-Smith) *A New Canon of English Poetry,* Barnes & Noble, 1967; *The Cold Flame* (based on tales of the Brothers Grimm), Hamish Hamilton, 1967; *The Christmas Book,* Dutton, 1968, 1972; *The Sayings of Dr. Johnson,* J. Baker, 1968; *The Angel and the Donkey* (juvenile), Hamish Hamilton, 1969, McGraw, 1970; *Maeldun the Voyager* (juvenile), Hamish Hamilton, 1971, Walck, 1972; *How the Moon Began: A Folk Tale from Grimm* (juvenile), Hamish Hamilton, 1972.

SIDELIGHTS: "My interests and upbringing are reflected in my poems for children."

HOBBIES AND OTHER INTERESTS: Music.

FOR MORE INFORMATION SEE: Brian Doyle, *The Who's Who of Children's Literature,* Schocken Books, 1968; *Horn Book,* August, 1969, December, 1970, October, 1972; *Third Book of Junior Authors,* edited by de Montreville and Hill, H. W. Wilson, 1972.

ANNA E. ROKEBY-THOMAS

ROKEBY-THOMAS, Anna E(lma) 1911-

PERSONAL: Born May 10, 1911, in Crieff, Ontario, Canada; daughter of Frederick Edwin (a farmer) and Jane Ann (McAninch) Roszell; married Howard R. Rokeby-Thomas (an Anglican minister), August 10, 1936; children: Emily Ann Nairne (Mrs. J. William McLean), David Earnest Roszell, Derwyn Evan Howard. *Education:* Guelph General Hospital School of Nursing, diploma, 1934; also attended Anglican Womens' College, 1935-36. *Religion:* Anglican Church of Canada. *Home:* 74 Jackson Ave., Kitchener, Ontario, Canada N2H 3P1.

CAREER: Victorian Order of Nurses, Guelph, Ontario, 1934-35; St. George's Mission, Cambridge Bay, Victory Island, Canadian Arctic, 1936-39; St. Thomas-Elgin General Hospital, St. Thomas, Ontario, 1952-60; Toronto General Hospital, Toronto, Ontario, 1960-65; writer, 1939—.

*WRITINGS—*For children: *Ningiyuk's Igloo World,* Moody, 1972; *Ning's Igloo Romance: A Sequel to Ningiyuk's Igloo World,* Moody, 1975. Contributor of articles and photographs of the Canadian Arctic to adult periodicals and stories to children's magazines since 1939. *Awards, honors:* Notable Canadian Children's Books exhibition, National Library of Canada, Ottawa, 1973, for *Ningiyuk's Igloo World.*

WORK IN PROGRESS: Short stories; a book.

SIDELIGHTS: "I was born on a farm in the lovely Ontario countryside. Our family was a large one and there was always a lot of fun and laughter—as well as hard work.

"With such a father as you to guide me, I know I can learn to be wise." ■ (From *Ning's Igloo Romance* by Anne E. Rokeby-Thomas. Illustrated by J.N. Howard.)

"As far back as I can remember I had a tendency to daydream and before I was eight years old I was making up stories in my imagination.

"My troubles started as I grew older and began writing the stories down on paper. I had the best parents in the world, but they thought my writings were utter foolishness and would get me nowhere. In spite of the fact that I excelled in school compositions they discouraged every writing attempt. Consequently, I did a lot of writing in hidden corners.

"A nursing career was approved for me and I went in training with my younger sister. My writing dreams lay dormant during those years. After my marriage, the ambition and desire to write flared up. I took night classes in writing and soon had the thrill of seeing both stories and articles in print.

"I was very fortunate to have a unique background to write about. We lived for some years among the primitive Eskimos and I made a vow then that I would write a book about an Eskimo girl and tell my readers what it is really like to live in an igloo. I have been able to do this. The story reads like one of my persistent dreams in a world of fantasy, but the background *is* authentic. I have given many lectures and addresses on the subject of the Canadian Arctic."

HOBBIES AND OTHER INTERESTS: Travel (Great Britain, Europe, and North America), gardening.

RYAN, Peter (Charles) 1939-

PERSONAL: Born November 18, 1939, in Harrogate, England; son of Charles Edmund (a brigadier general) and Joyce Mary (Dodgson) Ryan. *Education:* Trinity College, Dublin, B.A., 1963. *Home and office:* 11 Moore Park Rd., London S.W.6, England. *Agent:* Deborah Rogers, 5-11 Mortimer St., London W.1, England.

CAREER: British Broadcasting Corp., Television Service, London, England, member of production staff in science and current affairs departments, 1963-68; free-lance journalist, photographer, translator, and broadcaster, 1968—. *Member:* British Interplanetary Society (fellow), Geological Society (London; fellow), National Union of Journalists, Naval and Military Club.

WRITINGS: Invasion of the Moon, Penguin, 1969, revised edition, 1971; *Journey to the Planets,* Penguin, 1972, revised edition, 1973; *Planet Earth,* Penguin, 1972, revised edition, 1973, *The Ocean World,* Penguin, 1973; *UFOs and Other Worlds,* Penguin, 1975; *Solar System,* Allen Lane, 1978. Project editor for *Sunday Times,* 1973-74, editor of "The Facts of Life" series, 1974; technical editor for Bureau de Recherches Geologiques et Minieres (Saudi Arabia), 1975-76.

WORK IN PROGRESS: The Penguin Dictionary of Space, publication by Allen Lane and Penguin expected in 1979.

SIDELIGHTS: "The exploits of British comic-strip hero, Dan Dare and the writings of Arthur C. Clarke stimulated an early interest in space exploration. At the university I studied to become a geologist. When I graduated I was offered a French Government grant to study anthropology for one year at the Sorbonne but chose instead an equally tempting chance to learn how to produce science programming for television.

"After five years into the British Broadcasting Corporation, I became free-lance, writing and working with an illustrator, Ludek Pesek whom I met in Switzerland in 1969.

"I enjoy writing about space research although other subjects, including fiction, are also attractive."

PETER RYAN (at left)

It is difficult to imagine what a 70-metre-high wave looks like, but [this]. . .picture will give you some idea of what a "TSUNAMI" is, and the damage it can do. ■ (From *The Ocean World* by Peter Ryan. Illustrated by Ludek Pesek.)

SANDBERG, (Karin) Inger 1930-

PERSONAL: Born August 2, 1930, in Karlstad, Sweden; daughter of Johan and Hanna (a teacher; maiden name, Carlstedt) Erikson; married Lasse Sandberg (an artist), April 27, 1950; children: Lena, Niklas, Mathias. *Education:* Swedish Training College for Teachers, teacher's certificate, 1954. *Home:* Vaestra Raden 16, 65227 Karlstad, Sweden.

CAREER: Teacher in Karlstad, Sweden public schools, 1957-63; writer of books and of television and radio productions for children, 1963—. *Member:* Swedish Writers Association. *Awards, honors:* Swedish Author's Fund award, 1963; Karlstad culture prize, 1965; Hans Christian Andersen honorable mention and International Board on Books for Young People (IBBY) honorable mention, both 1966, and Leipzig International Book Exhibit award, 1971, all for *Niklas roeda dag;* Heffaklump award from *Expressen* newspaper (Sweden), 1969, for *Pappa, kom ut!;* Nils Holgersson Medal, 1973; Astrid Lindgren Prize, 1974.

WRITINGS—All illustrated by husband, Lasse Sandberg; all first published by Raben & Sjoegren, except as noted: *Faaret Ullrik faar medalj* (title means "Woolrik the Sheep Gets a Medal"), Eklund, 1953; *Jag maalar en . . .* (title means "I Paint a..."), Eklund, 1955; *Jonas bilen och aeventyret* (title means "Jonas the Car and the Adventure"), Geber, 1959.

Godnattsagor paa rullgardinen (title means "Bedtime Stories on the Blind"), Geber, 1960; *Filuren paa aeventyr* (title means "The Adventure of the Little Filur"), Geber, 1961; *Hemma hos mej* (title means "At My Place"), Geber, 1962; *Lena beraettar,* Geber, 1963, 3rd edition, 1971, translation by Patricia Crampton published as *Here's Lena,* Methuen, 1970; *Trollen i Lill-Skogen* (title means "The Trolls in the Little Wood"), Karlstad Town, 1963; *Niklas roeda dag,* Geber, 1964, 2nd edition, 1967, translation published as *Nicholas' Red Day,* Delacorte, 1967; *Barnens bildordlista* (title means "Children's Wordbook"), Skrivrit, 1965; *Den musikaliska myran* (title means "The Musical Ant"), Geber, 1965, 2nd edition, 1970; *En morgon i varuhuset* (title means "One Morning in the Department Store"), [Stockholm], 1965; *Lilla spoeket Laban,* Geber, 1965, 3rd edition, 1976, translation by Nancy S. Leupold published as *Little Ghost Godfrey,* Delacorte, 1968, translation by Kersti French published as *Little Spook,* Methuen, 1969; *Johan,* 1965, 3rd edition, 1970, translation by Patricia Crampton published as *Johan's Year,* Methuen, 1971.

Pojken med de Hundra bilarna, 1966, translation published as *The Boy With 100 Cars,* Delacorte, 1967; *Tomtens stadsresa* (title means "The Tomten Goes to Town"), General Post Office (Sweden), 1966; *En konstig foersta maj,* 1967; *Niklas oenskedjur,* 1967, translation by R. Sadler published as *Nicholas' Ideal Pet,* Sadler & Brown, 1968, published as *Nicholas' Favorite Pet,* Delacorte, 1969; *Pojken med de maanga husen,* 1968, translation published as *The Boy with Many Houses,* Delacorte, 1969; *Vi passar oss sjaelva* (title means "We Look after Ourselves"), Geber, 1968; *Pappa, kom ut!,* 1969, translation published as *Daddy Come Out!,* Sadler & Brown, 1970, published as *Come On Out, Daddy,*

Inger and Lasse Sandberg and family.

Little Anna had a terrible cold.
She had to stay in bed with a
Scarf around her neck.
She sneezed and sneezed.
■ (From *When Little Anna Had a Cold* by Inger and Lasse Sandberg. Illustrated by Lasse Sandberg.)

Delacorte, 1971; *Johan i 2:an*, 1969, 2nd edition, 1970, translation by Patricia Crampton published as *Johan at School*, Methuen, 1972; *Filurstjaernan* (title means "The Filurtar"), Geber, 1969.

Buffalo Bengt och indianerna, 1970, translation published as *Buffalo Bengt and the Indians*, Sadler & Brown, 1971; *Lena staar i koe* (title means "Lena Lines Up"), Geber, 1970; *Stora Tokboken* (title means "The Big Crazybook"), Geber, 1970; *Vad aer det som ryker?*, 1971, translation by Merloyd Lawrence published as *Where Does All That Smoke Come From?*, Delacorte, 1972; *Fred Strid krymper* (title means "Mr. Fred Strid Shrinks"), 1972; *Vi leker oeken, Froeken*, 1973, translation published as *The Desert Game*, Methuen, 1974, published as *Let's Play Desert*, Delacorte, 1974; *Hej, vaelkommen till mej!*, 1974, translation published as *Let's Be Friends*, Methuen, 1975; *Perry och osynlige Wrolf* (title means "Perry and the Invisible Wrolf"), 1975; *Var aer laanga farbrorns hatt?* (title means "Where's Tall Uncle's Hat?"), 1976.

Little Anna series: *Vad Anna fick se*, 1964, 4th edition, 1974, translation published as *What Anna Saw*, Lothrop, 1964; *Lilla Anna och trollerihatten*, 1965, 4th edition, 1976, translation published as *Anna and the Magic Hat*, Sadler & Brown, 1965, published as *Little Anna and the Magic Hat*, Lothrop, 1965; *Vad lilla Anna sparade paa*, 1965, 4th edi-

tion, 1974, translation published as *What Anna Saved*, Sadler & Brown, 1965, published as *What Little Anna Saved*, Lothrop, 1965; *Lilla Annas mama fyller aar*, 1966, 4th edition, 1974, translation published as *Little Anna's Mama Has a Birthday*, Sadler & Brown, 1965, published as *Little Anna's Mama Has a Birthday*, Lothrop, 1966; *Naer lilla Anna var foerkyld*, 1966, 4th edition, 1974, translation published as *When Anna Had a Cold*, Sadler & Brown, 1966, published as *When Little Anna Had a Cold*, Lothrop, 1966.

Lilla Anna och Laanga Farbrorn paa havet, 1971, translation published as *Little Anna and the Tall Uncle*, Methuen, 1973; *Var aer lilla Annas hund?*, 1972, translation published as *Where Is Little Anna's Dog?*, Methuen, 1974; *Lilla Annas julklapp*, 1972, 3rd edition, 1974, translation published as *Kate's Christmas Present*, A. & C. Black, 1974; *Lilla Anna flyttar saker*, 1972, 3rd edition, 1974, translation published as *Kate's Upside Down Day*, A. & C. Black, 1974; *Lilla Anna leker med bollar*, 1973, translation published as *Kate's Bouncy Ball*, A. & C. Black, 1974; *Lilla Anna kom och hjaelp!*, 1972, 2nd edition, 1974, translation published as *Kate, Kate Come and Help!*, A. & C. Black, 1974; *Lilla Anna i glada skolan* (title means "Little Anna in the Happy School"), 1975.

Mathias series: *Mathias bakar kakor*, 1968, 3rd edition, 1974, translation published as *Daniel and the Coconut Cakes*, A. & C. Black, 1973; *Mathias och trollet*, 1968, translation published as *Daniel's Mysterious Monster*, A. & C. Black, 1973; *Mathias maalar en . . .* , 1969, translation published as *Daniel Paints a Picture*, A. & C. Black, 1973; *Mathias hjaelper till*, 1969, 2nd edition, 1974, translation published as *Daniel's Helping Hand*, A. & C. Black, 1973.

Writer, with husband, of over 180 children's television and radio programs broadcast in Sweden. Contributor to Swedish journals and magazines.

WORK IN PROGRESS: A series of books about lilla spoeket Laban (the little spook) and his new sister, Labolina; two television series of five shows each; a film guide about open schools for television broadcast and use in a teacher's training program.

SIDELIGHTS: Inger Sandberg stated that although she left teaching thirteen years ago she is still very interested in education. She recently went to study teaching programs for dyslexic children in England, and she and her husband both give lectures to teachers about open schools and children's books.

FOR MORE INFORMATION SEE: Horn Book, December, 1969, October, 1973.

SANDBERG, Lasse (E. M.) 1924-

PERSONAL: Born February 17, 1924, in Stockholm, Sweden; married Inger Erikson (a teacher and author), April 27, 1950; children: Lena, Niklas, Mathias. *Education:* Attended Anders Beckman's Art School, 1948-49. *Home:* Vaestra Raden 16, 65227 Karlstad, Sweden.

CAREER: Began working as a press photographer; became a cartoonist for magazines and newspapers; illustrator of children's books, beginning 1953. *Awards, honors:* Elsa Beskow Plaque, 1965, for *Lilla Spoeket Laban;* Hans Christian Andersen honorable mention and International Board on Books for Young People (IBBY) honorable mention,

LASSE SANDBERG

both 1966, and Leipzig International Book Exhibit award, 1971, all for *Niklas roeda dag;* Heffaklump award from *Expressen* newspaper (Sweden), 1969, for *Pappa kom ut!.*

WRITINGS: Herr Sandberg ser pa England, Raben & Sjoegren, 1966; *Herr Sandberg ser pa sig sjaelv,* Raben & Sjoegren, 1969; *Gagatan Sverige,* Raben & Sjoegren, 1970.

Illustrator; all written by wife, Inger Sandberg; all first published by Raben & Sjoegren, except as noted: *Faaret Ullrik Faar medalj* (title means "Woolrik the Sheep Gets a Medal"), Eklund, 1953; *Jag maalar en . . .* (title means "I Paint a. . ."), Eklund, 1955; *Jonas bilen och aeventyret* (title means "Jonas the Car and the Adventure"), Geber, 1959.

Godnattsagor paa rullgardinen (title means "Bedtime Stories on the Blind"), Geber, 1960; *Filuren paa aeventyr* (title means "The Adventure of the Little Filur"), Geber, 1961; *Hemma hos mej* (title means "At My Place"), Geber, 1962; *Lena beraettar,* Geber, 1963, 3rd edition, 1971, translation by Patricia Crampton published as *Here's Lena,* Methuen, 1970; *Trollen i Lill-Skogen* (title means "The Trolls in the Little Wood"), Karlstad Town, 1963; *Niklas roeda dag,* Geber, 1964, 2nd edition, 1967, translation published as *Nicholas' Red Day,* Delacorte, 1967; *Barnens bildordlista* (title means "Children's Wordbook"), Skrivrit, 1965; *Den musikaliska myran* (title means "The Musical Ant"), Geber, 1965, 2nd edition, 1970; *En morgon i varuhuset* (title means "One Morning in the Department Store"), [Stockholm], 1965; *Lilla spoeket Laban,* Geber, 1965, 3rd edition, 1976, translation by Nancy S. Leupold published as *Little Ghost Godfrey,* Delacorte, 1968, translation by Kersti French published as *Little Spook,* Methuen, 1969; *Johan,* 1965, 3rd edition, 1970, translation by P. Crampton published as *Johan's Year,* Methuen, 1971.

Pojken med de Hundra bilarna, 1966, translation published as *The Boy with 100 Cars,* Delacorte, 1967; *Tomtens stadsresa* (title means "The Tomten Goes to Town"), General Post Office (Sweden), 1966; *En konstig foersta maj,* 1966; *Niklas oenskedjur,* 1967, translation by R. Sadler published as *Nicholas' Ideal Pet,* Sadler & Brown, 1968, published as *Nicholas' Favorite Pet,* Delacorte, 1969; *Pojken med de maanga husen,* 1968, translation published as *The Boy with Many Houses,* Delacorte, 1969; *Vi passar oss sjaelva* (title means "We Look after Ourselves"), Geber, 1968; *Pappa, kom ut!,* 1969, translation published as *Daddy Come Out!,* Sadler & Brown, 1970, published as *Come On Out, Daddy,* Delacorte, 1971; *Johan i 2: an,* 1969, 2nd edition, 1970, translation by P. Crampton published as *Johan at School,* Methuen, 1972; *Filurstjaernan* (title means "The Filurstar"), Geber, 1969.

Buffalo Bengt och indianerna, 1970, translation published as *Buffalo Bengt and the Indians,* Sadler & Brown, 1971; *Lena staar i koe* (title means "Lena Lines Up"), Geber, 1970; *Stora Tokboken* (title means "The Big Crazybook"), Geber, 1970; *Vad aer det som ryker?,* 1971, translation by Merloyd Lawrence published as *Where Does All That Smoke Come From?,* Delacorte, 1972; *Fred Strid krymper* (title means "Mr. Fred Strid Shrinks"), 1972; *Vi leker oeken, Froeken,* 1973, translation published as *The Desert Game,* Methuen, 1974, published as *Let's Play Desert,* Delacorte, 1974; *Hej, vaelkommen till mej!,* 1974, translation published as *Let's Be Friends,* Methuen, 1975; *Perry och osynlige Wrolf* (title means "Perry and the Invisible Wrolf"), 1975; *Var aer laanga farbrorns hatt?* (title means "Where's Tall Uncle's Hat?"), 1976.

Little Anna series: *Vad Anna fick se,* 1964, 4th edition, 1974, translation published as *What Anna Saw,* Lothrop, 1964; *Lilla Anna och trollerihatten,* 1965, 4th edition, 1976, translation published as *Anna and the Magic Hat,* Sadler & Brown, 1965, published as *Little Anna and the Magic Hat,* Lothrop, 1965; *Vad lilla Anna sparade paa,* 1965, 4th edition, 1974, translation published as *What Anna Saved,* Sadler & Brown, 1965, published as *What Little Anna Saved,* Lothrop, 1965; *Lilla Annas mama fyller aar,* 1966, 4th edition, 1974, translation published as *Little Anna's Mama Has a Birthday,* Sadler & Brown, 1965, Lothrop, 1966; *Naer lilla Anna var foerkyld,* 1966, 4th edition, 1974, translation published as *When Anna Had a Cold,* Sadler & Brown, 1966, published as *When Little Anna Had a Cold,* Lothrop, 1966.

Lilla Anna och Laanga Farbrorn paa havet, 1971, translation published as *Little Anna and the Tall Uncle,* Methuen, 1973; *Var aer lilla Annas hund?,* 1972, translation published as *Where Is Little Anna's Dog?,* Methuen, 1974; *Lilla Annas julklapp,* 1972, 3rd edition, 1974, translation published as *Kate's Christmas Present,* A. & C. Black, 1974; *Lilla Anna flyttar saker,* 1972, 3rd edition, 1974, translation published as *Kate's Upside Down Day,* A. & C. Black, 1974; *Lilla Anna leker med bollar,* 1973, translation published as *Kate's Bouncy Ball,* A. & C. Black, 1974; *Lilla Anna kom och hjaelp!,* 1972, 2nd edition, 1974, translation published as *Kate, Kate Come and Help!,* A. & C. Black, 1974; *Lilla Anna i glada skolan* (title means "Little Anna in the Happy School"), 1975.

Mathias series: *Mathias bakar kakor,* 1968, 3rd edition, 1974, translation published as *Daniel and the Coconut Cakes,* A. & C. Black, 1973; *.Mathias och trollet,* 1968, translation published as *Daniel's Mysterious Monster,* A. & C. Black, 1973; *Mathias maalar en . . . ,* 1969, translation published as *Daniel Paints a Picture*, A. & C. Black, 1973; *Mathias hjaelper till*, 1969, 2nd edition, 1974, translation published as *Daniel's Helping Hand*, A. & C. Black, 1973.

Writer, with wife, of over 180 children's television and radio programs broadcast in Sweden.

SIDELIGHTS: The books by Lasse Sandberg and his wife, Inger, have been published in many countries, including Germany, England, and Japan. Sandberg's illustrations are primarily done in full color and two colors. Many of the Sandbergs' earlier books were written to provide their own small children with easily identifiable stories.

In *Come On Out, Daddy!* the husband and wife team told the story of a small boy who wished his father were in a career other than art. A critic for *Publishers Weekly* observed, "Consistency can be a crashing bore, but not when something is consistently funny, like the picture books of the Sandbergs. . . . For small boys, this picture book will prove irresistible, especially if they are small boys who are car-crazy."

FOR MORE INFORMATION SEE: Lee Kingman, editor, *Illustrators of Children's Books, 1957-1966*, Horn Book, 1968; *Publishers Weekly*, March 29, 1971; Doris de Montreville, *Third Book of Junior Authors*, H. W. Wilson, 1972.

"All the fathers go fishing or play ball with their children," said Matthew. "I wish you had an ordinary job; then you wouldn't have to work on weekends. You ought to be like Peter's father."
■ (From *Come On Out, Daddy!* by Inger and Lasse Sandberg.)

SCHMIDT, Elizabeth   1915-

PERSONAL: Born June 26, 1915, in Ubly, Mich.; daughter of Warner J. (a teacher) and Eolah (Brown) Bates; married Eric J. Schmidt (an attorney), December 15, 1956; children: Karen (step-daughter; Mrs. Michael Burns). *Education:* Pratt Institute, B.F.A., 1942; Wayne State University, M.A., 1949. *Religion:* Episcopal. *Home:* 534 Silverado Drive, Tiburon, Calif. 94920.

CAREER: American Red Cross, Alaska and overseas, recreation worker, 1943-46; Meinzinger Art School, Detroit, Mich., 1947-49; Cass Technical High School, Detroit, Mich., art teacher, 1950-60; El Camino High School, South San Francisco, Calif., art teacher, 1962-77. Active in local community committee for preservation of park land. *Exhibitions*—group shows: Detroit Artist Market; Michigan Water Color Society; Marin County Water Color Society, October, 1977. *Member:* Marin County Water Color Society, Mill Valley Arts Guild. *Awards, honors:* Second place, wa-

With his long neck a dinosaur like Brontosaurus could easily have reached into the tallest branches for these vines. ■ (From *What Did the Dinosaurs Eat?* by Wilda S. Ross. Illustrated by Elizabeth Schmidt.)

ter color, Mador County Fair, 1961; merit award, water color, Richard Yip Hawaii Painting workshop, 1975; award of excellence, water color, Richard Yip Baja Painting workshop, 1976.

ILLUSTRATOR: Wilda Ross, *Who Lives in This Log?*, Coward, 1971; Wilda Ross, *What Did the Dinosaurs Eat?*, Coward, 1972. Water colors have appeared in *Ford Times* Magazine.

SIDELIGHTS: "My high school training in commercial art at Cass Technical High School was the greatest motivation for me as an art teacher and illustrator. Although I had many excellent teachers in art schools and college, Miss Mary L. Davis, at Cass, was the first to excite in me, real interest in art. A list of famous designers, painters and illustrators who were her students would form a 'Who's Who' in itself, including David Fredenthal, Jim Lee, Harry Bertoia and countless others. She created such compelling interest in drawing, painting and simply talking about art it was necessary for her to literally 'chase' her students home, long after school hours, so she herself could go to supper. She maintained an enormous file of pictures by every well known artist and illustrator, to which her students were constantly exposed. She was an avid reader herself, and encouraged her students to read widely, to carry sketch books, attend art exhibits and observe all phases of life around them.

"Upon graduation from high school during the depression years, I studied briefly at The School of Arts and Crafts in Detroit and then worked 'for my room and board,' teaching art in a mission school for mountain girls in North Carolina for two years. This experience, added to the fact that I came from a family of teachers, (my father and two of his brothers were school principals), made it natural for me to choose teaching as a career. After a year at Wayne State University, I attended Pratt Institute, majoring in art education.

"During my first year of teaching in Detroit, I, with some of my students, would sketch portraits of soldiers at the U.S.O. evenings. Wanting to do more for the war effort, I joined the American Red Cross as a recreation worker, supervising craft shops in army hospitals in Texas, Alaska and the Aleutians. Later I worked on the ships bringing back European war brides.

"When I returned to the states I became an instructor in design at Meinzinger Art School, which at that time had a large student body of ex-soldiers, studying under the 'G-I' bill.

"Following my two years at Meinzingers' I worked for a Masters degree at Wayne State University, doing a great amount of experimentation in serigraphy with William T. Woodward, an expert teacher and artist in graphic arts. During this time I also worked part time in an advertising art studio.

"When Mary L. Davis retired from teaching in 1950 I was asked to fill that vacancy. No one could really take the place of that vital person, but I did enjoy many years of teaching pen and ink, wash drawing and poster design at Cass Technical High School, then considered one of the country's outstanding schools.

"In 1956 I was married to Eric J. Schmidt who ran a boat yard and did commercial diving. Our first home was aboard his schooner, the *Wave*, which he had brought to Detroit from Chesapeake Bay. It was about a hundred years old, the oldest ship of its kind still afloat, and was docked at Grosse

ELIZABETH SCHMIDT

Ile, Michigan. Eric was attending evening law classes at Wayne State University and upon receiving his law degree we moved to San Francisco, where he was to become a maritime lawyer. His undergraduate work at the University of California had been in fine art, so we have enjoyed a mutual interest in outdoor painting on weekends and during summer camping trips. In recent years we have both attended many art workshops, conducted by Richard Yip, in outdoor water color painting techniques.

"Along with my teaching I have found time for occasional free-lance assignments, including two commissions for water colors from *Ford Times* Magazine. Enjoying water color and pen and ink as mediums, I had always wanted to apply them as techniques for book illustration. This opportunity came along when I had taken a leave of absence from teaching. Knowing Wilda Ross, the author, we were able to work closely together on the co-ordination of illustrations to text in her two books, *Who Lives in This Log?* and *What Did the Dinosaurs Eat?*, making numerous 'field trips' to woods and parks to see plants, trees and insects.

"Because an illustrator must be able to draw and paint a great variety of things, the more he has seen of the rich fabric of life the more insight he brings to his work. Many things in my own life have affected my outlook and accomplishments. I grew up in a large family of ten brothers and sisters. I experienced the problems of the depression years, requiring my working my way through school in a variety of jobs, such as waiting on tables, clerking in stores, assembly line factory work, camp counseling and recreation work with children in a settlement house. I have traveled widely, in all of the states including Alaska and Hawaii, to Cuba, Mexico, the Bahamas and Europe. I have enjoyed such hobbies as photography, crafts, sewing and the study of Spanish. These experiences, I believe, have all affected my art in some way.

"In June of 1977 I retired from teaching. Energies spent in developing skills and creativity with students can now be directed to my work in painting and illustration."

FOR MORE INFORMATION SEE: Independent Journal, Fall, 1972.

SEIDMAN, Laurence (Ivan) 1925-

PERSONAL: Surname is pronounced *Side*-man; born March 8, 1925, in New York, N.Y.; son of Leo (in business) and Ida (Witkin) Seidman; married Marion Nesler (a teacher of physically handicapped infants), June 12, 1947; children: Douglass, Susan, Leslie. *Education:* City College (now of the City University of New York), B.B.A., 1947; New York University, M.Ed., 1949, Ed. D., 1969. *Home:* 140 Hill Park Ave., Great Neck, N.Y. 11548. *Office:* School of Education, C.W. Post College, Long Island University, Greenvale, N.Y. 11548.

CAREER: Elementary school teacher in New York, N.Y., 1949-1951; Searingtown Elementary School, Albertson, Long Island, New York, 1956-1970; Long Island University, C.W. Post College, Greenvale, N.Y., associate professor of education, 1971—. *Military service:* U.S. Army, first aid man in Infantry, 1943-45; served in Italy; received Bronze Star.

WRITINGS: Once in the Saddle: The Cowboys' Frontier, 1866-1896, Knopf, 1973; *Fools of '49: The California Gold Rush, 1848-1856,* Knopf, 1976.

SIDELIGHTS: "My special field of interest is the utilization of folk songs and ballads to teach the humanities and the full range of our country's history. I have used folk songs as a vehicle to 'turn students on' and to get them excited about their heritage and traditions. Folk songs are a catalyst which open up students to emotional and intellectual exploration of their cultural and historic backgrounds. But they are more than just history. Put into their proper settings and time slots, folk songs lead to insights into the economic, social, political and moral issues of their day.

"I sing 'with' students, not 'for' students. I am not an entertainer, nor do I use an instrument. Anybody can sing, and when you sing for your own pleasure and interest, rather than for some one else or for a mark, it is a whole new ball game. I am not a music teacher, merely one of the folk. I give courses in 'The Ballad of America' which trains teachers to utilize folk songs and ballads in working with their classes. It is an area which transcends grade levels, age levels and subject areas. It is an interdisciplinary, multimedia approach, so that in my classes I will often have teachers from kindergarten through high school, as well as librarians and media people.

"It is through my interest in folk songs that I became a writer. The more I listened to and sang folk songs about cowboys, whalers, loggers and miners, the more I became curious about them and their life style. So I started reading

and the more I read, the more I understood and enjoyed the songs. I learned so much, that I decided to try it out with my students in my fifth grade class. And I've been singing ever since. I have sung with thousands of students of all ages and I have never met one who did not like to sing, once the pressure was off and he or she was singing for himself and because they found the song beautiful and attractive.

"I received my doctorate in the field of social studies preparing a handbook for teachers on the utilization of folk songs to interpret and teach our American history and heritage.

"In 1963-64 I took a year's sabbatical and, with the entire family, camped for a year in Europe and Africa, living in a tent and moving southward with the seasons—an exhilarating and rewarding experience.

"Our camping trip abroad has left us with many rich dividends. We really got to know people, made loads of friends with other campers and always dropped the invitation to 'stop in and see us if you're in New York.' As a result, just about everyone we met has come over to visit us. We've had campers stay at our house from Tasmania, New Zealand, Japan, and most of Europe. In return we have visited many of them in their homes and being a good correspondent, have kept up friendships for these many years. Our children feel that the world is their oyster and have many homes open to them when and if they travel abroad.

"Our experiences led us to sharing our home with an exchange student from Columbia, our son, Fernando Cadena. In return, my son, Douglass, spent two summers down in South America in Columbia and speaks Spanish fluently. Above all, we have memories of wonderful places and marvelous people and a conviction that people throughout the world share the same hopes, needs, desires and emotions differently, but we are much more alike than we are different."

HOBBIES AND OTHER INTERSTS: Hiking and camping.

SHARMA, Partap 1939-

PERSONAL: Born December 12, 1939, in Lahore, India (now Pakistan); son of Baij Nath (a civil engineer and farmer) and Dayawati (Pandit) Sharma; married Susan Amanda Pick, October 21, 1971; children: Kiran Namrita, Tara Natasha. *Education:* St. Xavier's College, Bombay, India, B.A. (honors), 1959. *Politics:* "Democratic, anti-censorship, but no political party." *Religion:* Hindu. *Home:* 105, Olympus Rd., Altamount Rd., Bombay 400 026, India. *Office:* Flat 5B, Block 6, Shyam Nivas, Bhulabhai Desai Rd., Bombay 400 026, India. *Agent:* Oliver Swan, Collier Associates, 280 Madison Ave., New York, N.Y. 10016.

CAREER: Indian National Theatre, Bombay, playwright and director of English drama, 1961—. Chief free-lance commentator for newsreels and documentaries produced by Films Division (Bombay), 1960— (also producer-director); host of "What's the Good Word?," a program for Television Centre (Bombay), 1975-76; actor in Hindi feature films.

MEMBER: Cine Artistes Association, Radio Advertisers and Producers Association of India, Commentators Guild, National Centre for the Performing Arts, Films Division Film Study Group, Club Mahabaleshwar, Amateur Riders Club. *Awards, honors:* Silver Gazelle from the President of

India, 1971, for lead role in feature film ''Phir Bhi'' (title means ''Even Then''), which won the National Award for the best Hindi film of the year. RAPA First Prize, 1976, for best voice in radio spots.

WRITINGS: A Touch of Brightness (three-act play; first produced in London at Royal Court Theatre, March 5, 1967), Grove, 1967; *The Surangini Tales* (juvenile), Harcourt, 1973; *Dog Detective Ranjha* (juvenile), Macmillan, 1977.

Plays: ''Bars Invisible,'' (three-acts, first produced in Bombay by the Indian National Theatre, June, 1961); ''The Word,'' (three-act, first produced for the Bombay Arts Festival by the Theatre Group, March, 1966); ''The Professor Has a Warcry,'' (five-acts, first produced in Bombay by the Impermanent Theatre, January, 1970); ''A Touch of Brightness,'' (three-acts, banned in India in 1965, ban revoked by Bombay High Court in 1972, meanwhile play produced and published abroad, eventually produced by Indian National Theatre in Bombay, August, 1973).

Work anthologized in *25 Years of Indian Independence,* edited by Jag Mohan, Vikas (Delhi), 1973; *Young Winter's Tales 5,* edited by M. R. Hodgkin, Macmillan (London),

Surangini was such a beautiful little maiden that Kalu the weaver felt his heart would break if she did not speak to him. ■ (From *The Surangini Tales* by Partap Sharma. Illustrated by Demi Hitz.)

1974; *Aspects of Indian Literature,* edited by Suresh Kohli, Vikas, 1975; *Young Winter's Tales 8,* edited by M. R. Hodgkin, Macmillan (London).

Contributor of stories and articles to magazines.

WORK IN PROGRESS: The last two novels of a trilogy touching on contemporary events in India; *The Passport Racket* (novel; volume I of a trilogy).

SIDELIGHTS: ''Stories are perhaps a way of making more coherent and comprehensible the bewildering complexity of the world. I learn and discover as I write and I try to share what I have understood. This began with me when I was a child, before I could read, and when I needed to deduce a story to explain the pictures in a book. But that is just the technique; the aim is to uncover an aspect of the truth. The truth isn't always palatable. Two of my documentaries and a play have been banned. The High Court reversed the ban on the play; it is now a text in three Indian universities.''

SOLONEVICH, George   1915-

PERSONAL: Born October 15, 1915, in Moscow, Russia; son of Ivan and Tamara (Vosskressenskaya) Solonevich; married Inga Donner (an artist); children: Mike, Ulita. *Education:* Attended Graphische Lehr und Versuchsanstalt

PARTAP SHARMA

Ornithomimus was about three times as tall as you are. ■ (From *Dinosaurs and More Dinosaurs* by M. Jean Craig. Illustrated by George Solonevich.)

(Vienna), Atheneum (Helsinki), and Vienna Academy (Vienna). *Home:* Route 7, Box 375, Roanoke, Va. 24018.

CAREER: Free-lance illustrator.

ILLUSTRATOR: Herbert Kondo, *Adventures In Space and Time: The Story of Relativity,* Holiday House, 1966; *The Moon Tonight,* Holt, 1967; Vladimar and Nada Kovalik, *Undersea World of Tomorrow,* Prentice, 1968; Jean M. Craig, *Dinosaurs & More Dinosaurs,* Scholastic, 1968; Martin L. Keen, *Hunting Fossils,* Messner, 1970; Mae B. Freeman, *Do You Know About Stars,* Random House, 1970; Jene Lyon, *Astronomy: Our Sun & It's Neighbors,* Western, 1974; and many others.

SIDELIGHTS: "Born in a wrong place at a wrong time: Moscow, Russia, 1915. Lived through three wars, one revolution, four dictators, concentration camps, jails, escapes, assassination attempts and other diversions of political life in Europe and South America. Against this background studying art was a rather restless undertaking.

"Went to five different schools in different countries and, later, in true European tradition, worked, with varying success in every conceivable art field: from cartooning to poster painting, from portraiture to landscape painting.

"After arriving in New York in 1953 became a successful magazine illustrator. When American illustration died, turned to book illustration and then, finally, found my niche in wildlife painting.

"Not feeling much affinity with New York, bought a delightful mountain valley in the Blue Ridge Mountains near Roanoke, Va. Here my wife Inga and I spent four years building an art school, where I for several years thereafter attempted to teach talented kids my very own technique—the 'Pickup.' But talented kids are rare and untalented ones boring. Wildlife started taking more and more of our time, so we quit teaching and now we both devote our main efforts to the pure, free and unencumbered art. Inga mostly sculpts, while I paint: wildlife, landscapes, an occasional portrait.

"I work in my own oil technique, the 'Pick-up.'"

The place had always fascinated her, ever since she could remember. Like all the Buxton folk, however, she respected the **NO TRESPASSING** sign and kept her distance, wondering why the "furriners" from Baltimore were so unfriendly. ■ (From *Taffy of Torpedo Junction* by Nell Wise Wechter. Illustrated by Mary Walker Sparks.)

GEORGE SOLONEVICH

SPARKS, Mary W. 1920-

PERSONAL: Born August 27, 1920, in Brown Summit, N.C.; daughter of Nestor Glenn (a farmer) and Mamie (Hawkins; a teacher) Walker; married Thomas G. Sparks (an oil company employee), June 17, 1955; children: Tommy, Margaret, Clement. *Education:* Elon College, B.A., 1941; University of Houston, M.E., 1952. *Politics:* Undeclared. *Religion:* Baptist. *Home:* Route 6, Box 494, Beaumont, Texas 77705. *Office:* Port Neches Groves High School, Port Neches, Texas.

CAREER: Haw River and Monticello public schools, N.C., elementary school teacher, 1941-45; Ketchikan City School, Ketchikan, Alas., junior high teacher, 1945-47; Nederland ISD, Nederland, Tex., elementary and high school teacher, 1948-54; Central Junior High School, Greensboro, N.C., elementary school teacher, 1954-56; Port Neches Groves High School, Port Neches, Tex., teacher, 1976—. *Exhibitions:* Elon College, Elon College, N.C., 1947; Nederland Methodist Church, Nederland, Tex., 1949.

ILLUSTRATOR: Nell W. Wechter, *Taffy of Torpedo Junction,* John Blair, 1973.

MARY W. SPARKS

STERN, Simon 1943-

PERSONAL: Born September 12, 1943, in London, England; son of Peter Francis and Honour (Sayer) Stern; married Sylvia Caveney (an author; teacher), 1972; children: Suzannah. *Education:* Attended London College of Printing & Graphic Arts, 1960. *Politics:* Left-wing. *Religion:* Humanist. *Home:* 19 Corringham Road, London, NW11, England.

CAREER: Free-lance book illustrator, 1969—. Worked for a number of publishers on production and design before going to free-lance. *Member:* Association of Illustrators, Society of Authors, National Union of Journalists.

WRITINGS—All self-illustrated: (Editor) *The Life and Fables of Aesop,* Taplinger, 1970; *Neptune's Treasure,* Methuen, 1972; *Moon Trip,* Methuen, 1973; *Jungle Journey,* Methuen, 1974; *Kidnapped,* Methuen, 1976; *The Hobyahs,* Prentice, 1977.

Illustrator: Ian Serraillier, *The Ballad of St. Simeon,* Kaye & Ward, 1970, Watts, 1971; Ian Serraillier, *The Bishop and the Devil,* Warne, 1971; Derek Sampson, *Grump and the Hairy Mammoth,* Methuen, 1971; Brian Earnshaw, *Dragonfall Five and the Royal Beast,* Methuen, 1972; Brian Earnshaw, *Dragonfall Five and the Space Cowboys,* Methuen, 1972, Lothrop, 1975; Brian Earnshaw, *Dragonfall Five and the Empty Planet,* Methuen, 1973, Lothrop, 1976; Derek Sampson, *Grump Strikes Back,* Methuen, 1973; Herbert Eisner, *The Monster Plant,* Methuen, 1974; Sylvia Caveney, *Smiler's Pram Ride,* Methuen, 1974; Brian Earnshaw, *Dragonfall Five and the Hijackers,* Methuen, 1974; Sylvia Caveney, *Where Am I?,* Sidgwick & Jackson, 1974, Lerner, 1976; Brenda Thompson, *The Children's Crusade,* Sidgwick & Jackson, 1974, Lerner, 1976; Brenda Thompson, *Pirates,* Sidgwick & Jackson, 1974, Lerner, 1976; Brenda Thompson, *The Winds That Blow,* Sidgwick & Jackson, 1975, Ler-

ner, 1976; Eva Ibbotson, *The Great Ghost Rescue,* Macmillan (London), 1975; Brian Earnshaw, *Dragonfall Five and the Master Mind,* Methuen, 1975; Sylvia Caveney, *Inside Mom: An Illustrated Account of Conception, Pregnancy and Childbirth,* Sidgwick & Jackson, 1976, St. Martin's, 1977; Sylvia Caveney, *Little Zip's Dressing-up Book,* Pelham Books, 1977; Sylvia Caveney, *Little Zip's Zoo Counting Book,* Pelham Books, 1977; Brian Earnshaw, *Dragonfall Five and the Super Horse,* Methuen, 1977. Author and illustrator of the "Captain Ketchup" series which appears in *Humpty-Dumpty.*

WORK IN PROGRESS: Researching, reading and illustrating folk-tales; *"Mrs. Vinegar,"* for Methuen and Prentice-Hall.

SIDELIGHTS: "I became interested in 'art' at the age of twelve. I chose book illustration because I like stories, don't like advertisements, and am not sufficiently obsessed for 'fine' art. As a child, I was given two huge books of Fairy Tales: a complete Grimm and a selection from Afanasev's Russian collection, and I hope one day to be a good enough illustrator to do some of them justice."

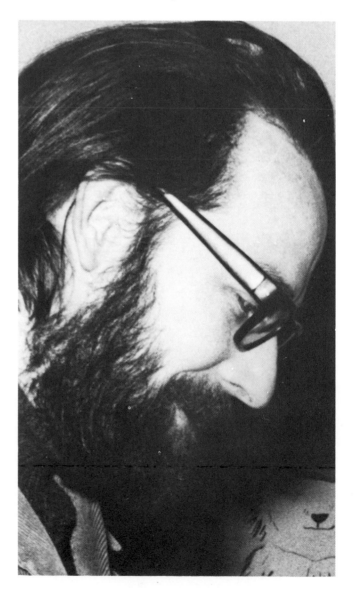

SIMON STERN

And Sir Quivernot got down from his charger and placed his foot in a dignified and dainty way on the dragon's corpse. ■ (From *Grummit the Dragon* by Honour Stern. Illustrated by Simon Stern.)

STERN by STERN

. . .John could just make out the dark tips of Ossian House's chimneys amongst its guarding firs. ■ (From *Ossian House* by A.C. Stewart. Jacket design by Simon Jeruchim.)

STEWART, A(gnes) C(harlotte)

PERSONAL: Born in Liverpool, England; married Robert Frederick Stewart (a mechanical engineer); children: Sheila Therese (Mrs. Andrew Philip Thomson). *Education:* Privately educated. *Politics:* "None: I despair of them all!" *Religion:* Church of England. *Home:* Knowetop, Corsock, Castle Douglas, Kirkcudbrightshire, Scotland, DG7 3EB.

CAREER: Writer. *Member:* Society of Women Writers and Journalists. *Awards, honors:* Edgar Allen Poe Award, from Mystery Writers of America for *Elizabeth's Tower,* 1972; award of merit, 1977, from Scottish Arts Council for *Beyond the Boundary.*

WRITINGS—All young adult novels: *The Boat in the Reeds* (illustrated by Christopher Brooker), Blackie & Son, 1960, Bradbury, 1970; *Falcon's Crag,* Blackie & Son, 1969; *The Quarry Line Mystery,* Faber, 1971, Nelson, 1973; *Elizabeth's Tower,* S. G. Phillips, 1972; *Dark Dove,* S. G. Phillips, 1974; *Ossian House,* Blackie & Son, 1974, S. G. Phillips, 1976; *Beyond the Boundary,* Blackie & Son, 1976; *Silas and Con,* Atheneum, 1977; *Brother Raimon Returns,* Blackie & Son, 1978.

WORK IN PROGRESS: A sequel to *Falcon's Crag;* research for a story about highland clearances.

SIDELIGHTS: "I grew up in a small seaside town in Cheshire, England, where the high spring tides often came over into our garden. My sole companion of my own age was my elder sister, as we were educated at first by a series of governesses. When I was in my teens we moved to a cottage in Kent and there my lifelong love of animals and gardens had a chance to develop. It was the first of a long series of country cottages peopled with a wide variety of animals, from my daughter's white mice, via guinea-pigs, hamsters, hens, ducks, geese, Siamese cats and goats to my favourites, retrievers, both labrador and flat-coated. Fortunately my husband—a mechanical engineer—and my daughter share my love of the country and animals.

"I cannot remember a time when I did not want to write but there never seemed any opportunity. Then my daughter went to boarding school and for a time gardens and animals gave place to a first-floor flat in a 400-year-old Dorset manor house and my only companions from eight-thirty until six were my two labradors. It could not have been a better place to start to write and I have continued to do so ever since.

"My daughter is now married and my husband and I live in a shepherd's cottage high amongst the Galloway hills in Scotland. We renovated it ourselves and it has one of the loveliest views anyone could wish for, and a garden and animals once again fill a large part of my life. I am very interested in wildlife too and seventy acres of marsh and moor which we own has been accepted by the Scottish Wildlife Trust as a nature reserve. We have planted eight acres of conifers as a windbreak, doing much of the planting ourselves, and made a mile-and-a-half long trail. Two small lochs provide homes for wild duck and winter quarters for whooper swans and also supply us with brown trout fishing.

"An added interest these last few years has been the lending of a bungalow I own to groups of physically handicapped children for holidays. I have always wanted to be able to do something of this kind and it has proved a very rewarding experience.

"When indoors, apart from writing, I cook and knit and I always must have something at hand to read. My husband paints—he did the end papers for *The Quarry Line Mystery*—and he types all my manuscripts. I write all my stories in long hand and then read them to my tape recorder—a great help in balancing the sentences.

"My writing naturally reflects my interests and the backgrounds of my stories are ones I know well and love. I began many of my books with no idea of what the plot would be; I just started with an idea, a scene or a character that interested me and wrote on—it was often more like writing down a story I was being told than inventing one. Any guidance or morals my stories may have, develop as a natural part of them, often unseen by me until later: they are never put in deliberately.

"I did not intend to write for young people, I began writing for my daughter and it went on from there. I have written adult stories that have been well-liked and kept for consideration but finally returned. I find a great satisfaction in writing books for young people and would not now wish to change.

"A well-known English critic once wrote: 'If I know and like a man I am careful never to read his books and if I enjoy a book I take pains to avoid meeting the author.' If this questionnaire is rather incomplete it is because I too strongly believe that authors and their work are things better kept apart. My books appear under my initials only to avoid my personal identity becoming imposed upon the story. Nothing about me can possibly be as interesting as a stranger in a tower, a mystery train running against signals or an invisible boy whistling in the Highland hills."

A.C. STEWART

Ian sat very still. Above the sound of the wind in the branches he could hear the pounding of his heart. ■ (From *The Boat in the Reeds* by A.C. Stewart. Illustrated by Christopher Brooker.)

STRATTON-PORTER, Gene   1863-1924

PERSONAL: Given name was Geneva Grace; born August 17, 1863, in Wabash County, Indiana; died December 6, 1924, in Los Angeles, California; daughter of Mark (a farmer) and Mary (Schellenbarger) Stratton; married Charles Darwin Porter (a chemist), April 21, 1886; children: Jeannette. *Education:* Educated privately. *Home:* Los Angeles, California.

CAREER: Novelist and naturalist. Her vast knowledge of natural history and photography brought her many journalistic positions. Photographic editor of *Recreation* for two years; natural history staff member of *Outing* for two years; specialist in natural history photography for *Photographic Times Annual Almanac* for four years.

WRITINGS: The Song of the Cardinal: A Love Story, Bobbs-Merrill, 1903, reissued, Grosset & Dunlap, 1953; *Freckles* (illustrated by E. Stetson Crawford), Doubleday, Page, 1904, reprinted, Scholarly Press, 1971 [other editions illustrated by Wladyslaw T. Benda, Doubleday, Page, 1912; Thomas Fogarty, Doubleday, Page, 1921; Ruth Ives, Junior Deluxe Editions, 1957; Michael Lowenbein, Whitman, 1965]; *What I Have Done with Birds,* Bobbs-Merrill, 1907, also published as *Friends in Feathers,* Doubleday, Page, 1917; *At the Foot of the Rainbow* (illustrated by Oliver Kemp), Outing Publishing, 1907; *Birds of the Bible,* Eaton & Mains, 1909; *A Girl of the Limberlost* (illustrated by W. T. Benda), Doubleday, Page, 1909, reissued, Brockhampton Press, 1959; *Music of the Wild,* Eaton & Mains, 1910; *The Harvester* (illustrated by W. L. Jacobs), Doubleday, Page, 1911; *Moths of the Limberlost,* Doubleday, Page, 1912; *After the Flood,* Bobbs-Merrill, 1912; *Laddie: A True Blue Story* (illustrated by Herman Pfeifer), Doubleday, Page, 1913; *Birds of the Limberlost,* Doubleday, Page, 1914.

Michael O'Halloran (illustrated by Frances Rogers), Doubleday, Page, 1915; *Morning Face* (self-illustrated), Doubleday, Page, 1916; *A Daughter of the Land,* Doubleday, Page, 1918; *Homing with the Birds: The History of a Lifetime of Personal Experiences with the Birds,* Doubleday, Page 1919; *Her Father's Daughter,* Doubleday, Page, 1921, reissued, Grosset & Dunlap, 1961; *The Fire Bird* (illustrated by Gordon Grant), Doubleday, Page, 1922; *Jesus of the Emerald* (poems; illustrated by Edward E. Winchell), Doubleday, Page, 1923; *The White Flag,* Doubleday, Page, 1923; *The Keeper of the Bees* (illustrated by G. Grant), Doubleday, Page, 1925, reissued, 1961; *Tales You Won't Believe,* Doubleday, Page, 1925; *Let Us Highly Resolve,* Doubleday, Page, 1927; *The Magic Garden* (illustrated by Lee Thayer), Doubleday, Page, 1927, reissued, Grosset & Dunlap, 1961.

ADAPTATIONS—Movies: "Michael O'Halloran," Gene Stratton Porter, 1923, Republic Pictures, 1937, Windsor Pictures, 1948; "Girl of the Limberlost," Gene Stratton Porter, 1924, Monogram Pictures, 1934, Columbia Pictures, 1945; "Keeper of the Bees," Gene Stratton Porter, 1925, Monogram Pictures, 1935, Columbia Pictures, 1947; "Laddie," Gene Stratton Porter, 1926, RKO Radio Pictures, 1935, RKO Pictures, 1940; "Any Man's Wife," based on *Michael O'Halloran,* Republic Pictures, 1937; "Romance of the Limberlost," based on *Girl of the Limberlost,* Monogram Pictures, 1938.

SIDELIGHTS: **August 17, 1863.** Born on a 240-acre Indiana farm named Hopewell. Christened Geneva Grace, Stratton was the youngest of twelve children. "No one wanted me; as there had been eleven of us, every one felt that was enough. [My sister] May was six years old and in school, and my mother thought there never would be any more babies. She was well as could be. She was growing ample and strong and making up for all she had missed while doing her best for the others. She had given away the cradle and divided the baby clothes among my big married sisters and brothers, and was having a fine time and enjoying herself the most she ever had in her life. The land was paid for long ago; the house she had planned, builded as she wanted it; she had a big team of matched grays and a carriage with side lamps and patent leather trimmings; and sometimes there was money in the bank. I do not know that there was very much, but any at all was a marvel, considering how many of us there were to feed, clothe, and send to college. Mother was forty-six and father was fifty; so they felt young enough yet to have a fine time and enjoy life, and just when things were going best, I announced that I was halfway over my journey to earth." [Gene Stratton Porter, *Laddie: A True Blue Story,* Doubleday, 1913.[1]]

"I was born on a farm and lived there until time to begin my schooling. I have had my part in everything that ever happened on a farm from making candles and pressing cracklings, to drying apples and dropping corn. . . . I was born near enough the close of the Civil War to have seen my people go through the hard times which ensued, and I saw my mother do it with pink on her cheeks and her eyes a-shine, her head held high, and getting a deal of enjoyment out of each day that she sanned and sewed and scoured because she believed in God and loved her neighbours, and she was always giving of herself in every way she could think of to try to bring a bit of joy into the lives of others, as well as to keep her own family continuously effervescing.

"Father was descended from a long line of ancestors of British blood. He was named for, and traced his origin to that Mark Stratton who married the famous beauty, Ann Hancock, and settled on Stratton Island, afterward corrupted to Staten, according to family tradition. From that point back for generations across sea he followed his line to that family of Strattons of which the Earl of Northbrooke is the present head. To his British traditions and the customs of his family my father clung with rigid tenacity, never swerving a particle through environment or association. He believed in God, in courtesy, in honour, in cleanliness, in beauty, in education. I have heard him say that he would rather see a child of his the author of a book of which he could be proud than on the throne of England—which was the strongest way he knew to express himself. His very first

earnings he spent for a book; when other men rested, he read; all his life he was a student, with the most tenacious memory of any man I ever knew intimately. He especially loved history—Rolland's, Wilson's, 'Outlines,' Hume, Macaulay, Gibbon, Prescott, Bancroft. He could quote all of them, paragraphs at a time, giving dates with unfailing accuracy. He could repeat the entire Bible, giving chapters and verses, save the books of generations; these he said were a waste of grey matter to learn. I never knew him to fail in telling where any verse quoted to him was to be found. . . .

"My father's mind was such a treasure-house that the greatest pity of his passing was that all he knew should perish with him. But it is scarcely fair to express it that way, for all his life, with no thought of fatigue or inconvenience to himself, he travelled miles uncounted to share what he had learned with those less fortunately situated by delivering sermons, lectures, talks on civic improvement and politics. He worshipped beauty: beautiful faces, souls, hearts; beautiful landscapes, trees, animals, flowers. He loved colour,—rich, bright colour and every variation down to the palest shades. . . .

"He was constantly reading aloud to us children and to visitors, descriptions of the great deeds of men. Two 'hair-raisers' I especially recall were the story of John Maynard, who piloted a burning boat to safety while he slowly roasted at the wheel, and the story of Clemanthe. My heart stops and my flesh creeps as I write these lines that bring back every inflection of my father's wonderful voice as he would cry, in imitation of the Captain, 'John Maynard' and then give the reply until it sank to a mere gasp—'Aye, aye, Sir!'

"His other especial favourite was the story of Clemanthe and her lover's immortal answer to her question, 'Shall we meet again?' I am convinced my father could equal a great actor in reciting that, for he believed in and loved that answer, and his heart thrilled to its depths when he repeated it.

"Strong meat this for babes, but it was the kind we had from the cradle to the day of leaving our home.

"I had very few books, only two or three of my own. The markets did not afford the miracles common to the children of to-day. In fact, books are now so numerous, so cheap, so bewildering in colour and make-up, that I sometimes think children lose their perspective and love none of them as I loved my few plain little ones, filled with short stories and poems, with almost no illustration. I had a storehouse in the school books of my elder brothers and sisters, especially in the series of McGuffy readers from One to Six. For pictures I was driven to the Bible, dictionary, magazines about sheep and cattle, and the historical works read by my father.

"As I grew older there were magazines and more books. The one volume in which my heart was enwrapped was a collection of masterpieces of fiction belonging to an older sister. It contained *Paul and Virginia, Undine, Picciola, The Vicar of Wakefield,* and *Pilgrim's Progress.* These I spelled out painstakingly, a word at a time, until I almost knew them by heart from reading and re-reading. They were exquisitely expressed and conceived stories, and they may have done much in forming high conceptions in my childish mind of what really constituted literature and of furthering the lofty ideals instilled by my parents.

"I had been drilled at home and I could understand any ordinary printed matter and spell quite well before I ever started to school. My first literary effort was printed in wobbly letters in the back of an old grammar. It was entitled 'Ode to the Moon,' not that I had any idea what an 'ode' was other than that I had heard it discussed in the family, together with epic and sonnet, as forms of poetic expression.

> "'Oh, Moon, thou art glorious,
> Over the darkness of night
> Thy beams shine victorious.
> Thou lightest the weary traveller's way,
> Guiding his feet till break of day.'"

[Jeannette Porter-Meehan, *Life and Letters of Gene Stratton Porter,* Doubleday, Doran, 1928.[2]]

School was an absolute torture for young Stratton, who was allowed to run wild on the farm. "No books or teachers were needed to tell me about flowing water and fish, how hawks raised their broods and kept house, about the softly cooing doves of the spice thickets, the cuckoos slipping snakelike in and out of the wild crab-apple bushes, or the brown thrush's weird call from the thorn bush. I knew what they said and did, but their names, where they came from, where they went when the wind blew and the snow fell—how was I going to find out that? Worse yet were the flowers, butterflies, and moths; they were mysteries past learning alone, and while the names I made up for them were pretty and suitable, I knew in all reason they wouldn't be the same in the books. I had to go [to school], but no one will ever know what it cost. . . .

"Schoolhouses are made wrong. If they must be, they should be built in a woods pasture beside a stream, where you could wade, swim, and be comfortable in summer, and slide and skate in winter. The windows should be cut to the floor, and stand wide open, so the birds and butterflies could pass through. You ought to learn your geography by climbing a hill, walking through a valley, wading creeks, making islands in them, and promontories, capes, and peninsulas along the bank. You should do your arithmetic sitting under trees adding hickorynuts, subtracting walnuts, multiplying butternuts, and dividing hazelnuts. You could use apples for fractions, and tin cups for liquid measure. You could spell everything in sight and this would teach you the words that are really used in the world. Every single one of us could spell incompatibility, but I never heard father, or the judge, or even the Bishop, put it in a speech."[1]

October, 1874. Family moved to Wabash, Indiana. Geneva changed her name to Geneve. "When I lived in Wabash, Indiana, I was bounded on the west by the Miami Reservation, who boasted descendants of Logan, although his immediate family was supposed to have been wiped out. John Logan, however, claimed a rather immediate relationship with the old Chief of the Mingoes. On the south we had old Chief Wacacoonah of the Meshingmesas and hundreds of his tribe among whom I circulated freely as a child, being well acquainted with the Chief's daughters, Nancy and Susan, and often having been entertained in the old Chief's home with my brother-in-law, who was an Indian Agent and the guardian for many members of these tribes."[2]

February, 1875. After seven years of invalidism, her mother died. "She was the mother of twelve lusty babies, all of whom she reared past eight years of age, losing two little

Stratton-Porter, as a child.

girls at that time as a result of scarlet fever and whooping-cough, too ugly a combination for even such a wonderful mother as she. With this brood on her hands, she found time to keep an immaculate house, to set a table renowned in her part of the state, to entertain with unfailing hospitality all who came to her door, to beautify her home with such means as she could command, to embroider and fashion clothing for her children by hand; but her great gift was conceded by all her ability for making things grow. At this she was wonderful. . . . There is a shaft of white stone standing at her head in a cemetery that belongs to her, on a corner of my father's land; but to me her real monument is a cedar of Lebanon . . . topping the brow of a little hill crossing the grounds. She carried the slips from Ohio where she had them of a man who had brought a tree, a tiny thing, from the Holy Land, and he gave her two little cuttings. She planted both this way, one in her dooryard and one in her cemetery. That tree must stand thirty feet tall now, and have a body two feet in circumference."[2]

1879. Entered high school. "Friday afternoon was always taken up with an exercise called 'Rhetoricals,'—a misnomer as a rule, but let that pass. Four years were required to complete the course, and each Friday afternoon the pupils of one of these years furnished entertainment for the assembled school faculty. Our subjects were assigned and we cordially disliked the essays, sketches, and stories we were compelled to write, always putting them off until the last minute and then scratching down anything that would serve and not cut our grades too badly. This particular day on which I was to have a paper, the subject assigned me was 'Mathematical Law.' I knew that mathematical laws were worked out with a precision that was something wonderful, one of the greatest of miracles. (I had heard of Kepler.) But I also knew that I never had passed any examination in Mathematics by more than the 'skin of my teeth,' and that the subject had been given me purposely, and as punishment, by a professor who understood me so little that she never took into consideration that such a course on her part could only result in making me dislike it more.

"I put off the work until my paper had been called for three times to undergo preliminary reading by the professor. I truly had not access to works from which to prepare a proper paper, either in the school or home library. On the other hand, I had a brother-in-law who was a college man and a mathematical shark, and from him I might have secured all the material I needed; but I detested the subject and the professor who had forced me to more of it than my daily wrestle with Trigonometry involved, so I came to Thursday night with excuses and not a line on paper. I was told to bring in my work Friday morning for her to glance over before I appeared on the platform with it. I went home in hot anger. Why in all this beautiful world wouldn't they help me to do the thing I could do, and let anyone of four members of the class who revelled in Mathematics do that subject? No doubt they had George Wilson, who could stand and solve mentally any proposition read to him, writing on migration or how to plant lilies! At study hour in the evening I was distracted, and there came a culmination.

"'I can't do a paper on Mathematics, and I won't!' I said stoutly. "But I will do such a paper on a subject I *can* write

about as will open their foolish eyes as to how wrong they are!'

"I picked up a pencil and began seeking some clue that would lead to a subject. My eyes fell on my loved book on the table before me, the most wonderful story of which was *Picciola,* by Saintine. Instantly I began to write. Breathlessly I wrote for hours. I exceeded the limit ten times over. I wrote pages on pages. The poor Italian Count, the victim of political offences, shut by Napoleon from the wonderful grounds, mansion, and life that were his, restricted to bare prison walls at Lenistrella, deprived of books, pen, paper, his one interest in life a little sprout of green, sprung no doubt from a seed dropped by a passing bird between the stone flagging of the prison yard before his window, had always deeply stirred my imagination. With him I had watched it through the years I had access to the book; with him I had prayed for it. I had broken into a cold sweat of fear when the jailer first menaced it; I had hated the wind that bent it roughly, and implored the sun, and sung a paean of joy at its budding and worshipped in awe before the thirty perfect blossoms. The Count had named it *Picciola,* the little one; to me also it was a personal possession—my little one. Well might that piece of work be proclaimed Saintine's masterpiece; no man could do a greater thing of its kind, and its kind happened to be kindred to my spirit. It was one of the things I knew more about than any teacher could teach me. That night we lived the life of our 'little one' over again, the Count and I, and never were our anxieties and joys more poignant. At midnight I laid down the pencil and read what I had written. I could make no corrections. I had given my heart's best blood. It represented my brain's finest imaginings; it came in a tide, and to touch it was sacrilege. I copied my work in ink, read it once

The edge of the Limberlost. ■ (From *Moths of the Limberlost* by Gene Stratton-Porter. Illustrated by the author.)

Limberlost Cabin, South.

more, and went to bed happy, in spite of my anxiety as to what would occur.

"Next morning I dared my crowd to see how long they could remain on the grounds and yet reach the room before the last toll of the bell. The scheme worked. Coming in so late, we frustrated the Principal, and she began the opening exercises without remembering my paper. At noon I carried it home and read it twice more instead of eating my dinner, and each time I loved it better and saw new beauty in it. Again I was as late as I possibly dared be, and not seeing me, the Principal did not remember my paper until she came to my name and subject on her programme near the close of the exercises, through which I sat in cold fear. If things went too far in school worse happened at home, as we children well understood. When she remembered my name, she looked at me meaningly, announced my inspiring mathematical subject and called my name. I arose, walked to the front and made my best bow to the Principal, to the faculty, and to my schoolmates. Then I turned to her and said: 'I waited until the last minute because I knew absolutely nothing about my subject' (the audience laughed and she was forced to smile, so I continued with growing hope), 'and I could find nothing either in the library here or at home, so last night I reviewed Saintine's masterpiece, *Picciola.*'

"Then instantly I began to read. I was almost paralysed at my audacity and with each word I expected to hear a terse little interruption: 'You may report at this office!' Imagine my amazement when what I did hear at the turning of the first page was: 'Stop a minute!' Of course I stopped, and Miss Mary Bird, whom I had christened at the first glimpse of her 'The Merry Bird,' left the room. A minute later she appeared with the Superintendent of the City Schools.

"'Begin again!' she said. 'Take your time.'

"I was too amazed to speak. Then thoughts came in a rush. *My paper was good.* It was as good as I had believed it. It was better than I had known. It was so good that an unprecedented thing had happened; the Superintendent of the schools had been called from his office to hear it read. I glanced at him in consternation. Professor Thomas was a kindly man and he smiled and nodded.

"'Go on!' he said.

"And maybe I didn't 'go on!' I lifted my proud head, opened the gates, and took that assembly room and the corps of teachers into our confidence, and the Count and I told them all that was in our hearts about a little flower that sprang between the paving-stones of a prison-yard. The Count and I were free spirits. From the book I had learned that. He got into political trouble through it, and I had got into mathematical trouble; and we told our troubles. One instant the room was in laughter; the next the boys turned their heads and the girls who had forgotten their handkerchiefs cried into their aprons, and were unashamed. At the turning of a sheet I stole a glance at the 'Supe,' as we called him. As the oil ran down Jacob's beard even into his lap, so the tears were running down the professor's beard even into his lap! For almost sixteen big foolscap pages I held them, and I was eager to go on and tell them more about it when I reached the last line. Never again was a subject assigned to me; and if I had that paper to-day, I know four editors who would pay me very well for it!"[2]

1883. Missed the last three months of school to nurse her ill sister. "Like Thoreau, I never worried over diplomas, and unlike most school children I studied harder after leaving school than ever before, and in a manner that did me real good. I never went to school again, and the best that can be said of what education I have is that it was strictly private. It was the very best kind in the world for me; the only

"If you had known about wonders like these in the days of your youth, Robert Comstock, could you ever have done the thing you did?" ■ (From *A Girl of the Limberlost* by Gene Stratton-Porter. Illustrated by W.T. Benda.)

possible kind that would not have ruined a person of my inclinations. I studied the things in which I was most interested, and whenever I had the opportunity, having at my command my brother's library and the libraries of the school and town. I have always been too thankful for words that circumstances saved my brain from being run through a groove in company with dozens of others of widely differing tastes and mentality. What measure of success I have had comes through preserving my individual point of view, method of expression, and the Spartan regulations of my childhood home. Whatever I have been able to do has been done through the line of education my father was able to give me, and through my parents' methods of rearing me."[2]

1886. Courted Charles D. Porter, a young druggist from Geneva, Indiana, who was responsible for the third change of her name from Geneve to Gene. She wrote to him: "How *glad* I am! I am going to be so good to you that you won't think there's anything *like* me. I am sure that so long as I am your little pet, Genie Girl will find the world as bright as love and tender care can make it. In your love I am *happy*; I know that *while* I am happy, I can make you so. Every day I think of something that I would love to do

to comfort, help, or entertain you. I will do all I can to run a home properly; but my *Big Job* is you. You are *mine* (this is for anybody who says you are not) now; it is my joy to take especial care of you, and I'll pet you and love you and *spoil* you all I please.

"I have been studying the plan of the house you sent very closely, and I have a very nice arrangement all clear, I would not think of building an addition, Mr. Porter; the house is too big already. I always notice that the closer quarters you put young married folks in, the happier they are. I am sure I can dispense with an addition and still so arrange matters as to make a very pleasant home. I know I seem young to take care of a house, and I'll very probably be able to run it better in ten years than I am now; but if I do the best I can, and you help and encourage me, I know I'll succeed."[2]

April 21, 1886. Married Charles Darwin Porter. She insisted on using her maiden name, joining it to her husband's surname with a hyphen. "I think a beautiful girl who is glad she *is* a woman, glad for the genuine, manly passion she will some day rouse, glad to be a wife and found a bright, attractive home and get her crown from the touch of baby hands, glad to be bright and lovely and sweet, to robe herself to *please,* and *forget* herself to *comfort*—well, there is something in such a life for woman that makes me stare at these strong-minded, bossy, cross, fussy, frowsy, woman's rights, political stump-speaking women in amazement. Truth to tell, I loathe them. They despise low necks because their own necks are scrawly; they despise bare arms because theirs are pimply; they rail at powder because a coat of white lead would not cover their blotches; they rave at men because no man would have them—or get sick of them if they did."[2]

July 5, 1887. Pregnant. "Yes, I am still happy—happier than I have ever been in my life before. It somehow came all at once, this great joy, and it has not calmed yet. What a great surpassing thing is this mother love that is creeping softly over me. I never could have imagined that I should stay here through the long days alone, in the heat, and yet bear it all with as sweet a smile as I ever had for my lover, for the sake of this little new life, and for the yet dearer sake of him whom I have so lovingly promised to comfort and make happy."[2]

Her only daughter, Jeannette, was born. "I have a beautiful little daughter; but I'm not any older, and I've got just as much fun in me as ever."[2]

With her husband, she designed and built a fourteen-room cabin on the edge of the great Limberlost Swamp in Northeastern Indiana. "I have seldom gotten more fun out of a given amount of money than I had in the building of a kitchen for Limberlost Cabin that represented, at the time which I built it, the level best I could do in accumulating comforts and conveniences for the cook. It was a big kitchen—big as an ordinary living room. Its north wall from floor to ceiling, with the exception of a door, was given over to a long case for brooms, carpet sweepers, dust pans, vacuum cleaners, and dust cloths; a cupboard above for the lamps and candles necessary when country electric service is interrupted by the falling of branches after heavy storms; and this same wall contained flour chests opening out on rollers with receptacles for corn meal and brown flour and white flour and buckwheat. Above, a long, wide board that could be drawn out upon which to spread cookies fresh from the oven, and cakes from the tins; and above that, shelves on to the highest reach, for essences and spices and seasonings and the myriad things a cook needs to have at hand for her convenience.

"Half the length of the west wall went into another huge cupboard for kitchen dishes above and larger utensils below. A big window gave a view of the west woods and the winding lake shore and the roadway, with a small table beneath it for the convenience of those using the kitchen.

"Against the east wall, the last word in Battle Creek gas ranges with six burners to accommodate cooking food to the extent of any crowd the Cabin ever sheltered. Level with the face of the cook, a small oven for cookies, pies, cakes, and biscuit. Below, a broiler for game, fish, and steak. Overhead, racks for conveniences, a steam cap, and below the cooking burners a huge oven for turkeys and the big roaster.

"And, in the middle of the kitchen, the piece de resistance, an article of my own devising into which I put many hours of figuring and much thought—a huge table, the top of which is a two-inch thick slab of golden oak covered with neatly laid zinc. Across one end, an eighteen inch wide slab of oak for pounding and cutting, covered by a cap of zinc to keep it dustless when not in use."[2]

Began to explore and photograph the Limberlost, which was a natural preserve of wild birds, plants and moths. The results appeared as articles in *Recreation* and *Outing*. "I was abnormally sensitive about trying to accomplish any given thing and failing. I had been taught in our home that it was black disgrace to undertake anything and fail. If you started, you simply must finish, and in good shape. My husband's drug store carried books and magazines, and it was impossible to take departments in any of them and not have it known, but few people in our locality read *Recreation* and *Outing*. None of them were interested in photography, and very few in Natural Science, so that what I was doing was not known."[2]

1903. First book, *The Song of the Cardinal*, published. "With a glad heart and with ideals lifted still higher by the warm praise given the literary value of this book, I determined to preserve myself from the sin of deterioration by ever going back and using amateur work after success came. So, on a roaring wood fire in my library, I cremated *Mademoiselle Dinvar*, the book modelled after *Lucille*; a romantic poem, 'The King'; two short novels; a book of poems; and three short stories. I thought I was doing the right thing then; now I am much afraid it was wanton sacrifice to a high ideal. Every day I use material I can write no better than I could then for either freshness or originality. The facility acquired by practice could have been used in re-writing."[2]

October, 1904. *Freckles* published. "With my first novel, after having been told by three publishers that it would sell barely enough to pay expenses if I left the Nature work in, my reply was to leave it as I thought a book should be written, and if it did not bring me over six hundred dollars, I would cut down my necessities to that sum and never lift my voice to complain. That was a good guess, for my first cheque from *Freckles* was exactly six hundred dollars, and I had many less than that, before, advertised like Pears' soap 'by its loving friends,' at seven years of age the book advanced on the line of best sellers."[2]

Freckles' face was white, with colorless lips, but in his eyes was the strength of undying courage. ■ (From *Freckles* by Gene Stratton-Porter. Illustrated by Ruth Ives.)

1904-1905. Wrote a series of bird articles for the *Ladies' Home Journal*.

An incident while studying a black vulture nest showed her tenacious dedication in portraying the wildlife of the swamp. "I shielded my camera in my arms, and before we reached the well I thought the conveyance would be torn to pieces. Starting out on foot, through the steaming fetid pools, through swarms of gnats, flies and mosquitoes and poisonous insects, keeping a watch for rattlesnakes, we sank ankle-deep at every step, and logs we thought solid broke beneath us. Our progress was a steady succession of prodding and pulling each other to the surface. Our clothing was wringing wet and exposed parts of our bodies lumpy with bites and stings. My husband found the tree, cleared an opening into the great prostrate log, traversed its unspeakable odors for nearly forty feet to its farthest recess and brought the baby and egg to the light in his leaf-like hat. We could endure the location only by dipping napkins into deodorant and binding them to our mouths and nostrils. Every third day for almost three months we made this trip. . . :" [*Smithsonian*, Volume 7, Number 1, April, 1976.[3]]

The time and care that Gene Stratton-Porter demanded of herself in her photographic work is evident in her prints.

Stratton-Porter and her car which she turned into a dray to search out specimens.

Their quality and crispness was so exceptional that the Eastman Kodak Company sent an executive to the Limberlost cabin to observe her methods of development. Stratton-Porter was too embarrassed to let him know that she used the family bathroom for a darkroom, stuffing rags around the doors and windows to make the room totally dark. For developing trays she appropriated the family turkey platters. Instead of confessing these "techniques" to Kodak, the photographer gave credit to her husband, a competent druggist, for his accurate mixing of the finest photographic chemicals money could buy—and to certain special qualities of the local water.

Working in the days before there were high-speed films, miniature cameras and telephoto lenses, Stratton-Porter lugged her forty pounds of camera equipment through snake-infested swamps, up trees and around quicksand to record at close range the life processes of her subjects. Somehow, through a trust nurtured with birds and other wildlife, she got her camera within a few feet of some of the most intimate moments in the lives of wild creatures.[3]

August, 1909. *Birds of the Bible,* a book which required exhaustive research, was published. "As I searched for material for this book, there slowly dawned upon me the sane and true things said of birds in the Bible as against the amazing statements of Aristotle, Pliny, and other writers of near the same period in Pagan nations. This led to the search for the dawn of bird history, and the very first picture preserved ever made of birds. It was a merry chase, and it led me around the world, through books and galleries and museums; but it was uplifting and inspiring work that I loved to do. By what I would have given for and thought of such a book in my childhood, I gauged what people might think now, and thereby made my one error in my judgment concerning my own work. I thought ministers would find

new meaning, beauty, proof of sanity, and truth in the Bible through it; I thought Sabbath School teachers would hail it as a Godsend in their work of interesting the young in the Bible; I thought every home honoured by the possession of a Bible would like these beautiful poetical and wonderful quotations sifted out for them and made tangible for them by photographs under one cover in a hand volume.

"So I urged my publisher to spare no pains or expense in making a beautiful book, and he did as I requested. I designed the cover of willow bark from a tree in Palestine with the head of a hoopoe protuding from the opening to its nest. After working unceasingly for many months myself and inciting my publisher to a triumph in book-maker's art, I waited for the Christian homes of the land to set the stamp of their approval on my long and difficult task. I wondered if anyone would dream, in examining those beautifully reproduced studies, that I had been compelled to handle and to literally burrow in poison ivy vines to secure studies of the brooding peacock; if they would suspect that I carried a mirror from a dresser-top and set it up in a barnyard to throw a ray of light through a window on to the nest of a swallow among the rafters of a barn; or guess what lice rained upon me from various nests, what mosquitoes and insects stung me, how perspiration almost blinded me, or how tired and dirty I came in each night from my day's work afield.

"But the people did not think any of the things I thought they would, and the book had a disappointingly slow sale."[2]

In the same month, *A Girl of the Limberlost* was published. "I am a creature so saturate with earth, water, and air that if I do not periodically work some of it out of my system in ink, my nearest and dearest cannot live with me. When such a time overtakes me, I write as the birds sing, because I must, and usually from the same source of inspiration. So my first book was one stretch of river bank and swamp that I knew, one bird and one old man with whom I was sufficiently intimate to record his true picture. Then, like Grandfather Squeers, I felt that I had the 'hang of it now and could do it ag'in.' So I wrote another book. I put in a little more swamp, several birds, and a few people I knew I could portray faithfully.

"It was then the mail-box business began. First, a wealthy club woman of a great city wrote me that she had read one of my books to a company of tired clerks, while they lunched at their noon rest hour, and it had brought to them a few minutes of country life so real that they begged for more. A nurse wrote from a hospital ward, for a man who had always lived in and loved the open and now, from spinal trouble, would never walk again, that my pictures of swamp and forest were so true he had lost himself for an hour in them. . . . The warden of a state reform school wrote that fifteen hundred sin-besmirched little souls in his care, shut for punishment from their natural inheritance of field and wood, were reading my books to rags because they scented freedom and found comfort in them. . . . And the dignified and scholarly Orren Root, sitting with his feet on the fender in the library of his beloved 'Hemlocks,' read one of my books one night and the next day wrote me: 'I have a severe cold this morning, because I got my feet very wet last night walking the trail with *Freckles,* but I am willing to risk pneumonia any time for another book like that.'

"I have such letters in heaps, from every class and condition of people, all the way from northern Canada to the lowest tip of Africa, all asking for more of the outdoors, as I see it, because my descriptions are absolutely real to them, and my characters recognized as transcriptions from life.

"So I wrote *A Girl of the Limberlost,* to carry to workers inside the city walls, to hospital cots, to those behind prison bars, and to scholars in their libraries, my story of earth and sky. Incidentally, I put in all the insects, flowers, vines, and trees, birds and animals that I know, and such human beings as I grow well enough acquainted with in my work in the woods, that I feel able to record a faithful study of their loves, pains, joys, temptations, and triumphs.

"This reduces my formula for a book to simplicity itself—an outdoor setting of land in which I have lived until . . . I know 'the procession of the year.' Then I people the location with the men and women who live there, and on my pages write down their story of joy and sorrow commingled as living among them I know it to be. This is the secret of any appeal that my work may make. I am nothing but a machine of transmission. If it be truth that my work does not conform to the ordinary standards of fiction-writing, it is probably because very little of what I write is fiction, and people know it.

"I live in the country and work in the woods, so no other location is possible for my backgrounds, and only the people with whom I come in daily contact there are suitable for my actors. Naturally, there come times when other locations and people are forced upon me, but I decline to admit that I have a working knowledge of them. And I want to say for such people as I put into books, that in the plain, old-fashioned country homes where I have lived, I have known such wealth of loving consideration, such fidelity between husband and wife, such obedience in children, such constancy to purpose, such whole-souled love for friends and neighbours, such absence of jealousy, pettiness, and rivalry, as my city critics do not know is in existence. I know that they do not know these things exist, else they would not question my chronicles of them. But much can be forgiven a critic when he attempts to criticize a life that he never lived, and a love that he never knew.

Laughing Kingfisher. ■ (From *Homing with the Birds* by Gene Stratton-Porter. Photos by the author.)

(From the movie "Freckles," starring Martin West and Carol Christensen. Copyright © 1960 Twentieth Century-Fox.)

(From the movie "Keeper of the Bees," starring Michael Duane and Gloria Henry. Produced by Columbia, 1947.)

(From the movie "Her First Romance," starring Alan Ladd. Copyright 1951 by Columbia Pictures.)

(From the movie "Laddie," starring Tim Holt. Produced by RKO Radio Pictures Incorporated, 1935.)

"And you're doing without it yourself to carry it to Laddie, I'll be bound!" cried the Princess. ■ (From *Laddie: A True Blue Story* by Gene Stratton-Porter. Illustrated by Herman Pfeifer.)

"I never could write a historical novel, because I want my history embellished with anything on earth save fiction, I could not write of society, because I know just enough about it to know that the more I know, the less I wish to know. I have read a few 'problem' novels and they appeal to me as a wandering over nasty, lawless subjects and situations of the most ancient type, under new names. There is nothing remaining for me but the woods, and the people I meet there.

"So for my boys behind bars, first of all, for my working girls, for my scholars, and friends of leisure, I 'aimed' to conjure up part of a swamp that I once knew, and set its flowers blooming, its birds singing, its wonderful creatures of night a-wing. And then I tried to tell a simple story of a girl in calico and cow-hide, who struggled until she reached the things she craved, even as once I struggled; of a woman who suffered many deaths for sins that she never committed, and found peace at last; of a man who had everything in life, yet kept himself clean, even as many men I know today, because they are too refined and proud to stoop to common, contaminating sin; of a man and woman who might have been anyone's Aunt Margaret and Uncle Wesley; of a little child that I fed, doctored, and quoted literally nine-tenths of his sayings and doings; and a couple of young people who found the best in themselves through suffering, as most of us suffer and find our better selves sooner or later; and sunshine at the end, as please God, it shall come to all of us who work and do the best we know.

"My critics say that these methods never can produce literature; yet it is in my memory that the scenes of real masterpieces are lands intimately known, and the characters are people who are daily familiar with the authors. It is my belief that no great book ever was written any other way, and that no literature truly characteristic of a nation is possible by any other method. As to whether my work is, or ever will be, literature, I never bother my head. Time, the hearts of my readers, and the files of my publishers, will find me my ultimate place. In the meantime, I shall have had the joy of my work, for to me it is joy unspeakable to make a swimming hole splash, squirrels bark, and nuts rattle down inside reform-school walls, or to set a bird singing, leaves rustling, and a cricket chirping beside hospital cots. As for my 'aim,' Cale Young recently put it into verse for me. He did not know that he did it for me, but I did the instant I saw it:

> "'I ask no more
> Than to restore
> To simple, homely things their former joy.'"[2]

February, 1909. Daughter, Jeannette, married.

1911. *The Harvester,* which had the largest sale of Porter's books, was published. "Of course, I am not quite a fool, so as deeply as I see into Nautre I also see human nature. I know its failings, its tendencies, its weaknesses, its failures, its blackest depths of crime even; and the people who feel called upon to spend their lives analysing, digging into and uncovering these depths of depravity have that privilege—more the pity! My life has been very fortunate in one glad way: For every bad man and woman I ever have known, I have met, lived with, and intimately known an overwhelming number of strictly clean, decent people, and *upon the lives of these I base what I write.* To say that this does not reproduce a picture true to life is as great a falsehood as was ever coined. It does. It produces a picture true to ideal life, to the best men and women can do at level best. It produces exactly such a picture as I opened my eyes upon at birth. There is not one tender, loving, thoughtful, chivalrous thing I described the *Harvester* as saying and doing that I have not seen my father and two of my brothers do constantly for my mother and sisters in my own home. My father was precisely such a man; and my mother adored him. One of my most distinct memories dates back to high-chair days when I sat between them thus elevated. Every day at meal time, from serving tea and dessert, my mother finished last. Every meal my father excused himself, came and stood back of her chair, and in the presence of his family gave tangible evidence of his regard for her by stroking her hair, patting her shoulder, kissing her lips, cheek, or brow, as the mood moved him. This particular day he was quizzical. He tilted back her head and laid his lips on a spot just where the base of her white throat spread to her breast, a spot honey sweet, as any of her dozen babies could have testified. With her head held against him he questioned: 'Mary, do you love me yet?'

"This instant I can see her form stiffen and straighten and hear her amazed and wondering voice: 'Why, *Mark,* I love you until I can scarcely keep my fingers off you!'

"Now what do I care for the newspaper or magazine critic yammering that there is not such a thing as a moral man, and that my pictures of life are sentimental and idealized. They are! And I glory in them. They are straight, living pictures from the lives of men and women of morals, honour, and loving-kindness. They form idealized pictures of life because they are copied from life where it touches religion, chastity, love, home, and hope of Heaven ultimately.

"Am I the only woman in this broad land so born and reared? Was my home the only one with a moral code and religious practice? Are there not homes by the thousand in which men and women are true to their highest ideals? I have seen and been in them by the hundred. Since the publication of *The Harvester* scores of men, even from across the sea, have written me that all their lives they have kept the law 'as a moral obligation to society at large and a matter of fastidious personal cleanliness,' as one man expressed it. . . .

"How a big majority of book critics and authors have come to believe and to teach that no book is *true to life* unless it is true to *the worst in life,* God knows; I do not, and I cannot find out. The only explanation that seems to reach the root of the matter at all lies in the fact that most of these critics are attached to magazines and newspapers where strenuous rush is the law, and the most of life they see, and that upon which they live and thrive, if they do live and thrive, is the sin, error, mistakes, the dreadful things men and women do in the wildest of city life when half mad with the insane rush. So they judge all life by what they see of it, never taking into consideration the big side they do *not* see and know. A critic is scarcely to be blamed for not believing in a life and love he never knew; yet surely it is poor judgment, to say the least, to judge all life by the atmosphere of the average city newspaper and magazine office.

"To deny that wrong and pitiful things exist in life is folly; but to believe that these things are made better by promiscuous discussion by people who fail to prove in their books that their viewpoint is either right, clean, or helpful, is close insanity. If there is to be any error on either side in a book, then God knows it is better that it should be on the side of pure sentiment and high ideals than on discussion in books of subjects that often serve to open to a large part of the world their first knowledge that such forms of sin, such profligate expenditure, such waste of life's best opportunities, exist.

"I happen to know that thousands of young people form their ideas of what they consider a wonderful and a desirable life to live from the books of half a dozen popular authors, and they would be infinitely better off if the Government actually censored books and forbade publication of those containing sensual and illegitimate situations which intimately describe how social and national law is broken by people of wealth and unbridled passions. There is one great beauty in idealized romance: reading it can make no one worse than he is. It may fire thousands to higher inspiration than they ever before have had."[2]

June, 1912. *Moths of the Limberlost* published. "The Fabre books are a part of my religion, but I cannot see that Fabre goes deeper, paints life history more accurately in the case of any insect he had studied than I do in *Moths of the Limberlost,* while my book has the added proof and attraction of the illustration. Yet France went wild over Fabre. I have a feeling very strongly entrenched that if I had made the mark I have on the homes of the United States in any country in Europe, or written and illustrated my seven Nature books, my reception would be very different for my Nature work.

"Scientists from the beginning have had no hesitation in using dead and pinned moth specimens for book illustra-

(From *Moths of the Limberlost* by Gene Stratton-Porter. Illustrated by the author.)

tions, despite the fact that the colours are faded, the wings in unnatural positions, and the body shrivelled. I would quite as soon accept the mummy of any particular member of the Rameses family I ever saw as a fair representative of the living man, as accept a mounted moth for a living one. All the illustrations in my moth book are made from living moths and caterpillars in perfectly natural positions in which they placed themselves."[2]

1913. *Laddie,* a novel that faithfully describes her childhood home, was published. "I could write no truer biography. To the contour of hill and field, to the last stripe on the wallpaper and knot on the door, that is the home in which I was born, the parents who reared me, the very words they said and the things they did, the exact circumstances of my birth, my brothers and sisters and some of my friends. There was no such person as 'Mrs. Freshett,' and some of the other neighbours described are fictitious, and a few of the things told never happened; but three-fourths of it is exact truth. If you will read 'Stratton' for 'Stanton,' 'Northbrooke' for 'Eastbrooke,' you will have the truth in the case as straight as I can tell it.

"I set out to paint the life of a child of real flesh and blood, not as a fancy picture, but straight from life. Now what is the exact truth concerning childhood? Are children pure, delicate, refined little angels? Are they indeed? The wildest fairy tale is not so wild as they implore you to make it, and when you tell them they must not say or do a thing, nine-

A Luna Courtship. ▪ (From *Moths of the Limberlost* by Gene Stratton-Porter. Illustrated by the author.)

tenths of them will, if it is humanly possible. It never appeared to me that the 'Sebethany Perkins incident' would be such a 'horror.' My editor warned me that it would be criticised; and I replied that it was absolutely true to childhood, and he let it stand as it was. I can feel the sick qualm to-day that I felt as I stood on that fence and bore witness to the fact that Sebethany had turned to stone. But did I go home when I warned that I would 'see something that I would sleep better not to see?' Not on your life! True to the savage and primal instincts in the heart of a very decently reared little girl under ten, I stuck right on that fence, and I saw for myself. But did I take any one's word for it? I did not.

"[A] criticism of *Laddie* by a minister of the Gospel was sent me in which he wrote of it as 'molasses fiction.' What a wonderful compliment! All the world loves sweets. Afield, bears as well as flies would drown in it. Molasses is more necessary to the happiness of human and beast than vinegar, and over-indulgence not nearly so harmful to the system. I am a molasses person myself. So is my family. So was my father's family. So are most of my friends—all of them who are happy, as a matter of fact. So I shall keep straight on writing of the love and joy of life I have found in the world, and when I have used the last drop of my molasses, I shall stop writing. Forever the acid of life will have to be doled out by those who have enough in their systems to be accustomed to it. God gave me a taste for sweets and the sales of the books I write prove that a few other people are similar to me in this.

"I have done every one of my books from my heart's best impulses, made them as clean and decent as I know how, and as beautiful and as interesting. I never have spared myself in the least degree, mind or body, when it came to giving the best I was able, and I never have considered money for a moment, more than that I had to live and could not do it by Nature books alone; so I lighten each Nature book with enough fiction to make it readable to those not interested in Nature work, sugar-coat their pill, so to speak. But to any fair-minded person my record proves that I have worked for love, not for money. In the beginning, when I knew the fate of any Nature book better than most folk, I deliberately chose to make my start with the work I loved, rather than with a book that would stand ten times the chance of being commercial."[2]

1913. Brother, Lemon Stratton, died. "The holidays were saddened for us by the death of my brother, 'Leon' of the *Laddie* book. I am proud to tell you that he had a jest in the face of such intolerable pain it sometimes left him senseless. Valvular leakage of the heart struck him suddenly, the result of an old wound in the Spanish War. He faced his Maker clear-eyed and unafraid, and crossed the Great Divide with serenity and dignity.

"I reached him in time for a good visit, but I could not see his grey face and swollen body. To me he was, and always will be, the picture I described in *Laddie* when he soberly flung those awful texts in the face of the church congregation. He went out like that, with the white light still on his brow.

"When I asked him if he would not like me to get a heart specialist, he said: 'My dear, there is no specialist special enough for such a blow-out as this—just put your ear to my chest and hear me soozle!'

Stratton-Porter in the swamp.

"I had to laugh even as I heard his poor heart running like a waterfall. To the very last he kept his doctor and nurses and friends laughing, and then said: 'It's all right,' and went to sleep.—Not a complaint; not a whimper; not a regret; but unafraid and 'all right.' I hope God will grant me grace to go unafraid and with as much dignity. Tears are not for him, for I believe I shall see him again. If not—'It's all right.'

"In his last will he left me his motherless little daughter of twelve, so I shall have one more little girl to love and help all I can."[2]

1915. "I have spent two happy weeks with my daughter and her babies in Philadelphia where I had a great time sitting on the floor building block houses and making up 'Sing-song' chants until I almost blistered my tongue. How the little brains grind! The older one wants to know if a camel has a hump so it can hump itself; why we don't walk on the ceiling, and what all the meat at the market comes out of. The baby tiny has three perfectly good new words, but no one has the slightest idea what they are. But her head and heart are all right. In a scuffle the other day she thought a little neighbour girl was hurting her big sister, and she picked up a small broom and waded into the fray quite valiantly.

"I named the older one 'Morning Face' almost at birth, partly because she is always smiling, even when she first wakens from sleep in the morning, or her nap in the after-

(From the movie "The Girl of the Limberlost," starring James Bell and Lillian Bronson. Copyright © 1964 by Screen Gems, Inc.)

(From the movie "Girl of the Limberlost." Produced by Columbia, 1945.)

noon; and partly because there is a wonder and a joy and a mystery which I never before saw so well pictured in the face of a child."[2]

October, 1916. *Morning Face* published. "The book is absolutely good Natural History as far as illustration is concerned, being the cream of years of field work saved to put in 'something good enough.' The text must be read in a sort of sing-song chant; the Natural History is right and true, I hope, lightened by gleams of humour which I find distressingly rare in books for children. This is the way I teach Natural History to the babies of my own family, and you would keenly enjoy watching the workings of their minds and seeing how their little faces light up as they become interested."[2]

1917. "The War has been a terror from the beginning, and now that it is taking our nearest and dearest, it comes home with a new meaning. From the start I have worked, and given, and have done all I knew how to do to help, but when I read that a battle is raging at Toul, and think of my sister's son Donald, in aviation there, to all I felt before is now added the deadly chill of apprehension that no one can know, until their own *flesh and blood are in it*. I have another nephew, a fine surgeon, who is to have charge of a base hospital near Paris, and several more who are ready to start the instant their call comes. I also have a man dispatch-riding, with the American division, who was my driver for over two years. Here in the woods, he of course had his room, and lived in my home. We put in three summers of field work, collecting, lifting, transplanting rare plants from where we motored to find them all over our State. He carried cameras and helped in picture work and drove my car. He was a straight, honest, brave lad, very quick; he could stop the car and be at the door with his arm ready to stay me, before I had moved to arise. He had no mother, and I mothered him as I do all boys; but not all are of such fine timbre, and respond to the effort one makes for them.

"The last work we did was to set a basket of painted trillium bulbs, sent to me by the pastor of a large Episcopal church in Pittsburgh; he is now a Chaplain with our troops, expecting to start to the front any day. We had a bargain. He collected for me in his country rambles, and during his vacation, I helped him get the Nature part of his sermons and lectures right; and gave him little hints about the wonders of Nature that he could use in his work. So William and I always set Dr. Frick's baskets with especial care. This last one we set the day before we went to Fort Wayne to start the boy on his way; and we both watered those trilliums with many hot tears. I may have many drivers, but I shall never have another William, and I doubt if he returns, for his first thought was never of William; it was always of some one else. So now we are in the War in earnest.

"My beautiful optimism is getting many a severe jolt these days; but I am going straight ahead doing the best I can. . . . One of the things which has puzzled me has been why, when there were whole armies of men exposed in camps and tents and insufficient buildings, we should have the most severe winter we have had in sixty years. Never have I heard of the winter of such length and severity as this. People have frozen in their homes for lack of coal, caused by the congestion of traffic in the heavy snows in the second place, in the *first* by wrong orders of coal to the companies the past summer; and many a soldier was frozen stiff in his tent, while hundreds died of pneumonia and kindred sickness. And we have had winters so mild that one could go without a wrap in January, and the roses leafed out. It surely is a difficult thing to understand."[2]

1918. *A Daughter of the Land* published. "I read proof with one eye and look out of the window with the other. Every minute I can spare from the book, or when I have to have a little fresh air and change, I have been out working with both hands to bring exquisite things from the surrounding swamps and marshes to add a spring touch to my flower woods. All the fall and winter stuff I planted seems to be coming on finely, but this is my first attempt to bring in spring things. I only have had a few days between galley and page proofs, but in that time I have gotten in several hundred exquisite plants, the man who did my forestry work has sent me several baskets of rare things, and a man who worked with me last year has been doing what he could alone, so that we total nearly a thousand roots set this spring, and I heartily wish it were ten."[2]

October, 1919. "I came out to California two weeks ago for a six months' rest and have been hard at work every minute getting settled to live and fighting a big heap of mail which always follows the publication of a new book. I had thought of going into a flat or apartment, but found myself in a city of near a million, the flats and apartments, no matter how lovely, rocking with the roll of traffic, jarring with noise, and reeking with the essential odour of many human beings living in close contact. Fresh from the woods, the combination of soapsuds, tobacco smoke, etc., was too much for my poor nostrils accustomed to nothing worse than a plain bed of muck, so I struck for the suburbs and a bungalow. Then to avoid the enormously inflated rents (they are asking from $250 up for bungalows that cost six thousand to build), I bought one of the critters and will take a chance on selling it when I finish with it. At the present minute that may not be soon. I sorter like this glorious sunshine, the pergola of Cherokes roses, the orange trees and blood red poinsettias, and the mocking birds tame as robins at home.

"If I had time to do it, I should be greatly interested in writing some sketches of travel in California. I see so much on the desert, in the canyons, and on the mountains that other writers have failed to mention, that I think I could do some quite interesting reading. I have no words in which to express what the ocean does to me, and the canyon does a bit deeper, and the desert deepest of all.

"Personally, I am feeling stronger and better than when I came to California. My doctor's orders were to keep quiet and to rest this winter. But the rest was not much of a success, as there are such a world of unusual and interesting things to see.

"In the afternoons and evenings this winter I have gone to many luncheons, receptions, dinners, and entertainments. A great many of the residents of California are cultured people of the East who have the wealth to come here and make their homes in a location where one can see the sea, desert, canyons, mountains, intensively cultivated orchards, and fields, all within a radius of forty miles of Los Angeles as a centre, much of it within ten or twelve. These people have money and leisure to do what they please, and none that I have met are pleasing to pamper themselves. They take their pleasures, but at the same time, they are going somewhere to raise a fund or give an entertainment for an orphans' home or crippled soldiers or unfortunate mothers. Mingled with these, one will meet actors, poets, authors, painters, sculptors, from all over the world, some

Wild Tiger Lilies. ■ (From *Moths of the Limberlost* by Gene Stratton-Porter. Illustrated by the author.)

of them attracted by the climate, some reproducing the scenery, some interested in moving pictures. Any one of them can stand on his feet and before any audience tell his story, sing his song, or explain what he is doing for the good of humanity, and why he is engineering his activities in the precise manner in which he is. I doubt if the life in this city can be equalled anywhere. It is a blaze of colour, a voice of rapture, a deep note of earnestness, a gay note of entertainment. Fine folk these artistic and creative people be! Some of them are self-seeking and selfish and pushing, as is the manner of humanity; but most of them are world-experienced, educated in adversity, a real treat.

"One never knows, when one starts out, what wonderful Nature picture or human experience one is going to meet. It is all intensely broadening and interesting. I cannot describe to you the splendour of some of the homes I have been in, the deliciousness of the food, or the beauty of the jewels and apparel. And these very folk are the ones who are helping every artistic and humane project, spending money like water over all sorts of institutions and projects for the benefit of humanity."[2]

April, 1922. "It seems to me that all of our writers have done better work since the War. This I absolutely know to be the case concerning poetry. There may be nothing epoch-making in what is being done in this country in the line of poetry at the present minute, but it certainly is a heart-moving, visionary, exquisitely beautiful brain product.

"Ever since I have been in California I have been taking an active hand at the profession of poetry myself. Before that

time it always had been a suppression, because I cannot remember the time when I was not interested in poetry and trying to write it, but I had some very discouraging advice when I was a youngster, on the strength of which I burned three books of poetry, one of which I would almost give my right hand to repossess to-day. So through the years, when anything became so insistent that I could not clear my mental decks for other action, I have written it and laid it away. Since coming to California, something in the wonderful air, the gorgeous colour on all hands, and the pronouncedly insistent rhythms of Nature, all have combined rather to force utterance.

"Last summer I sent some of my work to perhaps the most highly cultured man in America, Dr. Charles Wharton Stork, for seven years a professor of literature in Princeton University, a man who lectures in nine different capitals of Europe on English literature, in each country using its native tongue, a feat which I doubt if another man in America can perform. For the past seven years Dr. Stork has been the editor of *Contemporary Verse*, himself a poet and a writer of almost classic prose. He is held by many in New York to be the greatest living judge of poetry in this country. I sent him a bundle of my work and his reply came promptly and was very gracious indeed. His comment was, 'Why ask when you have only to command?' and he prefaced this with a statement that he had read many of my books and greatly enjoyed them.

"I was so encouraged by his verdict and that of two other critics to whom I sent the same things, that I have been moved to publication. The date of publication is set for the twenty-eighth of April; the title is *The Fire Bird*. For the great part the text is written in the rhythm of deep forest, but there are times when the wash of the sea and the winds of the canyons predominate. In every instance the Natural History, the tribal characteristics and customs are absolutely correct, while throughout I have made a strenuous endeavour in all cases to use that one word which better than any other will, to a nicety, convey a delicate shade of meaning, paint a picture, or sing a song. I have used very great care in the make-up of this book, having personally designed the cover, the front matter, and drawn the first crude draft of all the illustrations, in order that the book shall in all ways be true to Nature and to human nature.

"It is my first stepping-stone in an effort to establish for myself as high grade literary value as has any writer in this country, and I am asking the people who love me and who have cared for what I have done formerly, to enlist with me in this battle, and to do whatever lies in their power to help me.

"I am desperately tired . . . of having the high grade literary critics of the country give a second and at times a third class rating to my literary work because I would not write of complexes and rank materialism, which is merely another name for adultery. These critics are mostly men and they persist in handing the literary honours to men who put upon the pages of books pictures so rotten that were any one to attempt to translate them to the language of the screen, the world would throw up its hands in holy horror.

Porter with specimens of Wild Rose Pink and Buckeye Brown Marigold which she discovered.

"It is impossible for me ever to attain a high grade literary rating with these critics because of this. My satisfaction will have to lie in the fact that the high grade homes of the country, the cultured and refined people, do give me a first rating; and it is not sentimental women from whom I get it, but cultured and scholarly men in the highest walks of life. However, there is no reason why I should not make a first grade literary reputation, with poetry, which has been an obsession with me from childhood and which I have studied all my life in an effort to fit myself for such work."[2]

1922. Began to make motion pictures. "When you stop to consider that picture making is the third largest industry in the United States to-day and that a bad picture reaches more people than any other one medium, certainly it is worth while for the women who are trying to better conditions to take hold of the picture question and have a thorough understanding as to what their desires are in the matter of better pictures.

"And in this connection I should be mighty glad to see State Federations and the National Federation of Club Women hit some of the nasty books that are being produced to-day just as hard a blow as they would hit a nasty picture, and the same holds good of indecent dancing. Everybody seems to be aghast at the tendencies that are cropping up in our young people, and these objectionable tendencies are fostered by and developed from indecent pictures, indecent books, and indecent dances. The sexes are being allowed to mingle at too early an age. Plastic and impressionable youngsters who should be occupied with outdoor exercise and education are putting in their time at over-sexed shows and cheap dances, and in the reading of

Why is it, having once migrated, a grebe will not fly, even to save its life, until migration time comes again?
■ (From *Homing with the Birds* by Gene Stratton-Porter. Photos by the author.)

Gene Stratton-Porter displays nature-study gear in 1924, the year she died.

books and magazine stories that are appalling to any clean-minded mother.

"There are books for children, pictures for children, magazines for children, and there is music for children. You do not expect to allow your child to read *all* the books in your libraries, nor to understand *all* the music he hears, nor to attend *all* legitimate theatrical productions. Then why insist that you be able to take him to *all* moving pictures? There will be many not suitable for children, just as there will be books, music, plays, and magazines not suitable for children. Why insult the intelligence of a moving picture audience by making all pictures suitable for children?

"Parents must have some control over what 'movies' their children attend, just as they supervise their other forms of education and entertainment. There are many pictures made which are entirely proper for children and children should be restricted to those pictures. I should not like to believe that every time I went to see a moving picture, I was going to see one made for a child; for I think I am capable of understanding and appreciating an entertainment that a child is not. I do not believe any adult entertainment should be limited to the comprehension of a child, nor to that degree of intimate problems suited to childish minds and morals."[2]

August, 1923. *The White Flag* published. "I think possibly I wrote this book at this time because the critics are constantly telling me that I do not know life and that I will not tell the truth about things. So I felt that, in this one instance at least, I would show them that I did know life and that I could tell the truth about the seamy side of it as well as about the pleasant."[2]

December, 1923. *Jesus of the Emerald* published. "I came home exhausted with beauty and with wonder, physically tired, and rolled into bed. And immediately, this poem began coming. . . . Far into the night I had gone over it for the third time and then I punched up my pillows and tried to control my mentality, tried to settle down and go to sleep: and I found that sleep was impossible. I realized that while I had been working I had been praying; that I had been begging the Lord to help me to do a big thing, a beautiful thing, a thing that would be of benefit to the whole world, and as I lay there unable to sleep, this thought came to me: 'You have prayed the Lord for help. You feel that the poem as it stands in your mind is better than you could have done alone. Now perhaps the Lord does not want you to go to sleep and take the risk of forgetting.'

"So I got up and slipped into a heavy bathrobe and night sandals, and wrapping a big blanket around me, I went in to my desk because I could not use the typewriter without awaking my family and causing protest. So I sat down alone in my library and wrote out the poem. . . . When I finished I got up and pulled back the blind, and I could see down the Avenue to Sixth Street, and a little rosy finch was singing in the jacaranda tree under my window."[2]

1924. "This year I am writing each month for *Good Housekeeping* and I also greatly enjoy this work. I have made a practice of doing a book every other year, and a year ago I began with my own company, under my own supervision, to make pictures from my stories in order to get them on the screen with fidelity to themselves and to my idea of how a moving picture should be made.

"As the years go by, I can see myself changing. . . . I really am quite a respectable person by this time. Life has moulded me and hammered me and taught me and punished me and delighted me until I have deepened and broadened. . . .

"Unless I am on exhibition at some big public function, I am a plain and simply dressed woman, working from breakfast in the morning until noon and frequently all afternoon, and sometimes in the evening, trying to carry off the big job of monthly magazine serials, my mail, some degree of housekeeping, personal supervision of the making of pictures, and, at the present minute, the building of a summer house in Catalina and an all the year round workshop at Bel-Air, and if you do not believe that this is one woman's job, try it. I do take the time to put the best I have to give into each article as I write it. I think sometimes, when I look at the amount of work that I can perform in a day, that I had better keep my mouth shut on the question of health. It must be pretty good or I could not spend a day from six in the morning to six at night carrying stone and working on a fountain!

"I have long since decided that I so love California that this is the land in which I wish to finish my living and to do my dying."[2]

December 6, 1924. Died in Los Angeles in an automobile accident. During the last seventeen years of her life, Porter's books sold at the rate of 1,700 copies per day.

"In the economy of Nature nothing is ever lost. I cannot believe that the soul of men shall prove the one exception."[2]

FOR MORE INFORMATION SEE: Jeannette (Porter) Meehan, *Life and Letters of Gene Stratton-Porter,* Doubleday, Doran, 1928, reprinted, Kennikat, 1972; M. MacMullen, "Love's Old Sweetish Song," *Harper's,* October, 1947; Richard E. Banta, compiler, *Indiana Authors and Their Books, 1816-1916,* Wabash College Press, 1949; L. A. Johnson, "Cabin in Wildflower Woods," *Hobbies,* October, 1960; Brian Doyle, editor, *Who's Who of Children's Literature,* Schocken Books, 1968; D. Dahlke-Scott and M. Prewitt, "Writer's Crusade to Portray Spirit of Limberlost," *Smithsonian,* April, 1976.

SUTHERLAND, Margaret 1941-

PERSONAL: Born September 16, 1941, in Auckland, New Zealand; daughter of William Charles and Dorothy Genevieve (Bolton) Mansfield; married Alan Sutherland (a business consultant), December 12, 1959; children: Roger Anthony, Claire Frances, David Alan. *Education:* Attended high school in Auckland, New Zealand. *Religion:* "Subud." *Home:* 16 Manuka Rd., Titirangi, Auckland, New Zealand.

CAREER: Writer, 1968—.

WRITINGS: The Fledgling (novel), Heinemann, 1974; *Hello, I'm Karen* (juvenile), Methuen, 1974, Coward, 1976; *The Love Contract* (novel), Heinemann, 1976; *Getting Through* (stories), Heinemann, 1977.

SIDELIGHTS: "I like to write for pleasure and discovery. There are a lot of other things I enjoy, like music, animals, my home and family, and thinking about God. I am training to be a nurse. I started this before I got married, and did not

Karen loved to sit beside Mandy and the kittens, watching them as they played and rolled about, or slept. ■ (From *Hello I'm Karen* by Margaret Sutherland. Illustrated by Jane Paton.)

expect to be able to finish it. Now I know that if I don't mind working at it, I can do most things I am drawn to."

SWENSON, May 1919-

PERSONAL: Born May 28, 1919, in Logan, Utah; daughter of Dan Arthur (a teacher) and Anna M. (Helberg) Swenson. *Education:* Utah State University, B.S. *Home:* 73 Boulevard, Sea Cliff, N.Y. 11579.

CAREER: Poet, living in New York, N.Y., 1949—. Formerly worked as an editor for New Directions, New York, N.Y.; writer in residence at Purdue University, Lafayette, Ind., 1966-67. Has lectured and given readings at more than fifty American universities and colleges. *Awards, honors:* Poetry Introductions Prize, 1955; Robert Frost Poetry Fellowship for Bread Loaf Writers' Conference, 1957; Guggenheim fellowship, 1959; William Rose Benét Prize of the Poetry Society of America, 1959; Longview Foundation award, 1959; National Institute of Arts and Letters award, 1960; Amy Lowell Travelling Scholarship, 1960; Ford Foundation grant, 1964; Brandeis University Creative Arts Award, 1967; Rockefeller Writing fellowship, 1967; Distinguished Service Medal of Utah State University, 1967; Lucy Martin Donnelly Award of Bryn Mawr College, 1968; Shelley Poetry Award, 1968; National Endowment for the Arts grant, 1974.

MAY SWENSON

WRITINGS—Poetry: *Another Animal,* Scribner, 1954; *A Cage of Spines,* Rinehart, 1958; *To Mix With Time: New and Selected Poems,* Scribner, 1963; *Poems to Solve* (for children "14-up"), Scribner, 1966; *Half Sun Half Sleep* (new poems and her translations of six Swedish poets), Scribner, 1967; *Iconographs,* Scribner, 1970; *More Poems to Solve,* Scribner, 1971; *Windows and Stones* (translated from *Swedish Poems* by Tomas Transtromer), Pitt Press, 1972; *The Guess and Spell Coloring Book* (ages 5-10), Scribner, 1976; *New and Selected Things Taking Place,* Atlantic, 1978.

Plays: "The Floor" (one-act), first produced in New York at American Place Theater, May 11, 1966, on a triple bill with "23 Pat O'Brien Movies," by Bruce Jay Friedman, and "Miss Pete," by Andrew Glaze. The program title was "Doubles and Opposites."

Poems included in *A Treasury of Great Poems,* edited by Louis Untermeyer, Simon & Schuster, 1955; *New Poets 2,* Ballentine, 1957; *New Poets of England & America,* edited by Donald Hall, Robert Pack, and Louis Simpson, Meridian, 1957; *A Country in the Mind,* edited by Ray B. West, Angel Island Publications, 1962; *Twentieth-Century American Poetry,* edited by Conrad Aiken, Modern Library, 1963; *100 American Poems of the Twentieth Century,* Harcourt, 1963; *The Modern Poets,* edited by John Malcolm Brinnin and Bill Read, McGraw, 1963; *The New Modern Poetry,* edited by M. L. Rosenthal, Macmillan, 1967; *The New Yorker Book of Poems,* edited by Howard Moss, Viking,

1969; *Preferences,* edited by Richard Howard, Viking, 1974; *Western Wind,* edited by John F. Nims, Random House, 1974; and other anthologies. Poems also included in translation in anthologies published in Italy and Germany. Contributor of poetry, stories, and criticism to *Poetry, Nation, Saturday Review, Atlantic, Harper's, New Yorker, Southern Review, Hudson Review,* and other periodicals.

SIDELIGHTS: Swenson writes that the experience of poetry is "based in a craving to get through the curtains of things as they *appear,* to things as they *are,* and then into the larger, wilder space of things as they *are becoming.* This ambition involves a paradox: an instinctive belief in the senses as exquisite tools for this investigation and, at the same time, a suspicion about their crudeness." Although the senses may deceive and distort, the poet is nevertheless aware that deception is taking place and that there exists a reality whose nature must be apprehended other than sensually. This awareness leads Swenson to state: "Sometimes one gets the inkling that there are extrasenses as yet nameless, within the apperceptive system, if only one could differentiate them and identify their organs."

The poet's task then, becomes an incessant quest for a means of interpreting "the vastness of the unknown beyond his consciousness." Swenson continues: "The poet, tracing the edge of a great shadow whose outline shifts and varies, proving there is an invisible moving source of light behind, hopes (naively, in view of his ephemerality) to reach and touch the foot of that solid whatever-it-is that casts the shadow. If sometimes it seems he does touch it, it is only to be faced with a more distant, even less accessible mystery. Because all is movement—all is breathing change."

Among the "strategies and devices, the shamanism and sorcery this poet deploys," as Richard Howard admiringly describes them, is Miss Swenson's use of the riddle in *Poems to Solve.* The book may be enjoyed by both children and adults; the poems here are neither frivolous nor cute but another serious attempt to accommodate "the mystery that only when a thing is apprehended as something else can it be known as itself." Swenson writes of these poems: "It is essential, of course, with a device such as this to make not a riddle-pretending-to-be-a-poem but a poem that is also, and as if incidentally, a riddle—a solvable one. The aim is not to mystify or mislead but to clarify and make recognizable through the reader's own uncontaminated perceptions. By bringing into play the sensual apparatus of the reader, the poem causes him to realize the content eye-wise, ear-wise, taste, touch, and muscle-wise *before* beginning to cerebralize. The analyzing intellect ought not to be the first but the last tool that is applied to a poem, for applied alone, as it sometimes is, it can inhibit organic associative responses, can bypass initial curiosity and individual exploration, resulting in little more than a mechanistic contact with the poem."

May Swenson spent several summers at the Yaddo and MacDowell colonies. She has given poetry readings at the New York YM-YWHA Poetry Center, San Francisco Poetry Center, and before student audiences at various universities. She has recorded for "Today's Poets: Their Poems, Their Voices," Volume 2, Scholastic Records, 1968, and for the Library of Congress, Spoken Arts Records, Folkways Records, and others. In 1975 Caedmon issued a recording, "May Swenson Reads." Her poems have been set to music by Otto Leuning, Howard Swanson, Emerson Meyers, Joyce McKeel, and Warren Benson.

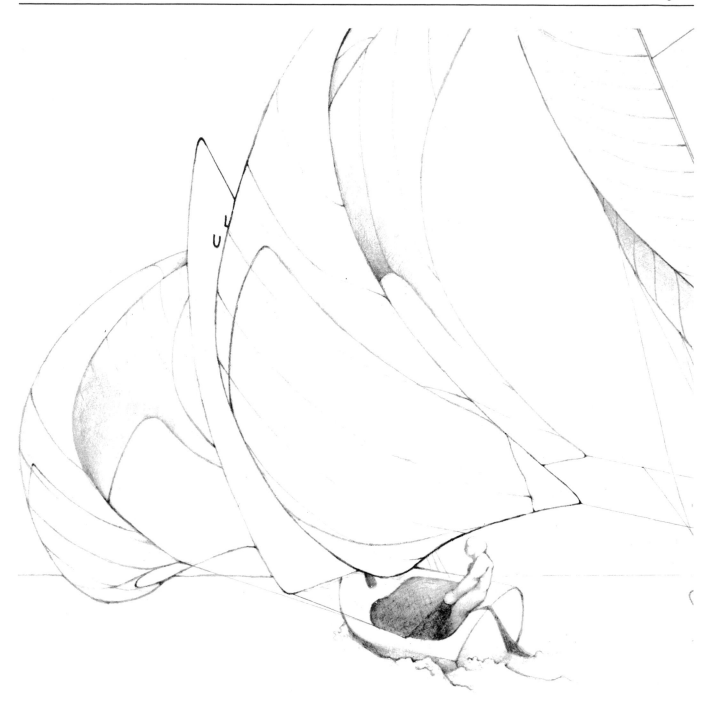

What looks like a flag gliding over water? ■ (From *The Guess and Spell Coloring Book* by May Swenson. Drawings by Lise Gladstone.)

FOR MORE INFORMATION SEE: Louis Untermeyer, editor, *A Treasury of Great Poems, English and American,* Simon & Schuster, 1955; John Malcolm Brinnin and Bill Read, editors, *The Modern Poets,* McGraw, 1963; Babette Deutsch, editor, *Poetry in Our Time,* 2nd edition, Doubleday, 1963; *New York Times Book Review,* September 1, 1963, May 7, 1967; Stephen Stepanchev, *American Poetry Since 1945,* Harper, 1965; Howard Nemerov, editor, *Poets on Poetry,* Basic Books, 1966; *Poems for Young Readers: Selections from Their Own Writing by Poets Attending the Houston Festival of Contemporary Poetry,* National Council of Teachers of English, 1966; *Tri-Quarterly,* fall, 1966; *Book Week,* June 4, 1967, and Volume 4, number 30; *Poetry,* December, 1967; *Craft Interview with May Swenson,* New York Quarterly, number 19, 1977; *American Poetry Review,*

March, April, 1978; Alicia Ostriker, *May Swenson and the Shapes of Speculation.*

TAKAKJIAN, Portia 1930- (Portia Johnston, Portia Wiesner, Portia Roach)

PERSONAL: Surname is pronounced Takjen; born December 10, 1930, in Los Angeles, Calif.; daughter of Le Roy (a professional musician) and Anne (Wiesner) Johnston; married first husband Asdur Takakjian, July 24, 1959 (divorced, 1970); married second husband David C. Roach (an oceanographer), September 3, 1977; children: Eric John, Kyle (first marriage). *Education:* Attended Pratt Insitute, Brook-

"More men have come from over the edge of the sea," she said to Pokatawer. "And with them is one boy." ▪ (From *Pocahontas* by Patricia Miles Martin. Illustrated by Portia Takakjian.)

lyn, N.Y., 1948-49. *Home and Office:* 10 Hester St., Piermont, N.Y. 10968. *Agent:* Al Colby, Graphic Art International, 60 West Main Street, Bergenfield, N.J.

CAREER: Stevens Biondi Decicco, New York, N.Y., illustrator, 1950-59; Lamont-Doherty Geological Observatory of Columbia University, New York, N.Y., illustrator, draftsman, 1970-77. Piermont Bi-Centennial Community, art director for Piermont History Book. *Exhibitions:* Collectors Gallery, New York, N.Y., 1958. *Member:* Nautical Re-

search Guild, Connecticut Marine Model Society Pilot, Mystic Seaport Steering Committee, New York Shipcraft Gui'd.

ILLUSTRATOR: Roland Gant, *French Folk and Fairy Tales,* Putnam, 1963; Patricia M. Martin, *Pocahontas,* Putnam, 1964. Has also illustrated many textbooks and teaching aides including an adventure series for Harcourt, 1968. Work has also appeared in *Metroviews* and *Readers Digest.*

WORK IN PROGRESS: An English literature series for McGraw-Hill; a book on model building with illustrations for Van Nostrand Rhineholt.

SIDELIGHTS: "I work almost exclusively in dyes. What line work I do is done in wolf pencil. I have a variety of styles but for those who look closely, the facial expressions are drawn in only one. This is the reason for a variety of pseudonyms. Clients have a tendency to pigeon hole you and my agent is aware of this. Ours has been a happy association for fifteen years. Unlike other complaints I've heard about the role of an agent, I don't think any one today can get along well without one. Too much time is required to do the job with precious little left over for running about trying to deal with secretaries let alone art editors.

"That crowd in the antiroom is probably a bevi of agents and a few art school graduates. My advice to the latter has been to get an agent if he'll take you. Unfortunately some schools do not prepare the future illustrator for the real world of illustration. We are beset with guidelines that at times, are unreal. Many of these students feel they can draw pretty pictures and they'll simply be bought, popped in a book, and voila! Instant success! Not so. You'll have to do a pile of illustrations you think are terrible and the client loves before you get one you both think is great. You have to be able to draw every ethnic group going and draw them well. It's about time as far as I'm concerned. Not too many years ago I can remember a glorious to-do with a publisher about the way blacks were being drawn. Fortunately the art editor and I won out. He was an x-POW with the marks inside and out and I suspect that was why he took up my cause. I like very much what I do in spite of all the rules one has to follow. I like children and I like to think that I'm 'coloring their world a little nicer' by giving them good illustration to spark their imagination and get them to read for fun.

"I was influenced by Leonardo Da Vinci. I spent hours drawing studies of hands and feet in my teens, and still doodle in like fashion. I always drew in perspective to the wonder of my kindergarten teacher. In fact I can remember one time when I received a rather poor mark for not drawing a house the way we had been shown to do it. I remember grumbling about "that wasn't how a house looked really" and swallowing down the tears when the class laughed at my funny looking house. My elephant skin started there. I'd been taught to draw officially, as soon as I could hold a pencil, by my mother. Her whole family were artists and the gift was passed on to me. It came as easily to me as writing until I broke an arm and had to learn to use the right hand. Today I use both.

"Strangely enough, my interests in ship model building have grown in scope during the last seventeen years. In the last five years I've been generally accepted among my male counterparts as someone who knows what they're doing. I've been represented in two major shows; one at the Hudson River Museum—'Man and the River,' and at the Schaefer Gallery at Mystic Seaport. I've taught classes for four years and have lectured on the subject as well. My first article, one of three, was published for the quarterly English journal, *Model Shipwright.*

"I have made numerous trips to Europe, but admittedly the last was to England for a round of all the Maritime Museums. The pencil and pad went with me as always. Some of the sketches made abroad are to me some of my best. I'm always in awe of its age. I love the old buildings and get a great deal of pleasure drawing them."

PORTIA TAKAKJIAN

Portia Takajian's works are included in the Kerlan collection at the University of Minnesota.

FOR MORE INFORMATION SEE: 1976 Bicentennial Directory Human Resources of New York State, Hudson Heritage House, 1976; *The Journal News* (Gannet News Service), April, 1976, December, 1976, April, 1977, December, 1977; *Newtown Bee,* January 28, 1977.

TAYLOR, Mildred D.

PERSONAL: Born in Jackson, Miss. *Education:* Attended University of Toledo; graduate study at University of Colorado. *Address:* c/o Dial Press, 1 Dag Hammarskjold Plaza, 245 East 47th St., New York, N.Y. 10017.

CAREER: Writer. English and history teacher with the Peace Corps in Ethiopia for two years. *Awards, honors: Song of the Trees* was named Outstanding Book of the Year by the *New York Times;* American Library Association Notable Book, 1976, National Book Award finalist, 1977, Newbery Medal, 1977, all for *Roll of Thunder, Hear My Cry.*

WRITINGS—Juvenile books: *Song of the Trees,* Dial, 1975; *Roll of Thunder, Hear My Cry,* Dial, 1976.

WORK IN PROGRESS: Two more books on the Logan family which will follow the children presented in her two earlier books into adulthood and through World War II.

SIDELIGHTS: "From as far back as I can remember my father taught me a different history from the one I learned in school. By the fireside in our Ohio home and in Mississippi, where I was born and where my father's family had lived since the days of slavery, I had heard about our past. . . . It was a history of ordinary people, some brave, some not so brave, but basically people who had done nothing more spectacular than survive in a society designed for their destruction. Some of the stories my father had learned from his parents and grandparents as they had learned them from theirs; others he told first-hand, having been involved in the

But Papa never divided the land in his mind; it was simply Logan land. For it he would work the long, hot summer pounding steel; Mama would teach and run the farm; Big Ma, in her sixties, would work like a woman of twenty in the fields and keep the house; and the boys and I would wear threadbare clothing washed to dishwater color; but always, the taxes and the mortgage would be paid. Papa said that one day I would understand. ■ (From *Roll of Thunder, Hear My Cry* by Mildred Taylor. Frontispiece by Jerry Pinkney.)

incidents himself. There was often humor in his stories, sometimes pathos, and frequently tragedy; but always the people were graced with a simple dignity that elevated them from the ordinary to the heroic.

"In those intervening years spent studying, traveling, and living in Africa and working with the Black student movement, I would find myself turning again and again to the stories I had heard in my childhood. I was deeply drawn to the roots of that inner world which I knew so well.... In this new book *Roll of Thunder, Hear My Cry* I included the teachings of my own childhood, the values and principles by which I and so many other Black children were reared, for I wanted to show a different kind of black world from the one so often seen. I wanted to show a family united in love and self-respect, and parents, strong and sensitive, attempting to guide their children successfully, without harming their spirits, through the hazardous maze of living in a discriminatory society.

"I also wanted to show the Black person as heroic. In my own school days, a class devoted to the history of Black people in the United States always caused me painful embarassment. This would not have been so if that history had been presented truly, showing the accomplishments of the Black race both in Africa and in this hemisphere.... It is my hope that to the children who read my books, the Logans will provide those heroes missing from the schoolbooks of my childhood, Black men, women, and children of whom they can be proud."

FOR MORE INFORMATION SEE: New York Times Book Review, November 16, 1975, November 21, 1976; *Kirkus Reviews,* September 15, 1976; *Commonweal,* November 19, 1976; *Horn Book,* December, 1976.

Terhune, at sixteen.

MILDRED D. TAYLOR

TERHUNE, Albert Payson   1872-1942

PERSONAL: Born December 21, 1872, in Newark, New Jersey; died February 18, 1942, at Sunnybank; son of Edward Payson Terhune (a clergyman) and Mary Virginia (Hawes) Terhune (a novelist who wrote under the pseudonym Marion Harland); married Lorraine Marguerite Bryson, January 10, 1898 (died); married Anice Morris Stockton (a composer and writer); children—first marriage: Lorraine Terhune Stevens. *Education:* Columbia University, A.B., 1893. *Home:* New York City and "Sunnybank," near Pompton Lakes, New Jersey.

CAREER: Member of the staff, New York *Evening World,* 1894-1916; writer; breeder of prize-winning collies. *Member:* Players, Adventurers, Dutch Treat, and Century clubs. *Awards, honors:* Medal of Excellence from Columbia University, 1933.

WRITINGS: Syria from the Saddle (nonfiction), Silver, Burdett, 1896; *Columbia Stories* (illustrated by Frederic Thornburgh), G. W. Dillingham, 1897; (with Marion Harland, pseudonym of his mother, Mary V. Hawes Terhune) *Dr. Dale* (novel), Dodd, 1900; *Caleb Conover, Railroader* (illustrated by Frank Parker), Authors and Newspapers Association, 1907; *The New Mayor* (adapted from the play, *The Man of the Hour,* by George Broadhurst), J. S. Ogilvie, 1907; *The World's Great Events* (first published as a series of articles in the New York *Evening World*), Dodd, 1908; *The Fighter,* F. F. Lovell, 1909.

A puppy needs an unbelievable amount of educating. It is a task to wear threadbare the teacher's patience and to do all kinds of things to the temper. Small wonder that many humans lose patience and temper during the process and idiotically resort to the whip, to the boot toe and to bellowing—in which case the puppy is never decently educated, but emerges from the process with a cowed and broken spirit or with an incurable streak of meanness that renders him worthless.

The Woman: A Novel (adapted from the play of the same name by William C. De Mille; illustrations by W. B. King), Bobbs-Merrill, 1912; *Around the World in Thirty Days: The Greatest Trip Ever Made*, Street & Smith, 1914; *Dad*, W. J. Watt, 1914; *The Story of Damon and Pythias* (adapted from the screenplay produced by Universal), Grosset, 1915; *Superwomen*, Moffat, Yard, 1916, 2nd edition, World Syndicate, 1931; *Dollars and Cents*, R. J. Shores, 1917; *The Years of the Locust*, R. J. Shores, 1917; *Fortune* (illustrated by W. Clinton Pette), Doubleday, Page, 1918; *Wonder Women in History*, Cassell, 1918; *Lad: A Dog*, Dutton, 1919, new edition (illustrated by Robert L. Dickey), 1926, later edition (illustrated by Ralph Ray), Grosset, 1950, adaptation by Bella Koral (illustrated by William Bartlett), Grosset, 1953, adaptation by Felix Sutton (illustrated by William Bartlett and Kathleen Elgin), Grosset, 1957, anniversary edition (illustrated by Sam Savitt), Dutton, 1959.

Bruce, Dutton, 1920; *Buff: A Collie, and Other Dog Stories*, G. H. Doran, 1921, reprinted, Grosset, 1961; *The Man in the Dark*, Dutton, 1921; *Black Caesar's Clan: A Florida Mystery Story*, G. H. Doran, 1922; *Black Gold*, G. H. Doran, 1922; *Further Adventures of Lad*, G. H. Doran, 1922, reprinted, Grosset, 1961, also published as *Dog Stories Every Child Should Know*, Doubleday, Doran, 1941; *His Dog*, Dutton, 1922; *The Amateur Inn*, G. H. Doran, 1923; *Lochinvar Luck*, G. H. Doran, 1923, reprinted, Grosset, 1961; *The Pest*, Dutton, 1923; *The Heart of a Dog* (illustrated by Marguerite Kirmse), G. H. Doran, 1924, reprinted, Doubleday, 1947, later edition (illustrated by Girard Goodenow), Junior Deluxe Editions, 1957; *Now That I'm Fifty* (memoirs), G. H. Doran, 1924; *The Tiger's Claw*, G. H. Doran, 1924; *Treve*, G. H. Doran, 1924, reprinted, Grosset, 1961.

Najib, G. H. Doran, 1925; *The Runaway Bag*, G. H. Doran, 1925; *Wolf*, G. H. Doran, 1925, reprinted, Grosset,

1961; *My Friend the Dog* (illustrated by Marguerite Kirmse), Harper, 1926, reprinted, Grosset, 1961; *Treasure*, Harper, 1926, published as *The Faith of a Collie*, Grosset, 1961; *Blundell's Last Guest: A Detective Story*, Chelsea House, 1927; *Bumps* (short stories), Harper, 1927; *The Luck of the Laird*, Harper, 1927, published as *A Highland Collie*, Grosset, 1962; *Gray Dawn*, Harper, 1927, reprinted, 1965; *Black Wings*, L. H. Allen, 1928; *Water!*, Harper, 1928; *Lad of Sunnybank*, Harper, 1929; *The Secret of Sea-Dream House*, Harper, 1929.

Proving Nothing (short stories), Harper, 1930; *To the Best of My Memory* (autobiography), Harper, 1930; *A Dog Named Chips*, Harper, 1931, published as *A Dog Named Chips: The Life and Adventures of a Mongrel Scamp*, Grosset, 1961; *Dog Book* (illustrated by Diana Thorne), Saalfield, 1932; *The Way of a Dog: Being the Further Adventures of Gray Dawn and Some Others*, Harper, 1932; *The Son of God*, Harper, 1932, 2nd edition, 1936; *The Book of Sunnybank* (illustrated with photographs by Margaret Bourke-White), Harper, 1934, published as *Sunnybank: Home of Lad*, Grosset, 1961; *Letters of Marque* (mystery novel), Harper, 1934.

Real Tales of Real Dogs (illustrated by Diana Thorne), Saalfield, 1935; *The Critter and Other Dogs*, Harper, 1936, reprinted, Grosset, 1961; *True Dog Stories* (illustrated by Diana Thorne), Saalfield, 1936; *A Book of Famous Dogs* (illustrated by Robert L. Dickey), Doubleday, Doran, 1937; Max J. Herzberg, editor, *The Terhune Omnibus* (illustrated with photographs by Margaret Bourke-White and frontispiece by Marguerite Kirmse), Harper, 1937, published as *The Best-Loved Dog Stories*, Grosset, 1954; *Unseen!*, Harper, 1937; *Grudge Mountain*, Harper, 1939, published in England as *The Mystery of Grudge Mountain*, Chapman, 1939, later published as *Dog of the High Sierras*, Grosset, 1961.

Dogs (illustrated by Kurt Wiese), Saalfield, 1940; *Loot!*, Harper, 1940, published as *Collie to the Rescue*, Grosset, 1952; (with wife, Anice M. S. Terhune) *Across the Line*, Dutton, 1945, reprinted, 1965.

Contributor: Harriet L. McClay and Helen Judson, editors, *Story Essays*, Holt, 1931; Ruth Lampland, editor, *Hobbies*

Time, patience, firmness, wisdom, temper control, gentleness—these be the six absolute essentials for training a puppy. Happy the human who is blessed with any three of these qualities. Lad, being only a dog, was abundantly possessed of all six. And he had need of them. ■ (From *Lad: A Dog* by Albert Payson Terhune. Illustrated by Sam Savitt.)

She had begun life, as far as any record can be found, tucked under the right arm of a mangy-looking man. The man stood on a New York street corner with her, when no policeman was in sight, and strolled along the busy shopping-block with an air of aloof preoccupation whenever a patrolman chanced to glance toward him. ■ (From *A Dog Named Chips* by Albert Payson Terhune. Illustrated by Robert L. Dickey.)

for *Everybody,* Harper, 1934; Thomas R. Cook, editor, *Essays in Modern Thought,* Heath, 1935; Iona Robertson Logie, editor, *Careers in the Making,* Harper, 1935; Trentwell M. White, editor, *How to Write for a Living,* Reynal, 1937; Victor Lasky, editor, *American Legion Reader,* Hawthorn Books, 1953.

Also author of the libretto *Nero* (comic opera; in collaboration with William C. De Mille), 1904; author of more than thirty motion picture scripts. Contributor of short stories, verse, and articles to various magazines, including *Smart Set, Good Housekeeping,* and *Reader's Digest.*

ADAPTATIONS—Films: "The Night of the Pub," 1920; "The Lotus Eater," 1921; "Grand Larceny," 1922; "Knockout Kelly," 1927; "His Dog," 1927; "Whom the Gods Destroy," Columbia Pictures, 1934 (based on his short story, "The Hero"); "Lad: A Dog," Warner Brothers, 1963 (based on his novel, *Lad: A Dog*).

(From the movie "Lad: A Dog," starring Angela Cartwright and Carroll O'Connor. Produced by Warner Bros. Pictures Corp., 1961.)

SIDELIGHTS: "I was born at Newark, New Jersey, on Saturday evening, **December 21, 1872.** My father was the Reverend Dr. Edward Payson Terhune. He was a clergyman. And he was infinitely more a Man. The greatest man I have known or shall know.

"My mother was a writer. She wrote under the pen name of 'Marion Harland.' This because, in her youth, her Virginia community deemed it shameful for a girl to write for publication.

"I was born on her forty-second birthday. My father was just a month her senior. I was the sixth and, by eight years, the youngest child." [Albert Payson Terhune, *To the Best of My Memory,* Harper, 1930[1]]

"In **1876,** my mother's lungs broke down. The doctors gave her the usual three months to live. (Why is it always three months—never two nor four?). My father left his church and took her and all of us to Italy. Two years later, she came home, cured, and in a rugged health that was to carry her past her ninety-first birthday.

"Once in the early months of her illness, when I girded at the Spartan fare and long sleep-hours she ordained for me, she made acidly joking reply that pretty soon I would have a lovely young stepmother with blue eyes and golden hair; who would let me sit up to all hours at night and who would give me all the candy and pastry I could gorge.

"That was enough. My imagination was fired. As my mother always had told me the truth, I knew this, too, must be true. Of course I didn't want her to die. But if she really had to—well, blue eyes and golden hair were an exquisite combination. And the thought of sitting up till midnight, and of gulping pounds of candy at breakfast every single morning, had a mighty lure.

"Ghoulishly I used to grin, on my mother's sickest days. Snarlingly I greeted the news that she was getting well. Tactfully I would turn the conversation, daily and hourly, toward my beautiful candy-dispensing young mother.

"Braggingly I babbled, to all and sundry, of the collie and the saddle-pony this darling young paragon was going to give me in addition to the sublimely indigestible diet that was to be mine. One evening I brought her into my prayers—and was scolded explosively for it.

"Years afterward my mother told me my unholy bliss in the prospect of her successor did more to make her resolve to get well than did all her medicines and the sweet Italian climate."[1]

1878. Returned to America after two years in Europe. Summered at Sunnybank. Wintered in Springfield, Mass.

"I had been dreaming much and blabbing more about Sunnybank during the past two years. It is the only place whereof I have dreamed and blabbed in my time, which

And now a lot of noisy and bothersome humans had invaded the quadrangle and wanted to paw him and pat him and praise him. Wherefore Lad at once got to his feet and stood aloofly disdainful of everything and everybody. He detested pawing, and, indeed, any outsider's handling. ■ (From "Lad: A Dog." Copyright 1961 by Warner Bros.)

loses none of its charm during years of absence. It was just as I remembered it; just as I had bragged of it to the children I played with in Europe.

"I remember photographically our return to Sunnybank after our two-year absence. It was in late September of 1878. To me the homecoming was chokingly poignant; so unbelievably rapturous that I had much trouble in remembering I was a hard-boiled man of early six and must not boo-hoo.

"For the rest of that winter we stayed here—my mother and one of my sisters and I—while my father was preaching in Springfield, Massachusetts, whither he had been called to the Old First Church. It was a splendid winter, livened by weekly visits from him. It was during that winter, too, that my father gave me my first—and last—lesson in the rottenness of ill-treating animals. I was only six. But the memory is as clear to me as though it had happened a year ago instead of five decades.

"I was playing with a litter of pointer puppies on the croquet lawn just in front of the house. It occurred to me that it would be the height of refined merriment to pick up one of the pups by his floppingly long ears and swing him to and fro, pendulum-fashion. I did it. The pup's whimpers of pain were most diverting.

"My father appeared, from nowhere in particular. Without a word, he picked me up by my own ample ears and swung me back and forth, twice; while I bellowed with hurt and rage. Then he set me down, still without speaking, and went indoors, leaving me there. I stood staring after him in white-hot hate. Never before had he been cruel to me or to any one else.

"Then, bit by bit, I stopped thinking how nice he would look with his bearded throat cut from ear to ear. Bit by bit it dawned on me that I was suffering precisely what the good little pointer pup must have suffered; that I had tortured the puppy in exactly the same way my father had tortured me.

"I stopped crying, I stood, thinking harder and more sanely than ever before in all my six years. For the first time I was putting myself in another's place—not at all a comforting thing to do. But it taught me more than would a ten-hour lecture on the swinishness of cruelty to the helpless.

"To the best of my recollection, that was the last time I felt the impulse toward wanton cruelty; or to tease something that had no chance to tease back."[1]

1879-1883. In Springfield. "Perhaps between six and twelve a boy does more real developing along certain lines, than at any other period. My course of reading helped to develop

(From the movie "Lad: A Dog." Produced by Warner Bros. Pictures Corp., 1961.)

me along a line that ought to have been helpful and was not. My father's library was comprehensive. I was allowed to wallow in it. I wallowed.

"Thus, not knowing I was delving into the classics, I read all of Shakespeare, all of Longfellow, seven of Scott's novels, Bryant's translation of *The Iliad,* Bayard Taylor's translation of Goethe's *Faust,* Percy's *Reliques,* much of Gibbon, more of Tennyson, before I was ten.

"Instead of profiting mentally by this mass of eagerly gorged and ill-digested literature, I tried to make practical application of much of it.

"Falstaff and Prince Hal and their gay adventures in holding up night travelers, and Robin Hood's escapades, caught tight hold of my imagination. I banded together a group of neighborhood boys and we set out to duplicate their feats.

"Not that we did any actual robbing, except of clotheslines for lariats and clothespoles for lances, and the raiding of a few orchards. But we made ourselves obnoxious in the vicinity of my Maple Street home by these twilight forays. As my father was a clergyman the brunt of the blame fell on me—where it belonged.

"I organized a band of outlaws in Blake's Woods—now a populous and houseful real-estate development, but then a forest—and, on the side, I drilled an Illiadesque legion of Trojans to defend Springfield against a hypothetical Greek fleet which was to sail up the Connecticut River at some unspecified date.

"To keep our hands in, we Trojans made hostile excursions into neighborhoods where less imaginative boys gave us grim welcome. Between times we Robin Hood gangsters broke the windows of robber barons on Avon Place—who did not know they were robber barons and who sent bills to my father for the cash damage done.

"Much of the applause—indeed the only applause—meted out to our deeds of derring-do was from the very little girls of the neighborhood, who lavished on me and my desperate brothers-at-arms such interesting plaudits as: 'Aren't you perfectly terrible!'

"Littlest and prettiest, but least admiring, of these tiny girls was Anice Stockton—the youngest pupil at Miss Kimball's School, on Mulberry Street, when I was the biggest and oldest boy there. There was an elfin charm and a queer loveliness and an honesty and a fearless spirit about Anice Stockton which used to make me by turns bragful and sheepish in her presence. She was not—is not—in the very least like any one else I have known. When I was twenty-eight, I went back to Massachusetts and married her.

"[Soon] I made a sad discovery about myself. My mother had taken me to New York to be outfitted for winter clothes. On her return she said gloomily to my two shocked sisters: 'He's only a little over six. *And he wears ten-year sizes in everything!*'

"That was the keynote. That was the theme of a curse that has been mine ever since. At six I was wearing ten-year sizes. At twelve I was wearing sixteen-year sizes. From the time I was sixteen, I never have been able to wear any ready-made garments, except only underclothes, shoes, and hats. Everything else has had to be built to my oversized self.

At once his ears went up, their tulip tips and the worriedly sympathetic glint in the eyes enlivening his whole expression. ■ (From *My Friend the Dog* by Albert Payson Terhune. Illustrated by Marguerite Kirmse.)

"Perhaps you think it must be a fine thing to stand six-feet-two-and-a-half in one's bare feet, and to have a fifty-inch chest and piano-mover shoulders, and to weigh two-hundred-and-twenty pounds or more? Well, it is not. Take that from me. It is NOT! It is as inconvenient, sartorially, as it would be to have a hump on one's back or only one arm.

"The man or boy of average size can be outfitted becomingly at any good department store or ready-made clothing place, and at almost fifty per cent less cost than can a giant like myself. Moreover, for the giant, hotel beds and the berths on shipboard and in Pullmans are things of horror.

"But, up from the age of six to twenty-odd these were minor bothers compared to the endless variations of: 'You are so large that you must be careful what you do and say. People will expect so much of you.' Just what it was that people would 'expect' of me I never have known. But morbidly I realized from the first that they weren't getting it."[1]

October 3, 1884. Moved from winter home in Springfield, Mass. to Brooklyn. "My father was much loved in Springfield, even if his family was not—least of all his trouble-seeking little son—and he was drawing a good salary there. Also he had refused calls to better churches in New York and elsewhere; and he was in no vital need of money. But there was ever something quixotically adventurous about him—something which made him battle for a losing cause when he might well have lived smugly upon a winning one. He was a fighter. And he was a Christian.

"The needs of the Brooklyn church, the hundred-to-one odds against success there, the joy of a clean uphill fight—all these stirred him to action. He accepted the call. Thereby he signed his own death-warrant—even if a deferred one.

"He went to Brooklyn at fifty-three—the strongest, most vigorous, most athletic, most sanguine of men. He left the First Reformed Church there in 1890—broken in health and in life; sick with the malady which later was to kill him; his buoyancy and athletic vigor forever gone in six years he had aged by a quarter-century.

"But he had achieved the task he had accepted. The church was free of debt and was on its feet. The pews were full. The revenues were high. He had changed an insolent ecclesiastical corpse into a prosperous Live One. He had 'fought the good fight.' He had finished his work. It had smashed him. But he had won. Few men have turned so certain a defeat into glorious victory. But as I said, it had smashed him."[1]

1889. Freshman at Columbia College. "In school-and-college days, my friends and I found Sunnybank a vacation paradise. I remember, in Freshman year at Columbia, I came out for the Thanksgiving three-day vacation, with [three classmates]. That Sunday—it was bitter cold—we went for a thirty-mile tramp through the mountains. We reached home, half-starved, just at nightfall.

"For dinner we had, among other things, an eighteen-pound turkey my mother had sent up here for us. We four didn't leave enough of that noble fowl for breakfast hash. Then, after lounging in front of the library fire for an hour or so, we took a fast three-mile cross-country run to settle our dinner and to make us sleepy. Such a feast and such exercise today would kill me out of hand.

"It had been planned that I should go to Yale, if, by some minor miracle, I could pass the entrance examinations. But when college time came my sisters both were married and my father was often away from home. Thus, my absence in New Haven would leave my mother alone. Loneliness was always a horror to her; though I think few humans have had less of it in their lives than had she. She dreaded the thought of spending so much time without companionship. She suggested that if I should go to Columbia instead of Yale I would be able to come home almost every night.

"Accordingly, I went to Columbia. Not because I wanted to, but because it was so ordered. I disliked the idea. Yale had been my desired goal ever since I was a child. Columbia, in those days, was referred to by students in out-of-town colleges as a day school; because it had no dormitory life.

"Looking back, I can see it was lucky for me that I was sent to a college whose president, Seth Low, was a friend of my parents and two of whose trustees were my father's boyhood chums. Without the pull involved by all this, I never could have won my useless Bachelor of Arts degree.

"For I have not yet passed my Freshman nor Sophomore mathematics exams, nor second-term Junior Greek, nor Senior Latin. If the archives of Columbia, between the years of 1889 and 1893, are open for inspection, any morbid investigator can verify the sad fact that there are at least six (perhaps more) unexpiated 'conditions' against my record. Yet I received the same sheepskin, and was graduated at the same time, as the hardest working and best students in my class."[1]

September, 1893. As a graduation present, traveled abroad with his mother. "After college I drifted through Europe for a while; then to the Near East. Egypt did not appeal to me, after a short sojourn. But Syria had a gripping hold on my imagination and on my heart as well.

"I crossed the Syrian wilderness on horseback and I swam the Jordan in flood (there were no railroad trains or Jordan bridges in those prehistoric days); I swam in the almost unswimmable Dead Sea where I bobbed about like an elongated cork and where the salt turned my hair and beard to the color of frost. I wandered into the Land of Moab; and for a space I 'went native' and lived with the outlaw El Kanah tribe of Bedouins.

"Oh, but it was a glorious time! All of it except when I worked my way into the Namaan House of Lepers, near Damascus, in the guise of a French physician; and when I tried a like adventure in invading a Moslem shrine near Hebron. Neither of those experiences had a single bright spot. Even now I don't enjoy thinking of them.

"But, for the rest, it was an epoch worth living for. I traveled by small private caravan, for the most part. My dragoman was Daoud Jamal. In later years—long after his death—I used Jamal and his amazing diction in my *Najib* yarns. As a young man Daoud had spent a year in America, and he had been in a Syrian venture at the Centennial at Philadelphia.

"I came home to Sunnybank. Here, to ease the galling inactivity, I wrote my first book, *Syria from the Saddle*. It was a vainglorious record of part of my Near East wanderings. The book was full of conceit and cockiness, of gleesome egotism. Also, at twenty-two, few men are brilliant travel writers.

"*Syria from the Saddle* went to twelve publishers. The twelfth accepted it. This unfortunate firm was Silver, Burdett & Company of Boston. I received an advance of fifty dollars—an advance which the sales never wholly covered. Yet the book won more laudatory reviews than anything else I have written. Perhaps on the same principle which makes an audience applaud a play acted by high school pupils and yawn at a better performance by professionals.

"I had begun writing when I was nineteen, during my Junior year at college. The *Columbia Spectator* offered a ten-dollar prize for the best short story written by an undergraduate. Brander Matthews was the judge. Mine was the only typed manuscript. Always I have had a morbid belief that that was why it won the ten-dollar award. For it was frightful drivel, even for a nineteen-year-old.

"The same year, I wrote a poem—not verse or doggerel, but a *poem* (though I called it a 'pome' until George Woodberry taught me the accepted pronunciation). I called it 'My Love and I.' Yes, it was that kind of poem. Since then I have written stuff of which I had less reason to be ashamed. I could not recite six lines of any of my later work, to save my soul. But every syllable of 'My Love and

I' is burned into my memory. I can't forget the measly thing any more than I could forget cutting off the fingers of a child.

"I sent it to *Lippincott's Magazine*, a leading worthwhile periodical in those days, with Julian Hawthorne and Amelie Rives and Clyde Fitch among its regular contributors. For some reason I cannot yet fathom, it was accepted. Stoddart, the editor, sent me a check for $20 for it.

"Life spread forth in one unmarred vista of success before me. I had written and polished 'My Love and I' in a single half day. Twenty-four lines; twenty dollars. By writing two such poems a day for five days a week and taking Saturdays and Sundays off, I could earn henceforth $200 a week. My future was assured. I set to work to realize on it.

"Two full years—two full years of steady scribbling—passed before anything else of mine was accepted anywhere.

"Apparently, there was some tricky catch in my calculations on the writing game. Apparently, too—though this was hard to credit—I was not to be my generation's immortal poet. Certain unholy limericks of mine, I am told, still are sung at Columbia. But, for the rest, my verse died, stillborn. I asked Richard Watson Gilder the reason. His answer was vividly frank: 'Because it is worthless.'"[1]

November, 1894. Became cub reporter for *Evening World*. Stayed until May 13, 1916. "One day it was my task to rewrite for its earliest edition a morning paper's story of the fourth Blank brother's suicide. I made casual mention that three elder brothers had killed themselves in the same way—a fact not recorded in any of the morning papers' clippings—and I received a scorching calldown from our city editor for not having played up that end of the story for what it really was worth, instead of dismissing it with a single line.

"Apparently when four brothers in succession shoot themselves, 'that is news,' even as when a man bites a dog; whereas a casual Brooklyn suicide is worth only three lines in the second day's evening papers."[1]

January 10, 1898. Eloped to Cazenovia, N.Y. with Lorraine Marguerite Bryson.

October 5, 1898. Only daughter, Lorraine Virginia was born. Wife died four days later.

September 2, 1901. Married Anice Morris Stockton. "When my wife and myself had come back from our wedding trip . . . we had taken account of our stock and found we had just eighteen dollars in the world. On the way from the station to our new West Eightieth Street flat, all our trunks and other luggage were stolen in one of the wholesale express-wagon robberies which were current. Thus we had begun married life with the first month's rent paid on our flat and with eighteen dollars in money and with the clothes we stood in.

"But somehow the situation, then, had seemed less appalling than pleasantly exhilarating. We had each other and we had our walk-up flat (the only reason we had chosen a flat on the fifth floor was because there was no sixth), and I had my office job, such as it was. What more did we need?

"It was a jolly little flat, all sunlight; though it was icy in winter and sometimes the roof leaked so generously that we had to sleep under umbrellas. Our cook was a dipsomaniac.

"We had been calmly certain that in a very few years we should be rich."[1]

November, 1901. Started doing work for extra money for *Evening World*. Did ghost pieces for famous names, translated articles from French periodicals, rewrote stories found in history books. Sold a weekly column "Up and Down with the Elevator Man," ran for year, also contributed to *Sunday World* and *Morning World*. "I had fooled myself into the idea that I was a moderately hard worker. But, . . . I took . . . stock and I realized I was a lazy failure. I must make a big change in my work and in my life itself, if ever I was to get anywhere. Especially if ever I was to get to Sunnybank.

"I was thirty-two years old, I had not one hundred dollars in the world, above my weekly pay—which had been boosted from $45 to $47.50. I was several thousand dollars in debt. I had no reasonable hope of doing better along the lines I was following.

"Once and again I had tried fiction writing. I had made barely enough by it to pay my typing bills. But I had been doing it only at odd times and when the spirit moved me. While youthful poverty may be amusing, there is no more humor in old-age poverty than in a malignant cancer. Fully a score of fellow-workers of my own age and even younger had died, leaving their wives penniless. I was not immortal. Also, a single long illness would wipe out not only my scant cash but my scantier credit; and might well leave me jobless.

"Something had to be done. Apart from robbing a bank—a line of endeavor for which I lacked the needful preliminary training—I saw no way to get ahead in the world except by forcing some kind of opening for myself as a fiction writer.

"Thenceforth, for several years, I set aside five hours a night, five nights a week, for this kind of work. After my nine-hour office day, I came home, got a shower and a rubdown; and, as soon as dinner was ended, I went to my desk and began writing. At first it was torment, to attack fresh toil at the jaded end of a nine-hour work period. But, bit by bit, I got into my stride. The stuff I turned out was pretty bad, but presently I found a sale for it."[1]

January, 1905. Anice came down with tuberculosis.

June, 1906. Witnessed murder of famous architect, Stanford White.

July 25, 1907. Reverend Dr. Terhune died. "The six years at the First Reformed Church had finished him for any protracted cleric work. He was broken; prematurely old.

"The rest of his days, up to his death . . . were spent either at Sunnybank—which he loved as I love it—or in preaching off and on, through charity, at churches which could not afford a regular pastor. He wanted to die in harness—and he did."[1]

1912. Purchased Sunnybank from his mother. "The old house has no definite architecture except of pleasant comfort. It had some eleven rooms when it was built. Then, as more children and more money drifted in, my parents made

The kitchen end of Sunnybank House. Photograph by Margaret Bourke-White.

the house larger. A room here and a wing there. Until now it had sixteen rooms, only one or two of them large; one or two perhaps unduly small.

"The beamed living room and the music room, I suppose, are one L-shaped room, divided as they are by an arch that goes almost from wall to wall.

"We like the living room. So do most of our guests, they tell us. One or two people do not. The wide fireplace's brick mantel and chimney piece rise to the ceiling. In front of the fire is the only couch in captivity long enough for me to stretch out to the full extent of my six-feet-two-and-a-half-inches. The Mistress had it made for me.

"It is nine feet long, over all, and with a seven-foot resting space between the overstuffed ends. It is nearly a foot deeper, too, than the average couch. One sinks into it with vast sense of well-being.

"It is dark brown. Brown is the general tone of the whole living room, for that matter, from the ancient Heppelwhite and Adam and Chippendale chairs and Sheraton desk—all handed down for God-knows-how-long in the Mistress's family—to the floor-to-ceiling clock which ticked out the hour of my great-grandsire's birth. It is a mellow room. A room that seems to me to be full of Peace.

"The firelight is reflected from the rows of silver trophies at one side of the brown wooden walls and from a heterogeneous mass of old weapons and armor on the wall behind the couch. On three sides of the room are built-in bookshelves reaching from the floor to the high diamond-paned windows. The books range from quaint calf-bound volumes and sets, of our grandparents' time, to the *New Oxford Dictionary* and the *Cambridge Shakespear.*" [Albert Payson Terhune, *The Book of Sunnybank,* Harper & Brothers, 1934²]

1915. "I wrote story after story for Ray Long; for all three of his magazines—the *Red Book* and the *Blue Book* and the now-defunct *Green Book*. Some months I had a story in all of them. Long kept his word as to the steady raising of my prices. Also, he printed my serial novels, *Dollars and Cents* and *The Years of the Locust* (both of them appearing soon afterward in book form and then as motion pictures), and one or two other serials; and a series of articles on famed actors and a series I called *The Woman Tamers*. For years after Long left the *Red Book* and came to New York as editor-in-chief for the Hearst magazines I continued to write for him.

"When he came East on business trips for the *Red Book,* Long would run out to Sunnybank for the weekend or for a few days' rest. Sometimes he came here to talk over story plots with me; sometimes just to loaf about with me in boat or car or woods. He had a way with animals, and our Sunnybank collies took to him almost at once. After a few visits, old Sunnybank Lad actually accepted him as a chum.

"Except for my wife and myself, in the order named, Lad hitherto had stood aloof from every one. He was coldly civil to our guests; but he kept out of their way as much as possible, avoiding their proffered pettings or cajoling words. One day, to every one's amazement, Lad walked up to Ray Long and laid his paw and his head on Long's knee. Long was laughingly proud of his conquest of the great dog's friendship. Thereafter, he and Lad were chums. Long grew tremendously fond of the big collie which so inexplicably had accepted him as a pal. One day he said to me: 'Bert, I wish you'd write me a story about Laddie.' The request flicked me on the raw. I made answer at some length. The answer was diatribe: 'What's the use?' I demanded. 'For ten years I've been begging editors to let me write dog stories. I know dogs—or I think I do. I've been studying them all my life, I want to write about them. But not an editor on earth will let me do it. Editors tell me the public isn't interested in dogs, and that all animal stories are out of date. Not one of them will give me a chance to tackle a dog yarn. What would be the sense of scribbling such a story and then having it rejected everywhere? I asked one editor to let me write a story about a bear, if he wouldn't let me write about a dog. He wouldn't. He told me the public 'wants something spicy.' So I offered to write a yarn about a cinnamon bear. But he couldn't see it. Why should I waste time writing you a story about Lad, when no editor has the wit to know that The Dog is as much a human emotion as love and hate and treasure-seeking? You wouldn't accept it.' 'Write it,' he bade me. 'I'll print it.'

"I wrote it. I called it 'His Mate.' It told of Lad's clash with a guest-collie, named Knave, and of the wooing of Lad's gold-white mate, Lady. I made no effort to humanize any of the dogs. I wrote of them as they were. The plot was simple; the actions and motives of the canine characters were normal. 'His Mate' appeared in the January, 1915, issue of the *Red Book*. Within three months four other editors wrote asking me for dog stories. That was the start.

"For this first six-thousand-word dog story I wrote at Ray Long's order, in 1914, I received $200. For the last six-thousand-word dog story I wrote at Ray Long's order, in 1923, I received $2,000—which was within $500 of the highest I have received from any editor for a single dog story."[1]

1916. Resigned from *Evening World;* moved to Sunnybank. Permanent home for the rest of his life. "During the last two years of my *Evening World* servitude, I had given up serious hope of sailing to any heights in literature. My last try at it in a magazine had been my year of work for Williard Huntington Wright on *Smart Set*. Once again, as I have said, I was to make a bid for it, in book form, when in 1917 I spent an entire summer writing and rewriting my novel, *Fortune*.

"I found I could make much more money as a scrawler of second-and-third rate stuff. While it is a noble thing to starve in a garret and to leave to posterity a few precious volumes which all folk praise and few read, yet to me there was something better worth while in grinding out work which brought me plenty of cash, if no high repute.

"I had known what it was to be hungry. I did not care to risk the experience again, either for myself or for those who depended on me. Deliberately, happily, I sold my highly putative literary birthright for a very actual and bounteous mess of pottage.

"I make no apology for this. There are a hundred-and-twenty million people in the United States. Even as the low-brow's dollar has the same spending qualities as has the dilettante's, so I think the lowbrow's literary approval is perhaps as well worth earning as is the *American Mercury's* or the *Saturday Review of Literature's*.

"I have not read a line written by Harold Bell Wright or by Zane Grey. I do not expect to read any of their work. But I do not believe either of those two men would have been able to pile up an avid reading public of millions of men and women for each of his books, unless those books had had as much merit in their own way as had anything of Walter Pater's or of D. H. Lawrence's or of Hergesheimer's; or of any other writer's, past or present, whom the *cognoscenti* extol and at whom the multitude yawn.

"Marlowe and Ben Jonson, whose plays could not draw large enough audiences to pay for heating the theater, sneered at Shakespeare as the cheap favorite of the groundlings.

"Marlowe is half-forgotten, today, except by the few of us who still find pleasure in his ill-built *Dr. Faustus* and *The Jew of Malta*, and one or two other neglected plays. Ben Jonson is remembered for a jumbled drama, almost never acted, *Every Man in His Humor*, and for a merrily indecent anecdote and for the claim that he wrote 'Drink To Me Only with Thine Eyes.' Shakespeare endures.

"God forbid that I should place Zane Grey or Harold Bell Wright on any such pinnacle of promised immortality! I say only that the public at large loves them and their kind; and that the public at large has shown no lasting devotion for any one of twenty writers whom the intelligentsia from time to time have acclaimed. Also that the enduring approval of

At the lily pool of Sunnybank. Photograph by Margaret Bourke-White.

the general public has more than once been proved correct by posterity.

"This [is a] windy preamble, to explain why I was not ashamed to sell the aforesaid and very problematical birthright for a mess of pottage which presently was to allow me to live as always I had longed to live and to do a thousand things that I never had dared hoped to be able to do."[1]

1918. Lad, the dog died. "The Sunnybank back porch at one end is a little more than two feet high from the ground. Some yards from this end are the steps, three or four of them, low and wide and easy. This porch is a gauge whereby I can tell the first active approach of old age in any of my collies.

"When I go out on the back porch from the house, any of the dogs that are in sight come running to greet me. They take the sheer side of the veranda in their stride with no semblance of effort.

"Then comes a day when one of them avoids the easy jump and trots along the walk on stiffening legs until he reaches the low flight of steps. He pads up these and thence trots along the porch toward me. He has gone many yards out of his way, sooner than to jump. And I know he is aging. I know it as well as he does.

"It is only a span of time, then, until I catch sometimes the sharply pathetic 'old dog look' in the eyes he lifts to mine. At first the look is momentary and it appears seldom. But in time it is permanent.

"And by that time he will not climb the flight of stairs to the second story of the house unless he is summoned. Also he is spending the bulk of his spare hours in sleeping.

"He knows how to take care of himself and how to save every savable atom of his fast-ebbing energy. Always except when the Mistress or I start out on a walk. Then, no matter what the effort or how hot or cold or wet the day, the gallant oldster is on his feet; gaily eager to go along. And when kindness makes us shut him in the house or in a kennel-yard, to save him the fatigue of the hike he used to find so easy, he mopes morosely and his age-sharpened feelings are cruelly hurt.

"Especially so was it with old Sunnybank Lad as age and weight began to encompass him. He had a mystic way of knowing when we were going for a walk. Wherever he might be lying, he would lumber heavily after us; straining every ancient muscle to catch up with us.

"I don't know how many times we turned back to the house, abandoning our hike, when we saw the toiling mahogany shape heaving its tired way up the drive in our wake—Lad, who once had been the swiftest and strongest of all our collies.

"I grant it was silly of us to abandon a bracing walk for the sake of humoring a pastworthy collie chum who loved us. But my own uncertain temper never went bad at such times. There would be chances for a thousand long walks after Laddie should be gone.

"Of late years, when younger people have gone far out of their way to be nice to my aging self and to ease down their speed to mine, the picture has risen unbidden to my memory of our turning back from our walks to salve Laddie's feelings.

"Perhaps the same principle obtains. Perhaps I am repaid in kind for my decency toward the outworn old Sunnybank Collie. Who knows?"[2]

1919. *Lad: A Dog* published. "I have told how I happened to begin writing dog stories. Having begun, I kept on. There was a strong demand for them, now that the early ones had scored.

"When Lad died, in September of 1918, I collected the ten or twelve yarns I had written about him; and I tried to sell the collection as a book under the name, *Lad: A Dog.*

"I queried the Doubleday-Page Company, which had published *Fortune* and which had an option on the next book I should write. The firm's literary adviser, Harry Maule, begged me not to send in *Lad: A Dog,* saying Doubleday-Page would not publish any dog stories as there was no sale for such stuff. He got the company to waive its right to my next volume, and I hunted elsewhere for a publisher whom I might induce to take my group of Lad tales.

"I was told that there had been no worthwhile dog books since *Bob, Son of Battle* and *The Call of the Wild,* and that the public did not want that kind of fiction. That book readers were no longer interested in dogs or in stories about

them. There was no demand; there was no possible profit. Any volume with a canine hero was foredoomed to fall flat.

"I knew there was a mistake, somewhere, in this line of argument. Magazine editors had said the same thing about short dog stories until Ray Long had begun publishing mine. Then they had been eager for them. I believed my Lad book would succeed, if only I could find a Ray Long of publishers.

"I found him. He was John Macrae, of E. P. Dutton & Company. Mr. Macrae read the story. Then he told me the character of Old Laddie himself appealed so strongly to him that he was going to take a chance on publishing the book. He did not look forward to a large sale; but he thought there might perhaps be enough readers to justify the venture.

"*Lad: A Dog* was published early in 1919, A few months later I had a letter from Mr. Macrae which began: 'Lad is on the rampage. He can't be stopped.'

"I don't know how many editions the book has gone through. I believe it was in its forty-somethingth; the last time I asked about it, two or three years ago. It passed the fifty thousand mark long before that time. After more than a decade it is still selling in its original $2 form, never yet having gone into the limbo of cheaper reprints."[1]

1923. Entered dogs for the first time at Westminster Kennel Club Show. "All my life I have made an intensive study of dogs. Thirty years ago I knew everything about them that could be known, and much more. After three decades of much closer study of them and their ways, I find to my dismay that I know almost nothing at all about them. I have scarcely scratched the surface. That is not false modesty. It is sickeningly true.

"The sum total of my canine knowledge and experience and observation is this: *Anything can happen; and usually it does.*

"Some day, in an access of honesty I shall substitute that great truth for my present smug kennel motto: *To win without boasting; to lose without excuses.*

"I have learned much from my dogs—far more than ever they have learned from me. But to this day there are a hundred things about their mentality—or its lack—that are scaled mysteries to me and to every other human.

"My dogs can read my mood, to a nicety. They can work out problems which call for genuine reasoning powers—there is no possible doubt of that. They can distinguish the engine-throb of my cars, a mile away, from the noise of all other cars. I have had two dogs—Wolf was one of them—that knew by some impossible psychic sense when my wife and I were starting home from a journey; or were planning to run up to Sunnybank from New York for the day, in winter. I have known dogs to show flashes of an intelligence which was more than human. But—

"I never yet knew a dog that had sense enough to unwind his own chain when he had tangled it around a tree or gotten it snarled in the brambles. I never knew a dog with the simple brain-power to lay a stick on a hearth-fire when the blaze flickered low—although such a dog loved the fire and had seen it replenished in that way a thousand times. I

ALBERT PAYSON TERHUNE

never knew a dog with sense enough to cease from worshipping a human fool.

"I can't work it out—this queer blend of super-and-subintelligence."[1]

1929-1939. Licensed American Kennel Club judge of Collie breed. "On my desk here in my study lies a certified five-generation pedigree of one of my best dogs; Champion Sunnybank Thane, admittedly the foremost show-collie of his day. In the fifth generation there are thirty-two names; the names of his great-great-great-grandparents.

"All thirty-two of Thane's great-great-great-grandparents were registered, in the infallible American Kennel Club Stud Book. Thus, the entire thirty-two were proven thorough-breds. I owned many of them. I judged several others at various dogshows. I have seen all of them, during the past fifteen years or so.

"I also have had thirty-two great-great-great-grandparents. Allowing the accepted average of three generations to a century, those thirty-two men and women were alive during the American Revolution. Indeed, their average birth date must have been somewhere around 1755.

"Do I know who all, or even half, of my thirty-two great-great-greats were? I do not. Nor do you know who yours were. I don't even know who half of my sixteen great-great-grandparents were; though they must have been alive during part of the nineteenth century.

"Nor, I think, do you know who half of your own great-greats were.

"Champion Sunnybank Thane's five-generation pedigree is one hundred per cent certain. My own five-or-even-four-generation pedigree is a mess."[2]

December 13, 1929. Terhune was hit by an auto, temporarily paralyzed, and bedridden for months.

1930. Went to England to recuperate. *To the Best of My Memory* published. "I had to map out a new plan of procedure, when I began work on my own account. I had noticed that a man who worked for himself had always either a Simon Legree or a loafer for a boss. It is so criminally easy to put off work to another day or to a later hour, when one is accountable to nobody but oneself for the completing of the day's task!

"Thus, from the start, I swore that I would have a Simon Legree and not an Easy Boss to guide my toil.

"I planned the hours that should be spent at my desk at steady typing; and I allowed nothing short of a catastrophe to change them. Again and again, on a morning when I knew the fish would be biting, I have told myself I needed a day off and that I would work the better for it. Whereat my Simon Legree self has answered: 'Get to your desk and stay there. Cut out the excuses.'

"Perhaps better men can write on inspiration and can afford to loaf through half of each day. I can't. A few weeks of it would turn me into an incurable idler. I scourge myself to work every morning at a certain time; and I stick at my desk until the day's task is finished. Often the work is so wretchedly poor that it must be torn up. But at least it has been done.

"I learned more about work-routine for writers from a few paragraphs in Anthony Trollope's autobiography than from every other inner and external source put together. Trollope likens a writer to a cobbler, as a mere artisan who must stick to his job all day and every day. He says that when an old-fashioned cobbler finished a pair of shoes, he laid the completed work aside with one hand while with the other he reached for a new sheet of leather. He says that a writer, finishing a story or an article or a book, should waste no time in rewarding himself by a spree or by a day's loafing; but should start at once on his next literary chore.

"To me, there is perfect wisdom in this advice. And infinitely greater men have adopted the same methods.

"The elder Alexandre Dumas, for example, set himself a certain number of pages to write—or to rewrite from the notes of Maquet or Gaillardet or others of his numberless collaborators—per day. Nor would he stop until every line on every one of these pages was written. On the very middle of a page—his last for the day—he completed *The Three Guardsmen*. He drew a line across the page's center; and under it he wrote these headlines: 'The Count of Monte Cristo! a Romance; by Alexandre Dumas.' Then he wrote the first half-page of *Monte Cristo* on the same sheet as the last half-page of *The Three Guardsmen*.

"To me, that is the acme of craftsmanship. You will note that neither of the two novels was a pot-boiler and that neither of them could be labeled as hackwork.

"Inspiration—or the will to work, which amounts to much the same thing—can be taught thus to come at call, and to be almost always at its best. I think the inspiration that cannot be trained to obey the summons of a writer is like a dog that cannot be trained to come to its master's call. The sooner both of them are gotten rid of, the better."[1]

1938. Cancer of the throat diagnosed. Proved malignant.

1941. Went into a coma, doctors didn't give him a chance to live, but he pulled out of it. "I have not been [old] long enough to keep from talking about it. Not long enough to keep from resenting it as I might resent some scurvy joke played on me.

"Age has not made me wise. But it has added yearly to my junk heap of experience and of observation until the blend of the two is beginning slowly to add up to something akin to a pseudo wisdom; something which is more interesting than useful to me.

"'The dunce who's sent to Rome excels the dunce who's kept at home' only because he has seen a thousand more new sights, met a thousand more people, heard a thousand unfamiliar truths and lies spoken and had a thousand new viewpoints forced upon him.

"Increasing Age is the Rome to which I have been sent. It has taught me much that the cleverest young homestayer does not know. I think that is how Age wins its unearned repute for wisdom.

"Not that the things I have discovered—most of them—are of the remotest value to me now. The envolving of an unhittable pitching delivery would not profit an elderly baseball player who is doubled up with chronic arthritis. Nor would a new-found knack of supreme marble-playing be an asset to an elderly banker. Get the idea?

"The Spaniards are a wise people, except perhaps as concerns their own welfare. And the Spaniards long ago summed up what I have been groping to say, in their bitterly true proverb: '*God gives walnuts to those who no longer have teeth to crack them.*'

"If one could always keep on feeling old, one would become resigned to the sorry state; as to a wooden leg or to a double set of false teeth. But one can't. At least *this* one can't.

". . . Possibly by the time I hobble past the eightieth milestone, I may have become used to the whole wretched thing and forget that once I was anything else. By then I may have acquired the foul mixture of exhaustion and bloodless apathy which folk miscall Philosophy."[2]

February 18, 1942. Died at Sunnybank. "A wonderful life it is, as perhaps I have said once or twice—or oftener. . . . We each have our own work, and we spend the bulk of every day at it. In addition to that, we have splendid times together—motoring, fishing, tramping, supervising the routine details of The Place, training the pups, and romping with our collie pack.

"When we have no guests, we arrange our meal-schedules as we choose to; breakfasting sometimes at half-past seven, sometimes at half-past ten. There is nobody to be inconvenienced. We can start off on a long or short vacation at a day's notice and when the fancy hits us. In brief, we can do precisely as we choose—and we do. Nobody who has not had to live for nearly half a century by rule of thumbs, and more or less at the behest of others, can appreciate the gorgeously endless relief which is ours in this kind of life."[1]

HOBBIES AND OTHER INTERESTS: "I am a crank on the subject of antique or strange weapons. For nearly forty years I have been collecting them, slowly and at intervals, in many parts of the world. I am much more of an enthusiast than an expert along this line. But I have picked up a few things that are good."[2]

FOR MORE INFORMATION SEE: Grant M. Overton, "Where the Plot Thickens," in *When Winter Comes to Main Street*, G. H. Doran, 1922; Albert Payson Terhune, *To the Best of My Memory*, Harper, 1930; Albert Payson Terhune, *The Book of Sunnybank*, Harper & Brothers, 1934; *Junior Book of Authors*, edited by Kunitz and Haycraft, H. W. Wilson, 1934; *The Bert Terhune I Knew*, Harper, 1943; Loring H. Dodd, *Celebrities at Our Hearthside*, Dresser, 1959; R. H. Boyle, "Kind and Canny Canines," *Sports Illustrated*, January 15, 1968; Kurt Unkelbach, *Albert Payson Terhune: The Master of Sunnybank*, Charterhouse Books, 1972; Irving Litvag, *The Master of Sunnybank*, Harper, 1977.

Obituaries: *New York Times*, February 19, 1942; *Newsweek*, March 2, 1942; *Time*, March 2, 1942; *Wilson Library Bulletin*, April, 1942; *Current Biography Yearbook 1942*.

THOMAS, Lowell (Jackson), Jr. 1923-

PERSONAL: Born October 6, 1923, in London, Eng.; son of Lowell Thomas (the journalist) and Frances (Ryan) Thomas; married Mary Taylor Pryor, May 20, 1950; children: Anne Frazier, David Lowell. *Education:* Dartmouth College, B.A., 1948; Princeton University, graduate study, 1951-52. *Politics:* Republican. *Religion:* Protestant. *Home:* 7022 Tanaina Dr., Anchorage, Alaska 99502.

LOWELL THOMAS, JR.

CAREER: Fox Movietone News, assistant cameraman, South America, 1939, Bradford Washburn Alaskan mountaineering expedition, 1940; lecturer, 1946—; assistant economist and photographer with Max Weston Thornburg, Turkey, 1947, Iran, 1948; worked in film production, Iran, 1949; organized the Tibet expedition with his father, Lowell Thomas, Sr., 1949; Cinerama Inc., South America, Africa, and Asia, field work, 1951-52, assistant producer, 1952-54; with his wife, Mary, wrote and filmed their travels by a small plane through Europe, Africa, and the Middle East, x954-55; "Flight to Adventure" television series, National Broadcasting Co., producer, 1956; "High Adventure" television series, producer and writer, 1957-59; producer of several documentary films, including "Adaq, King of Alaskan Seas," 1960, a film on the University of Alaska, 1964, and a film on Arctic oil exploration for Atlantic-Richfield Co., 1969; member of the Rockwell Polar Flight (first flight around the world over both poles), 1965; author; Alaska state senator, 1967-75; lieutenant governor of Alaska, 1975—. President of the Western Alaska council of the Boy Scouts of America; member of the board of directors, Salvation Army, Anchorage Unit; member of the Alaska Chamber of Commerce. *Military service:* U.S. Army Air Forces, Southeast Training Command, 1943-45; became first lieutenant.

MEMBER: Screen Actors Guild, Aircraft Owners and Pilots Association, Delta Kappa Epsilon, Marco Polo Club, Explorers' Club and Dutch Treat Club (both New York City), Bohemian Club (San Francisco), Rotary Club and Press Club (both Anchorage). *Awards, honors:* D. Litt., Scottsbluff College, 1969.

WRITINGS: Out of this World: Across the Himalayas to Tibet, Greystone Press, 1950; (with wife, Mary P. Thomas) *Our Flight to Adventure,* Doubleday, 1956; *The Silent War in Tibet,* Doubleday, 1959, reprinted, Greenwood Press, 1973; *The Dalai Lama,* Duell, Sloan, 1961; (editor) *The Trail of Ninety-Eight,* Duell, Sloan, 1962; (editor with father, Lowell Thomas, Sr.) *More Great True Adventures,* Hawthorn, 1963; *Lowell Thomas Jr.'s Adventures in National Country: A Guide to Florida,* Popular Library, 1966; (with L. Thomas, Sr.) *Famous First Flights That Changed History,* Doubleday, 1968.

SIDELIGHTS: At the age of fifteen, Lowell Thomas, Jr. acquired a job as an assistant cameraman for the Fox Movietone News and embarked on a career that has taken him from South America to Alaska. The world traveler has written several books about his expeditions around the globe, but his most recent book, *Famous First Flights That Changed History,* highlights the adventures of some of the early pioneers of air travel. The book was written in collaboration with his father, Lowell Thomas, Sr., and covers events from the first flight over the English Channel in 1909 to the 1965 jet flight over both poles.

TOLMIE, Ken(neth Donald) 1941-

PERSONAL: Born September 18, 1941, in Halifax, Nova Scotia, Canada; son of Archibald (a factory manager) and Evelyn (Murray) Tolmie; married Ruth MacKenzie (a librarian), August 8, 1962; children: Sarah Katherine, Jane Marianna. *Education:* Mount Allison University, B.F.A. (honors), 1962. *Home:* 115 South St., RR3 Bridgetown, Nova Scotia, Canada B0S 1C0.

KEN TOLMIE

The little egg said to the frog-on-a-log, 'Can I be like you, sir?' ■ (From *A Tale of an Egg* by Ken Tolmie. Illustrated by the author.)

TOLMIE

CAREER: Artist, illustrator, and writer. Member of board of directors of INAX Instruments; past chairman of Visual Arts Ottawa. Has had one-man shows in Ottawa, Toronto, and Halifax, and group shows and exhibitions in England and New York; his work is represented in collections at the National Gallery of Canada, Montreal Museum of Fine Arts, and private collections in the United States, Canada, and Europe. *Member:* Canadian Artists Representation.

WRITINGS: A Tale of an Egg (self-illustrated juvenile), Oberon, 1975.

Illustrator: Stuart MacKinnon, *The Welder's Arc,* Oberon, 1969; Mary Alice Downie, *The Fairy from the Green Sea,* Oberon, 1978.

SIDELIGHTS: Tolmie has lived and worked in England and Spain. He lived in Ontario for ten years. After travelling for a year in Canada, searching for the right place to settle in, he and his family are now living in Nova Scotia, in the first-settled area in North America. He has bought a beautiful Victorian home, with ample studio facilities, where he plans to continue painting, and writing, and illustrating books. He enjoys the quiet beauty of rural and small-town Nova Scotia, and is pleased to be settled in an area inbred with a real sense of historical time past.

Tolmie is primarily a painter of compelling and realistic images in tempera, and has recently developed a strong interest in illustrating and writing books. He feels that illustrations in children's literature must be clear, must concentrate on es-

sentials, and must be of a genuinely artistic quality. Children have a compelling interest in the detail of an image, and are put off by indecision and vagueness in illustrations, or indeed in anything.

FOR MORE INFORMATION SEE: In Review, Canadian Books for Children, Autumn, 1976.

VIGNA, Judith 1936-

PERSONAL: Surname is pronounced *Veen*-ya; born April 27, 1936, in Gedney, England; came to the United States in 1958, naturalized citizen, 1968; daughter of John (a physician) and Audrey Stephenson (Brackenridge) Pankhurst; married Arnaldo Vigna, December, 1960 (separated). *Education:* Attended St. Martin's School of Art, 1956, and School of Visual Arts, 1960; student at Queens College of the City University of New York, 1973—. *Residence:* Whitestone, N.Y. *Agent:* Curtis Brown Ltd., 575 Madison Ave., New York, N.Y. 10022.

CAREER: Lincolnshire Standard, Boston, England, journalist and artist, 1953-55; Dorville House, London, England, public relations assistant, 1955-57; Henry Morgan Co., Montreal, Quebec, advertising copywriter, 1957-58; Young & Rubicam, Inc., New York, N.Y., copywriter, 1958-65; free-lance writer and illustrator, 1965—. *Member:* Authors Guild of Authors League of America.

But the Superslobs said, "You can't go home, Jonathan James. You are a Superslob, and you belong with us." ■ (From *The Little Boy Who Loved Dirt and Almost Became a Superslob* by Judith Vigna. Illustrated by the author.)

WRITINGS—Self-illustrated children's books: *Gregory's Stitches*, Albert Whitman, 1974; *The Little Boy Who Loved Dirt and Almost Became a Superslob*, Albert Whitman, 1975; *Couldn't We Have a Turtle Instead?*, Albert Whitman, 1975; *Everyone Goes as a Pumpkin*, Albert Whitman, 1977; *Anyhow, I'm Glad I Tried*, Albert Whitman, 1978.

WORK IN PROGRESS: Stories for children, with emphasis on everyday childhood problems.

SIDELIGHTS: "An addiction to books as a child in England—particularly those of Beatrix Potter and Kenneth Grahame—motivated me early on to write and illustrate children's books, but I did not realize that ambition until quite recently.

"My goal, in putting together a picture-book, is to approach common childhood problems such as a new baby or loss of a precious possession, with a humorous touch that can help a child over a painful experience. Most of the situations I present in my books are dug up from my own childhood—remembering uncomfortable feelings, minor calamities (that seemed major at the time!)—or overwhelming joy. In trying to keep in touch with a child's feelings, I find it helpful to remember that many of the emotions we experience as adults are enormously intensified in children. Always acknowledging the marvelous sense of humor children have, I try to combine these emotions with a bit of fun and whimsy.

"Courses in psychology, a special interest in art therapy, plus some volunteer work with emotionally-disturbed children, have contributed to my background."

HOBBIES AND OTHER INTERESTS: Portrait painting, music, skiing, books, travel.

JUDITH VIGNA

LEONARD VOSBURGH

VOSBURGH, Leonard (W.) 1912-

PERSONAL: Born September 23, 1912, in Yonkers, N.Y.; son of Fredrick S. (an advertising salesman) and Helene (Horne) Vosburgh; married Alberta May Ewen (a secretary), October 20, 1945. *Education:* Attended Pratt Institute, two years; Art Students League, two years. *Home and Office:* 62 Mountain Avenue, North Plainfield, N.J. 07060.

CAREER: Free-lance book illustrator. Worked ten years as a free-lance advertising artist before turning to book illustration. *Exhibitions:* National Academy and American Water Color Society, 1949; also did nineteen pictures and murals for the State of Indiana for the American Revolution Bicentennial Exhibit of George Rogers Clark, 1976. *Awards, honors:* Received the *New York Times* 100 Outstanding Books of the Year for: *Barnum: Showman of America*, 1957, *Chingo Smith of the Erie Canal*, 1958, *Billy Yank and Johnny Reb*, 1959, *Fear in the Forest*, 1960, *My Cousin Abe*, 1962; *Chingo Smith of the Erie Canal* was also a *Herald Tribune* Honor Winner, 1961.

ILLUSTRATOR: Erna Oleson Xan, *Home for Good*, Ives Washburn, 1952; Frank B. Latham, *The Fighting Quaker*, Aladdin Books, 1953; Samuel H. Adams, *The Erie Canal*, Random House, 1953; Frederick A. Lane, *A Flag for Lafayette*, Aladdin Books, 1955; Frank B. Latham, *The Law or the Gun*, Aladdin Books, 1955; Alida Sims Malkus, *At the Battle of Gettysburg*, Grosset, 1955; Val Gendron, *Outlaw Voyage*, World, 1955; Andre Norton, *Yankee Privateer*, World, 1955; Polly Angell, *Andy Jackson*, Aladdin Books,

1956; Zachary Ball and Myra Fowler, *Wilderness Teacher*, Junior Literary Guild, 1956; Miriam Gilbert, *Eli Whitney: Master Craftsman*, Abingdon, 1956; Lorena A. Hickok, *The Story of Franklin D. Roosevelt*, Grosset, 1956; Robert N. Webb, *Richard the Lionhearted*, Grosset, 1957; Helen Wells, *Barnum: Showman of America*, McKay, 1957; Barnett Spratt, *Toppy and the Circuit Rider*, Abingdon, 1957; Samuel H. Adams, *Chingo Smith of the Erie Canal*, Random House, 1958; J. A. Rickard and Clyde Inez Martin, *Along Our Way*, W. S. Benson, 1958; P. Edward Ernest, *The Family Album of Favorite Poems*, Grosset, 1959; Earl S. Miers, *Billy Yank and Johnny Reb*, Rand McNally, 1959; Alfred Steinberg, *Daniel Webster*, Putnam, 1959.

Richard Deming, *American Spies*, A. Whitman, 1960; A. Conan Doyle, *The Sign of the Four*, Hart, 1960; Anya Seton, *Washington Irving*, Ballantine, 1960; Earl S. Miers, *When Grant Met Lee at Appomattox*, Grosset, 1960; Fredrika S. Smith, *Courageous Comrades*, Rand McNally, 1960; Cateau DeLeeuw, *Fear in the Forest*, T. Nelson, 1960; Arthur A. Gladd, *The Saracen Steed*, Dodd, 1960; Haydn S. Pearson, *New England Flavor*, Norton, 1961; Anne Ford, *Davy Crockett*, Putnam, 1961; Fairfax Downey, *Guns for General Washington*, T. Nelson, 1961; John Bunyan, *The Pilgrim's Progress*, Grosset, 1961; Doran Hurley, *John Hughes: Eagle of the Church*, P. J. Kennedy, 1961; *Galleys East*, Dodd, 1961; Earl S. Miers, *The Civil War*, Grosset, 1961; Earl S. Miers, *Ride to War*, Rutgers University Press, 1961; Nan H. Agle and Frances A. Bacon, *The Lords Baltimore*, Holt, 1962; *Navy Style*, T. Nelson, 1962; A Conan Doyle, *The Sign of the Four*, Hart, 1962; Nina B. Baker, *Nickels and Dimes*, Science Research Associates, 1962; Sigmund A. Lavine, *The Hayloft Inventor*, Science Research Associates, 1962; Robert N. Webb, *Florence Nightingale*, Grosset, 1962; Cateau De Leeuw, *The Proving Years*, T. Nelson, 1962; Aileen Fisher, *My Cousin Abe*, T. Nelson, 1962.

Pirates in Petticoats, McKay, 1963; *Andersen's Fairy Tales*, Grosset, 1963; Irving Robbin, *Guns*, Grosset, 1963; Felix Sutton, *The American Revolution*, Grosset, 1963; *Winning of the West*, Grosset, 1963; Harry Golden, *Forgotten Pioneers*, 1963; Cyril Harris, *Northern Exposure*, Norton, 1963; Walter Havinghurst, *Proud Prisoner*, Colonial Williamsburg, 1964; C. Virgil Jones, *Birth of Liberty: The Story of the James River*, Holt, 1964; Charles M. Wilson, *The Great Turkey Drive*, McKay, 1964; J. A. Rickard and Clyde Inez Martin, *Under Texas Skies*, W. S. Benson, 1964; Charles M. Wilson, *Crown Point: The Destiny Road*, McKay, 1965; Hertha Pauli, *Gateway to America*, McKay, 1965; Felix Sutton, *Discoverers of America*, Grosset, 1965; Lillian Budd, *Calico Row*, A. Whitman, 1965; Felix Sutton, *North American Indians*, Grosset, 1965; Irving Robbin, *Basic Inventions*, Grosset, 1965; Al Hine (editor), *This Land is Mine: An Anthology of American Vets*, Lippincott, 1965; Robert E. Alter, *Heroes in Blue and Gray*, A. Whitman, 1965; A. L. Todd, *Richard Montgomery*, McKay, 1966; Margaret Stanley-Wrench, *The Silver King*, Hawthorn, 1966; Lillian Budd, *Larry*, McKay, 1966.

Haydn S. Pearson, *The New England Year*, Norton, 1967; Allan Dwight, *To the Walls of Cartagena*, Colonial Williamsburg, 1967; Norah Smaridge, *The Tallest Lady in the World*, Hawthorn, 1967; Helen Marquis, *The Longest Day of the Year*, Meredith, 1969; Jessie Wiley Voils, *Summer on the Salt Fork*, Meredith, 1969; David Grubb, *The Golden Sickle*, World, 1969; Sol Holt and John R. O'Connor, *Exploring World History*, Globe, 1969; *The Americans*, American Heritage, 1970; *The Straggles*, Junior Literary Guild,

How we rode the next three days! First we thought of driving the cattle toward Harrisburg, but then we figured that was making ourselves Reb bait, so we looked for a wooded place in the other direction—toward Hanover. ■ (From *Billy Yank and Johnny Reb: How They Fought and Made Up* by Earl Schenck Miers. Illustrated by Leonard Vosburgh.)

The canal itself shared the prosperity. Every added mile brought in more tolls. ■ (From *The Erie Canal* by Samuel Hopkins Adams. Illustrated by Leonard Vosburgh.)

1970; Adele de Leeuw, *The Boy with Wings,* Nautilus, 1971; Ethelyn M. Parkinson, *Never Go Anywhere with Digby,* Abingdon, 1971; Ralph J. Kane and Jeffry A. Glover, *Inquiry U.S.A.,* Globe, 1971; *History of Texas: Texans All,* W. S. Benson, 1973. Illustrations have appeared in *Jack & Jill.*

WORK IN PROGRESS: Robert's Wonderful World, for the Methodist Publishing House, Nashville, Tenn.

SIDELIGHTS: "Born in Yonkers, New York, my early years were spent mostly in travel, father being an efficiency engineer. (Later on my father became an advertising salesman.) Five to six months was the longest we stayed in any one place. On reaching a new place, the first thing I did was to visit the local livery stables, these to me were the most interesting places, as all sorts of colorful characters hung around. I would pick up all kinds of discarded things, such as horse shoes, parts of wagons and one day carried a huge horse collar through the lobby of a hotel amid the stares of the people. For a time we lived near the Ohio River and remember very vividly the stern-wheel boats paddling back and forth. After ten years of traveling, we settled in North Plainfield, New Jersey where I attended the local schools. My grandparents lived in Plainfield and my Grandfather Horne and I had great talks together, he being a great reader, banjo player and conversationalist. Most of our chats were

of his boyhood in New York when 14th Street was once way uptown, stage coaches and hot potatoe men, etc.

"During summer vacations I worked on a farm in Palatine Bridge, New York. Living with my Aunt Susie, I have many wonderful memories of her and of riding on top of loads of hay, and looking down over the beautiful Mohawk Valley. My father's people settled in this section of the valley before the Revolutionary War. Peter Walden, an ancestor of mine, was given a grant of land by King George for being a faithful soldier. At the start of the Revolutionary War he joined the Patriots and fought for two years. In one skirmish he was scalped by one of Brandt's Indians and left for dead, but he lived to a great age, always wearing a little leather cap.

"The Mohawk Valley is rich in the history of Indians, Western migration, Erie Canal and the Revolution. My father as a boy often plowed up graves with their weapons, pottery, etc. Leaving school, I secured a position as a messenger for a lithograph firm in New York. Saw art work and met artists. At home I tried to copy their work with discouraging results. I needed professional training. Saved my money and entered Pratt Institute and afterwards Art Students League. Studied illustration under Harvey Dunn and Walter Biggs. Did all kinds of advertising art work for ten years, felt I was not progressing and asked myself what type of work would I enjoy doing the most. Here the experiences I had as a boy showed the direction to take. The past twenty-two years I have specialized in doing period and historical illustrations. At the last count I had illustrated ninety-one period and historical books. Have exhibited water colors at the National Academy and the American Water Color Society in New York City.

"I have been a small boat sailor for a number of years and in 1970 I designed a gaft-rigged cruising sloop and had it built by Curtis Applegarth in Oxford, Maryland."

FOR MORE INFORMATION SEE: Home News, North Plainfield, N.J., November 14, 1971.

WALDMAN, Bruce   1949-

PERSONAL: Born November 14, 1949, in the Bronx, N.Y.; son of Abraham (a businessman) and Jessie (Lea) Waldman. *Education:* Philadelphia College of Art, B.F.A., 1972; University of Buffalo, M.F.A., 1976. *Home:* 71 Chestnut Oval, Orangeburg, N.Y. 10962. *Office:* 7 East 17th St., New York, N.Y. 10003.

CAREER: Concerned Ecumenical Council of Greater Buffalo, Buffalo, N.Y., teacher, 1976; Lower Eastside Print Shop, New York, N.Y., teacher, 1977; Rockland Community College, Rockland, N.Y., teacher, 1977. *Exhibitions:* Rockland Foundation for the Arts, Rockland, N.Y., 1974-75; Niagara Community College, Niagara, N.Y., 1976; Lincoln Center for the Performing Arts, New York, N.Y., 1977; Metropolitan Museum of Art, New York, N.Y., 1977; 17th Street Gallery, New York, N.Y., 1977; Lower East

(From *Skunks* by Bernice Kohn Hunt. Illustrated by Bruce Waldman.)

Side Print Shop, New York, N.Y., 1977. *Member:* Society of Illustrators. *Awards, honors:* Grant for an animated film, Philadelphia College of Art; grant from the New York State Regence; grant for a three-man exhibit at Niagara Community College.

ILLUSTRATOR: B. Hunt, *Pigeons,* Prentice, 1972; B. Hunt, *Skunks,* Prentice, 1973; James Hoetker, *Hero Songs,* Scholastic, 1973; James Hoetker, *Epic Student Log,* Scholastic, 1973; Irving Stone, *The Agony and the Ecstacy,* Franklin Library, 1977. Also illustrated several short stories by Sir Arthur Conan Doyle and Edgar Allen Poe.

WORK IN PROGRESS: Illustrator of Arthur Miller, *Death of a Salesman,* for Penguin; illustrator of Arthur Miller, *The Crucible,* for Penguin.

SIDELIGHTS: "My interest in art started far back into my childhood. I've always drawn, and was encouraged to do so by my parents. Both my brother and sister are illustrators and my aunt is a printmaker."

WEIHS, Erika   1917-

PERSONAL: Surname pronounced wise; born November 4, 1917, in Vienna, Austria; daughter of Arthur S. (a woodworker and businessman) and Vilma (Friedman; a milliner) Foster; married Kurt Weihs (an artist; art director), June 6, 1942; children: Tom, John. *Education:* Attended Graphische Lehr und Versuchsanstalt, Vienna, Austria, 1934-

BRUCE WALDMAN

37; The Leonardo da Vince Art School, New York, N.Y. *Home:* 113 West 11th Street, New York, N.Y. 10011. *Agent:* Nettie King, 330 Woodland Place, Leonia, N.J. 07605. *Studio:* 24 East 21st Street, New York, N.Y. 10010.

CAREER: Painter; illustrator. Herbert Dubler Inc., New York, N.Y., designer of greeting cards (published under "ars sacra"), 1940-42; free-lance painter and illustrator, 1942—. *Exhibitions*—One-woman shows: Roko Gallery, New York, N.Y., 1950, 1961, 1963, 1967, 1970, 1974, 1976; Marist College, Poughkeepsie, N.Y., 1975; Jefferson Market Public Library, Greenwich, New York, N.Y., 1977; New York University, Loeb Student Center, New York, N.Y., 1972 (three-woman show), 1975 (two-woman show). Group shows: Tulsa Museum of Art, Tulsa, Okla.; Whitney Museum of American Art, New York, N.Y.; College of Medicine and Dentistry of New Jersey, Newark, N.J.; Nassau Community College, N.Y.; Georgetown College, Georgetown, Ky.; Tuskegee Institute, Tuskegee, Ala.; Ball State University, Muncie, Ind.; Wesleyan College, Macon, Ga.; Purdue University, Lafayette, Ind.; Carnegie Institute, Pittsburgh, Pa.; State Capitol Building, Albany, N.Y.; City Center, New York, N.Y.; Painters and Sculptors Society of New Jersey, Jersey City Museum and New York, N.Y.; American Veterans Society of Artists, New York, N.Y.; National Society of Painters, New York, N.Y.; Art Center of the Oranges, N.J.; Long Island Art League, N.Y.; Greater Fall River Art Association, Mass.; Art Association of Newport, R.I.; Village Art Center, New York, N.Y.; Allied Artists of America, New York, N.Y.; North Shore Community Arts Center, N.Y.; Lovisco Gallery, New York, N.Y., and Gloucester, Mass.; Community Gallery, New York, N.Y.; Quinata Gallery, Nantucket, Mass.; Katonah Gallery, Katonah, N.Y.; Dallas North Gallery, Dallas, Tex.; Golden Door Gallery, Pa.; Hinkley and Broehel Gallery, New York, N.Y.; Dulin Gallery, Tenn.; Obelisk Gallery, Washington, D.C. Exhibiting member of the National Association of Women Artists (traveling and New York, N.Y. exhibitions) and Audubon Artists. Works are in the permanent collections of Phoenix Museum of Art, Phoenix, Ariz.; The Laura Musser Museum, Muscatine, Iowa. *Member:* Audubon Artists, National Association of Woman Artists (oil jury chairperson, 1976, 1977), Artists Equity Association of N.Y., Inc. *Awards, honors:* National Asso-

(From *Count the Cats* by Erika Weihs. Illustrated by the author.)

ciation of Women Artists, Lillian Cotton Memorial Prize, 1971; Painters and Sculptors Society of New Jersey, 1971; National Association of Women Artists, Dr. Samuel Gelband Memorial Prize, 1978.

WRITINGS—Self-illustrated: *Count the Cats,* Doubleday, 1976.

Illustrator: *The Rolling Pancake and Other Nursery Tales,* L. B. Fischer, 1945; Alice Schneider (editor), *Tales of Many Lands,* Citadel, 1946; Johanna Spyri (author), Florence Hayes (adapter), *Heidi,* Random House, 1946; Florence Horn Bryan, *Susan B. Anthony,* Messner, 1947; Harpor, *The Magic Cricket Book,* Capitol, 1948; Ben Ross Berenberg, *The Snowman Book of Nursery Rhymes,* Capitol, 1948; Ben Ross Berenberg, *The Big Clock Book,* Capitol, 1949; Joseph Schrank, *The Cello in the Belly of the Plane,* Watts, 1954; Rudyard Kipling, *How the Camel Got His Hump,* Rand McNally, 1955; (co-illustrator) Carol Lane (compiler), *The Happy Hour Story Book,* Hart Book Co., 1955; Libby M. Klaperman, *Jeremy and the Torah,* Behrman House, 1956; Rudyard Kipling, *How the Rhinoceros*

Got His Skin, Rand McNally, 1956; Marion Belden Cook, *Terry's Ferry,* Dutton, 1957; *ABC,* A. Whitman, 1959.

Jane K. Lansing, *The Roly-Poly Policeman,* Hart Book Co., 1965; Edith G. Stull, *Good-Bye, Hello,* L. W. Singer Co., 1967; Shirley Rousseau Murphy, *The Sand Ponies,* Viking, 1967; Te Ata, *Indian Tales,* L. W. Singer Co., 1968; Michael Baker, *The Mountain and the Summerstars,* Harcourt, 1969; Harry Gersh, *When a Jew Celebrates,* Behrman House, 1971; Jules Harlow (editor) *Lessons From Our Living Past,* Behrman House, 1972; Seymour Rossel, *When a Jew Prays,* Behrman House, 1973; Francine Prose, *Stories From Our Living Past,* Behrman House, 1974; Seymour Rossel, *When a Jew Seeks Wisdom,* Behrman House, 1975; *Exploring Our Living Past,* Behrman House, 1978. Contributed illustrations to *The Book of Knowledge Annual,* The Grolier Society, 1947, 1958; *Busy Harbors,* Singer/Random House Literature Series, 1969; and magazines.

SIDELIGHTS: "I like to be in complete control over the visual part of a book. That is, be handed all the pertinent information plus the type-galleys and make a dummy with the

ERIKA WEIHS

type pasted in position and the illustrations sketched. I find this part the most exciting. Doing the finished art, especially that done in color separations, often becomes tedious.

"When I do illustrations in full color, I usually use acrylics or poster color. For the *Count the Cats* book I used children's crayons. Other books I have done in pen and ink, Wolff's carbon-pencil, guache, scratchboard. I feel that each story requires a different approach and technique and using a different medium changes one's style.

"Generally my style is flat, two dimensional. Although I am fascinated with unexpected results I get when I, for instance, do a monoprint, I really prefer a planned approach.

"I liked to draw as a young child and had encouragement from my mother and father and teachers throughout my school years. Going on to art school was a logical follow up.

"I was not a student of any one artist. Throughout my student years I was most moved by the work of Käthe Kollwitz. I also liked Egyptian Art. When I first came to the United States, it was Ben Shahn who most impressed me with his political paintings. I need to be moved emotionally, aesthetically, and/or intellectually by art to appreciate it. I am sure everything I ever saw has influenced me.

"I left Austria six months after the Nazi takeover, lived in England for over a year, also in Canada. But aside from that, I have hardly traveled, although I would love to.

"Periodically, I have a great need to be in the country; I need nature to restore me. I have plants I grow in the house, during the summer tomatoes and herbs on top of the roof (I lost my terrace to a demolition crew). My dream is to live in the country June through September, then to return to New York City for the balance of the year. I love the City. I love

the theater, contemporary dance, I am addicted to WBAI radio. My entering art school was preceded by my flunking mathematics, and Latin I believe . . . all this happened in a different place, at a different time—so very long ago."

WILDER, Laura Ingalls   1867-1957

PERSONAL: Born February 7, 1867, at Lake Pepin, Wisconsin; died January 10, 1957, in Mansfield, Missouri; buried in Mansfield Cemetery; daughter of Charles Philip and Caroline Lake (Quiner) Ingalls; married Almanzo J. Wilder, August 25, 1885; children: Rose Wilder Lane (an author). *Education:* Attended schools in Minnesota and the Dakota Territory. *Home:* Rocky Ridge Farm, Mansfield, Missouri.

CAREER: Teacher, beginning 1882; author, beginning 1926. *Awards, honors:* Runner-up for the Newbery Medal, 1938, for *On the Banks of Plum Creek,* and 1941, for *The Long Winter;* Pacific Northwest Library Association Young Readers' Choice Award, 1942, for *By the Shores of Silver Lake; Book World* Children's Spring Book Festival Award, 1943, for *These Happy Golden Years;* Laura Ingalls Wilder Award presented by the American Library Association, 1943, for the "Little House" books. (Since 1960 this award in her honor is made every five years to an outstanding author or illustrator of children's books.)

WRITINGS—All novels based on her own life; all published by Harper, except as noted: *Little House in the Big*

I was 2 years 4 months old when this picture was taken in April, 1889. I remember the picture-taking well, was impressed by the photographer's stupid pretense that there was a little bird in the camera. The photographer also kept putting my right hand on top of the left, and I kept changing them back because I wanted my carnelian ring to show. And in the end I won out. ■ (From *On the Way Home* by Laura Ingalls Wilder.)

(From the television series "Little House on the Prairie," starring Michael Landon and Melissa Sue Anderson. Produced by NBC.)

Woods (illustrated by Helen Sewell), 1932; *Farmer Boy* (illustrated by Sewell), 1933; *Little House on the Prairie* (illustrated by Sewell), 1935; *On the Banks of Plum Creek* (illustrated by Helen Sewell and Mildred Boyle), 1937; *By the Shores of Silver Lake* (illustrated by Sewell and Boyle), 1939, special edition, E. M. Hale, 1956; *The Long Winter* (illustrated by Sewell and Boyle), 1940; *Little Town on the Prairie* (illustrated by Sewell and Boyle), 1941; *These Happy Golden Years* (illustrated by Sewell and Boyle), 1943. Each of the above titles was published by Harper in a new edition, illustrated by Garth Williams, in 1953.

On the Way Home: The Diary of a Trip from South Dakota to Mansfield, Missouri, in 1894, edited by Rose Wilder Lane, Harper, 1962; *The First Four Years* (illustrated by Garth Williams), Harper, 1971; *West from Home: Letters of Laura Ingalls Wilder, San Francisco, 1915,* edited by Roger L. MacBride, Harper, 1974.

Contributor of articles to various magazines, including *Country Gentleman* and *McCall's.* Editor of the *Missouri Realist* for twelve years.

ADAPTATIONS—Television: "Little House on the Prairie" was a series for N.B.C. starring Michael Landon.

Recordings: "Little House in the Big Woods" was recorded by Julie Harris for Pathways of Sound, 1976.

SIDELIGHTS: **February 7, 1867.** Born in a log cabin at Lake Pepin, Wisconsin. "Bringing home the cows is the childhood memory that oftenest recurs to me. I think it is because the mind of a child is peculiarly attuned to the beauties of nature and the voices of the wildwood and the impression they made was deep.

"I am sure old Mother Nature talked to me in all the languages she knew when, as a child, I loitered along the cow paths forgetful of milking time and stern parents waiting, while I gathered wild flowers, waded in the creek, watched the squirrels hastening to their homes in the tree tops and listened to the sleepy twitterings of the birds.

"Many a time, instead of me finding the cows, they on their journey home unurged found me and took me home with them.

"I have never lost my childhood's delight in going after the cows. I still slip away from the other things for the sake of the walk through the pasture, down along the creek and over the hill to the farthest corner where the cows are usually found. . . . The voices of nature do not speak so plainly to us as we grow older, but I think it is because, in our busy lives, we neglect her until we grow out of sympathy. Our ears and eyes grow dull and beauties are lost to us that we should still enjoy.

"Life was not intended to be simply a round of work, no matter how interesting and important that work may be. A moment's pause to watch the glory of a sunrise or a sunset is soul-satisfying, while a bird's song will set the steps to

Swarms of little white butterflies hovered over the path. A dragon-fly with gauzy wings swiftly chased a gnat. On the stubble of cut grass the striped gophers were scampering. All at once they ran for their lives and dived into their holes. Then Laura saw a swift shadow and looked up at the eyes and the claws of a hawk overhead. But all the little gophers were safe in their holes. ■ (From *The Long Winter* by Laura Ingalls Wilder. Illustrated by Garth Williams.)

music all day long.'' [Donald Zochert, *Laura: The Life of Laura Ingalls Wilder,* Henry Regnery, 1976.[1]]

1870. Family moved west through Kansas, Minnesota, and Dakota Territory, homesteading. Finally settled in De Smet, South Dakota. ''My mother did not have to go out to work; she was married, my father was the provider. He got a day's work here and there; he could drive a team, he could carpenter, or paint, or spell a storekeeper at dinnertime, and once he was on a jury, downtown. My mother and I slept at Grandma's then, every night; the jury was kept under lock and key and my father could not come home. But he got his keep and two dollars every day for five straight weeks and he brought back all that money.

''I was seven years old and in the Second Reader at school but I had read the Third Reader and the Fourth and *Robinson Crusoe* and *Gulliver's Travels.* The Chicago *Inter-Ocean* came every week and after the grown-ups had read it, I did, I did not understand all of it, but I read it.'' [Laura Ingalls Wilder, *On the Way Home: The Diary of a Trip from South Dakota to Mansfield, Missouri, in 1884,* Harper, 1962.[2]]

October, 1880. The first blizzard of *The Long Winter.*

1882. Began to teach at the Bouchie School outside of De Smet at age fifteen. ''Even for fifteen, [I] was small; and now [I] felt very small.'' [Laura Ingalls Wilder, *These Happy Golden Years,* Harper, 1943.[3]]

Became engaged to Almanzo Wilder.

August 25, 1885. Married Almanzo James Wilder in De Smet. ''In the first few years of our marriage we experienced complete destruction of our crops by hail storms; the loss of our little house by fire; the loss of Almanzo's health from a stroke of paralysis and then the drought years of 1892-93-94.'' [From ''A Letter from Laura Ingalls Wilder,'' in *The Horn Book Magazine,* December, 1953.[4]]

''How heart breaking it was to watch the grain we had sown with such high hopes wither and yellow in the hot winds! And it was back breaking as well as heart breaking to carry water from the well to my garden and see it dry up despite all my efforts.

''I said at the time that hereafter I would sow the seed, but the Lord would give the increase if there was any, for I could not do my work and that of Providence also by sending rain upon the gardens of the just or the unjust.''[1]

December 5, 1886. Birth of her only child, Rose.

July 17, 1894. Family moved from South Dakota after severe droughts and the Panic of 1893 to Mansfield, Missouri, a 650-mile journey that lasted nearly six weeks.

''**July 23, 1894.** We crossed the James River and in twenty minutes we reached the top of the bluffs on the other side. We all stopped and looked back at the scene and I wished for an artist's hand or a poet's brain or even to be able to tell in good plain prose how beautiful it was. If I had been the Indians I would have scalped more white folks before I ever would have left it.

''I got my revolver fixed, then we had to spend so much time hunting for feed all over town that Mr. Cooley got to the ferry first.

''[**July 24, 1894**]. What is it about water that always affects a person? I never see a great river or lake but I think how I would like to see a world made and watch it through all its changes.

''Manly said he would just as soon own the whole of Nebraska as not, if it were fenced. Judging from all he has ever seen of the state it might do for pasture if he did not keep much stock. So far Nebraska reminds me of Lydia Locket's pocket, nothing in it, nothing on it, only binding round it. . . .

''The Hens are laying yet. Temperature 110°.

''**August 7.** On the road at 7:30, we crossed the line into Kansas at 10:28¼ exactly.

''[**August 14, 1894**]. We stopped to eat dinner about a mile from Topeka, then drove on through the city. There are a great many colored people in and around it. In North Topeka the street cars are electric, in South Topeka they are motor cars.

"The streets are asphaltum pavement and it is lovely to drive on, so soft and quiet that it doesn't seem real. It gives like rubber to the horses' feet. The caulks on their shoes make dents in it and slowly the dents fill up till the place is smooth again.

"**August 15.** Started at 7:20. Found a little black-and-tan dog in the road, lost. He is skin and bones, must have been starving, and is afraid of us. We stopped at several houses to ask, but nobody knew where he belonged so we are taking him along. The children delight to feed him milk. We have named him Fido.

"The Sante Fe Railroad hospital is in the north edge of North Ottawa, a large brick building. It looks very clean. In South Ottawa there is a handsome college building made of the native stone. In all the towns now there are many colored people.

"[**August 21**]. The country around Fort Scott looks like it might be a very good country. Crops are good where there are any, but there is lots of idle land and many places are gone bad. It seems that the people are shiftless; but you never can tell.

"A man said this country is worthless, and when Manly said that it looked to him like good land, he said, 'Oh yes, the land will raise anything that's planted but if you can't sell what you raise for enough to pay back the cost of raising it, what's the land worth?'

"[**August 22**]. We met seven emigrant wagons leaving Missouri. One family had a red bird, a mocking bird, and lot of canaries in cages hung under the canvas in the wagon with them. We had quite a chat and heard the mockingbird sing. We camped by a house in the woods.

"[**August 25**]. Well, we are in the Ozarks at last, just in the beginning of them, and they are beautiful. We passed along the foot of some hills and could look up their sides. The trees and rocks are lovely. Manly says we could almost live on the looks of them.

"We stopped for dinner just before we came to the prettiest part, by the side of a swiftly running stream, Turnback River. We forded it, through the shallow water all rippling and sparking.

"**August 29.** Left camp at 7:10. We are driving along a lively road through the woods, we are shaded by oak trees. The farther we go, the more we like this country. Parts of Nebraska and Kansas are well enough but Missouri is simply glorious. There Manly interrupted me to say, 'This is beautiful country.'

"They told him of a forty he can buy for $400, all cleared and into grass except five acres of woods and with a good ever-flowing spring, a comfortable log house and a barn.

"[**August 30, 1894**]. Some covered wagons came up behind us and we came up behind some ahead, all the teams going slowly holding back down hill and pulling up hill. At 11:30 we came into Mansfield in a long line of ten emigrant wagons."[2]

They settled in Mansfield at Rocky Ridge Farm, her final home. "We arrived in Mansfield, Missouri, with enough money to make payment on a rough, rocky forty acres of land and a little left to buy our food for a time. The only

It was a beautiful buggy, so black and shining, with glossy red spokes in the wheels. The seat was wide; at either end of it gleaming black supports slanted backward to the folded-down top behind, and the seat had a lazy-back, cushioned. Laura had never before been in a buggy so luxurious. ■ (From *These Happy Golden Years* by Laura Ingalls Wilder. Illustrated by Garth Williams.)

building on the land was a one-room log cabin with a rock fireplace, one door but no window, when the door was closed light came in between the logs of the walls where the mud chinking had fallen out. We lived there a year.

"Almanzo had recovered from the stroke but was not strong. He changed work with neighbors to build a log bar for his horses and a henhouse for a few hens."[4]

Spring, 1895. "In the Spring we planted a garden and together we cleared land of timber. I never could use an ax but I could handle one end of a cross-cut saw and pile brush ready to burn. Almanzo made rails and stove wood out of the trees we cut down. With the rails he fenced the land we cleared; the stove I hoed in the garden and tended my hens. We sold eggs and potatoes from our new-ground planting besides the wood and when we were able to buy a cow and a little pig we thought we were rich.

"After that it was much easier. We worked and saved from year to year, adding to our land until we owned 200 acres well improved; a fine herd of cows; good hogs and the best laying flock of hens in the country.

He was looking toward her. The wind stirred his fur and the moonlight seemed to run in and out of it.
■ (From *By the Shores of Silver Lake* by Laura Ingalls Wilder. Pictures by Garth Williams.)

"These years were not all filled with work. Rose walked three-quarters of a mile to school the second year and after and her schoolmates visited her on Saturdays. She and I played along the little creek near the house. We tamed the wild birds and squirrels; picked wild flowers and berries. Almanzo and I often went horseback riding over the hills and through the woods. And always we had our papers and books from the school library for reading in the evenings and on Sunday afternoons."[4]

"At long last I am beginning to learn that it is the sweet, simple things of life which are the real ones. . . . I believe we would be happier to have a personal revolution in our individual lives and go back to simpler living and more direct thinking. It is the simple things of life that make living worth while, the sweet fundamental things such as love and duty, work and rest and living close to nature.

"Life is complicated; people hurry and seem helpless. Notice the faces of the people who rush by on the streets or on our country roads. They nearly all have a strained, harassed look and any one you meet will tell you there is no time for anything anymore.

"The true way to live is to enjoy every moment as it passes and surely it is in the everyday things around us that the beauty of life lies. A Good New Year's resolution for all of us to make: To simplify our lives as much as possible."[1]

August 21, 1915. Began a trip from Mansfield to San Francisco to visit daughter, Rose, now a reporter and to see the Panama-Pacific International Exposition celebrating the opening of the Panama Canal.

"[**August 22, 1915**]. I sat all on the way [on the train] with a St. Louis German who smelled of beer and said V instead of W, but he was very kind and treated me to peaches and in the night it got cold and he woke me up, laying his extra coat very softly over me. He was old and gray-headed and a perfect gentleman. I'm going to find everyone kind and all the help I need, as usual.

"We should be in Denver but we are 198 miles away. Four hours and fifteen minutes late, but trying our best to make up the time. . . .

"[**August 23, 1915**]. It is queer-looking country, great hills of sand with the grass so thin over it that the sand shows through. Sand cliffs . . . and clumps of willows and cottonwoods along the river but not a tree anywhere else, just the sand hills rolling across in every direction. It must be the big ranch country. Every once in a while there will be a house and a barn and a windmill with corrals near. I can see bunches of horses and cattle farther away and bunches of calves nearer the barns. I counted fifty little calves in one bunch and there have been larger ones.

"All yesterday there was only one other woman in the car and she had her berth made up and stayed in it. There were three men. I asked one of them if he knew just where we were and so we got to talking. . . .

"The range is fenced up, you know. The land is so *flat*. This lawyer from Nebraska says it is *beautiful* and the old Frenchman and I smile at each other. He thinks it looks like a great country but not pretty. I don't like the lawyer chap even if he is a graduate of Harvard as he says. He talks too much with his mouth and takes much for granted. Sat down in the seat with me without being asked. I've frozen him out and my Frenchman has shook him and is talking with a very nice boy about the trip out of Denver. The Frenchman is on his way to San Francisco but stops over at Denver, while I go on. He was in Belgium just before the war and saw the Cathedral of Rheims, the one the Germans destroyed, you know, and that famous stained rose window that can never be replaced. He is about 75 years old and has told me of his wife who is a New Orleans Frenchwoman, and his mother who made several trips from New Orleans to Europe in sailing vessels when she was a girl.

"Oh, Dr. Fuson said to get me a pair of glasses for a dollar that would magnify so I could read while I'm away and when I come back he'll take me to the oculist that does his work and have him fix my eyes up right. . . .

"[**August 29, 1915**]. At Land's End I had my first view of the Pacific Ocean. To say it is beautiful does not half ex-

(From *These Happy Golden Years* by Laura Ingalls Wilder. Illustrated by Garth Williams.)

press it. It is simply beyond words. The water is such a deep wonderful blue and the sound of the waves breaking on the beach and their whisper as they flow back is something to dream about.

"We went down on the beach where the waves were breaking. There were crowds of people there and some of them were wading. I wanted to wade. Rose said she never had but she would, so we took off our shoes and stockings and left them on the warm sand . . . and went out to meet the waves. . . .

"The salt water tingled my feet and made them feel so good all the rest of the day, and just to think, the same water that bathes the shores of China and Japan came clear across the ocean and bathed my feet. In other words, I have washed my feet in the Pacific Ocean.

"The ocean is not ugly. It is beautiful and wonderful. You know I have never cared for cities but San Francisco is simply the most beautiful thing." [*West from Home: Letters of Laura Ingalls Wilder to Almanzo Wilder,* Harper, 1915.[5]]

She wrote her husband: "[**September 4, 1915**]. There is one building and courts that the city is planning to keep for a museum and park. [The Palace of Fine Arts, by the California architect Bernard Maybeck, is still a showplace at the San Francisco Marina.] This is where the most wonderful statuary is grouped along the walk and against the walls. 'The Pioneer Mother' is one—a life-size group on a pedestal so one looks up to it. A woman in a sunbonnet, of course pushed back to show her face, with her sleeves pushed up, guiding a boy and girl before her and sheltering

Photograph of Laura Ingalls Wilder, about two years after her stay in San Francisco.

and protecting them with her arms and pointing the way westward. It is wonderful and so true in detail. The shoe exposed is large and heavy and I'd swear it had been half-soled.

"[**September 13, 1915**]. . . . I do want to do a little writing with Rose to get the hang of it a little better so I can write something that perhaps I can sell.

"Don't buy the horse unless you are sure it is gentle. I do not want you hurt while I am gone or any other time for that matter. Could you get it on trial? What about getting a horse at a sale? . . .

"I am going to do the things I absolutely must do before I come home . . . such as going over some of my copy with Rose and going out to the Fair a couple more times, and then I am coming home. Rose is very busy with her copy and the house and all, so we do not accomplish much in a day. I am doing what she will let me to help me and to go play at the Fair with me. I am anxious to get back and take charge of the hens again. Believe me, there is no place like the country to live and I have not heard of anything so far that would lead me to give up Rocky Ridge for any other place.

"I want to go to Petaluma and see the chicken farm but that will cost something and I may not do that. Gee! It will be good to get busy again on my job.

The Wilders shortly after their marriage.

LAURA INGALLS WILDER

A long time ago, when all the grandfathers and grandmothers of today were little boys and little girls or very small babies, or perhaps not even born, Pa and Ma and Mary and Laura and Baby Carrie left their little house in the Big Woods of Wisconsin. ■ (From *Little House on the Prairie* by Laura Ingalls Wilder. Illustrated by Garth Williams.)

"[**September 21, 1915**]. . . . We came back through Butcher Town and passed the China Basin and up town again where we stopped at a moving picture show and saw Charlie Chaplin, who is horrid. I mean we saw him act in the pictures.

"The foghorn on Alcatraz is the most lonesome sound I ever heard and I don't see how the prisoners on the island stand it.

"Rose is running around town getting the material together for another story and I have just come back from seeing the Germans capture Przemys in a moving picture theater. The pictures are true, being actually taken on the ground. It is horrible because it looks so implacable, so absolutely without mercy.

"I am being as careful as I can and I am not for a minute losing sight of the difficulties at home or what I came for. Rose and I are blocking out a story of the Ozarks for me to finish when I get home. If I can only make it sell, it ought to help a lot and besides, I am learning so that I can write others for the magazines. If I can only get started at that, it will sell for a good deal more than farm stuff. We are slow about it, for Rose has to do the work that draws her pay. I do the housework so that she will have time to help me with my learning to write and to go with me to see things that I must see before I go away.

"I do enjoy being with Rose but I am so homesick it hurts. Rose has worked so hard to save the money to get me out for the visit that it seems a shame to leave before my ticket expires, but I am going to try and get things done so that I can come home the middle of October. . . .

"[**September 28, 1915**]. I am going to see the land around Mill Valley and find out all I can about it. Then if I come home by way of Los Angeles I will see about the country there, and at Pasadena, but I truly believe that when I come home and talk it all over with you we will decide to be satisfied where we are and figure out some way to cut down our work and retire right there. Gillette is trying to make me see how we could come out here and do scientific farming on a couple of acres at a great deal more profit, but we would have it all to learn and we are rather old dogs to learn new tricks, especially as we do not have to do so. The more I see here the more I think that I will come home and put all my attention on the chickens.

"I am getting some pointers on how to handle more of them for of course there will need to be more in order to get much from it, but if I can make a $1 a year on a hen there, why be to all the trouble to move out here and learn new conditions when that is about all they make here?

"Rose gave a little tea party for me yesterday, just a few of the girls and women who work on the Bulletin and who write. If you should see on the Margin of Life page a series of little stories, 'The People in Our Apartment House,' you may read them knowing that they are *true*. Rose is writing them and the 'little artist girl who lives in the basement' [Later to become Berta Hader, author-illustrator, with her husband, of children's books] makes the pictures. I like Rose's women friends very much. The men at the Bulletin office are only acquaintances. Some of them are very pleasant to meet and some I dislike very much. . . .

"[**September 29, 1915**]. The Australian exhibit was mostly wool and minerals. The New Zealand Building was near. Their exhibit was wood and woolen goods and moving pictures showing harvesting scenes, fishing scenes, surf bathing, loading of ships with oysters, hemp, wool, and cheeses for export. There was also a stock show showing their cattle and horses, in pictures I mean, and they were fine. Do you remember when we talked of going to New Zealand? I liked the pictures of the country very much.

"We met Rose in the Hawaiian Gardens in the Horticultural Building. They are a delightful combination of flowers and shrubs. . . . At one side is a balcony where a Hawaiian band plays and sings their native songs, which are lovely. The canaries have heard the music so long that at certain places they take up the tune and sing an accompaniment. It is beautiful.

Girls tied heavy veils over their faces when they went out in winter. But Almanzo was a boy, and his face was out in the frosty air. His cheeks were red as apples and his nose was redder than a cherry, and after he had walked a mile and a half he was glad to see the schoolhouse. ■ (From *Farmer Boy* by Laura Ingalls Wilder. Illustrated by Helen Sewell.)

"In the center of the space, which was nearly two hundred feet square, was a river and a waterfall. The waves were chains, the waterfall was chains on a windlass, and the broken water below the falls was chains. Everything about the exhibit was worked by electricity.

"To cap the day, as we came home on the streetcar a man sat near us who was chewing gum. He wore a stiff hat pulled down tight on his head and every time he chewed, his hat moved up and down fully two inches, up and down, up and down, with perfect regularity as though he were worked by electricity.

"[**October 6, 1915**]. The foghorns sound so mournful and distressed, like lost souls calling to each other through the void. (Of course, no one ever heard a lost soul calling, but that's the way it sounds.) It looks as though Russian Hill were afloat in a gray sea and Rose and I have taken the fancy that it is loosened from the rest of the land and floating across the sea to Japan. That is the feeling it gives one.

"[**October 9, 1915**]. The more I see of how Rose works the better satisfied I am to raise chickens. I intend to try to do some writing that will count, but I would not be driven by

the work as she is for anything and I do not see how she can stand it."[5]

November 20, 1915. Her first article appeared in *Missouri Realist*. It concerned modern food processing.

1926. Began to write the story of her prairie childhood.

1932. Publication of the first of the Little House books, *Little House in the Big Woods;* runner-up for the 1932 Newbery Award. "I thought that would end it. But what do you think? Children who read it wrote to me begging for more. I was amazed because I didn't know how to write. I went to little red schoolhouses all over the west and I was never graduated from anything.

"I have learned in this work that when I went as far back in my memory as I could and left my mind there awhile it would go farther back and still farther, bringing out of the dimness of the past things that were beyond my ordinary remembrance. Also, to my surprise, I have discovered that I have led a very interesting life."[1]

1932-43. The first eight books of the series published.

1949. Death of Almanzo, age 92.

1954. Creation of the Laura Ingalls Wilder Award by Children's Library Association. First recipient: Laura Ingalls Wilder.

January 10, 1957. Died in Mansfield, Missouri. As of 1976 over ten million copies of the Garth Williams edition of the "Little House" books have been sold.

FOR MORE INFORMATION SEE: M. Cimino, "Laura Ingalls Wilder," *Wilson Library Bulletin,* April, 1948; Elizabeth Rider Montgomery, *Story behind Modern Books,* Dodd, 1949; V. Kirkus, "Discovery of Laura Ingalls Wilder," *Horn Book,* December, 1953; "Letter from Laura Ingalls Wilder," *Horn Book,* December, 1953; "Letters to Laura Ingalls Wilder," *Horn Book,* December, 1953; J. D. Lindquist, "Tribute to Laura Ingalls Wilder," *Horn Book,* December, 1953; Garth Williams, "Illustrating the Little House Books," *Horn Book,* December, 1953; F. Flanagan, "Tribute to Laura Ingalls Wilder," *Elementary English,* April, 1957; Jane Muir, *Famous Modern American Women Writers,* Dodd, 1959; D. N. Anderson, "A Little More about Laura: Her Relatives in Wisconsin," *Elementary English,* May, 1964; W. J. Jacobs, "Frontier Faith Revisited," *Horn Book,* October, 1965; C. Kies, "Laura and Mary and the 3 R's," *Peabody Journal of Education,* September, 1966; Doris Kerns Eddins, *Teacher's Tribute to Laura Ingalls Wilder,* National Education Association, 1967; A. B. Potter, "Visit at Rocky Ridge Farm," *Instructor,* November, 1967; L. H. Mortensen, "Little Houses and Magnificent Mansions," *Elementary English,* May, 1968; Norah Smaridge, *Famous Modern Storytellers for Young People,* Dodd, 1969; C. Elliott, "Little Houses," *Time,* March 15, 1971; M. Ward, "Laura Ingalls Wilder: An Appreciation," *Elementary English,* October, 1973; Donald Zochert, *Laura: The Life of Laura Ingalls Wilder,* Henry Regnery, 1976.

Obituaries: *New York Times,* February 12, 1957; *Publishers Weekly,* February 25, 1957; *Wilson Library Bulletin,* April, 1957; *Current Biography Yearbook 1957.*

Laura Ingalls Wilder

LAURA INGALLS WILDER

SOMETHING ABOUT THE AUTHOR

CUMULATIVE INDEXES, VOLUMES 1-15
Illustrations and Authors

ILLUSTRATIONS INDEX

(In the following index, the number of the volume in which an illustrator's work appears is given *before* the colon, and the page on which it appears is given *after* the colon. For example, a drawing by Adams, Adrienne appears in Volume 2 on page 6, another drawing by her appears in Volume 3 on page 80, another drawing in Volume 8 on page 1, and another drawing in Volume 15 on page 107.)

316

Something about the Author • Volume 15

Mutchler, Dwight, *1:* 25
Myers, Bernice, *9:* 147
Myers, Lou, *11:* 2

Nakatani, Chiyoko, *12:* 124
Nason, Thomas W., *14:* 68
Navarra, Celeste Scala, *8:* 142
Naylor, Penelope, *10:* 104
Neebe, William, *7:* 93
Needler, Jerry, *12:* 93
Negri, Rocco, *3:* 213; *5:* 67;
    6: 91, 108; *12:* 159
Ness, Evaline, *1:* 164-165; *2:* 39;
    3: 8; *10:* 147; *12:* 53
Neville, Vera, *2:* 182
Newberry, Clare Turlay, *1:* 170
Newfeld, Frank, *14:* 121
Nicholson, William, *15:* 33-34
Niebrugge, Jane, *6:* 118
Nielsen, Jon, *6:* 100
Nielsen, Kay, *15:* 7
Ninon, *1:* 5
Nixon, K., *14:* 152
Noonan, Julia, *4:* 163; *7:* 207
Nordenskjold, Birgitta, *2:* 208
Norman, Michael, *12:* 117

Oakley, Graham, *8:* 112
Obligado, Lilian, *2:* 28, 66-67;
    6: 30; *14:* 179; *15:* 103
Obrant, Susan, *11:* 186
Oechsli, Kelly, *5:* 144-145; *7:* 115;
    8: 83, 183; *13:* 117
Ohlsson, Ib, *4:* 152; *7:* 57; *10:* 20;
    11: 90
Olschewski, Alfred, *7:* 172
Olsen, Ib Spang, *6:* 178-179
Olugebefola, Ademola, *15:* 205
O'Neil, Dan IV, *7:* 176
Ono, Chiyo, *7:* 97
Orbaan, Albert, *2:* 31; *5:* 65, 171;
    9: 8; *14:* 241
Ormsby, Virginia H., *11:* 187
Orozco, José Clemente, *9:* 177
Osmond, Edward, *10:* 111
O'Sullivan, Tom, *3:* 176; *4:* 55
Oughton, Taylor, *5:* 23
Overlie, George, *11:* 156
Owens, Carl, *2:* 35
Owens, Gail, *10:* 170; *12:* 157
Oxenbury, Helen, *3:* 150-151

Padgett, Jim, *12:* 165
Page, Homer, *14:* 145
Pak, *12:* 76
Palazzo, Tony, *3:* 152-153
Palladini, David, *4:* 113
Palmer, Heidi, *15:* 207
Palmer, Juliette, *6:* 89; *15:* 208
Panesis, Nicholas, *3:* 127
Papas, William, *11:* 223
Papish, Robin Lloyd, *10:* 80

Parker, Lewis, *2:* 179
Parker, Nancy Winslow, *10:* 113
Parker, Robert, *4:* 161; *5:* 74; *9:* 136
Parker, Robert Andrew, *11:* 81
Parnall, Peter, *5:* 137
Parrish, Maxfield,
    14: 160, 161, 164, 165
Parry, Marion, *13:* 176
Pascal, David, *14:* 174
Paterson, Diane, *13:* 116
Paton, Jane, *15:* 271
Payne, Joan Balfour, *1:* 118
Payson, Dale, *7:* 34; *9:* 151
Pederson, Sharleen, *12:* 92
Peet, Bill, *2:* 203
Peltier, Leslie C., *13:* 178
Pendle, Alexy, *7:* 159; *13:* 34
Peppe, Rodney, *4:* 164-165
Perl, Susan, *2:* 98; *4:* 231;
    5: 44-45, 118; *6:* 199; *8:* 137;
    12: 88
Pesek, Ludek, *15:* 237
Peterson, R. F., *7:* 101
Peterson, Russell, *7:* 130
Petie, Haris, *2:* 3; *10:* 41, 118;
    11: 227; *12:* 70
Peyton, K. M., *15:* 212
Pfeifer, Herman, *15:* 262
Phillips, Douglas, *1:* 19
Phillips, F. D., *6:* 202
"Phiz." *See* Browne, Hablot K.,
    15: 65
Picarella, Joseph, *13:* 147
Pickard, Charles, *12:* 38
Pienkowski, Jan, *6:* 183
Pimlott, John, *10:* 205
Pincus, Harriet, *4:* 186; *8:* 179
Pinkney, Jerry, *8:* 218; *10:* 40;
    15: 276
Pinkwater, Manus, *8:* 156
Pinto, Ralph, *10:* 131
Pitz, Henry C., *4:* 168
Pogany, Willy, *15:* 46, 49
Politi, Leo, *1:* 178; *4:* 53
Polseno, Jo, *1:* 53; *3:* 117; *5:* 114
Ponter, James, *5:* 204
Poortvliet, Rien, *6:* 212
Portal, Colette, *6:* 186; *11:* 203
Porter, George, *7:* 181
Potter, Miriam Clark, *3:* 162
Powers, Richard M., *1:* 230;
    3: 218; *7:* 194
Price, Christine, *2:* 247;
    3: 163, 253; *8:* 166
Price, Garrett, *1:* 76; *2:* 42
Prince, Leonora E., *7:* 170
Pudlo, *8:* 59
Purdy, Susan, *8:* 162
Puskas, James, *5:* 141
Pyk, Jan, *7:* 26

Quackenbush, Robert, *4:* 190;
    6: 166; *7:* 175, 178; *9:* 86;
    11: 65, 221
Quirk, Thomas, *12:* 81

Rackham, Arthur,
    15: 32, 78, 214-227
Rafilson, Sidney, *11:* 172
Raible, Alton, *1:* 202-203
Rand, Paul, *6:* 188
Rappaport, Eva, *6:* 190
Raskin, Ellen, *2:* 208-209; *4:* 142;
    13: 183
Rau, Margaret, *9:* 157
Ravielli, Anthony, *1:* 198; *3:* 168;
    11: 143
Ray, Deborah, *8:* 164
Ray, Ralph, *2:* 239; *5:* 73
Razzi, James, *10:* 127
Relf, Douglas, *3:* 63
Remi, Georges, *13:* 184
Renlie, Frank, *11:* 200
Reschofsky, Jean, *7:* 118
Rethi, Lili, *2:* 153
Reusswig, William, *3:* 267
Rey, H. A., *1:* 182
Reynolds, Doris, *5:* 71
Ribbons, Ian, *3:* 10
Rice, Elizabeth, *2:* 53, 214
Richardson, Ernest, *2:* 144
Rieniets, Judy King, *14:* 28
Riger, Bob, *2:* 166
Ringi, Kjell, *12:* 171
Rios, Tere. *See* Versace, Marie
Ripper, Charles L., *3:* 175
Rivkin, Jay, *15:* 230
Roach, Marilynne, *9:* 158
Roberts, Cliff, *4:* 126
Roberts, Doreen, *4:* 230
Robinson, Charles, *3:* 53; *5:* 14;
    6: 193; *7:* 150; *7:* 183; *8:* 38;
    9: 81; *13:* 188; *14:* 248-249
Robinson, Jerry, *3:* 262
Robinson, Joan G., *7:* 184
Rocker, Fermin, *7:* 34; *13:* 21
Rockwell, Anne, *5:* 147
Rockwell, Gail, *7:* 186
Roever, J. M., *4:* 119
Rogers, Carol, *2:* 262; *6:* 164
Rogers, Frances, *10:* 130
Rogers, William A.,
    15: 151, 153-154
Rojankovsky, Feodor, *6:* 134, 136;
    10: 183
Rose, Carl, *5:* 62
Rosenblum, Richard, *11:* 202
Ross, Clare, *3:* 123
Ross, John, *3:* 123
Roth, Arnold, *4:* 238
Rouille, M., *11:* 96
Rounds, Glen, *8:* 173; *9:* 171; *12:* 56
Rud, Borghild, *6:* 15
Ruffins, Reynold, *10:* 134-135
Ruth, Rod, *9:* 161
Ryden, Hope, *8:* 176

Sagsoorian, Paul, *12:* 183
Sampson, Katherine, *9:* 197
Samson, Anne S., *2:* 216
Sandberg, Lasse, *15:* 239, 241

AUTHOR INDEX

(In the following index, the number of the volume in which an author's sketch appears is given *before* the colon, and the page on which it appears is given *after* the colon. For example, the sketch of Aardema, Verna, appears in Volume 4 on page 1). This index includes references to *Yesterday's Authors of Books for Children*.

Bond, J. Harvey. *See*
  Winterbotham, R(ussell)
  R(obert), *10:* 198
Bond, Michael, *6:* 28
Bond, Ruskin, *14:* 43
Bonham, Barbara, *7:* 22
Bonham, Frank, *1:* 30
Bontemps, Arna, *2:* 32
Boone, Pat, *7:* 23
Borland, Hal, *5:* 22
Borland, Harold Glen. *See*
  Borland, Hal, *5:* 22
Bornstein, Ruth, *14:* 44
Borten, Helen Jacobson, *5:* 24
Borton, Elizabeth. *See* Trevino,
  Elizabeth B. de, *1:* 216
Bosco, Jack. *See* Holliday,
  Joseph, *11:* 137
Boshell, Gordon, *15:* 36
Boshinski, Blanche, *10:* 13
Bothwell, Jean, *2:* 34
Bottner, Barbara, *14:* 45
Bourne, Leslie. *See* Marshall,
  Evelyn, *11:* 172
Bova, Ben, *6:* 29
Bowen, Betty Morgan. *See* West,
  Betty, *11:* 233
Bowen, Catherine Drinker, *7:* 24
Boyle, Ann (Peters), *10:* 13
Boz. *See* Dickens, Charles, *15:* 55
Bradbury, Bianca, *3:* 25
Bradbury, Ray (Douglas), *11:* 29
Brady, Irene, *4:* 30
Bragdon, Elspeth, *6:* 30
Brandenberg, Aliki Liacouras, *2:* 36
Brandenberg, Franz, *8:* 14
Brandon, Brumsic, Jr., *9:* 25
Brandon, Curt. *See* Bishop,
  Curtis, *6:* 24
Branfield, John (Charles), *11:* 36
Branley, Franklyn M(ansfield),
  4: 32
Bratton, Helen, *4:* 34
Braymer, Marjorie, *6:* 31
Brecht, Edith, *6:* 32
Breck, Vivian. *See* Breckenfeld,
  Vivian Gurney, *1:* 33
Breckenfeld, Vivian Gurney, *1:* 33
Breda, Tjalmar. *See* DeJong,
  David C(ornel), *10:* 29
Breinburg, Petronella, *11:* 36
Brennan, Joseph L., *6:* 33
Brenner, Barbara (Johnes), *4:* 34
Brent, Stuart, *14:* 47
Brewster, Benjamin. *See* Folsom,
  Franklin, *5:* 67
Brewton, John E(dmund), *5:* 25
Brick, John, *10:* 14
Bridges, William (Andrew) *5:* 27
Bridwell, Norman, *4:* 36
Brier, Howard M(axwell), *8:* 15
Brimberg, Stanlee, *9:* 25
Brinckloe, Julie (Lorraine), *13:* 17
Brindel, June (Rachuy), *7:* 25
Brink, Carol Ryrie *1:* 34
Britt, Dell, *1:* 35

Brock, Betty, *7:* 27
Brock, Emma L(illian), *8:* 15
Brockett, Eleanor Hall, *10:* 15
Broderick, Dorothy M., *5:* 28
Brokamp, Marilyn, *10:* 15
Bronson, Lynn. *See* Lampman,
  Evelyn Sibley, *4:* 140
Brooks, Anita, *5:* 28
Brooks, Gwendolyn, *6:* 33
Brooks, Lester, *7:* 28
Brooks, Polly Schoyer, *12:* 63
Brosnan, James Patrick, *14:* 47
Brosnan, Jim. *See* Brosnan, James
  Patrick, *14:* 47
Broun, Emily. *See* Sterne, Emma
  Gelders, *6:* 205
Brower, Millicent, *8:* 16
Browin, Frances Williams, *5:* 30
Brown, Alexis. *See* Baumann,
  Amy (Brown), *10:* 9
Brown, Bill. *See* Brown,
  William L., *5:* 34
Brown, Billye Walker. *See*
  Cutchen, Billye Walker, *15:* 51
Brown, Bob. *See* Brown, Robert
  Joseph, *14:* 48
Brown, Dee (Alexander), *5:* 30
Brown, Eleanor Frances, *3:* 26
Brown, George Earl, *11:* 40
Brown, Irene Bennett, *3:* 27
Brown, Ivor, *5:* 31
Brown, Marc Tolon, *10:* 17
Brown, Marcia, *7:* 29
Brown, Margaret Wise, *YABC 2:* 9
Brown, Margery, *5:* 31
Brown, Marion Marsh, *6:* 35
Brown, Myra Berry, *6:* 36
Brown, Pamela, *5:* 33
Brown, Robert Joseph, *14:* 48
Brown, Rosalie (Gertrude) Moore,
  9: 26
Brown, William L(ouis), *5:* 34
Browning, Robert, *YABC 1:* 85
Brownjohn, Alan, *6:* 38
Bruce, Mary, *1:* 36
Bryant, Bernice (Morgan), *11:* 40
Bryson, Bernarda, *9:* 26
Buchan, John, *YABC 2:* 21
Buchwald, Art(hur), *10:* 18
Buchwald, Emilie, *7:* 31
Buck, Margaret Waring, *3:* 29
Buck, Pearl S(ydenstricker), *1:* 36
Buckeridge, Anthony, *6:* 38
Buckley, Helen E(lizabeth), *2:* 38
Buckmaster, Henrietta, *6:* 39
Budd, Lillian, *7:* 33
Buehr, Walter, *3:* 30
Bulla, Clyde Robert, *2:* 39
Burch, Robert J(oseph), *1:* 38
Burchard, Peter D(uncan), *5:* 34
Burchardt, Nellie, *7:* 33
Burford, Eleanor. *See* Hibbert,
  Eleanor, *2:* 134
Burger, Carl, *9:* 27
Burgess, Robert F(orrest), *4:* 38
Burgwyn, Mebane H., *7:* 34

Burland, C. A. *See* Burland,
  Cottie A., *5:* 36
Burland, Cottie A., *5:* 36
Burlingame, (William) Roger, *2:* 40
Burman, Ben Lucien, *6:* 40
Burn, Doris, *1:* 39
Burnett, Frances (Eliza) Hodgson,
  YABC 2: 32
Burnford, S. D. *See* Burnford,
  Sheila, *3:* 32
Burnford, Sheila, *3:* 32
Burns, Paul C., *5:* 37
Burns, Ray. *See* Burns, Raymond
  (Howard), *9:* 28
Burns, Raymond, *9:* 28
Burns, William A., *5:* 38
Burroughs, Polly, *2:* 41
Burt, Olive Woolley, *4:* 39
Burton, Hester, *7:* 35
Burton, Virginia Lee, *2:* 42
Burton, William H(enry), *11:* 42
Butler, Beverly, *7:* 37
Butters, Dorothy Gilman, *5:* 39
Butterworth, Oliver, *1:* 40
Butterworth, W(illiam)
  E(dmund III), *5:* 40
Byars, Betsy, *4:* 40
Byfield, Barbara Ninde, *8:* 19

Cable, Mary, *9:* 29
Cadwallader, Sharon, *7:* 38
Cain, Arthur H., *3:* 33
Cain, Christopher. *See* Fleming,
  Thomas J(ames), *8:* 19
Cairns, Trevor, *14:* 50
Caldwell, John C(ope), *7:* 38
Calhoun, Mary (Huiskamp), *2:* 44
Call, Hughie Florence, *1:* 41
Cameron, Edna M., *3:* 34
Cameron, Eleanor (Butler), *1:* 42
Cameron, Elizabeth. *See* Nowell,
  Elizabeth Cameron, *12:* 160
Cameron, Polly, *2:* 45
Camp, Walter (Chauncey),
  YABC 1: 92
Campbell, Ann R., *11:* 43
Campbell, Bruce. *See* Epstein,
  Samuel, *1:* 87
Campbell, Jane. *See* Edwards,
  Jane Campbell, *10:* 34
Campbell, R. W. *See* Campbell,
  Rosemae Wells, *1:* 44
Campbell, Rosemae Wells, *1:* 44
Canfield, Dorothy. *See* Fisher,
  Dorothy Canfield,
  YABC 1: 122
Canusi, Jose. *See* Barker, S.
  Omar, *10:* 8
Capps, Benjamin (Franklin), *9:* 30
Caras, Roger A(ndrew), *12:* 65
Carbonnier, Jeanne, *3:* 34
Carey, Ernestine Gilbreth, *2:* 45
Carini, Edward, *9:* 30
Carle, Eric, *4:* 41

Carleton, Captain L. C. *See* Ellis, Edward S(ylvester), *YABC 1:* 116

Carlisle, Clark, Jr. *See* Holding, James, *3:* 85

Carlsen, Ruth C(hristoffer), *2:* 47

Carlson, Bernice Wells, *8:* 19

Carlson, Dale Bick, *1:* 44

Carlson, Natalie Savage, *2:* 48

Carol, Bill J. *See* Knott, William Cecil, Jr., *3:* 94

Carpelan, Bo (Gustaf Bertelsson), *8:* 20

Carpenter, Allan, *3:* 35

Carpenter, Frances, *3:* 36

Carpenter, Patricia (Healy Evans), *11:* 43

Carr, Glyn. *See* Styles, Frank Showell, *10:* 167

Carr, Harriett Helen, *3:* 37

Carr, Mary Jane, *2:* 50

Carrick, Carol, *7:* 39

Carrick, Donald, *7:* 40

Carroll, Curt. *See* Bishop, Curtis, *6:* 24

Carroll, Latrobe, *7:* 40

Carroll, Laura. *See* Parr, Lucy, *10:* 115

Carroll, Lewis. *See* Dodgson, Charles Lutwidge, *YABC 2:* 297

Carse, Robert, *5:* 41

Carson, John F., *1:* 46

Carter, Dorothy Sharp, *8:* 21

Carter, Helene, *15:* 37

Carter, (William) Hodding, *2:* 51

Carter, Katharine J(ones), *2:* 52

Carter, Phyllis Ann. *See* Eberle, Irmengarde, *2:* 97

Carter, William E., *1:* 47

Cartner, William Carruthers, *11:* 44

Cartwright, Sally, *9:* 30

Cary. *See* Cary, Louis F(avreau), *9:* 31

Cary, Louis F(avreau), *9:* 31

Caryl, Jean. *See* Kaplan, Jean Caryl Korn, *10:* 62

Case, Marshal T(aylor), *9:* 33

Case, Michael. *See* Howard, Robert West, *5:* 85

Casewit, Curtis, *4:* 43

Casey, Brigid, *9:* 33

Casey, Winifred Rosen. *See* Rosen, Winifred, *8:* 169

Cason, Mabel Earp, *10:* 19

Cass, Joan E(velyn), *1:* 47

Cassel, Lili. *See* Wronker, Lili Cassell, *10:* 204

Cassel-Wronker, Lili. *See* Wronker, Lili Cassell, *10:* 204

Castellanos, Jane Mollie (Robinson), *9:* 34

Castillo, Edmund L., *1:* 50

Castle, Lee. *See* Ogan, Margaret E. (Nettles), *13:* 171

Caswell, Helen (Rayburn), *12:* 67

Catherall, Arthur, *3:* 38

Catlin, Wynelle, *13:* 19

Catton, (Charles) Bruce, *2:* 54

Catz, Max. *See* Glaser, Milton, *11:* 106

Caudill, Rebecca, *1:* 50

Causley, Charles, *3:* 39

Cavallo, Diana, *7:* 43

Cavanah, Frances, *1:* 52

Cavanna, Betty, *1:* 54

Cawley, Winifred, *13:* 20

Cebulash, Mel, *10:* 19

Ceder, Georgiana Dorcas, *10:* 21

Cerf, Bennett, *7:* 43

Cerf, Christopher (Bennett), *2:* 55

Cetin, Frank (Stanley), *2:* 55

Chadwick, Lester [Collective pseudonym], *1:* 55

Chaffee, Allen, *3:* 41

Chaffin, Lillie D(orton), *4:* 44

Chalmers, Mary, *6:* 41

Chambers, Aidan, *1:* 55

Chambers, Margaret Ada Eastwood, *2:* 56

Chambers, Peggy. *See* Chambers, Margaret, *2:* 56

Chandler, Edna Walker, *11:* 45

Chandler, Ruth Forbes, *2:* 56

Channel, A. R. *See* Catherall, Arthur, *3:* 38

Chapman, Allen [Collective pseudonym], *1:* 55

Chapman, (Constance) Elizabeth (Mann), *10:* 21

Chapman, Walker. *See* Silverberg, Robert, *13:* 206

Chappell, Warren, *6:* 42

Charlip, Remy, *4:* 46

Charlot, Jean, *8:* 22

Charmatz, Bill, *7:* 45

Charosh, Mannis, *5:* 42

Chase, Alice. *See* McHargue, Georgess, *4:* 152

Chase, Mary Ellen, *10:* 22

Chastain, Madye Lee, *4:* 48

Chauncy, Nan, *6:* 43

Chaundler, Christine, *1:* 56

Chen, Tony, *6:* 44

Chenault, Nell. *See* Smith, Linell Nash, *2:* 227

Cheney, Cora, *3:* 41

Cheney, Ted. *See* Cheney, Theodore Albert, *11:* 46

Cheney, Theodore Albert, *11:* 46

Chernoff, Goldie Taub, *10:* 23

Cherryholmes, Anne, *See* Price, Olive, *8:* 157

Chetin, Helen, *6:* 46

Chew, Ruth, *7:* 45

Chidsey, Donald Barr, *3:* 42

Childress, Alice, *7:* 46

Childs, (Halla) Fay (Cochrane), *1:* 56

Chimaera, *See* Farjeon, Eleanor, *2:* 103

Chipperfield, Joseph E(ugene), *2:* 57

Chittenden, Elizabeth F., *9:* 35

Chittum, Ida, *7:* 47

Chorao, (Ann Mc)Kay (Sproat), *8:* 24

Chrisman, Arthur Bowie, *YABC 1:* 94

Christensen, Gardell Dano, *1:* 57

Christgau, Alice Erickson, *13:* 21

Christian, Mary Blount, *9:* 35

Christopher, Matt(hew F.), *2:* 58

Chu, Daniel, *11:* 47

Chukovsky, Kornei (Ivanovich), *5:* 43

Church, Richard, *3:* 43

Churchill, E. Richard, *11:* 48

Chute, B(eatrice) J(oy), *2:* 59

Chute, Marchette (Gaylord), *1:* 58

Chwast, Jacqueline, *6:* 46

Ciardi, John (Anthony), *1:* 59

Clapp, Patricia, *4:* 50

Clare, Helen, *See* Hunter Blair, Pauline, *3:* 87

Clark, Ann Nolan, *4:* 51

Clark, Margaret Goff, *8:* 26

Clark, Mavis Thorpe, *8:* 27

Clark, Patricia (Finrow), *11:* 48

Clark, Ronald William, *2:* 60

Clark, Van D(eusen), *2:* 61

Clark, Virginia. *See* Gray, Patricia, *7:* 110

Clark, Walter Van Tilburg, *8:* 28

Clarke, Arthur C(harles), *13:* 22

Clarke, Clorinda, *7:* 48

Clarke, John. *See* Laklan, Carli, *5:* 100

Clarke, Mary Stetson, *5:* 46

Clarke, Michael. *See* Newlon, Clarke, *6:* 174

Clarke, Pauline. *See* Hunter Blair, Pauline, *3:* 87

Clarkson, Ewan, *9:* 36

Cleary, Beverly (Bunn), *2:* 62

Cleaver, Carole, *6:* 48

Cleishbotham, Jebediah. *See* Scott, Sir Walter, *YABC 2:* 280

Cleland, Mabel. *See* Widdemer, Mabel Cleland, *5:* 200

Clemens, Samuel Langhorne, *YABC 2:* 51

Clemons, Elizabeth. *See* Nowell, Elizabeth Cameron, *12:* 160

Clerk, N. W. *See* Lewis, C. S., *13:* 129

Cleven, Cathrine. *See* Cleven, Kathryn Seward, *2:* 64

Cleven, Kathryn Seward, *2:* 64

Clevin, Jörgen, *7:* 49

Clewes, Dorothy (Mary), *1:* 61

Clifford, Eth. *See* Rosenberg, Ethel, *3:* 176

Clifford, Harold B., *10:* 24

Clifford, Margaret Cort, *1:* 63

Clifford, Martin. *See* Hamilton, Charles Harold St. John, *13:* 77

Clifford, Peggy. *See* Clifford, Margaret Cort, *1:* 63

Finkel, George (Irvine), *8:* 59
Finlayson, Ann, *8:* 61
Firmin, Peter, *15:* 113
Fischbach, Julius, *10:* 43
Fisher, Aileen (Lucia), *1:* 92
Fisher, Dorothy Canfield,
    YABC 1: 122
Fisher, John (Oswald Hamilton),
    15: 115
Fisher, Laura Harrison, *5:* 67
Fisher, Leonard Everett, *4:* 84
Fitch, Clarke. *See* Sinclair, Upton
    (Beall), *9:* 168
Fitzgerald, F(rancis) A(nthony),
    15: 115
Fitzhardinge, Joan Margaret, *2:* 107
Fitzhugh, Louise, *1:* 94
Flack, Marjorie, *YABC 2:* 123
Fleischman, (Albert) Sid(ney),
    8: 61
Fleming, Alice Mulcahey, *9:* 67
Fleming, Ian (Lancaster), *9:* 67
Fleming, Thomas J(ames), *8:* 64
Fletcher, Charlie May, *3:* 70
Fletcher, Helen Jill, *13:* 36
Flexner, James Thomas, *9:* 70
Flitner, David P., *7:* 92
Floethe, Louise Lee, *4:* 87
Floethe, Richard, *4:* 89
Flood, Flash. *See* Robinson, Jan
    M., *6:* 194
Flora, James (Royer), *1:* 95
Flynn, Barbara, *9:* 71
Flynn, Jackson. *See* Shirreffs,
    Gordon D., *11:* 207
Folsom, Franklin (Brewster), *5:* 67
Forbes, Esther, *2:* 108
Forbes, Graham B. [Collective
    pseudonym], *1:* 97
Forbes, Kathryn. *See* McLean,
    Kathryn (Anderson), *9:* 140
Ford, Elbur. *See* Hibbert,
    Eleanor, *2:* 134
Ford, Marcia. *See* Radford, Ruby
    L., *6:* 186
Foreman, Michael, *2:* 110
Forrest, Sybil. *See* Markun,
    Patricia M(aloney), *15:* 189
Forester, C(ecil) S(cott), *13:* 38
Forman, Brenda, *4:* 90
Forman, James Douglas, *8:* 64
Forsee, (Frances) Aylesa, *1:* 97
Foster, Doris Van Liew, *10:* 44
Foster, E(lizabeth) C(onnell), *9:* 71
Foster, Elizabeth, *10:* 45
Foster, Elizabeth Vincent, *12:* 82
Foster, F. Blanche, *11:* 95
Foster, Genevieve (Stump), *2:* 111
Foster, John T(homas), *8:* 65
Foster, Laura Louise, *6:* 78
Fowke, Edith (Margaret), *14:* 59
Fox, Charles Philip, *12:* 83
Fox, Eleanor. *See* St. John, Wylly
    Folk, *10:* 132
Fox, Lorraine, *11:* 96
Fox, Michael Wilson, *15:* 117

Frances, Miss. *See* Horwich,
    Frances R., *11:* 142
Francis, Dorothy Brenner, *10:* 46
Francis, Pamela (Mary), *11:* 97
Frank, Josette, *10:* 47
Frankau, Mary Evelyn, *4:* 90
Frankel, Bernice, *9:* 72
Franklin, Harold, *13:* 53
Franklin, Steve. *See* Stevens,
    Franklin, *6:* 206
Franzén, Nils-Olof, *10:* 47
Frasconi, Antonio, *6:* 79
Frazier, Neta Lohnes, *7:* 94
French, Allen, *YABC 1:* 133
French, Dorothy Kayser, *5:* 69
French, Fiona, *6:* 81
French, Paul. *See* Asimov, Isaac,
    1: 15
Frewer, Glyn, *11:* 98
Frick, C. H. *See* Irwin, Constance
    Frick, *6:* 119
Frick, Constance. *See* Irwin,
    Constance Frick, *6:* 119
Friedlander, Joanne K(ohn), *9:* 73
Friedman, Estelle, *7:* 95
Friendlich, Dick. *See* Friendlich,
    Richard, *11:* 99
Friendlich, Richard J., *11:* 99
Friermood, Elisabeth Hamilton,
    5: 69
Friis, Babbis. *See* Friis-Baastad,
    Babbis, *7:* 95
Friis-Baastad, Babbis, *7:* 95
Friskey, Margaret Richards, *5:* 72
Fritz, Jean (Guttery), *1:* 98
Froman, Elizabeth Hull, *10:* 49
Froman, Robert (Winslow), *8:* 67
Frost, Lesley, *14:* 61
Frost, Robert (Lee), *14:* 63
Fry, Rosalie, *3:* 71
Fuchs, Erich, *6:* 84
Fujita, Tamao, *7:* 98
Fujiwara, Michiko, *15:* 120
Fuller, Catherine L(euthold), *9:* 73
Fuller, Iola. *See* McCoy, Iola
    Fuller, *3:* 120
Fuller, Lois Hamilton, *11:* 99
Funk, Thompson. *See* Funk, Tom,
    7: 98
Funk, Tom, *7:* 98
Funke, Lewis, *11:* 100

Gág, Wanda (Hazel), *YABC 1:* 135
Gage, Wilson. *See* Steele, Mary
    Q., *3:* 211
Gallant, Roy A(rthur), *4:* 91
Gallico, Paul, *13:* 53
Galt, Thomas Franklin, Jr., *5:* 72
Galt, Tom. *See* Galt, Thomas
    Franklin, Jr., *5:* 72
Gamerman, Martha, *15:* 121
Gannett, Ruth Stiles, *3:* 73
Gannon, Robert (Haines), *8:* 68
Garden, Nancy, *12:* 85

Gardner, Jeanne LeMonnier, *5:* 73
Gardner, Richard A., *13:* 64
Garfield, James B., *6:* 85
Garfield, Leon, *1:* 99
Garis, Howard R(oger), *13:* 67
Garnett, Eve C. R., *3:* 75
Garrison, Frederick. *See* Sinclair,
    Upton (Beall), *9:* 168
Garst, Doris Shannon, *1:* 100
Garst, Shannon. *See* Garst, Doris
    Shannon, *1:* 100
Garthwaite, Marion H., *7:* 100
Gates, Doris, *1:* 102
Gault, William Campbell, *8:* 69
Gay, Kathlyn, *9:* 74
Geis, Darlene, *7:* 101
Geisel, Theodor Seuss, *1:* 104
Geldart, William, *15:* 121
Gelinas, Paul J., *10:* 49
Gelman, Steve, *3:* 75
Gemming, Elizabeth, *11:* 104
Gentleman, David, *7:* 102
George, Jean Craighead, *2:* 112
George, John L(othar), *2:* 114
George, S(idney) C(harles), *11:* 104
Georgiou, Constantine, *7:* 102
Gibbs, Alonzo (Lawrence), *5:* 74
Gibson, Josephine. *See* Joslin,
    Sesyle, *2:* 158
Gidal, Sonia, *2:* 115
Gidal, Tim N(ahum), *2:* 116
Gilbert, (Agnes) Joan (Sewell),
    10: 50
Gilbert, Nan. *See* Gilbertson,
    Mildred, *2:* 116
Gilbert, Sara (Dulaney), *11:* 105
Gilbertson, Mildred Geiger, *2:* 116
Gilbreath, Alice (Thompson),
    12: 87
Gilbreth, Frank B., Jr., *2:* 117
Gilfond, Henry, *2:* 118
Gill, Derek L(ewis) T(heodore),
    9: 75
Gillett, Mary, *7:* 103
Gillette, Henry Sampson, *14:* 71
Gilman, Dorothy. *See* Dorothy
    Gilman Butters, *5:* 39
Gilman, Esther, *15:* 123
Gilson, Barbara. *See* Gilson,
    Charles James Louis,
    YABC 2: 124
Gilson, Charles James Louis,
    YABC 2: 124
Ginsburg, Mirra, *6:* 86
Giovanopoulos, Paul, *7:* 104
Gipson, Frederick B., *2:* 118
Gittings, Jo Manton, *3:* 76
Gittings, Robert, *6:* 88
Gladstone, Gary, *12:* 88
Glaser, Milton, *11:* 106
Glaspell, Susan, *YABC 2:* 125
Glazer, Tom, *9:* 76
Glick, Carl (Cannon), *14:* 72
Gliewe, Unada, *3:* 77
Glovach, Linda, *7:* 105
Glubok, Shirley, *6:* 89

Author Index